THE
FUNCTIONS
OF DREAMING

SUNY Series in Dream Studies
Robert L. Van de Castle, Editor

THE
FUNCTIONS
OF DREAMING

**Alan Moffitt, Milton Kramer,
and Robert Hoffmann,
editors**

STATE UNIVERSITY OF NEW YORK PRESS

Published by
State University of New York Press, Albany

For information, address State University of New York
Press, State University Plaza, Albany, N.Y., 12246

Production by Marilyn P. Semerad
Marketing by Fran Keneston

Library of Congress Cataloging in Publication Data

The Functions of dreaming / edited by Alan Moffitt, Milton Kramer,
    Robert Hoffmann.
        p.   cm. — (SUNY Series in dream studies)
    Includes bibliographical references and index.
    ISBN 0-7914-1297-0 (hard). — ISBN 0-7914-1298-9 (pbk.)
    1. Dreams.   I. Moffitt, Alan, 1939-   . II. Kramer, Milton, 1929-
    . III. Hoffmann, Robert, 1945-   . IV. Series.
    BF14078.F95   1993
    154.6'3—dc20   91–47539
                                                                   CIP

10 9 8 7 6 5 4 3 2 1

CONTENTS

Acknowledgments   vii

Contributors   ix

Introduction   1

1. Data Constraints on Theorizing About Dream Function
   David Foulkes   11

2. The Function of Dreaming in the Cycles of Cognition:
   A Biogenetic Structural Account............*John McManus,*
   Charles D. Laughlin, and *Jon Shearer*   21

3. A Model of Dreaming and Its Functional Significance:
   The State-Shift Hypothesis.........*Martha Koukkou* and
   Dietrich Lehmann   51

4. Connectionism and Sleep.....................*Gordon G. Globus*   119

5. The Selective Mood Regulatory Function of Dreaming:
   An Update and Revision...............*Milton Kramer*   139

6. Waking, Dreaming, and Self-Regulation.........*Sheila Purcell,*
   Alan Moffitt, and *Robert Hoffmann*   197

7. REM Sleep and Dreams as Mechanisms of the Recovery
   of Search Activity..............................*V. S. Rotenberg*   261

8. The Repetition of Dreams and Dream Elements: A Possible
   Clue to a Function of Dreams.........*G. William Domhoff*   293

v

9. Dreams and Adaptation to Contemporary Stress
David Koulack   321

10. REM Sleep and Learning: Some Recent Findings
Carlyle Smith   341

11. An Integrated Approach to Dream Theory: Contributions
from Sleep Research and Clinical Practice
Ramon Greenberg and *Chester Pearlman*   363

12. The "Royal Road" to the Unconscious Revisited: A
Signal Detection Model of Dream Function
Harry Fiss   381

13. The Impact of Dreams on Waking Thoughts and
Feelings.................*Don Kuiken* and *Shelley Sikora*   419

14. Reasons for Oneiromancy: Some Psychological Functions
of Conventional Dream Interpretation......*Waud H. Kracke*   477

15. "Pity the Bones by Wandering River which Still in
Lovers' Dreams Appear as Men"......*Robert Knox Dentan*
and *Laura J. McClusky*   489

16. Dreaming: Could We Do Without It? ......*John Antrobus*   549

Index   559

ACKNOWLEDGMENTS

The editors would like to acknowledge the support of an operating grant to the first editor from the Social Sciences and Humanities Research Council of Canada during the preparation of this volume, and to Carleton University for a sabbatical year during 1989-1990 for the first editor. Contributors to the present volume have been supported in their professional studies of dreaming and sleeping by their membership in the following associations and societies: the Association for the Study of Dreams, the Canadian Sleep Society, the Sleep Research Society and the European Sleep Research Society. For more information about these organizations write to: the Association for the Study of Dreams, Box 1600, Vienna, Virginia, 94117; the Canadian Sleep Society, Alistair MacLean, Ph.D., Psychology Department, Queen's University, Kingston, Ontario, K7L 3N6; the Sleep Research Society, 1600 14th Street North-west, Suite 300, Rochester, Minnesota, 55901-2200; the European Sleep Research Society, Dr. Dag Stenberg, Department of Physiology, Sil-tavuorenpenger 20 J, SF-00170 Helsinki, Finland.

We would also like to acknowledge the following for permission to reprint:

An excerpt from "Preludes" in *Collected Poems, 1909–1962* by T.S. Eliot, copyright 1936 by Harcourt Brace Jovanovich, Inc., copyright © 1964, 1963 by T. S. Eliot, reprinted by permission of the publisher.

An excerpt from the poems by E. Bronte (1985). Sometimes entitled "Sleep brings no joy," lines 1–12 from page 116 of E. Chitham and T. Winnifrith (Eds.). *Selected Bronte Poems*. New York: Basil Blackwell.

Figure 5.1 from W. Webb and Grune and Stratton (New York, 1968) from *Progress in Clinical Psychology*, vol. 8.

Figure 10.1 from C. Smith, L. Lapp and *Physiology and Behaviour* (1986).

Finally, the editors would like to express their deepest appreciation to their editorial assistant, Penny McGregor. Without her talent, dedication and resourcefulness, this volume would not have reached completion.

CONTRIBUTORS

John Antrobus, Ph.D. Department of Psychology, The City College of the City University of New York, New York, NY

Robert Knox Dentan, Ph.D. Departments of Anthropology and American Studies, State University of New York at Buffalo, Buffalo, NY.

William Domhoff, Ph.D. Departments of Psychology and Sociology, University of California Santa Cruz, Santa Cruz, CA

Harry Fiss, Ph.D. Department of Psychiatry, School of Medicine, University of Connecticut Health Center, Farmington, CT

David Foulkes, Ph.D. Atlanta, GA

Gordon G. Globus, M.D. Department of Psychiatry and Human Behavior, University of California Irvine Medical Center, Orange CA

Ramon Greenberg, M.D. Department of Psychiatry, Harvard Medical School, Massachusetts Mental Health Center, Boston, MA

Robert Hoffmann, Ph.D. Sleep Laboratory, Department of Psychology, Carleton University, Ottawa, Ontario

Martha Koukkou, M.D. Institute of EEG Brain Mapping, University Hospital of Psychiatry "Waldau", CH-3072 Bern, Switzerland

David Koulack, Ph.D. Department of Psychology, University of Manitoba, Winnipeg, Manitoba

Waud H. Kracke, Ph.D. Department of Anthropology, University of Illinois at Chicago, Chicago, IL

Milton Kramer, M.D. Sleep Disorders Center of Greater Cincinnati, Bethesda Oak Hospital, Cincinnati, Ohio

Don Kuiken, Ph.D. Department of Psychology, University of Alberta, Edmonton, Alberta

Charles D. Laughlin, Ph.D. Department of Sociology and Anthropology, Carleton University, Ottawa, Ontario

Dietrich Lehmann, M.D. Brain Mapping Laboratory, Department of Neurology, University Hospital, CH-8091 Zurich, Switzerland

Laura J. McClusky, M.A. Department of Anthropology, State University of New York at Buffalo, Buffalo, New York

John McManus, Ph.D. Philadelphia, Pennsylvania

Alan Moffitt, Ph.D. Sleep Laboratory, Department of Psychology, Carleton University, Ottawa, Ontario

Chester Pearlman, M.D. Boston VA Medical Center, Department of Psychiatry, Tufts University School of Medicine, Boston, Massachusetts

Sheila Purcell, Ph.D. Ottawa, Ontario

V.S. Rotenberg, M.D. Abarbanel Mental Health Center, Bat Yami, Israel

Jon Shearer, M.A. Ottawa, Ontario

Shelley Sikora, M.A. Department of Psychology, University of Alberta, Edmonton, Alberta

Carlyle Smith, Ph.D. Department of Psychology, Trent University, Peterborough, Ontario

INTRODUCTION

There is considerable disagreement among practitioners in the human and life sciences concerning the functional significance of dreaming even though the general outlines of the methodological requirements for a functional analysis of dreaming have been available for over a decade (Kramer, 1980). It might be tempting to attribute this disagreement to the successive difficulties during this century of psychoanalysis, psychiatry, sleep and dream psychophysiology and cognitive science to *"give an account"* of dreaming, in particular, a functional account explicating the goal-directed nature of such activity (Sternberg and Smith, 1988). Many cognitive scientists fail to see why they should be interested in sleeping and dreaming when they have it on good authority that dreaming is a biological epiphenomenon, random, meaningless and without goal direction. Epistemologically, dreaming has been regarded as a source of error rather than fact or truth just as ontologically it is a state of false consciousness (Malcom, 1959). Such views are not new. They can be found in the Nineteenth century, the Renaissance, and earlier (Lavie and Hobson, 1986; Ruprecht, 1990). There are, of course, those who disagree, then and now. For example, more than ten years ago Kramer (1982) argued that the functional significance of dream content on subsequent wakefulness was more likely to be affective than cognitive in nature.

The purpose of the present volume is to present a diverse collection of modern views of this perennial question by theoreticians, researchers, and practitioners of the human and life sciences. Not all those invited were able to participate. Therefore, the majority of the chapters that follow are positively disposed to the proposition that dreaming is functionally significant. We hope they stimulate new theory and research. We did not include contributions from the humanities because they were beyond our areas of competence as editors.

1

By *dreaming* we refer to any image, thought or feeling attributed by the dreamer to a preawakening state. The experience of dreaming and its recall vary within and among individuals across cultures along the following dimensions: frequency, quantity, quality, and type (Von Grunebaum and Callois, 1966). These dimensions of dreaming are culturally and historically universal, appearing during ontogeny at about three years of age, if not earlier (Foulkes, Chapter 1, this volume). Their emergence, development and transformation are strongly constrained by both biology and culture (Chapters 1–3, this volume). Thus, contributors to the present volume include anthropologists, psychologists, psychiatrists, neurologists, and biologists.

According to Fishbein (1976, p. 8) there are four possible classes of interpretations of the functional significance of such universals. These are presented in Table 1. The strongest class of interpretations assigns some function to dreaming at the time of its occurrence. The second class of interpretations views dreaming as not functionally significant at ⌐the time of its occurrence, but claims that it is necessary to build something that is functionally significant. The third class of interpretations views dreaming as not functionally significant by itself but in combination with other things it can build something that is functionally significant. The weakest interpretation assigns only an index or indicator function to dreaming and dream recall. This is dreaming as epihpenomenon, in which dreaming is a nonfunctional by-product of some other activity that is functionally significant. Such interpretations view dreaming as a

Table 1.

Classes of Interpretation of the Functional Significance of Dreaming

1.   The characteristic has survival value at that point in development
2.   The characteristic does not have survival value at that point in development, but it is necessary to build another characteristic that eventually will have high survival value.
3.   The characteristic does not have survival value at that point in development, but it will eventually be combined with other characteristics, the combination eventually having high survival value.
4.   The characteristic itself does not have high survival value, but it is the outcome of a characteristic that falls in one of the first three categories.
5.   The characteristic itself does not have high survival value, and it is not the outcome of a characteristic that falls in one of the first four categories.

Source: After Fishbein, 1976, p. 8.

window onto something else. A fifth possibility can be added suggesting that dreaming and dream recall have no function at all even as indices of other cultural, psychological, or biological processes.

All traditional and modern theories of dreaming, whether ideographic or nomothetic can be classified within these alternatives. Anthropological, developmental, personality and clinical theories usually emphasize the first three interpretations of Table 1, whereas cognitive, neurocognitive and biological theories tend to emphasize the fourth and the fifth possibilities. We call theories of dreaming that fall in the fourth and fifth categories *static functional theories*. Those falling in the first three categories are called *dynamic functional theories*. The details of dynamic functional theories differ. Their commonality resides in attributing some form of functional significance to variations within and among individuals within and among cultures in the dimensions of dreaming in the process of adaptation. The majority of the chapters in this book propose dynamic functional theories of dreaming. They differ in the extent to which dreaming is seen as having immediate or delayed causal consequences either alone or in combination with other psychological, developmental and cultural processes. In fact, functional dream theory is inconsistent only with assertions falling in the fourth and fifth categories of Table 1. Even apparently afunctional or antifunctional theories of dreaming such as the activation synthesis hypothesis (Hobson, 1988; Mamelak and Hobson, 1989), and various neural net theories (Crick and Mitchison, 1983, 1986; Hinton and Sejnowski, 1986) fall in the first three categories of Table 1. Part of the popular confusion on this point derives from the failure to appreciate that the apparent randomness of dreaming at the physiological level is neutral with respect to the functional significance of dreaming at the psychological level.

Dreaming can also index self-regulatory processes without participating in self-regulation—a category four interpretation of Table 1. The important question for indexical approaches to dreaming, and the distinguishing feature between them and interpretations that deny dreaming such a function concerns whether dreaming is a reliable epiphenomenon, not whether it is an epihenomenon. If reliable, dreaming can at least be granted the significance associated with category four interpretations. Although not centrally important for functional theories of dreaming, an indexical use of dreaming may throw significant light on the possible functional significance of other systems. Two recent examples are noteworthy. Gaines and Price-Williams (1990) have documented important differences among American and Balinese artists in how dreaming indexes and participates in the creative imagination in artists from these two cultures. Cuddy (1990) found that controlling statistically for prior sexual abuse eliminated gender differences in the frequency of experiencing nightmares. Indeed, the chapters of this book abound with examples of dreaming serving an indexical function. Often what is being indexed is the functional integrity of systems of adaptation that transcend dreaming and include it as a component. These will vary developmentally and cross culturally as Foulkes and McManus, Laughlin and Shearer (Chapters 1 and 2) suggest.

It is at this point that the supposed biologically based randomness of dreaming becomes important. The usual understanding, associated with various readings of the claims of the activation-synthesis hypothesis (Hobson, 1988; Hobson and McCarley, 1977; Mamelak and Hobson, 1989), that dreaming is both meaningless and functionless because it is random, is incorrect. For example, the Boltzmann machine model of sleeping, dreaming and waking self-regulation proposed by Hinton and Sejnowski (1986) sees dreaming as a random, REM-dependent process with immediate functional significance for wakefulness in the context of learning, relearning and self-regulation, a category one interpretation. The fact that dreaming is not random at the levels of content or process simply reinforces the point that randomness has nothing to do with the meaningfulness or the functional significance of dreaming. Crick and Mitchison (1983; 1986) have been widely misunderstood as having proposed an antifunctional theory of dreaming. This too is incorrect. For them, dreaming is error in a pattern recognition system serving an immediate adaptive function, when forgotten, in maintaining the sensitivity and selectivity of the pattern recognition system of waking consciousness. Dream recall for them is the propagation of error into the waking pattern recognition system with the potential to destabilize the functional integrity of that system. In the classification of Table 1, this is a category 1 explanation, sharpened by Occam's razor. Although their theory has not received wide support (see Globus, Chapter 4) and appears to be incorrect in detail (see Smith, Chapter 10), it has stimulated a great deal of rethinking of the functional significance of dreaming. In particular, their theory has provided one of the clearest rationales for cognitive science not to be interested in dreaming, except as a source of error to be minimized. It is hoped that the contents of this volume will provide reasons for a broader interest in the functional significance of dreaming and dream recall.

It is important to note that Crick and Mitchison's theory provides a good explanatory fit to the attitudes and values of a reasonably large number of individuals known to at least one of the editors. This editor once was informed by an acquaintance that, like Ruskin, the person hated dreaming and avoided it whenever possible. No dreaming as fountain of creativity for this person, not even dreaming as entertainment. Kramer (Kramer, Schoen, and Kinney, 1984) was the first to find a relation between dream repression and adaptation in a study of Chronic Delayed Post Traumatic Stress Disorder. Lavie and Kaminer (Kaminer and Lavie, 1989; Lavie and Kaminer, 1991) have reported similar findings in a study of the long term adaptation of victims of the holocaust. These findings suggest that Crick and Mitchison's theory may provide a tentative description of the adaptive significance of dream recall in the lives of some individuals even if the specific mechanisms they propose are incorrect.

Difficulties such as these indicate that an adequate theory of the functional significance of dreaming must account for both patterns of remembering as well as patterns of forgetting dreaming. These issues are addressed in Chapter 4 by Globus, who revises connectionist theory with dream remembering rather than dream forgetting as the focus; in Chapter 3 by Koukkou and Lehmann, who propose a neurobiological model of dreaming and dream recall; and in Chapter 2 by McManus, Laughlin and Shearer who propose an anthropologically informed neurobiological model of dreaming and waking.

Many of the chapters in the present volume indicate that dreaming is orderly and can be used to index other biological, psychological, and cultural processes (Kramer, 1982). In addition, the dynamics of dreaming appear to be implicated in the organization and functioning of self at the deepest levels within culture. The functions served are complex, including not only experiential, affective and cognitive aspects; they are also epistemic and meta-epistemic, having to do with knowing that we know and how we regard what we think we know (Doniger-O'Flaherty, 1984; Kitchener, 1983). The developmental psychology of dreaming within and among cultures is a major area of neglect deserving immediate attention. Ideographic, nomothetic and comparative studies of the development of dreaming are essential for this field of interest to progress (see Foulkes, Chapter 1). Only by establishing similarities and differences in the patterns of development of dreaming across cultures can we begin to comprehend the relative and interactive roles of biology and culture in the functional significance of dreaming and dream recall.

A systematic ambiguity runs through the collection of chapters in the present volume. Stage REM sleep and dreaming are widely regarded as natural synonyms by many. For others, the identification of stage REM sleep and dreaming is entirely wrongheaded. It incorrectly permits questions about the dreaming of infants and other species of mammals and avians and ignores the fact that we probably dream throughout sleep. For still others, dreaming is a human psychological process that can be properly discussed without reference to the underlying stage of sleep. The editors are aware of these differences and have not imposed an artificial unity where none exists. Getting the semantics straight is one of the important tasks for those interested in the functional significance of dreaming. Stewart and Tall (1983) have observed that it is a cardinal principal of mathematics not to throw away a good idea just because it does not work. It is much the same with the association of REM and dreaming. People are not going to give it up simply because it is not correct. The functional significance of dreaming may be independent of the functional significance of any stage of sleep (see Purcell, Moffitt, and Hoffmann, Chapter 6). On the other hand, even if dreaming is continuous throughout sleep, its functional range and significance may be contextually dependent on the stage of sleep during which it happens. Lucid dreaming, for example, occurs mainly during stage REM and descent stage 1 NREM sleep. Similarly, dreaming may enhance or interact with functions proposed for particular stages of sleep, such as the maintenance of search, memory, signal detection and problem solving during REM sleep (see Chapters 7, 10, 11, and 12). In this vein, Kramer (Chapter 5) has been successful in carefully delineating the mood regulating effects of dreams from the mood regulating effects of sleep. The interaction of dreaming with the REM sleep functions proposed by these authors opens interesting possibilities for further research and theory. The nature of the contextual dependency of the functions of dreaming on NREM sleep, especially when stages 2 and 4 are differentiated, remains to be determined (see Chapter 3).

Many chapters in the present volume testify that the boundary between waking and sleeping is causally permeable in both directions. Koulack's chapter explores the adaptive response of dreaming to stress. Greenberg and Pearlman explore dreaming as adaptive problem solving in response to challenges to the self. Moreover, the permeability of the sleep-wake boundary and, indeed, the nature of the waking and sleeping states are themselves bounded and shaped by cultural factors operating morphogenetically during ontogeny. Dentan and McKlusky

(Chapter 15) and Kracke (Chapter 14) indicate the range and roles of cultural interpretations of dreaming, whereas McManus, Laughlin, and Shearer (Chapter 2) argue that the functional significance of wakefulness, sleeping, and dreaming is shaped ontogenetically by culture. The claims of Malcom and Crick and Mitchison that dreaming is a source of error cannot be sustained. Dreams and their waking interpretations can be correct rather than erroneous. Lucid dreaming is a case in point, as are other examples in this volume of successful problem solving in dreams and as a result of dreaming. Whether and how the ability of dreaming to be referentially correct differs both within and among individuals and cultures over time are interesting topics for future research. Those individuals and cultures who do no such parsing of experience need to be further divided into those who can but do not, those who cannot, and those who will not. The functional significance of the forgetting of dream experience, in the form of incomprehension or nonrecall, is unlikely to be the same in these three groups, especially when considered across cultures. Developmental, cultural, and individual factors will form and limit the capacity of dreaming to parse certain forms of waking and sleeping experience. NREM dreaming emerges later in ontogeny, after five years of age, than REM dreaming, which emerges between three and five years. Lucid dreaming emerges later than both of these, sometimes as early as adolescence. However, many adults have never experienced lucid dreaming, so the emergence of this type of dreaming is not developmentally inevitabile. The emergence of dreaming during development is inevitable. If dreaming is an epiphenomenon, it is an inevitable epiphenomenon developmentally with the capacity to produce correct direct and indirect reference.

For the functions of dreaming to inevitably require forgetting during development in large numbers of individuals would require a cultural context considerably more hostile to dreaming than found in most cultures today, or an experiential context so traumatic that dream forgetting is not only the most appropriate adaptive response it is also the most desired, as when a person plagued by recurrent nightmares wishes the release of dreamless sleep. An interesting follow-up to Antobus's claim (Chapter 16) that we can do without dreaming might be to examine those who would like to but cannot. Domhoff (Chapter 8) deals with a related issue in his chapter on the functional significance of recurrent dreams, as do Kuiken and Sikora (Chapter 13) in a different manner by examining the impact of memorable dreams. Just as waking consciousness can be intrusive on dreaming, dreaming can be instrusive upon waking consciousness both cognitively and affectively (Chapters 5, 6, 9, and 13). It is with such dreaming that we approach category one and two explanations in the Fishbein scheme (Table 1), dreaming that has immediate or nearly immediate adaptive significance.

References

Cuddy, M. (1990). "Predicting Sexual Abuse from Dissociation, Somatization and Nightmares." Ph.D. dissertation, York University, Downsview, Ontario.

Crick, F., and Mitchison, G. (1983). "The Function of Dream Sleep." *Nature* 30: 111–114.

———. (1986). "REM Sleep and Neural Nets." *The Journal of Mind and Behavior* 5: 81–98.

Doniger-O'Flaherty, W. (1984). *Dreams, Illusions and Other Realities.* Chicago: University of Chicago Press.

Fishbein, H. (1976). *Evolution, Development and Children's Learning.* Goodyear Publishing Company, Inc.: Pacific Palisades, California.

Foulkes, D. (1985). *Dreaming: A Cognitive-Psychological analysis.* Hillsdale, N.J.: Lawrence Erlbaum Associates.

Gaines, R., and Price-Williams, D. (1990). "Dreams and Imaginative Processes in American and Balinese Artists." *Psychiatric Journal of the University of Ottawa* 15, no. 2: 107–110.

Hinton, G., and Sejnowski, T. (1986). "Learning and Relearning in Boltzmann Machines." In D. Rumelhart and J. McClelland (Eds.), *Parallel Distributed Processing*, vol. 1, pp. 282–317. Cambridge, Mass.: MIT Press.

Hobson, A. (1988). *The Dreaming Brain.* New York: Basic Books.

———, and McCarley, R. (1977). "The Brain as a Dream State Generator: An Activation-Synthesis Hypothesis of the Dream Process." *American Journal of Psychiatry* 134: 97–112.

Kaminer, H., and Lavie, P. (1989). "Dreaming and Long Term Adjustment to Severe Trauma." *Sleep Research* 18: 146.

Kitchener, K. (1983). "Cognition, Meta-Cognition and Epistemic Cognition." *Human Development* 26: 222–232.

Kramer, M. (1982). "The Psychology of the Dream: Art or Science." *Psychiatric Journal of the University of Ottawa* 7: 87–100.

Kramer, M. (1980). "The Function of Psychological Dreaming: a Preliminary Analysis." *5th European Congress of Sleep Research*, Amsterdam, Basil, Switzerland; Karger, pp. 182–185.

———, Schoen, L., and Kinney, L. (1984). "The Dream Experience in Dream Disturbed Vietnam Veterans." In B. Vanderkolk (Ed.), *Post Traumatic Stress Disorders: Psychological and Biological Sequellae.* Washington, D.C.: American Psychiatric Press.

Lavie, P., and Hobson, A. (1986). "Origin of Dreams: Anticipation of Modern Theories in the Philosophy and Physiology of the Eighteenth and Nineteenth Centuries." *Psychological Bulletin* 100, no. 2: 229–240.

———, and Kaminer, H. (1991). "Dreams that Poison Sleep: Dreaming in Holocaust Survivors." *Dreaming* 1, no. 1: 11–22.

Malcom, N. (1959). *Dreaming.* London: Routeledge and Kegan Paul.

Mamelak, A., and Hobson, A. (1989). "Dream Bizarreness as the Cognitive Correlate of Altered Neuronal Behavior in REM Sleep." *Journal of Cognitive Neuroscience* 1: 201–222.

Rupprecht, C. (1990). "Our Unacknowledged Ancestors: Dream Theorists of Antiquity, the Middle Ages and the Renaissance." *Psychiatric Journal of the University of Ottawa,* 15, no. 2: 117–122.

Stewart, I., and Tall, D. (1983). *Complex Analysis: The Hitchhiker's Guide to the Plane.* Cambridge: Cambridge University Press.

Sternberg, R. J., and Smith, E. E. (Eds.) (1988). *The Psychology of Human Thought.* Cambridge: Cambridge University Press.

Von Grunebaum, G., and Callois, R. (Eds.) (1966). *The Dream and Human Societies.* Berkeley: University of California Press.

1

David Foulkes ━━━━━━━━━━━━━━━

Data Constraints on Theorizing About Dream Function

It is not possible, within the format of this volume, to review systematically all of the empirical data that might bear on the question of dream function. I have tried elsewhere (Foulkes, 1985) to perform this task. Less theoretically cohesive accounts of the data of empirical dream psychology (e.g., Arkin, Antrobus, and Ellman, 1978; Ellman and Antrobus, 1991) are also readily available.

I take it as a matter of faith that any reasonable perspective on dream function must incorporate, or at least acknowledge, at minimum, the following sorts of data: (1) systematic observation of the contents and structure of dream reports collected under a sampling plan that is reasonably representative and under conditions where waking mnemonic loss or alteration is minimized; (2) systematic observation of the physiological/phenomenal states or conditions from which dreaming reliably is reported; (3) systematic observation of changes in dream contents and structure over the human life-span; and (4) systematic observation of the relationships of dream-report variables (incidence, contents, structure) with individual life-history variables (including experimental manipulations), with trait variables (e.g., character, cognitive status), and with sociocultural variables. What dreaming seems to be, in which states or conditions it seems to occur, how it seems to change during human development, and its relationships with other relevant variables surely must provide a good part of the foundation from which any plausible account of its function has to be elaborated.

In this spirit, I propose here to trace some functional implications of two sorts of underappreciated empirical observations about dreaming. *First,* it now seems apparent that dreaming is not limited to REM sleep, nor even to sleep itself; rather, dreaming seems to represent the mind's mode of conscious organization in any circumstance in which

11

external stimulation is reduced or occluded and voluntary control of consciousness is relinquished, while cognitive activation is maintained (Foulkes, 1985, ch. 2). *Second,* in early childhood, REM awakenings do not reliably generate dream recall, and there are indications that this failure may be one of dream generation rather than one of dream retrieval (ibid., 1985, ch. 3). Although it seems to me that these two classes of observation must have rich implications for the problem of dream function, neither has played much of a role in recent theorizing. For physiologically minded theorists, the multi-state basis of dreaming may be given lip service, but it likely is soon to be ignored as REM physiology is heralded as the explanation of all dream phenomena. Few theorists of any sort have made use of the ontogenetic data.

Blind Alleys

The *non*exclusive association of dream experience with REM sleep in mature humans reflects, first, the diffuse cerebral activation of the REM state, and, second, the presence of a level of conscious representational intelligence adequate to interpret nonconscious concomitants of this activation in a characteristic (narrative, world-simulating) way. However, because REM sleep is not the only state capable of supporting the sorts of brain activation and conscious mental organization associated with dreaming, then the function of dreaming cannot be identified with the function of REM sleep. Moreover, the ontogenetic observations in humans suggest that REM sleep must have arisen at a far more primitive evolutionary level than did the possibility of dreaming, which depends on a kind of representational intelligence generally lacking not only in other species but also in human infants.

The apparent late appearance (and puniness) of dreaming in the preschool years further suggests that dreaming, per se, can serve no significant functions in the regulation of relatively primitive behavioral systems. Other species share the behavioral systems, but not, presumably, the dreaming. Rather, if dreaming only emerges with the realization of representational intelligence and the kind of consciousness which it later entails, then one's search for systems functionally related to dreaming must begin at that higher plane of cognitive possibility.

However, it is likely that, even at this level, the search for teleologically construed functions of dreaming will prove fruitless. Traditionally, many laypersons and psychologists have evidenced a tendency to see design or purpose in dreaming: dreaming exists because it plays some critical role in life. The discovery of "a unique state of existence" (REM sleep) allegedly coextensive with dreaming may only have enhanced this teleological tendency. But it seems quite likely that REM dreaming could be only the fortuitous by-product of the evolution of other systems that independently have significant adaptive value (e.g., REM sleep, representational intelligence), but whose convergence in REM dreaming typically conveys few if any additional adaptive advantages. Further skepticism seems indicated by typical features of dreaming, including the apparently unsystematic way in which memory and knowledge are selected for realization in conscious dream imagery and the general night-to-night unpredictability of the substance of that imagery.

Effects

Function also can be construed as effect (Merton, 1957), and, in this sense, it would be quite remarkable were dreaming to be functionless. To spend, literally, years of our lives dreaming and to have nothing else at all thereby altered would imply a massive separation of dreaming from the rest of our existence. However, the major finding of the sort of systematic sampling that REM technology has permitted is just how closely connected our everyday dreaming seems to be with everything else that we do and are. Not only is it true that dream content generally simulates fairly well the texture of waking life, but it also is the case that waking individual differences (cognitive and characterological) tend to be directly reflected in dream experience. Thus, our dreaming existence is fully infused with the form and substance of our typical waking existence.

But is there evidence of comparable influence in wakefulness of our dream life? Are there waking consequences of the novel integrations that dreams achieve of their more familiar mnemonic sources? The evidence here is much less clear. For every anecdote of a waking life transformed by a remembered dream there must be at least as many instances of people who pride themselves on their summary dismissal of their dream life. That so many of our dreams are instantly forgotten also seems to pose a major problem. But clearly there could be effects that do not depend on waking *conscious* mediation, that is, the "remembered" dream. In fact, if as suggested earlier, the most significant functional relationships of dreaming are with other systems of symbolic processes, then any effects of dreaming would most likely be as invisible to ordinary consciousness as those systems themselves are. If dreaming's effects are largely at the level of the symbolic processes it engages, then these effects presumably will be elucidated only with considerably more difficult and subtle research than has yet seemed feasible, research in which there will be no plausible animal "models."

It has, of course, now become commonplace to propose "information processing" functions for dreaming and/or REM sleep. But the best evidence that REM sleep makes a difference in behavioral adaptation comes from subhumans in paradigms in which REM sleep deprivation affects learning or retention or in which novel adaptive demands lead to augmentation of REM sleep (e.g., Fishbein, 1981). It is by no means clear either that the kinds of performances required of animals in these studies or their level of mediation generalize well to humans or that dreaming as such could have anything to do with any animal's performance in any such situation. And in addition, it gives some pause for thought that compelling evidence has not been forthcoming for a role of REM sleep in specifically *human* information processing.

One would think that content reports of dreaming, reflecting information that obviously has been processed, might provide some clues as to information processing functions of human dreaming, but theorists typically start with memory (or, worse, the brain) and its alleged requirements, rather than with dream phenomenology. Clearly, we require more systematic analyses of which mnemonic representations are active during dreaming and of how they are being processed (e.g., Cavallero, Cicogna, and Bosinelli, 1988). Until such evidence is available, a major constraint on theorizing about dream function must be our ignorance about information processing in the dream itself.

Consciousness

The immediate function (effect) of dreaming is comparable to the immediate function of waking consciousness: making plausible sense of currently impinging or accessible information. All that is different about dreaming is the nature of this information. In the extreme case, the difference is between dreaming's diffusely active and unrelated mnemonic sources and waking's attentively focused and naturally patterned perceptual sources. But our best evidence now is that the cognitive interpretive system (Mandler, 1984) operating on information is, dreaming or waking, one and the same. This suggests that the search for "special" functions for dream consciousness may be misguided. To the degree that dream experience is different from waking experience, that difference only reflects the more dissociated sources of dreaming. The dissociation, in turn, reflects the requirement that we must lose both conscious self-awareness and conscious world-awareness to fall and stay asleep. Because sleep necessarily removes these two great sources of self-regulation, the dissociation of mental systems and contents from one another is inevitable.

It is testimony precisely to the continuity of dreaming and waking consciousness that dreams have many of the seemingly "curious" properties that they do. Waking consciousness presumably has evolved to reconcile two adaptive requirements: the construction of a *coherent* model of the world and the construction of a *faithful* model of the world. The strain between these two requirements must be considerably greater when informational inputs to consciousness are patterned neither by the environment nor by one's own intentions. That the generally coherent story lines of dreams end up with details that are almost always somewhat off-center, from the perspective of waking reality, indicates that, dreaming as in waking, coherence is not purchased at the total cost of fidelity. The informational sources available to dream consciousness do not, in fact, fit together very well. Dream consciousness makes the best story it can of them, nonetheless residually reflecting their diversity as well.

But why consciousness at all during sleep? Vertes (1984) proposed that non-REM sleep "rests" the brain, whereas REM sleep periodically "reawakens" it while permitting sleep to continue. The idea is that it is "detrimental" for the brain to remain for long, uninterrupted periods in a state of relative inactivity. We now know that for humans there is substantial capacity for conscious experience during non-REM sleep, as well as during REM sleep, where it reaches its fullest expression. Adaptively, however, the heightened activation of REM sleep has seemed something of a mixed blessing: although dreams arouse us, they also can disorient us. For other (dreamless) organisms, however, there may be no such cost attending REM arousal, whereas for the maturing human the adaptive benefits of conscious representational intelligence must far outweigh any side costs of dream-induced confusion which that intelligence permits.

Perhaps the significant continuity across species is that, during periods of prolonged inactivity and vulnerability, arousal is homeostatically regulated so that it becomes neither too low (corrected, for example, by periodic initiations of REM sleep and by episodic arousals from deep non-REM sleep associated with "night terrors") nor too high (corrected, for example, by awakenings from "anxiety dreams"), with the goal being to sustain the capacity for rapid engagement of whatever level of mentality a species typically employs in its adaptive encounters with the world.

Much evidence now suggests that the mentality we display in our REM dreaming is precisely the mentality we deploy in our more problematic encounters with waking reality: a mentality in which consciousness is constructing an evolving model of currently available information, a model that, in wakefulness, is at once sufficiently coherent to permit action and sufficiently sensitive to incoherence to forestall ignorant action.

Therefore, I believe that a conceptual realignment of questions about dream consciousness with those about waking consciousness may provide our best clues for inquiries into the functions of dream experience. In dreaming we do *not* have some unique cognitive configuration, which therefore might serve unique functions. Rather, the functions of dream consciousness may best be examined by considering the functions of consciousness more generally. Fortunately, after years of neglect, cognitive scientists now are beginning to address consciousness. Indeed, they have found that they must do so.

In human memory, for instance, to "remember" something is to become aware of it (Tulving, 1985). Thus, Tulving's (1983) concept of "conscious episodic recollection" best captures the sense of what we ordinarily mean when we say we remember. And, in the systematic study of human memory a number of significant, empirically based typologies seem to depend on a conscious vs. nonconscious distinction; for instance, declarative vs. procedural memory (Squire, 1986), explicit vs. implicit memory (Schacter, 1987), and effortful vs. automatic processing (Hasher and Zacks, 1979).

Both developmentally (e.g., Moscovitch, 1984) and neuropsychologically (e.g., Squire and Butters, 1984), it turns out that the most basic mnemonic distinction may be between memory with awareness and memory without awareness. As cognitive scientists tentatively turn toward the interface of cognition and affect, they also have acknowledged the theoretical primacy of an experiencing self (e.g., Mandler, 1984; Lewis and Michalson, 1983, 1984).

Thus, we also are beginning to see theoretical models of the role of consciousness in human information processing (e.g., Johnson-Laird, 1983; Mandler, 1984, 1985; Jackendoff, 1987). Although these models are by no means entirely compatible with one another, one point of moderate consensus is that consciousness must be a more skilled construction than automatic registration. This, in turn, implies cognitive prerequisites for our (human, adult) sort of consciousness, waking or sleeping, an implication entirely consistent with what we now know about the ontogeny of dream experience.

If consciousness (and, therefore, dreaming) is more a matter of active construction than of passive registration, then still another inconsistency bedevils reductionist theories that deduce human dreaming from the state of the cat's brain stem during REM sleep. Such theories take the sort of consciousness that permits dreaming to be a given across species, rather than being something itself highly problematic, requiring as much explanation as the dreaming so casually attributed to it. However, a good case can be made for the proposition that, however passive and mindless our *experience of dream events* may seem to be, *the ability to create dreams* in fact depends on an advanced and self-reflective consciousness generally lacking both in other species and in human infants (see Foulkes, 1990, for an elaboration of this view).

Dreaming and the Enlargement of Cognitive Psychology

In an especially incisive analysis, Foucault (1986) attacks the idea of "dream images." Images are, he says, the way by which we, awake, recollect the dream. Dreaming itself is a primary state of existence in a world—an imagined world, but a world nonetheless. This seems to me to be correct: although I now can have images of scenes from a lovely stay in the Black Forest, it seems to me very awkward to state that my stay in the Black Forest was experienced as "imagery." I did not experience imagery. I experienced the whole Black-Forest situation, including my place in it, my feelings and thoughts, and so forth.

This elemental phenomenological point links dreaming with consciousness in a broad sense—with "existence" or "experience." But in so doing, it seems to carry dreaming away from the possibility of cognitive psychological analysis. Cognitive psychologists study such things as "imagery," but there is a conspicuous lack of attention in the field to "existence."

If dreaming is a form of existence, something much more than the traditional conception of information processing (Globus, 1987), then whose province is it? Does it have to be abandoned to Dasein analysis? Does the road lead inevitably to some sort of mysticism? Were the skeptics right all along: dreaming lies beyond the grasp of empirical psychology? "Yes" answers, at this point, can only reflect failures of nerve and of effort. The efforts of the past few decades have transformed formerly intractable problems in psychology into ones that can at least be addressed meaningfully. This progress has come through young investigators challenging the narrower boundaries and presumptions of their elders. Dreaming can and should be a vehicle through which this process continues: if, for example, they come to see artificial intelligence as a limited and limiting model for psychology, then presumably they will move beyond it.

It is a disservice, whether by exponents or critics, to identify cognitive psychological approaches to dreaming with computational modeling or computer simulation. However "hot" this particular line now may seem to be (and many close students hold many reservations), there was a generic cognitive psychology before it came along (see, e.g., Humphrey, 1951; Johnson, 1955; Vinacke, 1952), and there will be one after it is gone. If a full account of human knowing and experiencing requires more than this one line permits, then we do not have to abandon either the subject matter or the rigor of our observation and thought, only that particular line of thinking.

There is something about dreaming that has always seemed to move people prematurely to forsake the possibility of disciplined empirical analysis. Indeed the signs are all about the United States now, as financial and intellectual support for systematic dream study has flagged, and a more whimsical, curiosity-centered, cottage industry of anything-goes dream "research" has moved in to fill the void. But this sort of regression is too easy; not only for its practitioners, who can pad their C.V.'s with minimal thought and effort, but also for cognitive psychology, which gets let off the hook. There is something too cozy about the symbiotic way in which cognitive psychologists passively write off dreaming to shrinks (or neuroscientists): if it is their thing, it is not our worry. Priority now in empirical dream psychology belongs precisely to challenging this unfortunate division of labor, this dichotomy of serious psychological study vs. either unserious psychological study or serious unpsychological study.

If dreaming cannot be written off, if it can be viewed and rigorously investigated within the framework of current varieties of cognitive psychology and cognitive science, then it may provide a goodly impetus for enlarging the scope of these fields. In dreaming, for example, feeling is a kind of knowing, a knowing of myself and a knowing of my environment. It is perhaps more difficult to erect artificial boundaries between this kind of knowing and other kinds of knowing in studying dream consciousness than in studying waking behavior. This is precisely why dreaming needs to be kept in a position of continuous challenge to anyone who claims to have a serious interest in human psychology. The challenge is this: if you cannot account for dreaming, you do not have it anywhere near right yet.

References

Arkin, A., Antrobus, J., and Ellman, S. (Eds.). (1978). *The Mind in Sleep: Psychology and Psychophysiology.* Hillsdale, N.J.: Lawrence Erlbaum Associates.

Cavallero, C., Cicogna, P., and Bosinelli, M. (1988). "Mnemonic Activation in Dream Production." In W. Koella, F. Obal, H. Schulz, and P. Visser (Eds.), *Sleep '86* pp. 91-94. Stuttgart: Gustav Fischer Verlag.

Ellman, S., and Antrobus, J. (Eds.). (1991). *The Mind in Sleep,* 2nd ed. Hillsdale, N.J.: Lawrence Erlbaum Associates.

Fishbein, W. (Ed.). (1981). *Sleep, Dreams and Memory.* New York: SP Medical and Scientific Books.

Foucault, M. (1986). "Dream, Imagination, and Existence." *Review of Existential Psycholoqy and Psychiatry,* 19: 29–78. [Original work published 1954]

Foulkes, D. (1985). *Dreaming: A Cognitive-Psychological Analysis.* Hillsdale, N.J.: Lawrence Erlbaum Associates.

————. (1990). "Dreaming and Consciousness." *European Journal of Cognitive Psychology* 2: 39–55.

Globus, G. (1987). *Dream Life, Waking Life: The Human Condition Through Dreams.* Albany: State University of New York Press.

Hasher, L., and Zacks, R. (1979). "Automatic and Effortful Processes in Memory." *Journal of Experimental Psychology: General,* 108, 356–388.

Humphrey, G. (1951). *Thinking: An Introduction to its Experimental Psychology.* London: Methuen and Co.

Jackendoff, R. (1987). *Consciousness and the Computational Mind.* Cambridge, Mass.: MIT Press.

Johnson, D. (1955). *The Psychology of Thought and Judgment.* New York: Harper & Brothers.

Johnson-Laird, P. (1983). *Mental Models: Towards a Cognitive Science of Language, Inference, and Consciousness.* Cambridge, Mass.: Harvard University Press.

Lewis, M., and Michalson, L. (1983). *Children's Emotions and Moods: Developmental Theory and Measurement.* New York: Plenum Press.

Lewis, M., and Michalson, L. (1984). "Emotion Without Feeling? Feeling Without Thinking?" *Contemporary Psychology,* 29: 919–920.

Mandler, G. (1984). *Mind and Body: Psychology of Emotion and Stress.* New York: W. W. Norton.

———. (1985). *Cognitive Psychology: An Essay in Cognitive Science.* Hillsdale, N.J.: Lawrence Erlbaum Associates.

Merton, R. (1957). *Social Theory and Social Structure,* rev. ed. Glencoe, Ill.: The Free Press.

Moscovitch, M. (Ed.) (1984). *Infant Memory: Its Relation to Normal and Pathological Memory in Humans and Other Animals.* New York: Plenum Press.

Schacter, D. (1987). "Implicit Memory: History and Current Status." *Journal of Experimental Psychology: Learning, Memory, and Cognition,* 13: 501–518.

Squire, L. (1986). "Mechanisms of Memory." *Science,* 232: 1612–1619.

——— and Butters, N. (Eds.). (1984). *Neuropsychology of Memory.* New York: Guilford Press.

Tulving, E. (1983). *Elements of Episodic Memory.* New York: Oxford University Press.

———. (1985). " Memory and Consciousness." *Canadian Psychology,* 26: 1–12.

Vertes, R. (1984). "Brainstem Control of the Events of REM Sleep." *Progress in Neurobiology,* 22: 241–288.

Vinacke, W. (1952). *The Psychology of Thinking.* New York: McGraw-Hill.

2

John McManus, Charles D. Laughlin,
and Jon Shearer ━━━━━━━━━━━━━━━━━━━━━━━━━

The Function of Dreaming in the Cycles of Cognition: A Biogenetic Structural Account

Dreaming is an integral part of the cyclical structure of cognized reality.[1] It is as essential to cognition as is thinking itself. Dreaming is, in fact, an aspect of thinking, without which what we normally associate with "thinking" becomes sterile, habitual, and distorted. Dreaming acts as a psychic glue to hold together the thought system and enrich it with the capacity for expansion and development. Dreaming is part of the infrastructure of the edifice of thought—so much so that to understand the function of dreaming we must develop a broader understanding about the organization and operation of consciousness and the brain. An exploration of the context of dreaming within the cycles of cognition will lead us to see that the function of dreaming is at the same time neurobiological and symbolic.

The Cognized Environment

Reality as we come to know it is a cognized entity and is formally constrained in its nature by the internal structures of the perceiving organism. Both the external world and the self, as we know them, are essentially symbolic models.[2] These models exist within the immensely intricate organization of the fibers composing our nervous system, especially within the cerebral cortex.[3] This system enters the world with an evolutionarily evolved basic structure, its components varying in their degree of openness or closedness to growth and modification. The nervous system is an organ within the developing cellular organization of living tissue, and as with the cellular structure in general, the nervous system follows an evolutionarily constrained course in its development.

But the nervous system performs unique functions within the organism. Among its other activities, it is the nervous system that knows.

Neurognosis

The course by which the nervous system comes to know about self and world is a well ordered one from beginning to end. The neural networks constituting our knowledge and experience have their developmental origin in initial *neurognostic*[4] structures that are present before, at, or just after birth, and the organization of which is largely genetically determined. Neonatal perceptual systems, for example, are neurognostically structured to apprehend and explore objects (Burnham 1987; Streri and Spelke 1988). Another good example of neurognostic structure is the bilateral asymmetry of cerebral functions, apparent in the anatomy of the fetal brain and producing an alternation between the digital-logical and temporal planning associations attributed to the left hemisphere and the analogue-metaphorical and atemporal gestalt associations attributed to the right hemisphere.

The developmental reorganization of these early structures is genetically regulated as well. Some potential organizations deteriorate, others become active, and still others remain relatively latent and undeveloped (see Changeux, 1985; Edelman, 1987; Varela, 1979). This selectivity is one reason why there is such remarkable plasticity in cognitive adaptation to the essentially chaotic and evolving nature of the self and the world.[5] There is a great deal of evidence that the relative richness or poverty of the outer operational environment has a determinant effect upon the complexity and growth of neural networks in ontogenesis (Diamond, 1988; Renner and Rosenzweig, 1987).

Autopoiesis and the Cognized Environment

The self and its environment are inextricably locked in an intricate dance, forever coupled in an increasingly complex process. The self alone is a relative abstraction from the matrix of its environment that comes to define itself through the emerging complexity of its own organization. Its principal attribute is the production and conservation of this self-organization while fulfilling the demands of adaptation to events in its environmental surroundings. Such a system is *autopoietic*, or self-generating.

We come to understand ourselves and our world in a symbolic way. We construct models of each through a complex process of neurological transformation. Models are organizations of neural tissue that grow and become more mature and ramified in their functioning. From an enormously complex system of such models we erect a *cognized environment.* The cognized environment is how we know and experience our self and our world, and yet the system of neurological transformations that mediate the cognized environment is part of the very world within which we are embedded and to which we must adapt in order to survive. Both the world and our self can be considered *transcendental* relative to our understanding—relative to our cognized environment. The internally constructed models that make up our cognized environment are to potential reality as maps are to geographical reality. Each element of our cognized environment and the total organized field of such elements is a symbolic correspondent of many of the forces impinging upon the organism. The sum total of these forces affecting the cognized environment may be termed the *operational environment.*[6] The operational environment is composed of both processes external to and affecting the self from without and processes internal to the organism, as well as interrelation between the two.

Our cognized environment may thus be considered an organization of neural models, and as such may be understood to be a hierarchically organized symbolic system. Within this system, networks of models are nested within other networks whose content is composed of symbolic transformations of forces affecting the tissues of the cognized environment. These transformations have their material reality in neural coordinations, or *entrainments,*[7] whose initial forms are neurognostic, whose eventual developmental complexity will be variable, and whose evocation may be environmentally linked. What we understand about our world, including ourselves, is the function of a set of entrainments of symbolic models that stabilize in organization while at the same time they operate to differentiate aspects of self and world and adapt to these aspects.[8]

Intentionality

The ongoing, moment-by-moment operation of the cognized environment is essentially *intentional* in organization; that is, neural networks tend to organize themselves about a phenomenal object. That phenomenal object is also mediated by a neural network and is, for the moment, the central focus of cognitive, affective, metabolic and motor operations for the organism (Neisser, 1976; pp. 20ff). Intentionality derives primarily from a characteristic dialogue between the prefrontal cortex (Fuster, 1980; Stuss and Benson, 1986) and the sensorial cortex of the human brain (Laughlin, 1986; 1988c; 1988d). Subsidiary structures entrained as a consequence of the dialogue between prefrontal and sensorial processes may be located over a wide expanse of cortical (e.g., parietal visual attention structures, right lobe imaginal structures, left lobe language processing structures), subcortical (e.g., hippocampal recognition structures, brain stem arousal structures, limbic emotional structures), and endocrinal (e.g., hypothalamic and pituitary structures) areas.

Experience[9] is a function of this intentional dialogue, and involves the constitution of a phenomenal world within the sensorium, the latter being a field of neural activity that arises and dissolves in temporally sequential epochs. These are coordinated with cognitive processes that associate meaning and form in a unitary frame (Laughlin, 1988d). The sensory and the cognitive-intentional aspects of experience are active products of neurological functioning, and they are exquisitely ordered in the service of abstract pattern recognition, both in moment-by-moment adult experience (Gibson, 1969) and in development from the earliest periods of pre- and perinatal consciousness (Chamberlain in Verny, 1987; Laughlin, 1990a; Parmalee and Sigman, 1983). The object of experience may be generated both externally via the sensory apparatus of the sensorium and internally via the imaginal structures of the sensorium.

The total field of experience arising each moment is mediated by what we call the *conscious network*, a continuously changing field of neural entrainments that may incorporate (re-entrain) any particular network one moment and exclude (disentrain) it the next (Laughlin et al., 1990). Conscious experience is not a simple function that may be located in one place in the brain—say in the hippocampus or in the frontal lobes. Rather it is produced by a complex and ever-changing pattern of neural activity occurring over a wide area of cortical and subcortical tissue.

The intensity of involvement of prefrontal processes is of prime importance in determining the quality of experience whether in waking, trance, dream or other state. Prefrontal involvement in conscious network may range along a continuum from *hypointentionality* (weak involvement of prefrontal processes; i.e., somnolence, bored, and dulled-out states) at one extreme through *intentionality* (the normal range of attention and awareness during waking consciousness) to *hyperintentionality* (intense involvement of prefrontal processes; i.e., meditative-contemplative states, absorption states, lucid dreaming [see below for definition of the latter]) at the other extreme. Among other factors, the intensity of intentionality will determine the extent of awareness present in waking or dreaming experience; that is, to what extent self-reflection, recognition, rational comprehension, energetic exploration, exercise of planning, continuity of experience, rational modulation of affect, and so forth are present to consciousness.

The cognized environment is therefore conceived as an "autopoietic" system (Maturana and Varela, 1980; Varela, 1979). The action or motor component of the cognized environment operates to control what arises within experience so as to fulfill anticipated events within the internal bounds of tolerance, a feedforward process we have termed the *empirical modification cycle,* or EMC (Laughlin and d'Aquili, 1974; pp. 84ff; see also Pribram, 1971; Neisser, 1976; Arbib 1972, Powers, 1973; Gray, 1982; and Varela, 1979, for consonant views). This feedforward process is required for learning and for transformation of models confronting the flux and ultimately incomprehensible complexity of a transcendental world.

The developmental interaction between neural models and the operational environment involves selection, growth, entrainment and re-entrainment, and hierarchical organization of initially neurognostic structures. Neural models become relatively fixed in organization and structure, and thus produce *creodes;* that is, become regularized, recursive, and predictable in cognitive content and response relative to the intentional object (Waddington, 1957; see also Piaget, 1971; 1985). It makes sense, therefore, to speak of an individual's cognized environment and its constituent models as an autopoietic system of creodes adapting to its operational environment. *Culture,* in this account, is conceived as socially patterned creodes in individual cognized environments, as well as the social procedures by means of which those creodes are established (Turner, 1983). The more important a particular pattern of entrainment is to a society, the more the society will impose related environmental conditions upon its young.

Neurognosis and Chronobiology

The functioning of the cognized environment, and indeed of the entire organism, depends upon a daily cycle of temporally structured, recurrent, and neurognostic patterns of entrainment. These patterns of activity are generally called *circadian rhythms* (Halberg, 1969; Moore-Ede, Sultzman, and Fuller 1982; Gooddy, 1988). The circadian system is characterized by (1) creodic subsystems that persist under a variety of external conditions, (2) creodes that exhibit a degree of closedness relative to external stimulation, (3) creodes driven by self-regulated oscillators that are typically (but not inevitably) coupled to each other, and (4) creodes that have the capacity to be entrained by factors in the outer operational environment which exhibit a given periodicity—these being termed *zeitgebers* (German for "time-givers"). *Zeitgebers* are events that drive the system through metabolic or sensory stimulation and that range in form from purely physical cues such as the light-dark cycle and diet to social cues like clock time and social rituals (Regal and Connolly, 1980; Zerubavel, 1981; 1985). The effect of changed routines and the application of physical and social *zeitgebers* may be to either disrupt the circadian system or bring it gradually into phase with external events (Folkard 1981).

One major circadian rhythm—and one closely allied to the sleep-wake cycle—is the core body temperature that has a range of 0.5 degrees Celsius with its lowest point typically in the early hours of the morning (around 3:00–5:00 a.m.). A pronounced rise in temperature takes place during the early waking hours, typically around 6:00 to 10:00 a.m., with a more gentle climb evident for the remainder of the day with a peak in the early evening around 8:00 p.m. Core body temperature and other such rhythms are now known to be due mainly to endogenous, rhythmically operating neuroendocrine systems that may be influenced, but not eliminated by exogenous *zeitgebers* (Aschoff, 1981; Moore-Ede et al., 1982; Suda, Hayaishi, and Nakagawa, 1979; Wever, 1979). For example, subjects placed in isolation, devoid of all temporal cues, tend to continue to exhibit a daily pattern of somatic functioning with a periodicity of slightly less than twenty-five hours.

The human species evolved as an essentially diurnal primate. That means that our species has developed a cognized environment and related somatic systems naturally oriented to adaptation to the external operational environment during daylight and rest and recuperation during the night. The core body temperature and the sleep-wake cycle that evolved to function in a diurnal animal can become desynchronized under certain circumstances (Wever, 1979; Moore-Ede et al., 1982), and this may lead to distinct adaptive problems such as those faced by night-shift workers (see Akerstedt, 1977; Monk and Folkard ,1983; Reinberg, et al., 1978; Shearer, 1982). It is now well established that the individual in modern society who is exposed to shift work is in a constant state of disruption of his or her internal oscillators so that total adaptation to the demands of shift-work is probably rare or nonexistent (see Lobban and Tredre, 1966). In other words, as diurnal animals, our internal functioning is radically disturbed when forced to become nocturnal (Naitoh, 1982; Akerstedt, 1982).

Among the problems faced by shift workers, none is more dramatic than sleep related deficits (see Kogi, 1982; Torii et al., 1982; Foret and Benoit, 1977). There is general agreement among most researchers that shift workers complain most often about sleep disturbances—primarily about sleep maintenance insomnia (difficulty staying asleep), sleep onset insomnia (difficulty getting to sleep) and shortened total sleep time

(Coleman, 1986; Harrington, 1978). EEG studies report similar findings (Dahlgren, 1981; Matsumoto, 1978; Torsvall, Akerstedt, and Gillberg, 1981). The reduction in total sleep time appears to be at the expense of stage 2 NREM and REM sleep, rather than slow wave sleep (stages 3 and 4), which is not significantly changed. Of interest here is the constant finding of shortened REM onset latencies, indicating that day sleep exhibits the same characteristics as lengthy morning naps or extended sleep with REM predominating and slow wave sleep reemerging (Karacan et al., 1970; Maron, Rechtschaffen, and Wolpert, 1964; Webb, 1982). In general, the data on sleep disturbances in shift workers concur with the view that sleep stage characteristics and the production of sleep fragmentation are, to a great extent, a function of circadian placement and length of the sleep period (Frese and Harwick, 1984; Naitoh, 1982; Webb and Agnew, 1974).

The circadian system, including the temporally patterned changes in the cognized environment, represents, then, an internal temporal order coproduced by internal oscillating creodes and by the afferent effects of *zeitgebers* in the environment. Numerous authorities have suggested that human well-being depends on the maintenance of this order and that repeated or long-lasting disturbances in the natural cycle may have detrimental effects upon functioning (see Akerstedt and Torsvall, 1978; Aschoff, 1978). We will suggest later that these data indicate quite clearly both the natural function of sleep and dreaming, and the human costs of disrupting that function. We must first, however, develop a greater appreciation of the symbolic function before returning to the crucial role of cycles in neurocognitive functioning.

Dreaming and the Symbolic Function

The biological functions of sleep are multifarious. Dreaming, as a special case of sleep function, is a natural and integral operation of the cyclical organization of cognition. The cognized environment maintains its organizational integrity through three coordinating functions or entrainments:

1. Reciprocal entrainment between the cognized environment and its external operational environment.
2. Reciprocal entrainments between the overall organization of the cognized environment and that of its constituent creodes.
3. Reciprocal entrainments among the constituent creodes.

Dreaming has an impact on and role within each of these coordinations. Its principal role lies with the third of these, coordination among the creodic networks constituting the overall cognized environment, and indirectly with the synchronization between the cognized environment and the operational environment. These coordinations are accomplished by dreaming within the cyclic functioning of the cognitive system, through a shift in balance of the architecture underlying the sensorium.

The architecture underlying the cognized environment is hypothesized to entail ever-changing patterns of entrainment arising within a field of potential entrainments defined by the three sets of architectural relations just discussed (Laughlin, et al., 1990): *hierarchical organization of the neural structures, bilateral asymmetry of cerebral functions, prefrontal-sensorial intentional polarity.* All three of these sets of relations influence the quality and intensity of intentionality; that is, the precise arrangement of associations and functions linked to the network operating between the prefrontal processes and the sensorial ones. All three therefore have an impact on the exact relationship between the cognized and operational environments. The intensity of intentionality is all-important in understanding the function of dreaming. For example, in hypointentional states in general, and those characteristic of dreaming among most Euroamerican adults:

1. The hierarchical control relations within the cognized environment would tend to break down and activity would center on more molecular structures and those lower in the system.

2. Nondominant hemispheric cortical functioning would tend to predominate; that is, emphasis would be on the imaginal, less logical functioning.

3. The balance of control in prefrontosensorial polarity would tend to shift toward the sensorial cortex and away from the prefrontal cortex.

As a general consequence of these operations, hypointentionality should

1. Lead to polysemic attribution of meaning to material experienced in the sensorium.

2. Emphasize transductive ("lateral," or "paleo") logic, which allows logically inconsistent elements or systems of meaning to coexist and interact.

3. Allow for metaphorical rather than logical representation of system activities.

4. Thereby lead to a greater probability of entrainment across networks constituting the cognized environment.

5. And increase the probability of internal cohesion of the cognized environment while actively adapting to the operational environment.

It is our contention that this process of structural transformation is exactly reflected by what most Euroamericans experience as dreaming. The typical Euroamerican dreaming experience is often characterized by poor recall during the waking state and among dream states, lack of thematic continuity between dream states (although this may be influenced during recall by interpretation), little or no control of dream themes or the exercise of planning between scenes. Dreaming is usually (but not always) free-wheeling and scattered in content, and in terms of exercise of will, the dream-ego is relatively passive (Hunt 1989). However, individuals who routinely experience lucid dreams (associated with more intense intentionality) may on occasion also experience dreams that are relatively fragmented in content and subjectively passive (Deborah Hillman, personal communication).

The adaptive functions of dreaming in this hypointentional sense are twofold: (1) dreaming primarily aids conservation and stability of the cognized environment by providing the means by which contradictory models may be assimilated to each other and entrained in a medium relatively free of logical constraints; (2) dreaming secondarily aids in expansion and development of the cognized environment by introducing new information, including previously contradictory information, to awareness by weaving that information into a greater fabric of entrainments arising within the three sets of relations discussed previously.

As suggested by our discussion of chronobiology, this set of functions of dreaming is seen as part of a more general cycle of functioning that is described by periodic fluctuations in patterns of entrainment constituting the cognized environment. This fluctuation of neural processing and entrainment ranges from (1) orientation toward adaptation to the external operational environment characterized by entrainments incorporating relatively higher intentionality, hierarchical control, dominant hemisphere logical faculties, and so on, to (2) orientation toward the demands of internal coordination incorporating relatively lower intentionality, hierarchical control, nondominant hemisphere imaginal faculties, and so on. Intermediate states ranging between these poles would include such states as relaxation, fantasy ("day dreaming") and play (see Laughlin and McManus, 1982, on the functions of play).

Penetration and the Symbolic Function

The development and activity of the cognized environment is thoroughly symbolic in nature. The *symbolic function* refers to the relationship between the sensorial object and the cognitive, neuroendocrine and other somatic processes organized about the object.[10] The symbolic function of the nervous system is that by which the whole network of models mediating the "meaning" of an object is *penetrated* by (i.e., becomes entrained to) the model mediating the sensory or imaginal object (Webber and Laughlin, 1979). The object, whether anticipated, imagined, or actual, is mediated by a network of cells that provides a partial meaning. The object is often referred to as a *symbol* when discussed in this context. The cognitive associations penetrated and intended upon the object—that is, the perceptual, conceptual, imaginal, affective, arousal, metabolic and motor networks that become configurationally entrained to the network formed between the prefrontal "subject" and the sensorial "object"—function to extend and elaborate the meaning of the object-as-symbol for the subject.

Homeomorphogenesis

These multiple, often complex entrainments tend (during development or enculturation) to form an intentional creode[11] with the object being alternatively its evocator (the object arises first and penetrates to its "meaning"), its fulfillment (the "meaning" goes looking for the object to complete itself), and its expression (the "meaning" uses the object to communicate itself). The communicative interaction between the various neurophysiological and other somatic systems that become entrained within the creode we term homeomorphogenesis.[12] For example, neuroendocrine systems may communicate unconscious biochemical transductions to cortical imaginal systems, the activity of which the individual may experience (or become aware of) in dream, trance, or fantasy. In turn, as new research in psychoneuroimmunology has shown (Ader, 1980), concentration on imagery may homeomorphogenically produce neuroimmunological transductions at the site of lesions, or produce enhanced production of endorphins to relieve pain (Prince, 1982).

All of the preceding applies directly to the function of dreaming, for dreaming is a thoroughly symbolic activity. Dreaming is a process that is neurological in nature and symbolic in cognitive content. Dream objects are symbolic elements associated with multiple, polysemic cognitive associations, much like a toy magnet held under a piece of paper may become the nexus of iron filings sprinkled on the paper. But in this case (and stretching the metaphor a bit), the iron filings may as easily fulfill themselves by producing and moving the magnet, as the magnet may evoke the iron filings. The activity of the iron filings may represent the ongoing neurological and somatic activities during sleep and the movements of the magnets the symbolic elements that constitute dreaming. The autopoietic dictate of self-conservation and self-generation pertain across the board and dreaming may be understood as a structured set of subprocesses which carry out an important and natural role in that more general process.

Cycles of Consciousness

One of the salient characteristics of the cognized environment is that it is experienced as a flow of recurring realities. The pattern of entrainments that mediate the cognized environment tend to cycle in a circadian manner, regulated by internal oscillators in interaction with external *zeitgebers*. Each moment of consciousness is a fresh re-entrainment of the conscious network that is constrained to the general limits of the circadian cycle and that may be experienced as anything from a continuity to a radical transformation relative to the moments that have gone before. Because the shifting entrainment of the conscious network manifests recurrent, gross temporal patterns, we may experience "chunks" of the cognized environment which we recognize as distinct. The circadian cycle of re-entrainment of the conscious network is neurognostically structured to address the dual demands of adaptation to the external operational environment and the organization of internal subsystems. This bipolarity relates both to the function of dreaming and to the stress (such as experienced by shift workers) that is produced by cultural interference with the natural alternation between external adaptive processing and internal adaptive processing.

Phases and Warps of Consciousness

Experience, as we have said, is constituted within the intentional dialogue between the prefrontal processes and sensorial processes of the brain. The total field of this dialogue is the conscious network, and awareness of bits of experience is a principle component of this field. Because the definitive characteristic of awareness is *re*collection, *re*membering, or *re*cognition of patterns in experience, awareness tacitly refers to a role played by knowledge in the constitution of experience. Furthermore, because the recursive quality of experience forms detectable patterns and may thus be cognized as such, reflexive knowledge about consciousness itself involves knowledge of experiential episodes. If an episode is perceived as a salient unit, then it may be cognized as distinct from other episodes, and perhaps labeled; for example, I am *awake, stoned, depressed, dreaming, angry, out of my body,* and so forth. These cognized episodes of experience, and their mediating neurocognitive entrainments, are called *phases of consciousness.* The points of experiential and neurophysiological transformation between phases are called *warps of consciousness* (Laughlin et al., 1986).

We hypothesize that phases of consciousness cycle on a circadian basis as a neurognostic alternation between those phases structured to optimally promote adaptation to the external operational environment (we call these *being awake* in our culture) and those phases designed to optimally promote adaptation, to each other, of subsystems within the internal operational environment (we call these *being asleep*). The intentionality (prefrontal-sensorial dialogue) of consciousness alternates between that configured about objects and relations in the external operational environment, and that configured about objects-as-symbols of internal accommodation.

Phase Attributes

Within the normal range of human consciousness, phases are rarely if ever recognized by their formal properties (e.g., structural complexity, predominant logical principles), however efficacious those properties may be in producing the phase. Furthermore, phases are never identified by the full complement of ever-changing information passing through the sensorium. Rather, phases are commonly defined on a small set of recurrent *phase attributes* that are recognized within the far greater set of available attributes. There are innumerable attributes of the experience of dreaming that could define a dream phase; yet, for example, in many cultures such as the Pukapuka (Beaglehole and Beaglehole, 1938; p. 307) the dream phase is interpreted as the period of the day during which the soul may move about in the world independent of the body and converse with rocks and spiders and other objects. Tibetan yogis, on the other hand, interpret the dream phase as illusory phenomena reflected in the mirror of the mind (Chang 1963). Of course, as we shall see, dream phases may be ignored and remain relatively ill defined as phases.

Phase attributes may be bodily sensations ("I am hungry," "I hurt here"), feelings ("I am angry"), sensory cues ("I am listening to music," "I am watching TV"), or activities ("I am jogging"). They may also involve characteristic relations among perceived objects ("I dreamed I was swimming at the bottom of the ocean"). Phases may be defined as well on qualities of thought: my thoughts are "discursive'" "scattered," "profound," "lucid," or "clever." The important point to remember is that societies typically define and socialize a set of possible phases of consciousness for their members who are socialized to recognize the appropriate attributes as definitive of their own and others' states of mind (see Tart, 1975). This conditioned recognition sets boundaries for culture members on the range of entrainments occurring during the cycle of consciousness. Part of the process of limiting the range of phases is by way of conditioning attention, thus culturally controlling the intentional processes.

Warps and Rituals

To understand the role of phases in consciousness, it is necessary to appreciate the vital importance of warps in producing and controlling phases. Although a phase is a discrete, cognized strip of unfolding experience dominating the sensorium, a warp has a causal influence on the organization of the phase succeeding it, and a causal influence on the cessation of the phase preceding it. A warp is a minuscule neurophysiological version of Victor Turner's (1979) *liminality:* an event standing between two cognized strips of experience (see also Gennep 1960). A liminal event is a sort of ritual-symbolic doorway or threshold (e.g., a rite of passage) between statuses. As a social activity, a liminal event may be much longer than a warp, but it is similar in being essentially antistructural and transformational in function. The warp is *disentraining* in nature and characterized by organizational chaos relative to the order of phases. For example, if one is "happy" one moment and "sad" the next, then somewhere between these two phases is a warp that involves the cessation of the happy phase and that produces the sad phase.

The liminal aspect of the warp metaphorically implies a kind of door or threshold through which the stream of consciousness must pass when it "leaves" one phase behind and "enters" another phase. There are three things to remember about warps: (1) warps are typically short in duration and consist of rapid neural *re-entrainment* of the conscious network, or some subsystem thereof; (2) although warps exhibit structural properties, most people are not aware of warps, but only of phases; and (3) warps may be induced by a large variety of *drivers* originating both internally and externally. It is apparent that if control of phases of consciousness is to be exercised by the individual or the society, the control must be exerted especially over warps and their driving mechanisms.

In other words, control must be exercised over the properties of consciousness *about which the individual is typically least aware.* Directing the intentional processes to the warps will often transform warps into phases, which will have the effect of transforming the organization and experiential properties of subsequent phases (see Tibetan dream yoga later). Moreover, ritualization of dream-related warps and "incubation" of dream content is a common feature in cultures that consider incorporating knowledge about and "power" from the dream experience important to healthy life (see O'Nell, 1976; Halifax, 1979; Grunebaum and Caillois, 1966; Tedlock, 1987a; Hillman, 1987; Laughlin, McManus, and d'Aquili, 1990).

It is therefore no coincidence that when control of alternative phases of consciousness is deemed salient and necessary, societies construct rituals—patterned activities replete with a variety of drivers (chanting, drumming, flickering lights, meditation objects, mnemonics, etc.)—and place them precisely at the warps (Turner, 1979; Gennep, 1960; Eliade, 1964; Grimes. 1982; McManus in d'Aquili et al., 1979). By focusing the intentional processes on culturally salient symbols, individual neurocognitive, affective, motor, and perceptual systems may be penetrated and re-entrained relative to socially desired goals (Laughlin, 1990c; Laughlin et al., 1986). And, as we shall see, such goals may involve integration of waking and dream consciousness.

Cross-Phasing

We have used the "flow" or "stream" of consciousness very loosely. Although sensory experiences appear to flow through consciousness, they are actually produced by the moment-by-moment re-entrainment of the networks making up the conscious network. The transfer of information across warps does not really involve the movement of something from "here" to "there," but rather requires a *minimal re-entrainment* of the networks mediating that information to the conscious network (see Varela, 1979). This transfer of continuity in the entrainments across warps we call *cross phasing* (Shearer, Moffitt, and Hoffman, 1979; Laughlin, et al., 1986; p. 120). This is literally what we mean when we say we *re*member a dream; there is some continuity of entrainment of conscious network between the dream phase and the waking phase. Some degree of cross phasing is a necessary, though not a sufficient, condition for integration within *polyphasic* consciousness (i.e., consciousness characterized by a multiphasic concept of self and world).

Cross phasing, of course, may be blocked or inhibited. The individual, or the whole social group for that matter, may be conditioned such that a minimal re-entrainment of neurocognitive systems does not occur across the warp. In that event, re-entrainment of the succeeding phase is insufficient for information pertaining to the preceding phase to be available to consciousness. This amounts to a conditioned amnesia in one phase of consciousness about what has happened in another phase of consciousness. For example, data on possession cults cross-culturally suggest that in some cultures such amnesia occurs between the possession state and the normal waking state (Bourguignon ,1976). More to the point, in some societies, such as our own, where dream recall in waking consciousness is discouraged or ignored as irrelevant to waking ego (Ullman, 1979, 1982), effective cross phasing is blocked and consciousness becomes conditioned into a state of *monophasia* (consciousness characterized by a concept of self and world generated from information gained largely from a single phase). It is important to recognize that *the enculturation of consciousness into monophasia or degrees of polyphasia is never fortuitous, but is a lawful consequence of how a society's culture is oriented vis-à-vis the inherent, neurognostic cycles of neurocognitive functioning* (see e.g., Hillman 1990.).

Types of Cultures Relative to Dreaming

Armed with both the chronobiological view of the cycles of conscious network entrainment, and the theory of cross phasing, it is theoretically possible to align societies on a continuum defined by the extent to which they (1) rely on polyphasic entrainment in their cultural view of the ego, or self-concept, and the world, or (2) encourage individual members via ritual to explore polyphasic experiences. For the sake of discussion, we can simplify this continuum by dividing it into four somewhat arbitrary types of culture and apply it to our analysis of the function of dreaming at the level of culture. We may thus speak of four types of culture relative to dreaming as follows.

1. Monophasic Cultures. Monophasic cultures are those that tend to value experiences occurring only in "normal" waking phases. These are cultures that effectively give credence to only those phases of consciousness that lie at the external adaptation pole of the circadian cycle. Exploration of dream and other alternative phases is typically proscribed, disparaged, or simply not socially facilitated in development. Blocked cross phasing is common in such cultures, especially when the group socializes members into a chronically stressful life-style. Institutional measures (such as schooling, religious training, family enculturation) may be taken to creodically limit the range of conscious network entrainments to only those having "practical" application in the "real" world. Individuals giving undue credence to dreams and other alternative phases may be labeled *abnormal, crazy, deviant, pathological, a sorcerer,* or *extraordinary*. This type of dream culture is associated with a materialist world-view.

Mainstream North American culture offers an example of monophasic culture, although there now exist movements that encourage the exploration of dreaming and the inclusion of dream experiences into a broader sense of self (Hillman, 1987; Tedlock, 1987b; p. 8–12).

2. Minimally Polyphasic Cultures. Minimally polyphasic cultures are those that seem oriented primarily toward waking phases, but that also give (often great) credence to the exploration of dreaming and other alternative phases. Exploration of dreaming may be institutionally encouraged via ritual, and emphasis is placed upon the proper interpretation of dream symbolism in terms comprehensible to the waking ego and within the context of the society's world view. The society may espouse a cosmology that gives meaning to dreaming and there may be dream specialists (or oneirocritics) that offer socially appropriate interpretations of dream experiences in strict accordance with the cosmology. There is little recognition of "flying" shamans and dream trips to multiple realities. Shamans, where they exist, are recognized for practical purposes such as healing, dream interpretation, divination, and so forth.

Dreams among Moroccans (Kilborne, 1974) are frequently interpreted by oneirocritics in such a way that they become "culturized" and socially appropriate to the interpreter. A similar pattern is apparent among the Mae Enga of New Guinea (Meggitt, 1962), where oneirocritics interpret dreams more in terms of the social situation of the dreamer than the literal content of the dream.

3. Fully Polyphasic Cultures. Fully polyphasic cultures are those whose cosmologies recognize multiple levels of reality, some or all of which may be explored via dreaming. All, or a portion, of the society's members are guided into dream experiences by way of ritual and instruction, perhaps under the aegis of a shaman or master adept. Extreme measures may be taken to produce alternative phases of consciousness, including what we in our culture would label *lucid dreaming*. Among these are formal meditation techniques, ingesting of psychotropic drugs, ordeals, fasting, pilgrimage to sacred places, and so on. Transpersonal experiences in dream and other phases are encouraged, actively sought, and highly valued. The dream-world or trance-world may well be valued more highly than the "mundane" world of "normal" waking consciousness. There are often a few individuals recognized as especially adept at entering "supramundane" realities and manipulating the "power" derived from such journeys for the benefit or detriment of others. This type of society tends to be nonmaterialistic in its cosmology, and although interpretation of dream experiences may be in cosmological terms, there is little emphasis on interpretation in waking ego terms; that is, experiences had in dream phases are fully meaningful as they occur.

According to Kracke (1979, 1987), everybody shares their dreams among the Kagwahiv of Brazil. Everyone may interact with supernatural beings, commune with a loved one and divine the future while dreaming. Moreover, shamans may actually influence future events while dreaming, as well as seek the aid of supernatural beings in healing and aid in the birth of a future shaman. The same pattern appears among the Kalapalo of Brazil (Basso, 1987; p. 88), who conceive of dreaming as a state of wandering of the dreambody and participation in events that inform the people of aspects of their self. Occasionally beings visit the dreamer and are the source of power and the ability to alter events, and they may lead to the dreamer becoming a shaman. Because the real world of spiritual forces is normally invisible in waking life, the Jivaro of Ecuador facilitate the encounter with supernatural souls with psychotropic drugs (Harner 1973) and then achieve union with the souls in a dream (Harner, 1962; p. 261).

4. Transcendental Polyphasic Cultures. These are cultures that are both fully polyphasic as just described and believe that exploration of dreaming and other alternative phases is a route to the realization of an ultimate Transcendental Experience (e.g., union with a godhead, experience of the essence of mind, void consciousness, enlightenment.). Exploration of the dream phases is not an end in itself, but rather a means to attaining an experience of that which is beyond, and perhaps the source of, phenomenal reality. Individuals who have attained the Transcendental Experience are held in high status as the greatest healers, guides, leaders, sages, and teachers—individuals who are wise relative to ultimate truth.

Tibetan dream yogis are taught to become aware of, open up, and control the hypnagogic warp between the waking phase and the sleep phase and the hypnopompic warp between the sleep phase and the waking phase (Chang, 1963). Awareness eventually transforms these warps into phenomenological phases that can be sustained for lengthy periods of time. The yogi is taught to transform his or her body into the form of their principal deity and to enter the hypnogogic and subsequent dream phases as the deity. This procedure involves the maintenance of an extraordinary degree of concentration and awareness throughout the dream phases (see also Laughlin, McManus and Shearer 1983).

Conclusions

In summary then, biogenetic structural theory holds (with Roffwarg, Muzio, and Dement, 1966; and others) that the function of dreaming is essentially developmental. We have seen that the primary task of the higher brain centers is to construct a cognized environment from the nascent, neurognostic structures of the pre- and perinatal nervous system. The cognized environment is a vast system of models pertaining to the "real world," or operational environment, including oneself as an organism. These models may be entrained to the conscious network to produce our moment-by-moment flow of experience. The models mediating experience operate within the field of associations entrained in the dialogue between the prefrontal intentional processes and the sensorial processes, and they become routinized in organization (form creodes) within cyclically recurring patterns of entrainment. These gross and recurring patterns of entrainment are recognized by their recurrent attributes, are usually cognized as recurrent by the individual, generally during enculturation by his or her society, and are experienced as phases of consciousness. Because our species has evolved as a diurnal primate, phases of consciousness tend to take on a daily, or circadian rhythm of recurrence that alternates between those specialized to encounter and cognize events in the outer operational environment (we call these *being awake* in our culture) and those specialized to establish a transformative, reorganizational and homeomorphogenic interaction between models and other somatic processes (we call this *being asleep* in our culture).

Although the biological functions of sleep are manifold (Hobson 1988), the function of dreaming itself may be seen as the symbolic fulfillment or evocation within the sensorium of transformative processes occurring in the main outside the bounds of conscious network. The feedback relations (homeomorphogenesis) between the symbolic play of dreaming and extrasensorial somatic processes is potentially a reciprocal one. But just how passive or active the conscious network will be in intending the sensorial play will vary from dream to dream, from individual to individual, and from society to society.

The extent of awareness within dream phases varies enormously, and it is the single most important variable in determining both (1) understanding in and of the dream, and (2) the locus of control of dream content. If awareness is hypointentional (weak involvement of prefrontal processes in conscious network), then the locus of control of dream experiences will lay with somatic processes largely outside the boundaries of the conscious network. At the other extreme, if awareness is intentional (within the "normal" range of waking involvement of pre-frontal processes in the conscious network mediating dreaming), then control of the dream experience may (but not necessarily) shift to conscious network. Of course, entrainments mediating dreaming may range on a continuum of prefrontal involvement between these extremes.

In other words, hypointentional entrainment in a dream phase will produce little awareness, and the content may be relatively dull, unclear, confusing, perhaps producing little cross-phase influence or memory in a subsequent phase of consciousness. Increased intentionality will tend to produce the opposite experience, characterized by vividness of sensory content, active awareness of theme and continuity, lucidity (i.e., awareness of dreaming while within the dream), comprehension of meaning and perhaps active involvement of the "dream ego" in controlling the dream content. Hyperintentionality (intense involvement of prefrontal processes) during dreaming may, for example, lead to the portaling experience (MacDonald, et al., 1988) in which intense concentration on some element of a scene produces a "doorway" that "opens up" into an entirely different scene, a very common experience among meditators and dream yogis. Under hyperintentional entrainment, the dream ego ceases to be a passive point of view in the dream and becomes an active, questing locus of control (see D. J. Hillman, 1987; LaBerge, 1981) that may facilitate the capacity for advanced exploration of one's own unconscious processes (Malamud, 1979).

The role of culture is enormous in preparing the individual to participate in and interpret experiences in multiple phases of consciousness (see, e.g., Eggan, 1955, on the Hopi). We have suggested that cultures may lie on a continuum from those tending to produce a monophasic orientation toward alternative phases to those that encourage transcendental exploration via alternative phases. Materialistic cultures tend to enculturate monophasic egos; that is, self-concepts informed primarily from memories accrued during waking phases of consciousness. Even when dream phases are not ignored as a source of experience, dreams are considered more like symbolic puzzles that must be decoded in terms comprehensible to the waking ego, than as experiences that are meaningful in their own right (J. Hillman 1979). By contrast, more spiritually inclined cultures tend to enculturate polyphasic egos; that is, those characterized by self-concepts informed from a variety of alternative phases of consciousness, including dream phases. In cultures that have developed advanced dream exploration as a means of verifying and vivifying their cosmology, experiences in the dream phase are meaningful to a polyphasic ego *from within the dream itself, and may not require later interpretation in the waking phase for comprehension and integration into the ego complex.*

We are *not* saying that dream phases function as a dialogue between, and reorganization of, internal systems only in polyphasic individuals and cultures. Rather, dream phases operate to reorganize internal systems whether or not the ego is polyphasic. The question is to what extent there is participation by higher cortical processes in all phases of consciousness. If there exists a severe discrepancy between the complexity of organization of conscious network in the waking phases and the complexity of organization of conscious network in the dream phases, then to that extent there will exist a fragmentation in the being between knowledge and intentionality about the external world, and knowledge and intentionality about the inner world. Moreover, as we have suggested for shift workers, the predominant orientation of intentionality toward external adaptation may actually produce stress-related deficits in the internal adaptation of somatic systems to each other. Adequate conditions for sleep and dreaming appear to be a requirement for basic health, and involvement of ego in the polyphasic unfolding of experience is probably a requirement for optimal health, and certainly for advanced spiritual development.

Notes

1. The authors wish to thank Deborah Jay Hillman and Pat Kolarik for their useful feedback.

2. When we speak of a model, we do not refer to either an ideal type or a description of a theory. A model is an actual organization of tissue the function of which is to constitute some aspect or aspects of the world before the mind (see Davis, Newburth, and Wegman, 1988; Purves, 1988).

3. The cortex is the phylogenetically newest part of the nervous system and forms a corrugated layer of tissue on the top of the brain. We agree with Doty (1975) that conscious processing is largely a cortical function.

4. The concept of neurognosis is complex and refers to the essential genetical component producing universal patterns of neural activity, and the experiential and behavioral concomitants of that activity; see Laughlin and d'Aquili (1974; ch. 5), Laughlin, McManus, and d'Aquili (1990; ch. 2) and d'Aquili, Laughlin, and McManus (1979; pp. 8ff).

5. See Varela (1979) on "structural coupling," Piaget (1985) on "adequation," Bateson (1979) on "coevolution," and van der Hammen (1988) on a structuralist account of evolution for consonant views on the coevolution of the organism and its environment.

6. We borrowed the concepts of cognized and operational environments from Rappaport (1968), but have changed their meaning substantially from his usage. For further elaboration of these concepts, see Laughlin and Brady (1978; p. 6), d'Aquili et al. (1979; pp. 12ff), Rubinstein,Laughlin, and McManus (1984; pp. 21ff), and Laughlin et al.(1990).

7 . *Entrainment* is a technical term in neurphysiology that means the linking of neural systems into larger configurations by way of dendritic-axonic-synaptic and endocrinological interconnections. Entrainments may be momentary or enduring. A change in a pattern of entrainment is termed *re-entrainment*.

8. The structure of models is not that of the part of the operational environment being modeled. Rather, we say that a model is more or less "adaptively isomorphic" with the operational environment (see d'Aquili, et al. 1979; p. 17). The term implies that models are partially isomorphic to at least the extent required for survival. *Isomorphic* means that the elements and relations composing the model are not the same as those of the noumenon being modeled. And just as there is more to a real airplane than there is to a model airplane, so too is there "transcendentally" more to the noumenon than there is to the model unless, of course, it is the network comprising the model that is itself the noumenon.

9. We mean by *experience* "that which arises before the subject" in consciousness (see Dilthey, 1976; Husserl, 1977). This includes perception, thought, imagination, intuition, affect, and sensation.

10. The biogenetic structuralist group has considered numerous issues relevant to the study of the symbolic function, including masquerade (Webber, Stephens, and Laughlin, 1983; Young-Laughlin and Laughlin, 1988), the evolution of brain and symbol (Laughlin, McManus, and Stephens, 1981), ritual (d'Aquili, 1983; d'Aquili and Laughlin, 1975; d'Aquili, Laughlin, and McManus, 1979; Laughlin, 1990c), myth and language (Laughlin and Stephens, 1980), exchange (Laughlin 1988a), play (Laughlin and McManus 1982), technology (Laughlin and Lepage, 1990), phenomenology (Laughlin 1988c, 1988d, 1990b; Laughlin, McManus and d'Aquili, 1990) and transpersonal experience (d'Aquili 1982; Laughlin, Chetelat and Sekar, 1985; Laughlin, McManus, and Webber 1984; Laughlin 1988b; Laughlin, McManus, and Shearer, 1983; Laughlin et al., 1986; MacDonald et al., 1988).

11. The enculturative process of developing meaning intended upon an object we have termed *semiosis* (see Laughlin and Stephens, 1980; p. 332).

12. The term *homeomorphogenesis* is a neologism we felt was required to focus analytical attention upon the communicative relationship between tissues and in the body. The term combines the concept of *morphogenesis* that has currency in some biological formulations (see e.g., Sheldrake 1981) and the root *homeo* (as in *homeomorphic*, meaning similar form or structure) to denote causally linked transformations of an isomorphic, but not the same kind in two or more subsystems.

References

Ader, R. (Ed.). (1980) *Psychoneuroimmunology.* New York: Academic Press.

Akerstedt, T. (1977) "Inversion of the Sleep Wakefulness Pattern: Effects on Circadian Variations in Psychophysiological Activation." *Ergonomics* 20: 459–474.

———. (1982). "Displacement of Sleep Period and Sleep Deprivation: Implications for Shift Work." *Human Neurobiology*, 1: 163–171.

——— and Torsvall, L. (1978). "Experimental Changes in Shift Schedules Their Effects on Well Being." *Ergonomics* 21: 849–856.

Arbib, M. A. (1972). *The Metaphorical Brain.* New York: John Wiley and Sons.

Aschoff, J. (1981). "Circadian Rhythms: Interface with and Dependence on Work-Rest Schedules." In L. C. Johnson, T. I. Pepas, W. P. Colquhouon, and M. J. Colligan (Eds.) *Biological Rhythms, Sleep and Shift Work* pp. 486–502. New York: Scientific Books.

———. (1978). "Features of Circadian Rhythms Relevant for the Design of Shift Schedules." *Ergonomics* 21: 739–754.

Basso, E. (1987). "The Implications of a Progressive Theory of Dreaming." In B. Tedlock (Ed.). *Dreaming: Anthropological and Psychological Interpretations.* Cambridge: Cambridge University Press.

Bateson, G. (1979). *Mind and Nature.* New York: E. P. Dutton.

Beaglehole, E., and Beaglehole, P. (1938). *Ethnology of the Pukapuka.* Honolulu: Bishop Museum Bulletin 150.

Bourguignon, E. (1976). *Possession.* San Francisco: Chandler and Sharp.

Burnham, D. K. (1987). "The Role of Movement in Object Perception by Infants." In B. E. McKenzie and R. H. Day (Eds.), *Perceptual Development in Early Infancy: Problems and Issues,* pp. 286–305. Hillsdale, N. J.: Lawrence Erlbaum Associates.

Chang, G. C. C. (1963). *Teachings of Tibetan Yoga.* Secaucus, N.J.: Citadel Press.

Changeux, J.-P. (1985). *Neuronal Man: The Biology of Mind.* Oxford: Oxford University Press.

Coleman, R. M. (1986). *Wide Awake at 3:00 A.M.* New York: W. H. Freeman.

Dahlgren, K. (1981). "Long Term Adjustment of Circadian Rhythms to a Rotating Shift Work Schedule." *Scandinavian Journal of Work and Environmental Health* 7: 141–151.

D'Aquili, E. G. (1982). "Senses of Reality in Science and Religion: A Neuroepistemological Perspective." *Zygon* , 17 no. 4: 361–384.

———. (1983). "The Myth-ritual Complex: A Biogenetic Structural Analysis." *Zygon,* 18 no. 3: 247–269.

——— and Laughlin, C. D. (1975). "The Biopsychological Determinants of Religious Ritual Behavior." *Zygon,* 10 no. 1: 32–58.

——— Laughlin, C. D., and McManus, J. (1979). *The Spectrum of Ritual.* New York: Columbia University Press.

Davis, J. L., Newburgh, R. W., and Wegman, E. J. (Eds.). (1988). *Brain Structure, Learning, and Memory.* Boulder, Colo.: Westview Press.

Diamond, M. C. (1988). *Enriched Heredity: The Impact of the Environment on the Anatomy of the Brain.* New York: The Free Press.

Dilthey, W. (1976). *Selected Writings,* ed. H. P. Rickman. London: Cambridge University Press.

Doty, R. W. (1975). "Consciousness from Matter." *Acta Neurobiol. Exp.,* 35: 791–804.

Edelman, G. (1987). *Neural Darwinism: The Theory of Neuronal Group Selection.* New York: Basic Books.

Eggan D. (1955). "The Personal Use of Myth in Dreams." *Journal of American Folklore* 17: 445–453.

Eliade, M. (1964). *Shamanism*. Princeton, N.J.: Princeton University Press.

Folkard, S. (1981). "Shift Work and Performance." In L. Johnson (Ed.), *Biological Rhythms and Performance*, pp. 483–492. New York: Scientific Books.

Foret, J., and Benoit, O. (1977). "Shift Work and Sleep." In P. Levin and W. P. Koella (Eds.), *Sleep 1976*, pp. 71–83. Basel: Krager.

Frese, M., and Hartwick, C. (1984). "Shift Work and the Length and Quality of Sleep." *Journal of Occupational Medicine* 26: 561–566.

Fuster, J. M. (1980). *The Prefrontal Cortex: Anatomy, Physiology, and Neuropsychology of the Frontal Lobe*. New York: Raven Press.

Gennep, A. L. van (1960). *The Rite of Passage*. Chicago: University of Chicago Press [originally published 1909].

Gibson, E. J. (1969). *Principles of Perceptual Learning and Development*. New York: Appleton-Century-Crofts.

Gooddy, W. (1988). *Time and the Nervous System*. New York: Praeger Publishing.

Gray, J. A. (1982). *The Neuropsychology of Anxiety*. Oxford: Oxford University Press.

Grimes, R. L. (1982). *Beginnings in Ritual Studies*. Washington, D.C.: University Press of America.

Grunebaum, G. E. von, and Caillois, R. (1966). *The Dream and Human Societies*. Berkeley: University of California Press.

Halberg, F. (1969). "Chronobiology." *Annual Review of Physiology* 31: 675–725.

Halifax, J. (1979). *Shamanic Voices*. New York: E. P. Dutton.

Harner, M. J. (1962). "Jivaro Souls." *American Anthropologist* 64: 258–272.

———. (1973). *The Jhivaro*. Garden City, N.Y.: Doubleday Books.

Harrington, J. M. (1978). *Shift Work and Health*. London: Her Majesty's Stationary Office.

Hillman, D. J. (1987). "Dream Work and Field Work: Linking Cultural Anthropology and the Current Dream Work Movement." In M.

Ullman and C. Limmer (Eds.), *Variety of Dream Experience*, pp. 117–141. New York: Continuum.

———. (1990). "Making Dreams Important: Grassroots Dream Appreciation Groups in American Culture." In S. Krippner (Ed.), *Language of the Night*. pp. 13–20. Los Angeles: Tarcher.

Hillman, J. (1979). *The Dream and the Underworld*. New York: Harper and Row.

Hobson, J. A. (1988). *The Dreaming Brain*. New York: Basic Books.

Hunt, H. (1989). *The Multiplicity of Dreams*. New Haven, Conn.: Yale University Press.

Husserl, E. (1977). *Cartesian Meditations: An Introduction to Phenomenology*. The Hague: Martinus Nijhoff.

Karacan, I., Williams, R. L., Finley, W. W., and Hursch, C. J. (1970). "The Effects of Naps on Nocturnal Sleep: Influence on the Need for Stage 1 REM and Stage 4 Sleep." *Biological Psychiatry* 2: 391–399.

Kilborne, B. (1974). "Dream Symbols and Culture Patterns: The Dream and Its Interpretation in Morocco." Ph.D. dissertation, University of Paris.

Kogi, K. (1982). "Sleep Problems in Night and Shift Work." *Journal of Human Erogology* 11 (suppl.): 217–232.

Kracke, W. (1979). "Dreaming in Kagwahiv: Psychic Uses of Dream Beliefs in an Amazonian Culture." *Psychoanalytic Study of Society*, pp. 119–171. New Haven, Conn.: Yale University Press.

———. (1987). "Myths in Dreams, Thought in Images: An Amazonian Contribution to the Psychoanalytic Theory of Primary Process." In B. Tedlock (Ed.), *Dreaming: Anthropological and Psychological Interpretations*, pp. 38–52. Cambridge: Cambridge University Press.

LaBerge, S. P. (1981). "Lucid Dreaming: Directing Action as It Happens." *Psychology Today* 15 no. 1: 48–57.

Laughlin, C. D. (1986). "Dots, Quanta, and the Necessity of the Phenomenological Reduction." Unpublished manuscript.

———. (1988a). "On the Spirit of the Gift." *Anthropologica* 27, nos. 1–2: 137–159 (delayed 1985 issue).

————. (1988b). "Transpersonal Anthropology: some Methodological Issues." *The Western Canadian Anthropologist* 5: 29–60.

————. (1988c). "The Prefrontosensorial Polarity Principle: Toward a Neurophenomenology of Intentionality." *Biological Forum* 81 no. 2: 243–260.

————. (1988d). "Time, Intentionality, and a Neurophenomenology of the Dot." Typescript.

————. (1989). "Pre- and Perinatal Anthropology: A Selective Review." *Pre- and Peri-Natal Psychology Journal* 3 no. 4: 261–296.

————. (1990a). "The Roots of Enculturation: The Challenge of Pre- and Perinatal Psychology for Ethnological Theory and Research." *Anthropologica* 31, 135–178.

————. (1990b). "The Mirror of the Brain: A Neurophenomenology of Mature Contemplation." Typescript.

————. (1990c). "Ritual and the Symbolic Function: A Summary of Biogenetic Structural Theory." *Journal of Ritual Studies* 4, no. 1: 15–39.

———— and Brady, I. A. (1978). *Extinction and Survival in Human Populations.* New York: Columbia University Press.

————, Chetelat, L. and Sekar, R. (1985). "Psychic Energy: A Biopsychological Explanation of a Cross-Cultural, Transpersonal Experience." Typescript.

———— and d'Aquili, E. G. (1974). *Biogenetic Structuralism.* New York: Columbia University Press.

———— and Lepage, A. (1990). "The Artifacts of Knowledge: A Biogenetic Structural Account of Symbol and Technology." *Anthropologie et Societes* 13 no. 2: 9–29 [in French].

———— and McManus, J. (1982). "The Biopsychological Determinants of Play and Games." in P. M. Rankin (Ed.), *Social Approaches to Sport* pp. 42–79. Rutherford, N.J.: Farleigh Dickinson University Press.

————, McManus, J. and d'Aquili, E. G. (1990). *Brain, Symbol and Experience: Toward a Neurophenomenology of Consciousness.* Boston: Shambhala New Science Library.

————, McManus, J., Rubinstein, R. A., and Shearer, J. (1986). "The Ritual Transformation of Experience." In N. K. Denzin (Ed.), *Studies in Symbolic Interaction* (Part A), pp. 107–136. Greenwich, Conn.: JAI Press.

————, McManus, J., and Shearer, J. (1983). "Dreams, Trance and Visions: What a Transpersonal Anthropology Might Look Like." *Phoenix: The Journal of Transpersonal Anthropology* 7 nos. 1–2: 141–159.

————, McManus, J., and Stephens, C. D. (1981). "A Model of Brain and Symbol." *Semiotica* 33, nos. 3–4: 211–236.

————, McManus, J., and Webber, M. (1984). "Neurognosis, Individuation and Tibetan Arising Yoga Practice." *Phoenix: The Journal of Transpersonal Anthropology* 8 nos. 1–2: 91–106.

———— and Stephens, C. D. (1980). "Symbolism, Canalization and P-Structure." In M. L. Foster and S. Brandis (Eds.), *Symbol as Sense.* New York: Academic Press.

Lobban, M. C., and Tredre, B. E. (1966). "Daily Rhythms of Renal Excretion in Human Subjects with Irregular Hours of Work." *Journal of Physiology* 185: 139–140.

MacDonald, G. F., Cove, J., Laughlin, C. D., and McManus, J. (1988). "Mirrors, Portals and Multiple Realities." *Zygon,* 24, no. 1: 39–63.

Malamud, J. (1979). "The Development of a Training Method for the Cultivation of 'Lucid' Awareness in Fantasy, Dreams, and Waking Life." Ph.D. dissertation, New York University.

Maron, L., Rechtechaffen, A., and Wolpert, E. A. (1964). "Sleep Cycle During Napping." *Archives of General Psychiatry* 11: 503–508.

Matsumoto, K. (1978). "Sleep Patterns in Hospital Nurses due to Shift Work: An EEG Study." *Waking and Sleeping* 2: 169–173.

Maturana, H., and Verela, F. (1980). *Autopoiesis and Cognition.* Boston: Reidel.

Meggitt, M. J. (1962). "Dream Interpretation Among the Mae Enga of New Guinea." *Southwestern Journal of Anthropology* 18: 216–229.

Monk, T. H., and Folkard, S. (1983). "Circadian Rhythms and Shift Work." In G. R. J. Hockey (Ed)., *Stress and Fatigue in Human Performance.* New York: John Wiley and Sons.

Moore-Ede, M. C., Sultzman, F. M., and Fuller, C. A. (1982). *The Clocks That Time Us.* Cambridge, Mass.: Harvard University Press.

Naitoh, P. (1982). "Chronobiologic Approach for Optimizing Human Performance." In F. M. Brown and R. C. Graeber (Eds.), *Rhythmic*

Aspects of Behavior, pp. 19–37. Hillsdale, N. J.: Lawrence Erlbaum Associates.

Neisser, U. (1976). *Cognition and Reality.* San Francisco: W. H. Freeman.

O'Nell, C. W. (1976). *Dreams, Culture and the Individual.* San Francisco: Chandler and Sharp.

Parmalee, A. and Sigman, M. (1983). "Perinatal brain development and behavior." In M. Haith and J. Campos (Eds.). *Handbook of Child Psychology: Volume 2: Infancy and Developmental Psychobiology.* New York: Wiley.

Paiget, J. (1971). *The Biology of Knowledge.* Chicago: University of Chicago Press.

———. (1985). *The Equilibration of Cognitive Structures.* Chicago: University of Chicago Press.

Powers, W. T. (1973). *Behavior: The Control of Perception.* Chicago: Aldine Books.

Pribram, K. H. (1971). *Languages of the Brain.* Englewood Cliffs: Prentice-Hall.

Prince, R. (1982). "The Endorphins: A Review of Psychological Anthropologists." *Ethos* 1: 303–316.

Purves, D. (1988). *Body and Brain: a Trophic Theory of Neural Connections.* Cambridge, Mass: Harvard University Press.

Rappaport, R. A. (1968). *Pigs for the Ancestors.* New Haven, Conn.: Yale University Press.

Regal, P. J., and Connolly, M. S. (1980). "Social Influences on Biological Rhythms." *Behavior* 72: 171–199.

Reinberg, A., Vieux, N., Ghata, J., Chaumont, A. J., and Laporte, A. (1978). "Circadian Rhythms Amplitude and Individual Ability to Adjust to Shift Work." *Ergonomics* 21: 763–766.

Renner, M. J., and Rosenzweig, M. R. (1987). *Enriched and Impoverished Environments.* New York: Springer-Verlag.

Roffwarg, H. P., Muzio, J. N., and Dement, W. C. (1966). "Ontogenetic Development of the Human Sleep-Dream Cycle." *Science* 152: 604–619.

Rubinstein, R. A., Laughlin, C. D., and McManus, J. (1984). *Science as Cognitive Process.* Philadelphia: University of Pennsylvania Press.

Shearer, J. (1982). "A Chronosociopsychological Approach to Shift Work." Ottawa: Carleton University Laboratory of Sleep and Chronopsychology, Working paper No. 3.

———, Moffitt, A., and Hoffmann, R. (1979). "Waking, Sleeping and Cross-Phase Transference." Paper presented at the annual meeting of the Canadian Ethnological society, Banff, Alberta.

Sheldrake, R. (1981). *A New Science of Life: The Hypothesis of Formative Causation.* Los Angeles: J. P. Tarcher.

Streri, A., and Spelke, E. S. (1988). "Haptic Perception of Objects in Infancy." *Cognitive Psychology* 20: 1–23.

Stuss, D. T., and Benson, D. F. (1986). *The Frontal Lobes.* New York: Raven.

Suda, M., Hayaishi, O., and Nakagawa, H. (Eds.). (1979). *Biological Rhythms and Their Central Mechanisms.* Amsterdam: Elsevier.

Tart, C. (1975). *States of Consciousness.* New York: E. P. Dutton.

Tedlock, B. (Ed.), (1978a). *Dreaming: Anthropological and Psychological Interpretations.* Cambridge: Cambridge University Press.

———. (1987b). "Dreaming and Dream Research." In B. Tedlock (Ed.), *Dreaming: Anthropological and Psychological Interpretations.* Cambridge: Cambridge University Press.

Torii, S., et al. (1982). "Effects of Night Shift on Sleep Patterns of Nurses." *Journal of Human Ergology* 11 (suppl.): 233–244.

Torsvall, L., Akerstedt, T., and Gillberg, M. (1981). "Age, Sleep and Irregular Work Hours: A Field Study with EEG Recording, Catecholamine Excretion and Self Rating." *Scadinavian Journal of Work and Environmental Health* 7: 196–203.

Turner, V. (1979). *Process, Performance and Pilgrimage.* New Delhi: Concept Publishing House.

———. (1983). "Body, Brain, and Culture." *Zygon* 18 no. 3: 221–245.

Ullman, M. (1979). "The Experiential Dream Group." In B. Wolman (Ed.), *Handbook of Dreams.* New York: Van Nostrand Reinhold.

———. (1982). "On Relearning the Forgotten Language: Deprofessionalizing the Dream." *Contemporary Psychoanalysis* 18 no. 1: 153–159.

van der Hammen, L. (1988). *Unfoldment and Manifestation.* The Hague: SPB Academic Publishing.

Varela, F. J. (1979). *Principles of Biological Autonomy*. New York: Elsevier-North Holland.

Verny, T. R. (Ed.). (1987). *Pre- and Perinatal Psychology: An Introduction.* New York: Human Sciences Press.

Waddington, C. H. (1957). *The Strategy of the Genes.* London: George Allen and Unwin.

Webb, W. B. (1982). "Sleep, Biological Rhythms, and Performance Research: An Introduction." In W. B. Webb (Ed.), *Biological Rhythms, Sleep and Performance*, pp. 1–29. New York: John Wiley and Sons.

———— and Agnew, H. (1974). "The Effects of Chronic Limitation of Sleep Length." *The Psychonomic Society* 6: 47–48.

Webber, M., and Laughlin, C. D. (1979). "The Mechanism of Symbolic Penetration." Department of Sociology-Anthropology Working Paper No. 79–8, Carleton University, Ottawa, Canada.

————, Stephens, C. D., and Laughlin, C. D. (1983). "Masks: A Reexamination, or Masks? You Mean They Affect the Brain?" In N. R. Crumrine and M. Halpin (Eds.), *The Power of Symbols*. Vancouver: University of British Columbia Press.

Wever, R. A. (1979). *The Circadian System of Man*. New York: Springer-Verlag.

Young-Laughlin, J., and Laughlin, C.D. (1988). "How Masks Work, or Masks Work How?" *Journal of Ritual Studies* 2 no. 1: 59–86.

Zerubavel, E. (1981). *Hidden Rhythms: Schedules and Calendars in Social Life*. Chicago: University of Chicago Press.

————. (1985). *The Seven Day Circle: The History and Meaning of the Week.* New York: The Free Press.

3

Martha Koukkou and Dietrich Lehmann ▬▬▬▬

A Model of Dreaming and Its Functional Significance: The State-Shift Hypothesis

1. Introduction

This chapter presents an outline of a heuristic model of the psychobiological brain processes (mental processes) that underlie the organization of human behavior in the different states of consciousness. It is an update and an extension of a proposed model of the psychophysiology of dreaming (Koukkou and Lehmann 1980; 1983b). The model is based on existing physiological (mainly EEG) and psychological experimental data and is focused on theoretical concepts. The aim is to formulate a broad framework for considering the psychobiological mechanisms that underlie mental processes during wakefulness and during sleep and for discussing their effects on the similarities and differences in the cognitive, emotional, and action (manifest behavioral) aspects of human existence in the different states of consciousness. We hope to show that it is not a "cognitive," or a "motivational," or a "physiological" model, but a model which integrates all dimensions of human existence.

The model is organized around recent applications of the information processing paradigm to the study of human behavior (for reviews, see. e.g., Anderson, 1981; Donchin, et al., 1986; Ellis and Hunt, 1983; Ingram and Kendall, 1986; Miller, 1982; Norman, 1981a). It suggests that there is a continuously recycling set of elementary, although complex, multifactorially defined and multiply interdependent psychophysiological operations—the "cycle of communication"—which is common to all states of consciousness for the organization of behavior. With this set of operations humans interact and communicate continuously with their internal and external realities. Using this set of operations, humans acquire and update continuously their knowledge about the internal and external realities, and on the other side they use this knowledge to organize and produce their—always psychologically and physiologically manifested—behavior. *Behavior* is defined as the continuous, dynamic, and selective readaptation to the "demands" of the complex, changing, and often unpredictable realities.

The reviewed data point to the basic role of the kind of knowledge stored in that memory space which is accessible to the cycle of communication at a given moment in time for the organization of current human behavior. The data suggest strongly that acquired knowledge is the "locus" of control of human behavior in all states of consciousness. They further bring evidence that the functional state of the brain as reflected in its electrical activity (EEG) at each moment in time defines which memory storage is accessible to and thus, which individual knowledge may be used by the cycle of communication for the organization of behavior. The arguments of the model are based on data and theories that suggest knowledge-implemented (memory-driven) and state-dependent brain operations for the organization of human behavior.

Accordingly, the major themes concern (1) the state-dependent brain mechanisms that implement the acquisition of knowledge, its integration into the already existing knowledge, and its retrieval and accessibility as well as the role of the brain's functional state in determining the accessible memory storages, (2) the role of accessible knowledge in controlling all aspects of behavior, and (3) the mechanisms by which the brain's electrically manifested functional state and hereby the accessible knowledge is continuously, dynamically, flexibly, selectively, and adaptively readjusted to the informational context of the momentary internal and external realities—the mechanisms of the shift or "no shift" of the brain's functional state. We propose that these mechanisms are the means for updating of the working memory, in other words, the mechanisms of semantic association (i.e., semantic priming or inhibition) and that they correspond to the mechanisms that underlie the orienting response and its "habituation." These themes are the building blocks for our understanding of the brain's operations (mental operations) that lead to the organization of human behavior in all states of consciousness; thus, also to dreaming and the distinctive characteristics of REM and NREM sleep mentation. The same building blocks and the resulting framework will be used to discuss dream generation, the coordination of sleep and the functional significance of sleep and dreaming. The proposed model does not invoke dream-specific brain processes or dream-specific sleep stages. It considers mental activity during sleep as resulting from the same basic set of operations (cycle of communication) with which the organization of human behavior is achieved in all states of consciousness. The functional and formal characteristics that differentiate REM from NREM sleep reports as well as REM reports, NREM reports, reports of hypnagogic hallucinations, of imagery, and of day dreaming from external reality-oriented and external reality-including wakeful mentation are accounted for by (1) the differences in the brain's functional state that precede the different reports, and (2) the differences in the brain's functional state between the state that precedes the report and the state during the report. Their effects on reported mentation and generally on behavior will be explained by the accessibility of different knowledge sets (context information) to the brain's operations of the cycle of communication during these different functional brain states. The degree of difference in cognitive-emotional and action style and the degree of impairment of retrieval of mental operations observed for mentations that took place during one state (e.g., REM sleep or sleep onset) and are recalled in another state (e.g., spontaneous or induced wakefulness) is a function of the magnitude of the difference between the two states defined by their respective EEG patterns.

Based on similarities in EEG patterns between some functional states of the awake brain during developmental stages with some functional states of the sleeping brain, we propose that some sleep stages—and this mainly after the age at which children can report dreams (Foulkes, 1982, 1983)—imply physiological regressions to earlier stages of development. This has two consequences. On the one hand, the information reaching the individual during sleep is initially treated with "childish" strategies ("primary process" rules). This is important for the maintenance of sleep so that its functions have time to occur. On the other hand, this physiological regression permits the comparison of the incoming information with the mnemonic contents of storages of earlier and actual developmental stages, and herewith its reevaluation in the light of biographically defined previous and recent experiences. If the result has been found to be important, the integration of the earlier and recent experiences is deposited in a storage that is accessible during wakefulness (storage of REM sleep). This serves the adaptive, assimilating reorganizing functions of sleep. The end effect is that new and previously acquired knowledge may be reconstructed and integrated in the knowledge of higher developmental levels and that sleep can be maintained because the input is treated with the imaginative and "permissive" strategies of childhood (compare Lehmann and Koukkou, 1990). This will be explained by the state dependency of information processing operations and their asymmetrical mode of functioning and by the shifts of the brain's functional states to higher arousal after receipt of important information. Within this framework, sleep, like wakefulness is considered as a multifactorially defined, cyclically recurring, but active, flexible, adaptive, and multidimensionally manifested phenomenon (e.g., Aschoff, 1965, 1980; Campbell, 1984; Hunt, 1989; Moruzzi, 1963, 1972; Webb, 1982). The aim of the physiological changes that accompany sleep and its different stages is considered to be the recurring installation of memory storages whose analysis strategies of the messages coming from the internal and external realities evaluate these messages in such a way that needs and functions of the organism that are concerned with its internal "household"—the functions of sleep —are given priority (Section 6).

These are not all completely novel ideas. Proposals with similarities in some aspects have been made by Antrobus (1987), Breger (1967), Foulkes (1982), Greenberg and Leiderman (1966), Hawkins (1966), Hunt (1989), Kosslyn (1980), Koulack and Goodenough (1976), Lowy (1942), and Palombo (1978). The main novel aspects of our model in its initial (Koukkou and Lehmann, 1980, 1983b) and in its present form is the kind of data, hypotheses, and research disciplines that we synthesize to formulate the model and support its assumptions, as well as some of the inferences of this synthesis for discussing psychophysiological mechanisms underlying sleep coordination, dream formation, and the functions of sleep and dreaming. The model has also been used to propose a mode of action of the therapeutic effect of dream interpretation (Koukkou and Lehmann 1980; 1983a) and to discuss forms of organization of human behavior that are studied by psychotherapists and psychiatrists; that is, neurotic and psychotic behavior (Koukkou, 1988; Koukkou-Lehmann, 1987; Koukkou and Lehmann, 1980; Koukkou and Manske, 1986).

We begin by describing the key concepts and operational definitions of the parts of the model; then we present an overview of the model and show how it can account for the formal characteristics of sleep mental activity, for dream generation and for the difficulties of dream retrieval during wakefulness. We end up by considering the application of the model to discuss the coordination of sleep and the physiological significance of sleep and of its subjectively recognizable concomitant, dreams.

2. The Systems Approach of the Organization of Human Behavior: The Cycle of Communication

From the perspectives of systems theory humans are in a continuous selective and dynamic interaction (communication) with their internal and external environments (realities) from which an enormous amount of information comes into their perceptual systems at every moment. Human behavior is the result of these interactions. We conceptualize as the internal environment the functional state of the body; that is, levels of functioning of the different systems (organs, hormonal, metabolic and vigilance conditions) and the sum of the individual's knowledge (some innate but most of it acquired; Section 3). The external environment is the social and physical environment of the individual. Thus, humans interact and communicate continuously with their knowledge, their body, and their social and physical environment.

These interactions, and thus human behavior, are coordinated by the central nervous system and reflect the integrative and cooperative functions of the entire brain. The brain is viewed as an adaptive information-processing system that operates with multiple feedback control loops. Its biological and psychological function is to acquire knowledge about the internal and external realities and about the outcome of the interaction with them, to update this knowledge continuously and to use this knowledge flexibly and dynamically to organize and coordinate behavior effectively in these environments. Thus, the brain is considered as an information processor, an information store, and information generator (e.g. Baumgartner, 1983; Bindra, 1980; Goldstein, 1983; Grossberg, 1986; Szentagothai, 1987). The human brain achieves these complex functions and thus produces behavior via the operations of the cycle of communication. The purpose of the communication with the internal and external realities is the continuous reevaluation of the informational significance of the messages coming from these realities for the momentary psychobiological priorities of the individual and the continuous readjustment (functional adaptation) of the whole organism (overt behavior manifestations, somatic, cognitive, and emotional aspects) to the recognized significance of these messages. The main determinant of this significance and thus of the characteristics of the functional adaptation is the previously acquired and momentarily accessible knowledge of the individual about similar messages in the past and about the effects of such messages on somatic, cognitive, and emotional functions.

The basic argument is that behavior coordinated by the brain as functional adaptation to the individually recognized significance of the internal and external realities is originally always purposeful (Sober, 1987). The main goal of this adaptation is the maintenance of the well-being of the individual as a living system in psychological (subjectively recognizable) and biological terms, and the removal of obstacles to this goal. Therefore, there is goal-directed behavior although no specific behavioral goals have been preprogrammed. This includes pursuit of goals that have been formulated on the basis of past experiences including acquired value systems.

2.1 The Functional Nature of the Cycle of Human Communication: The Initial Interpretation

Figure 3.1 sketches out the functional components (the operations) of the cycle of human communication. This heuristic schema does not present anatomical localizations but functional units. It implies however that the functional and structural nature of the cycle of communication

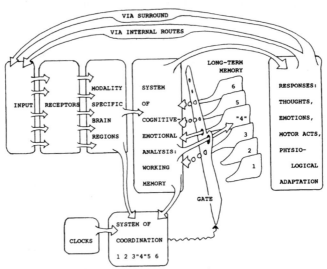

Fig. 3.1. Functional components of the human cycle of communication. The state-dependent interactions between Long-Term Memory and Working Memory are illustrated by the Gate area that is operated by the Coordinating System. In the figure, seven possible states are illustrated, more highly organized states having higher numbers. The momentary state is "4", providing optimal access for retrieval from and deposit to portion "4" of the Long Term memory; higher storages and the immediate lower neighbor can be partially read-out. Long-Term Memory store is shown as set of separate structures illustrating the functionally different, state-dependently accessible portions; physically, however, a common apparatus is to be assumed that is treated with different read-out modes. Flow of information shown by open channels, limited read-out indicated by broken channels.

corresponds to the functional and structural nature of the orienting response (Section 2.4).

Although many issues in the study of the brain's treatment of information and in the study of hemispheric specialization for cognitive-emotional functioning remain controversial, an integration permits the following formulations about the functions of the brain with which human behavior, defined as the selective adaptation to the individually recognized significance of the incoming information, is organized. The signals that continuously reach the receptors of all perceptual systems are transformed into the codes of each receptor and transferred in parallel pathways to the modality-specific brain regions. There, the signals are translated into the specific languages of the brain regions. The information from all specific regions converges then synchronously to the system of analysis of the amodal (personal) aspects of the information (in Figure 3.1, system of cognitive-emotional analysis). There, the sum of the available information from visceral and sensory channels is reencoded into the symbolic languages, verbal and nonverbal, and into the emotional languages of the individual's brain; that is, into the individual's acquired languages. Thereby is created a neuronal multimodal and multidimensional model of the momentary internal realities (thoughts, plans, goals, emotions, feelings, functions of the body) and of the external realities of the individual. This model arises out of the interaction between the information from the internal and external environments and the previously stored and momentary accessible knowledge about similar events (contents of working memory; Section 3.1). This occurs in parallel in many interactive neuronal sets—integrative, cooperative, holistic functions—of the neocortex of both hemispheres, each considering the cognitive and emotional informational aspects of the input for which it is specialized. In other words, this is the effective and dynamic synthesis, a multimodal pattern formation, between the new input and the set of activated (matched) mnemonic elements (memory set). The result is the neuronal model of the individual's reality. Related principles have also been used in computer technology (compare Stillings et al., 1987). Missing portions of the external inputs are filled in by the brain, using stored knowledge, to complete the "shape" of the perceived information (compare Lehmann and Koukkou, 1990). In sleep, because the external input is reduced by the preparation to go to sleep and because "childish" processing strategies are accessible (Sections 5 and 6), the "path" to the dreaming-like synthesis is open. Later discussion will show that state-dependent access to memory material (data, skills, and strategies) is a key point in these dynamic processes—dreaming being an extreme case in point.

Utilizing these brain functions, the individual knowledge-based neuronal model of the internal and external realities, the perceived information, is compared with the contents of working memory and incorporated into the matched memory representations, thus contributing to the updating of the individual's knowledge (e.g., Neves and Anderson, 1981; Norris, 1986; Rumelhart, et al, 1987; Section 3). This comparison terminates the sequence of the brain operations, which is called *preattentive processes* (Neisser, 1967), *information evaluation processes* (Duncan-Johnson, 1981; Hillyard and Kutas, 1983), or *initial interpretation of the information* (Norman, 1968). These processes have been studied by cognitive psychologists using psychological methods (e.g., Kahneman 1973, Schneider and Fisk, 1982, Shiffrin and Schneider, 1977) and by electrophysiologists using event-related EEG potential measurements (e.g., Brandeis and Lehmann, 1989; Donchin et al., 1986; Duncan-Johnson and Donchin, 1982; Hillyard and Kutas, 1983; Lehmann, 1984; Section 2.3).

The literature provides strong evidence that the pre-attentive processes (1) function in parallel for all externally as well as for all internally generated information (i.e., perceptions, thoughts, fantasies, emotions, memories, goals, body functions, feelings, etc.); (2) operate during all levels of consciousness, that is, during wakefulness and all sleep stages (Section 5); and (3) have an automatic access to the contents of working memory, that is, they operate with reflexive speed (Section 2.5). Therefore, humans cannot consciously follow the flow of these processes in their central nervous system. Only the results of these processes that correspond to the formation and manifestation of the initial answer may become available to awareness (e.g., Neisser, 1976; Posner and McLeod, 1982).

Specifically the pre-attentive processes lead (1) to the identification of the informational significance of the realities for the momentary psychobiological priorities of the receiving individual (pattern formation and pattern recognition); (2) to an estimation of the required demands for further information treatment, corresponding to the decision of which information processing mode (automatic or controlled or both) has to be used for this treatment (Sections 2.2 and 2.5); and (3) to the selection and initiation of the appropriate answer. The answer, a multidimensional response pattern, is relayed back to the central nervous system via internal (system of coordination) and external feedback control loops, thus informing it about the quality and the efficacy of the answer. The feedback information together with newly incoming signals leads to the updating of the contents of the working memory, in the literature treated also under the heading of "semantic association" and "semantic priming or inhibition" (e.g., Kohonen, 1978; Ratcliff and McKoon, 1988). The feedback and the new information both undergo the same sequences of information processing and both participate in the synthesis of the new model of the realities and in the construction of the next answer, and so forth.

Within the perspectives of the organization of human behavior that we follow, each information unit that has been identified by the pre-attentive processes is answered. This answer refers to the level of functioning of all systems of the organism. An answer is a change or a "no change" of the level of functioning of each system as compared to the level of functioning just prior to the start of the processing of the information (Koukkou and Lehmann, 1983b; 1987). The answer is subjectively perceivable in changes or no changes of cognition and emotion, and it is objectively measurable in changes or no changes of the level of function of all systems. Thus, as with all biological systems functional changes can be detected only when they are considered in relative, not in absolute terms, that is, by comparison with what existed before. The characteristics of this answer, which system will change its level of functioning and which will not, are continuously, dynamically, selectively, and individually redefined by the pre-attentive processes. The characteristics reflect the functional adaptation of the individual to the demands put on it by the momentary realities (the necessary coping dynamics) as evaluated against the accessible knowledge (contents of the working memory, the size of the memory set; Section 3.1). For our considerations, this functional adaptation is installed via the orienting response (Koukkou and Lehmann, 1987). Thus, the type and magnitude of the brain's functional adaptation is executed as the EEG component of a nonunitary, adaptive orienting response or as its "habituation"; it is installed via the system of coordination (Section 2.4 and 3.1).

Summarizing one can say that the operations of the cycle of communication generate and coordinate all dimensions of human behavior. These operations can be analyzed into three continuous, interdependent, dynamic, and complex sets of operations where each set depends on the previous one and initiates the next one. All three sets of operations are knowledge implemented. That means, their characteristics depend on the kind of previously acquired and momentarily accessible knowledge of the individual. These sets of operations are (1) the creation of the multidimensional neuronal model of the internal and external individual realities out of the interaction between incoming signals and momentarily accessible knowledge (pattern formation); (2) the evaluation of the significance of these realities for the momentary psychobiological priorities by matching against accessible knowledge (pattern recognition); and (3) selection and execution of the answer, which is a functional psychobiological adaptation to the recognized significance of these realities. The answer is relayed back to the central nervous system and together with new incoming messages participates in the formation of the next model of the realities, and so forth. Each of these complex processes is of course decomposable into component processes some of which have been described previously; more elementary ones cannot be considered here (e.g., Kandel and Schwartz, 1981, 1982).

Accordingly, each operation of the cycle of communication continuously produces analyses of the inputs; the results of these analyses, their outputs, are in turn inputs to subsequent stages of processing. This explains the continuity of behavioral organization. In this context human behavior is defined as the answer of the brain to perceived and evaluated multimodal and multidimensional information and is the result of a set of highly interactive, dynamic, context-directed, top-down cortical processes; it reflects at each moment the individually recognized significance of the incoming information. It manifests itself in perceptual, emotional, behavioral, and thought experiences and in physiological changes or "no changes"; that is, it always concerns both the psychological and biological aspects of human existence. Some of these aspects become conscious and some do not (Sections 2.1, 2.5).

2.2 Further Cognitive-Emotional Interpretation of the Information

Studies of human information processing show clearly that the initially perceived, identified, and answered information is further analyzed. During this analysis, the demands made by the momentary realities on the present psychobiological priorities of the individual (motivations, goals, momentary metabolic, hormonal, and generally homeostatic conditions and the level of vigilance) and the efficacy of the responses (of the psychobiological aspects of behavior) in coping with these demands are further evaluated in the light of other related information coming from the external and from the internal reality of the individual. These processes have been discussed in the literature under the headings of "further" or "cognitive interpretation of the incoming events" (Craik, 1979; Norman, 1984). We call them *further cognitive-emotional interpretation* to emphasize the position of our model that considers the mechanisms leading to the formation of human emotions and their role for the organization of behavior (Section 4).

In the context of our considerations the further cognitive-emotional interpretation of the momentary reality takes place with repeated cycles of communication, and its characteristics relate to the functional state of the brain as reflected in the scalp EEG during these processes (Sections 2.3 and 5). It takes place during wakefulness with both the automatic and the controlled information-processing mode. During sleep, all interactions of the individual with the internal and external realities take place with the automatic information-processing mode (Section 2.5). This mode, relying on automatized aspects of personal significance of the momentary realities, adapts the brain's functional state to the demands of these realities and hereby may maintain sleep or, when necessary, may change the depth of sleep or even introduce wakefulness (Sections 5 and 6).

2.3 Electrophysiology of Human Information Processing

Psychophysiologists have used the techniques of the event-related brain potentials (ERPs; e.g., Donchin, 1979; Donchin et al., 1983; 1986; Duncan-Johnson 1981; Näätänen, 1988), recently utilizing ERP mapping techniques (Brandeis and Lehmann, 1986, 1989; Lehmann, 1971) to examine processes within the brain in the time domain of milliseconds; that is, in the time between sensory inputs and behavioral outputs at the electrophysiological level. This research has identified brain electrical manifestations that signify the course of the human information-processing stages summarized as preattentive processes (e.g., Brandeis and Lehmann, 1986, 1989; Brown and Lehmann, 1979; Duncan-Johnson, 1981; Hillyard and Kutas, 1983; Loveless, 1983; Rohrbaugh, 1984; Section 2.1). The brain's response to analyzed information corresponds within the framework of our model to the EEG components of an adaptive, nonunitary orienting response (Section 2.4). This response has been studied with measurements of the EEG reactivity to signals of different informational value in within- and between-session repetitions, not only during wakefulness, but also during sleep (e.g. Beck, 1989; Bonnet, 1982; 1986; Harsh et al., 1987; Müller, 1986). It was found that the dimension of the initial EEG reactivity to "new" information relates to the quality of learning; it changes systematically as a function of changing contextual meaning, expectancy of and familiarity with the event. During learning and overlearning the information-induced EEG changes (the dimension of EEG reactivity) decrease with increasing familiarity with an event and a task; that is with better performance. The EEG reactivity is minimal or even abolished when the training procedure reaches automatic behavioral responses (Beck, 1989; Koukkou and Lehmann, 1987; Van Winsum, Segreant, and Geuze, 1984; Vogel, Broverman, and Klaiber, 1967). This means that when the linkage between the mnemonic representations of an event and of its response is automatized (Section 2.5), the response is selected and executed without the necessity of a change in the brain's functional state (see also Section 2.4).

Studies of information processing during behavioral and EEG sleep in humans demonstrated continued selective interaction with the environment. This is supported by event-related brain potential data, EEG reactivity measurements, and behavioral measurements (e.g., Badia, et al., 1985; McDonald, et al, 1975; Müller, 1986; Oswald, Taylor, and Treisman, 1960; Williams 1973; for a review see Bonnet, 1982; Pearlman, 1982). All studies show that humans are capable of correct behavioral responses during sleep based on knowledge acquired during wakefulness. The probability of correct responses decreases in the order stage 1, REM, stage 2, stage 3, and stage 4. Increasing motivation of the subjects participating in these studies increases response rate mainly for stimuli presented during stage 4 (Bonnet, 1982). Furthermore, several studies have shown (1) evidence of "habituation" of EEG reactivity and of other physiological responses during sleep (e.g., Firth, 1973; Oswald, et al, 1960); and (2) ability to discriminate during sleep (Williams, 1973). It is obvious that during sleep, information can be perceived, evaluated and properly utilized for the organization of sleep behavior (see also Section 6).

Well-learned skills (automatized responses to incoming information, Section 2.5) can be executed during sleep without awakening. The more familiar the subject is with a task, the better is its execution during sleep, and the smaller are the EEG changes associated with a good performance (e.g., Bonnet, 1982, 1986; Lehmann and Koukkou, 1974; Williams, 1973). A pertinent, very dramatic observation is the obvious ability of a sleep-walking person to process information in his or her habitual surroundings and to react to it "correctly" during the somnambulistic episode. The somnambulistic episodes occur during slow wave sleep EEG patterns, and very typically, the sleep walker is unable to recall the sleep walking events later during wakefulness (Jacobson et al,

1965). Awake recall of information received during sleep is possible only if a transient EEG wakefulness period occurs immediately following the arrival of this information (Emmons and Simon, 1956). The quality of recall is a function of the duration (Koukkou and Lehmann, 1968; Oltman et al., 1977) and degree (Lehmann and Koukkou, 1974; Moffitt et al., 1982) of the EEG wakefulness pattern that followed the arrival of the information during sleep.

These observations are in very good agreement with the results of dream recall studies that show that dream recall is a function of the amount of relative arousal before asking for dream recall out of sleep (Bonnet, 1982; Goodenough, 1978; Greenberg, 1981; Greenberg et al, 1983; Moffitt et al., 1982; Webb and Cartwright, 1978; Zimmermann, 1970). That is true for REM and NREM awakenings. REM awakenings resulting in dream recall show significantly different spectral EEG values than those resulting in no recall (Lehmann, Dumermuth, Lange, and Meier, 1981).

The EEG correlates of the further cognitive-emotional interpretation of incoming events (Section 2.2) have been studied with numerical computer-assisted analysis of short time series of EEG in relation to behavioral parameters or introspective experiences. These studies show that the EEG is a very sensitive indicator of internal state. Various relationships between brain states defined by EEG parameters and different types or classes of cognitive and emotional processing have been repeatedly reported using EEG epochs lasting from some seconds to a few minutes (e.g., Corsi-Cabrera et al, 1988; Ehrlichman and Wiener, 1980; Gevins et al., 1987; Lehmann, 1984; Lehmann and Koukkou, 1980; Lehmann, Koukkou, and Andreae, 1981; Libet, 1982; Machleidt, Gutjahr, and Mügge, 1989). In series of experiments we collected completely spontaneous and unconstrained thoughts during a no-task situation and analyzed 16 seconds of EEG before-the-thought reports. These studies showed systematic relations between the cognitive-emotional style expressed by the report and the brain's electrical state immediately before the report (Lehmann, Koukkou, and Andreae, 1981). Shorter EEG epochs in the range of very few seconds also show correlations with psychological functions. The typical "alpha" rhythm in relaxed human adults shows fluctuations of amplitude in the range of seconds that are related to fluctuations of sensitivity in visual perception, and fluctuations of the wave pattern in the same range of seconds that are related to fluctuations of choice reaction time (e.g., Gath, Lehmann, and Bar-On, 1983; Lehmann, 1980). However, classical EEG phenomena such as the

"K complex" (which occurs as an electric response to external information during sleep), and the previously mentioned studies of event-related brain potentials have made it likely that much shorter epochs might be functionally identifiable in the EEG, eventually down to the "single waves," electric manifestations in the tenth-of-a-second range.

Our studies on this micro-structure of the EEG and its functional and introspective correlates showed that such very brief states can be clearly identified. For these studies of micro-states, brain electric activity is not viewed as waveforms but as a continuous series of momentary electric landscapes (maps) at a typical rate of 128 or 256 maps/second. Over time, a given landscape tends to remain stable in its configuration, but periodically changes in polarity, which produces the temporal patterns of waveshapes in conventional EEG waveforms. A given landscape of the brain's momentary electric field can be assumed to represent the activity of a particular neuronal population and accordingly, a particular step or mode of information processing. A change of the momentary electric landscape must mean that a different neural population has become active and, hence, that a different step or mode of information processing is taking place. This leads to the possibility to identify momentary functional micro-states of brain activity on the basis of the spatial pattern of the momentary landscape of the brain's electric potential.

We examined recordings of spontaneous EEG data as to the duration of quasi-stable map landscapes; that is, as to the duration of the different functional micro-states. Mean duration over six normal subjects was 210 milliseconds, but 50 percent of the time was covered by states lasting longer than 323 milliseconds (Lehmann, Ozaki, and Pal, 1987). Behavior correlated with different types of micro-states (different momentary brain electric landscapes): choice reaction time to auditory stimuli differed significantly depending on the map landscape that existed at the moment of stimulus presentation; the results were similar in eight subjects (Lehmann et al, 1987). Moreover, different modes of spontaneous mentations were associated with significantly different landscapes of brain maps obtained immediately before the verbal report of the mentations. The subjects were instructed to report "what just went through their minds" whenever they heard a gentle prompt tone, given at irregular intervals twenty times within $1^1/_2$ hours. The reports were rated on various scales such as "visual imagery" vs "abstract thought," or "associated with emotions" vs "emotionally neutral," or "reality close" vs "reality remote." About 60 percent of all reports could be classed as imagery or abstract thought. The momentary EEG map immediately before the prompt signal was examined, and map landscape descriptors were extracted (two- or three-dimensional dipoles). The maps associated with the two classes of thoughts were significantly different over subjects (Figure 3 in Lehmann, 1989; Lehmann, Kofmel, and Weiss, 1990). Thus, the momentary brain electric field (the momentary brain micro-state) measured immediately before the subject is asked to report his or her experience, relates to the different qualities of human mentation (cognitive-emotional style, modality predominance like, for example, imagery mode and nonvisual mode of processing).

The brain electric micro-states are suggested to represent "atoms of thought," and their durations might reflect the probability that the given step of information processing can access the capacity-limited consciousness channel (as to minimum time for conscious experience, see Libet, 1982, 1985). We hypothesize that a change of micro-state reflects a completed cycle of preattentive processing. The concatenations of the short-lasting (subsecond to second range) micro-states may draw on a limited repertoire of micro-states. During different macro-states, these micro-state classes might be used with different frequencies, durations, or concatenation rules, thus accounting for the overall mean differences between macro-states, and also for a large variability of momentary processing strategies and memory accesses within a macro-state (day dream-type wake mentation, sleep onset hypnagogic hallucinations, and NREM and REM sleep dream mentation).

2.4 The Structural Nature of the Cycle of Communication: The Orienting Response and its EEG Components

In this section we propose that the developments of current research on the human orienting response and its functional significance for the organization of behavior suggest that the structural and functional nature of the orienting response is the structural and functional nature of the basic cycle of human communication. According to these developments the orienting response is a visceral but psychobiologically adaptive, nonunitary multidimensional response pattern. It is elicited by the preattentive processes in response to features of the multimodal input to the central nervous system that are identified as novel in contrast to the familiar, or as important in contrast to unimportant, or as unexpected in contrast to the expected (Lynn, 1966; Öhman, 1979; Pavlov, 1928; Pribram, 1979; Rohrbaugh, 1984; Sokolov, 1975; Spinks and Siddle, 1983; Stephenson and Siddle, 1983; Van Winsum et al, 1984; Velden, 1978). The orienting response includes event-related changes (components) in the central nervous system, in the vegetative and somatic systems, and in the subjectively and objectively recognizable behavior (i.e., in all aspects of the "answer" of the cycle of communication; Section 2.1). With repetition of information that elicited an orienting response, the different psychobiological components diminish and become differentially and selectively replaced by adaptive responses (in the literature often treated under the headings of "habituation," see e.g. Öhman, 1979; for a recent summary compare Turkkan, 1989), which, with further practice, may eventually become automatized and secondarily generalized (compare Shepard, 1986). These conclusions are based mainly on findings considering the so-called peripheral components of the orienting response.

Studies addressing directly the EEG components of the orienting response and its "habituation" are rare (see. e.g., Rohrbaugh, 1984). However, when the results of these studies are combined with results of EEG studies on attention, learning, overlearning, and performance (e.g., Beck, 1989; Brown and Lehmann, 1979; Corsi-Cabrera et al, 1988; Hillyard and Hansen, 1986; Koukkou, 1980; Koukkou-Lehmann, 1987; Koukkou and Lehmann, 1987; Lehmann, 1980; Lehmann et al., 1987; Van Winsum et al., 1984; see also Section 2.3), they also support at the EEG level the previously described view of the orienting response construct. They show that novel, intensive, important, and unexpected information elicits a shift of the brain's electrical state to more arousal. Appearance, form, intensity, duration, and topography of the event-related EEG changes (EEG reactivity) relate to learning and retrieval processes and change systematically as a function of changing contextual meaning, expectancy and familiarity with the event and as a function of increasing practice in "coping" with the event. Furthermore, there are clear within- and between-session changes that indicate functional adaptation ("habituation"). This is the case also for EEG reactivities elicited during sleep (Bonnet, 1982, 1986; Lehmann and Koukkou, 1974; Müller, 1986; and Section 5).

Therefore, it can be said that the structural nature of the orienting response corresponds to the structural nature of the cycle of communication. The orienting response provides the foundation for all of the organism's potential adjustments to the environmental information. It consists of the afferent system that carries information from all parts of the body and the deep cerebral regions to the various modality-specific and nonspecific cortical areas, where the mnemonic functions (memory in its broadest sense) have been localized; and it further consists of the efferent system that coordinates brain functions (functional states of the brain) and hereby memory functions, that is, accessible knowledge (Section 3.1), via the reticular formation (system of coordination; Figure 3.1) and coordinates movements and body organs by carrying neural messages (information) to the muscles and the organs. Accordingly, the functional specificity of the structural nature of the orienting response (of the cycle of communication) can be traced back to the afferent and efferent connections to the cortex. The cortex applies its integrative, holistic, cooperative functions (e.g., Baumgartner, 1983; Edelman, 1987) to the neural messages, extracts their individually defined momentary informational value and synthesizes the subjectively describable (thoughts, goals, plans, feelings, emotions, fantasies, etc.) and objectively measurable (overt behavior, physiology) "answers," based on both the interaction between incoming messages and previously acquired and momentarily accessible knowledge (see also Section 2.1).

In the light of these considerations the functional significance of the nonunitary orienting response with its graded manifestation is the adaptation of the level of functioning of the whole organism (change or no change of the level of functioning of each system), for efficient coping with the demands put on the organism by incoming externally and internally originated information (the latter including thoughts, memories, emotions, and fantasies). The demands of the incoming information are continuously reestimated by the preattentive processes that operate similarly in all levels of consciousness. The brain's functional adaptation is manifested in the form, strength, duration, and topography of event-related EEG changes or no changes. Within the framework of this model they reflect the updating of the individual's knowledge (contents of working memory; Section 3.1) to the contextual significance of the current internal and external realities (Koukkou-Lehmann, 1987; Koukkou and Lehmann, 1987; see also Donchin et al., 1983); this corresponds to the concept of semantic priming or inhibition and to the concept of shift or no shift of attention. Thus, the biological significance of the EEG components of a nonunitary, adaptive orienting response is the adaptation of the accessible knowledge to the momentary psychobiological priorities (motivation) of the individual. This is the case during all states of consciousness; that is, during wakefulness and during sleep (compare Section 5).

2.5 The Modes of Human Information Processing and the Concept of Automaticity

Recent concepts of attention and human information processing postulate that mental operations (brain functions) and thus the organization of human performance (psychologically and biologically manifested behavior) is realized with two different modes, referred to as automatic and consciously controlled processing (e.g., Neumann, 1984; Posner, 1982; Schneider and Shiffrin, 1977; Shiffrin and Schneider, 1977; Stillings et al., 1987). In the language of clinical psychology this distinction refers to the subjective experience that some mental processes require focused attention and therefore voluntary effort and others do not: for example, learning how to drive a car vs. driving a car when one is an experienced driver. The first is executed with the controlled mode and the latter with the automatic mode.

The controlled mode of processing is slow, flexibly allocated and regulated, and easily adapted, altered, or even reversed. It is highly demanding on attentional capacity and thus restricted by its limitations and leads to new learning. It operates only during wakefulness. It seems to have two main functions: (1) it provides the flexible and adaptable use and combination of knowledge for the organization of behavior in novel or important situations, and (2) it helps to maintain the focusing on goals during wakefulness as long as the realities do not offer information competing for the individual's attention. Both functions of the controlled information-processing mode are realized by the flexible adaptation of the individual's acquired knowledge (working memory's contents) to the contextual significance of the individual's external and internal realities (semantic priming or inhibition).

The automatic processing mode is fast, innate (reflexive stimulus-response relationships), or the result of extended practice, and it operates in all levels of consciousness; that is, during wakefulness and sleep. For the level of organization of complex human behavior, automatic processing refers only to the results of practice and is responsible for performance of well-learned behavior. Automatic processing requires and is the result of powerful long-term learning. What occurs in the organism as a result of practice is a coordination in memory (the formation of a sequence of tightly integrated associative functional connections) between the mnemonic representations of an event and a complex response (a skill or a strategy; Section 3) so that the identification of the event by the preattentive processes activates the response with reflexlike speed. Before the development of automaticity, these two (event and response; that is, functional adaptation) have been tried and slowly linked by attention-demanding acts that using the controlled information-processing mode, synthesize the response flexibly and dynamically, based on the individual's accessible knowledge and the new incoming information with repeated cycles of communication during the further cognitive-emotional interpretation of the information (Section 2.2). With increasing familiarity with event and response, the required amount of attention decreases and the accuracy and speed of responding increases. An automatized behavioral pattern, an active mastering has been developed, which may become secondarily generalized for similar events. Thus, functional differences of automatic as opposed to controlled processes are qualitative and not just a difference in degree (e.g., Logan, 1988; Schneider and Shiffrin, 1977; Shiffrin and Dumais, 1981; Shiffrin and Schneider, 1977).

Skills that are extensively practiced (automatized responses) can be performed in parallel; that is, simultaneously and with great accuracy and speed. This speed and the parallel form of automatized performance usually keeps the constituting elements of the performance hidden from conscious perception. Automatized processing relies on mechanisms for which conscious guidance is not necessary for successful execution. The actions may be executed without reference to and without control by consciousness (Neumann, 1984; Norman, 1981b; Schneider and Fisk, 1982). Thus, they can also be executed during sleep—the most illustrative example for the considerations of this chapter being human sleep walking (Jacobson et al., 1965; Section 5).

Under normal circumstances however, automatic processes are not independent of the person's current motivational state and general intentions, in spite of the possible lack of conscious awareness. Just the opposite: automatic processes facilitate accurate performance in the field of general intention because they rely on mnemonic representations of data, skills, and cognitive-emotional strategies (Section 3) that previous experiences had identified as necessary for the realization of this intention. Thus, being automatic does not mean that these operations lack control, but that they are controlled below the level of conscious awareness based on previously acquired knowledge. The earliest possible conscious awareness of an automatic operation is awareness of the selection or the execution of the response.

It is important to keep in mind that (1) mnemonic representation of different response categories can be attached (thus become automatized) to the mnemonic representation of the same event configurations (set of inputs) depending on the context and that (2) there are not only overt responses but also vegetative and other somatic responses, as well as complex mental operations like "attention" and "strategies" (cognitive-emotional) that can be attached in the brain's memory system as automatized response patterns to internally or externally originated information.

"Attention" as automatized response pattern is attached to mnemonic representations of sets of inputs to the memory system that have acquired an individually defined significance ("signal information"). In the context of our considerations an automatized attention response consists at the level of brain electrophysiology of a more or less intensive shift of the brain's EEG state to more arousal as compared to the brain's immediately preceding functional (EEG) state. An automatized attention response corresponds to the EEG component of the adaptive orienting response to individually significant information. All other automatized responses consist at the level of the brain's electrophysiology of a "no shift" in the EEG state as compared to the state just before (Section 2.3).

During wakefulness each shift in the brain's functional state to more arousal corresponds to a call of the controlled information-processing mode for the further treatment of the information that elicited this shift. All other aspects of the multimodal input to the brain are treated with the automatic information-processing mode based on previously acquired knowledge. Thus, during wakefulness where the human brain coordinates performance by using both information-processing modes in parallel, automatization sets free the capacity of the controlled information-processing mode for flexible interactions with individually significant aspects of the environment or with aspects with which the individual is not familiar.

During sleep all interactions with the internal and external realities are executed with the automatic information-processing mode. The preattentive operations of the cycle of communication based on knowledge stored during wakefulness in the momentary accessible store and in the higher ones (asymmetry of the state-dependent retrieval; Section 5) coordinate sleep behavior by using the automatic mode. This mode, when necessary (i.e., when signal information is recognized by the preattentive processes), may change the depth of sleep via automatized attention responses (i.e., shifts in the brain's functional state closer to wakefulness) and, if not sufficient, even may initiate wakefulness. In this way, the controlled information-processing mode can be used for coping with the signal information (compare Section 6.2).

3. Acquisition of Knowledge: The Human Memory System

All findings on which this model relies show clearly that the major determinant of the characteristics of human behavior is the sum of acquired knowledge. Acquired knowledge is the internal coordinate system continuously updated by current internally and externally generated information, and it is used to organize and control perception, cognition, emotion, and action; that is, complex human performance. The cycle of communication, which we have equated with the functional and structural nature of an adaptive, nonunitary orienting response, is the medium of the acquisition and updating of knowledge and of the manifestation of its effects on behavior. Acquisition of knowledge means acquiring mnemonic representations about the interactions with the environment. These representations enable the continuous remapping (a pattern formation) of the internal and external realities, the recognition and evaluation of their significance for the well-being of the individual (pattern recognition), and the formation of the appropriate responses. Thus, although the basic mechanisms of the organization of behavior—the operations of the cycle of communication—remain unchanged from birth to death and function equally in all states of consciousness, their effects on acquisition and updating of the individual's knowledge and on using this knowledge to form behavior varies as a function of the previously acquired and momentarily available knowledge (see also Koukkou and Lehmann, 1989). This explains the variability and individuality of human behavior and, for the scope of this article, of sleep mentation (Section 6).

We do not address the question of how the results of the individual interactions with the environments are maintained or represented in the brain so as to form later behavior. Common sense and all experimental findings suggest that whatever the physical instantiations of the mnemonic representations are, there can be no doubt that they are formed in the brain via the interaction with the environment. After all, there is no human being with a healthy brain and healthy executive organs who did not learn and use the language of his or her social environment to interact verbally with this environment. In this section we summarize the present state of the research on human memory (acquisition of knowledge) in general terms (e.g., Anderson, 1981; Ellis and Hunt, 1983; Morton, Hammersley, and Bekerian, 1985; see also Gorfein and Hoffman, 1987). In these terms human knowledge is stored in three mnemonic categories or memory representations: units of data, skills, and strategies.

Units of Data: Multimodal complex representations of past events and experiences. They originate from summary representations that generalize from details of the signals that gave rise to them and from their repetitions (e.g., Neisser, 1976; Rumelhart, 1980; Rumelhart et al., 1987; Stillings et al., 1987). They represent factual knowledge about the individual's realities. They constitute the knowledge basis. These representations include information about the internal (physiological, cognitive, and emotional) states existing at the time when an event is experienced and about the external context features surrounding the event.

Skills (Programs of Responses): These are particular memory representations of complex responses (specific sequences of actions) that are tightly bound to the mnemonic representations of particular input configurations (units of data). They are formed with intensive and mostly purposeful practice, based on the continuous interaction of the individual with specific internal and external environments (e.g., Neumann, 1984; Section 2.5).

Strategies (Procedural Knowledge): Cognitive-emotional strategies refer to knowledge about how to perform various mental activities in order to treat the physical, social, and internal realities (such as thoughts, memories, goals, emotions, signals for the body functions, metabolic, hormonal, and vigilance states) and their representations in memory in a systematic way (e.g., Anderson, 1981, 1985; Neisser, 1976; Section 2.5).

All three mnemonic categories are coded into all acquired languages of the individual; that is, into the symbolic (verbal and nonverbal) and emotional languages of the individual's brain (compare Section 4). They do not represent a one-to-one or an isomorphic correspondence with the features of the internal (e.g., thoughts and emotions) or external environment that gave rise to them (e.g., Baumgartner, 1983; Kandel and Schwartz, 1981, 1982; McClelland and Rumelhart, 1986; Pribram, 1971; Roitblat, 1982). They are dynamic phenomena that at each moment are resynthesized within the same or within more complex categories, based on the interaction between the inputs to the accessible memory storage and its activated representations, the contents of the working memory (Section 3.1). With each "use" they become updated (e.g., Anderson and Milson, 1989; Eich, 1982). Thus, the acquisition of human knowledge cannot be the acquisition of habits or the acquisition of simple connections between stimuli and responses. Furthermore, the memory representations—in contrast to some use of the concept in computer constructs—cannot be inert structures that are operated on by processes. They are dynamic functions of the cortical neuronal assemblies. All three mnemonic categories, when well learned, can be automatically triggered (with reflex-like speed) by the occurrence of given specific conditions in the current input and in the working memory; that is by the computation of a neuronal model of the internal and external realities similar to that one by which or for which they were originally developed (Section 2.5). Crucial missing portions of the external input are filled in out of the working memory's contents (compare Lehmann and Koukkou, 1990).

Human memory is assumed to consist of interconnected nodes, with each node representing a multidimensional concept (e.g., Atkinson and Shiffrin, 1968; Ellis and Hunt, 1983). With maturation of the individual and via the process of the continuous interaction with the environment, these nodes become more complex by building on previously stored mnemonic categories, and they become increasingly interassociated and interrelated with each other. Thus, the human memory system may be described as a very large capacity store that is organized in nodal structures. The nodes include control elements of signal representations. These control elements code important aspects of the events and experiences that gave rise to them (including emotional aspects) and are associatively related to context, to cognitive-emotional strategies developed to cope with such events, and to programs for responses (skills) as well as to response-evoking structures (e.g., Estes, 1973; Horton and Mills, 1984; Norman, 1986; Shiffrin and Schneider, 1977).

For our purposes, the human memory system is conceptualized in terms of functional separability of a continuum of memory stores (Baddeley, 1982; Morto, et al., 1985). Memory stores are viewed as arranged in a linear sequence of memory stores or in levels and sometimes in hierarchical tree structures (Atkinson and Shiffrin, 1968). The linearity of the order of memory stores (the levels) is mainly the result of the individual development. It has been proposed that the level structure of memory reflects the synaptogenesis and dendritogenesis that continue after birth (e.g., Akert, 1979; Edelman, 1987) and corresponds to the increase of the memory space with experience and maturation (e.g., Case, 1985). For our considerations, the increase in memory space, the level structure, is reflected in the developmental changes of the brain's electrical expression (EEG) (Koukkou and Lehmann, 1983b, 1989). Levels refer further to a temporal directionality of processing so that certain nodes (the less developed) activate other nodes (the more developed ones if they exist) but not vice versa (Shiffrin and Schneider, 1977; compare Section 5). The contents of each space, when well established, are activated automatically (Section 2.5); that is, quickly and reliably. When further "needed" or used, the contents of a given memory space are "copied" into the stores of the next level of development and provide the basis for the building of more complex nodal structures. The primacy of early experiences in "modulating" general behavior might be explained by this perspective.

Summarizing the functions of human memory, important conceptual distinctions exist between the functions that lead to inputs to, storage in, and retrieval from memory storages. Information entered into memory is continuously generated internally (thoughts, memories, emotions, goals, imaginations, signals from the body organs, metabolic and hormonal states, level of vigilance, etc.) and externally.

Storage, that is, mnemonic functions (building of memory representations), is an active phenomenon widely distributed in the cortical neuronal network. Memory representations are continuously and dynamically resynthesized (analysis by synthesis) via parallel processing by the holistic, integrative, and cooperative functions of the cortical neuronal assemblies, emerging from the interactions between already stored data and momentarily incoming internal and external signals (e.g., Anderson and Milson, 1989; Baumgartner, 1983; Grossberg, 1986; Kandel and Schwartz, 1982).

Storage in and retrieval out of the memory system is state-dependent and follows an asymmetric mode of function (Section 5). The mechanisms that allow fast and efficient search and access to memory (retrieval processes) have been discussed in the literature under the headings of spreading activation or under the headings of priming (e.g., Posner and McLeod, 1982; Ratcliff and McKoon, 1988). It has been repeatedly shown that retrieval relies on the coexistence of cues available at the time of storage with cues available at recall (e.g., Baddeley, 1982; Eich, 1980, 1986; Leventhal and Thomarken, 1986). Retrieval cues may be features of the external environment but may also be features of the internal state, that is, internal changes of a natural kind such as vigilance or hormonal and metabolic changes (Section 5), as well as thoughts and emotions (Eich, 1986; Mecklenbrauker and Hager, 1984). We are not consciously aware of all information stored in our memory system, not even all the currently accessible memory contents that are used by the automatic information-processing mode for the organization of the momentary performance (Section 2.5). Only when memory representations are activated (matched) during wakefulness by significant inputs or state changes, that is, when they are used by the controlled information-processing mode for the organization of behavior, do we become aware of their existence. At other times we or others notice the effects of knowledge on our performance although we are not aware of having purposefully acquired or used it (Bower, 1975).

3.1 Working Memory

Studies of human memory showed that at a given moment in time only a part of the total acquired knowledge (a part of the total memory storage) is accessible for current information processing. The activated contents of the currently accessible storage are called *working memory*. At a given moment in time working memory may include many different activated representations in different levels of analysis or only some specific ones (e.g., Anderson, 1985; Brainerd and Kingma, 1985; Craik and Lockhart, 1972; Ellis and Hunt, 1983; Horton and Mills, 1984; Stillings et al., 1987).

Working memory plays two somewhat distinct roles. First it acts as a selective window on long-term storage by making knowledge relevant to the current psychobiological priorities (motivational state) accessible to the cycle of communication for the organization of behavior. In other words, working memory offers its contents for the interpretation of incoming events, for evaluation of their significance for the momentary psychobiological priorities, for decision making, thinking, feeling, and handling, permitting the use of "appropriate" data units, skills, and cognitive-emotional strategies for coping with the momentary external and internal realities. Second it provides a storehouse for the integration and incorporation (storage) of incoming information relevant to the current motivational state (e.g., Shiffrin and Schneider, 1977). Thus, the contents of the working memory represent the momentarily activated set of facts available to the individual for guiding momentary behavior; that is, for perception, evaluation, and decision processes.

Accordingly, if the contents of the working memory are the basis for the organization of behavior, they have to be flexibly and continuously adapted to the changes of the internal and external realities of the individual. That means working memory has to be at each moment sufficiently rich in knowledge (1) to capture the familiarities and unfamiliarities of the individual's realities at the given moment, (2) to recognize the momentary individual psychobiological priorities and the demands put on these priorities by the momentary realities, and (3) to adapt the psychobiological responding in such a way that the momentarily valid priorities are not violated, but that, at the same time, significant aspects of event configurations are "adequately" treated. In other words, the working memory of a given moment includes acquired factual knowledge of the individual about himself or herself and about his or her internal and external realities as well as acquired skills and strategies (procedural knowledge) necessary to cope with such realities. Thus, working memory is not a fixed processing structure. It is dynamically and continuously reconfigured in the course of processing of information coming from the external environment and from all systems of the organism, and it is continuously readjusted to the momentary significance of such information; skills and strategies available in the working memory's contents play the major role (e.g., Shiffrin and Schneider, 1977; Ratcliff and McKoon, 1988). This description of the dynamics of working memory has similarities with the "concept of trace" proposed by McClelland and Rumelhart (1986) (compare also Edelman, 1987).

In the context of our considerations, the brain's functional state as reflected in the EEG at each moment in time defines the "size" of memory; that is, which memory storage is accessible and, thus, which portions of the individual's knowledge can be used for the conscious organization of behavior—executed via the controlled information-processing mode—or for the nonconscious (automatic) organization of behavior—executed via the automatic information-processing mode. The flexibility of the working memory is mediated by the continuous functional adaptation of the brain via automatized attention responses (Section 2.5). The required dimensions of this adaptation are at each moment reestimated by the preattentive processes and installed as the EEG components of the adaptive orienting response and its graded manifestation (shorter or longer lasting, more or less intensive shift or no shift in the brain's functional state; Section 2.4). This functional adaptation is constrained by the general determinants of the brain's functional state and by their momentary interactions (Section 5). The operations of the cycle of communication assess the environment continuously for its "significance." When the contents of the working memory do not suffice for the organization of adequate responses, they are revised by a shift of functional state. This is reflected by an EEG phenomenon, the "P300" at about 300 msec after an important event, and by the change of the EEG state. Donchin et al. (1986) suggested that the P300 is a manifestation of neural activity, produced whenever it becomes necessary to update the neuronal model that appears to be the basis of the ability of the nervous system to control behavior.

Working memory is thus a continuously and dynamically reconfigured (by the preattentive processes) and electrically manifested (by the EEG components of the orienting response) implementation of the brain's functional adaptation. This applies to all levels of consciousness between excitation, wakefulness, and sleep. It should be stressed again that the content of the working memory is not the content of consciousness. The experience of consciousness may lie in the subset of the content of working memory during wakefulness that is activated by input identified as important and thus given controlled processing as "attended to" (Shiffrin and Schneider, 1977). During sleep the recurrent appearance of the sleep stages corresponds to the recurrent opening of memory storages and thus to the formation of working memory contents that organize the interaction with the environment in such a way that sleep can be maintained and its functions maintain priority. The brain's functional state expressed in the EEG signature of REM sleep represents a working memory whose contents can to some extent be retrieved out of wakefulness (Section 6).

4. Emotions and Their Role for the Organization of Human Behavior

The role of the brain's information processing for the formation of emotions, and the position and the role of emotions (emotional aspects the internally and externally generated information and of their representations in memory) for the organization of behavior is not clear in the concepts and assumptions about human information processing. A number of recent publications discuss emotions and their relations to cognitive processes and to normal and abnormal behavior (e.g., Bower, 1981; Ciompi, 1982; Clark and Fiske, 1982; Greenberg and Safran, 1984; Ingram and Reed, 1986; Koukkou, 1988; Koukkou-Lehmann, 1987; Lazarus, 1982; Leventhal and Tomarken, 1986; Mandler, 1975; Mayer, 1986; Moser, 1983; Roth and Tucker, 1986).

The basic argument for our considerations is that human emotions emerge out of the same cooperative, integrative, holistic functions of the cortex that are the origin of all other subjectively perceivable components of behavior (perceptions, images, fantasies, thoughts, goals, plans, etc.) and all behaviorally and physiologically manifested components of behavior (compare Section 2.1). Accordingly, emotions neither precede nor follow cognition or action. This argument is based on the assumption that the mnemonic representations include not only information coming from the different modalities and from the internal states, but also information about their emotional qualities; that is, the mnemonic representations of acquired knowledge are coded into the acquired, symbolic, verbal and nonverbal, and into the emotional languages of the individual. Thus, activation of memory representations also activates emotions and vice versa. Cognition and affect are two indispensable subjective components of the individually synthesized reality, and they provide a perceivable link of the continuously functioning interaction of the individual with his or her realities (cycle of communication). There is no moment during life without subjectively experienced (cognitive-emotional), physiologically measurable, and behaviorally describable dimensions (compare, e.g., Greenberg and Safran, 1984; Leventhal, 1980). Some of these dimensions can be observed and studied without the individual's cooperation and some not.

The emotional qualities of incoming events (internal and external) and of their mnemonic representations emerge (1) out of the "quality" of the demands that these events impose on the well-functioning (the psychobiological well-being) of the developing individual at the moment of their first occurrences, (2) out of the consequences of these demands for the individual's well-being, (3) out of the efficacy with which originally innate response patterns by themselves or via modification of the quality of the interactions with the social environment contributed to the maintenance or the reinstallation of the individual's well-being, and (4) out of many repetitions of such combinations. Herewith, the personal aspects of the emotional qualities and consequences of the interactions with the internal and external realities and their mnemonic representations are formed. They lead to the development of the individual's emotional language. As we have seen, the neuronal model of the realities is continuously and dynamically resynthesized, based on the interaction between the incoming information and the accessible knowledge about similar events. Thus, at each moment in time the new emotional state is computed as one indispensable component of the multidimensional neuronal model of the individual's momentary internal and external realities. This component plays a decisive role for the choice of the information processing mode that will be used for the organization of behavior, and hereby it also plays a decisive role in the dimension of the working memory at each moment. As we have seen, the mnemonic representations of individually significant events become tightly connected with the mnemonic representations of attention responses. An attention response means a shift in the brain's functional state to more arousal and thus the change of the working memory's contents accessible to the cycle of communication (Section 5). In this way, individually defined significant aspects (emotional aspects) of memory representations may influence behavior and the quality of the individual's interaction with the realities. It has been shown that the personal significance of experiences influences retrieval processes (Bower, 1981; Mandler, 1975). This approach to emotions, in our opinion, helps to understand basic information processing in the area of affect in the same way in which cognition and organization of complex behavior is understood.

5. The Concept of Functional State of the Brain with State-Dependent Retrieval of Knowledge

The concept of global functional states of the brain has been a recurrent explicit or implicit theme in neurophysiological thinking, in assessment of levels of consciousness, in introspective experiences, in behavior studies, and in studies of psychopathology. Different states of the brain have been distinguished on scales with gross subdivisions such as childhood-adulthood, or wakefulness-sleep, but also in more finely graded scales such as relaxation-attention-excitation. Different descriptions have been used to define the different states. However, as the brain's functional states do not vary along only one dimension we need multifactorial descriptions. The concept of multifactorially defined functional states of the brain that are manifest in the scalp EEG and associated with state-dependent information processing operations are basic for our model. This concept is developed considering (1) the phenomenon of state-dependent retrieval and its relation to the brain's functional state as reflected in the scalp EEG, and (2) the research findings suggesting relations between the EEG states of the human brain and the cognitive-emotional and action styles as well as the brain's information processing operations, attention, learning, retrieval, and orienting (Sections 2.3, 2.4, and 2.5).

State-dependent retrieval or *state-specific memory* originally referred to the observation that events experienced and acquired in a particular drug state of the brain are optimally remembered when retention is tested in the same drug state that was present at the time of acquisition (Overton, 1979; Weingartner, 1978; for a recent review see Eich, 1986). This phenomenon has been studied with animals and humans and with a variety of centrally active drugs.

Eich (1986) summarized the chief characteristics of state-dependent retrieval considering human memory as follows. First, state-dependent retrieval has an asymmetrical mode of appearance, known as *dissociation of learning*. That means, events encoded in a drugged state are difficult to retrieve in the drug-free state, whereas events encoded in the drug-free state are not state-specific and can be retrieved in both drugged and drug-free states. Second, state-dependent retrieval is more likely to emerge when retention is accessed by means of a noncued procedure; the presence of reminder cues at the time of remembering diminishes dissociative effects (cues seem to function like "keys" that open or close memory storage; e.g., Eich, 1982; Ratcliff and McKoon, 1988). Third, well-learned behavior (automatized behavior; Section 2.5) is not state dependent. State-dependent retrieval is described in humans mainly for abstract (not automatized) concepts. Dreams also belong to such abstract concepts (Section 6). The model we presently propose includes the phenomenon of state-dependent retrieval (Figures 3.1 and 3.2).

There is no general agreement about the nature of the state-specific memory or state-dependent retrieval. However, because a review of the literature suggests clearly the importance of the retrieval context in determining what is or is not remembered, the phenomenon cannot be explained by failure or differences of consolidation. The evidence suggests that the differences are attributable to the quality of retrieval of information which is available in memory and accessible under some but not all conditions (Eich, 1986).

The demonstration of similar dissociations between acquisition and retrieval in humans without drug modification of the brain's functional state but in connection with internally and externally induced natural changes of this state are of special relevance for our considerations. State-dependent retrieval has been reported in healthy humans during state changes elicited by the environment, moods, and affective contexts (e.g., Bower, 1981; Teasdale and Russel, 1985), as a function of different times during daytime wakefulness (e.g., Holloway, 1978); and as a function of hormonal states (e.g., McGaugh, 1983). Furthermore, the concept of state-specific memory has been implicated in different disorders such as alcoholism, hyperreactivity, multiple personality, depression, epilepsy, and antiepileptic drugs as well as flashback phenomena of drug users (Reus, Weingartner, and Post, 1979; see also Eich, 1986; Koukkou, 1988). Drugs commonly employed in the treatment of psychiatric disorders, to our knowledge have not yet been tested for their ability to produce state-specific effects in human memory.

The review of the evidence of state-dependent retrieval in humans suggests clearly that all pharmacological and nonpharmacological situations that have been found to be connected with the phenomenon of state-dependent retrieval are characterized by EEG differences between the state of acquisition and the state of retrieval, where the state of acquisition was associated with slower mean EEG frequencies (less "aroused" state) than the state of retrieval (compare Figure 3.1; Koukkou and Lehmann, 1980, 1983b). Amnesia in hypnosis could also be a phenomenon based on state-dependent retrieval. According to the model there should be different EEG brain states during hypnosis and recall, and some recent findings on EEG during hypnosis have supported this assumption (e.g., Raikov, 1983).

Mental activity and experiences during sleep are difficult to recall during wakefulness. Furthermore, experiences during early stages of childhood development are impossible or difficult to recall in later stages of development and in adulthood (see Flavell, 1977; Hetherington and McIntare, 1975; Yussen, 1985). Both situations—sleep and early stages of development—are characterized by distinct differences in the EEG state of the brain and, more precisely, by slower EEG frequencies as compared with the adult's awake EEG. Retrieval difficulties for experiences of the first years of life increase with increasing age differences between storage and recall of an experience (e.g., Fivush, Gray, and Fromhoff, 1987). Retrieval difficulties of dreams or other experiences occurring during sleep increase with increasing vigilance difference between dream generation and dream report (e.g., Cartwright, 1981; Greenberg, 1981).

Accordingly, we proposed (Koukkou and Lehmann, 1980; 1983b) that the different functional brain states (EEG states) during sleep and early development also give rise to the phenomena of state-dependent memory storage and retrieval and generally to state-dependent information processing.

Wakeful thinking, emotions, and actions in early childhood (with its slow EEG frequencies) utilize strategies that differ from those used in adulthood (with its faster EEG frequencies), and it is well known that adult thinking and emotions during wakefulness (with its wakefulness EEG characteristics) show differences from adult thinking and emotions during dreaming (with its sleep EEG characteristics; Section 6). Furthermore, there are similarities between the cognitive-emotional style of childhood and dreaming (Piaget, 1962).

Based on these observations and the results of the studies showing close relations between cognitive-emotional styles and EEG micro-states during adult wakefulness (Section 2.3), we formulated the following. Different functional states of the brain reflect different neural functional states that are manifested in different EEG characteristics, have access to different assemblies of knowledge and different memory stores, and are associated with cognitive-emotional strategies that are state innate or have been acquired during a given state. In other words, the electrically manifested functional states of the brain define which memory storage is available and, thus, which kind of individual knowledge can be used by the cycle of communication for the organization of behavior at a given moment in time. Thus, operationally for each EEG state of the brain only a part of the total stored knowledge (total memory storages) is available (Figure 3.1) to influence the style of interaction with the environment.

Considering the finding that storage of new information is optimal in the state-associated store and retrieval of stored information is asymmetric, the reviewed relations of the EEG brain states to the phenomenon of state-dependent retrieval suggest the following. For a given functional state, retrieval is possible out of the storage of this state and out of storage associated with higher ranking, more complex organized states, but not out of storage of lower-ranking states. "Higher" states are those associated with EEG patterns similar to adult, healthy, and equilibrated wakefulness; that is, more developed, or more vigilant, or "better" regulated states in terms of metabolic and hormonal balance, or drug-free states. Thus, knowledge acquired during EEG states of the brain similar to adult wakefulness EEG states—implying higher-order storage—remains accessible to the cycle of communication when lower-order storage, that is, storage of less awake and less developed states, are open, but not the opposite. Accordingly, during sleep a wider spectrum of knowledge is potentially available for the evaluation of incoming information (compare Section 6). The accessibility of knowledge acquired in lower-order storage depends on the similarity between the EEG states at the times of experience and retrieval; that is, on the degree of match or mismatch between the EEG states. Changes of the EEG functional state of the brain in the direction of faster EEG frequencies (in the direction of adulthood or of more arousal) "close" the memory storages of less developed or less awake states (semantic inhibition) and herewith restrict the retrieval of information that has been encoded in these stages; at the same time these changes activate new storages and the shift-eliciting information is incorporated into the mnemonic contents of the newly opened storage and the knowledge of this storage is used for the further organization of behavior.

Thus, the EEG-defined functional state of the brain at each moment constrains the access to some knowledge and at the same time enables the access to other kinds of knowledge and thereby enables or constrains some kinds of cognitive-emotional and action styles; that is, the character and the quality of the interactions of the individual with his or her internal and external environment.

In consequence, mood states, an environment with specific significance to the individual, time during the day, hormonal states, levels of vigilance, and levels of development are associated with "proprietary" EEG states, and these by themselves function as retrieval cues. This can be explained by the "opening" and "closing" of memory storage (activation and disactivation of memory storage or content) by the changes of the brain's functional state. We have suggested these formulations also account for ordinary forgetting and behavioral changes in stress and panic and during depression (Koukkou, 1988; Koukkou and Lehmann, 1980, 1983b).

The human EEG recorded in wakefulness shows a shift of the dominant components to faster wave frequencies from birth to the end of puberty, with differences between brain regions in the rate of changes (Katada et al., 1981; Matousek and Petersen, 1973; Samson-Dollfus and Goldberg, 1979). During these ontogenetic EEG changes, (1) there is an enormous increase in the number of interactions between the cortical neurons (synaptogenesis and dendritogenesis that have been proposed to correspond to an increase of memory space; Akert, 1979; Edelman, 1987; Koukkou and Lehmann, 1987), and (2) there are changes in the cognitive-emotional and action (manifest behavioral) style of the developing individual. Generally speaking, the older the child, the more reality-including and reality-adaptive is its dealing with the environment (e.g., Flavell, 1977; Piaget, 1968; Reese, 1976; Yussen, 1985). At each age slower and faster EEG wave elements are combined in differing relations, and these relations fluctuate during a child's day, during which distinct fluctuations of cognitive-emotional and action style also can be observed. This means for the process of ontogenesis that in a given child during a day's wakefulness varying amounts of adult EEG patterns may be present and more or less mature behavior can be performed due to changes in the accessible knowledge. During the early stages of childhood development an enormous amount of knowledge is acquired. However, the mean age out of which adult humans can recall childhood experiences is the age of three to four years, an age when typical adult EEG patterns may be first seen for brief periods.

The alternation between wakefulness and sleep is also characterized by systematic EEG changes that go in the opposite direction than development. With decreasing levels of vigilance, there is a shift of the dominant EEG frequency components to lower frequencies. However, this shift is not homogenous. Slower and faster wave frequencies are combined in different relations, and these relations are different in different brain regions within and between conventionally defined sleep stages (e.g., Armitage et al., 1989; Borbely et al., 1981; Pivik, 1978). REM sleep, with its frequent dream reports, exhibits a wave frequency spectrum that is close to that of sleep stage 1 NREM and, to some extent, to wakefulness (e.g., Müller, 1986), but differs from it in interhemispheric EEG coherence (Dumermuth and Lehmann, 1981); REM sleep coherence is more "sleeplike."

Thus, the developmental changes of the EEG and their fluctuations during waking life have similarities with the changes of the adult EEG and their fluctuations during different sleep stages. With increasing age the mean EEG frequency increases, and with decreasing vigilance the mean EEG frequency decreases. Thus, during a person's (child, adolescent, adult) sleep varying amounts of less "developed" waking EEG patterns may be present. Based on these similarities, we have hypothesized that during sleep functional brain states of previous developmental stages are reinstalled. In this context, sleep implies repeated functional regressions to previous developmental stages; or in other words, during sleep humans go repeatedly through previous developmental (ontogenetic) functional states, and hereby they have access to knowledge (data, skills, and strategies) acquired or innate in the memory storage of these developmental stages. This corresponds to the functional significance of sleep and its psychological concomitant, the dream (Section 6). We do not conceive these EEG states as corresponding to conventional EEG sleep stages or years of age. We propose that brief epochs in the range of seconds or shorter as discussed earlier, represented by particular temporal patterns and spatial distributions of EEG potentials constitute a functional state (see Section 2.3).

For reasons of clarity, separate storage spaces that correspond to functional states are presented in Figure 3.1; one has to think, however, of a graded storage continuum. The different storage spaces do not imply different brain locations; the "space" is a common apparatus (cortex; Section 2.1) that operates in different functional states (neuronal functional states) or to which there is access from different directions or is treated with different tools. However, an ontogenetically defined time scale plays an additional role in the "amount" of storage space as we have mentioned earlier (compare also Section 3). The entire system in the illustration is shown in a functional state called 4; which implies that access to storage space 4 is open to the preattentive processes of the cycle of communication for perceptual categorization, identification, evaluation, for storage, and for the selection of the response. Storage spaces of higher order (which are indicated by higher numbers) are partially open for perceptual categorization, identification, evaluation, and selection of the response, but they are not accessible for storage; this illustrates the asymmetry of the phenomenon. Storage spaces of lower order, indicated by lower numbers, are not open for identification, recall, or storage, except that the next lower space is accessible for partial retrieval only.

The pivotal point of the model is that brain functioning is multifactorially defined and continuously reorganized and readjusted via the EEG components of the adaptive, nonunitary orienting response according to the informational demands put on the individual by the momentarily formed perceptions, thoughts, emotions, goals, motives, and so forth (the current analyzed information) and in relation to the brain's functional state just before the information's arrival. Possible functional readjustments are constrained by the general determinants of the brain's functional state, which are maturational age, internal clocks, metabolic and hormonal conditions, and by their relations at the given moment. Figure 3.2 summarizes these determinants and the mechanisms that mediate the interactions and their readjustments.

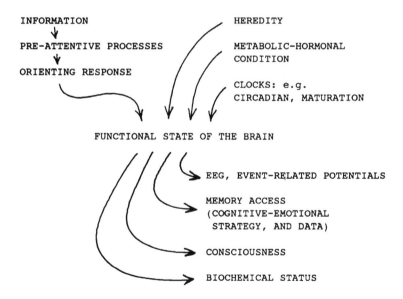

Figure 3.2. The momentary functional state of the brain, its determinants and its manifestations.

The brain's global functional states are conceived as a mosaic of many local functional states and reflect a certain organization of neural activity. Viewing the succession of global functional states over time, gross states such as sleep stages or wakefulness are seen as consisting of temporal sequences of global micro-states. Spontaneous state changes occur as a function of time, in principle governed by internal clocks (life cycle, hormonal cycle, circadian rhythms, 90-minute cycles, 5-second periods of fluctuation of attention, 10-Hz periodicity of human brain activity, etc.). These basic internal periodicities can be strongly influenced or even reset by readjustments of the state. Examples are the changes of the brain's electrical activity by individually significant information, its systematic changes during wakefulness and sleep by increasing familiarity with events; the increase of REM sleep time after days of stress, worry, and intense learning, and generally after emotionally demanding events during the day (e.g., Bloch, Hennevin, and Leconte, 1979; Greenberg, 1981; Greenberg et al., 1983; Hartmann, 1976; Smith, 1981).

Summarizing in the framework of our model: at each moment in time the preattentive processes of the cycle of communication, which operate continuously and similarly during all levels of consciousness, determine which features of the continuously re-created neuronal model of the internal and external realities must be answered with a shift of the brain's functional state to more arousal and which must not be followed by such a shift. The characteristics of this shift (intensity, duration, topography, etc.) are state dependent and at each moment are redefined by the preattentive processes out of the interaction between the current input to and the current contents of the working memory. These characteristics can be constrained by the general determinants of the brain's functional state and their momentary interactions. The shift or no shift in the brain's functional state is implemented via the EEG components of a nonunitary orienting response with an adaptive significance. It leads to a change or no change in the working memory's contents. In other words, it leads to the adaptation of the working memory's contents to the contextual significance of the momentary internal realities (e.g., thoughts and emotions, metabolic, hormonal, vigilance states) and of the external realities (e.g., important environments). This corresponds to the concepts of semantic priming or semantic inhibition (Section 2.4).

A shift to more arousal means for all states of consciousness that the preattentive processes recognized the whole set of inputs (the neuronal model of the realities) or some of its features as "new," unexpected, or important for the momentary psychobiological priorities. In other words, information that elicits emotion, surprise, curiosity, and so on, and information for which an automatized attention response is available in the working memory's contents (information that has "signal" characteristics) elicits a shift to more arousal. During healthy wakefulness this indicates the shift from the automatic to the controlled information-processing mode with its flexible, selective, and adaptive use of knowledge for the organization of behavior (Kahneman, 1973; Norman, 1976; Section 2.5). During sleep a shift in the brain's functional state to more arousal corresponds either to a clock-dependent change from NREM to REM stage or to the execution of an automatized "attention" response that has been established during wakefulness. In the latter case, the magnitude, form, and duration of this shift depends on the sleep stage. This state shift leads to the opening of higher-order memory storage for the further treatment of the signal information, resulting in state-dependent retrieval (semantic associations and priming), and at the same time leads to the shut-off of the lower-order storage (semantic inhibition). If in the light of the contents of the new storages the material again shows signal characteristics, the shift of the brain's functional state to more arousal may continue and, if necessary, may reach wakefulness. Thereby the controlled information-processing mode may be called up to cope with the signal information.

No shift in the brain's functional state means for all states of consciousness that the preattentive processes recognize the neuronal model of the momentary internal and external realities as familiar (i.e., as information for which automatized responses other than attention are available in the working memory's contents) or as unimportant for the momentary psychobiological priorities. In the case of familiarity, the automatized responses may be executed without changes of the brain's functional state. This means additionally that the further treatment of the information may take place also with the automatic information-processing mode based on the same working memory's contents . The concept of automaticity is used to explain the selective interactions with the internal and external environment during sleep and the formal characteristics of dreams (Section 6). Accordingly, in the context of the model, human behavior differs as a function of these factors: (1) functional state of the brain, (2) previously stored knowledge in the memory storage accessible from this functional state, and (3) context. These factors and their interactions may constrain or enlarge the spectrum of "solutions" available for tentative application to cope with the momentary realities.

Thus, they define the quality of the individual's cognitive-emotional and action style (the psychobiological pattern of behavior) at the given moment in time.

6. Dream Generation, Sleep Regulation and the Functions of Sleep

When considering the different kinds of dream reports in the literature, that is, reports collected in sleep laboratories, in analytic sessions, and from spontaneously remembered home dreams, it becomes obvious that sleep mentation can show all formal characteristics and qualities of human mentation. In other words, dreams can be unrealistic, bizarre, fantastic, discontinuous, with inadequate emotions but also realistic, plausible, continuous and with adequate emotions (e.g., Antrobus, 1978; Foulkes, 1985; Foulkes et al., 1988; Kramer, 1981; Schwartz, Weinstein, and Arkin, 1978; Strauch and Meier, 1989). The major differential characteristics of mentation reported out of sleep, however, remain an imagery (often visual but also multimodal) type of experience with hallucinatory self-participation and thus without self-awareness (the dreamer typically is not aware that he or she is dreaming; however, see also Purcell et al., 1986), and the lack of reference to momentary external reality. However, all these characteristics also can be experienced in different combinations during behavioral wakefulness, spontaneously as normal imagery (day dreaming, visualization), or as pathological imagery (schizophrenic imagery) and drug-induced imagery (e.g., Koukkou and Lehmann, 1976). Therefore, considering mechanisms of dream generation, we cannot expect the human brain to show characteristics which are not available to the system in wakefulness as well. Cases in point are the dreams of blind people, which do not include visual experiences (e.g., Kerr, Foulkes, and Schmidt, 1982; Schwartz et al., 1978), and children's sleep mentation reports that have been found to vary stylistically in accordance with developmental age and that can be first experienced as dreaming when the child has reached sufficient cognitive maturation in wakeful life (Foulkes, 1982). At the same time, however, we have to account for the characteristics that are more common in sleep mentation, for the difficulty of wakeful recall of dreams and for the characteristics of the brain's functional states associated with human sleep. Furthermore, because complete dream reports can be obtained not only from all sleep stages, but in particular well before the occurrence of a first REM stage (for a review of the evidence, see Foulkes, 1985), a general psychobiological theory of dream generation cannot be based on physiological features particular to one sleep stage. Nevertheless, such a theory has to propose an explanation not only for the differences between sleep mentation and wakeful mentation, but as well for the reported differences between REM and NREM dream reports and for the fact that the probability of dream recall in subsequent wakefulness varies as a function of the sleep stages out of which the reports were collected, indicative of state-dependent functions. The smaller the differences in the brain's functional state (as defined by the EEG) between the sleep state out of which the report was elicited and the state of wakefulness during which dream recall occurs, the better is the quality of recall (Cartwright, 1981); REM sleep, being similar in some aspects to waking (e.g., Feinberg and Floyd, 1982), is often found to be associated with better dream recall.

We propose that the general state dependency of the brain's information processing functions, the functional asymmetry of the state-dependent retrieval of memory material and their relations to the multifactorially defined and electrically manifested functional states of the brain as reviewed in Section 5 and Figures 3.1 and 3.2 account for the observed characteristics of dreaming. At the same time, such a suggestion permits an integration of the experimental findings and theoretical approaches concerning the determinants of sleep and the functions of sleep (see later).

6.1 Dream Generation

We define as a dream those results of sleep state-dependent types of cognitive-emotional interpretation of the sleeping individual's internal and external realities that are recallable and subjectively perceivable in subsequent wakefulness.

The flow of information to the central nervous system from the internal and external realities and the active, selective, and adaptive interactions with these realities are not interrupted by the change from waking to sleeping. The operations of the cycle of communication during sleep continue (1) to create neuronal models of the sleeping individual's momentary realities out of the interaction between incoming signals and momentarily accessible knowledge, (2) to evaluate the significance of these realities for the momentary psychobiological priorities, that is, for sleep and the present sleep stage, and (3) to select and execute the psychobiological "responses" (Figure 3.1 and Section 2.1). However, all aspects of these "responses" are changed by the alternation from wakefulness to sleep and the opposite. The subjective aspects of these "responses" that are recallable in wakefulness are the dreams.

During sleep, on the one side, the incoming external information has been actively eliminated or changed by the preparations to go to sleep. On the other side, the knowledge accessible to the cycle of communication for the creation of the neuronal model of the realities and their evaluation is changed because of the sleep-induced changes of the brain's functional state as reflected in the EEG. Accordingly, the continuously re-created neuronal models of the sleeping individual's internal and external realities are different from the models of wakefulness. They originate from the interaction between the contents of the sleep-stage-dependent portions of knowledge (knowledge stored in higher order storage is also accessible because of the functional asymmetry of the memory retrieval processes) and the incoming information during sleep, as synthesized by the cooperative, synergetic function of the neocortex (compare Hunt, 1989). They portray the reality of sleep as to its functional significance (see later). The resulting psychobiological answers to the sleep reality depict the functional adaptation to the necessity of sleep (functions of sleep) and can be recognized at the physiological level as maintenance or change of sleep stage, and at the psychological level as dreaming, or in experimental situations as responsiveness during sleep (e.g., Badia et al., 1985; Bonnet, 1982; Harsh et al., 1987; Koukkou and Lehmann, 1968; Lehmann and Koukkou, 1974).

Based on similarities in EEG patterns we have proposed that sleep implies physiological "regressions" to and thus the accessibility of memory stores of earlier stages of development. Considering dream generation, this regression means that data, skills and cognitive-emotional processing strategies that are innate to, or were acquired during, earlier developmental stages and stored in storage not directly accessible to waking adults become again available to the cycle of communication during sleep. Accordingly, dreams, being the result of a "regression" in information processing strategies and in quantity and quality of accessible knowledge, show properties that are common in cognitive-emotional treatment of realities in earlier developmental stages (Farnham-Diggory, 1972; Flavell, 1977; Freud, 1955; Piaget and Inhelder, 1969; compare Lehmann and Koukkou, 1990). That means (1) imagery characteristics with a high frequency of visual imagery, (2) strategies that "disregard" external reality, and (3) emotional aspects that very often are unspecific, neutral, or "inadequate" to the content. This corresponds to a "primary process"-like analysis of realities and within the framework of the model serves the maintenance and the functions of sleep (Section 6.2). These characteristics of dreaming are recognized only when considered in the light of adult awake knowledge. That is why in children's reports of sleep mentation we cannot expect to find characteristics that are not also available to their system in wakefulness. Sleep mentation of children can first be recognized as having occurred during sleep and meeting conventional characteristics of dreams during Piaget's preoperational period; reports of sleep mentation are in very close accordance with the wake mentation style of the developmental age (Foulkes, 1982, 1983). In general, the experience of specific types of dreams depends on previously acquired knowledge (Purcell et al., 1986).

Sleep is characterized physiologically by distinct patterns of the brain's electrical activity. These EEG patterns differ not only between wakefulness and sleep and from one sleep stage to another, but also show distinct short-term fluctuations during each sleep stage (e.g., Fein, Floyd, and Feinberg, 1981; Nakagawa, 1980). These fluctuations, indicative of shifts of state, reflect the result of the functional adaptation of the brain to incoming information (e.g., Badia et al., 1985; Harsh et al., 1987; Lehmann and Koukkou, 1974). Such state shifts correspond not only to background EEG fluctuations during sleep (e.g., Borbely, 1982) but also to the so-called phasic EEG events like Kappa complexes or vertex spikes (Pivik, 1978).

In the context of the model, each shorter or longer lasting, "spontaneous" or induced change of the brain's functional state implies changes in the memory contents accessible to the cycle of communication for the creation of the neuronal model of the momentary realities. When there is no spontaneous (clock time-induced) sleep stage change and when no information is recognized as individually important in the neuronal model of the sleeping individual's momentary reality, the brain's functional state (sleep stage) persists unchanged. That means that the sleep stage is "actively" maintained and that further related material is retrieved and associations are formed based on the contents of the accessible memory store and that the new associations are integrated in the memory store. Much of this processing may consist of image treatment in accordance with "childish" strategies (see also Lehmann and Koukkou, 1990). However, when important aspects are recognized in the neuronal model of the momentary reality or in the associations that are newly formed during sleep, a smaller or larger state shift toward wakefulness ensues as automatized attention response; the magnitude of this shift depending on the sleep stage. We have discussed the fact that the interaction with internal and external realities during sleep is accomplished with the automatic information-processing mode (Section 2.5).

A shift of the brain's functional state toward more arousal implies access to higher-order memory storage for the next cycle of communication. That means the activation of new associations, their storage in the newly opened storage, and at the same time the treatment of the momentary realities with more advanced cognitive-emotional strategies and the shut-off of access to lower-order storages. Hereby, the further treatment of the important information cannot take place by drawing on its entire original context material in the lower storage space (asymmetry of state-dependent retrieval). These continuously functioning, self-organizing features that use an unspecific new information or signal information label for installation of a state change can be viewed as a goal-directed unconscious mechanism with which Freud's concept of "dream work" (i.e., the mechanisms by means of which the manifest dream content is formed) can be psychobiologically explained. If, after evaluation of the newly created neuronal model of the realities in the light of the new contextual knowledge, important aspects are recognized again, the shift to more arousal is repeated and, if found necessary, may lead to complete waking. Hereby, the controlled information-processing mode can be used for coping with the important aspects of the realities, but under the sacrifice of access to some original context information. In this context, induced or clock-dependent state shifts account for the discontinuity of dream content.

Because interaction with the environment continues in all sleep stages and the sleeping individual continuously re-creates neuronal models of the sleep stage realities, important or unimportant aspects can emerge at each moment from the interaction between the sleep stage-dependent accessible knowledge and incoming information. Thus, very different portions of previously acquired data, skills, and cognitive-emotional strategies can become available in quick succession during sleep and can be used to create the sleeping individual's thoughts, emotions, and conclusions. This results in what may be described operationally as "unconscious decisions," comparable to automatic behavioral organization during wakefulness. Accordingly, the concept of automaticity as summarized in Section 2.5 may explain the interactions with the environment during sleep and the resulting subjective aspects; that is, the dreams. Recurrent dream themes are in this context the recurrent "openings" of memory stores where the mnemonic representations of the recurrent themes are stored as automatized (well-learned) material.

In other words, repeated clock-time and adaptive shifts of the brain's functional state, which means changes of the working memory's contents, during sleep will result in the formal characteristics of the dream narrative; that is, in "sleep-type" or "dream-type" mentation. The brain mechanisms that occur with state shifts are suggested to correspond to the concepts of repression, regression, distortion, condensation, censorship, and displacement of the psychoanalytical theory. The dream narrative may show unusual characteristics when compared with adult awake mentation, but it may also show characteristics that cannot be distinguished from awake mentation. In both cases however, according to the model, it is meaningful for the individual, because its contents reflect the interaction between the individual's past history and current motivational condition as defined by the recent wakeful priorities and by the current sleep necessity; that is, the functional significance of sleep (compare, e.g., Butler and Watson, 1985; Greenberg, 1981; Horne, 1988; Kramer, Schoen, and Kinney, 1987; Section 6.2).

Accordingly, within the framework of the model, dreaming is a continuous process, like mentation during wakefulness. It originates from the same psychobiological mechanisms (brain functions) from which all other subjectively perceived aspects of human existence originate in all vigilance states. It reflects the result of the active and selective interaction of the individual during sleep with his or her internal realities (sleep necessity, hormonal and metabolic state, experiences during the day, sleep-state dependent activated knowledge, etc.) and external realities (noise from the external environment, darkness, new sleep surroundings, etc.). Consequently, a dream can reflect an "effort of problem solving" in as much as there is a "problem." Otherwise, it reflects the continuous and selective interaction with the environment.

However, because during sleep a wider spectrum of the individual's knowledge is accessible (due to the reopening of the memory stores of earlier developmental stages and the continued access to the current ones), a wider spectrum of individual "solutions" is available for tentative application to new contextual or problem material. This is reflected in dream content. Thus, working with dreams in psychotherapy helps to gain insight into a wider spectrum of the individual's coping strategies (Koukkou and Lehmann, 1983a). Accordingly, this model of behavior generation (including dream generation) makes an all-knowing, details-recognizing agent unnecessary for the explanation of desired or unintended forgetting ("repression"). In other words, the model shows clearly that there is no need for an independently acting decision-making unit in "dream work" for the preservation of sleep. Along the lines of the model, sleep is preserved by the state-dependent treatment of information, which permits the evaluation of significance of the internal and external realities in the light of the contents of the current memory storage space and higher storage spaces, yet with "childish" strategies; that is, with strategies that permit an imagery- and fantasy-like treatment of information and that do not demand correction for external reality and reflection. Sleep is also preserved by the active reduction of external input by the preparation for sleep. Sleep preservation is necessary in order for its functions to have time to take place (Section 6.2).

Our model suggests further that no sleep stage is the locus of most or of all dream generation because the brain's information processing operations are not unique to wakefulness or to sleep or to one of the sleep stages such as REM sleep. At the same level of argumentation, however, the model suggests that there is no moment in healthy waking or asleep life without mentation. There are life stages, day stages, sleep stages, momentary stages, and so forth that are characterized by differences in their mentation styles. These differences are the result of the different knowledge that may exist (development) and can be used (state-dependency) by the cycle of communication to recognize and evaluate the momentary realities and to synthesize the adequate "responses."

The poor recall of sleep mentation (dreams) in subsequent wakefulness is accounted for by the phenomenon of state-dependent retrieval and its asymmetric mode of functioning. We have seen (Section 5) that in a functional state associated with sleep EEG patterns, retrieval is possible out of the storages of this state and out of storages associated with EEG patterns closer to wakefulness (good recognition in sleep for material encoded in wakefulness), but not the opposite (poor recognition in wakefulness of material received during sleep). Stage REM sleep with its wakefulness-closer EEG states (memory storage) accounts for the better recall of mentation occurring during this sleep stage in subsequent wakefulness. Furthermore, during narration of a dream when awake, a shift in functional state to more arousal due to recognition of some signal features in the dream content or due to an external input (e.g., telephone bell) might change the momentary state in such a way that recall of it in the newly attained higher state is not possible. The numerous differences in REM and NREM dream reports, that is, recallability, emotions, frequency, complexity, length, and so on, which have been described in the literature (e.g., Antrobus, 1983) are explained, on the one hand, by the numerous possible differences between the brain's functional state during the different sleep stages (which lead to differences in the accessible knowledge for analysis and evaluation of the information processed during different sleep stages) and, on the other hand, by the numerous possible differences between the brain's sleep states during a given mentation and the brain's wakeful states during recall of this mentation.

Specifically, we propose that the sources of the differences between REM dreams and NREM dreams, and in general, between awake and sleep mentations are twofold: (1) the sleep stage–related changes in the knowledge accessible to the cycle of communication, and (2) the degree of the functional distance between the state of dream formation (sleep mentation) and the state of dream recall. The physiological closeness of the REM stage storage to wakefulness storage and thus the ability to maintain access to information stored in REM stage storage out of wakefulness explains the better recall of sleep mentation that occurs during REM sleep.

Foulkes (1982) reported that dream narratives after REM awakenings are very rare in early childhood; he proposed that this indicates that REM sleep is "dreamless" in early childhood. The model presented in this paper explains the finding in the following way. The neonate and the child during the first years of life interact with the environment with the same cycle of communication as the adult and it produces mentation during wakefulness and during sleep. The knowledge, however, that the child uses to create the neuronal model of its realities during sleep is limited and is not very different from the knowledge available in wakefulness. Thus the resulting mentation cannot reach the characteristics of a dream mentation; that is, cannot become recognized as bizarre, fantastic, inadequate, discontinuous, and so on as compared to wakeful mentation. The same can be said for wakeful mentation during early development: it exists, of course, but its characteristics correspond to the age; that is, to the still relatively small quantity and restricted quality of existing knowledge (Koukkou and Lehmann, 1989). In other words, the interpretation of the internal and external realities of the young child during sleep is not so different from the interpretation of the realities during wakefulness. Thus, there are no salient differences between sleep and awake mentation to be recognized by the child as "occurring during sleep," and the child does not have the necessary knowledge to describe it in the way older children and adults would describe dream mentation.

In the light of these considerations, the brain's REM and NREM functional states during sleep in early development are not dreamless, just like wakefulness in early development is not "mentationless" or "interactionless." The apparent ontogenetic "dissociation" of REM sleep duration and the ability to report REM sleep dreams cannot indicate that the neonate and the small child do not dream or that REM is not related to dreaming. This apparent dissociation, in our opinion, should not be used as an argument against the relation between dream recall and stage REM sleep either. This relation has been confirmed many times and is in good agreement with all studies on the relations between EEG-defined functional states of the brain and learning and retrieval processes (Sections 2.3, 5, and 6.2). The studies suggest that stage REM states with their strong similarities with adult wakeful states have a special position for the organization of acquired knowledge within the knowledge-driven approach of the organization of human behavior. This does not imply, however, that stage REM states are specific dream-production states, but that they are states whose memory stores are close enough to adult awake states for successful retrieval of some of their contents (mentation during sleep) into consciousness during waking (Koukkou and Lehmann, 1983b; Sections 2.3 and 5).

6.2 The Determinants of Sleep (Sleep Regulation)

Common experiences and experimental evidence show clearly that there is an inherent flexibility and adaptability in the psychobiological functions which underlie the initiation and temporal organization of sleep. Sleep can, within limits, easily be extended, reduced, or replaced by wakefulness (e.g., Horne, 1988; Webb, 1982). The monophasic 24-hour-cycle and nocturnal placement of adult human sleep can be also replaced by a polyphasic temporal organization within a 24-hour day given an external reality that enables the initiation of sleep whenever needed (Campbell, 1984). The physiology of sleep and the dream contents are influenced by experiences during the day and by the importance of the information which reaches the individual during sleep (e.g., Greenberg, 1981; Lehmann and Koukkou, 1974; Oswald et al., 1960; Strauch, 1969). Furthermore, after days of intense learning or stress and worry and generally after emotionally demanding events during the day, a decrease of deeper sleep stages and an increase of REM sleep time or wakefulness time occurs (Greenberg, 1981; Greenberg et al., 1983; Hartmann, 1976). Thus, sleep and sleep stages as a set of the brain's macro-states are a cyclically reoccurring, but flexible and adaptive phenomenon. Accordingly, the determinant of sleep cannot consist of a primary center, or a primary substance, or a primary nonadaptive biological oscillator that determines timing and amount of sleep in general, or REM sleep in specific (compare, e.g., Feinberg and Floyd, 1982; Horne, 1988; Koella, 1988).

Within the framework of our model, all aspects of human existence and thus also sleep are multifactorially defined and multidimensionally manifested. They reflect the continuous, dynamic, selective, and adaptive interaction with the internal realities (psychobiological priorities and needs) and external realities. These interactions are coordinated by the brain via the operations of the cycle of communication. The cycle of communication functions with similar rules in all levels of consciousness and relies for the coordination of behavior on the individual's innate and acquired knowledge that is accessible at the given moment in time. Thus, considering the regulation of sleep, the model suggests the following. The assumed "oscillator" of the brain's level of vigilance (circadian rhythm) is one of the continuously and synergetically functioning determinants of the dynamic and selective balance between psychobiological priorities and needs—to which sleep "necessity," that is, the functions of sleep, belong—and the demands put on these priorities and needs by externally originated information. In other words, preprogramed is the "ability" to initiate and maintain the set of the brain's functional states that accompany sleep, when sleep is needed. This "necessity" of sleep—like all other necessities, for example, of food, at each moment is reestimated by the interaction between homeostatic and circadian factors. The initiation and maintenance of sleep, so that its functions can occur (the sleep necessity to be given priority), is controlled by the interaction between (1) the messages coming to the central nervous system from the internal and external realities, and (2) the individual's knowledge that is accessible for the analysis and evaluation of these messages. Accordingly, the experimental findings and the theoretical approaches integrated in the model suggest that sleep and its different stages is a multifactorially defined cyclically recurring, but flexible and adaptive phenomenon that is initiated, coordinated, modulated, maintained, or changed over longer or shorter time intervals actively via the operations of the cycle of communication.

6.3 The Functions of Sleep

Universal daily experience and experimental findings show that an individually defined and individually fluctuating minimum of daily sleep time is necessary for the maintenance of a psychobiological well-functioning and subjective well-being during wakefulness. The less this sleep time, the higher is the ensuing sleepiness and the more aggravating are the mood changes and the deterioration of performance. Therefore, the aim of sleep can be formulated to be the reinstatement of the brain's functional state that enables this well-functioning during wakefulness. That corresponds to the formulation that the function of sleep is the recovery of a condition of the brain that was present at the beginning of the previous period of wakefulness (e.g., Feinberg and Evarts, 1969; Moruzzi, 1972). The following have been specifically proposed as functions of sleep: (1) restorative synthetic functions (e.g., Adam and Oswald, 1977; Moruzzi, 1963) and (2) adaptive functions; that is, integration of new information into existing structures, matching and linking of significant past and present events, in other words, the reorganization of knowledge (e.g., Palombo, 1978, 1984; Pearlman, 1970; Shoen and Badia, 1984). For discussions about the different positions regarding sleep functions, see, for example, Bonnet, 1986; Horne, 1988; Miller, 1991; Pearlman, 1970; Webb, 1982.

Within the framework of the model, (1) the brain is considered an information processor, an information store, and an information generator that works in a state-dependent manner, and (2) sleep is considered as a multifactorially and dynamically defined adaptation of the brain's function (neuronal adaptation) to the "necessity" of sleep. This adaptation implies repeated physiological "regressions" to and the reopening of memory stores of earlier stages of development while maintaining access to memory stores of adult wakefulness (asymmetrical accessibility of knowledge). Accordingly, the sequential occurrence of gross sleep stages (NREM-REM) suggests a predefined program for a sequential but adaptively renewed access to memory stores of earlier levels of development. This serves both the maintenance of sleep and the realization of its restorative-adaptive functions. The information processing strategies of earlier development treat the incoming information during sleep with "childish" strategies. This means that the information is treated without reflection and without correction for external realities. Hereby sleep can be maintained, ensuring that there is time for its functions to occur.

The proposed mechanisms of state-dependent treatment and state-dependent retrieval of information and automatized "attention" responses to signal material found during sleep in memory stores of earlier developmental storages serve the adaptive function of sleep. They enable the accessibility and transfer of relevant information from "lower-" to "higher-"order storage spaces and hereby the reorganization of knowledge and assimilation of old material and coping strategies with new ones without inducing wakefulness. In this way, previously acquired knowledge (data, skills, and cognitive-emotional strategies) can be reviewed as to a potentially useful application to recent realities and can eventually be treated in consciousness as recalled dream content. Accordingly, knowledge once acquired and used by the individual for his or her interactions with the environment may become applicable again, and important aspects of past experiences can be incorporated into adult waking life. This is the mechanism through which working with dreams in psychotherapy can achieve therapeutic effects (Koukkou and Lehmann, 1983a; Koukkou and Leuzinger-Bohleber, 1992).

In this context, REM sleep with its optimal recall of dreaming attains a special physiological significance also for the brain's information handling. This significance, however, does not lie in the direct selecting, sorting, and consolidating of the new experiences received during recent waking life (as proposed by Shapiro, 1967, Koulack and Goodenough, 1976; Palombo, 1978; and Bloch et al., 1979), but in stage REM's neuronal organization that implies the use of memory stores whose contents are at least partially accessible during adult wakefulness. The phylogenesis of stage REM sleep (Tauber, 1974) with its systematic increase in more complex animals, and the ontogenesis of stage REM sleep with its decrease from birth to adulthood (i.e., with a decrease in the amount of previously acquired knowledge that has not yet been assimilated and integrated in the stores of adult wakefulness) supports this assumption.

Summary

The chapter presents a psychobiological model of human mental activity in different levels of consciousness. It combines existing experimental data and theoretical concepts. It considers mental processes during sleep (i.e., dreams) to be the result of brain mechanisms that function in all levels of consciousness/vigilance.

The model emphasizes the role of the brain mechanisms that concern learning, memory, and retrieval, and the mechanisms that give rise to the continuous, flexible, and adaptive readjustments of the brain's functional state to external and internal realities. The basic proposal considers that the brain's functional states during sleep and wakefulness are associated with differences in processing strategies, accessible memory stores, and EEG (brain electric activity) patterns. Basic brain states are brief, in the subsecond to second range. Different concatenations of the repertoire of states account for the variety of subjective experiences.

Shifts in functional state occur spontaneously (clock-driven) or as functional adaptations to processed information via the structural and functional aspects of the orienting response, and they cause the formal characteristics of dreams. Forgetting dreams is a function of the magnitude of the difference between functional states during storage and recall. Based on EEG similarities between sleep stages and developmental stages, brain states during sleep in adults are proposed to correspond functionally with waking states during childhood. Repeated functional regressions occur during sleep, opening access to older memory material and cognitive strategies unavailable during wakeful life. Thus, earlier experiences can be used on current problems. This dreamwork constitutes the biological significance of sleep.

References

Adam, K., and Oswald, I. (1977). "Sleep Is for Tissue Restoration." *Journal of the Royal College of Physicians of London* 11: 376–388.

Akert, K. (1979). "Probleme der Hinreifung." In R. Lempp (Ed.), *Teilleistungs-Störungen im Kindesalter*, pp. 12–32. Berne: Huber.

Anderson, J. R. (Ed.). (1981). *Cognitive Skills and Their Acquisition*. Hillsdale, N. J.: Lawrence Erlbaum Associates.

———. (1985). *Cognitive Psychology and Its Implications*, 2d ed. New York: W. H. Freeman.

——— and Milson, R. (1989). "Human Memory: An Adaptive Perspective." *Psychological Review* 96: 703–719.

Antrobus, J. (1978). "Dreaming for Cognition." In A. M. Arkin, J. S. Antrobus, and S. J. Ellman (Eds.), *The Mind in Sleep*, pp. 569–581. Hillsdale, N.J.: Lawrence Erlbaum Associates.

———. (1983). "REM and NREM Sleep Reports: Comparison of Word Frequencies by Cognitive Classes." *Psychophysiology* 20: 562–567.

———. (1987). "Cortical Hemisphere Asymmetry and Sleep Mentation." *Psychological Review* 94: 359–368.

Armitage, R., Hoffmann, R., Loewy, D., and Moffitt, A. (1989). "Variations in Period-Analysed EEG Asymmetry in REM and NREM Sleep." *Psychophysiology* 26: 329–336.

Aschoff, J. (1965). "Circadian Rhythms in Man." *Science* 148: 1427–1432.

———. (1980). "The Circadian System in Man." In D. T. Krieger and J. C. Hughes (Eds.), *Neuroendocrinology*, pp. 77–83. Sunderland, Maine: Sinauer Associates.

Atkinson, R. C., and Shiffrin, R. M. (1968). "Human Memory: A Proposed System and Its Control Processes." In K. W. Spence and J. T. Spence (Eds.), *The Psychology of Learning and Motivation: Advances in Research and Theory*, vol. 2, pp. 89–195. New York: Academic Press.

Badia, P., Harsh, J., Balkin, T., O'Rourke, D., and Burton, S. (1985). "Behavioral Control of Respiration in Sleep and Sleepiness Due to Signal-Induced Sleep Fragmentation." *Psychophysiology* 22: 517–524.

Baddeley, A. D. (1982). "Domains of Recollection." *Psychological Review* 89: 708–729.

Baumgartner, G. (1983). "Organization and Function of the Neocortex." *Neuroopthalmology* 3: 1–14.

Beck, H. (1989). "Spuren verbaler Gedächtnisbildung im Elektroenzephalogramm des Menschen." Ph.D. dissertation, University of Zurich.

Bindra, D. (1980). *The Brain's Mind. A Neuroscience Perspective on the Mind-Body Problem.* New York: Gardner Press.

Bloch, V., Hennevin, D., and Leconte, P. (1979). "Relationship Between Paradoxical Sleep and Memory Processes." In M. A. B. Brazier (Ed.), *Brain Mechanisms in Memory and Learning: From the Single Neuron to Man*, pp. 142–164. New York: Raven Press.

Bonnet, M. H. (1982). "Performance During Sleep." In W. B. Webb (Ed.), *Biological Rhythms, Sleep, and Performance*, pp. 205–237. New York: John Wiley and Sons.

———. (1986). "Performance and Sleepiness as a Function of Frequency and Placement of Sleep Disruption." *Psychophysiology* 23: 263–271.

Borbely, A. A. (1982). "A Two Process Model of Sleep Regulation." *Human Neurobiology* 1: 195–204.

———, Baumann, F., Brandeis, D., Strauch I., and Lehmann, D. (1981). "Sleep Deprivation: Effect on Sleep Stages and EEG Power Density in Man." *Electroencephalography and Clinical Neurophysiology* 51: 483–493.

Bower, G. H. (1975). "Cognitive Psychology: An Introduction." In W. E. Estes (Ed.), *Introduction to Concepts and Issues. Handbook of Learning and Cognitive Processes*, vol. 1, pp. 25–80. Hillsdale, N.J.: Lawrence Erlbaum Associates.

———. (1981). "Mood and Memory." *American Psychologist* 36: 129–148.

Brainerd, C. J., and Kingma, J. (1985). "On the Independence of Short-Term Memory and Working Memory in Cognitive Development." *Cognitive Psychology* 17: 210–247.

Brandeis, D., and Lehmann, D. (1986). "Event-Related Potentials of the Brain and Cognitive Processes: Approaches and Applications." *Neuropsychologia* 24: 151–168.

———. (1989). "Segments of Event-Related Potential Map Series Reveal Landscape Changes with Visual Attention and Subjective Contours." *Electroencephalography and Clinical Neurophysiology* 73: 507–519.

Breger, L. (1967). "Function of Dreams." *Journal of Abnormal Psychology* 72: 1–28.

Brown, W. S., and Lehmann, D. (1979). "Verb and Noun Meaning of Homophone Words Activate Different Cortical Generators: A Topographical Study of Evoked Potential Fields." *Experimental Brain Research* 46, Suppl. no. 2: 159–168.

Butler, S. F., and Watson, R. (1985). "Individual Differences in Memory for Dreams: The Role of Cognitive Skills." *Perceptual and Motor Skills* 61: 823–828.

Campbell, S. S. (1984). "Duration and Placement of Sleep in a 'Disentrained' Environment." *Psychophysiology* 1: 106–113.

Cartwright, R. D. (1981). "The Contribution of Research on Memory and Dreaming to a Twenty-Four-Hour Model of Cognitive Behavior." In W. Fishbein (Ed.), *Sleep, Dreams and Memory*, pp. 277–291. Lancaster: MTP Press.

Case, R. (1985). *Intellectual Development: Birth to Adulthood.* New York: Academic Press.

Ciompi, L. (1982). *Affektlogik.* Stuttgart: Klett-Cotta.

Clark, M. S., and Fiske, S. T. (1982). *Affect and Cognition.* Hillsdale, N.J.: Lawrence Erlbaum Associates.

Corsi-Cabrera, M., Gutierrez, S., Ramos, J., and Arce, C. (1988). "Interhemispheric Correlation of EEG Activity During Successful and Unsuccessful Cognitive Performance." *International Journal of Neuroscience* 39: 253–259.

Craik, F. I. M. (1979). "Human Memory." *Annual Review of Psychology* 30: 63–102.

——— and Lockhart R. S. (1972). "Levels of Processing: A Framework for Memory Research." *Journal of Verbal Learning and Verbal Behavior* 11: 671–684.

Donchin, E. (1979). "Event-Related Brain Potentials: A Tool in the Study of Human Information Processing." In H. Begleiter (Ed.), *Evoked Brain Potentials and Behavior*, pp. 13–88. New York: Plenum Press.

———, Karis, D. Bashore, T. R., Coles, M. G. H., and Gratton, G. (1986). "Cognititive Psychophysiology and Human Information Processing." In M. G. H. Coles, E. Donchin, and S. W. Porges (Eds.), *Psychophysiology: Systems, Processes, and Applications*, pp. 244–267. New York and London: Guilford Press.

———, McCarthy, G., Kutas, M., and Ritter, W. (1983). "Event-Related Brain Potentials in the Study of Consciousness." In R. J. Davidson, G. E. Schwartz, and D. Shapiro (Eds.), *Consciousness and Self Regulation* pp. 319–324. New York: Plenum Press.

Dumermuth, G., and Lehmann, D. (1981). "EEG Power and Coherence During Non-REM and REM Phases in Humans in All-Night Sleep Analyses." *European Neurology* 20: 429–434.

Duncan-Johnson, C. C. (1981). "P300 Latency: A New Metric of Information Processing." *Psychophysiology* 18: 207–215.

———— and Donchin, E. (1982). "The P300 Component of the Event-Related Brain Potentials as an Index of Information Processing." *Biological Psychology* 14: 1–52.

Edelman, G. M. (1987). *Neural Darwinism: The Theory of Neuronal Group Selection.* New York: Basic Books.

Ehrlichman, H., and Wiener, M. S. (1980). "EEG Asymmetry During Covert Mental Activity." *Psychophysiology* 17: 228–235.

Eich, J. E. (1980). "The Cue-Dependent Nature of State-Dependent Retrieval." *Memory and Cognition* 8: 157–173.

————. (1982). "A Composite Holographic Associative Recall Model." *Psychological Review* 89: 627–661.

————. (1986). "Epilepsy and State Specific Memory." *Acta Neurologica Scandinavia* 74 (Suppl. 109): 15–21.

Ellis, H. C., and Hunt, R. R. (1983). *Fundamentals of Human Memory and Cognition,* 3d ed. Dubuque, Iowa: W. C. Brown.

Emmons, W. H., and Simon, C. W. (1956). "The Non-Recall of Material Presented During Sleep." *American Journal of Psychology* 20: 76–81.

Estes, W. K. (1973). "Memory and Conditioning." In F. J. McGuigan and D. B. Lumsden (Ed.), *Contemporary Approaches to Conditioning and Learning,* pp. 278–286. Washington, D.C.: Winston.

Farnham-Diggory, S. (1972). "The Development of Equivalence Systems." In S. Farnham-Diggory (Ed.), *Information Processing in Children,* pp. 43–64. New York: Academic Press.

Fein, G., Floyd, T. C., and Feinberg, I. (1981). "Computer Measures of Sleep EEG Reliably Sort Visual Stage 2 Epochs by NREM Period of Origin." *Psychophysiology* 18: 686–693.

Feinberg, I., and Evarts, E. V. (1969). "Changing Concepts of the Function of Sleep: Discovery of Intense Brain Activity During Sleep Calls for Revision of Hypotheses as to Its Function." *Biological Psychiatry* 1: 331–348.

Feinberg, I., and Floyd, T. C. (1982). "The Regulation of Human Sleep." *Human Neurobiology* 1: 85–194.

Firth, H. (1973). "Habituation During Sleep." *Psychophysiology* 10: 43–51.

Fivush, R., Gray, J. T., and Fromhoff, F. A. (1987). "Two-Year-Olds Talk About the Past." *Cognitive Development* 2: 393–409.

Flavell, J. H. (1977). *Cognitive Development.* Englewood Cliffs, N.J.: Prentice-Hall.

Foulkes, D. (1982). *Children's Dreams: Longitudinal Studies.* New York: John Wiley and Sons.

———. (1983). "Cognitive Processes During Sleep: Evolutionary Aspects." In A. Mayes (Ed.), *Sleep Mechanisms and Functions in Humans and Animals—An Evolutionary Perspective*, pp. 313–337. Wokingham, England: Van Nostrand Reinhold.

———. (1985). *Dreaming: A Cognitive-Psychological Analysis.* Hillsdale, N.J.: Lawrence Erlbaum Associates.

———, Sullivan, B., Kerr, N.H., and Brown, L. (1988). "Appropriateness of Dream Feelings to Dreamed Situations." *Cognition and Emotion* 2: 29–39.

Freud, S. (1955). *The Interpretation of Dreams.* New York: Basic Books. [Original work, *Die Traumdeutung*, published Leipzig: Deuticke, 1900.]

Gath I., Lehmann, D., and Bar-On, E. (1983). "Fuzzy Clustering of EEG Signal and Vigilance Performance." *International Journal of Neuroscience* 20: 303–312.

Gevins, A. S., Morgan, N. H., Bressler, S. L., Cutillo, B. A., White, R. M., Illse, J., Greer, D. S., Doyle, J. C., and Zeitlin, G. M. (1987). "Human Neuroelectric Patterns Predict Performance Accuracy." *Science* 235: 580–585.

Goldstein, L. (1983). "Brain Functions and Behavior: On the Origin and Evolution of Their Relationships." *Advances in Biological Psychiatry* 13: 75–79.

Goodenough, D. R. (1978). "Dream Recall." In A. M. Arkin, J. S. Antrobus, and S. J. Ellman (Eds.), *The Mind in Sleep*, pp. 113–142. Hillsdale, N.J.: Lawrence Erlbaum Associates.

Gorfein, D. S., and Hofman, R. S. (Eds.). (1987). *Memory and Learning. The Ebbinghaus Centennial Conference.* Hillsdale, N.J.: Lawrence Erlbaum Associates.

Greenberg, R. (1981). "Dreams and REM-Sleep: an Integrative Approach." In W. Fishbein (Ed.), *Sleep, Dreams and Memory*, pp. 125–133. Lancaster: MTP Press.

—— and Leiderman, P. H. (1966). "Perceptions, the Dream Process and Memory: An Up-to-Date Version of Notes on a Mystic Writing Pad." *Comparative Psychiatry* 7: 517.

——, Pearlman, C., Schwartz, W. R., and Grossmann, H. Y. (1983). "Memory, Emotion, and REM Sleep." *Journal of Abnormal Psychology* 92: 378–381.

—— and Safran, J. D. (1984). "Integrating Affect and Cognition: A Perspective on the Process of Therapeutic Change." *Cognitive Therapy and Research* 8: 559–578.

Grossberg, S. (1986). "The Adaptive Self-Organization of Serial Order in Behavior: Speech, Language, and Motor Control." In E. C. Schwab and H. C. Nussbaum (Eds.), *Pattern Recognition by Humans and Machine vol 1. Speech Perception*, pp. 187–296. New York: Academic Press.

Harsh, J., Badia, P., O'Rourke D., Burton, S., Revis, C., and Magee, J. (1987). "Factors Related to Behavioral Control by Stimuli Presented During Sleep." *Psychophysiology* 24: 535–541.

Hartmann, E. (1976). *The Functions of Sleep*. New Haven, Conn.: Yale University Press.

Hetherington, E. M., and McIntare, T. W. (1975). "Developmental Psychology." *Annual Review of Psychology* 26: 97–136.

Hawkins, D. (1966). "A Review of Psychoanalytic Dream Theory in the Light of Recent Psycho-Physiological Studies of Sleep and Dreaming." *British Journal of Medical Psychology* 39: 85–104.

Hillyard, S. A., and Kutas, M. (1983). "Electrophysiology of Cognitive Processing." *Annual Review of Psychology* 34: 33–61.

—— and Hansen, J. C. (1986). "Attention: Electrophysiological Approaches." In M. G. H. Coles, E. Donchin, and S. W. Porges (Eds.), *Psychophysiology: Systems, Processes, and Applications*, pp. 227–243. New York: Guilford Press.

Holloway, F. A. (1978). "State Dependent Retrieval Based on Time of Day." In B. Ho, D. Richards, and D. Chute (Eds.), *Drug Discrimina-*

tion and State Dependent Learning, pp. 319–343. New York: Academic Press.

Horne, J. A. (1988). "Why We Sleep—The Function of Sleep and Sleepiness." In W. P. Koella, F. Obal, H. Schulz, and P. Visser (Eds.), *Sleep '86, Proceedings of the Eighth European Congress of Sleep Research*, pp. 44–47. Stuttgart and New York: Gustav Fischer Verlag.

Horton, D. L., and Mills, C. B. (1984). "Human Learning and Memory." *Annual Review of Psychology* 35: 361–394.

Hunt, H. T. (1989). *The Multiplicity of Dreams*. New Haven, Conn.: Yale University Press.

Ingram, R. E., and Kendall, P. S. (1986). "Cognitive Clinical Psychology: Implications of an Information Processing Perspective." In R. E. Ingram (Ed.), *Information Processing Approaches to Clinical Psychology*, pp. 3–22. New York: Academic Press.

Ingram, R. E., and Reed, M. R. (1986). "Information Encoding and Retrieval Processes in Depression: Findings, Issues, and Future Directions." In R. E. Ingram (Ed.), *Information Processing Approaches to Clinical Psychology*, pp. 132–150. New York: Academic Press.

Jacobson, A., Kales A., Lehmann D., and Zweizig, J. (1965). "Somnambulism: All Night Electroencephalographic Studies." *Science* 148: 975–977.

Kahneman, D. (1973). *Attention and Effort*. Englewood Cliffs, N.J.: Prentice-Hall.

Kandel, E. R., and Schwartz, J. H. (1981). *Principles of Neural Science*. New York: Elsevier-North Holland.

———. (1982). "Molecular Biology of Memory. Modulation of Transmitter Release." *Science* 218: 433–443.

Katada, A., Ozaki, H., Suzuki, H., and Suhara, K. (1981). "Developmental Characteristics of Normal and Mentally Retarded Children's EEG." *Electroencephalography and Clinical Neurophysiology* 52: 192–201.

Kerr, N. H., Foulkes, D., and Schmidt, M. (1982). "The Structure of Laboratory Dream Reports in Blind and Sighted Subjects." *Journal of Nervous and Mental Disease* 170: 286–294.

Koella, W. P. (1988). *Die Physiologie des Schlafes.* Stuttgart and New York: Gustav Fischer Verlag.

Kohonen, T. (1978). *Associative Memory: A System Theoretical Approach.* Berlin: Springer-Verlag.

Kosslyn, S. M. (1980). *Image and Mind.* Cambridge, Mass.: Harvard University Press.

Koukkou, M. (1980). "EEG Reactivity in Acute Schizophrenics Reflects Deviant (Ectropic) State Changes During Information Processing." In M. Koukkou, D. Lehmann, and J. Angst (Eds.), *Functional States of the Brain: Their Determinants,* pp. 265–290. Amsterdam: Elsevier.

———. (1988). "A Psychophysiological Information-Processing Model of Cognitive Dysfunction and Cognitive Treatment in Depression." In C. Perris, I. M. Blackburn, and H. Perris (Eds.), *Cognitive Psychotherapy,* pp. 80–97. Heidelberg: Springer-Verlag.

Koukkou-Lehmann, M. (1987). *Hirnmechanismen normalen und schizophrenen Denkens.* Berlin, Heidelberg, and New York: Springer-Verlag.

Koukkou, M., and Lehmann, D. (1968). "EEG and Memory Storage in Sleep Experiments with Humans." *Electroencephalography and Clinical Neurophysiology* 25: 455–462.

———. (1976). "Human EEG Spectra Before and During Cannabis Hallucinations." *Biological Psychiatry* 11: 663–677.

———. (1980). "Psychophysiologie des Träumens und der Neurosentherapie: Das Zustands-Wechsel-Modell." *Fortschritte der Neurologie, Psychiatrie und ihrer Grenzgebiete* 48: 324–350.

———. (1983a). "A Psychophysiological Model of Dreaming with Implications for the Therapeutic Effect of Dream Interpretation." In W. R. Minsel and W. Herff (Eds.), *Research on Psychotherapeutic Approaches (Proceedings of the First European Conference of Psychotherapy Research),* vol 2, pp. 27–34. Frankfurt and Circencester: Peter Lang.

———. (1983b). "Dreaming: The Functional State-Shift Hypothesis. A Neuropsychophysiological Model." *British Journal of Psychiatry* 142: 221–231.

———. (1987). "An Information-Processing Perspective of Psychophysiological Measurements." *Journal of Psychophysiology* 1: 109–112.

————. (1989). "Informationsverarbeitende Hirnprozesse und Kognitiv-emotionale Entwicklung: Eine Psychophysiologische Bertrachtung." In H. M. Weinmann (Hrsg.), *Aktuelle Neuropädiatrie 1988*, pp. 376–386. Heidelberg: Springer-Verlag.

Koukkou, M., and Leuzinger-Bohleber, M. (1992). "Psychoanalysis and Neuropsychophysiology: A New Understanding of Basic Psychoanalytic Concepts." In M. Leuzinger-Bohleber, H. Schneider, and R. Pfeifer (Eds.), *Two Butterflies on my Head—Psychoanalysis in the Interdisciplinary Scientific Dialogue*, pp. 133–181. Berlin: Springer.

Koukkou M., and Manske, W. (1986). "Functional States of the Brain and Schizophrenic States of Behavior." In C. Shagass, R. C. Josiassen, and R. A. Roemer (Eds.), *Brain Electrical Potentials and Psychopathology*, pp. 91–114. Amsterdam and New York: Elsevier.

Koulack, D., and Goodenough, D. R. (1976). "Dream Recall and Dream Recall Failure: An Arousal-Retrieval Model." *Psychological Bulletin* 83: 975–984.

Kramer, M. (1981). "Dream Content in Psychiatric Conditions: An Overview of Sleep Laboratory Studies." In C. Perris, G. Struwe, and B. Jansson (Eds.), *Biological Psychiatry 1981*, pp. 306–309. Amsterdam: Elsevier.

————, Schoen, L. S., and Kinney, L. (1987). "Nightmares in Vietnam Veterans." *Journal of the American Academy of Psychoanalysis* 15: 67–81.

Lazarus, R. S. (1982). "Thoughts on Relations Between Emotion and Cognition." *American Psychologist* 37: 1019–1024.

Lehmann, D. (1971). "Multichannel Topography of Human Alpha EEG Fields." *Electroencephalography and Clinical Neurophysiology* 31: 431–449.

————. (1980). "Fluctuations of Functional State: EEG Patterns and Perceptual and Cognitive Strategies." In M. Koukkou, D. Lehmann, and J. Angst (Eds.), *Functional States of the Brain: Their Determinants*, pp. 189–202. Amsterdam: Elsevier.

————. (1984). "EEG Assessment of Brain Activity: Spatial Aspects, Segmentation and Imagining." *International Journal of Psychophysiology* 1: 267–276.

————. (1989). "Spontaneous EEG Momentary Maps and FFT Power Maps." In D. Samson-Dollfus, J. D. Guieu, P. Etevenon, and J. Gotman (Eds.), *Statistics and Topography in Quantitative EEG*, pp. 27–48. Amsterdam: Elsevier.

————, Dumermuth, G., Lange, B., and Meier, C. A. (1981). "Dream Recall Related to EEG Spectral Power During REM Periods." *Sleep Research* 10: 151.

Lehmann, D., Kofmel, B. A., and Weiss, Y. (1990). "The Atoms of Thought: Momentary EEG State and Classes of Subjective Experiences During 'Day Dreaming'." *Brain Topography* 2: 247–248.

———— and Koukkou, M. (1974). "Computer Analysis of EEG Wakefulness Sleep Patterns During Learning of Novel and Familiar Sentences." *Electroencephalography and Clinical Neurophysiology* 37: 73–84.

———— and Koukkou, M. (1980). "Classes of Spontaneous Private Experiences, and Ongoing Human EEG Activity." In G. Pfurtscheller, P. Buser, F. Lopes da Silva, and H. Petsche (Eds.), *Rhythmic EEG Activities and Cortical Functioning*, pp. 289–297. Amsterdam: Elsevier.

———— and Koukkou, M. (1990). "Brain States of Visual Imagery and Dream Generation." In R. G. Kunzendorf and A. A. Sheikh (Eds.), *The Psychophysiology of Mental Imagery: Theory, Research and Applications*, pp. 109–131. Farmdale: Baywood.

————, Koukkou, M., and Andrea, A. (1981). "Classes of Day-Dream Mentation and EEG Power Spectra." *Sleep Research* 10: 152.

————, Ozaki, H., and Pal, I. (1987). "EEG Alpha Map Series: Brain Micro-States by Space Oriented Adaptive Segmentation." *Electroencephalography and Clinical Neurophysiology* 67: 271–288.

Leventhal, H. (1980). "Toward a Comprehensive Theory of Emotion. *Advances in Experimental Social Psychology* 13: 139–207.

———— and Tomarken, A. J. (1986). "Emotion: Today's Problems." *Annual Review of Psychology* 37: 565–610.

Libet, B. (1982). "Brain Stimulation in the Study of Neuronal Functions for Consciousness Experience." *Human Neurobiology* 1: 235–242.

————. (1985). "Unconscious Cerebral Initiative and the Role of Conscious Will in Voluntary Action." *The Behavioral and Brain Sciences* 8: 529–566.

Logan, G. D. (1988). "Toward an Instance Theory of Automatization." *Psychological Review* 95: 492–527.

Loveless, N. (1983). "The Orienting Response and Evoked Potentials in Man." In D. Siddle (Ed.), *Orienting and Habituation: Perspectives in Human Research*, pp. 71–108. New York: John Wiley and Sons.

Lowy, S. (1942). *Biological and Psychological Foundations of Dream Interpretation*. London: Keegan Paul Trench, Trubner.

Lynn, R. (1966). *Attention, Arousal, and the Orientation Reaction*. International Series of Monographs in Experimental Psychology, Vol. 3. Oxford: Pergamon Press.

Machleidt, W., Gutjahr, L., Mügge, A. (1989). *Grundgefühle*. Berlin and Heidelberg: Springer-Verlag.

Mandler, G. (1975). *Mind and Emotion*. New York: John Wiley and Sons.

Matousek, M., and Peterson, I. (1973). "Frequency Analysis of the EEG in Normal Children and Adolescents." In P. Kellaway and I. Petersen (Eds.), *Automation of Clinical Electroencephalography*, pp. 75–102. New York: Raven Press.

Mayer, J. D. (1986). "How Mood Influences Cognition." In N. E. Sharkey (Ed.), *Advances in Cognitive Sciences*, pp. 290–314. New York: John Wiley and Associates.

McClelland, J. L., and Rumelhart, D. E. (1986). "A Distributed Model of Human Learning and Memory." In J. L. McClelland, D. E. Rumelhart, and the PDP Research Group (Eds.), *Parallel Distributed Processing: Psychological and Biological Models*, vol. 2, pp. 170–215. Cambridge, Mass.: MIT Press.

McDonald, D. G., Schicht, W. W., Frazier, R. E., Shollenberger, H. D., and Edwards, D. J. (1975). "Studies of Information Processing in Sleep." *Psychophysiology* 12: 624–629.

McGaugh, J. L. (1983). "Hormonal Influences on Memory." *Annual Review of Psychology* 34: 297–324.

Mecklenbrauker, S., and Hager, W. (1984). "Effects of Mood on Memory: Experimental Tests of a Mood-State-Dependency Retrieval Hypothesis and of a Mood-Congruity Hypothesis." *Psychological Research* 46: 355–376.

Miller, J. (1982). "Discrete versus Continuous Stage Models of Human Information Processing. In Search of Partial Output." *Journal of Experimental Psychology: Human Perception and Performance* 8: 273–296.

Miller, L. (1991). *Freud's Brain: Neuropsychodynamic Foundations of Psychoanalysis.* New York: Guilford Press.

Moffitt, A., Hoffmann, R., Wells, R., Armitage, R., Pigeau, R., and Shearer, J. (1982). "Individual Differences Among Pre- and Post-Awakening EEG Correlates of Dream Reports Following Arousal from Different Stages of Sleep." *The Psychiatric Journal of the University of Ottawa* 7: 111–125.

Morton, J., Hammersley, R. H., and Bekerian, D. A. (1985). "Headed Records: A Model for Memory and Its Failures." *Cognition* 20: 1–23.

Moruzzi, G. (1963). "Active Processes in the Brain Stem During Sleep." *The Harvey Lectures Series* 58: 233–297. New York: Academic Press.

———. (1972). "The Sleep-Waking Cycle." *Reviews of Physiology* 64: 1–165.

Moser, U. (1983). "Beiträge zu einer Psychoanalytischen Theorie der Affekte." *Berichte aus der Interdisziplinären Konfliktforschungsstelle Nr. 10.* Zurich: Institute of Psychology, University of Zurich.

Müller, C. C. (1986). "Stimulierte Verarbeitungsprozesse im Schlaf-EEG." Ph.D. disertation, University of Zurich.

Näätänen, R. (1988). "Implications of ERP Data for Psychological Theories of Attention." *Biological Psychology* 26: 117–163.

Nakagawa, Y. (1980). "Continuous Observation of EEG Patterns at Night and in Daytime of Normal Subjects Under Restrained Conditions. I. Quiescent State when Lying Down." *Electroencephalography and Clinical Neurophysiology* 49: 524–537.

Neisser, U. (1967). *Cognitive Psychology.* New York: Appleton-Century-Crofts.

———. (1976). *Cognition and Reality: Principles and Implications of Cognitive Psychology.* San Francisco: W. H. Freeman.

Neumann, O. (1984). "Automatic Processing: A Review of Recent Findings and a Plea for an Old Theory." In W. Prinz and A. F. Sanders (Eds.), *Cognition and Motor Processes*, p. 255–293. Heidelberg: Springer-Verlag.

Neves, D. M., and Anderson, J. R. (1981). "Knowledge Compilation: Mechanisms for the Automatization of Cognitive Skills." In J. R. Anderson (Ed.), *Cognitive Skills and Their Acquisition*, pp. 57–84. Hillsdale, N.J.: Lawrence Erlbaum Associates.

Norman, D. A. (1968). "Toward a Theory of Memory and Attention." *Psychological Review* 75: 522–536.

———. (1976). *Memory and Attention. An Introduction to Human Information Processing*. New York: John Wiley and Sons.

———. (1981a). "Twelve Issues for Cognitive Science." In D. A. Norman (Ed.), *Perspectives on Cognitive Science*, pp. 265–295. Hillsdale, N.J.: Lawrence Erlbaum Associates.

———. (1981b). "Categorization of Action Slips." *Psychological Review* 88: 1–15.

———. (1984). "Theories and Models in Cognitive Psychology." In E. Donchin (Ed.), *Cognitive Psychophysiology: The Carmel Conferences*, vol. 1, pp. 119–138. Hillsdale, N.J.: Lawrence Erlbaum Associates.

———. (1986). "Reflection on Cognition and Parallel Distributed Processing." In J. L. McClelland, D. E. Rumelhart, and the PDP Research Group (Eds.), *Parallel Distributed Processing*, vol. 2, pp. 531–546. Cambridge, Mass.: MIT Press.

Norris, D. (1986). "Word Recognition: Context Effects Without Priming." *Cognition* 22: 93–136.

Öhman, A. (1979). "The Orienting Response, Attention, and Learning: An Information-Processing Perspective." In H. D. Kimmel, E. H. van Olst, and J. F. Orlebeke (Eds.), *The Orienting Reflex in Humans*, pp. 443–472. Hillsdale, N.J.: Lawrence Erlbaum Associates.

Oltman, P. K., Goodenough, D. R., Koulack, D., Maclin, E., Schroeder, H. R., and Flannagan, M. J. (1977). "Short-Term Memory During Stage-2-Sleep." *Psychophysiology* 14: 439–444.

Oswald, I., Taylor, A. M., and Treisman, M. (1960). "Discriminative Responses to Stimulation During Human Sleep." *Brain* 83: 440–453.

Overton, D. A. (1979). "Drug Discrimination Training with Progressively Lowered Doses." *Science* 205: 720–721.

Palombo S. R. (1978). *Dreaming and Memory.* New York: Basic Books.

———. (1984). "Recovery of Early Memories Associated with Reported Dream Imagery." *American Journal of Psychiatry* 141: 1508–1511.

Pavlov, I. P. (1928). *Lectures on Conditioned Reflexes.* New York: International Publishers.

Pearlman, C. A. (1970). "The Adaptive Function of Dreaming." *International Psychiatry Clinics* 7: 329–334.

———. (1982). "Sleep Structure Variation and Performance." In W. B. Webb (Ed.), *Biological Rhythms, Sleep, and Performance*, pp. 147–173. New York: John Wiley and Sons.

Paiget, J. (1962). *Play, Dreams and Imitation in Childhood.* London: Routledge and Kegan.

———. (1968). *On the Development of Memory and Identity.* Barre, Mass.: Clark University Press.

——— and Inhelder, B. (1969). *The Psychology of the Child.* New York: Basic Books.

Pivik, K. T. (1978). "Tonic States and Phasic Events in Relation to Sleep Mentation." In A. M. Arkin, J. S. Antrobus, and S. J. Ellman (Eds.), *The Mind in Sleep*, pp. 128–142. Hillsdale, N.J.: Lawrence Erlbaum Associates.

Posner, M. I, (1982). "Cumulative Development of Attentional Theory." *American Journal of Psychology* 37: 168–179.

——— and McLeod, P. (1982). "Information-Processing Models—In Search of Elementary Operations." *Annual Review of Psychology* 33: 477–514.

Pribram, K. H. (1971). *Languages of the Brain. Experimental Paradoxes and Principles in Neurophysiology.* Englewood Cliffs, N.J.: Prentice-Hall.

———. (1979). "The Orienting Reaction: Key to Brain-Presentational Mechanisms." In H. D. Kimmel, E. H. van Olst, and J. F. Orlebeke

(Eds.), *The Orienting Reflex in Humans*, pp. 3–20. Hillsdale, N.J.: Lawrence Erlbaum Associates.

Purcell, S., Mullington, J., Moffitt, A., Hoffmann, R., and Pigeau, R. (1986). "Dream Self-Reflectedness as a Learned Cognitive Skill." *Sleep* 9: 423–437.

Raikov, V. L. (1983). "EEG Recordings of Experiments in Hypnotic Age Regression." *Imagination, Cognition and Personality* 3: 115–132.

Ratcliff, R., and McKoon, G. (1988). "A Retrieval Theory of Priming in Memory." *Psychological Review* 95: 385–408.

Reese, H. W. (1976). "The Development of Memory: Life-Span Perspectives." In H. W. Reese (Ed.), *Advances in Child Development and Behavior*, pp. 38–52. New York: Academic Press.

Reus, V. I., Weingartner, H., and Post, R. M. (1979). "Clinical Implications of State-Dependent Learning." *American Journal of Psychiatry* 136: 927–931.

Rohrbaugh, J. W. (1984). "The Orienting Reflex: Performance and Central Nervous System Manifestations." In R. Parasuraman and D. R. Davies (Eds.), *Varieties of Attention*, pp. 323–373. New York: Academic Press.

Roitblat, H. L. (1982). "The Meaning of Representation in Animal Memory." *The Behavioral and Brain Sciences* 5: 353–406.

Roth, D. L., and Tucker, D. M. (1986). "Neural Systems in the Emotional Control of Information Processing." In R.E. Ingram (Ed.), *Information Processing Approaches to Clinical Psychology*, pp. 77–94. New York: Academic Press.

Rumelhart, D. E. (1980). "Schemata: The Building Blocks of Cognition." In R. Spiro, B. Bruce, and W. Brewer (Eds), *Theoretical Issues in Reading Comprehension*, pp. 33–58. Hillsdale, N.J.: Lawrence Erlbaum Associates.

———, Smolensky, P., McClelland, J. L., and Hinton, G. E. (1987). "Schemata and Sequential Thought Processes in PDP Models." In J. L. McClelland, D. E. Rumelhart, and the PDP Research Group (Eds.), *Parallel Distributed Processing*, vol. 2, pp. 17–57. Cambridge, Mass.: MIT Press.

Samson-Dollfus, D., and Goldberg, P. (1979). "Electroencephalographic Quantification of Time Domain Analysis in Normal 5–7 Year-Old Children." *Electroencephalography and Clinical Neurophysiology* 46: 147–154.

Schneider, W., and Fisk, A. D. (1982). "Concurrent Automatic and Controlled Visual Search: Can Processing Occur Without Resource Cost?" *Journal of Experimental Psychology (Learning, Memory and Cognition)* 8: 261–278.

———— and Shiffrin, R. M. (1977). "Controlled and Automatic Human Information Processing: I. Detection Search and Attention." *Psychological Review* 84: 1–66.

Schwartz, D. G., Weinstein, L. N., and Arkin, A. M. (1978). "Qualitative Aspects of Sleep Mentation." In A. M. Arkin, J. S. Antrobus, and S. J. Ellman (Eds.), *The Mind in Sleep: Psychology and Psychophysiology*, pp. 143–241. Hillsdale, N.J.: Lawrence Erlbaum Associates.

Shapiro, A. (1967). "Dreaming and the Physiology of Sleep." *Experimental Neurology* 19: 56–81.

Shepard, R. N. (1986). "Discrimination and Generalization in Identification and Classification: Comment on Nosofsky." *Journal of Experimental Psychology, General* 115: 58–61.

Shiffrin, R. M., and Dumais, S. T. (1981). "The Development of Automatism." In J. R. Anderson (Ed.), *Cognitive Skills and Their Acquisition*, pp. 111–140. Hillsdale, N.J.: Lawrence Erlbaum Associates.

Shiffrin, R. M., and Schneider, W. (1977). "Controlled and Automatic Human Information Processing: II. Perceptual Learning, Automatic Attending, and a General Theory." *Psychological Review* 84: 127–190.

Shoen, L. S., and Badia, P. (1984). "Facilitated Recall Following REM and NREM Naps." *Psychophysiology* 21: 299–306.

Smith, C. (1981). "Learning and Sleep States in the Rat." In W. Fishbein (Ed.), *Sleep, Dreams and Memory*, pp. 19–35. Lancaster: MTP Press.

Sober, E. (1987). "What Is Adaptationism?" In J. Dupré (Ed.), *The Latest on the Best: Essays on Evolution and Optimality*, pp. 105–118. Cambridge, Mass.: MIT Press.

Sokolov, E. N. (1975). "The Neuronal Mechanisms of the Orienting Reflex." In E. N. Sokolov and O. S. Vinogradova (Eds.), *Neuronal Mechanisms of the Orienting Reflex*, pp. 217–235. New York: John Wiley and Sons.

Spinks, J. A., and Siddle, D. (1983). "The Functional Significance of the Orienting Response." In D. Siddle (Ed.), *Orienting and Habituation: Perspectives in Human Research*, pp. 237–314. New York: John Wiley and Sons.

Stephenson, D., and Siddle, D. (1983). "Theories of Habituation." In D. Siddle (Ed.), *Orienting and Habituation: Perspectives in Human Research*, pp. 183–236. New York: John Wiley and Sons.

Stillings, N. A., Feinstein, M. H., Garfield, J. L., Rissland, E. L., Rosenbaum, D. A., Weisler, S. E., and Baker-Ward, L. (1987). *Cognitive Science. An Introduction.* Cambridge, Mass.: MIT Press.

Strauch, I. (1969). "Psychological Aspects of Dream Recall." Paper presented at the Symposium on Sleep and Dreaming, Nineteenth International Congress of Psychology, London.

———— and Meier, B. (1989). "Das Emotionale Erleben im REM-Traum." *Schweizerische Zeitschrift für Psychologie* 48: 233–240.

Szentagothai, J. (1987). "The Brain-Mind Relationship." In B. Gulyas (Ed.), *The Brain-Mind Problem: Philosophical and Neurophysiological Approaches*, pp. 61–78. Assen/Maastricht: Leuven University Press.

Tauber, E. S. (1974). "Phylogeny of Sleep." In E. D. Weitzman (Ed.), *Advances in Sleep Research*, vol. 1, pp. 132–174. New York: Spectrum.

Teasdale, J. D., and Russel, M. L. (1985). "Differential Effects of Induced Mood on Recall of Positive, Negative and Neutral Words." *British Journal of Clinical Psychology* 58: 138–146.

Turkkan, J. S. (1989). "Classical Conditioning: The New Hegemony." *Behavioral and Brain Sciences* 12: 121–161.

Van Winsum, W., Segreant, J., and Geuze, R. (1984). "The Functional Significance of Event-Related Desynchronization of Alpha Rhythm in Attentional and Activating Tasks." *Electroencephalography and Clinical Neurophysiology* 58: 519–524.

Velden, M. (1978). "Some Necessary Revisions of the Neuronal Model Concepts of the Orienting Response." *Psychophysiology* 15: 181–185.

Vogel, W., Broverman, D. M., and Klaiber, E. L. (1967). "EEG and Mental Abilities." *Electroencephalography and Clinical Neurophysiology* 24: 166–175.

Webb, E. B. (1982). "Sleep and Biological Rhythms." In W. B. Webb (Ed.), *Biological Rhythms, Sleep, and Performance*, pp. 87–110. New York: John E. Wiley and Sons.

―――― and Cartwright, R. (1978). "Sleep and Dreams." *Annual Review of Psychology* 29: 223–252.

Weingartner, H. (1978). "Human State-Dependent Learning." In B. T. Ho, D. W. Richards, and D. L. Chute (Eds.), *Drug Discrimination and State-Dependent Learning*, pp. 361–383. New York: Academic Press.

Williams, H. L. (1973). "Information Processing During Sleep." In W. P. Koella and P. Levin (Eds.), *Sleep*, pp. 36–43. Basel: Karger.

Yussen, S. (1985). *The Growth of Reflection in Children*. Orlando, Fla.: Academic.

Zimmermann, W. B. (1970). "Sleep Mentation and Auditory Awakening Thresholds." *Psychophysiology* 6: 540–549.

4

Gordon G. Globus ▬▬▬▬▬▬▬▬▬▬▬▬

Connectionism and Sleep

I want to develop here a connectionist theory of sleep and consider sleep function in that light. That is, I apply connectionist ideas about neural networks to sleep and sleep function. I first give an informal development of connectionism and the "self-organizing mind" and then, in the next section, relate it to sleep. Crick and Mitchison's (1983) connectionist account of REM sleep function is critiqued, and finally, I present the idea that one functional role for REM sleep is to decrease the residual "tuning bias" of neural networks, which widens their possibilities for the upcoming day.

Connectionism

It is helpful to keep in mind the distinction between cognitive science and brain science. Brain science studies the actual neural hardware of the brain whereas cognitive science is concerned with the abstract machine physically instantiated in the neural hardware. For cognitive science, the "mind" is stipulated to be an abstract "virtual" machine. The abstract machine might have indefinitely many hardware realizations. Until the recent development of connectionism it was widely believed that the brain and the digital computer realized the same abstract machine (the "Turing machine").

"Connectionism" is an approach to the mind as an abstract machine based on parallel distributed processing principles rather than the serial local processing of ordinary computers (Rumelhart, McClelland, and the PDP Research Group, 1986; McClelland, Rumelhart, and the PDP Research Group, 1986). The key idea of connectionism is that the machine is a net of richly interconnected nodes that variously influence each other. When disturbed by input the whole net becomes activated and spontaneously reorganizes toward a consensus of nodal influences. This spontaneous unprogrammed movement of the net toward self-consistency is the self-organizing property of the connectionist machine. Such a spontaneous holistic process is in sharp contrast to the serial rule-governed transformation of representations in computerlike computational devices.

Connectionism includes a range of approaches (which is not surprising, given the recency of connectionism's development). I focus on constraint satisfaction machines here. The present version has certain idiosyncracies; it is especially influenced by Maturana and Varela (1980, 1987) in that the network is seen as fundamentally *self-organizing*. Furthermore, my version emphasizes the "holistic" properties of connectionist neural networks ("C-networks") presumably realized in the brain. I shall think of C-networks as layered for perception, thought, and action. I also conceptualize C-networks as having a rich dynamic architecture, like the neural case, rather than the relatively simple static networks presently technologically realized by cumbersome modeling on computers. Finally, I develop a richer view of mind than is present in the literature of connectionism, factoring in instinctual, affective, and intentional components.

In C-networks there is a tremendous fanning-in of influence on any node of the network and a tremendous fanning-out of influence from any node to the rest of the network. C-networks are accordingly *holistic* in this homely sense: everything seems pretty quickly to effect somewhat just about everything. Thus the whole influences the part and is influenced by the parts, due to the rich interconnectivity.

The activity of a node in a C-network (firing of a neuron in the brain case) depends on the varying influences on it. The influence of a node's activity may be excitatory or inhibitory, extending over the node's sphere of influence. The strength of the connections between nodes (the "connection weights") constrains the influence of nodes on one another, and accordingly determines the C-network's response to input. In learning, excitatory and inhibitory connection strengths are adjusted, learning effects the connection weights. These connection strengths that shape the excitatory and inhibitory influences of nodes upon one another encode the C-networks' knowledge. There is no program of serial rule-governed steps acting on input, as in a computer, but only a disturbed, fluidly reorganizing whole, constrained in its reorganizing movement by its connection weights.

C-networks are dynamical systems, governed by sets of coupled nonlinear differential equations. As *dynamical systems*, an analogy can be made to thermodynamics; equations of the same form apply. Input disturbs the networks, and they begin spontaneously to reorganize themselves. In the reorganization, a global quantity over the whole network decreases. This global quantity, which Hopfield and Tank (1986) call the *computational energy*, decreases as the network comes into harmonious balance after disturbance. (Smolensky 1986, has formalized this movement of C-networks toward coherent "harmony" and calls his type of C-network, which is a recognition device, the *harmonium*.) Let us try to understand this coherent balance, this "harmony principle," at the level of the nodes, for it is a key property of C-networks: by governing the "computations," the movement toward self-consistency replaces the program in computer computation. So rather than a deterministic mechanical operation under programmed rules, the harmony principle coarsely steers a probabilistic operation.

Each node, by virtue of its excitatory and inhibitory connections, specifies a pattern in its sphere of influence. Each node "wants" certain nodes to be active and others inactive. To the extent that its specifications are met at each connection, that node is in harmony with the network. Thus node A that excites (or inhibits) node B is in harmony with B if B is in fact excited (or inhibited). In functioning, then, a best consensus across all the nodes is worked out, to maximize the self-consistent harmony of the whole. The sum of the harmony across all nodes determines the computational energy: increasing harmony gives decreasing computational energy and vice versa.

When input first disturbs the nodes, the computational energy is high. Then the network begins to adjust so as to increase the harmony. A stable state or cycle typically settles out. Whatever the network relaxes into is associated with a certain statistical probability; on different runs the network settles differently. Then with a change in input to the relaxed state, C-networks are again moved out of their low computational energy states. The C-networks are disturbed by such input change and may relax toward different low energy states, always proceeding probabilisticaly toward balance under the harmony principle.

All possible C-network states can be represented as points in an *N*-dimensional vector space, where the dimensions represent the state variables. A two-dimensional slice can be taken through the *N*-dimensional space that is chosen to contain states of special interest. The computational energy of the state at each point gives a third dimension, resulting in an "energy landscape." Maximal and minimal values for the computational energy can be represented as peaks and basins on the energy landscape; in the self-organizing process the network state tends to move downhill. Peaks and basins on the slice through the N-dimension-al vector space are, functionally speaking, "repellors" and "attractors." The networks' spontaneous self-organization toward low computational energy is represented in the energy landscape by a line settling in a basin-attractor.

Noise (the "computational temperature" in the thermodynamic analogy) is a crucial parameter in the movement toward harmony. Noise disturbs. When noise is decreased slowly (the "temperature" cooled by "simulated annealing") the network will with high probability settle into its very best minimum energy; with high noise, the network may settle into a somewhat lower coherence state with a higher computational energy, or even jump unpredictably from attractor to attractor. Noise is thus an important controlling variable of C-networks: *decrease signal-noise ratio (S/N) and the network shows the range of its possibilities,* as low probability states may settle out.

It is crucial in understanding C-networks to appreciate the role of inhibitory connections between units. To highlight this, let us take the C-network unit to be a "couplet" of components that act and are acted upon in unison. (In a richer version there would be a cluster of neurons composing the functional unit.) One member of the couplet is excitatory in its influence and the other member is inhibitory. Now for each cou-plet in the C-network the excitatory component exerts its influence to produce a certain pattern of activation in the network. Each couplet is in competition with many other couplets, whose excitatory components strive to bring about their own characteristic network pattern. If there were no inhibitory component, then a disturbance at any point of the network would quickly fan out through the whole network resulting in high intensity noise that carried no information.

Furthermore, without inhibition *the excitatory influence of different couplets tends to overlap.* Artificial basins are formed in the confluence, basins that disappear when inhibition sculpts unit influence more sharply. These spurious basins may be deep enough to form powerful secondary attractors that are "parasitic"; at the extreme, whatever state the network is perturbed into by input, the network settles into the para-sitic attractor. (Hoffman, 1986, nicely calls them *black holes.*)

In the vector space representation, as we saw, each pattern over the network is a point in an *N*-dimensional space. The network's evolution over time is a line in vector space to a stable point (or limit cycle). This space is stochastic: any line that we might happen to draw is associated with a certain probability. The excitatory-inhibitory ratio (E/I), like noise, is thus a crucial controlling variable of C-networks: *as E/I rises high probability parasitic attractors can take over the network.*

With this background we can now focus on the various sources of constraint. We have already considered the connection weights (presumably determined both genetically and through learning) as constraining the self-organizing process. Input is also a constraint; different inputs disturb in different ways. There is a *disturbance structure,* which is as much a constraint on the self-organizing process as the connection weights. (Of course, the connection weights change slowly through learning, whereas the disturbance structure changes quickly with the input flux from the environment.) Through its structure sensory input poses a problem; that is, by raising computational energy the input constraint makes a particular "demand" that the networks reorganize. So input both disturbs and constrains.

Another crucially important constraint is due to *tuning* of the nets (McClelland, 1985). Tuning can be conceptualized in various ways but for present purposes I propose that tuning affects a certain class of connection weights. In addition to the static connection weights already discussed that change relatively slowly in learning, there are also highly variable connection weights that change fluidly. These variable connection weights are tunable and provide a fluid constraint on the self-organizing process. For example, blocking synaptic reuptake increases available neurotransmitter and functionally increases the weight.

The tuning system is modular in organization. Each of the three internal modules considered here—drive, affect and intentionality (meaning)—tune (prime) all three layers of the C-network. Tuning the perceptual layer determines which inputs are permitted to disturb the C-networks; functionally the tuning constraint filters the input. So when sexually aroused we are disposed to perceive sexual objects, when depressed we see the world "through a glass darkly," and our meanings prescribe the possible worlds that limit what world we might perceive. Tuning the thought layer provides the *context* for thought. When sexually aroused we have sexy thoughts, when depressed our thought takes on a pessimistic tone, and intentionality provides the horizon of meanings within which thought proceeds. Tuning the action layer provides the goal orientation. When sexually aroused we are disposed to take certain sexual actions, when depressed we are disposed to inaction, and our meanings set the plans that guide action. These behavioral dispositions are encoded as constraints in the action layer produced by instinctual, affective and intentional tuning.

So there are a number of sources of functionally distinct constraint in C-networks: (1) sensory input from the surround posing problems, (2) instinctual tuning, (3) affect-mood tuning, and (4) intentional (meaning) tuning. In addition there is a relatively static constraint: (5) innate and learned connection strengths. Finally, (6) current state is a constraint. *Thus reality, instinctual drive, intentionality, affect-mood, knowledge, and current state come together in a self-organizing process that seeks to satisfy these constraints.* The consensus network state that settles out of the self-organizing process is thus an optimizing solution to a multiple constraint satisfaction problem.

C-Networks During Sleep

In this part of the discussion, the understanding of C-networks developed above is applied to the states of waking and sleep, where sleep has two phases: REM and NREM. We shall look at these states and phases in connectionist terms. Can they be distinguished by E/I, S/N, and the constraints just discussed? Table 1 proposes that these connectionist properties do parse out with these states and phases of ordinary being.

Table 4.1
States and Phases of Ordinary Being

States	Waking	Sleep	
Phases		REM	NREM
Controlling Variables:			
Activation	high	high	low
S/N	high	low	high
E/I	low	high	low
Constraints:			
Sensory	high	low	low
Intentional	high	high	low
Instinctual	high	high	low
Affective	high	high	low
Knowledge	high	high	low

Let us consider Table 4.1 in detail. Waking (W) is a highly activated state that is fully constrained by environment, tuning, and learning. Waking is a low noise state (high S/N) for optimal efficiency and has high inhibition (low E/I) that prevents the formation of spurious attractors.

NREM is deactivated and unconstrained by the environment; it is polar to waking in these characteristics. Furthermore, the other constraints are barely operational because of the general deactivation. Like waking, NREM is a low-noise, high-inhibition state (at least compared to REM, if not entirely equal to W). So NREM could be a kind of free-wheeling version of waking, unmodulated by the environment, if it were not for the low activation, which slows everything to a crawl. Of course, NREM is not completely turned down. At times there may be enough activation to produce dreams, but these are typically not full-fledged dramatic dreams (Foulkes, 1985). (As we shall see, network conditions change sharply in REM.) It is interesting that insomniacs will complain of thinking all night long, although their sleep may appear surprisingly normal, electrophysiologically speaking (Coleman, 1986). Here the level of arousal may be enough that a level of cognition persists during NREM.

REM is activated like W, but unconstrained by sensory input, like NREM. Activating input in REM is presumably random (Hobson and McCarley, 1977). Crucially in REM, *the process changes to high noise and low inhibition.* We have a free-wheeling version of W, but S/N is down and E/I is up, so there are special operative characteristics of the C-networks compared to W and NREM. Freud distinguished W processing as the "secondary process" and this REM kind of processing as the "primary process."

The shift in functioning from W or NREM to REM is associated with changes in neuromodulators. Noradrenergic and serotonergic systems shut off during REM sleep (Hobson, Lydic and Baghoyan, 1986; Mamelak and Hobson, 1989). Norepinephrine (NE) is thought to modulate S/N, improving signal to noise (Oades, 1985; Madison and Nicoll, 1986; Kolta, Diop and Reader, 1987). So in REM, with NE neurons off, noise would relatively increase. Furthermore, NE facilitates gamma-amino butyric acid (GABA) which is inhibitory (Woodward et al., 1979; Waterhouse, Moises, and Woodward, 1980; Sessler, Cheng, and Waterhouse, 1988). So another possible consequence of NE neurons shutoff in REM is a fall in GABAergic activity and a consequent decrease in inhibition. The shutdown of serotonin (5HT) also disinhibits forebrain activity (Mamelak and Hobson, 1989). Whatever the final neurochemical details, however, the general idea is attractive: *crucial neurochemical changes* (perhaps decreased S/N and increased E/I *during REM sleep shift fundamental parameters of network processing.*

At Freud's level of discussion —the mental apparatus — the neuromodulatory change of REM is reflected in a shift to the primary process. We now want to see if high noise and low inhibition during REM would explain the peculiar characteristics of dream mentation (see also Globus, 1989.)

The easiest way to see the argument, I think, is to recall the three dimensional or "energy landscape" (Smolensky, 1988), with the vertical axis representing the computational energy of the network state represented on the plane. Imagine a marble rolling across the energy landscape with its peaks and basins. The path of the ball represents the succession of states of the self-organizing system. The tendency of the ball is to move downhill and settle in a basin. But the various input disturbances are continually changing, so the ball in fact follows an erratic course, never settling into a basin for too long (unless "obsessed"). Furthermore, the movement of the ball is not strictly determined but is stochastic: there are various possible paths through vector space with their associated probabilities. This picture is further complicated by fluctuation in the energy landscape due to tuning.

Now let us recall what happens to this image when noise increases and inhibition decreases in REM. With decreased inhibition there is a tendency for a confluence of basins to form a spurious basin. If one basin represented the memory MemI and the other MemII, the confluence would represent shared features between MemI and MemII. Many basins might be confluent, forming a powerful parasitic attractor.

But this sounds very much like the dream characteristic Freud called *condensation.* Dream elements stand in for a number of latent thought elements, so that the dream material is condensed in comparison to the unconscious thoughts. Decreased inhibition thus would account for the dream characteristic of condensation: the parasitic attraction of the confluence stands for a number of contributing attractors. In dream interpretation along Freudian lines, we surmise the contributing attractors from their confluence, which is the condensation.

We also saw earlier that increased noise brings lower probability settlements. Whereas, in W, a state in the vicinity of MemI would in great likelihood settle into that basin, thereby recovering the memory encoded there, in REM, a state in the vicinity of MemI might perchance settle into some other related basin. But this is akin to Freud's "displacement," in which the psychical intensity that belongs to one memory is transferred to a related memory. In both, what was a less probable memory becomes realized.

The increasing noise of REM sleep also has the effect of destabilizing the network. With increased noise the ball in our image has a tendency to unpredictably "jump" from one basin to another. This would account for the abrupt thematic discontinuities, so characteristic of dreams, where we say with some surprise, "And the next thing I knew . . ."

The freedom from environmental constraint during REM explains what Rechtschaffen calls the *single-mindedness* of dreams, our typical absorption in the dream events. Consider what is going on. The networks are randomly activated, certain intentional, instinctual, and affective tunings left salient at the end of the day become operative, and the networks begin to reorganize. The intentional, drive, affective, and knowledge constraints are fully operative, but these are no longer reined in by the powerful constraint due to external "reality"; the networks are left to their own devices. The networks accordingly are ruled (single-mindedly) by the internal constraints, with occasional "jumps" to a different basin because of the high noise.

Now it is quite interesting, once thematized, that our general store of knowledge seems to be available both waking and dreaming. We find ourselves in strange places during dreams and manage to get along, however harrowing it might be, using what we know. In NREM sleep this knowledge is not much used, consistent with the unexcited character of NREM sleep: we tend to circle tediously round a group of thoughts (like a limit cycle in dynamical systems), getting nowhere. In REM sleep, by way of contrast, it may be that our knowledge even increases (that is, less probable solutions become available).

The position just developed should be contrasted with that of Mamelak and Hobson (1989), who also discuss the effect of neuromodulatory changes in REM sleep on neural networks and the consequences for dream cognition, but distinguish their network model from connectionist models. Of crucial importance, their focus is on error and chance —on the "error output" of neural networks that respond incorrectly because of aminergic demodulation and on the forced bifurcation of the networks due to spontaneous bursts of phasic pontogeniculooccipital (PGO) activity. Because for them error and chance rule dream cognition, the dream is at its deepest level meaningless, as Hobson and McCarley (1977) had argued previously.

The present view, in diametric contrast, finds the dream essentially meaningful in that a good solution is found to a multiple constraint satisfaction problem. Chance enters to a certain extent in that the self-organizing process is probabilistic, and the less probable enters with decreased signal-noise ratio, but the basic tendency is always for a self-consistency that meaningfully harmonizes incompatible constraints. So the dream is presented here as intrinsically problem solving on physiological grounds, whereas for Mamelak and Hobson (1989) the dream reflects deficient physiological information processing. Although the issue is not presently empirically decidable, it is important to appreciate that dreams conceived as deeply meaningful and creatively problem solving are fully compatible with biological mechanisms.

To summarize, we have taken sleep to be a unitary phenomenon, bifurcating into REM and NREM phases, in which there is a profound disconnection between the brain and its surroundings. The networks disengage from sensory input and are uninclined to produce motor output. So in sleep the C-networks run on their own, uninfluenced by interaction with the surroundings. Seen against W, NREM is a deactivated waking, whereas REM is as activated as waking, but certain network parameters are crucially shifted (suggested: increased E/I and decreased S/N in REM compared to W) so that the mind follows a "primary process." REM and W also differ crucially over the activating signals, which are random for REM and ordered for W. Random activation with shifted E/I and S/N greatly alters network properties: the networks thus operating reveal themselves in their products, our dreams. It is likely too simplistic to say that decreased NE, 5HT and GABA activity during REM modulates network parameters so that they process differently—a primary process—but the more general point remains: neurochemical modulation of C-network processing is straightforwardly conceivable and neurochemical changes in REM accordingly could account for the peculiarities of dreaming mentation.

The Function of Sleep: A Critique of Crick and Mitchison

I confine my discussion of the sleep function to C-networks. It must be remembered, of course, that sleep is integrated to the whole organism, and so its functions are manifold. My limit is to see what sleep does for the C-networks.

Now NREM function does not seem as puzzling as REM function. That the C-networks deactivate and go off line for a while, might allow for network maintenance or might even have no network function at all (although benefiting other systems and the total organism). REM is curiouser, a periodic activation that punctuates sleep, when the brain is aroused by random stimulation and operates with shifts in crucial network parameters.

Crick and Mitchison have considered connectionist nets during sleep and proposed that the function of REM is an unlearning that prunes overcrowded networks (1983). Their position is hardnosedly antipsychological and emphasizes *random* activation of memories as the basis for dream construction. (The biological monster Freud, 1953, thought he had slain in Chapter One of his dream book rises again in the work of Crick and Mitchison.) Let us consider the core of their story.

A problem crops up when memories are "stored" in the network. In the vector space representation memories are located in basin-attractors; memory recall is the process of settling into a basin. Memories as such are not actually stored, as in a computer. What is stored is connection weights, and memories are constructed by the net's process in accordance with the weights. When the number of memories thus "stored" gets up around 15 percent of the total number of nodes in the network, there is overcrowding and spurious memories arise. With overcrowding, there is overlap in the memory networks, so that parasitic attractors are formed in the overlap. The way to clean up this problem is to randomly perturb the network while changing the sign of the learning rule ("unlearning"). Such random unlearning rids the overcrowded network of parasitic states.

Just so in REM, Crick and Mitchison hold. The memory networks are overcrowded at the end of the day and parasitic attractors are formed. *In REM the networks are randomly activated with a negative learning rule*, and parasitic attractors that might lead to false obsession with spurious memories are thereby eradicated. The dream just reflects this random activation of memories in the unlearning process, to which a narrative function gives a superficial coherence.

Crick and Mitchison point to a dream life peculiarity that they think nicely supports their theory. Dreams are punctuated by abrupt thematic discontinuities, where our dream life radically shifts and we say surprisedly in the recounting, "And the next thing I knew . . ." Such radical thematic discontinuity, Crick and Mitchison hold, reflects the underlying random process. When a new memory randomly comes up for unlearning, it is taken up into the dream, forcing a thematic shift. The seeming coherence of dreams is a narrative attempt to link what are really random materials. It is as if the REM sleepy ego has to "make the best of a bad job," as Hobson and McCarley (1977, p. 1347) say, or as if it were a *bricoleur* (Edelson, 1973), a jack-of-all-trades who enterprisingly uses whatever materials happen to be at hand to fashion a solution. (For a more general critique of this view, see Globus 1987.)

This is not a full-fledged connectionist theory of dreams, it should be noted. *The dream is a by-product of something going on in C-networks* for Crick and Mitchison. They are explicit that they have nothing to say, connectionist or otherwise, about the narrative function that takes the memories randomly served up and fashions them into the dream. The dream is a mere epiphenomenon according to this view, at most revealing something about the dreamer's narrative tendencies. What is really going on, though, is a good, clean, biological process of housekeeping. In any case I think this theory is found wrong, once we bother to look at dream material. (And it takes no fancy interpretation, either.) I shall illustrate with one of my own dreams, which shows that there is a consistent underlying continuity across thematic discontinuities. (See also Globus, 1991.)

I dreamt that I was at my bank, trying to get some money out, but I was frustrated. There was construction going on and I couldn't find a teller. *The next thing I knew* I was in a room on the second floor, seeing an antiquity on display, a powerful male figure, which was for sale. I was debating with myself whether to buy the impressive statue, when a buyer from the east walked in and said he had purchased it for a client in Belgium. I left the bank somewhat ruefully at losing out on the statue to head for my car and *the next thing I knew* I was driving off-road with my wife in a barren desert. It was scary and then the car just stopped running in the middle of nowhere. We got out of the car to look at our desperate situation and I spied in the far distance what (improbably) looked to be a Tibetan monastery with a large gate and some tiny figures just visible. I said solemnly to my wife, "These are Buddha people." *The next thing I knew* my wife and children and I were entering the gates of the monastery. The children became engrossed in some activity and my wife and I strolled on, observing the bustling monastery life. Then my wife told me she had decided to join this community and went off. I was left wandering the monastery, filled with deep grief on having lost my wife and children.

This dream contains three thematic discontinuities. The shift from hometown main street to the desert was strikingly abrupt. The issue is this: does the dream randomly change course at these thematic discontinuities or is there a persistent underlying theme across the discontinuities?

The memories on which this dream is based seem quite clearly related to recent waking experiences. I had in fact recently been to my bank to get money. When I walked down the street afterward I noticed that where there had previously been an elegant bank furnished with beautiful antiques, there was now construction, a breaking up of the space into tourist shops. I had recalled at the time the magnificent flower, plant, and antique store that the bank had previously displaced at that site, briefly mourned the destructive effect of "progress," and then continued down the street. So banks, construction, and my great aesthetic love for antiquities were "day residue" for me that might be randomly stimulated during REM, *pace* Crick and Mitchison.

Further, my old car having stopped running was in fact very much on my mind. I had recently bought another car, which I thought fit my image far less well, and I was reluctantly feeling that it was time to sell my ancient indisposed 1960 model. And I had ridden over a bumpy dirt road that day too, at the start of vacation. And the very evening of the dream I had had some thoughts about giving up the struggle of academia and living a spiritual life. Furthermore I had recently seen in a magazine a photograph of a Tibetan scene (the Dalai Lama's palace in Lhasa) very much like one of the scenes I saw when we first strolled around the monastery. These recent waking experiences might be thought to provide more random material for the dream *bricoleur* to piece together, just as Crick and Mitchison say.

The problem for the Crick and Mitchison story, however, is that these memories are not a random collection but have an inner meaningful coherence: they symbolize my major attachments, which in the dream are presented as lost. For openers I am trying to get my money, but I cannot because of the construction. My memory of being at the bank might just happen to be randomly stimulated, I suppose, but surely the bank symbolizes one of my major attachments. I cannot get my money, which symbolizes material loss. Then there is a thematic shift to the second floor and the antiquity (male archetype) for sale. Note that even though there is a thematic shift, there is not a new memory, which the Crick and Mitchison theory calls for. My memory of the original wonderful antique store and my sense of aesthetic loss are integral to the memory complex that includes going to the bank. So here is a case where the supposed thematic shift–random memory relation does not hold. What does hold across the transition is the issue of attachment and loss, first material and then aesthetic.

Then there is the thematic discontinuity where I leave the main street of my hometown and abruptly find myself driving bumpily across the desert until my car stops. I suppose the memory of driving a bumpy dirt road with my wife and children to a vacation house that day might have been randomly selected, but surely a car stopping is not randomly chosen. My public image is very much tied up with my old faded yet classic car. (Friends had protested my announcement of intending to sell it, "But that car is *you!*") So the memory across this thematic transition is not random but symbolizes my loss of image.

Finally there is the thematic shift to the Tibetan monastery that appears improbably in the barren desert. Note that this shift began *before* the dream discontinuity. (I discern the monastery in the far distance and say there are Buddha people and *then* the next thing I know I am entering the monastery with my wife and children.) The memory here has to do with my inauthentic musing about taking up the spiritual life. I have always been attracted to Tibetan Buddhism and am fond of quoting Buddha to psychotherapy supervisees, "Attachment is the root cause of suffering!" So the memories of living a spiritual life and the Tibetan scene (the palace that symbolizes the Tibetan people's loss after the Chinese occupation) are not random either; these memories above all have to do with attachment and loss. And at the end of the dream, symbolization breaks down: I actually lose my wife and children and am plunged into grief.

Even minor dream details are related to attachment and loss. Although my bank does not have a second floor, the building with the former bank under construction did. There is only one thing I know about that second floor, which I have never visited. I once knew someone who had a very fine office on that floor (which to his dismay he lost when the landlord succeeded in evicting him). What always comes to mind in connection with this person when occasionally he crosses my mind is this story from years ago: his live-in girlfriend went back to Europe supposedly to visit her family and he never heard from her again. That memory always evokes a strong empathic response in me. So even the detail of the second floor is related to memories of attachment and loss; it presages the loss of my wife at the end of the dream.

My dream, then, is not constructed from randomly chosen memories superficially stitched together by a narrative. Instead what seems to happen is that my inauthentic fantasy about living a spiritual life—giving up attachments—gets authentically carried out in my dream, but symbolically. My main categories of attachment are symbolized by memories having to do with materialism, aesthetics, image, family, and still other attachments (which I have not mentioned) and these are all presented as relinquished in the dream. Such a dream is an exquisite construction, an existential whole despite the superficial thematic discontinuities, not something superficially put together by a haphazard, REM-sleepy ego making the best of a bad job.

I think that anyone who takes his or her own dreams seriously, or works seriously with the dreams of others, will easily confirm what clinicians know (but that Crick and Mitchison who disdain working at the "clinical bench" never find out): that there is a coherence to the memories across seeming radical thematic discontinuities in dreams and that the thematic shifts in dreams do not parse with changes in memories. To simply ridicule dream "interpretation," as Crick and Mitchison (1986, p. 245) do, is dogmatic, and avoids coming to grips with the insufficiency of their theory as a model of mental functioning during the REM phase of sleep.

The Function of Sleep for C-Networks

Rejecting Crick and Mitchison's account, then, of REM's function as unlearning in the service of clearing out artifactual network obsessions, what other network function might REM serve? I want to develop the idea that *a function of the REM phase of sleep is to decrease tuning bias on the C-networks.*

One additional idea will be required though. (Shades of Freud's "libidinal cathexes.") Let us go through the story again, but a little more fully. As we proceed through W on our world line, we have many, many urges, feelings and meanings throughout the day; in present terms, the internal modules continually tune the networks during waking. By the end of the day, as we prepare for sleep, the tunings that were operational do not all have equivalent status: some of them are more easily reactivated, viz., tunings having to do with unrequited urges, unresolved feelings, and highly significant meanings, even meanings whose significance is unconscious. So certain tunings at the end of the day are left with lowered thresholds of arousal, and these lowered thresholds are carried into sleep.

Now comes the random disturbance of the REM phase of sleep. Recall that the brain's C-networks are disconnected from the world surround on both sensory and motor sides in REM as well as NREM phases. The networks are disturbed into activity and "do their own thing" according to their intrinsic properties. "Their own thing" is *ex hypothesi* a self-organizing process.

One of the modules that gets activated and tunes during REM (and sometimes spontaneously in NREM, at times of restless partial arousal) is the intentional module. When the intentional tuning module gets randomly activated, the context of meanings that thereby becomes operational and tunes is just those meanings with lowered thresholds of arousal that were left more salient at the end of the day (whatever the reasons for the salience, Freudian or not, turn out to be). Similarly for the other two modules, low-threshold urges and feelings are aroused by the random activation and begin to tune. All of this modular tuning constrains the networks. The networks thus attuned begin to self-organize toward self-consistency under the disturbing random activation. So there are intentional, instinctual, affective and knowledge constraints operational, as in W, but input is random rather than ordered by the world surroundings, and tuning depends on residuals rather than being freshly modulated by input order. The result of the self-organizing process thus disturbed and constrained under REM sleep conditions is the dream.

Here is where the Freudian notion is added: tuning activity serves to raise the threshold of the tunings (cf. discharge libidinal cathexis). What is going on is not random learning under a negative Hebb's Rule (i.e., unlearning) but a restoring of unbiased activation thresholds through use. The salient low-threshold meanings, motivations, and feelings get caught up in the random activation and with their activity their threshold rises; everything tends to equalize in probability. Throughout the periodic disturbances of REM, the state of the networks moves toward decreasing the computational energy, toward self-consistency. The REM phase accordingly brings the networks toward a state of harmony without bias, so that they are optimally open to all possibilities, to whatever the day might bring. I agree with Crick and Mitchison that dreaming frees us from obsession, however, obsession not with memories but with meanings, urges, and feelings, and not because spurious attractors are rooted out but because the networks are freed of tuning bias, thereby increasing the range of possibility. So the REM phases of sleep decrease bias and increase possibility, promoting openness, which is a salutary way to prepare for the new day.

Summary

Two states of ordinary being, waking (W) and sleep (S), and the two phases of S, REM and NREM, have been considered.

In W the connectionist networks (C-networks) are activated and functioning optimally, with a high signal-noise ratio (S/N) and a low excitation-inhibition ratio (E/I). The networks self-organize to disturbing and constraining sensory input—under intentional (meaning), instinctual, affective, knowledge and present state constraints—and relax into self-consistent states that emit output.

In S the C-networks are disconnected from the environment on both input and output sides, which serves manifold functions. In the NREM phase of S, there is deactivation, whereas in the REM phase there is activation, like W, but the activation is random. Further, S/N falls and E/I rises in REM compared to W, as a function of shifts in neurochemical modulation (possibly decreased norepinephrine, serotonin, and GABA, which effectively decreases S/N and increases E/I). With this shift in crucial parameters of network functioning, the networks process very differently in REM—Freud's "primary process"—compared to W (the "secondary process").

The function of NREM is primarily for the whole organism and its nonneural systems; perhaps there is necessary maintenance of C-networks accomplished when deactivated during NREM but there is no network function per se.

The function of the REM phase is not random unlearning that frees overcrowded networks of spurious obsession, as Crick and Mitchison (1983) hold, because the clinical-phenomenological study of dreams shows that the memories on which the dream is based are not random but related even across radical thematic discontinuities. I suggest instead that at least one important network function of REM is to decrease residual intentional, instinctual, and affective tuning bias so that the networks are open to wider possibility on waking.

References

Coleman, R. (1986). *Wide Awake at 3:00 A.M.* New York: W. H. Freeman and Co.

Crick, F., and Mitchison, G. (1983). "The Function of Dream Sleep." *Nature* 304: 111–114.

———. (1986). "REM Sleep and Neural Nets." *The Journal of Mind and Behavior* 7: 229–250.

Edelson, M. (1973). "Language and Dreams." *The Psychoanalytic Study of the Child* 27: 203–282.

Foulkes, D. (1985). *Dreaming: A Cognitive-Psychological Analysis.* Hillsdale, N.J.: Lawrence Erlbaum Associates.

Freud, S. (1953). "The Interpretation of Dreams." In J. Strachey (Ed. and Trans.), *The Standard Edition of the Complete Psychological Works of Sigmund Freud*, vols. 4 and 5. London: The Hogarth Press. [Original work published 1900].

Globus, G. (1987). *Dream Life, Wake Life.* Albany: State University of New York Press.

———. (1989). "Connectionism and the Dreaming Mind." *Journal of Mind and Behavior* 10: 179–195.

———. (1991). "Dream Content: Random or Meaningful?" *Dreaming* 1 no. 1: 27–40.

Hobson, J. A., and McCarley, R. W. (1977). "The Brain as a Dream State Generator: An Activation-Synthesis Hypothesis of the Dream Process." *American Journal of Psychiatry* 134: 1335–1348.

Hobson, J. A., Lydic, R., and Baghdoyan, H. A. (1986). "Evolving Concepts of Sleep Cycle Generation: From Brain Centers to Neuronal Populations." *The Behavioral and Brain Sciences* 9: 371–448.

Hoffman, R. E. (1986). "Computer Simulations of Neural Information Processing and the Schizophrenia-Mania Dichotomy." *Archives of General Psychiatry* 44: 178–188.

Hopfield, J. J., and Tank, D. W. (1986). "Computing with Neural Circuits: A Model." *Science* 223: 625–633.

Kolta, A., Diop, L., and Reader, T. A. (1987). "Noradrenergic Effects on Rat Visual Cortex: Single-Cell Microiontophoretic Studies of Alpha-2 Adrenergic Receptors." *Life Science* 41: 281–289.

Madison, D. V., and Nicoll, R. A. (1986). "Actions of Noradrenaline Recorded Intracellularly in Rat Hippocampal CA1 Pyramidal Neurones, in Vitro." *Journal of Physiology* 372: 221–224.

Mamelak, A. N., and Hobson, J. A. (1989). "Dream Bizarreness as the Cognitive Correlate of Altered Neuronal Behavior in REM Sleep." *Journal of Cognitive Neuroscience* 1: 201–222.

Maturana, H. R., and Varela, F. J. (1980). *Autopoiesis and Cognition: The Realization of the Living.* Dordrechet: Reidel.

————. (1987). *The Tree of Knowledge: The Biological Roots of Human Understanding.* Boston: Shambhala.

McClelland, J. L. (1985). "Putting Knowledge in Its Place: A Scheme for Programming Parallel Processing Structures on the Fly." *Cognitive Science* 9: 113–146.

————, Rumelhart, D. E., and the PDP Research Group. (1986). *Parallel Distributed Processing: Explorations in the Microstructure of Cognition,* vol. 2. Cambridge, Mass.: MIT Press, Bradford Books.

Oades, R. D. (1985). "The Role of Noradrenaline in Tuning and Dopamine in Switching Between Signals in the CNS." *Neuroscience and Biobehavioral Reviews* 9: 261–282.

Rumelhart, D. E., McClelland, J. L., and the PDP Research Group. (1986). *Parallel Distributed Processing: Explorations in the Microstructure of Cognition,* vol 1. Cambridge, Mass.: MIT Press. Bradford Books.

Sessler, F. M., Cheng, J., and Waterhouse, B. D. (1988). "Electrophysiological Actions of Norepinephrine in Rat Lateral Hypothalamus. I. Norepinephrine-Induced Modulation of LH Neuronal Responsiveness to Afferent Synaptic Inputs and Putative Neurotransmitters." *Brain Research* 446: 77–89.

Smolensky, P. (1986). "Information Processing in Dynamical Systems: Foundations of Harmony Theory." In D. E. Rumelhart, J. L. McClelland, and the PDP Research Group (Eds.), *Parallel Distributed Processing,* vol. 1, pp. 194–281. Cambridge, Mass.: MIT Press.

————. (1988). "On the Proper Treatment of Connectionism." *Behavioral and Brain Sciences* 11: 123.

Waterhouse, B. D., Moises, H. C., and Woodward, D. J. (1980). "Noradrenergic Modulation of Somatosensory Cortical Neuronal

Responses to Iontophoretically Applied Putative Neurotransmitters." *Experimental Neurology* 69: 30–49.

Woodward, D. J., Moises, H. C., Waterhouse, B. D., Hoffer, B. J., and Freedman, R. (1979). "Modulatory Actions of Norepinephrine in the Central Nervous System." *Federation Proceedings* 38: 2109–2116.

5

Milton Kramer ■■■■■■■■■■■■■■■■

The Selective Mood Regulatory Function of Dreaming: An Update and Revision

The Theory of Dream Function

An Introduction

The present chapter presents a particular attempt to construct a theory of the function of psychological dreaming. This undertaking presupposes a more general theory of dream functioning of which a particular theory, in this case the Selective mood Regulatory Theory of Dreaming, is a case in point. It is essential to begin by exploring the more general question of dream function in order to understand the problems involved before proceeding to a particular theory of the function of dreaming.

A caveat is in order. The issues related to the role of internal mental processes in a causal behavioral chain will not be explored (Sternberg and Smith, 1988). The dominant position in the cognitive sciences is a monistic one in which the Hobbesian materialistic view has captured the day and the dualistic Cartesian position resides in the realm of mystical ideas (Dellarosa, 1988). Unfortunately, the evidence for a holistic view is not compelling (Hobson, 1988; Reiser, 1984). The cognitive sciences deal little, if at all, with non-goal directed, emotionally related, so-called non-determined thinking (Smith, 1988). In the present essay I will describe events as mentally caused, leaving open the more fundamental issues of what one means by a mental cause. However, issues related to mental causation in dreaming do need to be addressed.

The Functions of Dreaming: A Distinction

It is necessary to distinguish two senses in which the concept of function can be applied to psychological dreaming. The concept of function can be used either in the sense of *what* the dream does or *how* the dream is constructed (Breger, 1967). If one explores the consequences of dreaming, one is interested in what the dream does. What is the effect or result of dreaming? In this sense of function, one is concerned with the dream as an independent variable and with subsequent waking thought or behavior as the dependent variable. Leveton (1961) has suggested that dreams can be viewed as the "night residue" that helps precipitate the consequent waking behavior.

Function can be used in another sense to describe how things are made. In the case of psychological dreaming, the function of dreaming also relates to the construction and organization of the dream. What contents are selected, by what rules and how are they melded together? These are the questions the *how* function of dreaming addresses. Studies that examine the mode by which presleep elements and elements from memory are selected (Piccione et al., 1977) and enter, directly or by transformation (Witkin & Lewis, 1967), into the dream, which describe the interconnection of the parts of the dream (Klinger, 1971), and which delineate the sequential development of the dream across the REM period (Kramer, Roth, and Czaya, 1975) and across the night (Kramer, McQuarrie, and Bonnet, 1980; Kramer et al., 1964) are all examples of the *how* function of dreaming. From the perspective of dream construction, the dream is the dependent measure.

The two aspects of dream function, what the dream achieves—its effects or consequences—and how the dream is constructed and organized, are often related. Freud (1955) clearly related the two. The dream for Freud was constructed in response to a disturbing infantile wish to provide a disguised gratification of the wish that resulted in the protection of the continuity of sleep. This infantile wish may be seen as the independent variable and the disguised gratification as the dependent variable. The dream work was postulated by Freud as the mechanism for constructing the dream in which the disguised gratification occurred. The dream experience of disguised gratification then becomes the independent variable with sleep protection as the consequent dependent variable.

The distinction between the dream as independent and dependent variable has been explored by others (Cartwright, 1978; Fiss, 1979). Unfortunately, the distinction has not been consistently applied, and evidence for the *what* of dream function often has been confused with evidence for the *how* of dream formation.

The Theory of Adaptive Dream Function

Those theories of psychological dreaming that specify a consequent function may be considered adaptive in nature. Such theories espouse either an assimilative or accommodative function for dreaming (Piaget, 1962).

Theories of dreaming that view dream function as assimilative are more likely to be able to account for the totality of the dream experience. In these assimilative theories, the dreaming process functions automatically, outside of conscious awareness; that is, without recall and secondary reworking. These theories generally have the dream achieve some corrective (Kramer and Roth, 1973b) or reductive goal (French, 1952).

In the accommodative theories of dream function, the dreamer is altered as a result of the dream experience (Jung, 1974). The dream is a special experience that has the potential for a significant and often decisive impact on the dreamer's life. In the accommodative theories of dream function, the dream must become conscious, enter awareness, and be "understood" to have its transforming effects.

It is possible, if not probable, that the dream serves both an assimilative and accommodative function. It may be that those dreams that are recalled are related to more significant events of the moment (Cohen, 1974; Trinder and Kramer, 1971) and carry the potential for the transforming experience either in themselves or in conjunction with a waking exploration. Meanwhile, the bulk of dreaming would be continuing, outside of awareness, to achieve the more modest reductive assimilative goal.

Criteria for Demonstrating a Function for Dreams

To adequately pursue a function for psychological dreaming, one needs to pursue both the *how* of dream formation and the *what* of dream consequence. Either alone is only half the story. Therefore, a complete theory of psychological dreaming needs to place the dream between the waking events that preceded and the waking events that follow it. This wake-dream-wake paradigm needs to be the basis for exploring the function of dreaming.

If one can manipulate aspects of the presleep experience and the dream experience itself, the possibility for demonstrating an effect on the dream and on subsequent wakefulness becomes possible. It has been shown to a greater or lesser degree that dream content can be directly manipulated (Tart, 1979). For example, presleep suggestion to dream about certain topics or specific dreams has been effective (Meier, 1967). Posthypnotic suggestions to have certain kinds of dreams have also met with some success (Schrotter, 1959). Paradigms that have conditioned subjects to respond when a certain type of dream is occurring have also been accomplished (Cartwright, and Lamberg, 1992). Further, dreams can be directly manipulated. Stimuli introduced during REM sleep have been shown to effect dreaming systematically (Castaldo and Holzman, 1969). Also, dream content can probably be altered by prior REM deprivation with an intensity increase in the rebound condition (Firth, 1974). The systematic exploration of some if not all of these manipulations might well permit us to gain sufficient control over the dreaming process to manipulate it effectively either as a dependent or independent variable.

If one can alter various aspects of the dream experience, the possibility for demonstrating an effect on subsequent wakefulness then exists. However, one needs to have some idea in what aspect of subsequent wakefulness one might expect to see some change caused by the dream.

The variables to examine in wakefulness that are likely to be effective in influencing dream content or to be subsequently influenced by dream content are those of an affective rather than cognitive nature (Ekstrand et al., 1977). The waking experiences most likely to appear in dreams are those with an affective charge (Piccione et al., 1977). The link of waking life to dreams is more likely to be an affective rather than a cognitive one (Kramer, Roth, and Palmer, 1976). In examining the wake-sleep-wake continuum, we should look for the relationship between presleep affective states and the consequent dream experience and then to complete the sequence, the relationship of dreaming to the affective state of the dreamer the following morning.

The Core Observation

The Contribution of REM Physiology

Freud (1955) has proposed that dreaming serves to protect the continuity of sleep. Taking our lead from this proposal, the physiological study of REM sleep (the mental content of which will be taken as our paradigm for psychological dreaming) has contributed two observations that buttress this suggestion. First, if the dream is related to maintaining sleep and if the longer one sleeps the more likely one is to wake up, after the initial settling down process, then the distribution of REM sleep across the usual sleep period is appropriate: it is positively accelerated, more of it occurring later in the night (Webb, 1969, see Figure 5.I). The second observation about the dream's role in the continuity of sleep relates to the frequent finding that a period of dreaming sleep, REM sleep, often ends in a brief arousal. In a study we did in ten subjects,

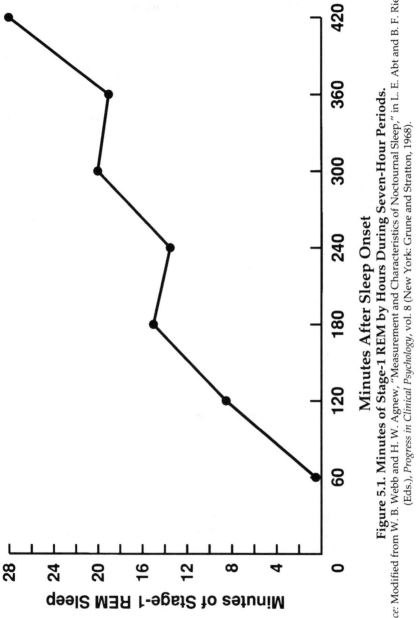

Minutes After Sleep Onset

Figure 5.1. Minutes of Stage-1 REM by Hours During Seven-Hour Periods.

Source: Modified from W. B. Webb and H. W. Agnew, "Measurement and Characteristics of Noctournal Sleep," in L. E. Abt and B. F. Riess (Eds.), *Progress in Clinical Psychology*, vol. 8 (New York: Grune and Stratton, 1968).

studied one night each, 90 percent of the REM periods ended in a brief arousal of less than 15 seconds. Overwhelmingly, as for most of sleep, there is no memory for this brief arousal.

Dreaming sleep is properly placed in the night to support a role in the continuity of sleep. And dreaming sleep is related to arousals as most periods of dreaming sleep end in a brief arousal. One is encouraged by these observations to explore a relationship between dreaming and the continuity of sleep.

Some dreams appear to disturb sleep, not protect its continuity. It may be useful to provide an example of such a dream. This might serve as a vehicle to concretize some of the problems the dream experience poses, as well as some of the factors that predispose one to having a disturbing dream, that stimulate its appearance. The dream that disturbs sleep tests Freud's proposal that the dream protects sleep.

The following disturbing dream was reported by a 26-year-old man who was a patient in a Veterans Administration hospital.

> "I dreamed I was back in Vietnam and I had thrown a grenade into one of the Vietnamese huts. I went inside and there was one of the babies blown up all over the inside of the hut. I woke up and was terrified, nauseated, and crying."

The dream is troubling and leads to an awakening associated with negative affect and the recall of a prior troubling dream (Kramer and Roth, 1977).

It is worth noting that many dreams have no accompanying feeling, and in those from which some feeling tone is reported, a negative feeling is more common than a positive one (Hall and Van de Castle, 1966). The romantic notion of the "land of dreamy dreams" (Gilchrist, 1981) is not borne out by the experience of dreaming.

In a study (Taub et al., 1978) that compared a recalled dream with a recalled nightmare with the subject's concept of a nightmare, the least intense emotional experience was the recalled dream and the concept of the nightmare was described with the most intense affect. A successful dream has muted feelings as its usual accompaniment.

The Intensity of Dreaming

The intensity of the dream experience shows a systematic development across the REM period (Kramer et al., 1975). We awakened four subjects at various time points after the onset of REM (0.5, 2.5, 5.0, 10, 20, and 30 minutes). We did this for the second and fourth REM periods until we had two data points for each subject at each time point. Dream reports were collected from the last 10 seconds prior to awakening and were rated along a number of dimensions on a dream intensity questionnaire (DIQ), including recall, activity, emotion, anxiety, clarity, pleasantness, fright, violence-hostility, dramatic quality, distortion, relationship to personal life, and logic. As we found no content difference between the second and fourth REM periods, the data were combined at each time point from the two. A one-way analysis of variance was performed on the total matrix of raw scores for each of the twelve dimensions of the DIQ at the five time points (0.5 minutes was dropped as there was too little data). The overall effect of time was significant. Post hoc tests showed that dream reports collected at 5 minutes were different from those from 10 minutes, and reports collected after 20 minutes of REM were different from those at 30 minutes, but reports from 10 and 20 minutes intervals did not differ.

The development of dream content across the REM period is primarily linear. However, we did show a plateau between content collected 10 and 20 minutes into REM periods (Kramer et al., 1975; see Figure 5.2). This ebb and flow in dream content fits the eye movement pattern described by Aserinsky (1971), which we have replicated (Johnson et al., 1980; (see Figure 5.3). Aserinsky speculated that dream content might ebb and flow in keeping with the pattern of eye movement activity, which our findings do indeed support (Kramer et al., 1975).

Dreaming: An Emotional Surge

The rise and fall in the intensity of affect and content across the dream period is consonant with the possibility that during REM sleep there is a surge of emotion. We speculate that a function of dreaming is to contain or attempt to contain this surge.

Several questions need to be explored. Is the recallability of a dream influenced by the relative success of the dream process in containing the emotional surge occurring during REM sleep? Does the arousal after a dream period lead to the awakening of the "nightmare" because the "intensity" surge exceeds the integrative capacity of the dream experience? These are questions that need to be pursued. The variability and magnitude of alterations in autonomic function reflected in changes in heart rate, blood pressure, and respiration associated with the REM period may also point to the affective nature of the REM experience (Freemon, 1972). Efforts to connect content with variability in

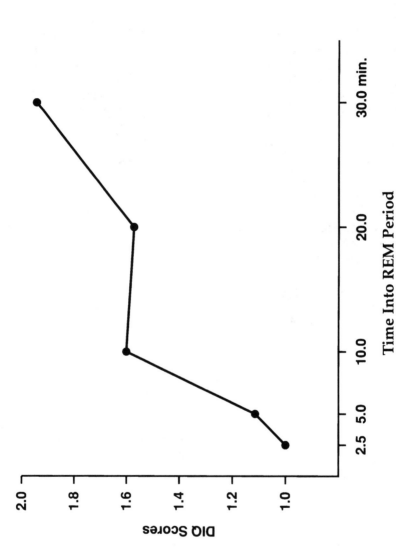

Figure 5.2. Mean Dream Intensity Questionnaire (DIQ) Scores as a Function of Time into REM.

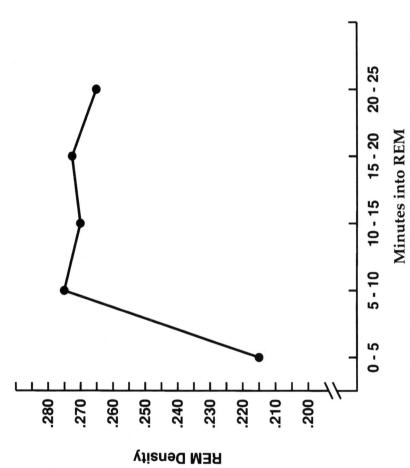

Figure 5.3. REM Density vs. Time into the REM Period.

autonomic variables have been minimally successful (Hauri and Van de Castle, 1973). Nevertheless, the autonomic functions during REM sleep are experiencing fluctuations in keeping with an emotional surge.

When the integrative (sleep maintaining) function of the dream is successful, the dream does not enter awareness. The dream is encompassed in the amnesia that is sleep, and the function of such a dream is subsumed under an assimilative function for dreaming.

Dream Function: Containment of the Emotional Surge

What factors might influence or determine the success of the capacity of the dream experience in containing the emotional surge of the REM period and keep the dreamer asleep and without dream recall? Is the attempt to contain the emotional surge related to the content of the dream experience, to the preoccupation with and ability of the dreamer to recall dreams, to the emotional condition (psychopathology, predispositional states) of the dreamer, or to the responsivity of the dreamer to the dream experience (heightened arousal levels)?

Subjects who reported two or more experiences of disturbed dreaming (nightmares) per week were compared to a group of vivid dreamers (Kramer, Schoen, and Kinney, 1984a). The nightmare sufferers had the same content categories in their dreams and with about equal frequencies as the vivid dreamers. The integrative capacity of dreaming is not simply influenced by the content of the dream.

The ability to recall dreams is not the determiner of the ability to integrate the emotional surge experienced during REM sleep. Vivid dreamers actually reported much higher dream recall in general than the subjects with nightmares (89 percent vs. 54 percent). Vivid dreaming may index a partial failure, on a continuing basis, of the capacity to manage the emotional surge during dreaming sleep. However, if the nightmare was intrinsically related to the dream experience per se, one might expect recall to be higher in the chronic nightmare sufferer than in the vivid dreamer.

There does seem to be a predispositional factor determining the capacity of the dreamer to contain the emotional surge that occurs during REM sleep. The nightmare sufferers in our study had higher scores on all the MMPI scales and on emotionally based scales of the Cornell Medical Index, and they had a greater number of prior psychiatric hospitalizations. They felt that the occurrence of disturbed dreams on a given night was related to current feelings (e.g., anger, sensitivity, and general emotion). The emotional state of the person in whom the dream occurs appears to be a determinant of the integrative capacity of these dreams in containing the emotional surge occurring during REM sleep.

The emotional responsivity of the dreamer to the dream experience is another factor that reflects the predispositional issue in determining the success or failure of the integrative function of dreaming in containing the emotional surge that occurs during REM sleep. Nightmare sufferers, more than vivid dreamers, are described by others as more responsive and more frightened during sleep, apparently in response to their dreams.

The integrative failure that is apparently reflected in an increased responsivity in the nightmare sufferer is confirmed in a study of chronic delayed post-traumatic stress disorder (CDPTSD) patients who have frequent nightmares (Kinney and Kramer, 1985). When these CDPTSD patients were given an above-threshold tone during sleep they responded in 93 percent of trials whereas the response rate in a group of control subjects was only 52 percent. Clearly, the CDPTSD patients are more responsive, and these are people who, indeed, are more emotionally troubled. This suggests the notion that predispositional issues (psychopathology) may alter the responsivity to dreaming of the dreamer. This change in responsivity may be based on a difficulty in containing "internal emotional forces" during sleep.

It is of interest to note that the work with chronic delayed post-traumatic stress disorder sufferers did indeed suggest that their increased responsivity was internal. In an awakening threshold study (Schoen, Kramer, and Kinney, 1984), in which an ascending method of awakening was used, it was found that the chronic delayed post-traumatic stress disorder sufferer had a higher awakening threshold compared to controls. If the CDPTSD patients were being externally vigilant one would have expected a lower threshold. The fact that the CDPTSD patient's threshold is higher suggested that they are indeed internally vigilant.

In the previous above threshold study (Kinney and Kramer, 1985), the CDPTSD patients had a much higher rate of failure to identify the source of the disturbing stimulus than control subjects. The chronic delayed post-traumatic stress disordered patients were unable to identify the source of the disruption 92 percent of the time, whereas the control subjects were unable to identify the source 60 percent of the time. Again, this would support a greater internal focus of attention in the chronic delayed post-traumatic stress disordered patients as a possible explanation for their almost total failure to identify the source of their sleep disruption.

During the dream, there is evidence, both psychologically and physiologically, of an emotional surge that rises and falls across the REM period. If the dream is successful, a brief arousal occurs for which there *is* no memory. If the dreamer is emotionally troubled and therefore hyperresponsive on either a transient or chronic basis, this predisposition has, as an associated feature, a failure of the dream to contain the emotional surge and the likelihood of a dream recall or a frightening awakening is enhanced. The capacity to contain the emotional surge of the dream is determined by the "soil," the affective state of the dreamer, that the dream falls on at the time of dreaming.

It is clear that the emotional surge within a dream period is inextricably linked to the intensity of the dream and probably to the intensity of the physiological variables such as eye movement, heart rate, blood pressure, and respiration that occur during the dream period (Freemon, 1972). These observations suggest that an examination of both the waking affective and mental state as they relate to dreaming would be appropriate.

Mood Before and After Sleep

An Introduction

The core observation in approaching the function of dreaming has led to a view that the dream, as Freud (1955) had suggested, serves to protect the continuity of sleep by containing the repeated emotional surge that occurs during dreaming sleep. This observation draws our attention to the relationship of dreaming in particular and sleep in general to the emotional-affective state of the individual.

It is apparent to even the casual observer that there is an intimate connection between sleep and how one feels, one's subjective state, one's mood or affective condition. The likelihood of obtaining a good night's sleep is generally credited to the subjective state of the person prior to going to sleep, and how one feels in the morning often is believed to be the consequence of the quality and quantity of the sleep that preceded it. Sleep, if one is trying to understand its function, is best seen as placed between two periods of wakefulness. Prior wakefulness impacts sleep and sleep impacts subsequent wakefulness.

How depressed or anxious one is before going to sleep has been shown to alter how well one sleeps (Rimon, Fujita, and Takahata, 1986;

Rosa, Bonnet, and Kramer, 1983). From a psychological perspective, the more intense emotional experiences of the day (Piccione et al., 1977) and the thoughts one has before going to sleep (Kramer, Moshiri, and Scharf, 1982; Piccione et al., 1977) are likely to appear in the dream of a subsequent night's sleep. Sleep is clearly responsive to the experiences that precede it during the day.

The physiological and psychological aspects of sleep are also related to the waking activity of the next day. How well one performs on various psychomotor tasks following a night's sleep is influenced by even small alterations in the number of hours of prior sleep; for example, decrements in performance can be shown with even a 1 hour reduction in prior sleep (Wilkinson, 1968). Feeling states on arising in the morning are more predictive of the performance that day than are hours of total sleep (Johnson et al., 1990). Also, mental activity in the morning is linked to the dreams of the prior night (Kramer et al., 1982). There is a thematic continuity between the dreams of the night and spontaneous verbal behavior obtained the following morning. Wakefulness is clearly responsive to the experiences during the sleep that preceeded it.

It appears that sleep is linked to both prior and subsequent wakefulness. Sleep, in both its physiological and psychological aspects, is linked to wakefulness; how one feels before and after sleep is connected to the intervening period of sleep.

The possibility that sleep functions to alter the subjective state, for example, how one feels, one's mood, seems plausible. An exploration of the sleep-mood interaction should look at the relationship of both the psychology and physiology of sleep to waking mood.

A systematic study of the mood-sleep relationship was undertaken. The approach was to utilize standard measures of mood, sleep psychology, and sleep physiology, beginning with relatively normal situations and then extending the observations to more extreme circumstances. Mood was chosen because sleep and subjective state appear to be closely related. Mood appears to vary from day to day, across the day and well might bear a relationship to both dreams and sleep physiology.

The Measurement of Mood

The mood measurement device utilized in these studies was the Clyde Mood Scale (see Table 5.1). This (Clyde, 1963) is a forty-eight item adjective checklist that yields scores on six factors: friendly, aggressive, clear thinking, sleepy, unhappy, and dizzy (anxious). It was necessary to establish that the scale was reliable, sensitive to change in mood from night to morning, and further, that the repeated use of the scale did not lead to stereotypy across days; that is, that it continued to be sensitive to mood change (Kramer and Roth, 1973b).

Mood scores were collected from eight normal male subjects who slept for fifteen consecutive nights in the sleep laboratory (Kramer and Roth, 1973b). The six mood subscales were found to be independent, that is, not intercorrelated, and the level of mood subscale scores obtained were similar to published norms (Clyde, 1963). The mean and variability of mood subscale scores from the first and last third of the fifteen day observation period were not different. The scale, as applied, was capturing the same subjective states as described by Clyde. The subscales were indeed independent aspects of mood and the responses did not show adaptation across the observation period as the mean level and variability remained the same.

Table 5.1
Principal Items Included in Each Factor on the Clyde Mood Scale

Factor	Four Principal Items
Friendly	Good natured
	Pleasant
	Kind
	Warmhearted
Aggressive	Boastful
	Forceful
	Rude
	Sarcastic
Clear thinking	Efficient
	Alert
	Clear thinking
	Able to concentrate
Sleepy	Sleepy
	Drowsy
	Fatigued
	Tired
Unhappy	Sad
	Downhearted
	Troubled
	Worried
Dizzy (Anxious)	Sick to the stomach
	Dizzy
	Jittery
	Shaky

Mood Difference Across the Night

The means and standard deviations of the mood subscale scores at night and in the morning of the eight subjects who slept for fifteen consecutive nights in the laboratory were different from each other, decreasing from night to morning (Kramer and Roth, 1973b) (see Figure 5.4). If these differences were related to the psychology and/or physiology of sleep, then sleep might play a role in mood regulation.

The possible influence of age, setting (sleep location), sex of the subject, hypnotic drug use, or dream awakening on mood change before and after sleep was explored before examining the relationship of mood difference to aspects of the intervening sleep. The influence of these variables tests the stability of the night-morning mood difference we found (Kramer and Roth, 1973b).

Two additional studies in the laboratory of night-morning mood differences over fifteen to twenty nights found identical results (Roth, Kramer and Roehrs, 1976). In the first study the age of the subject varied (20–70) while in the second study the age of the subjects were all the same (20–25). In both studies it was found that the mood at night was different than the mood in the morning both in mean level and variability. The Unhappy and Friendly subscales decrease while the Sleepy subscale increased from night to morning (the apparent paradoxical change in Sleepy was related to how close to awakening the testing occurred).

The possibility exists that the change in mood from night to morning is a function of the setting in which the subject slept (Roehrs et al., 1973). The structure and regimentation of the laboratory may have determined the result. A comparison to subjects sleeping at home was needed. Mood scales before and after sleep in eleven male college subjects who slept in the laboratory for fifteen consecutive nights were compared to those of twelve male college students who slept at home for fifteen consecutive nights. The results for both were the same. Again, mean mood and variability is higher at night than in the morning. Further, on post hoc tests the Friendly mood subscale showed a statistically significant decrease in both groups and the Unhappy mood subscale showed a decrease in the group that slept at home. The location, where one sleeps, does not effect the mood changes seen from night to morning.

There is reason to believe that the affective state in men and women is different (Cattell, 1973) and that their sleep (Williams, Karacan, and Hursch, 1974) and dream patterns (Winget and Kramer, 1979)

154

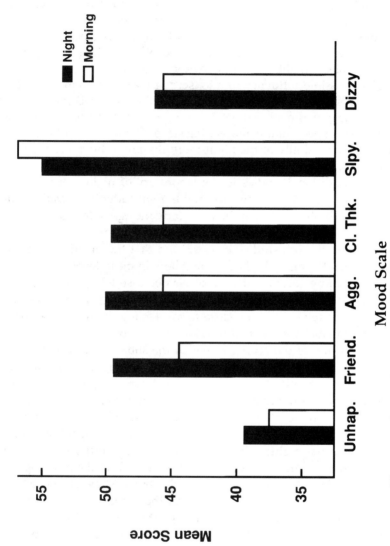

Figure 5.4. Mean Clyde Mood Subscales, Night and Morning Ss=8.

are also different. Mood change from night to morning was examined in a group of men and women (Lysaght, Kramer, and Roth, 1979). Twelve male and twelve female college students completed Clyde Mood Scales before and after sleep for fifteen consecutive days while sleeping at home. There was a significant decrease in mood from night to morning in both groups. On post hoc tests, Friendly and Unhappy decreased in men with Sleepy showing a trend to decrease, whereas in women Friendly and Sleepy showed a significant decrease while Unhappy showed a trend to decrease. Mood changes across the night are not influenced by the sex of the person. Mood changes are similar in men and women across the night.

The change in mood on the Clyde Mood Scale from night to morning was again demonstrated in a study of twelve men ages 25–35 who slept for nine consecutive nights, all of whom took a hypnotic drug (Schwartz, Kramer, and Roth, 1974). On post hoc tests only the Sleepy mood subscale showed a statistical change, an increase, from night to morning. Of interest in this study was the fact that the systematic night-morning mood difference was demonstrated in only nine nights of study and in patients taking a centrally active medication.

The process of awakening a subject from each REM period does not alter the relationship between night and morning mood (unpublished data). Twelve male subjects who slept for twenty consecutive nights in the sleep laboratory and were awakened from the end of each of the first four REM periods filled out Clyde Mood scales before and after sleeping in the laboratory. On post hoc testing the Friendly, Aggressive, and Clear Thinking mood subscales decreased significantly while Unhappy showed a trend to decrease and Sleepy a trend to increase.

The results of our studies of pre- and postsleep mood relationships lead to the conclusion that how one feels before going to sleep and on awakening the following morning are systematically different from each other. The intensity and variability of various aspects of how one feels decreases from night to morning (see Tables 5.2, 5.3 and 5.4). This is true in the laboratory (Kramer and Roth, 1973b; Roehrs et al., 1973), at home (Lysaght et al., 1979), across a wide age range (20–70) (Roth, Kramer, and Roehrs, 1976), for both men and women (Lysaght et al., 1979), and whether the subjects were participants in a hypnotic drug study (Schwartz et al., 1974) or were awakened for dream collection (unpublished data).

Mood Predictability Across the Night

How stable a person's mood is in general and from day to day remains a question. Do various aspects of mood (subjective state) vary systematically from night to morning for each individual (much as the dream content of one person is different from that of another)? Also, does the mood of an individual from night to night vary in a systematic manner (as does dream content) (Kramer, Hlasny, Jacobs, and Roth, 1976)? To examine these two questions we studied the night and morning mood scores on the Clyde Mood Scale from four groups of individuals (fifty-two in all), three female (*n* = 40) and one male (*n* = 12), three studies in the laboratory and one at home (female) for 15 to 21 consecutive nights (three studies), or non-consecutive nights (one study) (Kramer, 1991) (see Table 5.5).

Table 5.2
Summary of Mood Studies
Mean Scores: Main Effects and Interactions (ANOVA)

	Baseline[1]	Age[2]	Sex[3]	Drug[4]	Dream Awakenings[5]
Moods	.001	.001	.001	.01	.001
Time	.001	.001	.005	.05	.05
Mood x Time	.05	.01	.05	.01	.001

1 Kramer and Roth, 1973b.
2 Roth, Kramer, and Roehrs, 1976
3 Lysaght et al., 1979
4 Schwartz et al., 1974
5 Kramer, unpublished data

Table 5.3
Summary of Mood Studies,
Standard Deviations: Main Effects and Interactions (ANOVA)

	Baseline[1]	Age[2]	Sex[3]	Dream Awakenings[4]
Moods	.01	.01	.005	.001
Time	.05	.05	.001	NS
Mood x Time	NS	NS	NS	.02

1 Kramer and Roth, 1973b
2 Roth, Kramer, and Roehrs, 1976
3 Lysaght et al., 1979
4 Kramer, unpublished data

Table 5.4
Summary of Mood Studies,
Mean Scores: Post Hoc Tests and Direction of Change

	Friendly	Aggressive	Unhappy	Sleepy	Clear Thinking	Anxious
Baseline[1]	↓ **	↓	↓ **	↑ *	↓	↓
Age[2]	↓ **	↓	↓ **	↑ **	↓	↓
Home-Male[3]	↓ **	↑	↓ **	↓ *	↑	↓
Home-Female[3]	↓ **	↓	↓ *	↓ **	↑	↑
Dream Awakenings[4]	↓ ***	↓ ***	↓ *	↑ *	↓ ***	↑
Drug[5]	↓	↓	↓	↑ **	↓	↑
Appropriate Direction	6/6	5/6	6/6	4/6	4/6	3/6
Stat. Sig.	5/6	1/6	5/6	6/6	1/6	0/6

*$p<.10$. **$p<.05$. ***$p<.01$.

[1]Kramer and Roth, 1973b.

[2]Roth, Kramer, and Roehrs, 1976.

[3]Lysaght et al., 1979.

[4]Kramer, unpublished data.

[5]Schwartz et al., 1974.

Table 5.5
Mood Studies: Variables

	Subjects	Sex	Location	Nights	Continuous
Study A	14	F	Laboratory	17	No
Study B	15	F	Home	21	Yes
Study C	11	F	Laboratory	20	Yes
Study D	12	M	Laboratory	20	Yes

Two correlations were done for each of the four groups. First, a between-subject Pearson product moment correlation was done (Downie and Heath, 1970). The mood subscale scores at night and in the morning were averaged for each subject in each group and the single night and morning scores for each subject in each of four groups were correlated. The correlation on each mood subscale score (Friendly, Aggressive, Unhappy, Sleepy, Clear Thinking, Anxious, and Average Intensity) was averaged, after a Z transform, across the four studies. Second, a within-subject Pearson product moment correlation for each of the subscales was done, averaged across the subjects in each group, and then across four groups, again using a Z transform. The between-subject correlation captures the trait aspect of mood whereas the within-subject correlations are more likely to capture the state aspect of mood.

Table 5.6
Correlation (Between Subjects) of Average Night to Morning
Mood Subscale Scores

	Friendly	Aggres-sive	Unhappy	Sleepy	Clear Thinking	Anxious	Average
Study A	.95***	.94***	.95***	.72**	.93***	.88***	.75**
Study B	.93***	.84***	.88***	.15	.80***	.53*	.93***
Study C	.98***	.92***	.78**	-.26	.78**	.59	.87***
Study D	.62*	.97***	.94***	.27	.94***	.27	.88***
Mean	.93***	.95***	.90***	.26	.88***	.62*	.87***

*p<.05. **p<.01. ***p<.001.

The trait aspect of mood, mood stability in general, as measured by various subscales of the Clyde Mood Scale is summarized in Table 5.6. This correlation is obtained by separately averaging night and morning scores for each subject and correlating these scores across subjects. In the twenty-eight correlations of the four studies, twenty-three are statistically significant. The level of correlation is very high, with twenty-one of twenty-eight being .72 and above. The mean subscale correlations across the four studies for each of the subscale scores showed that two, Sleepy and Anxious, are low ($r = .26$ and $.62$) while five, Friendly, Aggressive, Unhappy, Clear Thinking, and the Average scale subscores, are high ($r = .87$ to $.95$, see Table 5.6).

The state aspect of mood, mood variability from day to day, as measured by the various subscales of the Clyde Mood Scale is summarized in Table 5.7. This table shows the result of correlating the night and morning score of each subject on each of the seven Clyde Mood subscales, then averaging that score across the subjects within each study and then across all four studies. It is apparent that the within-subject correlations are low and not significant; only two of twenty-eight were significant and the mean correlation over all four studies for each subscale varies between .03 and .29.

Table 5.7
Correlation (Within Subjects) of Average Night to Morning
Mood Subscale Scores

	Friendly	Aggres-sive	Unhappy	Sleepy	Clear Thinking	Anxious	Average
Study A	.26	.19	.25	.09	.16	.14	.30
Study B	.18	.18	.46*	.04	.34	.23	.43*
Study C	.23	.11	.29	-.09	.13	.11	.07
Study D	.19	.25	.13	.08	.23	.14	.15
Mean	.22	.18	.29	.03	.22	.16	.24

*$p<.05$.

It is of interest to examine the frequency and distribution of significant correlations at the individual level in the four studies. In these studies, out of 364 correlations (52 subjects times 7 subscales = 364 correlations), 88 were statistically significant when only 18 would be expected by chance at the 5 percent level, if all the correlations were independent. There is reason to believe from other studies that the subscales are indeed independent, as in five studies the main effect of mood is statistically significant at the .01 to .001 level (see Table 5.2).

Some 24 percent (88/364) of the individual night to morning correlations were significant ($p < .05$). The distribution across studies was 19 percent (19/98) of the correlations in the first study (A) were statistically significant, 30 percent (32/105) in the second study (B), 25 percent (19/77) in the third study (C), and 21 percent (18/84) in the fourth study (D) (see Table 5.8).

Table 5.8
Number and Percentage of Subjects Who Show at Least One Statistically
Significant (Within Subject) Night to Morning Mood Subscale Correlation

	Number of Subjects	Subjects with at least one stat. sig. correlation	Percentage
Study A	14	9	64
Study B	15	15	100
Study C	11	8	73
Study D	12	10	83
Total	52	42	81

Do all the subjects show at least one statistically significant relationship between night and morning mood scores? Not all, but most do. Some forty-two or 81 percent of the subjects show at least one such relationship between mood before and after sleep whereas 19 percent, ten of the fifty-two, do not (see Table 5.8). The eighty-eight statistically significant correlations are distributed over the forty-two subjects so that sixteen have one, thirteen have two, nine have three, one has four, and three have five.

In Table 5.9 the number of subjects with a significant within subject correlation for each subscale in each of the studies is given. The largest number of significant correlations is with the Unhappy mood subscale. Some twenty-two of the fifty-two subjects (42 percent) show a significant correlation of night and morning scores for Unhappy. The lowest number of significant correlations is with Sleepy, with only eight of the fifty-two subjects (15 percent) showing a significant correlation.

Table 5.9

Number and Percentage of Subjects with a Statistically Significant Correlation on a Night to Morning Mood Subscale Score (Within Subjects)

	Friendly	Aggres-sive	Unhappy	Sleepy	Clear Thinking	Anxious	Average
Study A	3(21%)	2(14%)	5(36%)	1(7%)	2(14%)	3(21%)	3(21%)
Study B	3(20%)	5(33%)	8(53%)	2(13%)	5(33%)	3(20%)	6(40%)
Study C	4(36%)	1(9%)	6(55%)	2(18%)	3(27%)	2(18%)	1(9%)
Study D	3(25%)	3(25%)	3(25%)	3(25%)	3(25%)	2(17%)	1(8%)
Total	13(25%)	11(21%)	22(42%)	8(15%)	13(25%)	10(19%)	11(21%)

The number and percentage of nights in each study on each mood subscale score that showed a decrease from night to morning is shown in Tables 5.10 and 5.11. Some 999 night and morning mood subscores were obtained in the four studies. Five of the mood subscales (Friendly, Aggressive, Unhappy, Clear Thinking, and Average Intensity) showed a subscale score decrease in over 50 percent of nights (64, 59, 62, 56, and 63 percent). The Sleepy and Anxious subscale scores showed a decrease in just under 50 percent of nights (49 and 47 percent).

The number and percentage of subjects showing a decrease in mood subscale scores in at least 50 percent of nights in each study is summarized in Table 5.12. On the Average (intensity) subscale, 81 percent of subjects showed a decrease in intensity of mood on at least 50 percent of nights. On individual subscales, 76 percent of the subjects showed the decrease in at least 50 percent of nights on the Aggressive subscale, 74 percent on the Unhappy subscale, 69 percent on Friendly, 63 percent on Clear Thinking, 46 percent on Sleepy, and 41 percent on the Anxious subscale.

Table 5.10
Number of Night to Morning Mood Scale Pairs for Each Subscale
That Decreased from Night to Morning

	Friendly	Aggres-sive	Unhappy	Sleepy	Clear Thinking	Anxious	Average
Study A[1]	149.5	124.5	147	115.5	152.5	115	155.5
Study B[2]	140	148	144	222	103	108	161
Study C[3]	179.5	161	169	56.5	149	130.5	141
Study D[4]	169	157.5	158.5	93	154.5	119.5	167.5
Total[5]	638	591	618.5	487	559	473	625

[1]N=238.
[2]N=315.
[3]N=217.
[4]N=229.
[5]N=999.

Table 5.11
Percentage of Night to Morning Mood Score Pairs for Each
Subscale That Decreased from Night to Morning

	Friendly	Aggres-sive	Unhappy	Sleepy	Clear Thinking	Anxious	Average
Study A	63%	52%	62%	49%	64%	48%	65%
Study B	44%	47%	46%	70%	33%	34%	51%
Study C	83%	74%	78%	26%	69%	60%	65%
Study D	74%	69%	69%	41%	67%	52%	73%
Mean	64%	59%	62%	49%	56%	47%	63%

In the series of studies looking at the predictive relationship between pre- and postsleep mood, both between and within subjects, we found a series of systematic relationships. How one feels along a number of dimensions (Friendly, Aggressive, Unhappy, Clear Thinking and Anxious) before and after sleeping is different (see Tables 5.2, 5.3 and 5.4) but highly correlated from night to morning, that is, specific to the individual (see Table 5.6). For example, how Friendly one is on average at night and in the morning is specific for that individual, different from other people, and a trait aspect of the person. And the particular aspects of subjective state (mood) on a day to day basis that are systematic, that is, correlated from night to morning, for a given individual are unique for that individual. One person may have a systematic relationship from night to morning across days in how Unhappy he feels, while another may have it in how Aggressive she feels. In most people, the night to day aspect of mood that correlates most often across days is the Unhappy aspect of mood (See Table 5.9).

Table 5.12
Number of Subjects Showing Change (Decrease) in Mood Subscale
Scores in 50 Percent of the Nights

	Friendly	Aggres- sive	Unhappy	Sleepy	Clear Thinking	Anxious	Average
Study A	10(71%)	10 (71%)	10.5(75%)	5.5(39%)	13 (93%)	6 (43%)	12(86%)
Study B	5(33%)	8 (53%)	7 (47%)	13 (87%)	2 (13%)	2 (13%)	10(67%)
Study C	11(100%)	11 (100%)	10 (91%)	2 (18%)	8.5(77%)	7.5(68%)	10(91%)
Study D	10(83%)	11.5(96%)	11 (92%)	3.5(29%)	9.5(79%)	6 (50%)	10(83%)
Total	36(69%)	39.5(76%)	38.5(74%)	24 (46%)	33 (63%)	21.5(41%)	42(81%)

Mood Change and Sleep Deprivation

Up to this point the mood scales taken daily, before and after sleep, have been described as if any difference found could be due only to the intervening sleep. A moment's reflection would suggest that the difference between a mood scale taken in the morning and one taken at night could just as well be attributed to the period of intervening wakefulness as to the intervening sleep. Are morning and night moods different because last night's mood is different than this morning's mood or are they different because this morning's mood is different from tonight's mood?

To explore the issue of whether the mood change was related to intervening sleep or intervening wakefulness, two sleep deprivation studies were done. In the first study (Roth, Kramer, and Lutz, 1976), the subjects slept at home at baseline, were kept awake in a group for one night in the laboratory and slept at home on the recovery night. Mood scales were collected before and after usual sleep times. Three mood subscales were affected by sleep deprivation. The Sleepy and Aggressive mood subscale scores were higher following deprivation than at baseline or recovery and the Friendly mood subscale was higher after deprivation than at baseline but not different than from recovery.

The sleep deprivation experience was repeated in the laboratory with twelve college-age men using two periods of deprivation, 40 hours (one night) and 64 hours (two nights) (Vaccarino et al., 1981). The subjects completed Clyde Mood Scales at the usual bedtime and wake-up time. With increasing sleep deprivation, subjects showed increased scores on the Sleepy and Anxious subscales and decreasing scores on the Clear Thinking subscales. Recovery occurred after one night's sleep. Changes in the Friendly subscales were unsystematic and unrelated to the deprivation experience. No changes were found in the Aggressive and Unhappy subscales.

Mood is sensitive to even one night of sleep deprivation. This supports the position that the mood changes described are related to the intervening sleep process. The aspects of mood that appear to be sensitive to sleep loss are Sleepy, Clear Thinking and Anxious. Changes in Friendly and Aggressive are perhaps more related to the social experience of the deprivation in the two experiments as the subjects were either in a group situation or alone in the sleep laboratory.

The decrease in Friendly in all the normal sleep-through studies may well be related to the social isolation of the sleep period (Kramer and Roth, 1973b; Roehrs et al., 1973; Roth, Kramer and Lutz, 1976). The decrease in the Unhappy mood subscale in normative sleep-through studies remains to be explained (Lysaght et al., 1979; Roehrs et al., 1973; Roth, Kramer and Roehrs, 1976).

Mood Change Across the Day

The mood change from night to morning, based on the deprivation experiments, did appear to be related to the intervening sleep. This is not to say that mood does not change from morning to night. To explore the issue, mood change across the day was studied and clear changes in mood were found (Lysaght et al., 1978). The Cheerful, Energetic and General Activation mood scales were maximal at noon and minimal at bedtime, whereas Inert-Fatigue and Deactivation mood sleep scales were maximal at bedtime and minimal at noon. The time course of the daytime mood change is not the same as that of the diurnal temperature curve. The activation-deactivation scales seem to be phase advanced about four hours from that of the temperature curve.

These changes in mood, with low activity maximal at bedtime and high activity at noon support the conclusion that the mood changes we found in the previous studies are sleep related as a different pattern of mood change seems to occur during the day. However, the daytime mood pattern is related to the night-morning pattern. Importantly, the mood pattern is not a simple epiphenomenon to that of a diurnal temperature curve.

Mood and Daytime Performance

To be sure that mood had some real life significance, the relationship between mood and performance was examined in two studies. In twelve subjects who had ingested various amounts of hypnotic compounds, correlations were obtained between performance on cognitive and psychomotor tasks done 3.5, 10.0, and 22.5 hours after ingestion and the scores on the six mood subscales of the Clyde Mood Scale (Lutz, Kramer, and Roth, 1975). Five of the six mood subscales showed a significant correlation with performance measures (Sleepy -.53, Clear Thinking .38, Friendly .36, Unhappy .33, and Aggressive .18).

In the second study (Rosa, Bonnet, Warm, and Kramer, 1981), twelve normal subjects who were sleep deprived for 40 and 64 hours (one and two nights) and who had shown clear-cut changes in mood also had performance decrements after 40 hours, which continued through the second night. Performance returned to normal fairly rapidly after one night's sleep.

Johnson has also shown that there is a relationship between subjective state and performance (Johnson et al., 1990). Postsleep mood scales correlate better with performance than do objective measures of sleepiness or the number of hours of prior sleep.

We have shown (1) that mood is different before and after sleep, (2) that the level and variability of mood decreases from night to morning, (3) that the change in mood is due to the intervening sleep, (4) that the Friendly, Unhappy and Sleepy aspects of mood show the most systematic change across the night, (5) that almost all aspects of mood (six of seven) show a highly predictable relationship from night to morning, (6) that most subjects (81 percent) have at least one significant mood subscale correlation from night to morning across sleep, (7) that mood correlations from night to morning across days occur most often with the Unhappy mood subscale (42 percent of subjects) and least often with the Sleepy mood subscale (15 percent), and (8) that on the majority of days (63 percent) a decrease occurs in mean mood intensity from night to morning.

Mental Content Before, After and During Sleep

An Introduction

If the dream is related to the affective condition of the individual, does it show a series of changes similar to what we found in our studies of mood? An examination of the dream content of various groups and individuals will be explored to test the assumption that dreams vary analogously to mood.

Dream Differences Between Groups

Demographic variables such as sex, age, race, marital status and social class are powerful psychological factors that have many important covariates both cognitive and affective. It is not unreasonable to expect that the dream might well reflect these differences in its content and feeling.

We examined dream reports of a representative sample of 300 adults in the city of Cincinnati (Kramer, Winget, and Whitman, 1971). The reports were scored using both the Hall–Van de Castle and Gottschalk–Gleser content scoring systems. We found that the five major demographic variables did have associated dream content. The greatest number of significant content differences was associated with the sex of the dreamer (ten). The age of the dreamer (four), and the race, marital status, and social class of the dreamer (three each) were less discriminating.

Let me illustrate a few of these associations. Women reported more dreams and had more characters and emotions in their dreams. Men had more aggression and achievement striving with success in their dreams. People between 21 and 34 had more guilt in their dreams, and people over 65 had more death anxiety in their dreams. Those of the lower social class had more characters in their dreams than those of the upper class. Whites had more covert hostility than blacks. The divorced and widowed had more death concerns than either single or married people.

It seems, then, that demographic variables are associated with dream content differences, both cognitive and affective. Among demographic variables, the sex of the dreamer seems to be the most important organizer of dream content. It is surprising to see that such an important factor in our society as race does not seem to be any more important in organizing dream content than are age, social class, or marital status. Given the important role of sex in determining dream content, and that emotion is a distinguishing characteristic between men and women in their dreams, the potential importance of a mood-dream content relationship is underlined. However mood change across the night does not appear to be different in men and women (Lysaght et al., 1979).

We have also examined the laboratory collected dreams of young white men and women and observed a number of significant dream content differences (Kramer, Kinney, and Scharf, 1983a). For example, men have more male characters and fullness references in their dreams and women have more thinking and intensity references in their dreams. These observations support the finding that sex is a powerful organizer of dream content.

Dream content is a regular process since one finds differences where there are psychological differences. As these demographic groups are known to have significant cognitive and affective differences, differences in dream content is what one would expect.

We have noted in both laboratory and non-laboratory studies that the dreams of various patient groups are different from each other (Kramer, Baldrige, Whitman, Ornstein, and Smith, 1969; Kramer and Roth, 1973a). In both the non-laboratory and laboratory studies, we were able to show that the dreams of Schizophrenics are different from the dreams of the Depressed. One significant difference was that the Depressed dreamed more about family members and the Schizophrenics about strangers. Another difference was that Schizophrenics have more apprehension in their dreams.

In a laboratory study of Vietnam veterans with disturbed dreaming, all of whom had chronic delayed post-traumatic stress disorders, dream content was clearly different from a group of Vietnam combat veterans who did not have CDPTSD. Fifty percent of the dreams of the patient group were manifestly about their military experience, while none of the control group had dreams with military experience (Kramer, Schoen, and Kinney, 1984b).

It is clear that at a group level, utilizing both laboratory and non-laboratory collected dreams, the dream reflects psychological differences, cognitive and affective, in both normal and disturbed populations. This lends support to the dream report being an organized, non-random event that has the specificity and variability to be potentially relatable to sleep related mood changes. The dreams associated with demographic and illness variables clearly reflect the subjective state of the person. It may be that the mood state of the individual is related to these dream content differences.

Dream Differences Between and Within Individuals

From the viewpoint of clinicians, the important questions about dreaming relate to their manifestations at the individual level. The crucial issue is whether the dream is organized at the individual level; that is, can discriminations be made between individuals and between nights of the same individual, as we found in our studies of mood before and after sleep (See above).

We examined the dreams of normal and schizophrenic individuals to see if the dreams of individuals within each group could be distinguished (Kramer, Hlasny, Jacobs and Roth, 1976). Judges were given fifteen dreams from each of five normal subjects. They were able to sort the dreams correctly at a highly significant level. They were able to do a similar exercise with the dreams of Schizophrenics with slightly less accuracy but still at levels well beyond chance. This discrimination was made based on the dream itself, independent of any knowledge of the dreamer. The dreams of individuals are distinguishable, one from the other, whether the person is normal or psychiatrically ill.

The dreams of an individual are increasingly predictive from night to night (Kramer and Roth, 1979). We collected dreams from subjects from the end of each REM period for twenty consecutive nights. Dream content measurement showed a modest (.46) but significant night to night predictability over two weeks. The mean level of predictability in the second week was .50 and in the first .22, suggesting an adaptation effect over this time period. Night 19 was found to be highly predictive of night 20 ($r = .80$) and greater than nights 1–2 ($r = .05$) and 10–11 ($r = .30$), both of which were nonpredictive.

The next level of orderliness was to see if the dreams of one night could be discriminated from the dreams of another night within the same individual (Kramer, et al., 1976). Judges were given five nights of three dreams each from ten normal subjects and five nights of three dreams each from five schizophrenic subjects. The judges were able to sort the dreams by night within a subject or patient well beyond chance levels. The dreams of a given individual are different night to night.

The clinical technique of searching for a day residue and exploring its relationship to the subsequent night's dreams has considerable empirical foundation. We have shown that the emotionally more intense experience of the day is represented in the dreams of the night (Piccione et al., 1977), and now we have shown that the dreams of a night are separate from those of another night, implying a thematic connection within a night's dreaming. Dreams are different between individuals, and they are different by nights within an individual.

Dream Differences Across the Night

The next question related to whether there was an organization to the dreams across the night from REM period to REM period. We pursued the matter by examining REM periods across the night (Kramer, McQuarrie, and Bonnet, 1981). We examined the dreams from twenty-two subjects who slept in the laboratory for twenty consecutive nights and had their dreams collected from the first four REM periods of the night. We found that the word count of REM 1 was less than 2, and 3 was less than 4, but that 2 and 3 were not distinguishable. Eight of twenty-two content categories showed a change across the night with word length held constant. We found content changes across almost all periods, four from 1 to 2 and five from 2 to 3, but none from 3 to 4.

Looking at mean scores of the significant variables across the night from REM period to REM period, the primary pattern of change is linear. However, in the three significant character variables, total characters, single characters, and female characters, there was a nonsignificant decrease in mean content level in REM period 4, which was suggestive of the inverted U-shaped function, namely tension accumulation, discharge, and regression, postulated for dream problem solving across the night (see Subsection on "The Sequential Dream Pattern" later in this chapter).

There is clear support for a systematic dream content change across the night. The possibility that dream content may be processed across the night is suggested by the many content differences found in REM periods across the night.

Dreaming and Waking Thought

We wanted to see if dreaming and waking thought were related. Was the processing of dream content across the night, that our study of REM period content differences implied (Kramer, McQuarrie and Bonnet, 1981), potentially linked to waking mental content? Were the preoccupations (current concerns) of the individual that are reflected in his or her dreams linked to waking thought?

We decided that Thematic Apperception Test (TAT) stories, a waking fantasy production, might be appropriate for comparison to dreams to examine the nature of a waking dreaming connection (Kramer Roth and Palmer, 1976). We collected the dreams from each of the first four

REM periods of twenty-four subjects who slept three non-consecutive nights in the laboratory. These subjects each gave responses to ten TAT cards. The TAT stories and dreams were scored utilizing a 6 point scale on ten of the twenty need-press variables described by Murray. The rank order intensity score correlation of the group for the ten need-press variables for dreams and TAT stories was .72 and was significant at the 5 percent level. The highest three items on the TAT were dominance, aggression, and affiliation; and for the dreams affiliation, dominance, and achievement. The lowest three items on the TAT were counteraction, deference, and order, and for the dreams, counteraction, deference, and sex. The intensity of dreams and TAT stories are similar. Fantasy products from the waking and sleep states are highly related.

In another investigation we examined the relationship of mental content obtained immediately before and after going to sleep to the intervening dream (Kramer, Roth, Arand, and Bonnet, 1981). We saw this more as a test of the state relationship between dreaming and waking thought as contrasted to the TAT story, which we saw as more of a trait relationship. Forty subjects slept for three nonconsecutive nights in the sleep laboratory and had their dreams collected from the first four REM periods. Prior to going to sleep and on awakening in the morning they were asked to speak into a tape recorder on any subject of their choice for five minutes. The verbal samples and the dream reports were scored for characters (eight scales), descriptive elements (three scales), activities (five scales), environmental press (one scale), and emotions (one scale) of the Hall-Van de Castle Dream Content Scoring System. Correlations were done comparing the subjects' scores on each of the eighteen scales. Nine of the scales were significant with a significant mean correlation of .38. The distribution of the eighteen correlations was significantly different from zero. Dream content and the waking psychological parameters are indeed related, thereby demonstrating a state relationship between dreaming and waking thought.

There had not been a study of coherence within and connectedness between dreaming and waking thought; that is, are dreams and waking thought similarly related within each domain as well as between domains? We attempted to explore this issue as it would be a direct examination of content relatedness utilizing the wake-sleep-wake paradigm (Kramer et al., 1982).

We studied the dreams of twenty subjects who slept in the sleep laboratory for three nonconsecutive nights and had their dreams collected from the end of each of the first four REM periods. Prior to going to sleep and after awakening in the morning, they gave 5-minute verbal samples. The content of the verbal samples and dreams were examined for thematic similarities and percentage similarities by individuals and nights were determined. By individuals, the verbal samples showed a connection among themselves in 95 percent of the cases whereas the dreams showed connectedness in 75 percent of individuals. These proportions of similarity are significantly different at the 5 percent level. Night verbal samples are thematically connected to the dreams that follow in 85 percent of individuals, and dreams are connected to morning verbal samples in 70 percent of individuals. This difference is not statistically significant. The inferences one may draw from this study are that waking thought is more coherently organized than dreaming thought, that dreams may be more reactive than they are proactive, and that there is a thematic connection across the wake-sleep-wake continuum.

The Similarity of Change in Dream Content and Mood

Dreams vary in a manner analogous to if not identical with that of mood. Dreams reflect psychological differences in demographically and psychopathologically different populations in which affective differences may well exist. Dreams of individuals are different from one another and the dreams of an individual are different night to night. The mood of individuals are different from each other, and mood also varies from night to night within an individual.

Dream content changes in a linear fashion across the night. Analogously, mood is different at night than in the morning, changing across the night.

Dream content and waking (fantasy) thought are related and show both trait and state relationships. Mood changes across the day are different from but potentially related to the change in mood across the night.

Mental content is related from presleep wakefulness to dreams to postsleep wakefulness so that the processing of content across the night could be occurring. Interestingly, three dream content character scales show the rise and fall in frequency, that is, the tension accumulation, discharge and regression pattern, one would expect if a problem solving function were operating in REM sleep.

The Dream's Responsiveness to the Emotional State of the Dreamer

The dream report, as reflected in its discriminating qualities, is an organized event and, importantly, is responsive to a number of influences. We now report on a number of studies that have explored the influence of various emotionally significant experiences on dream content. These studies underline the reactive nature of the dream as a dependent variable. The dream is responsive to the emotional condition (mood) of the dreamer.

Emotionally Significant Waking Experiences Influence Dream Content

We have explored the influence of daytime activities on the dreams of the night (Piccione et al., 1977). Seven subjects slept for ten nights each in the laboratory and had their dreams collected from each REM period. On the day prior to sleeping in the laboratory, the subjects filled out a daily activity report (DAR) and an emotional tone report (ETR) each hour. Judges were unable to match the dreams of the subjects to either the DAR or the ETR reports. Judges then were given the matched DAR and dreams and asked to pick the activities of the day most represented in the dreams. A comparison of the ETR with those DAR events chosen showed that the higher, more intense, scores were associated with the events chosen as being incorporated in the dreams. Daily activities that judges rated as most prevalent in the night's dream were the activities the subject had given the highest emotional rating. Dream content is most concerned with and influenced by the activities of the day that are accompanied by the more intense emotional tones.

Pursuing a similar issue as to what events of the day appeared in the night's dreams, we attempted to select an event of emotional significance to the subject, arguing that such an event ought to be represented in the dreams of the subject. We reasoned that the beginning and ending of an experience are events of high emotional charge (Kramer, Roth, and Cisco, 1977). We predicted that coming into and leaving the sleep laboratory across an experimental period of twenty days was such an event. We thought that we should be able to tell the first nights from the last nights better than the middle nights from each other. The judges were able to discriminate the dreams of nights 1 and 20 and 3 and 18 at statistically significant levels ($p < .02$ and $p < .05$), but not nights 5–16, 7–14, 9–12 or 10–11.

We wondered if the laboratory experience itself might have an influence on the content of subjects' dreams. Whitman had reported a study of the dreams of experimental subjects which showed women have rape fantasies and men have exploitation fantasies while sleeping in the sleep laboratory (Whitman et al., 1962). The laboratory itself then may be a powerful force affecting dreams.

We reasoned that if the laboratory is such a strong emotional stimulus, it ought to appear in the dreams of the subjects. We examined 754 dreams collected from fourteen subjects who slept for twenty consecutive nights in the sleep laboratory ((Piccione, Thomas, Roth, and Kramer, 1976). Dreams were scored for references to the laboratory and then analyzed to see whether any change (adaptation or sensitization) occurred across the twenty nights.

There was no decrease across the twenty nights in the percent of dreams that reflected laboratory incorporation either when comparing the first night (39 percent) to all other nights (34 percent) or when comparing nights 1–5 (33 percent) to subsequent five night blocks (28 percent, 33 percent, and 33 percent). This consistently high level of incorporation suggests that the laboratory remains a potent stimulus across the twenty nights.

The percentage of incorporation varied greatly from night to night, from a low 2 percent on night 5 to a high of 44 percent on night 10. The variability of the first ten nights (S.D. = 24.6 percent) was compared to the variability of the second ten nights (S.D. = 13.5 percent). Although variability was lower on the second ten nights, the two variability measures were not statistically different. The interpersonal situation remains a potent force in a patient's life. Twenty days in the laboratory reflected only the suggestion of adaptation.

Emotionally Significant Interpersonal Situations are Reflected in Dreams

We have examined the interpersonal relationships in the sleep laboratory to explore their effect on dreaming, speculating that this interpersonal situation with its emotional charge might be a significant influence on dream content. In a study of dream recall, subjects reported REM awakening content to a technician at night and then to a psychiatrist in the morning (Whitman, Kramer, and Baldridge, 1963a).

We noted that some dreams were reported at night to the technician that were not reported in the morning to the psychiatrist and some were reported in the morning that had not been reported at night.

Selective reporting related to the interpersonal situation was apparent in the case of a male patient who reported dreams that reflected his masculine adequacy to the psychiatrist in the morning; for example, helping a woman or dating women other than his wife. However, anxious dreams reflecting his homosexual fears, say, of closeness to a man or being examined and penetrated by a man, were reported to the technician at night but not to the psychiatrist in the morning. For a female subject, dreams criticizing the technician were presented to the psychiatrist in the morning, whereas dreams reflecting her sexual concerns and doubts about the psychiatrist's adequacy were reported in the laboratory to the technician but not to the psychiatrist.

The dream content in both cases related to aspects of the patients' psychology but also to the interpersonal relationship between the dreamer and dream listener. Unacceptable aspects of the dreamer were withheld from the psychiatrist. Whether the content was suppressed or repressed cannot be assessed. However, it seems apparent that the content with its explicit or implicit meaning appeared to determine which dreams were and were not reported.

Clearly the interpersonal context in which the dream was experienced and to whom it was to be reported influenced what dream was selected for reporting. Again, the affective state of the dreamer influenced the content and reporting of the dream.

We followed our lead that studying the dreams of patients might reveal the effect of the interpersonal context on dreaming by examining the relationship of dreaming in patient-therapist dyads (Whitman, Kramer, and Baldridge, 1963b). We had ten therapist and patient pairs sleep in the laboratory at about the same time. To enhance the meaning of the patient to the therapist, we chose the night before the therapist was to discuss his patient at a supervisory case conference. The patients did dream about the therapists 41 percent of the time, but the therapists dreamed about the patients only 14 percent of the time. The therapists however, dreamed about the supervisory conference in 42 percent of their dreams and about the experimental situation in 54 percent

What started out to be a study of patient-therapist dyads became a study of the direction of emotional preoccupation. The patient is concerned about the therapist, the therapist is concerned about supervision and the experimental situation. A third of the dreams reported by the supervisors concerned the research group. Each of the groups studied dreamed of the next "higher" observing group. The *New Yorker* magazine, commenting on the study, saw the participants as a bunch of "sleepy social climbers". One's emotional preoccupations do indeed influence and focus one's dreams.

In the third experiment of this series examining the effect on dreams of various interpersonal situations, we looked at the effect of varying the sex of the experimenter on the content of the subject's dreams (Fox et al., 1968). We were able to show that more groups appeared in dreams when the experimenter-subject pair was of different sexes compared to when the pair was of the same sex.

In addition, thematically different issues were explored depending on the nature of the subject-experimenter relationship. A female subject, a nurse, used the imagery of intravenous (IV) infusions to capture the difference in the two relationships. With a male experimenter, the IV in three dreams was running fine; whereas with a female experimenter, the tubing was disconnected in one dream and the IV had run dry in another.

We have explored the influence of the emotional preoccupation (principal current concern) of the dreamer as a significant, if not primary, influence on the content of the subject's subsequent dreams. We have shown that the more intense emotional experiences of the day are more apt to appear in dreams, that experiences likely to be emotionally laden are likely to be represented in dreams, and that the emotional nature of the interpersonal situation is a determinant of several variables, such as which dream is chosen for reporting, which of a number of situations is chosen for focus in dreams, and how an ongoing relationship in the laboratory (the relationship to the experimenter) is elaborated. In summary, the principal waking current emotional concern is structuring and influencing of dream content.

Drug Treatment and Affective State

Given that the emotional (affective) component seemed so determining of dream content and that dream content seemed so responsive to personal manipulations such as the beginning and ending of an experience and who the person is who hears and collects the dream, we chose to use a nonpersonal manipulation of affective state to see if dream content could be altered. We examined the laboratory collected dreams of ten depressed patients before and after successful treatment with an antidepressant (Kramer et al., 1968). We observed that after short-term treatment (one week), hostility and anxiety in their dreams were increased, and by the end of four weeks when the patients had recovered from their depression, hostility, anxiety, and intimacy had decreased and heterosexuality and motility had increased in their dreams. Most important, drugs that effect the emotional-affective dimension of the patient's life altered (influenced) dream content.

The Concomitant Manipulation of the Dream

We have been successful in altering the ongoing dream itself by introducing emotionally significant material during the dream-REM process (Kinney, Kramer, and Bonnet, 1981; Kramer, Kinney, and Scharf, 1983b). This is the most direct (experimental) demonstration of the dream's response to affective influence.

In two experiments, we exposed subjects once during a REM period, in their own voice, to a name of high meaning (H = family member or friend), and on another occasion to a name of lower meaning (L = an unfamiliar name). High-meaning names were incorporated significantly more often ($\bar{x}$ H = 49 percent) than low-meaning names ($\bar{x}$ L = 8 percent), although recall of hearing the names is the same ($\bar{x}$ H = 19 percent, $\bar{x}$ L = 17 percent). Further, general dream recall was the same in both conditions.

Meaningful names did appear more often in dreams than low-meaning names ($p < .05$). The dream can indeed be directly influenced by a significant, meaningful stimulus.

It is clear that the dream is responsive to a number of affective influences. The dream responds to the emotional experiences of the prior days, the effect of new and continuing experiences (beginning and ending, the laboratory itself), important interpersonal situations (therapy, supervision and to whom dreams are reported at night in the laboratory), mood altering drugs and hearing significant names during dreaming.

The Relationship Between Mood and Dreams

Having established that sleep and mood (subjective state) are related and having evidence that dreams are related to the individual's waking subjective state, and that dreams are reactive to the emotional state of the dreamer an exploration of the relationship between mood change across the night and dream content seemed appropriate. If dreams contain or alter affective state, dream content and mood change should be related.

The Mood Change-Dream Content Relationship: A Pilot Study

In a pilot study, two men were studied who slept for twenty consecutive nights in the sleep laboratory (Kramer and Roth, 1973b). The Clyde Mood Scale was administered before sleep and upon arising in the morning. Their dreams were collected from the end of the first four REM periods of each night. The dreams were content scored utilizing thirty-one scales of the Hall–Van de Castle dream content scoring system: twelve character scales, nine activity scales and twenty descriptive element scales (Hall and Van de Castle, 1966). Each of the six mood subscales of the Clyde Mood Scale (Unhappy, Friendly, Aggressive, Sleepy, Clear Thinking, and Dizzy or Anxious) were correlated with each content scale for each subject. Overall, 372 correlations were done (6 mood subscales × 31 content subscales × 2 subjects). At the 5 percent level, three times the number of significant correlations were obtained than would have been expected by chance (54 obtained versus 18.6 expected by chance, $p < .001$). The largest number of correlations was obtained with the Unhappy mood subscale (23 versus 3.1, ($p < .001$) and the character subscales (27 versus 7.2, ($p < .001$). The greatest numbers of correlations were between the Unhappy mood subscale and the character scales (14 versus 1.2 $p < 001$). The nature of this relation was such that the more characters of any type that appeared in the dreams the greater the decrease in the Unhappy subscale from night to morning.

This pilot study was of great interest as it was the Unhappy mood subscale that related best to dream content, and this was one of the three subscales that consistently showed a significant change from night to morning in the sleep through studies. The other scales that showed consistent change were the Friendly and Sleepy subscales. These findings led to a more extensive study of dream-mood relationships.

A Confirmation of the Mood Change-Dream Content Relationship

The mood change–dream content relationship was studied in twelve additional male subjects who slept for twenty consecutive nights in the sleep laboratory, filled out Clyde Mood Scales before and after sleep and had their dreams collected from each of the first four REM periods of the night (Kramer and Roth, 1980). The dreams were scored for eight character subscales, nine activity subscales, and fifteen descriptive element scales of the Hall-Van de Castle Dream Content Scoring System. The scores on each mood subscale were correlated with each content scale in each subject ($32 \times 6 \times 12 = 2,304$ correlations). The number of significant correlations obtained was compared to the number expected at the 5 percent level using a chi square statistic.

Mood change and dream content were significantly related (219 significant correlations versus 115 expected by chance, $p < .001$). A significant relationship to dream content was found for five of the six mood subscales: Unhappy (54 significant correlations), Sleepy (35), Aggressive (35) and Dizzy (Anxious) (34, $p < .001$) and Clear Thinking (31, $p < .01$). However, the distribution of mood–dream content correlations across the mood subscales was not random ($p < .001$) and one, the Unhappy mood subscale, had significantly more correlations than the others ($p <$

.01). Again, as in the mood-dream pilot study, the Unhappy mood subscale seems to have a particular connection to dream content.

A significant relationship to mood change across the night was found for the character subscales (60 versus 29) the descriptive elements subscales (100–54) and the activity subscales (59–32) (chi square, $p < .001$ for all three). The distribution of significant mood subscale correlations across the three content scale categories is what would be expected by chance. However, only within the character scale are the correlations unevenly distributed ($p < .01$). Again, only the Unhappy mood subscale had a different and greater than chance ($p < .01$) number of correlations with the Character scales. As was found in the pilot study, it is the Character-Unhappy mood subscale link that shows the greatest (most systematic) relationship.

At this point the evidence indicates (1) that mood before and after sleep is different; (2) that the level and variability of mood decreases from night to morning; (3) that the change in mood is due to the intervening sleep; (4) that it is the Friendly, Unhappy, and Sleepy aspects of mood that show the most systematic change from night to morning; (5) that almost all aspects of mood (six of seven) show a highly predictable relationship from night to morning; (6) that most subjects (81 percent) have at least one significant mood subscale correlation from night to morning; (7) that mood correlations from night to morning across days occur most often with the Unhappy mood subscale (42 percent of subjects); (8) that on the majority of days (63 percent) a decrease in mean mood intensity occurs across the night; (9) that the change in various aspects of mood across the night is related to the dream content of the night; and (10) that the change in the Unhappy mood subscale across the night is related to the characters that appear in the dreams of the night.

A Caveat

A caveat is in order. A series of explorations were undertaken to examine the relationship between dream content and pre- and postsleep mood in two comparable groups (Rosa, Kramer, Bonnet, and Thomas, 1981). In one study, mood dream content correlations were established in a group of subjects (six men and six women), and it was shown that a similar set of correlations did not appear in a comparable group (six men–five women). These subjects all slept for twenty nights in the sleep laboratory taking Clyde Moods before and after sleep and had their dreams collected from the first four REM periods of the night. Another aspect of these studies was to select sixteen subjects (8 men and 8 women) from the previous group of twenty-three and select high and low mood score nights and test for dream content differences. Again, no differences were found. These approaches failed to extend our demonstration of dream content–mood relationships. It is possible that the nature of the dream content-mood correlation is subject dependent and to expect replication across groups for exactly the same correlations may not be reasonable. (See Tables 5.7 and 5.9, which show that night-morning mood correlations are subject specific.) And, the relationships between dream content and mood within a subject on a single night may not show an adequate degree of difference.

Dream Content Change in Depressive Illness

By examining dream content in patients who have a major mood change, namely depressed patients, further light may be shed on the mood change–dream content relationship. It has been shown that dream content is different in the depressed and, further, that dream content changes with changes in the depressed state.

The masochistic dream type described by Beck, who felt it was specific to depressed patients, did indeed occur in the dreams of depressed patients whose dreams were collected in the laboratory (Kramer, Trinder, Whitman and Baldridge, 1969). In two studies (Kramer, Baldridge, Whitman, Ornstein, and Smith, 1969; Kramer, Trinder, and Roth, 1972), a nonlaboratory one and laboratory one, the typical dream character of the depressed was a family member, and this was different than for the Schizophrenic, whose typical dream character was a stranger. Apparently the character type who appears in the dream is related to significant psychological aspects of the dreamer. This underscores the importance to dreaming of the character aspect of the dream experience. This aspect of the dream related most specifically to the most particular mood change across the night; namely, the decrease in the Unhappy mood subscale. Unhappiness is the aspect of mood that on the surface would be most related to depression.

The content of the dream can be shown to change with changes in the depressed state. In a sleep laboratory study of depressed patients who were treated with an antidepressant, it was shown that their dream content changed when their depression improved (Kramer et al., 1968). Hostility and anxiety decrease in the dreams of the depressed whereas intimacy and heterosexuality increase when the depression lifts. In another study (Kramer, Brunner, and Trinder, 1971), a single case report, dream content was different in the manic and depressed phases of a Manic Depressive illness. Interestingly, the depressed phase had an increased incidence of happy emotions and recurrent dreams occurred at the transition point between the manic and depressed phases of the illness.

These studies lend support to the notion that a change in affective state (mood) is related to changes in dream content. This theme of change is central to the thesis that mood change from night to morning is related to changes in the content of the intervening dreams.

The Relationship Between Mood and the Physiology of Sleep

It is necessary to examine the relationship of the physiology of sleep, as represented in sleep stages and total sleep time, to mood change across the night in order to explore any overlap with changes in mood that have been attributed to dreaming. Is it possible that similar changes in similar mood subscales would occur in relationship to the physiology of sleep? To search for this possibility, mood changes across the night were examined in relation to some of the physiological parameters of sleep.

Sleep Deprivation and Mood Change

Total sleep deprivation studies were clearly linked to alterations in mood (Roth, Kramer, and Lutz, 1976; Vaccarino et al., 1981). There was an increase in Sleepy and Dizzy (anxious) mood subscale scores and a decrease in Clear Thinking scores with one night's sleep deprivation, all of which intensifies with the second night of sleep loss.

Sleep loss alters how one feels. Is there a relationship between all or parts (stages) of sleep and mood? Webb has suggested that REM deprivation results in a hyper-responsive state and stage 4 deprivation results in a hypo-responsive state. Both are associated with reduced ego controls (Webb, 1969). If there is a relationship between the physiology of sleep and mood, is it similar to or different from what was found for dream content and mood?

Mood Change and Sleep Physiology

Six male subjects slept in the sleep laboratory for fifteen consecutive nights, filled out Clyde Mood Scales before and after sleep and had their sleep monitored electrophysiologically (Kramer and Roth, 1973b). The difference in mood scores (night minus morning) on each of the Clyde Mood subscales was correlated with five physiological measures of aspects of sleep: total sleep time, total REM time, stage 3–4 time, stage 2 time, and number of awakenings (6 x 6 x 5 = 180 correlations).

Three times the number of correlations between mood and sleep physiology were found than would have been expected by chance (26 versus 9, $p < .001$). The largest number of significant correlations found were with the Sleepy mood subscale (7 versus 1.5, $p < .001$) and total sleep time (11 versus 1.8, $p < .001$). The largest number of significant correlations was between Sleepy and total sleep time (4.0 versus 0.3, $p < .01$). Sleepy, in previous studies, has not been found to be related to the content of dreaming (Kramer and Roth, 1980). Mood change across the night was related to aspects of the physiology of sleep.

The mood-sleep physiology relationship was examined in a second study in which eleven college-age men slept for fifteen consecutive nights in the laboratory, filled out Clyde Mood Scales before and after sleep, and had their sleep recorded electrophysiologicaly (Kramer, Roehrs, and Roth, 1976). The sleep records were scored for total sleep time, stage 1 time, stage 2 time, stage 3–4 time, stage REM time, sleep latency and REM latency.

In this replication sleep study, the seven sleep variables were used, in a multiple regression analysis, to predict the six mood subscales. Significant correlations were found for four of the six scales; in two, Sleepy and Friendly, $r = .42$ ($p < .01$) and in two, Aggressive and Clear Thinking, $r = .26$ ($p < .05$). Unhappy and Dizzy (Anxious) ($r = .22$ and $.20$, respectively) have nonsignificant correlations. When tested to see if any of the correlations were different from each other the two highest, Sleepy and Friendly, were different from the two lowest, Unhappy and Dizzy (Anxious).

Analyses were performed to see which of the seven variables were predictive of which aspects of mood. The partial correlations showed stage 2 time, stage 3–4 time, and sleep latency were significantly predictive of the change in the Sleepy and Friendly mood subscale scores.

It is worthwhile to note that the mood subscale most particularly related to dream content, Unhappy, is not predicted by the sleep physiology parameters. And further, the non-REM aspects of sleep physiology are predictive of mood changes across the night and that the subscales most involved with the physiology of sleep are Sleepy and Friendly.

Mood Change and REM Physiology

Hartmann has found that REM time was increased in depressed patients, implying that a relationship should exist between the Unhappy mood subscale and REM time (Hartmann et al., 1969). Unhappy mood, measured by the Clyde Mood Scale, in normals is related to REM dream content, not to any physiological aspect of REM, either time or latency. Eleven men slept for fifteen consecutive nights in the laboratory and had Clyde Moods taken before and after sleep, filled out an MMPI, and had their sleep electrophysiologically monitored. No relationship was found in these eleven subjects either between their presleep Unhappy Mood subscale score or their score on the Depression scale of the MMPI and the amount of REM time they had (Kramer, Roehrs, and Roth, 1972). In normal subjects, Unhappy mood is related to the content of REM dreams not to the amount of REM time.

Clinical States Alter Sleep Physiology and Dream Content

Significant clinical states show systematic sleep physiology changes as well as dream content changes. Clinically, it has been found that anxious patients have trouble getting to sleep whereas depressed patients have trouble staying asleep. In a sleep laboratory study, it was found that anxious subjects take longer to fall asleep, have more arousals and less total sleep time (Rosa et al., 1983). Depressed patients, studied in the laboratory, show changes in their sleep physiology, particularly earlier REM onset, increased REM density, and frequent arousals (Rimon et al., 1986). Dream content is different in depressed and schizophrenic patients (Kramer, et al., 1969; Kramer and Roth, 1973a) and in patients with CDPTSD (Kramer et al., 1984b).

Dream Content and Sleep Physiology are Related to Different Aspects of Mood

Dream content and sleep physiology are related to the mood change that occurs across the night. A comparison of the distribution of significant correlations across mood subscales for dream content categories and sleep physiological parameters, based on two pilot studies in normal subjects, suggests a differential relationship (Kramer and Roth, 1973b). The fifty-four significant dream content mood correlations obtained are found primarily in the Unhappy (43 percent), Aggressive (16 percent), and Friendly (15 percent) subscales. The twenty-six significant sleep physiological parameter mood subscale correlations are related to changes in the Sleepy (27 percent), Dizzy (Anxious) (25 percent), and Clear Thinking (19 percent) mood subscales.

Conclusion

The data to this point suggest that sleep has a relationship to mood change across the night. The data further suggest that sleep physiology and sleep psychology may be differentially related to various sub-aspects of mood. From a physiological point of view, how sleepy one feels relates to the amount of sleep, particularly non-REM sleep, one has obtained. From a psychological point of view, how happy one feels in the morning is related to who one dreams about at night. People are important to us, even in our dreams.

The mood regulatory function of sleep is suggested by the fact that the mood at night is different from the mood in the morning; specifically, both the mean level and variability of mood decrease from night to morning. There is a "funneling action" across sleep whereby mood decreases in intensity and variability. The activities during sleep, both physiological and psychological, are "corrective"; as if a thermostat is operating to move the mood level toward a central and lower point. In this sense the dream, which seems particularly involved with one aspect of mood, that is, Unhappy, is a selective affective (mood) regulator which functions as an "emotional thermostat." Similarly, the physiological aspect of sleep, especially non-REM sleep, is related to the Sleepy aspects of mood. Apparently, non-REM sleep also acts as a selective mood regulator.

Problem Solving: The Dream Mechanism for Mood Change

Introduction

If dreaming is to function to protect sleep by absorbing the emotional surge that appears to occur during REM sleep, then dreaming ought to be related to the emotional state of the dreamer. That is indeed the case: changes in emotional state across the night are related to the content of the dream (see the earlier subsections on the mood change–dream content relationship).

There are multiple dream periods across the night that are part of the periodicity of REM sleep. These multiple dreams of the night are related to the emotional preoccupations or current concerns of the dreamer. As pre- and postsleep mood is related to the intervening dreams and sleep physiology of the night, so is the dream content of the multiple REM periods of the night related to what is on the dreamer's mind before and after sleeping (Kramer, Roth and Palmer, 1976; Kramer, Roth, Arand and Bonnet, 1981; Kramer, Moshiri and Scharf, 1982).

As mental content is thematically related across the wake-dream-wake sequence, the linear change in dream content across the night (REM periods) is such that the processing of mental content (and its emotional concomitant) could be occurring. For example, three dream content character scales show the rise and fall across the REM periods of the night that one might expect if dreaming was engaged in a problem solving activity. (See the Section on "Mental Content Before, After, and During Sleep").

Patterns of Problem Solving

Two principal patterns of thematic dream development across the night are discernible (Kramer et al., 1964): one of a progressive-sequential type in which problems are stated, worked on, and resolved; and the other a repetitive-traumatic type in which the problem is simply restated and no progress occurs.

The effectiveness of the night's dreaming varies from night to night within the same subject. This may be a result of the differential pattern of dreaming across the night. If one has experienced a progressive-sequential dream pattern there may be a positive alteration in the emotional state of the dreamer. The problem solving that takes place is emotional in nature. If the problem that one goes to sleep with is simply restated and not "solved," then a less successful night's dreaming has occurred. It could be through this mechanism of "problem solving" or failure to "problem solve" that the affective alteration takes place (French and Fromm, 1964). This may also be concomitant with the change in the degree of unhappiness across the night and related to the appearance of appropriate character types in the dream.

It may be useful to illustrate the patterns of dream development from a subject who slept in the experimental dream-sleep laboratory and who showed both patterns of dreaming. Subjects do show both patterns, which suggests there is not universal success in altering the emotional preoccupations of the previous day (See Table 5.10) This may account for some of the variability in how one feels on awakening in the morning.

The Progressive-Sequential Dream Pattern

The progressive-sequential pattern shows an alternating ascendancy of disturbing and reactive motives and a concomitant tension accumulation, discharge and regression pattern. This is the inverted U shaped pattern described as associated with a successful night's dreaming. Each dream report obtained was from a REM period awakening.

Female Subject - Dream Night #6 (Kramer et al., 1964)

(6-1): "This little girl was asleep. She was being real cute, prolonging things for money or to stay in the hospital longer."

(6-2): "I passed Frank's wife in a car. She saw me come . . . she pulled away. I got kind of mad. I decided that it didn't make any difference . . . ."

(6-3): "I was playing tennis. I hit it back real hard. We won the game."

(6-4): "A patient didn't need the doctor after all. She started out thinking she needed a doctor but she didn't. She had a big bandage on her stomach."

(6-5): "Doctor was not able to treat patient because he was not properly licensed. The patient is planning to use surgery against the doctor."

Interpretation

(6-1): The thematic pattern seems to be that the subject wished to depend on or cling to the doctor and hospital even if she had to claim illness, but the "cuteness" revealed a seductive motive as well.

(6-2): The subject expressed, vis-à-vis the wife of a friend, the feared and expected rejection which she tried to minimize.

(6-3): This dream can be seen as a turning point in that the victory in the tennis game appears to discharge effectively the tension generated by the conflict between a wish to be close to the doctor-experimenter for care and love (the disturbing motive) and the feared rebuff or abandonment (reactive motive). She switched to successful competition where she won with a partner. The inference was that whatever she was struggling with has been conquered.

(6-4): The victory with a partner in the previous dream permitted her to deny her need for the doctor which she admitted she once had, and there was evidence that the need continued (the bandage).

(6-5): The recognition of the continuing repressed need for the doctor for care and love (6-4) caused her to intensify her rejection of him by being critical of the doctor's qualifications and expressing her wish to get even or hurt him. It was the familiar double assertion: "Not only do I not need you, but you're no good anyway".

The sequential pattern in this series expressed a dependent-sexual longing toward the experimenter-doctor that led to a feared (expected) rejection by the wife-mother in the second dream. The conflict was mastered in the third dream by an aggressive victory with her own partner. The fourth dream revealed a rejection of the previous need although a recognition is present that the need still existed. In the last dream of the night a more intense rejection in the form of an attack on a doctor served further to deny the need.

The Repetitive-Traumatic Dream Pattern

The repetitive-traumatic pattern involves a restatement of the conflict, often in different settings and at different levels of regression, with different degrees of concreteness or abstraction. Some interrelationship is suggested but this is predominantly a basic restatement within a narrow range without the progression seen in the sequential dream pattern.

Female Subject - Dream Night #3 (Kramer et al., 1964)

(3-1): "Somebody was lost. It was a dog and they were trying to find out where it lived. A little kid or somebody couldn't tell where he lived. It wasn't my dog, though. I wasn't lost. This person who was lost was always fumbling around leading everybody else around because he didn't know what he was doing. Some boy, I think. Somehow we had telephone numbers trying to find the right one. It was supposed to be that little boy that was lost."

(3-2): "They filled up the car. There wasn't enough room, unless I went back with the people we went back with before. I could go back with someone else. The place we were going was an orphanage some place, some house, a place like that."

(3-3): "I was dreaming about visiting, I think it was some EEG laboratory, or something like that where the mothers could leave their children, and they could go shopping. I doubt whether they could, there wouldn't be enough room for all of these people."

Interpretation

(3-1): The boy (associations = experimenter) was seen as lost and misleading others. Not she, but the boy was lost. There was concern in the dream that she was going to be misled by the experimenter because of his inexperience so she tried to call home.

(3-2): In a setting of abandonment (orphanage) she hoped anxiously there would be room for her to return home. She had a ride home, but the car was crowded.

(3-3): She was in the laboratory temporarily and her mother was going to return for her (implied). There wasn't enough room.

In all the dreams of the night, the subject dealt with her fear of being abandoned and her method of recontacting her family: calling on the phone, riding in a car, or being picked up.

These patterns are elaborations or specifications of the general thesis that dreams may subserve a problem solving function (French and Fromm, 1964). It may be through this effort at "emotional problem solving" that the dream succeeds in or fails to contain the emotional surge that leads to the arousal-awakening that is the hallmark of dreaming. Difficulty in emotional problem solving in waking life is certainly more characteristic of the psychopathologically disturbed who have been found to be more responsive to the arousal-awakening after a REM period and who report more "bad dreams."

Sleep is generally a successful process, although there is much concern expressed about a disturbed night's sleep. Given that the process is generally successful, one would expect to see the progressive-sequential pattern occur more often than the repetitive-traumatic one, and that was the case in the two laboratory subjects studied (50 percent versus 32 percent) (Kramer et al., 1964). It was in 63% of nights the average mood intensity score decreased in our sleep-through studies. (See Table 5.11)

Conclusion

If the progressive-sequential pattern is more common, one ought to see content change across the REM periods of the night. This was indeed found when the dreams were analyzed of twenty-two subjects who slept for twenty consecutive nights in the dream-sleep laboratory and had dream content collections from each REM period of the night (Kramer, McQuarrie, and Bonnet, 1981). Word count and dream content showed systematic and statistically significant change across the night. Particularly, three character variables showed an increase and decrease across the night in keeping with the inverted U-shaped curve that the progressive-sequential pattern describes. Also, it is the character variable that is best correlated with change on the Unhappy dimension of mood across the night (Kramer and Roth, 1980).

There is evidence from a number of studies that dreams are a regular and orderly process (Kramer, 1982). Dreams of individuals are distinguishable one from another. Dreams of the same person from one night are separable from the dreams of another night. And, dreams of one night are correlated to the dreams of the next night. All of these relationships lend support to the notion that the dreams of a night are focused on a single topic, whether processed in a progressive-sequential or repetitive-traumatic manner. Dreams are unique to the individual dreamer.

The emotional preoccupations or current concerns of the dreamer, assessed from TAT stories (Kramer, Roth and Palmer, 1976) and presleep and postsleep verbal samples (Kramer et al., 1981), are significantly correlated with the content of a night's dreams. Thematically (Kramer et al., 1982), the dream content is linked both to the current concerns of the subject presleep and to the emotional preoccupation of the dreamer the subsequent morning. The notion of a content processing of emotionally relevant material by the dreamer during dreams is supported by these observations. The current emotional concern of an individual is relatable across the waking-sleeping- (dream)- waking continuum.

Concluding Summary

Theories of dreaming need to address dreams that go on automatically, outside of awareness, and those that enter awareness and potentially have the capacity for a more direct effect on the dreamer's consciousness (Kramer, 1981). One needs both an assimilative and accommodative theory of dreaming. The former being reductive and the latter being potentially transforming.

The *selective mood regulatory theory of dreaming* is an example of an assimilative theory of dream function. The dream functions to contain the affective surge that occurs during REM sleep. If successful, one has no memory for dreaming and sleep proceeds essentially undisturbed. If partially unsuccessful, a dream recall occurs that, if conditions are right, becomes a disturbing dream, a nightmare, with a troubled awakening.

Mood changes systematically from night to morning. Dreams, which reflect the waking emotional preoccupations of the dreamer, change across the night, and are linked to the emotional preoccupations of the dreamer the next morning. A successful night's dreaming, which occurs about 60 percent of the time, is the result of a progressive-sequential, figurative problem solving occurring across the night. A successful night's dreaming has as a consequence an increase in happiness by having the proper number or type of characters appear in the night's dreaming.

The experience of the recalled dream, which depends to a degree on a troubled state in the dreamer, opens the possibility for an extension of this assimilative, reductive view to encompass some degree of transformation, of accommodation as well. States of disturbance increase the likelihood of change. Dreaming that enters awareness can become the object of attention for the dreamer and lead to change in the dreamer, to an enhancement in self-knowledge. The technique of dream translation (Kramer and Roth, 1977) can facilitate the process of change.

References

Aserinsky, E. (1971). "Rapid Eye Movement Density and Pattern in the Sleep of Normal Young Adults." *Psychophysiology* 8: 361–375.

Breger, L. (1967). "The Function of Dreams." *Journal of Abnormal Psychology Monograph* 72: 1–18.

Cartwright, R. D. (1978). *A Primer on Sleep and Dreaming*. Reading, Mass., and London: Addison-Wesley.

———— and Lamberg, L. (1992). *Crisis Dreaming: Using Your Dreams to Solve Your Problems*. New York: Harper Collins.

Castaldo, V., and Holzman, R. (1969). "The Effects of Hearing One's Voice on Dreaming Content: Replication." *Journal of Nervous and Mental Disease* 148: 78–82.

Cattell, R. D. (1973). *Personality and Mood by Questionnaire*. San Francisco: Jossey-Bass.

Clyde, D. (1963). *Manual for the Clyde-Mood Scale*. Miami, Fl.: Biometric Laboratory, University of Miami.

Cohen, D. B. (1974). "Toward a Theory of Dream Recall." *Psychological Bulletin* 81: 138–154.

Dellarosa, D. (1988). "A History of Thinking." In R. J. Sternberg and E. E. Smith (Eds.), *The Psychology of Human Thought*, pp. 1–18. Cambridge: Cambridge University Press.

Downie, N. M., and Heath R. W. (1970). *Basic Statistical Methods*. New York: Harper and Row.

Ekstrand, B., Barrett, T., West, J., and Maier, W. (1977). "The Effect of Sleep on Human Long-Term Memory." In R. Drucker-Colin and J. L. McGaugh (Eds.), *Neurobiology of Sleep and Memory*, pp. 419–438. New York: Academic Press.

Firth, H. (1974). "Sleeping Pills and Dream Content." *British Journal of Psychiatry* 124: 547–553.

Fiss, H. (1979). "Current Dream Research: A Psychobiological Perspective." In B. Wolman (Ed.), *Handbook of Dreams.* pp. 20–75. New York: Van Nostrand Reinhold.

Fox, R., Kramer, M., Baldridge, B., Whitman, R., and Ornstein, P. (1968). "The Experimenter Variable in Dream Research." *Diseases of the Nervous System* 29: 698–701.

Freemon, F. (1972). *Sleep Research: A Critical Review.* Springfield, Ill.: Charles C Thomas.

French, T. M. (1952; 1953; 1958). *The Integration of Behavior*, vols. 1–3. Chicago: University of Chicago Press.

———— and Fromm, E. (1964). *Dream Interpretation.* New York: Basic Books.

Freud, S. (1955). *The Interpretation of Dreams.* New York: Basic Books.

Gilchrist, E. (1981). *In the Land of Dreamy Dreams.* Fayetteville: University of Arkansas Press.

Hall, C., and Van de Castle, R. (1966). *The Content Analysis of Dreams.* New York: Appleton-Century-Crofts.

Hartmann, E., Baekeland, F., Zwilling, G., and How, P. (1969). "Long and Short Sleepers: Preliminary Results." *Psychophysiology* 6: 255.

Hauri, P., and Van de Castle, R. L. (1973). "Psychophysiological Parallels in Dreams." *Psychosomatic Medicine* 35: 297–308.

Hobson, J. A. (1988). *The Dreaming Brain.* New York: Basic Books.

Johnson, B., Kramer, M., Bonnet, M., Roth, T., and Jansen, T. (1980). "The Effect of Ketazolam on Ocular Motility During Sleep. *Current Therapeutic Research* 28: 792–799.

Johnson, L. C., Spinweber, C. L., Gomez, S. A., and Matteson, L. T. (1990). "Daytime Sleepiness, Performance, Mood, Nocturnal Sleep: The Effect of Benzodiazepine and Caffeine on Their Relationship." *Sleep* 13: 121–135.

Jung, C. G. (1974). *Dreams.* Princeton, N.J.: Princeton University Press.

Klinger, E. (1971). *Structure and Functions of Fantasy.* New York: Wiley-Interscience.

Kinney, L., and Kramer, M. (1985). "Sleep and Sleep Responsivity in Disturbed Dreamers." *Sleep Research* 14: 178.

Kinney, L., Kramer, M., and Bonnet, M. (1981). "Dream Incorporation of Meaningful Names." *Sleep Research* 10: 157.

Kramer, M. (1981). "The Function of Psychological Dreaming: A Preliminary Analysis." In W. P. Koella (Ed.), *Sleep 1980, Fifth European Congress* Sleep Research, Amsterdam, 1980, pp. 182–185. Basel: S. Karger.

———. (1982). "The Psychology of the Dream: Art or Science." *Psychiatric Journal of the University of Ottawa* 7: 87–100.

———. (1992). "Mood Change from Night to Morning." *Sleep Research* 21: 153.

———, Baldridge, B., Whitman, R., Ornstein, P., and Smith, P. (1969). "An Exploration of the Manifest Dream in Schizophrenic and Depressed Patients." *Diseases of the Nervous System (Suppl.)* 30: 126–130.

———, Brunner, R., and Trinder, J. (1971). "Discussion of Miller and Buckley. Dream Changes in a Manic-Depressive Cycle." In J. H. Masserman (Ed.), *Science and Psychoanalysis*, pp. 138–151. New York: Grune and Stratton.

———, Hlasny, R., Jacobs, G., and Roth, T. (1976). "Do Dreams Have Meaning? An Empirical Inquiry." *American Journal of Psychiatry* 133: 778–781.

———, Kinney, L., and Scharf, M. (1983a). "Sex Differences in Dreams." *Psychiatric Journal of the University of Ottawa* 8: 1–4.

———, Kinney, L., and Scharf, M. (1983b). "Dream Incorporation and Dream Function." In W. P. Koella (Ed.). *Sleep 1982*, Sixth European Congress on Sleep Research, Zurich, 1982; pp. 369–371. Basel: S. Karger.

———, McQuarrie, E., and Bonnet, M. (1980). "Dream Differences as a Function of REM Period." *Sleep Research* 9: 155.

———, McQuarrie, E., and Bonnet, M. (1981). "Problem Solving in Dreaming: An Empirical Test." In W. P. Koella (Ed), *Sleep 1980*, Fifth, European Congress on Sleep Research, Amsterdam, 1980, pp. 174–178. Basel: S. Karger.

———, Moshiri, A., and Scharf, M. (1982). "The Organization of Mental Content in and Between the Waking and Dream State." *Sleep Research* 11: 106.

————, Roehrs, T., and Roth, T. (1972). "The Relationship Between Sleep and Mood." *Sleep Research* 1: 193.

————, Roehrs, T., and Roth, T. (1976). "Mood Change and the Physiology of Sleep." *Comprehensive Psychiatry* 17: 161–165.

———— and Roth, T. (1973a). "A Comparison of Dream Content in Dream Reports of Schizophrenic and Depressive Patient Groups." *Comprehensive Psychiatry* 14: 325–329.

———— and Roth, T. (1973b). "The Mood-Regulating Function of Sleep." In W. P. Koella and P. Levin (Eds.). *Sleep: Physiology, Biochemistry, Psychology, Pharmocology, Clinical Implications.* First European Contress on Sleep Research, Basel, *1972*, p. 563–571. Basel: S. Karger.

———— and Roth, T. (1977). "Dream Translation." *Israel Annals of Psychiatry and Related Disciplines* 15: 336–351.

———— and Roth, T. (1979). "The Stability and Variability of Dreaming." *Sleep* 1: 319–325.

————— and Roth, T. (1980). "The Relationship of Dream Content to Night-Morning Mood Change." In L. Popoviciu, B. Asgian, and G. Badin (Eds.), *Sleep 1978,* Fourth European Congress on Sleep Research, Tigre-Migres, 1978, pp. 621–624. Basel: S. Karger.

————, Roth, T., Arand, D., and Bonnet, M. (1981). "Waking and Dreaming Mentation: A Test of Their Interrelationship." *Neuroscience Letters* 22: 83–86.

————, Roth, T., and Cisco, J. (1977). "The Meaningfulness of Dreams." In W. P. Koella and P. Levin (Eds.). *Sleep 1976,* Third European Congress on Sleep Research, Montpellier, 1976, pp. 324–326. Basel: S. Karger.

————, Roth, T., and Czaya, J. (1975). "Dream Development Within a REM Period." In P. Levin and W. P. Koella (Eds.). *Sleep 1974,* Second European Congress on Sleep Research, Rome, 1974, pp. 406–408. Basel: S. Karger.

————, Roth, T., and Palmer, T. (1976). "The Psychological Nature of the REM Dream Report and T.A.T. Stories." *Psychiatric Journal of the University of Ottawa* 1: 128–135.

————, Schoen, L. S., and Kinney, L. (1984a). "Psychological and Behavioral Features of Disturbed Dreamers." *Psychiatric Journal of the University of Ottawa* 9: 102–106.

————, Schoen, L., and Kinney, L. (1984b). "The Dream Experience in Dream Disturbed Vietnam Veterans." In B. Vanderkolk (Ed.), *Post Traumatic Stress Disorders: Psychological and Biological Sequellae.* Washington, D.C.: American Psychiatric Press.

————, M., Trinder, J., and Roth, T. (1972). "Dream Content Analysis of Male Schizophrenic Patients." *Canadian Psychiatric Association Journal* 17: 251–257.

————, Trinder, J., Whitman, R., and Baldridge, B. J. (1969). "The Incidence of Masochistic Dreams in the Night Collected Dreams of Depressed Subjects." *Psychophysiology* 16: 250.

————, Whitman, R., Baldridge, B., and Lansky, L. (1964). "Patterns of Dreaming: The Interrelationship of the Dreams of a Night." *Journal of Nervous and Mental Diseases* 139: 426–439.

————, Whitman, R., Baldridge, B., and Ornstein, P. (1968). "Drugs and Dreams III: The Effects of Imipramine on the Dreams of the Depressed." *American Journal of Psychiatry* 124: 1385–1392.

————, Winget, C., and Whitman, R. (1971). "A City Dreams: A Survey Approach to Normative Dream Content." *American Journal of Psychiatry* 127: 1350–1356.

Leveton, A. F. (1961). "The Night Residue." *International Journal of Psychoanalysis* 42: 506–616.

Lutz, T., Kramer, M., and Roth, T. (1975). "The Relationship Between Mood and Performance." *Sleep Research* 4: 152.

Lysaght, K., Kramer, M., and Roth, T. (1979). "Mood Differences Before and After Sleep: A Test of Its Generalizability." *Sleep Research* 8: 168.

Lysaght, R., Roth, T., Kramer, M., and Salis, P. (1978). "Variations in Subjective State and Body Temperature Across the Day." *Sleep Research* 7: 308.

Meier, C. A. (1967). *Ancient Incubation and Modern Psychotherapy.* Evanston, Ill.: Northwestern University Press.

Piaget J. (1962). *Play Dreams and Imitation in Childhood.* New York: W. W. Norton.

Piccone, P., Jacobs, G., Kramer, M., and Roth, T. (1977). "The Relationship Between Daily Activities, Emotions and Dream Content." *Sleep Research* 6: 133.

Piccione, P., Thomas, S., Roth, T., and Kramer, M. (1976). "Incorporation of the Laboratory Situation in Dreams." *Sleep Research* 5: 120.

Reiser, M. F. (1984). *Mind, Brain, Body.* New York: Basic Books.

Rimon, R., Fujita, M., and Takahata, N. (1986). "Mood Alterations and Sleep." *Japanese Journal of Psychiatry and Neurology* 40: 153–159.

Roehrs, T., Kramer, M., Lefton, W., Lutz, T., and Roth, T. (1973). "Mood Before and After Sleep." *Sleep Research* 2: 95.

Rosa, R., Bonnet, M., and Kramer, M. (1983). "The Relationship of Sleep and Anxiety in Anxious Subjects." *Biological Psychiatry* 16: 119–126.

Rosa, R., Bonnet, M., Warm, J., and Kramer, M. (1981). "Recovery of Performance During Sleep Following Sleep Deprivation." *Sleep Research* 10: 264.

Rosa, R., Kramer, M., Bonnet, M., and Thomas, J. (1981). "The Relationship of Dream Content to Pre- and Post-Sleep Mood." *Sleep Research* 10: 153.

Roth, T., Kramer, M., and Lutz, T. (1976). "The Effects of Sleep Deprivation on Mood." *Psychiatric Journal of the University of Ottawa* 1: 136–139.

Roth, T., Kramer, M., and Roehrs, T. (1976). "Mood Before and After Sleep." *Psychiatric Journal of the University of Ottawa* 1: 123–127.

Schrotter, K. (1959). "Experimental Dreams." In D. Rappaport (Ed.). *Organization and Pathology of Thought* pp. 234–248. New York: Columbia University Press.

Schoen, L. S., Kramer, M., and Kinney, L. (1984). "Auditory Thresholds in the Dream Disturbed." *Sleep Research* 13: 102.

Schwartz, J., Kramer, M., and Roth. T. (1974). "Triazolam: A New Benzodiazepine Hypnotic and Its Effect on Mood." *Current Therapeutic Research,* 16: 964–970.

Smith, E. E. (1988). "Concepts and Thought." In R. J. Sternberg and E. E. Smith (Eds.), *The Psychology of Human Thought,* pp. 19–49. Cambridge: Cambridge University Press.

Sternberg, R. J., and Smith, E. E. (Eds.). (1988). *The Psycholoy of Human Thought.* Cambridge Cambridge University Press.

Tart, C. T. (1979). "From Spontaneous Event to Lucidity: A Review of Attempts to Consciously Control Nocturnal Dreaming." In B. Wolman (Ed.), *Handbook of Dreams*, pp. 226–288. New York: Van Nostrand Reinhold.

Taub, J., Kramer, M., Arand, D., and Jacobs, G. (1978)."Nightmare Dreams and Nightmare Confabulations." *Comprehensive Psychiatry* 19: 285–291.

Trinder, J., and Kramer, M. (1971). "Dream Recall." *American Journal of Psychiatry* 128: 76–81.

Vaccarino, P., Rosa, R., Bonnet, M., and Kramer, M. (1981). "The Effect of 40 and 64 Hours of Sleep Deprivation and Recovery on Mood." *Sleep Research* 10: 269.

Webb, W. B. (1969). "Partial and Differential Sleep Deprivation." In A. Kales (Ed.), *Sleep Physiology and Pathology: A Symposium.* Philadelphia: J. B. Lippincott Co.

—— and Agnew, H. W. (1968). "Measurement and Characteristics of Nocturnal Sleep." In L. A. Abt and B. F. Reiss (Eds.), *Progress in Clinical Psychology*, vol. 8, pp. 2–27. New York: Grune and Stratton.

Whitman, R., Kramer, M., and Baldridge, B. (1963a). "Which Dream Does the Patient Tell?" *Archives of General Psychiatry* 8: 277–282.

Whitman, R., Kramer, M., and Baldridge, B. (1963b). "Experimental Study of Supervision of Psychotherapy." *Archives of General Psychiatry* 9: 529–535.

Whitman, R., Pierce, C., Mass, J., and Baldridge, B. (1962). "The Dreams of the Experimental Subject." *Journal of Nervous and Mental Diseases* 134: 431–439.

Wilkinson, W. B. (1968). "Sleep Deprivation: Performance Tests for Partial and Selective Sleep Deprivation." In L. A. Abt, and B. F. Riess (Eds.), *Progress in Clinical Psychology*, vol. 17, pp. 28–43. New York: Grune and Stratton.

Williams, R., Karacan, I., and Hursch, C. (1974). *EEG of Human Sleep; Clinical Applications.* New York: John Wiley and Sons.

Winget, C., and Kramer, M. (1979). *Dimensions of Dreams.* Gainesville: University Presses of Florida.

Witkin, H. A., and Lewis, H. B. (1967). "Presleep Experiences and Dreams." In H. A. Witkin and H. B. Lewis, *Experimental Studies of Dreaming,* pp. 148–201. New York: Random House.

6

Sheila Purcell, Alan Moffitt, and Robert Hoffmann ━━━━━━━━━━━━

Waking, Dreaming, and Self-Regulation*

Introduction: The Magic Curtain

T heories of dreaming extending back over the centuries have supported every form of extravagance in terms of what can or cannot be done in dreams, and in waking as a result of dreaming. The sleep-wake boundary has been seen as a magic curtain across which lie knowledge of the future, the universe, truth or madness, delusion and error. The advent of the sleep laboratory and the discovery of REM sleep were milestones in the grounding of dream theory within scientific methodology. Current theories of the organization, structure and functions of dreaming are based on more systematically collected empirical data. Unfortunately, in countering the magic curtain effect and the excesses of prescientific theorizing, current academic dream theory is more than just conservative. It has regularly reduced dreaming to a "nothing-but" phenomenon, particularly concerning the question of the functions of dreaming. At its most expansive, scientific theorizing defines dreaming in terms of cognitive deficiencies not shared by normal waking consciousness. These limits, largely framed as dream isolation and suspension of self-regulatory functions, have become overly constraining in the light of new findings for which present theories cannot account.

The foci of this chapter are on (1) the capacity of the dream ego for two kinds of competence during dreaming and (2) on the interrelation of waking and sleeping mentation. The first kind of competence is dream self-reflection, self thinking about self, where self takes self (or an aspect

*Preparation of this chapter and the research it reports were supported by operating grants from the Social Sciences and Humanities Research Council of Canada to A. Moffitt, Laboratory of Sleep and Chronopsychology, Department of Psychology, Carleton University, Ottawa, Ontario, Canada.

197

of self) as an object of awareness. The most metacognitive dream self-reflection found in the dream literature is awareness of dreaming while dreaming and even noticing that one is noticing dreaming while dreaming (Kitchener, 1983; Moffitt et al., 1988), usually referred to as lucid dreaming (LaBerge, 1985; Van Eeden, 1972). In this case, the dreamer takes the entire state of consciousness during dreaming as an object of awareness. The second kind of dreaming competence, a conative vector that can also culminate in lucid dreaming, is that of intentionality or dream control. When this ability is noticed by the dreamer within the dream, lucidity can be triggered (Garfield, 1974). Dream control may occur in the presence of lucidity or it may not. Similarly, lucidity can also trigger dream control. The following dream is an example of lucid dream control:

> I dreamed I was having dinner with a rather uptight group of psychologists when a woman across the table suddenly started recriminating with me for leaving the world of the academic elite and lowering my standards to those of the Sunday newspapers. I protested that this was an exaggeration and that I believed that the layman was entitled to at least some of our ideas, especially as he was paying for our research. At this she literally spat across the table that I was bringing the whole profession into disrepute, that we must maintain some vestige of authority, and so on. My fury rose to such a pitch that I had an irresistible desire to beat her up, and no sooner had I become aware of this desire than I realized with the utmost clarity that I was dreaming and could do exactly what I wanted because dream bodies cannot get hurt.
>
> So leaning across the table, I grabbed her by the hair, punched her face, and knocked her front teeth out. This inspired me to further violence and with an exhilaration I have never previously experienced, I dragged her onto the floor and began to beat up her body in the same way. Of course she fought back and I can still feel the slashing of her fingernails across my cheek and the kicks of what felt like hobnailed boots on my back. At last I detected the waning of her strength, and the fight was over. Then the scene changed, and I found myself in another room walking toward this woman, who was now transformed and wearing a nurse's uniform. As we approached each other, I reminded myself that I must not magically change the events of my lucid dream but allow them to happen spontaneously and observe the outcome. I noticed that she was smiling now and that her front teeth were back in place. She then put out her arms to me in a friendly gesture, and we hugged each other.

I woke up with a great sense of well-being . . ." (Faraday, 1973, pp. 300–301)

Finally, we will examine ways of influencing dream self-reflective-ness and control from the waking perspective and the effects of such manipulations on dreaming and subsequent waking. The point of view we will attempt to establish is that waking and dreaming can be regard-ed as an autopoietic system, mutually causal, codetermining and coe-volving (Maturana & Varela, 1980; Varela, 1979). Varela (1979) has char-acterized the organization of autopoietic systems as follows:

> An autopoietic system is organized . . . as a network of processes of pro-duction . . . of components that produces the components that: (1) through their interactions and transformations continuously regenerate and realize the network of processes . . . that produced them; and (2) constitute it ... as a concrete unity in the space in which they exist by specifying the topolog-ical domain of its realization as such a network. (Varela, 1979)

Deficiency Views of Dreaming

Since the turn of the century (Freud, 1953, originally 1900), the pre-dominant conception has been that dreaming is cognitively deficient rel-ative to normal waking consciousness. This view has regularly used as examples the "fact" that the dreamer can neither be self-reflective nor intentional (Globus, 1987, p. 12). For example,

> The sleeping self has no pragmatic interest whatsoever in transforming its largely confused perceptions into a state of partial clarity and distinctness, in other words to transform them into apperceptions. . . . The dreamer, however, has no freedom of discretion, no arbitrariness in mastering the chances, no possibility of filling in empty anticipations. The nightmare, for instance, shows clearly the inescapableness of the happening in the world of dream and the powerlessness of the dreamer to influence it. . . . Yet among these activities [of mind] there are none of apperceiving and of volition. The life of the dream is without purpose and object. (Schutz, 1962, pp. 240–242).

The Freudian notion of suspension of ego control during "unconscious-ness," as sleep is often thought to be (e.g., Malcolm, 1959), provides a common theoretical framework for cognitive deficiency views that vary in extremity. In hard terms, Hartmann (1973) stresses aspects of normal waking consciousness that subserve "feedback-interactive self-guid-ance—associated with a continuing sense of self over time" (p. 148) which he claims are "entirely absent" during dreaming. This view artic-ulates a passive conception of dreaming characterized by a general lack of intentionality and an inability to self-reflect (Hilgard, 1977). A softer version refers to reduced needs for overt action and relaxation of volun-tary control and critical evaluation (e.g., Cartwright, 1980, p. 242; Wasserman and Ballif, 1984–85). Rechtschaffen (1978) describes statisti-cally normative dreaming as single-minded and isolated from other sys-tems of consciousness. He cites as evidence for "massive nonreflective-ness" the typical lack of dream lucidity, the lack of imagination in the dreamer while slavishly attending to dream story events for long peri-ods, and the generally poor recall of dreams. He suggests that these manifestations are due to the relative isolation of dreams from stimulus input, autonomic activity, organismic state, and motor output. He rea-sons that dream isolation must therefore serve the underlying functions of dreaming by suspending ego control.

A similar position is expressed in the state-shift theory of Koukkou and Lehmann (1983), a psychophysiological theory of dreaming rooted in the psychoanalytic assumption that dreams are regressions. It posits deficits in terms of activation-arousal. Their fundamental observation is that the fastest EEG patterns are generated by the vigilant adult brain. Consequently, slower EEG patterns represent lower levels of vigilance and temporary regressions to brain states associated with earlier devel-opmental stages. Thus, the lower frequency of integrated electric activity found in sleep is theoretically reflected in decreased functional complex-ity of information processing relative to waking. Consistent with the deficiency tradition, consciousness is equated with waking, and the impossibility of self-reflective dreaming is stated unequivocally (Koukkou and Lehmann, 1983).

Another example of a deficiency theory is the activation-synthesis hypothesis (Hobson, 1988; Mamelak and Hobson, 1989; McCarley and Hoffman, 1981), which equates dreaming with REM sleep physiology. The equation of REM sleep with dreaming is untenable in the light of non-REM dreaming (Foulkes, 1962; Moffitt et al., 1982; Morel, Hoff-mann, and Moffitt, 1990; Vogel cited in Weiss, 1986, p. 9). Nevertheless the theory stresses initial activation in the brain stem at the expense of accounting for the moderating and controlling influences of cortical feedback on dreaming (Foulkes, cited in Rechtschaffen, 1983). Accord-ing to this theory, the conscious correlates of brain stem commands for oculomotor and somatomotor movement (corollary discharge information) constitute the matrix from which dream experience is elaborated (McCarley and Hoffman, 1981). In this theory, all dream events begin as physiological accidents. The REM sleep activation of a hypothetical brain stem pattern generator is necessary for dream activity. Because these patterns are either instinctual or developed during waking, dream activities for which there is no brain stem pattern generator are left unexplained. It then becomes difficult to explain creative or recombinatory aspects of dream behavior that require the dream to act on its own output, such as lucidity or learning to fly (Green, 1968, 1990; Hunt, 1989; LaBerge, 1985). Dreams are seen as bizarre because they are the outcome of certain random physiological events imposed on a radically altered tonic physiological background during sleep. The dreamer does not control or learn to control dream events either from waking or during dreaming. In this view, the sleeping forebrain is making the best of a bad job. Indeed, Hobson (1988) allows that dreaming might serve the function of entertainment, but if taken too seriously might be a serious source of error in waking.

Crick and Mitchison (1983, 1986; Crick, 1988) have advanced a theory of dreaming based on some assumptions from artificial intelligence, neural net theories, and the activation-synthesis hypothesis. Based on certain computer models of brain functioning, the waking state is seen as processing information in a consistently rational and logical manner. This unlikely view of normal waking consciousness, popular in the field of artificial intelligence, tends to pervade cognitive science (Gardner, 1985, p. 44) and gives rise to views of dreaming as the irrational excitations of noise in a cybernetic system. In their view, the sleeping brain dreams in order to dispose of this noise. To recall dreams is contrary to their biological purpose, which is to eliminate such noise. Therefore, dream recall is dysfunctional from this point of view.

As varied as the deficiency theories are, they hold considerable sway and have in common a view of waking and dreaming as largely discontinuous with one another. The cognitive superiority of the waking mind is not seen as accessible to an isolated dream state. For some, the processes and products of dreaming and dream recall are generally viewed as inconsequential or even harmful. For others, the purported cognitive deficiencies of the dream state are intrinsic to its functional significance.

An Alternative View: The Consciously Self-Regulating Dream Ego

The preceding view imposes arbitrary ceilings on the cognitive and conative aspects of lived dream experience compared to waking. This view has not been shared by all researchers. Some point to the sheer fact of dream recall as evidence for conscious processes during sleep (Fiss, 1983; Stoyva and Kamiya, 1968) and as an antidote to the widespread view that waking and sleeping correspond to conscious and unconscious processes (Freud, 1953). Some have sought to investigate the continuity rather than discontinuity of mentation across the sleep-wake boundary. However, the continuity literature is highly dispersed and has not usually focused on conscious dream cognition and intentionality by the dream ego. Rather, dreaming has been seen as the intelligent result of some dream planning processor (e.g., Foulkes, 1978, 1979; Foulkes and Schmidt, 1983), as unconscious information processing (Foulkes, 1985, Kuiken, 1981, 1986; Hinton and Sejnowski, 1986), as metaphor (Antrobus, 1977), as a visual transduction of cognition (Hall, 1966) and as the biological basis of poetry and the imagination (Jones, 1980; 1987).

Those studies that look at cognitive complexity within the dream ego typically do so outside a continuity context. Conceptually some of these studies relate to the research reported in the present chapter in a tangential way, articulating low to moderate levels of self-reflectiveness and intentional behavior. For example, the dreamer might be described as present and active, and possibly speaking (Bosinelli, Cicogna, and Molinari, 1974; Weinstein, Schwartz, and Ellman, 1988). However, these studies are embedded within a tonic-phasic research paradigm that uses only small fragments of dream reports (Foulkes and Pope, 1973; Molinari and Foulkes, 1969) and that use scales with very limited psychometric properties such as limited range and largely nominal categories (Bosinelli et al., 1974; Foulkes cited in Winget and Kramer, 1979, pp. 114–116).

A few studies have looked at whole dream reports from the point of view of a consciously functional dream ego (e.g., Hendricks and Cartwright, 1978; Karle et al., 1980). Adelson (1959) for example, found that women who were high in literary creativity had dreams that showed more detachment, reflectiveness, multiple perspectives, bizarreness, dream control, and self-transformations than noninventive women whose stereotyped dreams were characterized by banality, single-mindedness, and brevity. In this case, the cognitive complexity of dream experience was not seen as deficient relative to waking, but rather as a function of an individual difference variable that was continuous for individuals across waking and sleeping. Domino (1976) found almost identical results in his study of waking creativity and primary process dream mechanisms, the main difference being Domino's Freudian (primary process) interpretation of what other theorists (Globus, 1987; Jones, 1980, 1987; Jung, 1974; Rossi, 1972, 1986) would call *creative dreaming*. In a similar vein, Snyder (1970), in a large scale study of REM dreams, noted the ongoing background reflectiveness that was similar to waking. A classic small survey by Green (1968) on lucid dreaming went largely unnoticed for years in the scientific dream community, much the way observations anomalous to orthodoxy often do (Child, 1985; Kuhn, 1970; Ullman, Krippner, and Vaughn, 1973, 1989). Green's book documents self-reflective and intentional dreaming in some of their most impressive forms.

The Impact on Measurement

When these two fundamentally different versions of dream experience, a passive, cognitively deficient dream ego versus a self-reflective and intentionally functional dream ego, are weighed in terms of their impact on research it is clear that the deficiency assumption has carried the day. For example, Winget and Kramer's (1979) compendium of available dream scales demonstrates that scaling emphases for dream ego function have been on pathology, symptomatology, and consistency with waking reality. The extent to which the functioning of the dream self is measured is that self-representation should be adequate and realistic; it should be involved in dream events; and its aggressive behavior should be appropriate. Almost no mention is made of any form of metacognition, with the exception of Foulkes's nominal categories of secondary cognitive elaboration (SCE), one of which is a fundamental articulation of dream self-reflection, "awareness of one's mental processes as an object of consciousness" (Winget and Kramer, 1979, p. 115). The SCE categories themselves appear to have minimal psychometric properties.

For the most part, dream researchers have been looking at dreams through a narrow aperture, precluding the observation of higher-level dream cognition and conation and restricting the variety and range of dream experiences and their waking consequences that can enter into theory. The problem is compounded when restricted data on average dreaming in a nondream culture such as our own are generalized to a species-wide theory of dreaming (Cartwright, 1977; Cohen, 1979; Jones, 1980; Rechtschaffen, 1978). Resulting theories are likely to underestimate the range and variability of dreamers' abilities while dreaming and the effects of dreaming on waking functioning.

The capacity for people to demonstrate metacognitive dreaming and to learn to transfer these abilities from waking to dreaming and from dreaming to waking might be illuminated through theoretical and research attention to individual differences. For example, the modest differences in dreaming and waking cognitive styles between frequent and infrequent dream recallers (Austin, 1971; Bone, 1968; Bone and Corlett, 1968; Bone, Nelson, and McAllister, 1970; Cernovsky, 1984; Cohen, 1974; Cory et al., 1975; Domhoff and Gerson, 1967; Goodenough et al., 1974; Lewis et al. 1966; Moffitt, Hoffmann, and Galloway, 1990; Schonbar, 1965; Sheldrake and Cormack, 1974; Witkin and Lewis, 1967) probably extend to differences in dream self-reflectiveness (Purcell et al., 1986) and dream control (Wallin, 1977). The study of extreme groups is a design tool that can contribute to the illumination of cognitive and conative processes during dreaming. Similarly, the development of psychometrics which reflect the broader range of dream functioning reported in the phenomenological literature is required (e.g., Green, 1968; Garfield, 1974, 1979).

The Advent of Lucid Dream Research

The investigation of lucid and intentional dreaming has been initiated in the last decade (Gackenbach, 1978; Hearne, 1978; LaBerge, 1980; Malamud, 1979; Tart, 1979; Wallin, 1977), challenging the established view that such events did not occur or had no place in a theory of normal dreaming because they were vanishingly rare (Rechtschaffen, 1978). This line of research has continued to develop although it is still outside the mainstream (Blackmore, 1982; Dane, 1984; Fenwick et al., 1984; LaBerge, 1985; LaBerge and Gackenbach, 1986; McCarley and Hoffman, 1981; Ogilvie et al., 1982; Purcell, et al., 1986; Tholey, 1983; Tyson, Ogilvie, and Hunt, 1984; Hunt, 1984; 1989).

The main findings of the research on lucid dreaming have established that awareness of dreaming while dreaming is an empirically observable event. Subjects can be taught to signal the onset of lucidity in a way that is reliably recognizable from the polygraph record (Dane, 1984; Hearne, 1978; LaBerge, 1980; LaBerge et al., 1981; Fenwick et al., 1984). This is done by exploiting the naturally occurring eye movements of REM sleep, so that the subject executes a prearranged pattern of such movements when first aware of the dream state. It has been found that (1) lucid dreaming is much more prevalent than imagined a few years ago (Blackmore, 1985; Dement, cited in LaBerge, 1980; Gackenbach, 1978; McCarley and Hoffman, 1981); (2) that most people (58 percent) dream lucidly at least once in their lives and that many (21 percent) do so quite frequently (Snyder and Gackenbach, 1988); (3) that lucidity and intentional dreaming can be learned (Dane, 1984; Doyle, 1984; LaBerge et al., 1981; Purcell et al., 1986; Tholey, 1983; Wallin, 1977); (4) that there are individual differences involved in the development of the skill (Blackmore, 1982; Gackenbach, 1978; Purcell et al., 1986); and (5) that there is considerable potential for lucidity and intentionality while dreaming in terms of the purposive interruption or transformation of nightmares, and for waking self-exploration and insight (Brylowski, 1990; Faraday, 1974; Green, 1968; Malamud, 1979; Purcell et al., 1986; Tart, 1979; Garfield, 1974; Orr et al., 1968).

Responses to Lucid Dream Research

So far few attempts have been made to account for lucid and intentional dream phenomena theoretically or to index such processes psychometrically. Usually, the theoretical attempts still bear the stamp of the deficiency tradition by maintaining the dichotomy between ordinary and nonordinary dreaming (Hunt, 1982; Gackenbach and Bosveld, 1989; Tart, 1979) or by explaining lucidity nonpsychologically in terms of biological accident (McCarley and Hoffman, 1981). Some attempts at conceptualizing and scaling lucid phenomena (Garfield cited in Gackenbach, 1978) or combined lucid-control phenomena (Gackenbach and Bosveld, 1989; Malamud, 1979) explicate the range of lucid phenomena with lessened emphasis on the prelucid processes that precede them. For example, Tart's (1975, 1979) "discrete altered states of consciousness" model has been the one most commonly applied to lucidity, explicitly by Hunt (1982) and implicitly by others (LaBerge, 1985; Foulkes, 1985; Rechtschaffen, 1978) through the concept of "nonordinary" dreaming. Tart (1979) emphasizes the intentional or control aspects of lucid dreaming, so that for experimental purposes the dream can become an independent variable. LaBerge has made extensive use of this research paradigm in his study of lucid dreaming. However, the discrete states concept has the disadvantage of creating obstructive conceptual boundaries. Although claims of special or transcendent knowledge are seldom explicitly made, the idea of discrete altered states still invokes discontinuities in natural experiencing and creates the theoretical problem of transitions (Feldman, 1980, pp.1–6). For example, Tart (1979) insists on lengthy lucid episodes with waking levels of cognitive skill, complete memory for normal waking consciousness, and dream control as central to the definition of lucid dreaming as a discrete altered state. This conception ignores the incremental advances in these skills found in virtually all the theoretical and empirical lucidity literature (Dane, 1984; Garfield, 1974, 1976, 1979; Green, 1968; Malamud, 1979; Ogilvie et al., 1982, 1983; Purcell et al., 1986; Rossi, 1972; 1986). In other words, the phenomena may not be as discrete as they are continuous.

The most recent attempt to construct a cognitive theory of dreaming (Foulkes, 1985) has made little use of the research on highly self-reflective and intentional dreaming.

> First, lucid dreaming is quite rare—it is the exception that proves the rule of our generally unreflective and involuntary dreaming. Second, because lucid dreaming is, on the face of it, a different mental organization from ordinary dreaming, it's not likely to be similar to ordinary dreaming in all other respects besides lucidity. Thus, the idea that self-conscious lucid dreamers can be trained to signal to us during sleep about what dreaming is really like has an inherent limitation. Since the system is no longer the same system, the observations may not be pertinent to ordinary non-reflective dreaming. Third, by the same token, however, the study of lucid dreaming can, more indirectly, help in the understanding of typical (unre-flective, involuntary) dreaming. Lucid dreaming is a natural (or contrived) experiment in which certain features of ordinary dreaming are altered. By determining the consequences of that alteration on the whole nature of dream experience, we may be able to determine the role of absent self-awareness in ordinary dreaming. (Foulkes, 1985, pp. 44–45).

The rarity of lucidity assumed by some authors (e.g., Foulkes, 1985; Rechtschaffen, 1978) is a bogus objection to its validity for a theory of dreaming (Gackenbach, 1978; LaBerge and Gackenbach, 1986; Dement cited in LaBerge, 1980; Reed, 1978; Snyder and Gackenbach, 1988; Tart, 1979). Moreover, experimental studies indicate that a conservative estimate of 1 to 3 percent of all dreams recalled by young adults from REM sleep are lucid (McCarley and Hoffman, 1981; Purcell et al., 1986). Mainstream insensitivity to lucid dreaming as part of normal dreaming (Foulkes, 1985, p. 44; Rechtschaffen, 1978) has inadvertently been encouraged by lucidity researchers who themselves contribute to an artificial polarization of lucid and nonlucid dreaming. The habit creates the problem of stranding the act of "noticing," as in lucidity, outside a theory of normal dreaming. The problem of unnecessary dichotomization is also extended to dream control by virtue of its association with lucid dreaming. Additionally, the presence of intentional processes in so-called ordinary dreaming seems to have virtually escaped research notice.

Several lines of influence may account for these oversights. One is the Freudian legacy which sees the sleep-wake boundary as congruent with consciousness versus unconsciousness. Another is the assumption that ego control is suspended during sleep, a notion that caused Rechtschaffen (1978) to posit dream isolation from other systems of consciousness as a prerequisite to the functional significance of dreaming. Foulkes's model therefore emphasizes intentionality in the dream generation mechanism rather than in the dream ego (Foulkes, 1978; Foulkes and Schmidt, 1983; Griffin and Foulkes, 1977). In addition, an emphasis on content rather than process has characterized dream research, although this emphasis is changing. Another influence is the tendency toward overly reductionist physiologizing in accounting for dream phenomenology (e.g., Crick, 1988; Crick and Mitchison, 1983, 1986; McCarley and Hoffman, 1981). Yet another is the comparison of dream mentation with a biased view of waking mentation in cognitive science stressing those voluntary deductive and inductive mental processes that can be successfully modeled by computers and neural net theory (Gardner, 1985; Hopfield, 1982; McClelland and Rumelhart, 1986; Rumelhart and McClelland, 1986). Another is the lack of good instrumentation for evaluating assumptions about dream volitional processes (Winget and Kramer, 1979). Foulkes (1985, p. 18) acknowledges the bias in the word "involuntary" when applied to dreaming, but then proceeds as if the qualification had no implications.

> being able to take the dream where you want it implies the return of voluntary self-regulation, whose presence makes lucid dreaming rather different than unlucid dreaming. Furthermore, such control is difficult to achieve (and uneasily managed even when it is achieved), which makes it unlikely that it characterizes much garden variety dreaming, with its absence of voluntary regulation. (Foulkes, 1985, p. 150)

The dichotomization of continuous phenomena may have finished bearing fruit. A strategy with a better yield would be one that does not create divisive boundaries, but simply broadens the range of possible observations. We were able to find only one theory of the interrelation of waking and dreaming that was compatible with this logic. Rossi's (1972) phenomenological theory of self-reflectiveness in dreaming and waking emerged from his work as a clinician. The theory is developmental and dialectical in the sense that there are stages in the development of self-reflectiveness, the attainment of which require the presence of a feedback loop between dreaming and waking consciousness such as that provided by some psychotherapies (Corriere et al., 1980; Rossi, 1972, 1986) or dream workers (Delaney, 1979; Garfield, 1979; Ullman, 1979). The basic mechanism for this feedback loop is attention to the recalled dream. Rossi begins with the assumption common to Jungian, existential and humanistic thought that dreams and fantasies reflect aspects of our phenomenal world. In other words, they reflect us as do mirrors; they self-reflect. Thus their function is to be attended to (Rossi, 1972, 1986) or noticed (Moffitt et al., 1988). Self-reflection during waking and dreaming can then be seen as components of the same phenomenological process. For Rossi, the process of psychological differentiation occurs through self-reflection because attention facilitates noticing, which in turn enables insight. These processes constitute resources toward the range of behavioral choices perceived by the dreamer, whether in waking or in dreaming. Through further self-reflection the implications of behavior can then feed back on subsequent cognition and behavior. Conversely, this process can be under-used. In Rossi's terms, "When the dream seems to be nothing more than a repetition of routine daily activities, the autonomous process is not sufficiently engaged; the dreamer's conscious identity is too rigid and tends to block out the inner processes of creative change and development" (Rossi, p. 162). When dreaming is ignored, "this endogenous process of psychological growth, change, and transformation" (ibid., p. 142) is dormant and dreaming is banal. This curtails the development of self-actualizing behavior that evolves from autonomous to consciously modulated processes. According to Rossi the human capacity to learn self-reflection is requisite to structure the original psychological experience of dreaming into new patterns of awareness and behavior. This is due to information transfer among states, that is, recalling dreams and attending to dreaming during waking. Like Jones (1980), Rossi sees dreams as filled with possibilities, some tried and true for the dreamer, some overworked and even dysfunctional. Others are new, alien, untried, and provide opportunities for the expansion of choice. Bizarreness then, is an indicator of change; single-mindedness and banality are indicators of stasis in this theory. Rossi's approach emphasizes a continuity of dialectical conscious processes between waking and dreaming. His theory of self-reflectiveness is framed in clinical and humanistic terms, but it is easily reframed for experimental use.

Self-Reflectiveness

Self-reflectiveness can be conceived as a self-organized subject-object relation where both subject and object of attention are the self. In other words, a self-organized, recursively nested deployment of attention is the cognitive basis for an explanation of lucid and intentional dreaming. Rossi's thinking is consistent with a systems perspective in that he sees dreaming and waking as co-determining, coevolving processes. Both occur spontaneously, but the initial kick (Murayama, 1963) that sets this coevolution in motion is noticing the dream, first from waking, and increasingly from within the dream itself (Moffitt et al., 1988).

Rossi describes a sequence of dream processes he claims are developmentally ordered on the self-reflectiveness dimension, beginning with ego-absent dreams and culminating in multilevel awareness by the dream ego. The dimension depicts the gradual differentiation of each level of awareness. Progress through the stages from none to two or more levels of awareness oscillates between categories. For example, the dreamer may put himself or herself in a position of objectivity or distance that sets up the likelihood of his or her reflecting on events (level 4), even though explicit reflections occur at the next level (level 5). Similarly, the dreamer may experience two different ways of being (e.g., a change in age or role, level 6), but the simultaneous awareness of the two roles or ages and so on, occurs at the next level (level 7). Gradually, Rossi unfolds the dimension of "levels of awareness" (self-reflection) from none to many. More specifically, (1) in the simplest case the dream contains no people or personal objects, nor associations that the dreamer can recognize. After this point, (2) people and personal associations are present, but the dreamer is not. The next stage (3) represents most of normative dreaming wherein dreamers are single-minded or completely caught up in the dream drama with no other perspective on themselves or their actions. Because the awake person often makes the (self-reflective) connection between such dreams and his or her own emotional needs in daily life, these dreams are said to contain the potential for self-awareness, were waking attention directed toward them. At the next stage, (4) the dreamer is largely an observer in the dream, but not a participant. At this point, a self-reflective process within the actual dream is beginning to be evident. From there, (5) the dream may develop such that soliloquies and dialogues occur, about which Rossi claims,

> the discriminating power of the word apparently evolves from the imagery of the dream drama and greatly enhances the clarity and significance of self-reflection. Verbal associations form cognitive networks binding more autonomous processes of emotion and imagery for the construction and stabilization of new states of awareness. The word in dreams thus touches upon a growing edge of the personality, a place where awareness is expanding and a new identity is being synthesized. (1972, p. 133)

At the next level of self-awareness, (6) the dreamer may experience multiple states of being within the dream. He or she may experience two or more self-images in the same dream, each of which represents a different state or way of being, for example, role changes, different chronological stages, metamorphoses, and more. Finally, (7) multiple levels as opposed to states of awareness appear in the dream at the same time. In this category, the dreamer is fully self-reflective. "Examination of one's thoughts, feelings or behavior in a dream implies that one is taking one's self as a subject for observation" (Rossi, 1972, p. 139). The experiencing self and the examining or observing self express two simultaneous levels of awareness. Bizarreness represents a different perspective from the dreamer's, and as such is a "multiple levels" dream. Rossi states that a perspective or level of awareness very different from one adhered to in everyday life is quite naturally grotesque, weird or idiosyncratic, and that what is common and expected in dreams is ordinary only from the perspective of one's daily habitual and single-minded frame of reference. Rossi's category of most highly self-reflective (multilevel) dreams interestingly contains nearly every form of prelucidity and lucid dreaming mentioned in the descriptive literature, such as the dream within a dream, deja vu, analyzing a dream while dreaming, and dream control. Rossi does not delineate dream evolution beyond the multiple-levels category; his intentions were more theoretical and therapeutic than psychometric. The main contribution of his work toward the present discussion is a psychological account of how dreaming and waking coevolve and participate in the processes of psychological differentiation through the person's capacity to self-reflect.

The Psychometric Response
Scaling Dream Self-Reflectiveness

The only published experiments using Rossi's theory, to the authors' knowledge, were done by the authors (Purcell et al., 1986), who chose to see the difficulty of dream deficiency as at least partially resolvable by a metric based on a self-reflectiveness dimension. The authors made certain modifications to Rossi's sequence for their research purposes (see Table 6.1). They wanted to use spontaneous dream reports only, without any waking associative material from subjects to make a conservative evaluation of self-reflectiveness within dreaming. Therefore they excluded the use of interpretation, inference, or association from the dreamer's waking perspective as part of the scoring. For example, bizarreness was limited to that bizarreness noticed by the dreamer within the dream and appearing spontaneously in the dream report. Consistent with the phenomenological method, dream scorers made no judgment as to what is bizarre (category 7) and simply scored those occasions where the dreamer spontaneously reported awareness of the oddity during the dream.

There was an additional reason for this modification. There is a self-contradictory element concerning bizarreness in Rossi's multiple levels category of dream self-reflectiveness. From Rossi's humanistic phenomenological perspective, bizarreness is not an objective absolute (categories defined by therapist or experimenter), but rather a relative and subjective judgment defined only in the dreamer's terms. For our experimental purposes a potential error lies in the fact that this judgment may come from the dreamer's waking state, whereas it is more theoretically consistent if it comes from the judgment of the dreamer within the dream. Otherwise, it is not a within-dream self-organized state comparable to the other types of multilevel (category 7) dreaming enumerated by Rossi. Bizarreness without concurrent recognition of it as bizarreness would at most be an example of multiple states (category 6), and at least, demonstrate the dreamer's single-minded lack of conscious integration of the multiple perspectives. Support for this position resides in the theoretical and empirical fact of prelucidity (Green, 1968; McCarley and Hoffman, 1981; Ogilvie et al., 1982; Purcell et al., 1986). The critical attitude adopted by the dreamer toward what he or she is dreaming constitutes the various forms of prelucidity (Green, 1968), that also make up Rossi's multilevel awareness category.

Table 6.1

Self-reflectiveness Scale Categories in Abbreviated Form.

CATEGORY	PROCESS LEVEL
1.	Dreamer not in dream; objects unfamiliar; no people
2.	Dreamer not in dream; people or familiar objects present
3.	Dreamer completely involved in dream drama; no other perspective
4.	Dreamer present predominantly as observer
5.	Dreamer thinks over an idea or has definite communication with someone
6.	Dreamer undergoes a transformation of body, role, emotion, age, and so forth
7.	Dreamer has multiple levels of awareness: simultaneous participating and observing; dream within a dream; noticing oddities while dreaming
8.	Dreamer has significant control in or control over dream story, can wake up deliberately
9.	Dreamer can consciously reflect on the fact that he or she is dreaming.

Notes: For Rossi (1972), dream control, prelucidity and lucidity are all examples of dreams with multiple levels of awareness (here, category 7). We have assigned these dreams additional categories (8 and 9) because of our research interests. We have restricted our use of bizarreness to those oddities that are recognized as odd by the dreamer within the dream. We have similarly restricted transformations (category 6) to those in the dreamer only, excluding those in the environment or of other dream characters.

Following Green's (1968) explication of prelucidity and lucidity, we further differentiated these categories from the general multilevel category where Rossi stopped. Control over the dream and finally, lucid dreaming constituted the upper end of the sequence (categories 8 and 9). Category 7 remained for those multilevel dream events that logically require less self-reflectiveness, such as watching and participating simultaneously or recognizing a dream oddity without concluding that one is dreaming. The range of these lucid-control categories could be further extended and elaborated if it suited research purposes (e.g., Malamud, 1979). An abbreviated version of the self-reflectiveness scale we use can be found in Table 6.1.

In the Purcell et al. (1986) laboratory study, significant but small differences in self-reflectiveness were found between the dream reports of REM and stage 2 and between frequent and infrequent dream recallers. The dream ego is slightly more self-reflective in dreams reported following stage REM awakenings than from stages 2 and 4, which do not differ. The home dream diary experiment of Purcell et al. (1986)

however, did not examine individual differences in dream recall, sampling randomly from a normal population of university students. It was found that dream self-reflectiveness in baseline (untreated) subjects was identical to that of laboratory subjects collapsed across sleep stages. It was also found that dream self-reflectiveness could be increased in at least three different ways: through increasing simple attention to dreaming, through posthypnotic suggestion, and through rehearsal of attention patterning schemata learned during wakefulness (Clerc, 1983). When waking attention predisposed dreaming attention to specific reflections (especially noticing a dream oddity within the dream), awareness of dreaming frequently ensued. Self-reflectiveness was reasonably normally distributed in baseline and attention control subjects. These results suggested that a view of lucidity as dichotomous, as either present or not, is better replaced by a continuous process of self-reflection that includes lucid dreaming. The resulting shift for a general theory is that dreaming is more self-reflective than is generally thought and could possibly be much more so were cultural entrainment mechanisms operating to enhance this dream process. (Doniger O'Flaherty, 1984; Laughlin et al., 1986; O'Nell, 1976; Purcell et al., 1986; Tedlock, 1987).

Intentionality

It is in the context of this approach that a psychometrically adequate scale for intentional dreaming was sought. The Dream Control Scale (see later) permits an empirical evaluation of the standard view that dreaming is deficient in voluntary processes. As with the Dream Self-Reflectiveness Scale, dream control is seen as a quasi-continuous variable rather than a dichotomous one. This view allows for a depolarization of how intentional processes have been conceptualized; that is, dream control is either present or absent or that the presence of dream control distinguishes the dream as nonordinary.

In view of Green's (1968) and Garfield's (1974) delineation of two main lines along which lucid dreaming may develop (through developing dream control, and through developing a critical attitude to what is dreamed), these two vectors may be scaled separately. On Rossi's continuum, dream control is seen only in its final form as a multiple-level form of dreaming, largely without developmental antecedents. For some authors what may represent a lack of intention through failure to be involved (Corriere & Hart, 1977; Mahrer, 1971) represents the beginnings of a detached perspective for Rossi and appears in category 4. However, his emphasis is more on the cognitive-insight or attentional dimension, which he calls *self-reflectiveness*. The phenomenological and ideographic literature, however, suggest that the evolution of dream control has its own scalable sequence.

Dream Control

By *dream control* we mean the extent to which the dreamer's intentionality is operative in determining dream events. Control by the dreamer within the dream (called *intentional dreaming* by Wallin, 1977) is not to be confused with the phenomenon of experimenter control, a research paradigm that sees dream control as a subject's successful incorporation of content elements of presleep stimuli presented by the experimenter (see Domhoff, 1985; Tart, 1965, 1979 for reviews). The focus here is on the process by which the dreamer comes to respond to dream-generated events and situations by perceiving behavioral options and acting to bring about an outcome that suits the dreamer. When a dreamer becomes conscious that his or her world is a dream world, he or she may or may not intentionally exploit this awareness by flying, experimenting, transmuting the body, or otherwise interacting with the dream experience (Chang, 1963; Gackenbach and Bosveld, 1989; Garfield, 1979; Gillespie, 1986; Green, 1968; LaBerge, 1985; Tart, 1979). The dreamer may even follow plans concocted during wakefulness (A. Brown, 1936; Green, 1968; Hearne, 1982; LaBerge, 1985; Tart, 1979). This freedom to choose, influence, or control dream structure and events, including the conscious decision not to exercise such control, is spontaneous but can be enhanced by learning, expands with practice, and includes the acquisition of many dream skills. In fact, a classical learning curve has been used to describe the acquisition of control over lucid dream duration (Garfield, 1976). It also appears that in some individuals intentional processes can become enhanced with autosuggestion and practice in the absence of lucidity (Doyle, 1984; Garfield, 1974; Malamud, 1979), with psychotherapy (Hendricks and Cartwright, 1978; Corriere and Hart, 1977; Corriere et al., 1980; Mahrer, 1971), with psychodrama techniques (Wallin, 1977), and group support (Garfield, 1974; Greenleaf, 1973; Hart, 1971; Wallin, 1977). These intentional processes have been referred to as prelucid control (Ogilvie et al., 1982), implying a range of intentional functioning during dreaming worthy of investigation.

Observations regarding lucidity and lucid control emerged empirically (Green, 1968) in the absence of a theoretical framework within which they might fit. These phenomena clearly did not square with prevailing notions of the unconscious that were based on sleep and the suspension of ego control (Freud, 1953). The cognitive (attentional and intentional) deficiencies which are corollary to such a conception of the dream state leaves dreams with high levels of ego functioning as oddities beyond accounting, just as with self-reflectiveness (Foulkes, 1985; Freud, 1953; Rechtschaffen, 1978). By default, self-reflective dreaming was seen dichotomously as either present or absent, and dream control seems to have suffered the same fate. Green's (1968) concept of prelucidity and Rossi's (1972) dimensional concept of self-reflectiveness point the way to a more continuous and dialectical view of the development and dynamics of dream control. The view taken here is that dream control as a single unitary category requires further delineating.

Although the amazing range of dream control possible in the lucid dream state has been apparent for some time (Chang, 1963; LaBerge, 1985; Tart, 1979), Green (1968; 1990), Garfield (1974), and to some extent Rossi (1972, 1986) were struck with prelucid forms of dream control. Garfield (1974), who became proficient at intentional dreaming before she developed habitual lucid dreaming, states:

> Only two of the systems [for developing dream control] require high consciousness during the dream state: lucid dreamers and Yogi dreamers. You need some degree of dream consciousness to recognize that you are supposed to confront danger rather than run (in a dream). Lucidity is unimportant in the other systems and hence may limit their usefulness. You can shape your dreams without high consciousness, but the more aware you become of your dream state while you are in it, the more you will be able to actively relate to it and use it to your benefit. (p. 205).

For many authors, the importance of lucidity resides in its capacity to enhance dream control. Control is seen as play or therapeutic treatment (Faraday, 1973; Garfield, 1974), as a scientific tool for the advancement of psychophysiology (Green, 1968; LaBerge, 1985; Tart, 1979), and philosophically, as a tool for the ultimate recognition of all mental phenomena as problematic and perhaps illusory (Chang, 1963; Doniger O'Flaherty, 1984).

Although dream control typically accompanies a stabilized capacity for lucidity, its development also appears to precede lucidity in some people (Garfield, 1974; Wallin, 1977). Dream control and lucidity appear to be complementary and interactive in that the emergence of one typically leads to the emergence of the other, and each capacity is maximized in the presence of the other. Nevertheless, however highly inter-active they may be, the mechanisms of noticing and acting are not the same and their variations do not lie on the same dimension.

Rossi's construct of self-reflectiveness can be seen as enumerating levels of awareness. For him, dream control involves more than one level of awareness (dreaming and controlling dreaming) and is therefore a complex form of dream metacognition, as is lucid dreaming. It occu-pies one high-level category and the development of intentionality is not otherwise mapped. What for some authors represents low control, that is, lack of involvement and hence the denial of the opportunity for mas-tery (Corriere et al., 1980; Hendricks and Cartwright, 1978; Mahrer, 1971), for Rossi represents the beginnings of a detached perspective and an opportunity for self-reflectiveness. The alternative view is that the dreamer attempts to cope with dream situations in a manner similar to waking. Thus, involvement, courage, effort, expressiveness, mastery, success and self-reflectiveness all vary, often independently. The net conclusion is that perceiving and acting require separate scale measures on logical and functional grounds. In addition, such scales might pro-vide normative data for describing the nature and range of those human abilities necessary for the further development of a psychological theory of dreaming.

The Development of a Scale for Dream Control

On the basis of the empirical and clinical literature, the dream con-trol dimension can be ordered as it occurs without lucidity (control "in" the dream), and as it progresses around and after the attainment of lucidity (control "over" the dream). On such a scale, prelucid control precedes awareness of control logically, ontologically, and ontogeneti-cally (Garfield, 1974; Green, 1968; Malamud, 1979; Berkson, 1980). Dreams in a normal population vary in the degree of control in the dream situation where the dreamer might demonstrate control of his or her own actions and on the environment (Brenneis, 1970; Hall and Van de Castle, 1966; Sheldrake and Cormack, 1974). An example of a low cat-egory on this dimension occurs when, for example, dream characters, but not the dreamer, are carriers of the dream action (Corriere and Hart, 1977; Mahrer, 1971). Control in the dream then increases until the dreamer is carrier of the action, responding effectively to dream situa-tions. Power and luminosity (peak experiencing) may be expressed by the dreamer in the fully successful dream (Corriere et al., 1980; Hunt, 1989).

Control "over" is seen as a higher order of control than control "in." The ability for control over dreaming develops in some dreamers who can compose dreams (Garfield, 1974), or change an element in a recurring nightmare (Halliday, 1982; Tart, 1979; Wallin, 1977) or choose to awaken from them entirely (Green, 1968; Orr et al., 1968). In Jung's (1974) sense, the dreamer is the scene, the player, the producer, and so forth. When acting as though one knows this, one has control over one's dream. When one notices this, he can become lucid. This degree of control is usually a precursor to lucid dreaming ability. When one knows it is one's own dream, his role as "owner" of it has been found to expand the magnitude of one's control over dream events (Gackenbach and Bosveld, 1989; LaBerge, 1985), the morphology and capabilities of one's own body (Chang, 1963), and one's command of cognitive abilities (Green, 1968; Tart, 1979; Van Eeden, 1972). The dreaming self is consciously and intentionally participating in the processes of dream formation puzzled over by Cartwright (1974, p. 388), Foulkes and Schmidt (1983), and Globus (1987).

Available Scales

An instrument was needed that would evaluate the level of dream control expressed in the dream report. The procedure for instrument development was taken from F. Brown (1970). A review of available scales showed that none were well suited to the present purposes on theoretical or psychometric grounds, although some were partially suitable. For example, Ogilvie et al. (1982) looked at nonlucid, prelucid, and lucid dreams in terms of whether control was present or absent. In contrast to this tri-level approach to dream control, we make the assumption that dream control is a more or less continuous variable with a much larger theoretical range (Chang, 1963; McCarley and Hoffmann, 1981).

This ordinal view is consistent with Brenneis (Winget and Kramer, 1979, p. 96) who sees dream control as one of thirty-four dimensions of ego style. This three-point scale sees dream events as (1) entirely within the dreamer's control, (2) at some point out of such control, and (3) completely out of such control, and it forms a basis for an ordinal scale. The range, however, is restricted from a psychometric perspective and is perhaps too general to ensure interrater reliability. Moreover, the issue of control over the dream is not addressed. This was the only scale of dream control per se that was found in the literature at the time we conducted our research, reported later.

Brenneis (1970) used similar three-point scales describing other dimensions of ego style that could easily be seen as aspects or strands of a control dimension such as centrality-involvement, activity level, effort-exertion and feeling expressiveness-assertiveness. Such strands present the possibility of multi-dimensional scaling if they summed additively to the construct of dream control. This assumption was rejected on the grounds that the dream depends for its coherence on the interaction and fit of these strands. Not only is the whole greater than the sum of its parts theoretically, but from a psychometric perspective it was thought that raters might compound their error variance with several scales per dream when one might do. The Self-Reflectiveness scale (Purcell et al., 1986) adapted from Rossi (1972) served as a model at this choice point.

We took the view that the construct's name was dream control and that it referred to a cluster of empirically related dream behaviors determined by an underlying factor, that is, volition-intentionality. What varies is the degree to which the dreamer's intention or action is cognitively developed and acted upon with success for the dreamer, although these may not be well explicated in the spontaneous dream report. The solution taken here to the philosophical conundrum of determining intentional action was the development of certain textual criteria for scoring each level on a nine-point dream control scale. These criteria were based predominantly on those of Brenneis's thirty-four dimensions of ego style that were related to control: centrality-involvement, activity level, effort and feeling expressiveness. Similar three- and five-point scales of these dream traits by other researchers were used to help develop and expand the criteria for each level of the scale. Level descriptions for centrality-involvement were adapted also from Breger, Hunter and Lane (cited in Winget and Kramer, 1979, p. 146) and Cappon (cited in Winget and Kramer, 1979, p. 96). Descriptions of level of feeling expressiveness were adapted also from Breger and his colleagues and from Corriere et al. (1980, pp. 192–193). What constitutes activity was adapted from Hall and Van de Castle (1966) as well as the notion of failure-success.

These scales formed the basis for categories 1–7 of the control scale, to which nonlucid control over and lucid control added two more categories (see Table 6.2). No attempt was made to discriminate a range of lucid control categories due to the much lower frequency of lucid dreams, although this could be done should it suit an experimenter's purposes.

Table 6.2

Dream Control Scale Categories in Abbreviated Form.

CATEGORY	PROCESS LEVEL
1.	The dreamer is not present in the dream. (e.g., the police chased a man down an alley)
2.	The dreamer is present in the dream as an observer and reporter of events but does not participate, or report his or her own thoughts and feelings on dream events. (e.g., I watched the police chase a man down an alley)
3.	The dreamer is present predominantly as observer, although he or she may express private responses to dream events or may engage in some minimal peripheral activity (e.g. I watched the police chase a man down my alley and wondered if he were innocent or guilty)
4.	The dreamer is central or a main protagonist but control or expressiveness is minimal and the dreamer is weak and ineffectual. (e.g., the police were chasing me; I was cornered in an alley with no chance of escape)
5.	The dreamer has some impact due to more effort or more success than in category 4 (e.g., the police were chasing me for something I didn't do and they were getting closer the faster I ran)
6.	The dreamer gains control over the dream situation to a large extent, but not maximally; solutions may be banal, temporary, incomplete. (e.g. ,the police were chasing me down an alley; I hid behind a door)
7.	The dreamer gains full control of himself or herself and the dream situation and may express strong good feelings (e.g., the police were chasing me down an alley, but I was able to out run them all and scaled the wall easily; I laughed when I realized I had lost them)
8.	The dreamer has control "over" (as opposed to control "in") the dream or part of it or may manipulate dream mechanics as would a film director; an explicit statement of awareness of dreaming while dreaming is absent, (e.g., the police were close on my heels, but I thought of a secret hiding place that was quite far off; I slowed the dream down to give myself a head start, and I got to safety in plenty of time)
9.	The dreamer exerts or attempts to exert control over dream events or outcomes in the context of dream lucidity, or awareness of dreaming while dreaming (e.g., as soon as I realized I was dreaming, all the anxiety of this chase left me; I turned and faced the police and they all smiled at me.

Dreaming to Waking Transfer Effects

Although it seems clear that the idea of dream isolation has been greatly overstated, the other side of the coin concerning transfer or carry-over effects from dreaming to waking are definitely underresearched "in the light of all the theoretical speculation about what dreams are supposed to accomplish" (Cohen, 1979, p. 271). Cartwright frames the questions of transfer effects this way:

> Waking mental life can operate in any number of modes, receiving and retrieving data from different sources in different combinations. Do these differences have consequences for how night time thought is distributed, and does this in turn affect the deployment of attention in the subsequent waking activity, or are these independent non-interactional states? Are the affective memory schemas reorganized on the basis of the endogenous experience of the dreams or are these state-dependent systems? Are there dream residues as well as day residues and where should we look for their effects? (In Fishbein, 1980, p. 244).

Like Cartwright, many researchers (e.g., Cohen, 1979, p. 164; Kramer, 1982; Sirois-Berliss and DeKoninck, 1982; Wasserman and Ballif, 1984–85) emphasize the affective carry over effects of dreaming. Foulkes (1982) has noted that dreams generate experience that provides the dreamer with the opportunity for an affective response, rather than affect causing the dream. To follow through on Foulkes's conclusion, symbolization in dream awareness of the affective response (Hendricks and Cartwright, 1978) constitutes cognitive competence developed in the dream state that is available to the waking state through the mechanism of attention to the recalled dream (Hall, 1966; Rossi, 1972; 1986). Cohen (1979, p. 271) notes that waking tasks that measure carry-over effects from dreaming to waking are as yet relatively undeveloped (mood carry over is an exception, e.g., Kramer and Roth, 1980; Sirois-Berliss and DeKoninck, 1982). As Weiss (1986) and Foulkes (1985) have pointed out, REM deprivation has been the dominant paradigm for investigating such effects by inferring them from behavioral deficits. This approach is methodologically problematic and has been disappointing in terms of information yield (see Foulkes, 1985, for a review). Another more direct approach might be to use dreams and subjective reports of dreaming to waking transfer effects as data, thus evaluating the less systematically collected impressions of clinicians and dream workers regarding specific kinds of transfer effects (e.g. Delaney, 1979;

Rossi, 1972, 1986). Doyle (1984) has shown that the dream competence taught to subjects enabling them to have more pleasurable dreams, an aspect of dream control, was still in effect at a six-month follow-up. Wallin (1977) found that subjects who were successful in changing their dreaming differed from unsuccessful subjects on posttest questionnaires in that they had dramatic experiences of insight during the study. Successful subjects experienced a reduced discrepancy between images of self and self-ideal. They found they wanted less control from and over others and found greater ease in interpersonal relations. Again, these effects were still present at a follow-up interview.

Cohen (1979, p. 271), Delaney (1979), and Garfield (1974) all suggest presleep dream incubation as a good possibility for obtaining transfer effects from dreaming to waking; for example, concerning problem solving or a current concern. In Delaney's training groups, she noticed how flexible dreams are in responding to entrainment originating from normal waking consciousness and from the hypnagogic period. This is the transfer of competence from waking to dreaming illustrated by other researchers (Doyle, 1984; Purcell et al., 1986; Wallin, 1977). Delaney has also noted the return effects from dreaming to waking so that dreams can answer questions, provide creative ideas and solutions, rehearse skills needed in waking, and generate insight, in addition to altering moods.

The Study[*]

This section reports an investigation of the transfer of attentional skills across the sleep-wake boundary with reference to the metacognitive processes of self-reflectiveness and dream control. The aim of the research was to extend the empirical and theoretical reach of the studies of Purcell et al. (1986). In addition to altering the treatment conditions of that experiment, the current study included an individual difference variable, self-reported variation in the frequency of dream recall. It was anticipated that frequent dream recallers would experience greater waking to dreaming transfer effects than infrequent dream recallers. A three-week data collection period was used to enable the teaching and learning of self-reflective and dream control skills and to provide subjects with a sufficiently lengthy experimental period to enable the post-experimental evaluation of dreaming to waking transfer effects. The groups in the experiment were an untreated control group (baseline), an

---

[*]Conducted by the first author in partial fulfillment of the requirements for the Ph.D. degree, Faculty of Graduate Studies and Research, Carleton University.

attention-placebo aimed at focusing attention on detailed dream recall (attention control), and a schema group designed to develop dream lucidity and control. Differential patterns of response by the dream ego were expected to emerge as a function of treatment conditions, gender, self-reported frequency of dream recall, and their interactions. Finally, a questionnaire was used to examine the effects of the dream manipulations on subsequent waking attitudes, beliefs, and behaviors.

Method

Subjects

Subjects were recruited from a large population of psychology undergraduates, predominately young adults, who had been assigned randomly to course sections by the university registrar. On the basis of an initial questionnaire given to 445 students, 95 subjects completed the experiment: 27 male frequent recallers, 27 female frequent recallers, 22 male infrequent recallers, and 19 female infrequent recallers. Frequent dream recallers recalled dreams four times a week or more; infrequent dream recallers, once a week or less.

Instruments

Initial questionnaire. The purpose of this instrument was to elicit demographic and pretest information to facilitate subject selection and assignment to groups on the basis of gender and self-reported frequency of dream recall. The query regarding frequency of recall was embedded among items about other aspects of dream experience.

Report skills questionnaire. This was a training instrument designed to remind subjects about detailed dream reporting and cultivate general attentiveness to dreaming during the experiment. Items queried the presence of various kinds of dream details such as color, speech, and emotion. This instrument appeared on the reverse side of dream log sheets for subjects in attention control and schema groups. They were asked to fill out the questionnaire for each dream report.

Dream self-reflectiveness scale. Table 6.1 (see earlier) presents a brief version of this scale. A manual (available from the authors) based on this instrument was used by judges to score all dreams on self-reflectiveness.

Dream control scale. Table 6.2 (see earlier) presents a brief version of this scale. A manual (available from the authors) based on this instrument was used by judges to score all dreams for level of dream control.

Dreaming to waking transfer effects. Table 6.4, later, will show results from the posttest. These items were extracted from Delaney's (1979) Appendix, which discusses the results of keeping of a dream diary. Items queried the effects of dreaming on subsequent waking, which subjects rated on a scale from 1–7. Ratings on individual items were used as scores to evaluate the effects of different types of dreaming to waking transfer effects. No groups were tutored in these items or had such effects suggested to them. This instrument was designed to gather data on what kinds of dreaming to waking transfer effects subjects themselves report noticing, with the expectation that such effects would be more apparent for subjects who have attended most to dreaming. It was decided that it was unnecessary to disguise from subjects the obvious purpose of the questions for two reasons. One was the improbability of being able to do so after an experiment that was very intensively about dreaming. Another was the protection afforded by a randomized research design with control groups (Campbell and Stanley, 1963) so that the information about differential carry-over effects resides in the differences in group scores. With this design protection, the contaminating effects of a pretest were avoided.

Procedure

The three experimental conditions were baseline, attention control, and schema groups, similar to those described in Purcell et al. (1986) but with several modifications (details of treatment conditions are available from the authors). No suggestions of dreaming to waking transfer effects were made in any group. Handouts were given to treatment subjects to increase the efficacy of treatment sessions and thus compensate for the increased treatment load without extending the session time. Baseline subjects were required to report to the experimenter weekly instead of just at the end of the experiment, as in Purcell et al. (1986), to maintain better participation by these subjects. Similarly, treatment subjects always had to make up missed sessions. This was done in person rather than over the phone, because the latter may have inadvertently encouraged less participation in the earlier study. Posttesting for dreaming to waking transfer effects was also introduced at the end of the experiment.

All subjects were asked to write dream reports at home for a three-week period upon awakening from sleep each morning. They were told that any experience during sleep constitutes a dream to override privately held definitions of the term. To avoid a response bias on the basis of social desirability, subjects were told that the experimenter was investigating dreams as they actually occurred and that any editing to make dreams more coherent or presentable was contrary to experimental purposes. Subjects were asked to avoid discussing the experiment with others. At the end of the experiment they filled out the posttest and were debriefed. Differential instructions for groups were as follows.

Baseline: (N = 32; 9 male frequent recallers, 9 female frequent recallers, 8 male infrequent recallers, 6 female infrequent recallers) Subjects were asked to keep a dream log without further instruction. They were given dream log sheets without a report skills questionnaire on the reverse side. Subjects met with the experimenter once a week, long enough to hand in the week's dream reports and collect additional log sheets as needed. At the end of three weeks they handed in their final dreams, filled out the posttest questionnaire on dreaming to waking transfer effects, and were debriefed about the purposes of the experiment.

Attention Control: (N = 30; 9 male frequent recallers, 8 female frequent recallers, 6 male infrequent recallers, 7 female infrequent recallers) In addition to dream collection, subjects were asked to fill out a report skills questionnaire (available from the authors) on the back of each dream report after writing each dream. Weekly half-hour meetings with the experimenter dealt with detailed reporting of dreams and answering questions subjects had about making their reports.

Schema: (N = 33; 9 male frequent recallers, 10 female frequent recallers, 8 male infrequent recallers, 6 female infrequent recallers). In addition to dream collection, subjects filled out a report skills questionnaire for each dream during week 1, a dream control questionnaire during week 2 and a self-reflectiveness rating scale during week 3 (see Purcell, 1987). Subjects also wore a leather bracelet during the experimental period, which served as a cue for schema rehearsal whenever it was noticed during the day (Clerc, 1983). Schemata were learned at weekly half-hour meetings with the experimenter and were given as handouts. The first schema involved questioning the present state of consciousness and reminding oneself that this same question can be posed during dreaming. Further schemata were designed to predispose the subjects' attention toward noticing certain targeted dream situations and processes, such as learning to notice oddities and to notice opportunities for choice in behavioral expression (specific instructions can be found in Purcell, 1987). At the same time as the posttest, subjects in this group wrote answers to questions about their degree of compliance with the experimental requests.

Scoring of dream protocols. A training set of fifty dreams was used to train four judges, two for each of the Self-Reflectiveness and Control Scales. The experimenter was the third rater for each scale. The dreams collected during the experimental period were typed with minor editing. This was felt necessary because treatment subjects had a tendency to discuss aspects of their dreams at the end of the report reflecting treatment discussions or questions on the reverse side of the report. Because this verbiage was not part of the actual dream report, it was eliminated to avoid artificially inflating word counts. Reports were shuffled and given to raters with no identifying labels. After scoring the dreams in blocks of 200, judges met to submit their ratings and discuss those which did not meet the scoring criterion of exact agreement by two out of three judges on the first independent round. Dreams not easily agreed upon by this procedure were given the score accorded by the middle judge although the option remained open to report a dream as unscorable and omit it from the data analysis if this seemed more appropriate.

Hypotheses

1. Main effects of treatment. First, it was expected that as attention to dream processes increased, dream self-reflectiveness scores would increase. (1) Significant group differences were predicted for mean self-reflectiveness scores. This mean was expected to be highest in the schema group, followed by the attention control, then the baseline group. (2). The schema group's treatment was expected to produce significantly more lucid dreams from more lucid dreamers than attention control and baseline group' conditions.

Second, dream control was expected to increase as a function of learning to notice opportunities for alternatives in behavioral expression during dreaming. The schema group was expected to have significantly higher dream control scores than attention control and baseline groups.

Third, it was expected that group differences on the dreaming to waking posttest would be significant. Mean scores were anticipated to be highest from schema subjects, followed by the attention control, then the baseline subjects.

Main effects of pre-experimental self-reported frequency of dream recall. A significant main effect for self-reported frequency of dream recall was expected. (1) For dream self-reflectiveness, frequent recallers were expected to have significantly higher scores than infrequent recallers. (2) For dream control, frequent recallers were expected to have higher scores than infrequent recallers. (3) For dreaming to waking transfer effects, frequent recallers were expected to have higher scores than infrequent recallers.

Treatment by frequency of recall interaction. It was expected that individual differences in dream self-reflectiveness, dream control, and dreaming to waking transfer effects would be attenuated as a function of increased attention to dream processes. (1) Mean differences in dream self-reflectiveness between frequent and infrequent recallers were expected to be significant in the baseline group, but were not expected to be significant in the schema group. (2) Mean differences in dream control between frequent and infrequent recallers were expected to be significant in the baseline group but were not expected to be significant in the schema group. (3) No hypotheses were formulated concerning treatment by individual differences interactions for the dreaming to waking posttest.

Results

The average age of the subjects was 24.8 years with a minimum of 19 and a maximum of 45 years. Interrater reliability was considered satisfactory for nine-point scales. Of the 1212 dreams that were collected, 1144 or 94.4 percent reached the scoring criterion of exact agreement by two out of three raters on the first round of independent ratings of the dream Self-Reflectiveness Scale. The remaining 5.6 percent were resolved by discussion. On the first round of independent ratings, 1083 reports or 89.36 percent reached the scoring criterion for the Dream Control Scale. The remaining 10.6 percent were resolved by discussion.

The correlation between the two scales over the 1212 dreams was .41 ($p < .001$). The degree of association varied with treatment condition. It was low in the baseline group's condition ($r = .32, p < .001$), vanished in the attention control group's condition ($r = .09, p < .10$), and became stronger in the schema group's condition ($r = .57, p < .001$).

Waking to Dreaming Transfer Effects

Dream Self-reflectiveness (DSR): Dream self-reflectiveness was taught only to the Schema group in only one treatment session, during the third week of data collection. There was a small but significant main effect of treatment on DSR scores, $F(2, 82) = 5.83, p < .001$. The Student-Neuman-Keuls test of mean differences showed that both the attention control ($\bar{x}$ = 5.1) and schema ($\bar{x}$ = 5.5) groups had significantly higher scores than the baseline group ($\bar{x}$ = 4.6), suggesting that both treatments increase dream self-reflectiveness. The Attention Control and Schema groups did not differ. In addition, there was a small but significant main effect for gender, F (1, 82) = 5.04, $p < .03$), with females ($\bar{x}$ = 5.2) having higher overall scores on the dream self-reflectiveness measure than males ($\bar{x}$ = 4.9). This same analysis performed on subject means calculated excluding lucid dreams yielded the same results: small but significant main effects for treatment, $F(2, 82)$ = 5.12, $p < .005$, and gender, $F(1, 82)$ = 7.30, $p < .008$, with schema and attention control subjects having significantly higher DSR means than baseline subjects, and females having significantly higher DSR means than males.

The DSR scale distributions for treatment groups (see Figure 6.1) were the same as Study 2 of Purcell et al. (1986) in all but one respect. Baseline subjects performed differently in the two studies, showing fewer DSR category 3 dreams in the present study with a corresponding increase in other categories. Consequently DSR means for the baseline group were higher in the present study (4.6 as opposed to 3.7). The mean word count of their dream reports was higher (102 as opposed to 65). This outcome can be interpreted as the result of more carefully maintained motivation to participate by the baseline subjects in the present experiment.

Figure 6.1 shows that the greatest representation in DSR category 7, noticing oddities, was due to the attention control group's condition. The least was due to the baseline group's condition, with schema subjects falling in between. Schema subjects show the greatest representation in DSR category 9, lucid dreaming.

The hypothesized interaction of treatment and self-reported frequency of recall on DSR scores was not significant, nor was the main effect of self-reported frequency of recall. However, as can be seen from Figure 6.2, frequent and infrequent recallers were significantly different in the distributions of their dreams across DSR scale categories, $\chi^2(8)$ = 18.69, $p < .02$. More dreams of infrequent recallers were scored as DSR 3, single-minded involvement, whereas more dreams of frequent recallers were scored as DSR 5, involving thought or speech. There was no difference in the number of lucid dreams reported by frequent and infrequent recallers. It should be remembered, however, that although such distributions describe information lost in subject means, assumptions of independence are violated.

228

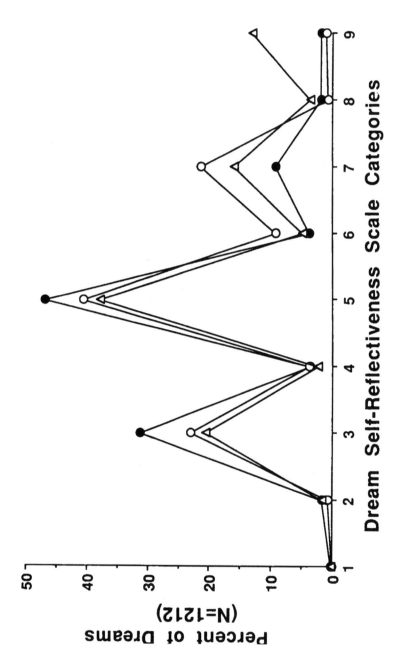

Figure 6.1. Distributions of dreams (%) Across Dream Self-Reflectiveness Scale Categories for Baseline (•), Attention Control (○), and Schema (△) groups.

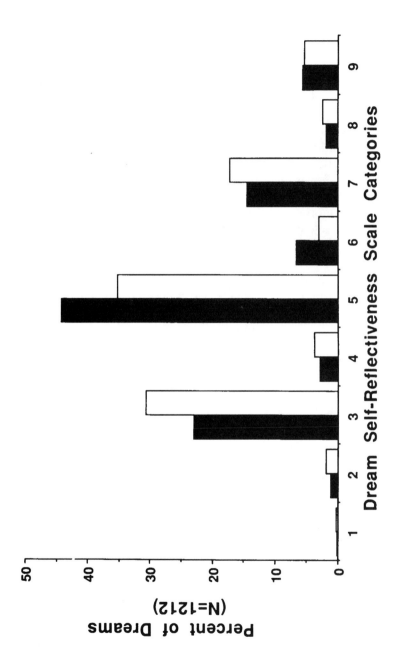

Figure 6.2. Distributions of Dreams (%) Across Dream Self-Reflectiveness Scale Categories for Frequent (■) and Infrequent Recallers (□)

When the recall variable was based on the actual frequency of recall during the experiment, little support for the hypothesized interaction between frequency of recall and treatment was found. A median split of subjects within each treatment group was performed and used as an independent variable along with treatment and gender in a 3 x 2 x 2 ANOVA. In this posthoc analysis, treatment effects were significant, the gender difference was not significant, and higher recallers ($\bar{x}$ = 5.1) had slightly but significantly higher DSR scores than lower recallers ($\bar{x}$ = 4.8), $F(1, 82)$ = 5.07, $p < .03$. The expected interaction between observed frequency of recall and treatment groups was not significant.

ANOVA with weekly DSR scores used as a repeated measure showed a significant interaction of treatment and the repeated DSR measure, $F(4, 128)$ = 4.28, $p < .003$, which is depicted in Figure 6.3. It can be seen that attention control subjects performed like schema subjects during the first week, but dropped to levels more comparable to baseline subjects during weeks 2 and 3. Tests of simple main effects demonstrated significant differences between groups for each week of the experiment. During the first week, $F(2, 87)$ = 9.80, $p < .001$, both the schema and attention control groups had higher DSR means than the baseline group (Student-Neuman-Keuls). Week 2 dreams, $F(2, 82)$ = 7.77, $p < .01$, were significantly more self-reflective in the schema group than in other groups, and the same pattern was significant for week 3 dreams, $F(2, 82)$ = 9.93, $p < .001$.

Lucid Dreaming: Subjects with lucid dreams had significantly higher mean scores on the Dream Self-Reflectiveness scale when the lucid dreams (DSR 9) were removed from subject means, $t(92)$ = 2.70, $p < .008$. Similarly, lucid dreamers had significantly higher mean scores on the Dream Control scale when the lucid control category (DC 9) was removed from subject means, $t(92)$ = 1.98, $p < .05$.

Analysis of the number of lucid and nonlucid dreamers across groups showed a significant group difference, $\chi^2 (2)$ = 17.17, $p < .001$) which was clearly attributable to the 50 percent of schema subjects who reported one or more lucid dreams. It can be seen from Table 6.3 that the spontaneous incidence of lucid dreams in baseline and attention control subjects was about 1 percent, which is the rate commonly observed (McCarley and Hoffman, 1981; Purcell et al., 1986). The rate of 13.1 percent observed in the Schema group is substantially above the spontaneous rate.

A test of association between the presence or absence of lucidity and the experimentally observed dichotomy of higher and lower rates of

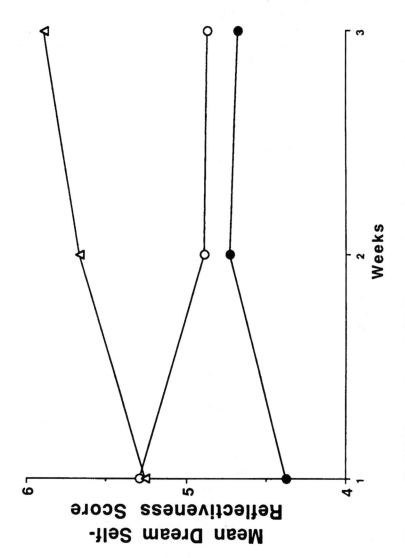

Figure 6.3. Weekly Means on Dream Self-Reflectiveness Scores for Baseline (•), Attention Control (○), and Schema (△) groups (*N* = 76)

recall was significant, χ^2 (1) = 4.57, $p < .03$. Those subjects in the schema group who achieved lucidity tended to be those with highest rates of recall during the experimental period. Those who were experiencing good rates of recall prior to the experiment did not show a significant tendency to develop lucidity during the experiment. Finally, lucid dreamers showed greater dreaming to waking transfer effects than other subjects, discussed later with other posttest findings.

Table 6.3
Rates of lucid dreaming under different treatment conditions.

	Baseline Group (N = 32, dreams = 433)	Attention-Control Group (N = 30, dreams = 345)	Schema Group (N = 32, dreams = 434)
No. lucid Dreamers	4 (12.5%)	3 (10.0%)	16 (50%)
No. lucid dreams	7 (1.62%)	3 (0.90%)	57 (13.13%)

Lucid Dream Phenomenology: Lucid dreams were examined for the presence or absence of rehearsed schemata, where lucidity was the contingent response, and comparisons were made of baseline and attention control subjects' dreams with schema subjects' dreams. Fisher's Exact Test shows that the schema dream reports contained significantly more triggers than dreams from the other groups, which tended not to include triggers to lucidity ($p = .02$). Successful triggers that did appear in spontaneous lucid dreams were one instance of recognizing a dream oddity, one flying dream, and one dream experienced as an out-of-body experience. In the schema group, subjects with multiple lucid dreams tended to use the same trigger nearly every time, and typically this was the recognition of a dream oddity. Twenty-four lucid episodes were triggered by the recognition of a dream oddity. Eleven lucid dreams contained references to the experiment, and on four of these occasions, this triggered the lucid episode. There were four lucid dreams triggered by the recognition of a recurring dream sequence, three were stress induced, and two were falling dreams. One dreamer became lucid when he arrived at a certain place in which he had arranged with a friend in the waking state to meet in the dream state. Eighteen schema subjects' lucid dreams had no trigger evident in the report.

Dream Control (DC): Dream control (DC) was taught only to the schema group in only one treatment session, during the second week of data collection. The treatment difference was significant as a main effect, $F(2, 82) = 3.84, p < .03$). The Student-Neuman-Keuls test of mean differences showed that the schema group ($\bar{x} = 5.2$) had slightly but significantly more dream control in their reports than did either the baseline ($\bar{x} = 4.8$) or the attention control subjects ($\bar{x} = 4.9$), consistent with the fact that dream control was taught only to Schema subjects. There was a significant main effect for self-reported frequency of dream recall, with frequent recallers ($\bar{x} = 5.1$) demonstrating more dream control than infrequent recallers ($\bar{x} = 4.8$), $F(1, 82) = 6.07, p < .02$. Figure 6.4 shows the distributions of all dreams across DC scale categories for frequent and infrequent recallers. These distributions are significantly different, $\chi^2 (8) = 20.05, p < .01$. As can be seen, the distributions are more normally distributed than DSR scale scores (see Figure 6.2). Infrequent recallers have more dreams categorized as DC 1, 2, 4, and 8. Frequent recallers show more dreams in DC categories 5, 6, 7, and 9.

There was a significant three-way interaction between treatment, gender, and self-reported frequency of recall for Dream Control Scale scores, $F(2, 82) = 4.29, p < .02$. Female frequent recallers and male infrequent recallers in the schema group were most responsive to dream control instruction. Male frequent recallers and female infrequent recallers in the attention control and schema groups did not differ from subjects in conditions with no dream control instruction. However, tests of simple main effects failed to find any mean significantly different from any other.

Analysis of variance of dream control scores using weekly means as a repeated measure showed a significant effect of time on dream control as a main effect, $F(2, 128) = 7.40, p < .001$, that is, dream control means showed an overall linear increase across weeks for all subjects. *T*-tests comparing these means showed that the overall week three mean was significantly greater than the week two mean, $t(77) = 2.27, p < .03$, and also greater than the week 1 mean, $t(82) = 3.70, p < .001$.

The two-way interaction of treatment with the repeated measure (weekly DC means) was also significant, $F(4, 128) = 2.55, p < .04$, at both week 2, $F(2, 79) = 4.08, p < .02$, and 3, $F(2, 79) = 8.14, p < .001$. Schema subjects demonstrated significantly more dream control than either baseline or attention control subjects on both weeks. The biggest increase in dream control was in the schema group during week 2 when dream control instruction took place. However, there was a significant

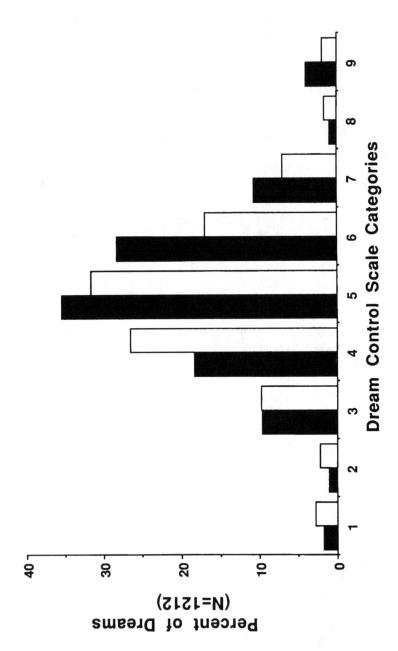

Figure 6.4. Distributions of Dreams (%) Across Dream Control Scale Categories for Frequent (■) and Infrequent Recallers (▢)

three-way interaction of treatment, weeks and self-reported frequency of recall, $F(4, 128) = 3.20$, $p < .02$, see Figure 6.5. In the baseline group, frequent-infrequent differences in dream control did not reach significance until week 3, $F(1, 27) = 7.38$, $p < .01$. In the Attention Control condition, frequent recallers had higher scores than infrequent recallers at week 1, $F(1, 27) = 11.35$, $p < .002$; at week 2 there was no difference, and by week 3 infrequent recallers had significantly greater dream control than frequent recallers, $F(1, 24) = 6.78$, $p < .02$. Significant frequent-infrequent recaller differences were not observed in the Schema group at any time.

When frequency of recall observed in the experiment (median split) was used as the independent measure in the overall factorial ANOVA, there were significant main effects for treatment, $F(2, 82) = 5.70$, $p < .01$, and observed frequency of recall, $F(1, 82) = 5.97$, $p < .02$. No other main effects or interactions were significant. The means for observed higher and lower recallers (5.2 and 4.8, respectively) were very close to those for self-reported frequent and infrequent recallers (5.1 and 4.8, respectively).

Dreaming to Waking Transfer Effects

Rate of Dream Recall: A 3 x 2 x 2 factorial ANOVA (treatments, self-reported recall, and gender) was performed on observed frequencies of dream recall during the experiment. The only significant effect was the main effect for the self-reported trait of frequency of recall, $F(1, 82) = 38.20$, $p < .001$. However, this accounted for only 30.6 percent of the variance in observed dream recall frequency, demonstrating that subjects' habits of recall are variable and are altered by the experiment even in the baseline condition. Observed rates of dream recall were consistent with self-report in frequent recallers (five times a week or more), and greater than expected in infrequent recallers. The average infrequent recaller reported 2.7 dreams per week compared with a preexperimental rate of once a week or less, therefore reaching rates of reporting consistent with average or mid-range recallers (Moffitt et al., 1990). Repeated measures ANOVA using observed recall rates as the dependent measure found significantly greater dream recall during the first enthusiastic week of the experiment for all subjects, but particularly in high recallers, $F(2, 164) = 3.39$, $p < .04$, although infrequent recallers maintain mid-recaller rates and frequent recallers maintain high rates.

Word Count: Groups differed significantly in the length of their reports, $F(1, 82) = 5.05$, $p < .01$. The Student-Neuman- Keuls test of mean

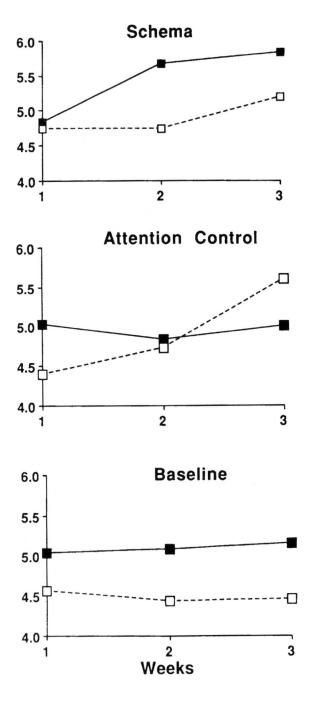

Figure 6.5. Mean Dream Control Scores Across Weeks for Frequent (■) and Infrequent Recallers (□) as a Function of Treatment Group

differences showed that schema ($\bar{x}$ = 139) and attention control ($\bar{x}$ = 132) subjects had longer dream reports than did baseline subjects ($\bar{x}$ = 110). Repeated measures analysis shows a small but significant decline in word counts after the first week for subjects overall, $F(2, 128) = 3.30, p <$ .04. These results replicate those in Purcell et al. (1986). There was no significant effect for self-reported frequency of recall. However, the post-hoc use of observed recall frequency in this analysis did reveal a significant effect for frequency of recall on word count, $F(1, 82) = 5.42, p$ < .02. Average length for observed higher recallers was 138 words and for observed lower recallers, 114 words.

Post-test Dreaming to Waking Transfer Effects: ANOVAs using gender and self-reported frequency of recall as independent variables were conducted within each group, with the addition of lucidity-nonlucidity in the Schema group. Table 6.4 presents the significant effects of these analyses. Effects of frequency of recall were found on four questions: 3, 5, 6, and 9. In the baseline condition, infrequent recallers correctly reported recalling dreams more than usual compared to frequent recallers (question 5). Also in the baseline group, frequent recallers reported greater consequences for action during waking than infrequent recallers (question 6). In the attention control group, frequent recallers more often awoke in "moods" during the experiment than infrequent recallers (question 3). This can be interpreted in part as a negative result of the task demands of this experimental condition. However, frequent recallers in the Attention Control group also reported greater confusion about their waking life as a result of dreaming than infrequent recallers (question 9). Apparently self-reported frequent dream recallers experience some negative effects from the generalized procedure of detailed dream reporting, which calls even greater attention to their dream life. However, those subjects who responded to lucid dream induction in the schema group, which was clearly an effect of treatment, did experience greater dreaming to waking transfer effects than their nonlucid dreaming counterparts in the same condition. This fact indicates that even though the lucidity variable cannot be used in an overall ANOVA for all groups, there were dreaming to waking transfer effects in lucid dreamers as a result of treatment. These effects were found in four of ten items: question 1, a greater effect of recording dreams upon waking life, particularly for male frequent recallers who were also lucid dreamers; question 2, lucid dreamers reported greater awareness of dreams becoming more interesting than prior to the experiment; question 9, lucid dreamers experienced less confusion about a waking issue after waking from a dream about it; question 10, lucid dreamers experienced greater understanding of waking issues as a result of writing out their dream reports. Evidently, lucid dreaming had positive waking effects that were both cognitive and motivational in nature.

Table 6.4
Dreaming Effects Questionnaire (Post test)

1. Recording my dreams has had (no effect . . . a lot of effect) on my waking life.
   Attention Control: gender*(male $\bar{x}$ = 2.73, female $\bar{x}$= 3.67)
   Schema: lucidity by frequent/infrequent by gender* (see Table 6.5)
2. My dreams have started to become more interesting to me (false . . . true).
   Schema: lucidity** (lucid $\bar{x}$ = 5.81, nonlucid $\bar{x}$ = 4.06)
3. During the experiment I noticed I awakened in "moods" more often than usual (false . . . true).
   Attention Control: frequent-infrequent* (frequent $\bar{x}$ = 3.65, infrequent $\bar{x}$ = 2.38)
4. During the course of the experiment I woke up with ideas or solutions to problems, or ideas and solutions appeared in my dreams (never . . . frequently).
5. My frequency of dream recall during the experiment was (less . . . more) than usual.
   Baseline: frequent-infrequent** (frequent $\bar{x}$ = 3.61, infrequent $\bar{x}$ = 5.43)
6. During the experiment I woke up from a dream with an "impression" of something I should do, like an urge to action (never . . . frequently).
   Baseline: frequent-infrequent* (frequent $\bar{x}$ = 3.39, infrequent $\bar{x}$ = 2.29)
7. During the experiment I "rehearsed" some action in a dream that I was later able to execute (never . . . frequently).
8. Sometimes a dream had the effect of helping me see things in my waking life more clearly (never . . . frequently).
9. Sometimes a dream had the effect of confusing me about some aspect of my waking life (never . . . frequently).
   Attention Control: frequent-infrequent* (frequent $\bar{x}$ = 4.35, infrequent $\bar{x}$ = 3.23); gender* (male $\bar{x}$ = 3.27, female $\bar{x}$ = 4.47); frequent-infrequent by gender* (see Table 6.6).
   Schema: lucidity** (lucid $\bar{x}$= 2.50, nonlucid $\bar{x}$ = 4.44).
10. Writing down a dream sometimes helped me see a clue or angle on waking life that I hadn't noticed before (never . . . frequently).
    Schema: lucidity* (lucid $\bar{x}$ = 4.69, nonlucid $\bar{x}$ = 3.31).

Rating Scale:1 2 3 4 5 6 7
** $p < .01$
* $p < .05$

Discussion

The results of the study have essentially replicated and extended the findings of Study 2 in Purcell et al. (1986). Base rates of dream self-reflectiveness, including lucid dreaming and dream control are now established for young adult psychology undergraduates. These processes can be enhanced through waking entrainment of attention and intention. Differences between frequent and infrequent recallers can be understood largely in terms of performance rather than competence differences. Although alterations in self-reflectiveness resulted from the intentional experimental treatments in the schema condition, unexpected increases in dream control across the duration of the experiment were observed to occur spontaneously for infrequent recallers in the attention control placebo condition. Finally, attention to dreaming was shown to have both positive and negative effects on subsequent waking cognition and feeling, depending on the methods used to manipulate waking attention and intention.

Table 6.5

Schema Group: Lucidity by Frequent-Infrequent by Gender Interaction for Question 1.

	Frequent	Infrequent
Lucid:		
Male	5.00	2.00
Female	4.25	3.50
Nonlucid:		
Male	2.83	3.75
Female	5.50	2.25

Table 6.6

Attention Control: Frequent-Infrequent by Gender Interaction for Question 9

	Frequent	Infrequent
Male	4.22	1.83
Female	4.50	4.43

The distributions of dreams in the baseline group across both scales show that self-reflection and intentional action occur naturally and substantially in the dream state, and that the degree to which attention and action systems are operative vary, as they do in waking. Spontaneous and uninfluenced dreaming demonstrates a range of self-reflectiveness from none to fully lucid awareness of state. Spontaneous dreaming also demonstrates a range of intentional functioning from none to control over the generation of some dream events. In the vast majority of spontaneous dreams the dreamer is moderately self-reflective and moderately effective in his or her actions.

The correlation between DSR and DC Scales was significant but low, .32 in the baseline condition. This reflects the fact that the constructs of dream self-reflectiveness and dream control are largely independent. The covariation was eliminated by increasing attention to dreaming in the attention control condition, where there was no correlation between scales ($r = .09$). Conversely, the correlation between DSR and DC scales was increased by increasing the interaction between attentional and intentional systems as was the case in the schema condition where the correlation was significant but moderate ($r = .57$). Self-reflective and intentional behaviors are largely independent functions within the self-regulatory system. These results support the natural occurrence of self-regulatory functions in dream experience. Two of these are the self-reflective and control systems which are largely independent but potentially interdependent. At the highest levels of these capacities, each may be maximized in the presence of the other.

Dream self-reflectiveness and dream control can be reliably measured. The measurement scales appear to adequately approximate the continuous constructs they represent. The Dream Control Scale is particularly satisfactory with regard to its psychometric properties. The dream Self-Reflectiveness Scale, although satisfactory, could be improved by broadening the description of categories 4 and 6. This could be done without distorting the theoretical framework underlying the scale. Several results support the construct validity of lucid dreaming on the DSR dimension. Lucid subjects had higher DSR means than non-lucid dreamers, even when their lucid dreams were excluded. Also, dream phenomenology shows that they clearly used cues to trigger lucidity, cues that emerge in categories 7 and 8. In addition, the mechanism of attention to dream detail that constituted the attention control group's treatment resulted in significantly more category 7 dreams (two levels of awareness) than occurred in the baseline group.

More general empirical support for the scaled theoretical dimension comes from the fact that the scale results generally conform to theoretically derived expectations.

The effects of individual differences in dream recall rates, whether self-reported or empirically determined during the experiment, are generally small, even when significant, and do not interact with treatments. This is especially true for the results concerning self-reflectiveness, where the main impact of individual differences in recall during the experiment was associated with lucid dreams. Individuals with higher rates of recall during the experiment were more likely to have a lucid dream. However, the occurrence of lucidity during the experiment had little or nothing to do with preexperimental self-reported variations in habitual rates of home dream recall. The treatment procedures for the induction of lucid dreams appear to be quite effective, with about 50 percent of the subjects in the schema group reporting at least one lucid dream during the experiment. This can be interpreted as a result of the reorganization of the schemata governing the interrelations between the orientation response and other semantic systems during dreaming. The effects of self-reported variations in the frequency of dream recall are more prominent for dream control than for dream self-reflectiveness, but even here the magnitude of the main effect in most analyses is small. Of much greater theoretical interest is the finding of a significant interaction of treatments, groups and weeks, attributable to an unanticipated increase in dream control across the duration of the experiment by infrequent recallers in the attention control group (see Figure 6.5). This is a spontaneous effect. It was not taught or suggested in the experimental protocol. It reveals that simply paying more attention to dreaming and to detailed dream reporting is sufficient to produce a spontaneous change in this conative vector for these subjects. Why this effect occurred only for infrequent recallers remains unknown. It is probably a motivational effect and it presents an interesting avenue for further research. Nevertheless, these findings, and the others discussed previously, support the claim that individual differences in habitual rates of home dream recall and dream content represent performance rather than competence differences. This point is further illustrated in a comparison of the performance of the baseline groups in this experiment and in the Purcell et al. (1986) experiment. In the present experiment the performance of the baseline group was considerably higher than in the previous experiment with respect to average level of dream self-reflectiveness and average length of dream reports. These differences are probably complex, resulting from the better techniques used in the present experiment to maintain motivation in the baseline group and also to the increased notoriety of and interest in our dream research program by the undergraduate student population since our previous experiment (Purcell et al., 1986). It is also worth noting that these factors operate against finding significant treatment effects in this experiment.

The average score for all questions on the posttest dreaming to waking questionnaire was 3.7, suggesting measurable dreaming to waking transfer effects that could be increased in experiments specifically designed to do so. Effects in the present experiment are due to paying attention to dreaming in various forms. The practice effect is more evident in those who recalled more dreams as a preexperimental trait or who experienced lucidity during the experiment. Three questions, 4, 7, and 8, showed no power to discriminate between groups in the experiment. Question 4 refers to dream problem solving, question 7 to the dream rehearsal of an action that improves the waking performance of an action, and question 8 to seeing things in life more clearly. It may be that these questions need more specific presleep deployment of attention to be effective, as is implied by the clinical, dream-work and anecdotal literature. Overall, the results show that positive and negative cognitive and motivational dreaming to waking transfer effects do occur in all groups, and occur maximally in subjects who responded maximally to the specific conditions of the experiment.

The results regarding gender are minimal. Self-reflectiveness is significantly greater in the dreams of females than males, but the differences are small and may be minimally interesting theoretically. No gender differences were found for dream control. The effects of gender were somewhat more prominent concerning dreaming to waking transfer effects. The experience of lucid dreams during the experiment appeared to differentially enhance the effect of dreams upon waking life for male frequent recallers (see Table 6.5). Conversely, male infrequent recallers in the attention control group experienced less confusion about a waking issue as a result of dreaming than the other subjects in this group. In other words, the effects of gender alone or in interaction were more prominent on dreaming to waking than on waking to dreaming transfer effects.

Summary. (1) First, metacognition and epistemic cognition in both self-reflective and intentional forms is not exclusive to waking. Both occur spontaneously in dreaming and are apparently relatively normally distributed. Lucid awareness of dreaming while dreaming occurs spontaneously in about 1 percent of dreams of university students. Some of these spontaneously lucid dreams are characterized by high-level dream control. Second, individual differences in frequency of dream recall influence levels of self-reflectiveness and control in spontaneous dreaming. The effects of individual differences in self-reflectiveness are attenuated when attention is educated to dream processes. Rather, similar processes of self-regulation occur between and within waking and dreaming. Extant levels of these forms of dream metacognition and epistemic cognition can be increased by increasing attention to the dream process and content during waking. It appears that such dream skills can be learned by the appropriate deployment of waking attention. Third, there is questionnaire evidence that dream experience can directly inform a waking perspective.

Implications. The present demonstration of the range of dream control and dream self-reflectiveness is evidence that ego control is not suspended during dreaming as is commonly thought. The dream ego interacts with the dream environment revealing a breadth of self-regulatory activity. In addition, these abilities may be expanded through both intentional and spontaneous learning. It appears evident that the notion of dream isolation (Rechtschaffen, 1978) has been overextended and that dream processes are responsive to attentional and intentional influences from waking. This has been demonstrated in a short time period for a young population, minimally invested in dreaming, yet relatively open to learning.

The evidence for dreaming to waking transfer effects further weakens the idea of such extremely state specific cognition as is posited by the notion of isolation (Rechtschaffen, 1978) or necessary regression (Koukkou and Lehmann, 1983). Through the mechanisms of attention and intention specifically deployed from waking, dreaming can demonstrate greater metacognitive and epistemic capacity. The state-shift theory of Koukkou and Lehmann (1983) is brilliant in terms of its conceptualization of states that are so similar to one another that they shift via the orienting response in a way that is virtually continuous. This theory is compatible with the present characterizations of self-reflectiveness and intentionality in that increments in both may well consist of orienting responses to information in the dream that would not normally evoke such a response. It is possible to orient to both the occurrence and the recognition of bizarreness within the dream, and the functional state may shift due to this orientation. Similarly, a state shift undoubtedly occurs when the dream is recognized as such and the dreamer orients to this new insight. The research on the electrophysiology of lucid dreaming shows that it usually occurs in the most activated periods of REM sleep and is thus consistent with Koukkou and Lehmann's association of the orienting response at the time of a state shift with increased activation. The inconsistency in the state-shift theory is its psychoanalytically derived reductionism with regard to dream cognition. The present data do not support the idea of all dreams as regressions to developmentally earlier levels of functioning, incapable of self-reflection and intentional action. Rather, they suggest that during most dreaming the connection of the orienting response system to the sensorimitor, affective, semantic and pragmatic systems governing attention and action are inhibited, rather than regressed. As a result, bizarreness, improbabilities, and unexpected transformations go unnoticed and opportunities for choice in action are missed in the dream. Specific waking deployment of attention and intention directed at the process as well as the content of dreaming can differentially alter the form and amount of inhibition of the interrelation of the orientation, affective, semantic and pragmatic systems. The implication for the activation-synthesis hypothesis (Hobson, 1988; McCarley and Hoffman, 1981; Mamelak and Hobson, 1989) is that a greater role in dream generation must be given to cortical feedback and the interaction of top-down and bottom-up processes (Rumelhart, 1980). There are similar implications for Crick and Mitchison's idea that recalled dreams are necessarily maladaptive. Negative consequences during waking appear to result from an intensification of dreaming related to content and detail rather than to process. More technically, in terms of Hinton and Sejnowski's (1986) neural net theory the results of the present study indicate that the routines governing the computation of weighting functions for hidden units are not state specific. Moreover, hidden units must and do model their own activity during sleep, an activity that appears to affect the operation of hidden units during waking as well. Moreover, the results of the present study strongly suggest that schema theory (Rumelhart, 1980) can be extended to include cross-state schema induction (a process defined as "some aspect of the system sensitive to the recurrence of configurations of schemata that do not, at the time they occur, match any existing schemata," p. 54) as a "natural part of a schema-based system" (p. 54).

The experiment demonstrates several aspects of the mechanisms by which information is transferred between waking and dreaming and becomes common to both states. The results are supportive of a feedback loop between states, mediated by attention and intention, by which both states can coevolve (Rossi, 1972, 1986). According to the approach developed in this paper, this coevolution can account for some of the differences among men and women and frequent and infrequent dream recallers in habitual rates of recall. Frequent recallers can be regarded as habitually more "state interdependent" than infrequent recallers. However, in both groups, and especially infrequent recallers, the isolation between states (Rechtschaffen, 1978) can be overridden by mutual access to broadening information bases achieved through attention to dreaming and dream reporting. This mutual causal learning effect increases the cognitive and experiential range of each state by virtue of the increasing overlap and interaction with the other state. Rather than a domain of experience and cognition that is state specific, the sleep-dream system in these individuals can move to relatively greater state interdependence with waking in experience, cognition, and affect. The expression of dream intentionality is enhanced among infrequent recallers by the simple device of more attentive reporting of dream details. The enhancement of dream self-reflectiveness up to and including lucidity is facilitated by explicit tuition, including the priming of some generalized cognitive and procedural schemata during waking (Rumelhart, 1980).

The experimental use of frequent and infrequent recallers was helpful in establishing some validity for the notion of state interdependence. The tendency found in the empirical literature for frequent recallers to be more psychologically differentiated (Goodenough et al., 1974) or more cognitively flexible and creative than low recallers has been extended to their dreaming in some studies (Fitch and Armitage, 1989; Purcell et al., 1986; Sheldrake and Cormack, 1974; Wallin, 1977), and this extension is replicated and extended by the present results. In particular, the sensitivity of dream praxis in infrequent recallers to paying more attention to dream reporting is an undocumented difference between frequent and infrequent recallers. Schema induction procedures, however, attenuated preexperimental individual differences. These results are interpreted as supporting Rossi's (1972, 1986) claim that there are complex dialectical relations between waking and sleeping. This waking-dreaming continuity is the basis for attempting to influence dream processes from the vantage point of waking through the mechanism of educating attention. Posttest findings that frequent recallers report significantly more dreaming to waking transfer effects than infrequent recallers are an additional aspect of the mutual causal system put forward here. Waking attention to dreams and their various aspects feeds back on subsequent dreaming, which in turn feeds back on subsequent waking. The measurement scales used in this experiment show that this feedback is concerned with abstract high level self-regulatory processes such as self-reflectiveness and intentionality. It may well involve other such processes as well. The data reveal a picture of psychological organization that is dynamic, self-regulating and ready for reorganization in some individuals when attention is allotted. These results are in keeping with a control systems approach (Carver and Scheier, 1981), which can aid in the interpretation of gender, treatment, and individual differences in recall. From this perspective, cognizance of oneself as an individual and monitoring one's own behavior are necessary for self-regulation. The same reasoning, that is, that self-attention promotes self-regulation, guides clinical approaches to personality change (e.g., Rossi, 1972, 1986). The present experiment reveals these same processes in dreaming and aspects of their relation to waking processes. From this view, self-regulatory processes that go on in both states are related and subsumed under the larger self-regulatory system, which is the whole individual, not simply the waking individual.

A control systems approach is based on the function of feedback relations. Many such loops are negative; that is, their goal is discrepancy reduction and the return to a desired state. The positive feedback loops inferred by Rossi (1972; 1986) and from the present results deal with discrepancy enhancement. The process by which a discrepancy becomes noticeable (e.g., noticing bizarreness), makes a difference, or constitutes new information is the process of differentiation or, simply, of learning (Rumelhart, 1980). Carver and Shreier (1981) review studies in social psychology that show that increased self-focus facilitates self-regulation of behavior. Similarly, a trained redeployment of attention to their dreams (self-focus) in both frequent and infrequent recallers begins to destabilize this individual difference, as shown in the attention control and schema conditions. Both of these in turn have an impact on the differential effects of dreaming upon waking.

Conclusions

We have shown that dreams provide much opportunity for volition, action, self-expression, and self-reflectiveness, and that the dream ego responds to dream situations the best it can. Not only are attentional and intentional systems variably operative in dreaming, as they are in waking, but the dreamer is an active participant in the dream creation process through an active, spontaneous conscious encounter with his or her phenomenal world in both waking and sleeping. The present results indicate that the inhibitory constraints on this process are implicit in the organization of the dreamer rather than the dreaming. The lifting of these constraints, their reorganization, can be effected through the mechanisms of attention and intention on what is to be reorganized. The constraints on this response are therefore not implicit in dreaming itself, although this view of dreaming has been widely held.

The demonstrations of dream self-regulation made possible by the Dream Self-Reflectiveness and Dream Control Scales would have been difficult previously, in the near absence of adequate instrumentation. The lack of such instrumentation was embedded in a conception of dreaming that did not permit seeing similarities and interrelations between waking and dreaming experience, to the point of calling abilities perceived as exclusively waking ones "anomalous" and "nonordinary" when they occur during dreaming. The reasoning and the results of the present chapter confirm and extend a suggestion we made elsewhere, that some of the functions of dreaming include the creation of knowledge based on experience and experience based on knowledge (Moffitt et al., 1988). The results reported here support this interpretation. Thus, dreaming serves both epistemological and ontological functions. Moreover, the manner of interaction of these functions is dialectical. Dream lucidity increases the waking cognitive consequences of dreaming, whereas intensification of the dream reporting process can increase waking cognitive confusion. In all cases, dreaming has measurable waking cognitive consequences.

Future Directions

It is clear from the preceding that there is a need for a theoretical heuristic that encompasses both sleeping and waking mental activity and their interrelation, transcending the sleep-wake boundary. Similarly, there is a need for theory concerning the source of human consciousness. Dreaming is a phenomenon of consciousness just as consciousness is a phenomenon of dreaming. Thus, the question of consciousness itself must be addressed. These concerns have led us to explore the work of Maturana and Varela (1980; Varela, 1979) and the concept of autopoietic systemic reflection. Briefly, we conceive of the mind-brain as a system that must take care of itself synchronically and diachronically, both waking and sleeping. It must maintain itself, monitor itself, and make decisions about the validity of its own functioning. Further, it must do this without the aid of a homunculus. From this point of view, consciousness is a property of the mind-brain as a self-organizing system. This has led us to develop the idea of systemic reflection as an extension of the notion of self reflection. Systemic reflection includes all processes involved in the mind-brain keeping track of itself for the purpose of successful functioning both organizationally and adaptively. Conscious experience then is one manifestation of the mind-brain keeping track of itself. During waking hours when sensorimotor adaptation is usually primary, systemic reflection directs itself to that task. During sleep, systemic reflection is freed from the constraints of sensorimotor adaptation. Instead, the mind-brain is operating with regard to internally motivated organizational demands. Being awake and mobile places demands on the system for adaptive functioning and orienting to new stimuli in the environment. This is typically the psychological state studied by cognitive and behavioral psychologists. However, adaptive demands on the system may be relaxed, resulting in behavioral inactivity, an inhibition of the normal relations governing the interrelation of the orienting, affective, semantic and pragmatic systems, and a transition to a mode of mental functioning dominated by organizational constraints. The normal manifestation of this is daydreaming during wakefulness and dreaming during sleep. We differ from Piaget, for example, by placing dreaming under the rubric of the functional invariant of organization rather than assimilation in the context of adaptation. Piaget appears to have viewed dreaming as an assimilative mode in the context of adaptive functioning (Piaget, 1962). In this we think he was in error. Just as waking is predominately concerned with adaptation, sleep is predominately concerned with organization. The forms of consciousness during dreaming are manifestations of autopoietic systemic reflection in the mind-brain system during sleep, just as awareness, metacognition and epistemic cognition (Kitchener, 1983; Doniger O'Flaherty, 1984) are manifestations of autopoietic systemic reflection in the mind-brain system during waking. We conclude that the forms of organization and interrelation of systemic reflection during waking and sleeping are autopoietic, entailing functional relations in ontology, epistemology and praxis. Moreover, as in all sufficiently complex symbolic systems, all schemata involved in systemic reflection are "first-class" objects; that is, there is no principled distinction between program and data. Each can be either, as needed. It is on this basis that complex symbolic systems, such as the autopoietic systems governing the interrelation of self-reflectiveness and intentionality between waking and dreaming, become self-modifying. Such systems are deeply recursive both in theory (Springer and Friedman, 1989) and in fact, as the results of the study show. Thus, we disagree with formulations that necessarily regard waking cognition as program and dreaming as data (Crick and Mitchison, 1983, 1986; Foulkes, 1982; Kohlberg, 1969). Our results suggest that the mind-brain systems involved in regulating the interrelation of systemic reflection during waking and dreaming are open to cultural, group and individual entrainment mechanisms, intentional and unintentional, formal and informal, at the levels of habit (the baseline group) and design (the attention control and schema groups) for both the process and content of dreaming and the effects of these upon subsequent waking thought and affect.

References

Adelson, J. (1959). "Creativity and the Dream." *Merrill-Palmer Quarterly* 6: 92–97.

Antrobus, J. (1977). "The Dream as Metaphor: An Information Processing and Learning Model." *Journal of Mental Imagery* 2: 327–338.

Austin, M. (1971). "Dream Recall and the Bias of Intellectual Ability." *Nature* 231: 59–60.

Berkson, D. (1980). "Interviews with Handicapped, Slow Learner and Normal Children About Their Dream Experiences: A Comparative Study." B.A. Thesis, Carleton University.

Blackmore, S. (1982). "Out-of-Body Experiences, Lucid Dreams, and Imagery: Two Surveys." *Journal of the American Society for Psychical Research* 76: 301–317.

———. (1985). "Lucid Dreams and Viewpoints in Imagery: Two Studies." *Lucidity Letter* 4 2: 34–42.

Bone, R. (1968). "Extraversion, Neuroticism and Dream Recall." *Psychological Reports* 23: 922.

——— and Corlett, F. (1968). "Brief Report: Frequency of Dream Recall, Creativity, and a Control for Anxiety." *Psychological Reports* 22: 1355–1356.

————, Nelson, A., and McAllister, D. (1970). "Dream Recall and Re-spression-Sensitization." *Psychological Reports* 27: 766.

Bosinelli, M., Cicogna, P., and Molinari, S. (1974). "The Tonic-Phasic Model and the Feeling of Self-Participation in Different Stages of Sleep." *Italian Journal of Psychology* 1: 35–65.

Brenneis, C. (1970). "Male and Female Ego-Modalities in Manifest Dream Content." *Journal of Abnormal Psychology* 76: 434–442.

Brown, A. (1936). "Dreams in Which the Dreamer Knows He is Asleep." *Journal of Abnormal and Social Psychology* 31: 59–66.

Brown, F. (1970). *Principles of Educational and Psychological Testing*. Hinsdale, Ill.: Dryden Press.

Brylowski, A. (1990). "Nightmares in Crisis: Clinical Applications of Lucid Dreaming Techniques." *Psychiatric Journal of the University of Ottawa* 15 2: 79–84.

Campbell, D., and Stanley, J. (1963). "Experimental and Quasi-Experimental Designs for Research on Teaching." In N. Gage (Ed.), *Handbook of Research on Teaching*, pp. 171–246. Chicago: Rand and McNally.

Cartwright, R. (1974). "The Influence of a Conscious Wish on Dreams: A Methodological Study of Dream Meaning and Function." *Journal of Abnormal Psychology* 83, no 4: 387–393.

————. (1977). *Night-Life: Explorations in Dreaming*. Engelwood Cliffs, N.J. Prentice-Hall.

————. (1980). "The Contribution of Research on Memory and Dreaming to a 24-Hour Model of Cognitive Behavior." In W. Fishbein (Ed.), *Sleep, Dreams and Memory*, pp. 239–247. New York: Spectrum Book Publications.

Carver, C., and Scheier, M. (1981). *Attention and Self-Regulation: A Control-Theory Approach to Human Behavior*. New York: Springer-Verlag.

Cernovsky, Z. (1984). "Dream Recall and Attitude Toward Dreams." *Perceptual and Motor Skills* 58: 911–914.

Chang, G. (1963). *Teachings of Tibetan Yoga*. Secaucus, N.J.: Citadel Press.

Child, L. (1985). "Psychology and Anomalous Observations: The Question of ESP in Dreams." *American Psychologist* 40 no. 1: 1219–1230.

Clerc, O. (1983). "Natural Induction of Lucid Dreams." *Lucidity Letter* 2, no. 1: 4–5.

Cohen, D. (1974). "Toward a Theory of Dream Recall." *Psychological Bulletin* 81: 135–154.

———. (1979). *Sleep and Dreaming.* Toronto: Pergamon Press.

Corriere, R., and Hart, J. (1977). *The Dream Makers.* New York: Funk and Wagnalls.

Corriere, R., Karle, W., Woldenberg, L., and Hart, J. (1980). *Dreaming and Waking.* Culver City, Cal.: Peace Press.

Cory, T., Ormistan, D., Simmel, E., and Dainoff, M. (1975). "Predicting the Frequency of Dream Recall." *Journal of Abnormal Psychology* 84: 261–266.

Crick, F. (1988). "Neural Networks and REM Sleep." *Bioscience Reports* no. 8, 6: 531–535.

——— and Mitchison, G. (1983). "The Function of Dream Sleep." *Nature* 304, no. 14: 111–114.

——— and Mitchison, G. (1986). "REM Sleep and Neural Nets." In R. Haskell (Ed.), *The Journal of Mind and Behavior* (Special Issue:) 7, nos. 2 and 3: 229–249; 99–119.

Dane, J. (1984). "A Comparison of Waking Instructions and Post-Hypnotic Suggestion for Lucid Dream Induction." Ph.D. dissertation, Georgia State University.

Delaney, G. (1979). *Living Your Dreams.* San Francisco: Harper and Row.

Domhoff, W. (1985). *The Mystique of Dreams: A Search for Utopia Through Senoi Dream Theory.* Berkeley: University of California Press.

——— and Gerson, A. (1967). "Replication and Critique of Three Studies on Personality Correlates of Dream Recall." *Journal of Consulting Psychology* 31, no. 4: 431.

Domino, G. (1976). "Primary Process Thinking in Dream Reports as Related to Creative Achievement." *Journal of Consulting and Clinical Psychology* 44: 929–932.

Doniger O'Flaherty, W. (1984). *Dreams, Illusions and Other Realities.* Chicago: University of Chicago Press.

Doyle, M. (1984). "Enhancing Dream Pleasure with Senoi Strategy." *Journal of Clinical Psychology* 40, no. 2: 467–474.

Faraday, A. (1973). *Dream Power.* New York: Berkeley Medallion Books.

———. (1974). *The Dream Game.* New York: Harper and Row.

Feldman, D. (1980). *Beyond Universals in Cognitive Development.* Norwood, N.J.: Ablex Publishing Corp.

Fenwick, P., Schatzman, M., Worsley, A., and Adams, J. (1984). "Lucid Dreaming: Correspondence Between Dreamed and Actual Events in One Subject During REM Sleep." *Biological Psychology* 18: 243–252.

Fishbein, W. (Ed.). (1980). *Sleep, Dreams and Memory.* New York: SP Medical and Scientific Books.

Fiss, H. (1983). "Toward a Clinically Relevant Experimental Psychology of Dreaming." *Hillside Journal of Clinical Psychiatry* 5, no. 2: 147–159.

Fitch, T., and Armitage, R. (1989). "Variations in Cognitive Style Among High and Low Frequency Dream Recallers." *Personality and Individual Differences* 10, no. 8: 869–875.

Foulkes, D. (1962). "Dream Reports from Different Stages of Sleep." *Journal of Abnormal Psychology* 65: 14–25.

———. (1978). *The Grammar of Dreams.* New York: Basic Books.

———. (1979). "Children's Dreams." In B. B. Wolman (Ed.), *Handbook of Dreams*, pp. 131–167. Toronto: Van Nostrand Reinhold.

———. (1982). "REM-Dream Perspectives on the Development of Affect and Cognition." *Psychiatric Journal of the University of Ottawa* 7, no. 2: 48–55.

———. (1985). *Dreaming: A Cognitive Psychological Analysis.* Hillsdale, N.J.: Laurence Erlbaum Associates.

——— and Pope, R. (1973). "Primary Visual Experience and Secondary Cognitive Elaboration in Stage REM: A Modest Confirmation and Extension." *Perceptual and Motor Skills* 37: 107–118.

———— and Schmidt, M. (1983). "Temporal Sequence and Unit Composition in Dream Reports from Different Stages of Sleep." *Sleep* 6, no. 3: 265–280.

Freud, S. (1953). "The Interpretation of Dreams." In J. Strachey (Ed. and Trans.), *The Standard Edition of the Complete Psychological Works of Sigmund Freud*, vols. 4 and 5. London: Hogarth Press. [Original work published 1900.]

Gackenbach, J. (1978). *A Personality and Cognitive Style Analysis of Lucid Dreaming*. Ph.D. dissertation, Virginia Commonwealth University.

———— and Bosveld, J. (1989). *Control Your Dreams*. New York: Harper and Row.

Gardner, H. (1985). *The Mind's New Science: A History of the Cognitive Revolution*. New York: Basic Books.

Garfield, P. (1974). *Creative Dreaming*. New York: Ballantine Books.

————. (1976). "Psychological Concommitants of the Lucid Dream State." *Sleep Research* 5: 183.

————. (1979). *Pathway to Ecstasy*. New York: Holt, Rhinehart and Winston.

Gillespie, G. (1986). "Ordinary Dreams, Lucid Dreams and Mystical Experiences." *Lucidity Letter* 5, no. 1: 27–30.

Globus, G. (1987). *Dream Life, Wake Life*. Albany: State University of New York Press.

Goodenough, D., Witkin, H., Lewis, H., Koulack, D., and Cohen, H. (1974). "Repression, Interference and Field Dependence as Factors in Dream Forgetting." *Journal of Abnormal Psychology* 83: 32–44.

Green, C. (1968). *Lucid Dreams*. Oxford: Institute of Psychophysical Research.

————. (1990). "Waking Dreams and Other Metachoric Experiences." *Psychiatric Journal of the University of Ottawa*, 15, no. 2: 123–128.

Greenleaf, E. (1973). "Senoi Dream Groups." *Psychotherapy: Theory Research and Practice* 10, no. 3: 218–222.

Griffin, M., and Foulkes, D. (1977). "Deliberate Presleep Control of Dream Content: An Experimental Study." *Perceptual and Motor Skills* 45: 660–662.

Hall, C. (1966). *The Meaning of Dreams.* New York: McGraw-Hill.

——— and Van de Castle, R. (1966). *The Content Analysis of Dreams.* New York: Appleton-Century-Crofts.

Halliday, G. (1982). "Direct Alteration of a Traumatic Nightmare." *Perceptual and Motor Skills* 54: 413–414.

Hart, J. (1971). "Dreams in the Classroom." *Experiment and Innovation: New Directions in Education at the University of California* 4: 51–66.

Hartmann, E. (1973). *The Functions of Sleep.* New Haven, Conn., and London: Yale University Press.

Hearne, K. (1978). *Lucid Dreams: An Electrophysiological and Psychological Study.* Ph.D. dissertation, University of Liverpool.

———. (1982). "Effects of Performing Certain Set Tasks in the Lucid-Dream State." *Perceptual and Motor Skills* 54: 259–262.

Hendricks, M., and Cartwright, R. (1978). "Experiencing Level in Dreams: An Individual Difference Variable." *Psychotherapy: Theory, Research and Practice* 15, no. 3: 292–298.

Hilgard, E. (1977). *Divided Consciousness: Multiple Controls in Human Thought and Action.* New York: John Wiley and Sons.

Hinton, G., and Sejnowski, T. (1986). "Learning and Relearning in Boltzmann Machines." In D. Rumelhart and J. McClelland (Eds.), *Parallel Distributed Processing: Explorations in the Microstructures of Cognition. Vol. 1. Foundations*, pp. 282–317. Cambridge, Mass. MIT Press.

Hobson, A. (1988). *The Dreaming Brain.* New York: Basic Books.

Hopfield, J. (1982). "Neural Networks and Physical Systems with Emergent Collective Computational Abilities." *Proceedings of the National Academy of Sciences* 79: 2554–2558.

Hunt, H. (1982). "Forms of Dreaming." *Perceptual and Motor Skills*, Monograph Supplement I-V54.

———. (1984). "A Cognitive Psychology of Mystical and Altered State Experience." *Perceptual and Motor Skills*, Monograph Supplement I-V58.

———. (1989). *The Multiplicity of Dreams*. New Haven, Conn.: Yale University Press.

Jones, R. (1980). *The Dream Poet*. Cambridge, Mass.: Schenkman Publishing Co.

———. (1987). "Dream and Metaphor." *Psychiatric Journal of the University of Ottawa* 12, no. 2: 87–92.

Jung, C. (1974). *Dreams*. Princeton, N.J.: Princeton University Press.

Karle, W., Corriere, R., Hart, J., and Woldenberg, L., (1980). "The Functional Analysis of Dreams: A New Theory of Dreaming." *Journal of Clinical Psychology* 36: 5–78.

Kitchener, K., (1983). "Cognition, Metacognition and Epistemic Cognition." *Human Development* 26: 222–232.

Kohlberg, L. (1969). "Stage and Sequence: The Cognitive-Developmental Approach to Socialization." In D. Goslin (Ed.), *Handbook of Socialization Theory and Research*, pp. 346–480. Chicago: Rand McNally.

Koukkou, M., and Lehmann, D. (1983). "Dreaming: The Functional State-Shift Hypothesis." *British Journal of Psychiatry* 142: 221–231.

Kramer, M. (1982). "The Psychology of the Dream: Art or Science?" *Psychiatric Journal of the University of Ottawa* 7, no. 2: 87–100.

——— and Roth, T. (1980). "The Relationship of Dream Content to Night-Morning Mood Change." *Sleep,* Fourth European Congress on Sleep Research, pp. 621–624. Basel: S. Karger.

Kuhn, T. (1970). *The Structure of Scientific Revolution*, 2d ed. Chicago: University of Chicago Press.

Kuiken, D. (1981). "Self-Consciousness as a Component and Correlate of Focusing Ability." In E. Klinger (Ed.) *Imagery Vol. 2. Concepts, Results, and Applications*, pp. 231–238. New York: Plenum Press.

———. (1986). "Dreams and Self-Knowledge." In J. Gackenbach (Ed.), *Sleep and Dreams: A Sourcebook*, pp. 225–250. New York: Garland Publications.

LaBerge, S. (1980). *Lucid Dreaming: An Exploratory Study of Consciousness During Sleep*. Ph.D. dissertation, Stanford University.

———. (1985). *Lucid Dreaming*. Boston: J. P. Tarcher.

——— and Gackenbach, J. (1986). "Lucid Dreaming." In B. Wolman and M. Ullman (Eds.), *Handbook of States of Consciousness*, pp. 159–198. New York: Van Nostrand Reinhold.

———, Nagel, L., Dement, W., and Zarcone, V. (1981). "Lucid Dreaming Verified by Volitional Communication During REM Sleep." *Perceptual and Motor Skills* 52: 727–732.

Laughlin, C., McManus, J., Rubenstein, R., and Shearer, J. (1986). "The Ritual Transformation of Experience." *Studies in Symbolic Interaction* 7 (Part A): 107–136.

Lewis, H., Goodenough, D., Shapiro, A., and Slesar, I. (1966). "Individual Differences in Dream Recall." *Journal of Abnormal Psychology* 71: 52–59.

Mahrer, A. (1971). "Personal Life Change Through Systematic Use of Dreams." *Psychotherapy: Theory Research and Practice* 8, no. 4: 328–332.

Malamud, J. (1979). *The Development of a Training Method for the Cultivation of "lucid" Awareness in Fantasy, Dreams and Waking Life*. Ph.D. dissertation, New York University.

Malcolm, N. (1959). *Dreaming*. London: Routledge and Kegan Paul.

Mamelak, A., and Hobson, A. (1989). "Dream Bizarreness as the Cognitive Correlate of Altered Neuronal Behavior in REM Sleep." *Journal of Cognitive Neuroscience* 1: 201–222.

Maturana, H., and Varela, F. J. (1980). *Autopiesis and Cognition*. Dordrecht: D. Reidel.

McCarley, R., and Hoffman, E. (1981). "REM Sleep Dreams and the Activation-Synthesis Hypothesis." *American Journal of Psychiatry* 138, no. 7: 904–912.

McClelland, J., and Rumelhart, D. (Eds.). (1986). *Parallel Distributed Processing: Explorations in the Microstructure of Cognition*. Vol. 2. *Psychological and Biological Models*. Cambridge, Mass.: MIT Press.

Moffitt, A., Hoffmann, R., and Galloway, S. (1990). "Dream Recall: Imagination, Illusion and Tough-Mindedness." *Psychiatric Journal of the University of Ottawa* 15, no. 2: 66–72.

Moffitt, A., Hoffmann, R., Mullington, J., Purcell, R., Pigeau, R., and Wells, R. (1988). "Dream Psychology: Operating in the Dark." In J. Gackenbach and S. LaBerge (Eds.), *Conscious Mind, Sleeping Brain: Perspectives on Lucid Dreaming*, pp. 429–439. New York: Plenum Press.

Moffitt, A., Hoffmann, R., Wells, R., Armitage, R., Pigeau, R., and Shearer, J. (1982). "Individual Differences Among Pre- and Post-Awakening EEG Correlates of Dream Reports Following Arousals from Different Stages of Sleep." *The Psychiatric Journal of the University of Ottawa* 7, no. 2: 111–125.

Molinari, S., and Foulkes, D. (1969). "Tonic and Phasic Events During Sleep: Psychological Correlates and Implications." *Perceptual and Motor Skills* 29: 343–368.

Morel, C., Hoffmann, R., and Moffitt, A. (1990). "EEG Correlates of Dream Recall and Nonrecall from Stage 2 Awakenings Throughout the Night." *Sleep Research* 19: 137.

Murayama, M. (1963). "The Second Cybernetics: Deviation Amplifying Mutual Causal Processes." *American Scientist* 51, 2: 164–179.

Oglivie, R., Hunt, H., Kushniruk, A., and Newman, J. (1983). "Lucid Dreams and the Arousal Continuum." Lucidity Letter 2, no. 2: 1–2.

Oglivie, R., Hunt, H., Tyson, P., Lunescue, M., and Jeakins, D. (1982). "Lucid Dreaming and Alpha Activity: A Preliminary Report." *Perceptual and Motor Skills* 55: 795–808.

O'Nell, C. (1976). *Dreams, Culture and the Individual.* San Francisco: Chandler and Sharp.

Orr, W., Dozier, J., Green, L., and Cromwell, R. (1968). "Self-Induced Waking: Changes in Dreams and Sleep Patterns." *Comprehensive Psychiatry* 9: 499–506.

Piaget, J. (1962). *Play, Dreams and Imitation in Childhood.* New York: W. W. Norton.

Purcell, S. (1987). "The Education of Attention to Dreaming in High and Low Frequency Dream Recallers: The Effects of Dream Self-Reflectiveness, Lucidity and Control." Ph.D. dissertation, Carleton University.

———, Mullington, J., Moffitt, A., Hoffmann, R., and Pigeau, R. (1986). "Dream Self-Reflectiveness as a Learned Cognitive Skill." *Sleep* 9, no. 3: 423–437.

Rechtschaffen, A. (1978). "The Single-Mindedness and Isolation of Dreams." *Sleep* 1, no. 1: 97–109.

———. (1983). "General Discussion: Dream Psychophysiology." In M. Chase and E. Whitman (Eds.), *Sleep Disorders: Basic and Clinical Research*, pp. 401–413. New York: Spectrum Publications.

Reed, H. (1978). "Meditation and Lucid Dreaming." *Sundance Community Dream Journal* 2, no. 2: 237–238.

Rossi, E. (1972). *Dreams and the Growth of Personality*. New York: Pergamon Press.

———. (1986). *Dreams and the Growth of Personality*, 2d ed. New York: Bruner Mazel.

Rumelhart, D. (1980). "Schemata: The Building Blocks of Cognition." In B. Bruce and W. Brewer (Eds.), *Theoretical Issues in Reading Comprehension*, pp. 33–58. Hillsdale: N.J.: Lawrence Erlbaum Associates.

——— and McClelland, J. (Eds.). (1986). *Parallel Distributed Processing: Explorations in the Microstructure of Cognition*. Volume 1. *Foundations*. Cambridge, Mass.: MIT Press.

Schonbar, R. (1965). "Differential Dream Recall Frequency as a Component of 'Life Style'." *Journal of Consulting Psychology* 29, no. 5: 468–474.

Schutz, A. (1962) "On Multiple Realities." In M. Natanson (Ed.), *The Problem of Social Reality: Collected papers of Alfred Schutz*, vol. 1, pp. 207–259. The Hague: Martinus Nijhoff.

Sheldrake, P., and Cormack, M. (1974). "Cyclicity in Dreaming: Patterns in Dream Preoccupations for Men and Women." *International Journal of Chronobiology* 2: 217–221.

Sirois-Berliss, M., and DeKoninck, J. (1982). "Menstrual Stress and Dreams: Adaptation or Interference?" *Psychiatric Journal of the University of Ottawa* 7, no. 2: 77–86.

Snyder, F. (1970). "The Phenomenology of Dreaming." In L. Madow and L. Snow (Eds.), *The Psychodynamic Implications of the Physiological Studies on Dreams*, pp. 124–151. Springfield, Ill.: Charles C Thomas.

Snyder, T., and Gackenbach, J. (1988). "Individual Differences Associated with Lucid Dreaming." In J. Gackenbach and S. LaBerge (Eds.), *Conscious Mind, Sleeping Brain*, pp. 221–259. New York: Plenum Press.

Springer, G., and Friedman, D. (1989). *Scheme and the Art of Programming.* Cambridge, Mass.: MIT Press.

Stoyva, J., and Kamiya, A. (1968). "Electrophysiological Studies of Dreaming as the Prototype of a New Strategy in the Study of Consciousness." *Psychological Review* 75: 192–205.

Tart, C. (1965). "Toward Experimental Control of Dreaming: A Review of the Literature." *Psychological Bulletin* 64: 81–95.

———. (1975). *States of Consciousness.* New York: E. P. Dutton.

———. (1979). "From Spontaneous Event to Lucidity: A Review of Attempts to Consciously Control Nocturnal Dreaming." In B. Wolman (Ed.), *Handbook of Dreams*, pp. 226–268. New York: Van Nostrand Rhinehold.

Tedlock, B. (1987). *Dreaming: Anthropological and Psychological Interpretations.* Cambridge: Cambridge University Press.

Tholey, P. (1983). "Techniques for Inducing and Manipulating Lucid Dreams." *Perceptual and Motor Skills* 57: 79–90.

Tyson, P., Oglivie, R., and Hunt, H. (1984). "Lucid, Prelucid and Nonlucid Dreams Related to the Amount of EEG Alpha Activity During REM Sleep." *Psychophysiology* 21, no. 4: 442–451.

Ullman, M. (1979). "The Experiential Dream Group." In B. Wolman (Ed.), *Handbook of Dreams: Research, Theory and Applications*, pp. 406–423. New York: Van Nostrand Reinhold.

———, Krippner, S., and Vaughan, A. (1973). *Dream Telepathy.* New York: Macmillan

———, Krippner, S., and Vaughn, A. (1989). *Dream Telepathy*, 2d ed. Jefferson, N.C.: McFarland and Co.

Varela, F. (1979). *Principles of Biological Autonomy*, p. 13. New York: North Holland.

Van Eeden, F. (1972). "A Study of Dreams." In C. Tart (Ed.), *Altered States of Consciousness*, pp. 146–160. New York: Anchor Books. [Originally published in 1913.]

Wallin, J. (1977). "Intentional Dreaming." Ph.D. dissertation, The Wright Institute.

Wasserman, I., and Ballif, B. (1984–85). "Perceived Interactions Between the Dream and the Waking Divisions of Consciousness." *Imagination, Cognition and Personality* 4, no. 1: 3–13.

Weiss, L. (1986). *Dream Analysis in Psychotherapy*. New York: Pergamon Press.

Weinstein, L., Schwartz, D., and Ellman, S. (1988). "The Development of Scales to Measure the Experience of Self-Participation in Sleep." *Sleep* 11, no. 5: 437–447.

Winget, C., and Kramer, M. (1979). *Dimensions of Dreams*. Gainesville: University Presses of Florida.

Witkin, H. A., and Goodenough, D. R. (1981). *Cognitive Styles: Essence and Origins*. New York: International Universities Press, Inc.

Witkin, H., and Lewis, H. (Eds.). (1967). *Experimental Studies of Dreaming*. New York: Random House.

7

V. S. Rotenberg ━━━━━━━━━━━━━━━━━━━━━

REM Sleep and Dreams as Mechanisms of the Recovery of Search Activity

The present chapter develops and deepens the basic propositions of the conception of search activity (Arshavsky and Rotenberg, 1976; Rotenberg and Arshavsky, 1979a; 1979b; 1984; Rotenberg, 1982; 1984), integrating the character of the subject's behavior in ordinary and stressful situations, the body's resistance to disease and stress, and the functional designation of REM sleep.

No complex system can be explained by the specific features of its elements. On the contrary, the system determines the function of the elements. This proposition is particularly appropriate when applied to living systems. It follows from this proposition that the departure point in the study of highly organized biological systems, animals and humans, should be their integral behavior and the psychological activity that regulates it. The character of integral behavior determines the state and function of individual physiological systems. This is particularly true of the function of REM sleep and dreams, because any conception purporting to explain their functional relevance should be psychophysical in its nature (i.e., consider both the physiological and the psychological processes occurring in REM sleep) and should apply equally to humans and higher mammals. Such a conception can be constructed only with due account of the specific functional features of behavior, because the general strategy and basic tendencies of behavior determines the correlation between the various functional systems of the organism designed to ensure this behavior.

An adequate behavior classification should meet the following requirements: (1) the types identified on its basis should be relatively easy and reliably determined in simple experiments; (2) it should not be excessively detailed. Although detailed classification systems create greater accuracy and subtlety of behavior description, a more important factor gets lost, specifically the correlation with the physiological and biochemical changes in the organism. Biological systems are less differentiated than psychological systems. Therefore not every psychological state can be correlated with a strictly definite and unique physiological pattern. On the contrary, similar biological changes may correspond to different behavioral forms and psychological states.

The author and his colleague have proposed a new behavioral classification satisfying these requirements on the basis of their own systematic research using both animals and humans (Arshavsky and Rotenberg, 1976, 1978; Rotenberg, 1984). This classification is based on the principle of biological relevance of search activity, which influences the success of the subject's activity in general and the body's resistance to stress, diseases, and various other harmful factors.

By search activity is understood activity designed to change the situation or the subject's attitude to it in the absence of a definite forecast of the results of such activity (i.e., in the case of pragmatic indefiniteness), but with constant monitoring of the results at all stages of activity.

This definition makes it clear that certain behavioral categories cannot be classed with search behavior. This primarily applies to all forms of stereotyped behavior having a quite definite forecast of results. For example, panicky behavior at first glance may seem to imitate search behavior but differ from it by the disturbance of the feedback between the activity and its regulation. Really, during a panic the results of the activity are not considered at any stage and cannot be used for the correction of behavior. No line of activity can be traced to its conclusion and panicky behavior easily becomes imitative, approaching stereotyped behavior. Finally, the antipode of search behavior is the state of renunciation of search, which in animals may assume the form of freezing or imaginary death.

Search behaviors in animals are categorized as all types of active defense behavior (both aggression and active avoidance) as well as the active self-stimulation of the brain zones of positive reinforcement. Such self-stimulation is a complex multicomponent behavior, which includes appetence, aversion, and search activity proper (Grastyan, 1976). It has been shown that self-stimulation is obtainable from the same brain structures whose forcible stimulation creates orientative-exploratory behavior; the duration of self-stimulation correlates with the manifestness of the general exploratory reaction of the animal being stimulated (Schiff, Rusak, and Block, 1971); self-stimulation is in competitive relations with stereotyped behavior (Wauquier, 1980), and teaching self-stimulation to dog pups prompts them to develop search behavior (Kassil and Vatayeva, 1981). Naturally, search behavior also includes orientative-exploratory behavior, which particularly often manifests itself in an open-field test: the more manifest the exploratory behavior, the more frequently the animal comes out into the open-field center.

In many mammals (cats, rats, etc.) the electrophysiological correlate of search behavior is synchronous high-amplitude theta-rhythm of the hippocampus. It regularly accompanies search behavior (Simonov, 1981). None of the existing hypotheses pertaining to the functional relevance of this rhythm contradicts the following assumption: search activity plays a great role in teaching, in directed attention, in behavior planning, in the organization of arbitrary motor acts, and in the selective memorizing of information (Rotenberg, 1984). Nevertheless, the identification of purely behavioral criteria of search presents certain difficulties. At first glance, an animal's search activity can be reflected in its motor activity. Indeed, search frequently manifests itself in exploratory behavior. But the notion of "search" is broader than the notion of "exploratory behavior," and identification of search behavior with motor behavior may lead to serious errors.

First, search can proceed without any manifestations in the motor sphere if the movements pose a threat or, according to the conditions of the experiment, involve a punishment. The temporary inhibition of overt behavior at the encounter with a new, surprising, or emotionally significant situation is a very well-studied phenomenon (Gray, 1982; Morrison, 1982). During such inhibition intense reappraisal of the situation proceeds; that is, search behavior. Passive avoidance works. For example, in the Porsolt Test intense search activity characterizes the rats that find the shallowest place in the pool sooner than others, where they can maintain immobility resting on their tails. Conversely, less adapted rats inclined to panicky behavior spend a much longer time performing exhausting movements around the pool (Hawkins et al., 1980). This unproductive chaotic activity appears to be inversely correlated with search activity. Moreover, exclusive orientation to motor activity without consideration of the entire context of the situation and the research conditions frequently leads to the erroneous identification of such salutary passive avoidance with the reaction of surrender (renunciation of search) of the freezing type.

Tracing the boundaries of search activity in humans is a still more complex problem, where psychological processes unaccompanied by overt behavior play a still greater role. Among humans, search manifests itself in the planning, fantasizing, and rethinking of the situation. In addition, the hallucinatory emotional experiences and delirium of psychic patients are classed with perversely oriented but very intensive search activity (Rotenberg, 1982). Therefore, in humans, just as in animals, it is simpler to indicate states and forms of behavior that undoubtedly do not contain the search activity component. Into this category falls stereotyped behavior with an exact forecast of results. However, it is difficult to determine such behavior operationally and separate it from the entire behavior context. The state of renunciation of search can be identified with greater definiteness. Above all, this includes various forms of depression and the reaction of surrender, which Engel and Shmale (1967) have called *give-up–giving-up*. Within the same category lies unproductive, neurotic anxiety similar to the freezing reaction (anticipation of a catastrophe) in animals. In keeping with psychodynamic conceptions, the author assumes that neurotic anxiety is a consequence of the repression of an unacceptable motive from consciousness. The repression can be regarded as a purely human variant of renunciation of search of the modes of realization of the unacceptable motive in behavior and modes of integration of it with other, realized behavioral orientations. The difference between productive emotional tension (the normal anxiety of a healthy individual in a state of stress), instrumental in mobilizing all psychological and physical resources to overcome obstacles, and unproductive emotional tension (in particular, neurotic anxiety) that hampers successful activity is determined by the presence or absence of search activity in the structure of emotional tension.

Search and renunciation of search influence the body's resistance to stress and other harmful factors in an opposite manner. The author's research (Rotenberg and Arshavsky, 1979a; 1979b), as well as publications of many other authors (Simonov, 1981; Seligman, 1975; Anisman, Ritch, and Sklar, 1981), has shown that search behavior raises the body's resistance and stress resistance and blocks the development of stress diseases and artificially induced pathology such as experimental epilepsy, anaphylactic shock, hypertension, myocardial infarction, cardiac rhythm disturbances, Parkinsonlike neuroleptic syndrome, the implantation of malignant tumors, addiction to alcohol, and so on. Renunciation of search furthers the development of all these forms of pathology, reduces the body's biological resistance and may cause death. Appropriate experiments on animals are extensively described in the author's previous publications (Rotenberg and Arshavsky, 1979b; Rotenberg 1984).

Therefore, this chapter will outline similar facts obtained in research on humans.

More and more new facts show that the emergence and development of psychosomatic diseases, including ischemic heart disease, myocardial infarction, malignant tumors, and duodenal ulcers very frequently follow overt or covert depression (Glass and Carver, 1980; M. Weiss, 1985; Justice, 1986; Appels, 1979). Both constructive aggressiveness analogous to creative activity and destructive aggressiveness directed outward reduce the risk of psychosomatic diseases, whereas the deficit of aggressiveness corresponding to the notion of "renunciation of search" increases this risk (Ammon, Ammon, and Griepenstroh, 1982). This stands in good agreement with data about the competitive relations between depression and aggressive behavior (Pittman and Pittman, 1979; Harrel and Hayness, 1978) and with experimental data showing that aggressive behavior during stress prevents the development of somatic disturbances (J. Weiss, 1977). Undesirable and uncontrolled changes in life further the development of somatic diseases (Mullen and Sulls, 1982). The absence of control over the situation is one of the key factors in the development of learned helplessness (Seligman, 1975); that is, in renunciation of search. Individuals who withstand emotional stress very well and do not fall ill afterward exhibit more constructive relations with the world and clear aims. They are fighters having a pronounced motivation of achievement (Kobasa, 1979). At the same time, the impossibility of coping with a stressful situation leads to the inhibition of active behavior (i.e., to a renunciation of search) accompanied by the activation of the hypothalamus–pituitary body–adrenal cortex system. Such a combination of pronounced stress with the blockade of active search behavior soon leads to the development of peptic ulcers (Kukleta, 1979). This is the watershed between stress and distress (Selye, 1974). The latter stems from a loss of control over the situation, a drop in resistance, and relative predominance of the activity of the pituitary body–adrenal cortex system (Henry and Stephens, 1977). In the author's opinion, the transition of stress as a reaction of increased mobilization geared to overcome difficulties of life into distress leading to illness and death reflects a qualitative change of the character of behavior and a replacement of search activity with a state of renunciation of search (Rotenberg, 1984).

The body's resistance declines in the case of renunciation of search in stressful situations unacceptable to the subject and also in the case of any weakening of search behavior. Individuals with high indices on the anhedonia scale (apathy and lack of initiative) die a natural death earlier than individuals with low indices on this scale (Watson and Kugala, 1978). On the other hand, even prolonged and very intense stress unaccompanied by a reaction of surrender not only does not reduce the body's resistance, but may even raise it. For example during the Second World War participants in military operations or individuals who did hard work in the rear showed a drop in the rate of disease compared to the prewar period (Natelson, 1983). Furthermore, concentration camp inmates who lived to see their release (in the main, people who retained the ability to resist, even if only inwardly) exhibited the disappearance of the symptoms of their precamp psychosomatic diseases.

Thus, the old dilemma, whether stress is useful or harmful is solved depending on the degree of manifestness of search activity during stress. But if search activity is of such great biological relevance and renunciation of search leads to illness and death, why has the latter regressive behavior survived in the course of evolution and what makes it emerge?

All higher mammals including humans, at the early stages of ontogenesis inevitably experience helplessness determined by the relatively slow development of the central nervous system and all mechanisms (nervous, hormonal, and vegetative) that ensure subsequent search behavior. Naturally, during the early stages of ontogenesis such a state cannot be called renunciation of search. It is normal and inevitable and the only accessible form of a defense reaction for an immature organism. The organism thus acquires an early experience of passive reaction, an experience of helplessness. Both this experience and the ways to overcome it are of colossal relevance to the individual's entire subsequent life. In the case of a correct attitude of the primary group, above all the mother, this early experience of helplessness can be successfully and painlessly overcome. The child, gradually feeling constant support will pass on to increasingly active behavior. The child's first steps toward the development of search activity must proceed under the constant protection of the mother who helps the child overcome fear of new situations, fear that consolidates the experience of passive reaction. All injuries in early childhood, from the physical separation from the mother to insufficient emotional contact with her and the feeling of insufficient protectedness due to strained relations between the parents can consolidate the experience of primary helplessness and fear of the newness of situations and of the need for search behavior. The imprinting mechanism may lead to the development of a state of renunciation of

search in an adult, especially if the emotional problems encountered in some way resemble conflicts of early childhood. Thus readiness for the development of neuroses and psychosomatic illnesses is formed. It is exactly from these general biological positions, the relations between early helplessness and the formation of search activity, that the author proposes considering the Freudian theory of the role of early psychotraumatizing situations in the entire subsequent development of the individual. Regressive behavior in the cases of neuroses and psychosomatic illnessses according to Freud is indeed a regression towards a biologically earlier state of passiveness and helplessness that assumes the form of renunciation of search. However, as the physiological mechanisms of search behavior mature, the child should gain increasing independence and be induced to practice independently overcoming obstacles. The very fact of such overcoming, of the broadening of possibilities, exercises a powerful reinforcing effect, developing a search requirement in the child. The existence of an independent search requirement is proved by experiments in which animals are placed in artificial "ideal" conditions in which all their primary requirements (in food, partners, and play) are satisfied and yet they make efforts to escape from this "paradise" into an unknown and potentially dangerous expanse in spite of their fear of it.

If an independent requirement for search activity is not shaped, in time throughout later life search behavior may emerge only as a forced reaction to complex situations, will be colored by negative emotions, and may fairly easily yield to the state of renunciation of search. At this early stage two opposite conditions may equally suppress the development of the search requirement, constant (invariable) negative reinforcement and invariable positive reinforcement. In the former case any activity, above all search activity, is depreciated in the subject's eyes and perceived as senseless and leading to punishment. The child soon learns that search is dangerous. In the latter case, when all desires are satisfied immediately and without sufficient effort, the search activity requirement is not formed because it is superfluous. If the search requirement is not sufficiently developed then subsequently at maturity even moderately stressful situations and minor obstacles to the achievement of an aim may cause a reaction of surrender.

However, a search requirement does not guarantee the stable preservation of search activity either. Even when this requirement is pronounced, renunciation may occur if failures come in close succession and acquire greater relevance than the aims the child strives to achieve

and are greater than the positive reinforcement from search itself. On the other hand, the more pronounced the search requirement and the higher the search activity, the more difficult it is to suppress and evolve learned helplessness because search itself, irrespective of its final results, can come to represent an independent value and bring pleasure, as in the case of creation. It can be assumed that in the animals and humans in which learned helplessness can never be evolved (according to Seligman, this category accounts for 20 percent among dogs) early experience has ensured a high level of search activity.

Renunciation of search is also possible when the status quo fully satisfies the subject. The basic aims are achieved without search behavior on the basis of developed behavioral stereotypes and search even poses the threat of a loss of what is already achieved. In these conditions the subject is motivated to make no search. If such a motivation emerges in an individual with a high original search requirement, he or she will develop an inner conflict. The search requirement will be frustrated, and if no modes of realization are found for it, the mounting inner tension may result in psychological and somatic disturbances. Perhaps this is the mechanism of the diseases of achievement that emerge on the crest of success after the individual abruptly breaks off the search efforts.

When the search requirement is not great, the cessation of search activity is not perceived subjectively as a stress creator. Furthermore, such a cessation may be accompanied by a feeling of relief or relaxation. However, the body's resistance to various harmful factors then decreases and the organism becomes more vulnerable. In addition, easy success, taken as natural, decreases the productivity of efforts (Tiggeman, 1981).

The author's psychological research, carried out jointly with I. S. Korostelyova has confirmed these theoretical conceptions, supplementing them with concrete data. It was established that in the case of systematic negative reinforcement a serious factor of the risk of prompt surrender is the predominance in the individual of the fixation on the obstacle as a reaction to frustration (Rosenzweig, 1935) combined with a low aggregate motivation of achievement (Heckhausen, 1977). In healthy subjects prolonged negative reinforcement changes the type of reaction to frustration in the direction of an increase of fixation on the obstacles. In psychosomatic patients characterized by gastric and duodenal ulcers and malignant tumors this type of reaction, even outside emotional stress, is much more pronounced than in healthy individuals. The

dominance in the achievement motivation structure of the motive of avoidance provokes greater emotional tension in the course of negative reinforcement. This may also play a serious role in bringing about a renunciation of search. The similar level of the two motives (the motive of the achievement of success and the motive of the avoidance of failure) create prerequisites for an inner motivational conflict and, combined with a low aggregate motivation, determine tendencies toward early attempts to stop activity. The decline of the ability to forecast results and the insufficiently expressed striving to use various means of achieving an aim, coupled with an inner motivational conflict, create conditions for a renunciation of search. Any impossibility to satisfy a powerful need eventually entails a renunciation of search and illness (see McClelland, 1982).

At the same time, the greatest resistance to the development of a reaction of surrender during the stress due to negative reinforcement is found in subjects with a predominant desire to overcome obstacles. Combined with a high aggregate motivation for achievement, such a desire to overcome obstacles can be assessed as a manifestation of a high degree of expression of search activity, especially if the motive of the achievement of success clearly dominates the motive of the avoidance of failure.

The question of the physiological mechanisms of search behavior has no final solution so far. Undoubtedly, an appreciable role in the brain system regulating these behavioral forms is played by the hypothalamus (Rotenberg and Arshavsky, 1979b) and the hippocampus (Simonov, 1981). Apparently, the frontal brain lobe is of essential importance. The biochemical mechanisms of search behavior are also studied insufficiently but there are reasons to believe that the brain's catecholamine system is closely connected with search behavior. Learned helplessness accompanied by somatic disturbances emerges when the brain catecholamine level drops (Seligman, 1975). An artificial reduction of catecholamine levels by tetrabenazine speeds behavioral depression whereas the prevention of depletion by MAO inhibitors raises stress resistance, restoring the animal's ability for an active reaction to stress (Katz, Roth and Carrol, 1981). The neuroleptic blockade of the postsynaptic receptors of the catecholamine system also weakens search behavior (Rotenberg, 1988a; Wauquier, 1980). In animals that cannot control the stressful situation the brain norepinephrine level drops particularly low and they show the greatest distress (Lehnert et al., 1984; Kohno et al., 1983). Substances blocking brain epinephrine metabolism impede the teaching of complex avoidance to an animal (Archer, Jonsson, and Ross, 1985). Finally, the locus coeruleus plays a major role in the organization of various forms of search behavior (Paul and Van Dongen, 1981).

On the basis of all the preceding facts the following hypothesis has been advanced (Rotenberg, 1984). Search activity can begin in the presence of a certain critical level of the brain catecholamines (in particular, norepinephrine and dopamine) that are utilized in the course of search. Search activity itself, once it begins, stimulates the synthesis of the brain catecholamines and ensures their necessary or even excessive amount. In the case of acute stress it is exactly the rise in the brain norepinephrine content that is connected with search activity (Stone, 1975; Stone and Platt, 1982).

Thus the more pronounced the search activity, the sooner the expenditure of the catecholamines necessary to maintain the search behavior is compensated. The functional task of such a system with positive feedback (the more intense is the search, the more intense the expenditure and synthesis of the catecholamines and the more intense the search) is to support search activity. But if this system is to start working at the very outset, the brain catecholamine level must be above a critical level. If it drops below that level, search behavior becomes impossible.

In a state of renunciation of search this system does not function. Furthermore, in this state that manifests itself in unproductive emotional tension, the catecholamine expenditure climbs possibly due to the drop in its reuptake (as presumably happens in the case of a chronic stress). Thus, a vicious circle forms: renunciation of search, a drop in the brain catecholamine level followed by a deepening of the renunciation of search.

This vicious circle is formed whenever there is a drop in search activity, whatever the reason. This makes it interesting to discuss the ideas of Zuckerman (1984), who assumes that the optimal level of behavioral activation and adaptation corresponds to a moderate activation of the brain catecholamine system. A low level of this system's activity corresponds to primary depression, secondary anxiety, and the inhibition of active behavior.

An excessively high level of activity of the same system corresponds to the anxiety-panic behavior and secondary neurotic depression. Because it is difficult to imagine a depression combined with a high level of activity of the brain catecholamine system, the present author proposes the following modification of this scheme. The activity of the brain catecholamine system becomes "excessive" when, and only when, for some reason the subject fails to maintain search behavior, yielding to panicky (stereotyped) behavior. This happens in particular when there is a threat of frustration of vital requirements and fear of the consequences of failure disintegrates all behavior. However, panicky behavior is not search behavior, as shown previously. Consequently, it does not restore the brain catecholamine level. The expenditure of catecholamines exceeds their synthesis, and eventually there comes a pronounced drop in their levels and a secondary depression develops. The same is characteristic of neurotic anxiety that, just as with panic, is dominated by agitated behavior. In terms of the author's conception, a deficit of search behavior is common to panic, neurotic anxiety, and depression. The difference is that panic and anxiety reflect the process of constant decline of the brain catecholamine level, whereas depression is the result of this decline. Consequently, in the case of any form of renunciation of search, if it is not overcome and does not give way to search behavior by the activation of compensatory mechanisms or a change in life circumstances, eventually depression develops. This proposition is confirmed by clinical observations. The present hypothesis is also supported by the fact that the state of panic is arrested by tranquilizers of the benzodiazepine series to a lesser extent than by tricyclic antidepressants, which block the reuptake of norepinephrine (Shekhan, Ballenger, and Jacobson, 1980). The foregoing makes it clear that the most characteristic aspect of search activity is the biological relevance of the very process of search, whatever its pragmatic results. Search is necessary for the preservation of good health, irrespective of the degree of satisfaction with the situation and the presence or absence of frustration and formal symptoms of stress. Search activity is not a means, but an end. It performs a protective function, even if the search object is unattainable.

Herein lies the basic difference between the conception of search activity and the conception of coping behavior (Coyne and Lazarus, 1980). Herein, too, lies the difference between the conception of search activity and the conception of Engel and Shmale (1967), who focused attention on one pole of behavior; the give-up–giving-up complex. Another difference is the inclusion in search behavior of a wider scope of phenomena than is usually understood by coping behavior, in particular, spontaneous creative activity and orientative-exploratory behavior. It is also of basic importance that, according to this conception, search activity is not only a mechanism of ensuring adaptation, but also a mechanism of the development of the individual, a mechanism of one's self-realization and consequently, an important factor behind the progress of the population as a whole. The elimination of individuals inclined toward renunciation of search maintains search behavior in the population, without which its entire development will stop.

But if search behavior really plays such a vital role in adaptation and development, there must be a fundamental mechanism permitting compensation for the biologically, psychologically, and socially harmful state of renunciation of search and ensuring the restoration of search activity. Such a mechanism is REM sleep and the accompanying dreams (Rotenberg, 1984). Arguments supporting this assertion follow.

First, experiments on animals have shown that the behavioral forms that include a search component (active-defense behavior and self-stimulation) are accompanied by a reduction of REM sleep without its subsequent rebound; that is, there is a drop in the REM sleep requirement (Putkonen and Putkonen, 1971; Cohen et al., 1975). Conversely, the state of renunciation of search, caused by the stimulation of the ventromedial nuclei of the hypothalamus almost doubles the REM sleep requirement and the percentage of this sleep phase in rats (Rotenberg and Arshavsky, 1979a, 1979b). Rats that display low activity in a stressful situation requiring active behavior show a higher percentage of REM sleep and prefer alcohol to glucose. The latter fact furnishes an additional proof of the inclination toward the renunciation of search. The taking of alcohol increases behavioral activity and shortens REM sleep in these animals (Viglinskaya and Burov, 1987). The process of adaptation to a stressful situation gradually shortens REM sleep (Sinton and Jouvet, 1983), which enables these authors to regard the lengthening of REM sleep at the encounter with a threatening situation as part of the coping strategy.

In top-class athletes REM sleep grows longer after considerable athletic failures that may cause a reaction of surrender (Rotenberg and Arshavsky, 1979a). On the postexamination night REM sleep lasts longer only in students who show signs of unproductive emotional tension. Specifically, the vegetative and electromyographic indices of emotional tension remain high after the examination and intellectual problems are solved hastily and with mistakes. After a sleep with an extensive REM phase the signs of such tension disappear (Rotenberg and Arshavsky, 1979a).

The subjects in whom REM sleep lengthens in the course of intensive learning of a foreign language did not display mounting stress (De Koninck et al., 1975). REM sleep deprivation exercises a particularly negative effect on the solution of creative problems (Lewin and Glaubmann, 1975).

Second, the REM sleep requirement, determined by the latency to REM sleep and by an increase of the REM sleep period in the first cycles, is increased in the cases of depression (Reynolds and Kupfer, 1988) and neurotic anxiety (Greenberg, Pearlman, and Campel, 1972). The REM sleep period is longer in long sleepers (Hartmann, 1973). Long sleepers are characterized by a higher sensitivity level, an inclination toward subdepressive reactions and a rise in the MMPI clinical scales compared to short sleepers (Wagner and Mooney, 1975). High sensitivity to anxiety sources and a disposition to depressive reactions is also characteristic of narcoleptic patients who show a constantly high REM sleep requirement (Beutler et al., 1981).

At the same time, highly reactive individuals with a pronounced type A pattern show a shorter total sleep duration (Hicks et al., 1980), the latter exhibiting the closest correlation with the REM sleep duration.

REM sleep, just like total sleep duration, abruptly shortens in a state of high creative activity as well as in pathological states with high but unproductive search activity such as mania and acute psychosis with psychoproductive symptomatics (Mendelson, Gillin and Wyatt, 1977). The author's research carried out jointly with I. S. Korostelyova and V. V. Kulikovsky also confirms these regularities. The percentage of REM sleep in subjects working in strained conditions of high responsibility negatively correlates with the magnitude of pure motivation of achievement (by Heckhausen, i.e., with the difference between the motive of the achievement of success and the motive of the avoidance of failure). The closer the indices of these motives, the greater the REM sleep percentage. REM sleep percentage also directly correlates with the degree of expression of trait anxiety and the motive of the avoidance of failure, with the presentiment of failure in activity and with the need to avoid failure. It has been shown earlier that the conflict of motives and the relative predominance of the motivation of the avoidance of failure predispose toward a reaction of surrender in the case of prolonged negative reinforcement. Consequently, psychophysiological research confirms that in the case of a combination of factors capable of bringing about a state of renunciation of search there is a compensatory rise in the REM sleep requirement. The ratio of the REM sleep duration in the first two cycles to the delta-sleep duration can be regarded as a quantitative indicator of the degree of expression of renunciation of search. In the case of depression and neurotic anxiety this indicator rises and in the case of productive emotional tension it drops (Rotenberg, 1980; Rotenberg and Arshavsky, 1979a).

Third, the hippocampal theta-rhythm, typical of search behavior in waking, is found during REM sleep. Correlations between the degree of expression of the theta-rhythm in waking and in sleep fully confirm the author's hypothesis: the more the theta-rhythm is found in waking, the less it is expressed in REM sleep. Furthermore, if in the course of REM sleep deprivation it becomes possible to induce active-defense or exploratory behavior characterized by the hippocampal theta-rhythm, the subsequent compensatory REM sleep "rebound" may not set in at all; that is, the REM sleep requirement declines (Oniani and Lortkipanidze, 1985). In the absence of the hippocampal theta-rhythm in the course of REM sleep deprivation there is a great REM sleep "rebound" in the restorative sleep. This suggests that the role of REM sleep in the compensation for the state of renunciation of search is largely determined by the intensity of search activity during dreams.

In agreement with this conception is the fact that during the early stages of ontogenesis of newborn babies, in the absence of prerequisites for overt search behavior the greatest proportion of sleep is active sleep whose many indicators resemble those of the REM sleep of adults. Research shows that the monoamine reuptake blockers sharply suppress active sleep in early ontogenesis and these animals, when adult show longer REM sleep than controls as well as a higher amplitude of the hippocampal theta-rhythm in REM sleep (Mirmiran et al., 1981). These animals display signs of higher emotionality (fear) in waking, faster learning of passive avoidance, and weaker sexual and exploratory behavior. It can be assumed that the suppression of activated sleep in early ontogenesis for a long period reinforces the position of helplessness, natural at this stage, which manifests itself in the behavior of an adult. The REM sleep increase reflects the insufficiently successful tendency to overcome this position.

Fourth, one of the strongest arguments in favor of this hypothesis is the results of the investigation of animal behavior during REM sleep without muscular atonia, the result of a local impairment of the locus coeruleus (Jouvet and Delorme, 1965; Morrison 1982). Meticulous analysis has shown that the most common component of this behavior, orientative, search, attacking, or agitated is search activity as understood by the author. Simultaneously, exploratory open-field behavior is activated in waking. From these facts Morrison draws the conclusion that the impairment of the locus coeruleus disturbs the brain system that in a normal state inhibits locomotor behavior in an emotionally significant situation. In the author's view, this phenomenon can be more accurately described as the inhibition of the overt locomotor manifestation of search activity. Thus, these experiments furnish direct proof of pronounced search activity in REM sleep. Also, it is possible that the increase of the locomotor component of search behavior in waking after destruction of the locus coeruleus is at least partly connected with partial REM sleep deprivation because animals that "participated" in their own dreams wake up during REM sleep more often than the controls. Similarly, motor agitation after REM sleep deprivation is a very well-known fact.

Fifth, the psychological analysis of the processes taking place in human dreams is also consistent with the hypothesis. Currently the best developed and argued conception of the functional relevance of dreams has been proposed by Greenberg (1987). According to this conception, dreams integrate incoming information with previous experience in such a way as to help the subject with the current situation. After successful dreams the subject's position in relation to the complex situation in waking grows stronger, and after unsuccessful dreams it weakens. In Greenberg's opinion, there is a direct connection between the content of the dreams and the emotional problem that is brought out by psychoanalysis. However, experience shows that this connection is not always so clear. In many cases it can be only a question of analogies. Even in the example cited by Greenberg (1987) this connection is conventional and based on image transformations: the rollback of the car in which the subject climbs a hill in his dreams is, after all, only a conventional analogue of fear of regressive relations of dependence. In their earlier publications Greenberg and Pearlman (1979) expressed an idea that appears to be broader: in a dream a pressing emotional problem can be substituted for by another, connected with it not so much semantically as by emotional relevance. This substituting problem, unlike the actual one can be solved. However, in that case the operating basis of dreams is not the successful result of the solution of the problem but the very process of solution itself. For what is the sense of solving a conventional problem in dreams if this solution cannot be directly carried over to the actual problem in waking? In the author's terminology, the process of search has its own relevance. Then the concrete problem and its conceptual aspect are inessential: the process of search can be stimulated by problems bearing no relation to reality. All that is important is that the search should not lead to a deadlock and that there should be no renunciation of search in the dreams themselves. In this sense the observations of Greenberg and Pearlman (1979) are of extraordinary importance. They have pointed out that in individuals with disturbed psychological adaptation their dreams show a regularly manifesting reaction of surrender before insuperable difficulties and that there is a certain connection between these reactions of surrender in sleep and in waking. In the author's opinion, this connection consists of the fact that renunciation of search for a solution to a problem situation in dreams not only does not compensate for the state of renunciation of search in waking, but even deepens it. For example, individuals who successfully cope with emotional problems display more pronounced positive motives in the concluding dream compared to those who in such cases exhibit a reaction of depression (Cartwright et al., 1984).

The research of the author (Rotenberg, 1980, 1988b, 1988c) as well as of Cohen (1977) shows that in ordinary conditions individuals having high sensitivity and neuroticism the entire functional REM sleep-dreams system operates with higher tension, showing a higher REM sleep requirement and more saturated and emotionally significant dreams than individuals having low neuroticism. In cases of additional emotional load or after REM sleep deprivation in individuals with a low sensitivity level, the activity of this system rises by way of compensation whereas individuals with high sensitivity frequently exhibit a disruption of adaptation, and the activity of the entire system decreases (reduction of dream recall, awakening after REM sleep, and its shrinkage following more unpleasant dreams than before). The author assumes that it is the result of the extension of the state of renunciation of search to the dreaming process as well.

What presumably are the biochemical aspects of the compensatory, restorative effect of REM sleep on search activity? If search activity is to begin in REM sleep, the level of the brain catecholamines, primarily norepinephrine, must exceed a certain critical value as in waking. In natural conditions, when neurotoxic substances are not used and thus do not destroy the catecholaminergic neurons, the drop in the level of norepinephrine and other catecholamines to a critical level and below is due mainly to a renunciation of search. This means that the latter state begins before the brain catecholamines reach the critical level. For REM sleep and dreams this level is presumably lower than for waking. Indirectly, this assumption is confirmed by the fact that a lower level of cerebral activation in general is sufficient for the effective functioning of image, right-hemispheric thinking than for logical-sign thinking. Dreams are dominated by image thinking (Rotenberg, 1985a; 1985b). Gaillard (1985) confirms that the realization of REM sleep necessitates a lower activity of the brain noradrenergic system than the realization of waking. Consequently, when in a state of renunciation of search waking changes into sleep, the brain catecholamine level is already too low for the restoration of search behavior in waking (with the preservation of the conditions that have brought about the renunciation of search), but it is still high enough for search to begin in dreams. Furthermore, the transition to sleep points to withdrawal from the situation that caused the reaction of surrender.

This means that there is a temporary removal of the factors that deepen this state and the reserves for search activity are not yet exhausted. Conditions are created for search in REM sleep to perform its compensatory function and for the system with a positive feedback, described earlier, to go into action. Most significant, a compensation of the search activity deficit not only takes place during REM sleep, but also the restoration of the possibilities for this activity during subsequent waking, which is even more important.

With due account of all these circumstances, the plunge into the inner world of dreams in principle may create such optimal conditions for search activity that a mechanism limiting this activity becomes necessary. Otherwise the dreams may, "on the principle of self-repayment," last indefinitely long, hampering the transition to NREM sleep and waking. Gaillard (1985) describes one of such limiting mechanisms—stimulation of alpha-two adrenoreceptors that decrease the ejection of norepinephrine and easily suppress REM sleep. However, waking is suppressed only in the case of much higher doses of stimulators whereas the blockade of alpha-two adrenoreceptors either leaves the REM sleep unaffected or lengthens it much less than waking. REM sleep is much more sensitive than waking to the stimulation of alpha-two adrenoreceptors, and the regulatory mechanism with the participation of these receptors limits the lengthening of REM sleep.

The proposed hypothesis concerning the functional role of REM sleep and dreaming helps explain the following contradiction. It is known that unavoidable aversive stimulation with multiple repetitions during the twenty-four hour period soon leads to a reaction of surrender, causing learned helplessness. In addition, this correlates with the drop in brain catecholamine levels (Swenson and Vogel, 1983; Kohno et. al., 1983; Lehnert et. al., 1984). However, if the same hour-long stress regularly recurs for many days, that is, the stress acquires a chronic character but is limited in time, fairly soon both behavioral and somatic adaptation occur and the brain catecholamine system activity goes back to the original level (Stone and Platt, 1982). Possibly this is due to the fact that in the intervals between the stress stimulation the animal sleeps and the REM sleep performs its compensatory function. The alternative explanation is that in the case of chronic stress the system maintaining the brain catecholamine level reshapes in such a way that the drop of this level immediately activates the feedback system, which stimulates catecholamine synthesis. But if this were really so, after a while the stress impact would immediately have to intensify the norepinephrine ejection. In the meantime, the opposite takes place: norepinephrine ejection increases in the conditions of peace, in the intervals between the stress impacts, whereas during the action of stress itself, however many times it recurs the catecholamine ejection decreases (Stone and Platt, 1982). In terms of the author's hypothesis this is explained as follows: the irremovable aversive stress provokes a reaction of surrender and a drop in the brain catecholamine system activity, and REM sleep in the intervals restores this activity.

Thus, REM sleep requirement rises in the case of renunciation of search in waking and a decline of the brain catecholamine system activity. If the drop in the brain catecholamine level then does not reach a critical point REM sleep grows longer and the search in dreams intensifies. If the brain catecholamine level falls below a critical level due to long and strong aversive impacts, including those preventing the onset of sleep or due to pharmacological interventions the very activation of the compensatory search in REM sleep becomes impossible. The author sees in this the reason for a nonlinear relationship between the REM sleep duration and the dose of preparations that change the brain catecholamine level: a moderate decrease of this level activates the mechanisms starting search activity in REM sleep and lengthening the REM sleep; a rise of this level corresponding to high search activity lowers the REM sleep requirement and leads to its reduction even without the subsequent rebound, and the excessive drop in the brain catecholamine level inhibits search activity in REM sleep and can also cause its reduction. This nonlinear relationship corresponds exactly to the nonlinear relationship between the degree of manifestness of depression and REM sleep: when the leading MMPI scale depression rises from 65 to 75 T points REM sleep grows longer (compared to the magnitude of this scale of up to 65 T points). When the scale score grows further REM becomes reduced (Rotenberg, 1988c). But even when REM duration does not change, REM sleep in fact loses its functional designation and undergoes a qualitative change. The physiological and biochemical mechanisms ensuring the emergence of REM sleep do not fully coincide with the mechanisms ensuring search activity in REM sleep. In dreams, as in waking, the feeling of helplessness and unproductive anxiety begins to dominate, the individual's active position in dreams is absent, the number of dreams recalled decreases, the dynamics of vegetative indices changes (the rise in the pulse frequency in REM sleep and the reduction of the GSR are less pronounced), the heart contraction frequency correlates with the negative emotional experiences in them rather than with the degree of the individual's participation in the dreams, and so forth (Rotenberg, 1988b). Similar qualitative changes in REM sleep and dreams in the cases of depression have been established by Berger, Reimann, and Lauer (1988) and by Escalate (1986). All these changes are signs of the weakening of search activity in REM sleep. This sleep may then become not simply useless, but even harmful: during REM sleep in which the renunciation of search continues the brain catecholamine reserves become further exhausted instead of refilling. This changes REM sleep from a mechanism of compensation into an important mechanism of pathogenesis (Rotenberg, 1980, 1988b, 1988c). Apparently, a serious role in this functional disturbance is played by the weakening of image thinking (Rotenberg, 1985a, 1985b). Perhaps this is the reason for the positive effect of the deprivation of REM sleep (and of sleep in general) in the case of some forms of depression and Parkinsonism (Vogel, 1979; Wehr and Sack, 1988). Such deprivation breaks the vicious circle when the state of renunciation of search, having developed in waking, deepens still more in REM sleep.

The problem of the functional adequacy of the REM sleep-dreams system is among the basic problems in the search activity conception. The ideas about the role of functional defectiveness of this system in the mechanisms of the development of neuroses, depressions, and psychosomatic disturbances, first advanced by the author (Rotenberg and Biniaurisvili, 1973), have been gaining increasing confirmation in recent research. For instance, Berger, Reimann, and Lauer (1988) have shown that in healthy individuals acute and brief emotional stress does not change the sleep structure (duration of the REM sleep and the latency of the first REM sleep episode) if there is a change in the character of dreams in the first REM sleep episodes. These become more alarming and aggressive and are characterized by the dreamer's more active participation in his or her own dreams compared to the research outside stress. However, in the last REM sleep episode the mood restores, which apparently shows the compensatory-adaptive role of the REM sleep processes. Yet qualitative changes in REM sleep alone may be found to be not enough. In subjects who react to stress by unproductive anxiety after stress the duration of the REM sleep increases, above all, in its first two cycles (Rotenberg and Arshavsky, 1979a; Rotenberg and Alexeyev, 1981). If the lengthening of the REM sleep is not enough to compensate for its qualitative inadequacy, there is a growing threat of psychosomatic or psychological disturbance. This should draw attention to the fact that in patients with cardiac pathology who are administered intensive therapy the increase of the phasic oculomotor activity in the REM sleep takes place before an increase in the delta-sleep duration (Broughton and Baron, 1973); that is, the restoration of the functional adequacy of the REM sleep is found to be a major adaptation factor. The positive curative effect in the cases of depression is yielded not by the deprivation of REM sleep as such, but by the deprivation of functionally inadequate REM sleep. This formulation of the question makes it clear that the direct comparison of the results of REM sleep deprivation in the cases of depression with the effect of REM sleep deprivation in animals is not justified. The well-known proposition that REM sleep deprivation in animals activates their behavior needs serious refinement. First, such activation is not observed in all forms of deprivation. If the deprivation follows a method other than that of Jouvet (i.e., is not administered on a water-surrounded platform) but in comfortable conditions by the direct stimulation of the reticular formation of the truncus cerebri (Rotenberg, Kovalzon, and Tsibulsky, 1986) or if active-defense and orientative behavior is provoked at the deprivation (Oniani and Lortkipanidze, 1985), there is neither a pronounced behavioral change nor distress symptoms. If the deprivation follows the Jouvet method the activating effect on behavior is observed only at the relatively early deprivation stages when the animal was removed from the platform and placed for some time in a substantially less stressful open-field situation or in the conditions of self-stimulation. After longer deprivation periods animals display a drop in their activity and physical resistance. They may even die. Mollenhour, Voorhees, and Davis (1977) show that the number of aggressive behavioral reactions increases only for ninety-six hours of the deprivation period and then declines. These authors have assumed that prolonged REM sleep deprivation leads to the exhaustion of the brain catecholamines, as imipramine, which raises the activity of the cate-cholamine system, improves the learning of active avoidance in some animals even after 120 hours of deprivation.

This point of view fully coincides with the author's theoretical ideas. Indeed, the conditions of REM sleep deprivation according to Jouvet should provoke the reaction of renunciation of search: the frustra-tion of the need for activity, above all search activity when this method is used, combines with the irremovable aversive impacts connected with the fall into the water at the onset of every REM sleep episode. Compen-sation for this state in REM sleep is impossible due to the REM sleep deprivation. Only during relatively early deprivation stages when the animals are temporarily taken out of this stressful situation to an open field with more favorable conditions does the rebound of frustrated activity, its compensatory increase, which manifests itself in behavioral agitation, appear. The author assumes that the recent series of experi-ments of Rechtschaffen et al., (1983) can also be explained exactly in these terms.

Compared to the classical REM sleep deprivation procedure according to Jouvet, Rechtschaffen's procedure at first glance permits equating the control and experimental animals by the deprivation condi-tions and avoiding excessive stress for both groups. The control and the test animals are forced to make efforts to avoid getting into the water an equal number of times a day. But the test animals do so whenever they fall asleep or enter into the REM sleep phase, whereas in the control rats such plunges are not connected with sleep and they have a chance to make up for lost sleep while the experimental animals are awake. Thus, the fundamental difference between the groups is confined to the fact that the experimental group is deprived of all sleep or of certain stages, and this eventually leads to the death of the animals. There is a high direct correlation between the duration of survival and the degree of intactness of REM sleep. Before they died the test animals showed pro-nounced distress symptoms and a high energy expenditure. The same lethal consequences follow from total sleep deprivation, from selective full REM sleep deprivation, and from a similar deprivation of high-amplitude NREM sleep (Everson et al., 1986).

This may give the impression that only sleep deprivation is respon-sible for all physiological changes and the death of the test animals. However, in the author's opinion, this is not quite so. The author assumes that the deprivation conditions according to Rechtschaffen and according to Jouvet have much more in common than it seems at first glance. Indeed, the test animals plunge into the water whenever they need sleep or its certain stages. Thus, the actual requirement for sleep or for certain stages of sleep is frustrated. In the course of such frustration the animal learns the inexorability of punishment. Naturally, each time it can eventually escape the water, but it cannot prevent the very fact of frustration used as punishment. What can be easily coped with in waking is more agonizing when sleep is greatly needed. A control animal does not develop an experience of the inexorability of punishment at every attempt to satisfy its sleep requirement, whereas an experimental animal forms exactly such an experience, eventually leading to learned helplessness. In such a case REM sleep as the compensatory mechanism related to search behavior is suppressed. In the case of selective deprivation of high-amplitude NREM sleep a rivalry is created between the requirement for NREM sleep due to the deprivation itself and the great REM sleep requirement due to the conditions of deprivation (the development of learned helplessness). Such a rivalry shortens the REM sleep in these animals compared to the control group. This makes interesting Rechtschaffen's observation that, even among the control animals in the gravest functional state was the rat that showed the shortest REM sleep. Thus, in the final analysis, the lethal effect of the deprivation of sleep and its individual stages is due to a combination of conditions that provoke the state of renunciation of search and simultaneously impede the use of the REM sleep compensatory mechanism. This conclusion is indirectly supported by the results of the study of postdeprivation restorative sleep. To the authors' own surprise, both after the selective REM sleep deprivation and after the total deprivation of all sleep, the animals showed, above all, a compensatory "rebound" of only the REM sleep. Only the rats administered the selective deprivation of the high-amplitude NREM phase in the restorative sleep exhibited NREM rebound, but in these cases, too, the NREM sleep rebound appears together with an almost equally intensive REM sleep rebound (Everson et al., 1987).

In the author's view, the outlined ideas concerning the function of REM sleep and dreams can help solve many debatable problems of sleep psychophysiology. Among such problems, in particular, is the role of sleep in memory and learning processes.

It has been shown that REM sleep grows longer at certain stages of the solution of emotionally significant complex problems, which the animal or human subject is originally unprepared to handle, called *unprepared learning* (McGrath and Cohen, 1978). REM sleep deprivation carried out directly after such learning greatly impedes it. The author proposes the following interpretation of these facts: a complex problem that the subject is not ready to solve (Seligman, 1970) may cause a renunciation of search with much greater probability than a simple one, especially at the early stages of the solution when failures prevail over successes. If the state of renunciation of search is not overcome by REM sleep, this state itself will make it impossible to find the right solution or keep it in memory. Therefore, the lengthening of the REM sleep directly before the critical point in the learning, after which the animal fully develops the habit, is not surprising. However, in some cases the lengthening of REM sleep may be found to be not enough to compensate for the state of renunciation of search, especially if the REM sleep is functionally inadequate. In these cases it may increase more in the animals that are the least successful in forming the new habit. On the other hand, not all animals exhibit a reaction of renunciation of search encountering complex problems, and some, on the contrary, may display a reaction of surrender even facing simple problems. Hence, the basic possibility of polymorphism and ambiguity of sleep changes in these conditions.

Short-time sleep deprivation by the Jouvet method, as said earlier, leads to the frustration of search behavior and its rebound after the deprivation is removed. The high level of motor activity and the high excitability of the central nervous system in such cases may not simply further the learning of simple active avoidance, but even may interfere with passive avoidance. This may determine divergences between research findings. REM sleep deprivation following the learning of complex forms of behavior disturbs those compensatory mechanisms of self-regulation that help overcome the state of renunciation of search. This state remains and upsets the processes of information retention. For example, it is known that depression and unproductive anxiety negatively interfere with learning.

Finally, another paradoxical fact is the absence of REM sleep in such a highly developed animal as the dolphin (Mukhametov, 1988). The author sees only one explanation for this phenomenon. In the natural conditions the dolphin maintains constant active interaction with the environment, a state of constant search. This contact with the environment continues unabated throughout twenty-four hours since the dolphin sleeps now with its left, now with its right hemisphere, one of the two remaining constantly awake. Apparently, the state of renunciation of search is not biologically inherent in a dolphin. Hence, the absence of REM sleep in this animal. An indirect confirmation of this hypothesis is the fact that dolphins find it very difficult to adapt themselves to forms of captivity that limit the possibility of active behavior. If they fail to go over to a new behavior type, such as active interaction with the experimenter, these highly intellectual animals soon die.

The proposed conception makes it possible not only to put together the results of vastly different investigations into one system, but also to eliminate a number of contradictions between them.

References

Ammon, G., Ammon, G., and Griepenstroh, D. (1982). "Behandlungsmethodik und Widerstand von der traditionellen Psychoanalyse zur dynamyschen Psychiatrie." In G. Ammon (Ed.), *Handbuch der Dynamischen Psychiatrie*, pp. 351–406. Munich and Basel. Ernst Reinhardt Verlag.

Anisman, H., Ritch, M., and Sklar, L. (1981). "Noradrenergic and Dopaminergic Interactions in Escape Behavior Analysis of Uncontrollable Stress Effect." *Psychopharmacology*, 74, nos. 3–4: 263–268.

Appels, A. (1979). "Myocardial Infarction and Depression. A Cross-Validation of Dreyfuss Findings." *Activitas Nervosa Superior* 21, no. 1: 65–66.

Archer, T., Jonsson, G., and Ross, S. (1985). "Active and Passive Avoidance Following the Administration of Systemic DSP4, Xylamine or p-Chloramphetamine." *Behavioral and Neural Biology* 43: 238–249.

Arshavsky, V. V., and Rotenberg, V. (1976). "Search Activity and Its Influence on Experimental and Clinical Pathology." *Zhurnal Vysshey Nervnoy Deyatelnosti* 26: 424–428.

―――. (1978). "Different Types of Behavioural Reactions and Emotional States and Their Influence on Pathophysiological and Clinical Syndromes." *Uspekhi Fiziologicheskikh Nauk* 3: 49–72.

Berger, M., Riemann, D., and Lauer, C. (1988). "The Effects of Presleep Stress on Subsequent Sleep EEG and Dreams in Healthy Subjects and Depressed Patients." *Sleep '86*, pp, 84–86. Stuttgart and New York: Gustav Fischer Verlag.

Beutler, L., Ware, J., Karacan, I., and Thornby, J. (1981). "Differentiating Psychological Characteristics of Patients with Sleep Apnea and Narcolepsy." *Sleep* 4: 39–47.

Broughton, R., and Baron, R. (1973). "Sleep of Acute Coronary Patients in an Open Ward Type Intensive Care Unit." *Sleep Research* 2: 144.

Cartwright, R., Lloyd, S., Knight, S., and Trenholme, I. (1984). "Broken Dreams: A Study of the Effects of Divorce and Depression on Dream Content." *Psychiatry* 47: 251–259.

Cohen, D. (1977). "Neuroticism and Dreaming Sleep: A Case for Interactionism." *British Journal of Social and Clinical Psychology* 16: 153–163.

Cohen, H., Edelman, A., Bowen, R., and Delmont, W. (1975). "Sleep and Self-Stimulation in the Rat." Abstracts of the Eleventh Annual Meeting, APSS, New York, p. 75.

Coyne, J., and Lazarus, R. (1980). "Cognitive Style, Stress Perception and Coping." In I. Kutash and L. Schlesinger (Eds.). *Handbook on Stress and Anxiety: Contemporary Knowledge, Theory and Treatment.* San Francisco: Jossey-Bass.

De Koninck, J., Proulx, G., Prevost F., and Healey, T. (1975). "Intensive Language Learning and REM Sleep." Paper presented at the Annual Meeting of the Association for the Psychophysiological Study of Sleep, Edinburgh.

Engel, G., and Shmale, A. (1967). "Psychoanalytic Theory of Somatic Disorders." *Journal of the American Psychoanalytic Association* 15: 344–365.

Escalate, J. (1986). "REM-EEG Sleep in Masked Depression." *Journal de Psychiatrie Biologique et Therapeutique* 22: 24–26.

Everson, C., Bergmann, B., Fang, V., Leutch, C., Obermeyer, W., Refetoff, S., Schoeller, D., and Rechtschaffen, A. (1987). "Physiological and Biochemical Effects of Total Sleep Deprivation in the Rat." In M. Chase, D. McGuinty, and G. Crane (Eds.). *Sleep Research*, vol. 15, p. 216. Los Angeles: Brain Information Service/Brain Research Institute, UCLA.

Everson, C., Kushida, C., Bergmann, B., Gilliland, M., Pilcher, J., Fang, V., and Rechtschaffen, A. (1987). "Recovery from Chronic Sleep Deprivation in the Rat." In M. Chase, D. Mcguinty, C. O'Connor

(Eds.). *Sleep Research*, vol. 16, p. 521. Los Angeles: Brain Information Service/Brain Research Institute, UCLA.

Gaillard, J. (1985). "Involvement of Noradrenaline in Wakefulness and Paradoxical Sleep." In A. Wauquier, J. M. Gaillard, J. M. Monti, and M. Radulovacki (Eds.), *Sleep: Neurotransmitter and Neuromodulators*, pp. 57–67. New York: Raven Press.

Glass, D., and Carver, C. (1980). "Helplessness and the Coronary-Prone Personality." In J. Garber and M. Seligman (Eds.), *Human Helplessness, Theory and Applications*, pp. 223–244. New York and London: Academic Press.

Grastyan, E. (1976). "Motivation and Reinforcement." *Acta Physiologica Academiae Scientarum Hungaricae* 48, no. 4: 299–322.

Gray, J. (1982). *The Neurophychology of Anxiety: An Enquiry into the Functions of the Septohippocampal System*. Oxford: Oxford University Press.

Greenberg, R. (1987). "Self-Psychology and Dreams: The Merging of Different Perspectives." *Psychiatric Journal of the University of Ottawa* 12, no 2: 98–102.

———— and Pearlman, C. (1979). "The Private Language of the Dream." In J. Natterson (Ed.), *The Dream in Clinical Practice*, pp. 85–96. New York: Jason Aronson.

————, Pearlman, C., and Campel, D. (1972). "War Neuroses and the Adaptive Function of REM Sleep." *British Journal of Medicine and Psychology* 45: 27–33.

Harrel E., and Hayness, J. (1978). "Reversal of Learned Helplessness by Peripheral Arousal." *Psychological Reports* 43: 1211–1217.

Hartmann, E. (1973). "Functions of Sleep." In U. Jovanovic (Ed.), *The Nature of Sleep*, pp. 238–252. Stuttgart: Gustav Fischer Verlag.

Hawkins, J., Phillips, N., Moore, J., Gilliland, M., Dunbar, S., and Hicks, R. (1980). "Emotionality and REMD: A Rat Swimming Model." *Physiology and Behavior* 25: 167–171.

Heckhausen, H. (1977). "Achievement Motivation and Its Constructs: A Cognitive Model." *Motivation and Emotion* 1: 283–329.

Henry, I., and Stephens P. (1977). *Stress, Health and the Social Environment.* New York: Springer-Verlag.

Hicks, R., Allen, J., Armogida, R., Gilliland, M., and Pellegrini, R. (1980). "Reduction in Sleep Duration and Type A Behavior." *Bulletin of the Psychonomic Society* 16: 109–110.

Jouvet, M., and Delorme, J. (1965). "Locus coeruleus et sommeil paradoxical." *Current Research of Social Biology* [Paris] 159: 895–899.

Justice B. (1986). "Evidence of Psychosocial Influence in Disease Onset." *The Cancer Bulletin* 38, no. 5: 241–244.

Kassil, V., and Vatayeva, L. (1981). "Search Activity and Choice of Occupation on the Different Stages of Ontogenesis." In P. V. Simonov and G. Gasanov (Eds.), *Search Activity, Motivation and Sleep* [in Russian], pp. 13–15. Baku.

Katz, R., Roth, K., and Carrol, B. (1981). "Acute and Chronic Stress Effects on Open Field Activity in the Rat: Implication for a Model of Depression." *Neuroscience Biobehavioral Reviews* 5: 247–251.

Kobasa, S. (1979). "Stressful Life Events, Personality and Health. An Inquiry into Hardiness." *Journal of Personality and Social Psychology* 31: 1–11.

Kohno, Y., Hoaki, Y., Glavin, G., Nagaca, B., Tanaka, M., Tsuda, A., and Nagasaki, N. (1983). "Regional Rat Brain NA Turnover in Response to Restraint Stress." *Pharmacology, Biochemistry and Behavior* 19, no. 2: 287–290.

Kukleta, M. (1979). "System of Behavioral Inhibition in a Stress Situation: Possible Role in Neurosis." *Activitas Nervosa Superior* [Prague] 21, no. 1: 32–33.

Lehnert, H., Reinstein, D., Strowbridge, B., and Wurtman, R. (1984). "Neurochemical and Behavioral Consequences of Acute Uncontrollable Stress: Effect of Dietary Tyrosine." *Brain Research* 303; 215–223.

Lewin, F., and Glaubmann, H. (1975). "The Effects of REM Deprivation: Is It Detrimental, Beneficial or Neutral?" *Psychophysiology* 12, no. 3: 349–353.

McClelland, D. (1982). "The Need for Power, Sympathetic Activation and Illness." *Motivation and Emotion* 6, no. 1: 31–41.

McGrath, M., and Cohen, D. (1978). "REM Sleep Facilitation of Adaptive Waking Behaviour: A Review of the Literature." *Psychological Bulletin* 85, no. 1: 24–57.

Mendelson, W., Gillin, J., and Wyatt, R. (1977). *Human Sleep and Its Disorders*. New York: Plenum Press.

Mirmiran, M., Van de Poll, N., Corner, M., Van Oyen, H., and Bour, H. (1981). "Suppression of Active Sleep by Chronic Treatment with Chlorimipramine During Early Postnatal Development: Effect upon Adult Sleep and Behavior in the Rat." *Brain Research* 204: 129–146.

Mollenhour, M., Voorhees, J., and Davis, S. (1977). "Sleepy and Hostile: The Effects of REM Sleep Deprivation on Shock-Elicited Aggression." *Animal Learning and Behaviour* 5, no. 21: 148–152.

Morrison, A. (1982). "Central Activity States: Overview." In A. L. Beckman (Ed.), *The Neural Basis of Behavior*, pp. 3–17. New York: Spectrum Publications Medical and Scientific Books.

Mukhametov, L. (1988). "The Absence of Paradoxical Sleep in Dolphins." In W. P. Koella, F. Obal, H. Schulz, and Pl. Visser (Eds.), *Sleep '86*, pp. 154–156. Stuttgart and New York: Gustav Fischer Verlag.

Mullen, B., and Sulls, J. (1982). "'Know Thyself': Stressful Life Changes and the Ameliorative Effects of Private Self-Consciousness." *Journal of Experimental Social Psychology* 18: 43–55.

Natelson, B. (1983). "Stress, Predisposition and the Onset of Serious Disease: Implication About Psychosomatic Etiology." *Neuroscience and Biobehavioral Reviews* 7, no. 4: 511–528.

Oniani, T., and Lortkipanidze, N. (1985). "Effect of Paradoxical Sleep Deprivation on the Learning and Memory." In T. N. Oniani (Ed.), *Neurophysiology of Motivation, Memory and Sleep-Wakefulness Cycle*, pp. 214–234. Tbilisi: Metsniereba.

Paul, A., and Van Dongen, G. (1981). "The Human Locus Coeruleus in Neurology and Psychiatry." *Progress in Neurobiology* 17: 97–139.

Pittman, N., and Pittman, T. (1979). "Effects of Amount of Helplessness Training and Internal-External Locus of Control on Mood and Performance." *Journal of Personality and Social Psychology* 37, no. 1: 39–47.

Putkonen, P., and Putkonen, A. (1971). "Suppression of Paradoxical Sleep Following Hypothalamic Defence Reactions in Cats During Normal Conditions and Recovery from P.S. Deprivation." *Brain Research* 26: 334–347.

Rechtschaffen, A., Gilliland, M., Bergmann, B., and Winter, J. (1983). "Physiological Correlates of Prolonged Sleep Deprivation in Rats." *Science* 221: 182–184.

Reynolds, C., and Kupfer, D. (1988). "Sleep in Depression." In R. Williams, I. Karacan, and C. Moore (Eds.), *Sleep Disorders, Diagnosis and Treatment*, pp. 147–164. New York: J. Wiley and Sons.

Rosenzweig, S. (1935). "A Test for Types of Reaction to Frustration." *American Journal of Orthopsychiatry* 5: 395–403.

Rotenberg, V. (1980). "Sensitivity, Neuroticism and Sleep Disturbance: Some Controversial Problems." *Waking and Sleeping* 4: 271–279.

———. (1982). "Schizophrenie im Lichte des Konzepts der Suchaktivitat: Psychophysiologischer Aspekte." *Dyamische Psychiatrie* 72, 73: 10–20.

———. (1984). "Search Activity in the Context of Psychosomatic Disturbances, of Brain Monoamines and REM Sleep Function." *Pavlovian Journal of Biological Science* 19: 1–15.

———. (1985a). "Dream: A Special State of Consciousness." In A. Prangishvili, A. Sherozia, and F. Bassin (Eds.), *The Unconscious, Nature, Functions, Methods of Study*, vol. 4, pp. 211–223. Tbilisi: Metsniereba.

———. (1985b). "Sleep Dreams, Cerebral Dominance and Creation." *Pavlovian Journal of Biological Science* 20, no. 2: 53–58.

———. (1988a). "Das Neuroleptische Syndrom im Lichte der Verhaltens-Neurochemie." *Dynamische Psychiatrie* 108, 109: 36–42.

———. (1988b). "Functional Deficiency of REM Sleep and Its Role in the Pathogenesis of Neurotic and Psychosomatic Disturbances." *Pavolovian Journal of Biological Science* 23, no. 1: 1–3.

———. (1988c). "The Nature of Non-Linear Relationship Between the Individual's Present State and His Sleep Structure." In W. Koella, F. Obal, H. Schulz, and P. Visser (Eds.). *Sleep '86*, pp. 134–137. Stuttgart and New York: Gustav Fischer Verlag.

——— and Arshavsky, V. (1979a). "REM Sleep, Stress and Search Activity." *Waking and Sleeping* 3: 235–244.

——— and Arshavsky, V. (1979b). "Search Activity and Its Impact on Experimental and Clinical Pathology." *Activitas Nervosa Superior* 21, no. 2: 105–115.

——— and Arshavsky, V. V. (1984). *Search Activity and Adaptation.* Moscow: Nauka Publishers.

——— and Alexeyev, V. (1981). "Essential Hypertension: A Psycho-Somatic Feature or a Psycho-Somatic Disease? A Differential Analysis of Cases in Terms of Search Activity Concept." *Dynamic Psychiatry* 68: 129–139.

——— and Binaiurisvili, R. (1973). "Psychophysiological Investigation into Night Sleep." *Zhurnal Vysshey Nervnoy Deyatelnosti* 26: 424–428.

———, Kovalzon, V., and Tsibulsky, V. (1986). "Paradoxical Sleep-Protection from Stress." *Science in the USSR* 2: 45–51.

Schiff, B., Rusak, B., and Block, R. (1971). "The Determination of Reinforcing Intracranial Stimulation: An Ecological Approach." *Physiology and Behavior* 7, no. 2: 215–220.

Seligman, M. (1970). "On the Generality of the Laws of Learning." *Psychological Review* 77: 406–418.

———. (1975). *Helplessness. On Depression, Development and Death.* San Francisco: W. H. Greeman.

———. (1982). "Learned Helplessness and Life-Span Development." Paper presented at the International Conference of Life-Course Research on Human Development. Max-Planck Institute, West Berlin.

Selye, H. (1974). *Stress Without Distress.* Philadelphia, New York: J. B. Lippincott.

Shekhan, D., Ballenger, J., and Jacobsen, G. (1980). "Treatment of Endogenous Anxiety with Phobic, Hysterical and Hypochondrial Symptoms." *Archives of General Psychiatry* 37: 51–59.

Simonov, P. (1981). *The Emotional Brain* [in Russian]. Moscow: Nauka Publishers.

Sinton, C., and Jouvet, M. (1983). "Paradoxical Sleep and Coping with Environmental Change." *Behavioral Brain Research* 9, no. 2: 151–164.

Stone, E. (1975). "Stress and Catecholamines." In A. Friedhoff (Ed.), *Catecholamines and Behavior*, vol. 2, pp. 31–71. New York: Plenum Press.

Stone, E., and Platt, E. (1982). "Brain Adrenergic Receptors and Resistance to Stress." *Brain Research* 237: 405–414.

Swenson, R., and Vogel, W. (1983). "Plasma Catecholamine and Corticosterone as Well as Brain Catecholamine Changes During Coping in Rats Exposed to Stressful Footshock." *Pharmacology and Biochemistry of Behavior* 18, no. 5: 689–693.

Tiggeman, M. (1981). "Noncontingent Success Versus Noncontingent Failure and Learned Helplessness." *Journal of Psychology* 109: 233–238.

Viglinskaya, I., and Burov, Y. (1987). "Possible Correlation Between the Level of Alcohol Motivation and the Electrophysiological Sleep Patterns in Rats." *Bulletin of Experimental Biology and Medicine* 103: 394–396.

Vogel, G. (1979). "REM Sleep and the Prevention of Endogenous Depression." *Waking and Sleeping* 3: 313–318.

Wagner, M., and Mooney, D. (1975). "Personality Characteristics of Long and Short Sleepers." *Journal of Clinical Psychology*, 31, no. 3: 434–436.

Watson, C., and Kugala, (1978). "Anhedonia and Death." *Psychological Reports* 43: 1120–1122.

Wauquier, A. (1980). "The Pharmacology of Catecholamine Involvement in the Neural Mechanisms of Reward." *Acta Neurobiologiae Experimentalis* 40: 665–686.

Wehr, T., and Sack, D. (1988). "The Relevance of Sleep Research to Affective Illness." In W. Koella, F. Obal, H. Schulz, and P. Visser (Eds.),

Sleep '86, pp. 207–211. Stuttgart and New York: Gustav Fischer Verlag.

Weiss, J. (1977). "Psychological and Behavioral Influences on Gastrointenstinal Lesions in Animal Models." In J. Maser and M. Seligman (Eds.), *Psychopathology: Experimental Models*, pp. 232–269. San Francisco: W. H. Freeman.

Weiss, M. (1985). "Type A Behaviour in a Population of Berlin, GDR: Its Relation to Personality and Sociological Variables and Association to Coronary Heart Disease." *Activitas Nervosa Superior* 27, no. 1: 1–72.

Zuckerman, M. (1984). "Sensation-Seeking: A Comparative Approach to a Human Trait." *Behavioral and Brain Sciences* 7, no. 3: 413–471.

8

G. William Domhoff ▬▬▬▬▬▬▬▬▬▬▬▬

The Repetition of Dreams and Dream Elements: A Possible Clue to a Function of Dreams

I must admit at the outset that I am wary of any argument about the "function" of anything. Functional arguments are notoriously hard to test or refute, and thus they abound on every subject, including dreams. All of the functional arguments I have read to date concerning dreams seem about equally plausible, and of course dreams (and dreaming) could have more than one function (cf., Hunt, 1986; Moffitt and Hoffman, 1987).

Even worse, it might be that dreams have no function at all. REM sleep seems to have functions, but dreaming and REM sleep are not the same thing (e.g., Hall, 1967; Pivik, 1978; Foulkes and Schmidt, 1983). Thinking can be said to have a problem-solving function, generally speaking, but not all forms of thinking have this or any other function, and dreaming as a form of thinking in sleep or sleep-related states may be among those kinds of thinking without any function. It may be that dreams, although they contain consistent age, gender, and cross-cultural similarities and differences, are merely throw-away productions that happen to be revealing about both the human condition and individual personality (e.g., Hall and Nordby, 1972). Hunt (1986) captured the point well in saying that dreams may not have a function "but rather many potential uses or lines of articulation" (p. 214).

Despite all this backing and filling, I try nonetheless to work up to the question of dream function in this chapter, and I do so in a way that has become somewhat unusual in the past few decades. Rather than looking at the process of dreaming or the nature of REM sleep, I will suggest that certain features of dream content might be a possible clue to at least one function of dreams. The main premises on which I rely in my argument are familiar and basic, but I have not seen them presented in the literature in quite the way I will organize them. Or, to put it another way, if I have borrowed this way of supporting a well-known claim for dream function, I have repressed the source.

My argument derives primarily from Hall and Van De Castle's (1966, pp. 13–14) notion that the intensity of a preoccupation can be inferred from the frequency with which a particular dream character or dream activity appears. Generalizing this notion to include the frequency of certain types of dreams as well as dream elements, this leads to the general psychodynamic view of dreams as dealing, with "emotional preoccupations" (Kramer, 1982) or "unfinished business," which may include infantile wishes, undeveloped archetypes, societally repressed insights, future challenges, or incomplete gestalts.

If there is anything new to my argument, it stems from the fact that I want to look at the function of dreams by constructing a continuum that I call the *repetition dimension*. It runs from repeated dreams to repeated themes and elements in dreams. This continuum begins at one extreme with traumatic dreams that reproduce overwhelming experiences again and again, to the great discomfort of the dreamers. The continuum then moves to the recurrent dreams that puzzle or frighten many people at one time or another in their lives, but do not always seem to be directly tied to any particular experience. From recurrent dreams it is only a small jump to repetitive themes within long dream series, examples of which will be given in the main body of the chapter. The continuum ends with the mundane characters, activities, and objects that appear in ordinary dreams consistently over decades in long dream series, or appear more frequently in an individual or group's dreams than might be expected on the basis of norms for dream content (Hall and Van De Castle, 1966).

Somewhere along this continuum it might be possible to find a place for common or typical dreams, that is, a type of dream a great many people around the world report they have had at least once. Chase dreams, falling dreams, flying dreams, and nudity dreams are examples of such typical dreams (e.g., Harris, 1948; Hall, 1955; Griffith, Miyago, and Tago, 1958; Kramer, Winget, and Whitman, 1971). However, as my focus is on repetition by individuals or certain types of people (e.g., Vietnam veterans, children), I will not deal with common dreams in this chapter.

So far, then, all I have said is that we may find a clue to one possible function of dreams if we look at repetitive dream content. What I do in the following sections is examine what we know about traumatic dreams, recurrent dreams, repeated themes, and frequent dream elements to see if any common thread emerges. I argue tentatively throughout the chapter that the findings support the idea that dreams are an attempt at resolving emotional preoccupations, as others have suggested (e.g., Hall, 1953a; French and Fromm, 1964; Breger, 1967; Cartwright, 1977; Delaney, 1979; Kramer, 1982; Hartmann, 1984; Fiss, 1986). I leave open the question of whether this is an evolutionary function of dreams or a use discovered later by shamans and psychoanalysts as culture developed in history.

At the very least, this chapter poses a new question for dream theorists. Just as no theory of cognition should be taken seriously if it cannot encompass dreaming, as Antrobus (1978) and Foulkes (1985) have argued, so too should no theory of dreams be taken seriously if it cannot deal with the repetition dimension that I show to be very prominent in dreams and dream content.

Traumatic Dreams

Traumatic dreams, now understood as a major symptom of post-traumatic stress disorder, are experienced by soldiers in war, people engulfed in natural catastrophes, individuals involved in terrible accidents, and men, women, and children who have been raped or assaulted. They are notable because they tend to repeat the traumatic event in all its emotional detail and horror. People suffering from traumatic dreams often dread the thought of going to sleep.

Despite the dramatic and overwhelming nature of traumatic dreams, they have not been at the center of theoretical attention. They are often seen as atypical and peripheral. Freud's thinking may be the ideal example on this point. Although he was well aware of the role of infantile trauma in neuroses almost from the outset of his work, traumatic dreams did not figure at all in *The Interpretation of Dreams* (1953, originally published in 1900). Instead, he came to his insights there through analyzing free associations to everyday dreams that were complex and puzzling. Just how far traumatic dreams were from his attention can be seen in the fact that he began his theoretical argument about dreams as wish fulfillments by pointing to the most simple of dreams, namely, children's short dreams of things they longed for the day before.

In the years between 1900 and 1914 many critics suggested that certain types of dreams, such as anxiety and punishment dreams, did not fit the theory. But Freud vigorously argued that there were indeed wishes underlying these seemingly nonwishful dreams. It was only due to new material on "war neurosis" dreams brought to his attention during World War I that he came to believe there was a type of dream that may not fit his theory. Indeed, this realization was one reason for the major changes he made in his instinct theory after the war (Freud, 1955).

Still, when it came to dream theory, Freud (1955, p. 13) put war neurosis dreams to the side by saying that "the function of dreaming, like so much else, is upset in this condition [traumatic neuroses] and diverted from its purposes." In his final formulation on dreams, he admitted that traumatic dreams did not fit his theory but nonetheless stuck with the old theory by saying that in rare situations a more basic mechanism aimed at mastering overwhelming stimuli took control of psychic functioning (Freud, 1955, p. 32; 1964, p. 29).

In a way, then, my argument begins where Freud left off the second time around, with traumatic dreams and the phenomenon of repetition. Contrary to Freud, I am saying that we should not start with the easiest of dreams, young children's short dreams, which we now can suspect may be in any case mere sleeptalking during NREM sleep or brief awakenings on the basis of Foulkes's (1982, pp. 44–47) finding of virtually no dream recall in children under age 5 studied in the laboratory. Instead, we should begin with the most difficult of dreams, traumatic dreams, and search for a theory that encompasses them as well as wish fulfillment dreams.

The most systematic studies on traumatic dreams concern Vietnam veterans because they can be studied in large numbers due to their common experience; then too, they also make themselves available to researchers through VA hospitals. It is this work that makes it possible to go beyond a mere summation of a wide variety of individual instances in a search for generalizations. Focusing primarily on research by Hartmann (1984) and his associates and Kramer, Schoen, and Kinney (1987), which also summarizes and utilizes earlier studies by many investigators, the following things can be said about traumatic dreams and those who suffer them. First, the combat soldiers who suffer later from traumatic dreams were younger, less educated, and more likely to be emotionally involved with a close buddy who was killed or injured as compared with nonsufferers with similar combat experiences. Those who did not have such dreams put up a wall between themselves and other people while in Vietnam; they decided very early not to get close to anyone (Hartmann, 1984, p. 209).

Second, the dreams begin to change slightly over time as the person recovers, gradually incorporating other elements and becoming less like the exact experience. Put another way, the traumatic dreams slowly come to resemble ordinary dreams (Hartmann, 1984, p. 219). Third, there seems to be a decline in traumatic dreams if they are discussed in groups with other veterans who suffer from them (Wilmer, 1982). Hartmann (1984, pp. 238–239) notes that early discussion also seems to decrease such dreams in those who suffer from other kinds of traumas as well.

Finally, it is noteworthy that those who have recovered often suffer a relapse to the old dream content when faced with new stressors. Kramer, Schoen, and Kinney (1987) provide good examples of this phenomenon for veterans dealing with marital disruption; war scenes from the past then return with all their pain and anxiety. Thus, "the Vietnam experience serves as a metaphor to express the difficulties" (Kramer, Schoen, and Kinney, 1987, p. 79). It is at this point that we can see how the study of traumatic dreams and their aftermath illuminates the general study of dreams, for dreams as a metaphoric expression of our conceptions and emotional preoccupations is an important strand of dream theorizing (Hall, 1953b, 1953c; Antrobus, 1977; Baylor, 1981; Baylor and Deslauriers, 1985).

I draw the following implications from the work on traumatic dreams. First, such dreams should not be put aside as exceptions of one sort or another. They are legitimate, "real" dreams that occur in all stages of sleep, including REM, and they are experienced as dreamlike by the dreamers. Second, these dreams deal, quite obviously, with emotional problems that have overwhelmed the person. They are about emotional events that people cannot "handle" or "assimilate" or "master," to use several different words that capture aspects of the difficult experience we are here trying to comprehend. Somehow the person's defenses were down or overwhelmed; something was able to get in under the radar and wreak havoc with normal psychic functioning. Third, to the degree that the experience gradually is assimilated, to that degree the dreams decrease in frequency and become altered in content. Fourth, the way in which the experience sometimes reappears when new problems arise suggests that the old traumas have become metaphors for new stressful situations.

Traumatic dreams, then, reflect a preoccupation with problems we have not resolved. This is a possible starting point for a theory of dream function. Before making too much of one type of dream, however, it is necessary to look at the closest relative of traumatic dreams, the recurrent dream, to see what conclusions can be drawn from studying it.

Recurrent Dreams

Recurrent dreams have not been studied with the depth and intensity of traumatic dreams. Most of the studies have been clinical-anecdotal in nature or based on brief surveys. However, the combined results of several of these studies provide the basis for generalizations and inferences about recurrent dreams (LaRue, 1970; Cartwright and Romanek, 1978; Robbins and Houshi, 1983; D'Andrade, 1985).

On questionnaires, 50 to 65 percent of college students report that they have experienced a recurrent dream at one time or another in their lives (Cartwright and Romanek, 1978; Robbins and Houshi, 1983; D'Andrade, 1985). There is great variation in the length of the period in which they occur, ranging from a few months to decades. There also is great variation in the frequency with which the dream appears within that time period—from once or twice a week to once or twice a year (D'Andrade, 1985).

Recurrent dreams are most often reported to begin in childhood. Adolescence is also a frequent time of onset, with only a few beginning in adulthood (Robbins and Houshi, 1983; D'Andrade, 1985). The affective tone of recurrent dreams is negative in 60–70 percent of the cases, making them in that sense very reminiscent of traumatic dreams (Cartwright and Romanek, 1978). Two content analyses find that recurrent dreams are much more likely than ordinary dreams to contain only the dreamer (LaRue, 1970; D'Andrade, 1985). The most frequent content theme of recurrent dreams is being attacked or chased, accounting for 43 percent of recurrent dreams in one study:

> A content analysis of the recurrent dreams that students reported revealed that only one type of dream occurred with any frequency, an anxiety dream in which the dreamer was being threatened or pursued. The threatening agents were wild animals, monsters, burglars, or nature forces such as storms, fires, or floods. The dreamer was watching, hiding, or running away. (Robbins and Houshi, 1983, p. 263)

Recurrent dreams are often reported to begin at times of stress, such as the death of a loved one, separation from parents, or the divorce of parents. However, the content usually does not reflect the stress situation directly. The following recurrent dream, reported by a woman in college as beginning at age 14 when she left her mother's house to live with her father and stepmother, is typical in this regard, as well as in its lack of any characters except the dreamer:

> I am asleep in my bed at home. I know I'm in bed, in my room—but I have no tangible sensations in regard to my surroundings. It is pitch black and like a vacuum. There is a vague feeling of dizziness. A large, hairy (masculine) hand reaches out and pushes me into my closet. The door cannot be opened. The hand sets the closet on fire and I suffocate and die in the heat and smoke. (LaRue, 1970, p. 7)

Still, there are occasional recurrent dreams that deal exactly with the emotional problem facing the dreamer, as with a virgin woman who was anguished about whether or not to sleep with her boyfriend. In the dream she is making love with her boyfriend: "The dream is very active and does not involve climax, merely tension, fear and a subsequent shame and day of headaches on awakening" (LaRue, 1970, p. 4).

Not all subjects can link the onset of recurrent dreams to a stressful event, but the possibility that the stressful event is sometimes forgotten or repressed is demonstrated in a hypnoanalytic study of a recurrent dream from a 31 year old woman hospitalized with conversion hysteria (Moss, Thompson, and Nolte, 1962). Described by the authors as a classic case such as might have been seen by Freud at the turn of the century, the patient volunteered a recurrent dream that puzzled her but seemed to be related to her lifelong fear of death:

> She walked into her bedroom and there in the dark stood a small furry white dog. Though it tried to be friendly and snuggle up to her, she was very frightened. She edged out of the bedroom and when the dog tried to follow, she managed to close the door. (The dream would invariably awaken her and she would sleep the remainder of the night on the living room sofa.) (Moss , Thompson, and Nolte, 1962, p. 63)

There is reason to believe from clinical studies and surveys that recurrent dreams often disappear when the problem is resolved (Cartwright, 1979). Systematic evidence related to this observation has been provided by Brown and Donderi (1986), who gave a battery of well-being measures to recurrent dreamers, former recurrent dreamers, and non-recurrent dreamers. They found that the current recurrent dreamers scored significantly lower on well-being measures than former recurrent dreamers. They also found that the everyday dreams of the current recurrent dreamers contained "larger proportions of aggressive, anxious, and dysphoric dream content, relative to the other two groups" (Brown and Donderi, 1986, p. 619).

The conclusion I draw from this work on recurrent dreams is that most of them are very similar to traumatic dreams. More exactly, they are watered-down versions of traumatic dreams. They have their origins in some sort of stressful situation, usually in childhood or adolescence, they are repeated, and they are mostly unpleasant. They differ from the traumatic dreams of those diagnosed with post-traumatic stress disorder in that they usually are not a reexperiencing of the stressful situation. Instead, they seem to be more metaphoric in content, with wild animals, untamed nature, monsters, or scary strangers chasing, attacking, or entrapping the dreamer.

Still, the fact that all recurrent dreams cannot be tied to obvious stressors, as in the case of traumatic dreams, presents a problem for linking the repetition dimension with emotional preoccupation. In some instances the stressors may be buried, as with Moss, Thompson, and Nolte's (1962) hysterical patient, but findings from a study of an unusual type of recurrent dream suggest a new angle: what is ordinary for some people may be stressful for others. The unusual recurrent dreams to which I refer are the nightmares of the small number of people who suffer from lifelong nightmares. These dreams and those who dream them have been studied by Hartmann (1984) through psychiatric interviews and a battery of psychological tests with fifty subjects. The subjects were the most extreme from among many who responded to a newspaper ad asking for interviews with those who suffer from frequent nightmares.

Although lifelong nightmare sufferers do not have exactly the same nightmare each time, there tends to be a thematic pattern that makes the nightmares very similar to recurrent dreams. As Hartmann (1984, p. 61) notes, "Some of the subjects described having had 'some form of this nightmare' or 'something like this' many times." Moreover, there are only a few themes that make up most nightmares for most of the subjects. As was found with the college students who reported recurrent dreams in the aforementioned survey studies (e.g. Robbins and Houshi, 1983; D'Andrade, 1985), by far the most important theme is of being chased and attacked.

Typically, a subject would recall childhood nightmares in which he or she was chased by a monster, something big, strange, and unknown.

Later on, the chaser was more likely to be a large unidentified man, a group of frightening people, a gang, or a troop of Nazis. Often, the dreamer was not only chased, but attacked, or hurt in some way. Sometimes there was only a threat that something would happen and the dreamer awakened in fright. However, in many cases the dreamer was actually caught, beaten, stabbed, shot, or mutilated (Hartmann, 1984, p. 60).

In terms of their content, as well as in their repetition and emotional intensity, the nightmares of those who are lifelong sufferers from an early age are very similar to traumatic dreams. And yet, these people do not recall any obvious traumas. Nor do they suffer from excessive anxiety, anger, or guilt according to personality tests and psychiatric appraisals. Instead, they are relatively normal people who work mainly as artists, teachers, and therapists; some are in graduate school. They are creative and service-oriented people who responded to the ads because they wanted to help others by helping science.

What seemed to differentiate these people from various control groups utilized by Hartmann was their extreme sensitivity and openness from early childhood onward. They were likely to be upset by little things as children; they thought of themselves from the start as unusual and they seemed to be exceptionally self-conscious and aware for youngsters. Hartmann concludes that these people remain especially "thin skinned," as the common expression goes, whereas most of us are rather "thick skinned." Hartmann makes the contrast in terms of thick and thin "boundaries" and provides many examples of how this distinction holds, whether it be in the rejection of rigid sex roles or the lack of strong psychological defenses.

These findings suggest that there is a small percentage of highly sensitive people for whom many everyday experiences are in effect highly traumatic. Their genetic make-up or early life experiences have made daily life for them like a combat zone that is comparable to what Vietnam was for average people who were not old enough or sophisticated enough to put on hard personal shells. If we conceive of the thin-thick dimension of the human personality interacting with a dimension of experience that ranges from very nonthreatening to overwhelming, then we can begin to see that all dreams might be reactions to traumatic experiences, even if the traumatic experience for some people is no more than thinking about an interview with a potential employer. Put another way, what is traumatic is a relative matter, and all dreams therefore may be seen as dealing with traumatic experiences of differing degrees.

The findings on recurrent dreams thus seem to reinforce the idea that dreams are an attempt to deal with our emotional preoccupations. However, a theory based on traumatic dreams and recurrent dreams is not broad enough—there are too many people who do not report having either of these types of dreams, and there are too many dreams that are neither traumatic nor recurrent. It is therefore necessary to search for the repetition dimension in the everyday dreams of everyday dreamers.

Repetitive Dream Themes

Clinical researchers, especially Jungians, have given us some intimations of the degree to which certain themes may repeat themselves in dreams. However, it was Hall's systematic work with long dream series, some stretching over several decades, that revealed just how pervasive and consistent repeated themes are in dreams. I would go so far as to call the finding astonishing and suggest that they are not fully appreciated for their theoretical implications.

Hall analyzed about 20 series of over 100 dreams, some of which are reported in Hall and Nordby (1972, pp. 80–102), others of which are unpublished (e.g., Hall, 1982). All show the same general results. Perhaps the most persuasive of the published findings concern a woman who gave herself the code name Dorothea. She wrote down 649 dreams over a fifty-year period, the first in 1912 when she was 25 years old, the last used in the analysis in 1963 when she was 76 years old (Smith and Hall, 1964, p. 66; Hall and Nordby, 1972, p. 82). Ten themes appeared with considerable regularity in Dorothea's dreams. Six appeared with basically the same frequency throughout the entire fifty years. In one out of every five dreams she was eating or thinking of food. The loss of an object, usually her purse, occurred in one out of every six dreams. Dorothea was in a small or disorderly room, or her room was being invaded by others, in every tenth dream. Another 10 percent of her dreams involved the dreamer and her mother. She was going to the toilet in one out of every twelve dreams, and she was late, concerned about being late, or missing a bus or train in one out of every sixteen dreams (Hall and Nordby, 1972, p. 83). These six themes alone account for at least part of the content in about 70 percent of her dreams.

In addition, three themes declined over the years and one showed an increase followed by a decrease. She dreamed more of being ill in her younger years, when she was in fact more often ill. She also dreamed more of traveling, which she actually did more of at that time. There were also more babies in her dreams when she was younger. Being left out, not waited on, or ignored was the theme that increased in frequency as she grew into middle age, then declined in her later years. Hall and Nordby (1972, p. 83) suggest that her middle years were a problem for her in terms of being left out because she was unmarried and "also because, being a woman, her professional advancement had not been as rapid as she deserved."

However, it is not really possible to attempt to explain in any detail how these themes might relate to stresses in Dorothea's life. This is simply because we do not know enough about her beyond the fact that she grew up in a large missionary family in China, came back to the United States as a teenager, earned a Ph.D. in psychology at age 38, taught in a normal school that became a university for many years before retiring, and had no interest in any of the psychodynamic theories of dreams (Smith and Hall, 1964, p. 66). She just liked to write down her dreams in her diary and had done nothing with them until she wrote to ask Hall in 1963 if he wanted them. The important point to be drawn from this series is the sheer repetition of themes over five decades, for this appears to have echoes, however emotionally faint, of traumatic dreams and recurrent dreams.

One of Hall's (1982) unpublished analyses provides an opportunity to suggest that the themes discovered in a long dream series can be connected with traumatic experiences. This analysis of 449 dreams covers "only" sixteen years, but the themes are unusual and they can be organized in some instances in such a way as to yield inferences about their possible origins. In addition, Hall was able to learn a good deal about this person after the dreams were analyzed. The subject of this analysis, called *T* by Hall, wrote Hall the following letter in the late 1970s:

> May I say how much I have enjoyed your books about dreams. I have utilized them as I sought help through psychotherapy to moderate certain character defects.
>
> I have reached the age where I am aware of my own mortality. I have probably 2,000 dreams written down through the nights over sixteen years. Some are typed. Some are in handwriting. If you're interested in such a group of dreams, I will type them out and send them to you (Hall, 1982, p. 2)

Hall wrote back that he would like to see a few of the typed dreams before he decided whether to do anything with the series. The letter and typed dreams that came back convinced Hall he was dealing with a literate and reasonable person. In addition, the dreams were interesting because they were so bizarre, a feature of a dream series that is more atypical than the common image of dreams might lead one to expect.

Hall then asked for half the dreams, including the first and last hundred and ones from all other years. The dreamer, who had greatly overestimated the number of dreams in his collection, sent back 449 dreams. Later he sent the remaining 514 on his own initiative (Hall, 1982, p. 3). The analysis to be presented here was completed before the second half of the dreams arrived. Our careful reading of the remaining dreams convinced Hall and me that they are no different in their thematic content from those Hall analyzed.

As Hall later learned, T was indeed to all outward appearances a normal and satisfied person. In his early fifties at the time he first contacted Hall, he was a law enforcement official who had earned a degree in creative writing since his retirement. He was married, and his two grown children were doing well. He reported that psychotherapy had helped him with his tendency toward anxiety, anger, and depression—he no longer became so angry with authority figures, he did not become depressed, and he was a "recovering alcoholic," who had not had a drink in seventeen years. He had stopped the womanizing of his earlier years and controlled his compulsive gambling.

But one thing did not change between 1963 and 1979, and that was his dreams. The same themes were present in the first hundred dreams as in the last hundred (Hall, 1982, pp. 64–65), and they are very different from what is found in most dream series. The five main themes for our purposes here are (1) the overbearing but seductive mother; (2) the weak but lovable father; (3) the dangerous homosexual who makes advances and must be attacked; (4) males with female characteristics and females with male characteristics; and finally (5) metamorphoses of all kinds and descriptions, including men into women, women into men, humans into animals, young into old, and objects into animals and people. When these themes are then looked at in the context of the fifty-four dreams where he is a child or teenager, feels like a child, or is back in his boyhood home, it becomes possible to make some very strong inferences about the early problems that probably led to the consistent themes in his dreams.

There are thirty-one dreams where his mother appears and twenty-six with his father present. The mother is variously "depicted as being insincere, self-pitying, overbearing, cold, quarrelsome, rude, and contemptuous," and in only one dream, where she consoles T, is she presented in a positive way (Hall, 1982, p. 14). In one dream she turns into a werewolf and in another characteristic dream T is trying to break free as she clings and holds tight to him, demanding to be kissed.

Conversely, T's love for his father is demonstrated in five dreams, and in four dreams the father is helpful and concerned in regard to T. There are three dreams where the father acts as a moral authority, but five in which he is weak, passive, or inadequate, sometimes in relation to T's mother. In one dream T sucks his father's penis and in another dream T notices that his father has no penis.

Homosexuals are extremely rare in the dreams of heterosexuals, but T has twenty-eight dreams in which they appear. Usually they approach him and make advances toward him; he is disgusted or frightened, and he tries to repulse them, sometimes quite violently with a knife or other weapon. There are also eleven dreams in which T is surprised or confused by women with penises, men with breasts, or men without penises. In one such dream, "a beautiful woman appeared naked with a penis. My feelings are confusion, disbelief in what I saw." T makes advances toward her, but she rejects him; he keeps asking her if she has a penis. Then, "she shows it to me growing out of her left breast. She described how she made it by pushing a small stick or object into her breast. It is like the hard penis of an eight or ten year old boy" (Hall, 1982, pp. 34–35).

There are seventy-three metamorphoses in T's dreams, and they are far more varied and far less benign than those found in Ovid's *Metamorphoses*. Of the most relevance to this brief summary of the study are the twelve dreams where a man changes into a woman, or vice versa. In two of these twelve, T himself makes the change. Sometimes there is an age change as well as a gender change, as when an enemy soldier changes into a 15-year-old girl or a 10-year-old girl changes into T (Hall, 1982, pp. 39–40).

Taken as a whole, the unusual themes in this dream series suggested to Hall that T was plagued by three emotionally troubling questions: Am I male or female? Am I heterosexual or homosexual? Am I an adult or a child? (Hall, 1982, p. 41). T's conception of his mother as overbearing in contrast to his father as passive may have been one cause of these questions, but his regression dreams—where he is a youngster, feels childish, or is back in his parents' home—also suggest that he may have suffered some traumatic homosexual experiences as well. From among the several dreams where he is an actual child in the dream, the following five seem to bring together a number of the earlier themes drawn from dreams where he is an adult:

> "There was a grandmother-type woman on a bed. If some event occurred, or I did something properly, I would get to sleep all night with her. Then someone had me by the hand and was pulling me away from her. I knew that he was a homosexual." T then changes into a man and beats the homosexual with a crowbar.
>
> T's young brother climbs into bed with T, curls up close to him, and says how much he loves T.
>
> T has taken on feminine mannerisms and is treated with contempt by his mother.
>
> A fat man makes sexual advances toward T, and T hits him. The man is not hurt and begins to suck on T's breast.
>
> A strange old man smeared semen on him, grabbed the bottom of his scrotum between two fingernails, and pinched him. It hurt but T could not escape.

Hall concludes as follows about these regression dreams:

> ...each of them seems to contain the revival of an actual experience, a reliving of that experience. The dream is not a fantasy, something made up out of whole cloth. The details may be altered, elaborated, or distorted from the original experience but the essential theme of the dream happened to T at some previous time in his life. It may be T's conception of what happened; nevertheless, it is a conception of something that did happen (Hall, 1982, p. 53)

Put another way, Hall hypothesizes that T did suffer humiliation at the hands of his mother, was pained by the passivity of his father, and did have youthful homosexual experiences with an older man or a brother of about his own age. What makes it possible to make these inferences is the large number of dreams, including the large number of regression dreams in which the various themes in the dream series also occur.

Although T readily agreed with the characterization of his mother and father, he did not recall ever having been involved in homosexual behavior. In the reply in which he discussed this issue he seemed to be very upset by Hall's suggestion. Hall, who never met T, drew back from quizzing him any further because he did not want to cause T any problems. He made extra efforts to disguise T's exact age, geographical location, and former occupation so that his private printing of the analysis could not possibly lead anyone to recognize the dreamer. In short, this case can only be described as suggestive support for my claims because one key inference could not be fully studied.

The analysis of 1,368 dreams from a four-year period reported by a man in his mid-thirties who turned out to be a child molester did give Hall the opportunity to make an inference about an early childhood trauma that was corroborated by the dreamer. The inference was made on the basis of certain repeated themes and the complete absence of any mention of his father, making the case more of a clinical analysis and raising the complicated issue of whether or not zero or near-zero appearances of expected themes or characters also can be used to infer a traumatic experience. Knowing nothing about the man at the start except his age and involvement with a psychotherapist, Hall quickly inferred the infantile nature of the dreamer's sexuality from his wide range of sexual practices and objects, and the large number of friendly and sexual interactions with children. There was a greater focus on young girls as compared to boys (Bell and Hall, 1971, pp. 20–24, 33–34; Hall and Nordby, 1972, pp. 30–31).

Urinating and defecating were very frequent themes in these dreams. There also was a theme of gender confusion in which women had penises or beards, or disguised themselves as men. At the same time, the dreamer sometimes saw himself as a woman. In addition, there was a high incidence of various kinds of holes, openings, and tunnels, and the dreamer usually entered them, explored them in some way, or continued to focus on them. From these varying themes Hall concluded that the man had poor impulse control, confusion about gender, and a particular concern with the nature of female genitals, with the latter inference based on a symbolic interpretation of the curiosity about holes and tunnels. Further, Hall guessed that the man was a child molester whose primary desire was to look at the genitals of little girls. All of these inferences, along with others, proved correct according to the therapist and the dreamer (Bell and Hall, 1971, pp. 26–27, 36–37, 40–41, 50–52; Hall and Nordby, 1972, pp. 39–41, 109–110).

However, it was the total lack of any reference to the father, in contrast to a disproportionate number of dreams about his mother and sister, that led Hall to suspect either the absence of a father or a traumatic experience with the father. To check the possibility that a traumatic experience was the cause of the zero frequency, Hall searched for possible symbolic substitutes for the father. The following dream about an anthropomorphized bull was the final reason for guessing that the dreamer had himself been molested as a child by the father:

> A bull that seemed to have human intelligence came behind me and held me against him. I did not like his advances and I sensed that he wanted to have sexual relations with me. So I broke away from him" (Hall and Nordby, 1972; Bell and Hall, 1971, p. 136).

Confirming the interpretation, the dreamer reported that he had been forced to perform fellatio on his father for several years beginning at around age 4. He said he enjoyed the experience at the time, but came to have severe guilt feelings about it later on. Hall concluded that the dreamer's child molesting was an attempt to deal with this earlier trauma as well as to experience the pleasures of it (Bell and Hall, 1971, pp. 73–76, 90).

Although there were no references to his father in the dreams he had over the four-year period he wrote them down, it turned out that he had told the psychotherapist of an age-regression dream from his adolescence that did include his father. It was a dream he says he may have had more than once, and it was very similar to his memory of the traumatic seduction except that fellatio does not occur:

> I was a young boy, four years old. The room, the carpet were all familiar. My father was there. Something happened before the climax, but it's difficult to remember. My father was walking toward me, staring like a hypnotist. I was frightened that if I backed up I'd fall off the edge or something. I woke up on the floor next to the bed. (Bell and Hall, 1971, p. 76)

This dream also raises the question of when the consistency of dreams establishes itself in the developmental cycle. Most of the long dream series analyzed by Hall came from adults, and most of the information we have on the dreams of children and adolescents is cross sectional. Foulkes's (1982) longitudinal study of children 3 to 8 and 9 to 14 showed changes similar to what we might expect from cross-sectional data, but there is no data I know of that might speak to the question of when repeated themes stabilize.

I do not want to make too much out of the child molester case because it is somewhat conjectural and based to some extent on symbolic interpretations. Put another way, my primary concern is to explore a repetition continuum that might provide a basis some day for thinking in terms of metaphorical (symbolic) interpretations, not to use symbolic interpretations to establish the continuum. Nevertheless, the isolation of a specific trauma through the investigation of a dream series is noteworthy enough to encourage other investigators to do similar analyses.

Clearly, more work needs to be done within long dream series on the connection between repetitive themes (and the absence of expected themes) and specific traumas. In particular, it might be very useful to see if different themes can be found at different age levels of age-regression dreams, as suggested in T's dreams. For now, though, I think the cases of T and the child molester, when seen in the light of consistent themes in other long dream series, provide the basis for concluding that repetitive themes in dreams are very likely the residues of experiences that were emotionally upsetting, thereby linking repetitive dream themes with traumatic dreams and recurrent dreams. It is now time for the acid test—to see if and how the usual content of ordinary dreams from average dreamers might relate to the repetition dimension.

Repeated Dreams Elements

Most clinical theorists, with the exception of Jung (1974) and French and Fromm (1964), tend to focus on one dream at a time, and they attempt to understand each dream in terms of material from outside of it—events of the previous day, biographical information, free associations, amplifications, or the acting out of the dream. Such an approach does not lend itself to finding that a person dreams consistently about certain elements or has higher frequencies for some dream elements than most people.

The quantitative content analysis system developed by Hall (1951; 1953a; 1969) and his associates (Hall and Van De Castle, 1966; Hall and Nordby, 1972) takes a different tack. By constructing carefully defined categories for settings, objects, emotions, characters, activities, social interactions, and many other elements in dreams, and then tabulating frequencies for each of these categories, this method provides a way to study dreams without going outside the dreams themselves. And, contrary to some criticisms of the method (Rupprecht, 1985, pp. 203–206; Garfield, 1988, pp. 26–31), it is not gender biased in its construction or findings. Comparable results with the system on women's dreams collected and scored by women (Dudley and Fangalori, 1987; Tonay, 1990–91) demonstrate this fact even though it is true (Rupprecht, 1985, p. 203) that Hall's theoretical interpretations of his empirical findings, which many of us do not share, are in terms of orthodox psychoanalytic theory and culturally sanctioned roles. Nor does the Hall–Van De Castle system merely end up "confirming the obvious" and yielding "only culturally common material," as Cartwright (1986, pp. 412–413) asserts in suggesting that new approaches be tried "before abandoning the quest for whether dreams are truly unique."

Instead, quantitative content analysis has led to many reliable and interesting findings about dreams, including gender differences, simply by comparing dreams with other dreams, either other dreams in a long dream series or with norms derived from the dreams of many different people. It is now known, for example, that in most countries around the world men in general dream twice as often about men as they do about women, whereas most women dream equally about women and men (Hall and Domhoff, 1963a; Hall and Van De Castle, 1966; Hall, 1984). It is also known that men in the United States tend to have more aggressive than friendly interactions with other men and more friendly than aggressive interactions with women, whereas most American women tend to have equal amounts of friendly and aggressive interactions with both men and women (Hall and Domhoff, 1962, 1963b, 1964; Hall and Van De Castle, 1966; Hall et al., 1982). These findings lend themselves to many possible interpretations, but it does not seem correct to call them "sexist" when they are the completely unexpected result of an objective scoring system and do not have negative implications about women. Nor do they seem to reflect any obvious cultural expectations.

To relate the quantitative findings on repeated elements to personal preoccupations, Hall and Van De Castle (1966, pp. 12–14) make the crucial assumption mentioned at the beginning of the chapter. They postulate that the frequency with which an element appears is an indicator of how intensely the dreamer feels about either the element itself or the emotional preoccupation for which the element is a metaphor. In effect, this assumption, which is supported by every personality study Hall and his associates have done (Hall and Nordby, 1972, pp. 103–127), also underlies the discussions in the earlier sections. I have generalized the Hall–Van De Castle assumption to explore the repetition dimension.

The repetition of elements in dreams can be demonstrated in two different ways. First, there is repetition in long dream series, where the comparison is of earlier with later dreams. Second, it is possible to compare the dream of an individual, or a class of individuals such as children, with norms. These norms are based on five dreams from each of 100 male and female college students between the ages of 18 and 25 who attended Western Reserve University and Baldwin Wallace College between 1947 and 1950 (Hall and Van De Castle, 1966, pp. 158-194). They have been updated with men and women at the University of Cincinnati (Riechers, Kramer, and Trinder, 1970) and the University of Richmond (Hall et al., 1982), and with women students at Salem College (Dudley and Swank, 1990) and the University of California, Berkeley (Tonay, 1990–91) with the finding that there have been very few changes.

Before looking at how short dream series or the dreams of a given group compare with the norms, however, it is useful to supplement the previous section on repetitive themes in long dream series by looking at the repetition of specific elements in two long dream series not previously discussed. First, Maria kept a record of her dreams when she was single in her early twenties and then again in her sixties when she was widowed and all her other relatives were also dead. As Hall and Nordby (1972, p. 84) summarize:

> Virtually all the frequencies were the same in the two sets of dreams. There were the same number of males and females, and the same kinds of objects. There was the same proportion of friendly and aggressive interactions with each class of character. There were even the same number of prominent persons and Negroes in the two sets of dreams. There was an amazing amount of consistency despite a forty-year difference in age.

Not all categories remained constant, however. When she was younger, Maria was more often a victim of aggression, especially from males, but in her sixties she was more often the aggressor. Parenthetically, "Maria felt this change was due to more self-confidence and assertiveness," which would mean that the change fits with a change in her preoccupation with herself as a weak person (Hall and Nordby, 1972, p. 84). There also was a great decline in sex dreams, which may have reflected an operation that left her with "no sexual outlets whatsoever" (Hall and Nordby, 1972, p. 84).

The dreams of Jeffrey cover a twenty-five-year period between the ages of 37 and 62. Here, too, most categories remained constant in their frequencies even though Jeffrey moved from one coast to another, left his wife and "came out" as a homosexual, and retired from his teaching position. Once again, as with Maria, there were some gradual changes. More strangers began to appear in his dreams after he left his wife and family, and the number of sex dreams increased, which paralleled an increased number of sexual outlets (Hall and Nordby, 1972, p. 84). However, even some of the changes occurred within a context of consistency. For example, he dreamed of a more narrow range of male characters, but the overall ratio of male to female characters in his dreams remained the same: "Fewer characters in a class are compensated by more frequent appearances of each character" (Hall and Nordby, 1972, p. 91).

We like to think of dreams as irregular and infinitely varied, but as the findings on repeated themes and repeated elements in long dream series clearly establish, dreams are in fact extremely regular and repetitive. Even if this were the only contribution of quantitative content analysis, which it is not, the method would have contributed far more than conceded in the aforementioned comments by Cartwright (1986, p. 412).

Comparing the dreams of children with those of adults provides a way to show how norms can reveal a type of repetition in dreams. First, children are much more likely to have aggressions and misfortunes in their dreams, with misfortunes being defined as any accident, illness, or loss not caused by some other character in the dream and over which the dreamer has no control. Second, children are four times as likely as adults to be victims of aggressions rather than instigators. Third, there are many more animals in children's dreams, and these animals very often are the characters that attack the dreamer (Hall and Nordby, 1972, pp. 19–22, 86). Finally, there is twice as much apprehension in children's dreams (Van De Castle, 1971, pp. 37–38). Taken together, these results suggest that children are more afraid than adults of being hurt, lost, or attacked. I use this example of course because I hope it makes intuitive sense to most readers.

The dreams of Franz Kafka contain repetitive elements that seem to reveal his major preoccupations as compared with the typical man. Hall and Lind (1970) culled thirty-seven dreams from the diaries and letters of Kafka that had been published in English up until that time. They found that Kafka differed from the Hall and Van De Castle male norms, and from most male dream series, in that there was less sex, less aggression, less involvement in the aggression that did occur, and less involvement in a variety of activities as compared with other dream characters. In addition, there was a heightened concern with watching or looking, whether as a spectator or as a person who is unable to look. These high frequencies, in conjunction with the low frequencies on sex, aggression, and dreamer-involved activities, suggest that Kafka was a passive person. The content of his diaries and the testimony of his friends provide abundant evidence for that inference (Hall and Lind, 1970, pp. 47–48).

Then too, Kafka is three times as likely as the average male dreamer to make reference to the body or body parts; for example, hair, eyes, face, extremities, or internal organs. Moreover, the bodies are often disfigured. There is also a greater mention of clothing and of nudity. These findings together suggest that Kafka was preoccupied with his body, and that indeed turned out to be the case. Although he was a handsome six-footer, he thought of himself as skinny and weak, and compared himself unfavorably to his more muscular father. There are constant aspersions about his body in his diaries, and one of his friends wrote that "every imperfection of the body tormented him, even, for example, scurf [dandruff], or constipation, or a toe that was not properly formed" (Hall and Lind, 1970, pp. 41–42). Kafka was a fastidious dresser who also concerned himself with what other people were wearing. He was interested in the nudist movement and in natural health practices (Hall and Lind, 1970, pp. 42–43).

Other elements in Kafka's dreams relate to his personality and waking concerns, but they need not detain us here. The passivity and preoccupation with the body that can be inferred from high or low scores in a number of categories are the most striking features of Kafka's dreams.

Freud's dreams as reported in *The Interpretation of Dreams* (1953) also have some unusual differences from those of the typical man. In the twenty-eight available dreams analyzed by Hall and Domhoff (1968) most of the aggression occurs with females and most of the friendliness with other men, which is just the opposite of the usual male pattern reported at the outset of this section. Freud is also much more likely to be befriended by the males than he is to befriend them in his dreams, whereas most males give as much friendship as they receive. Hall and Domhoff (1968) conclude that Freud had a passive attitude toward men and a hostile attitude toward women, inferences that are amply supported in Ernest Jones's (1953, 1955, 1957) three volume biography.

These kinds of findings, and many more that could be recounted, are all provocative, and they all point in the same direction—we dream about our emotional preoccupations, about what bugs us. Sometimes the "traumatic" starting point of a dream is the simple fact that the dreamer is a vulnerable child; from this fact come age differences in dreams. Other times the "problem" is that the dreamer is male or female, with all the burdens, expectations, and dangers that either of the sex roles entails; from this come gender differences in dream content, whether due to biology, culture, or a complex interaction of the two that varies the importance of biology and culture from one gender difference to the next. Sometimes the problems are more personal, or individual, and thus we have traumatic dreams, recurrent dreams, repetitive themes, and atypical frequencies on some dream elements for some dreamers.

The only problems with the findings from quantitative content analysis is convincing dream theorists to take them seriously and to think about their implications. That is why Hall and Van De Castle (1966, pp. 3–8) anticipate the widespread aversion to quantification on the part of dream researchers and deal carefully with the likely objections to content analysis.

Conclusion

It has been my contention that there is an overlooked dimension that runs from the most dramatic and frightening of dreams to some of the most mundane elements in everyday dreams. I have tried to demonstrate this claim by using findings from the literature on traumatic dreams, recurrent dreams, lifelong nightmares, long dream series, and quantitative content analysis.

I have concluded from an examination of such literature that repetition does indicate preoccupation with a problem in all these different instances. We dream about emotional hang-ups, fixations, unfinished personal business. The occasional intellectual, creative, or lucid dream is a rarity. With this conclusion we move very close to the domain of functions, however that multifaceted term is defined. I am in effect suggesting that dreams can be seen as attempts at comprehending our emotional problems. They attempt to deal with our personal preoccupations, and that is why they are more unpleasant than pleasant, more confusing than transparent.

This conclusion about problem resolving is nothing new. It has been suggested in one form or another by others using different kinds of research evidence (e.g., Breger, 1967; Cartwright, 1977, 1979; Delaney, 1979; Hartmann, 1984, p. 215; Fiss, 1986). All this chapter has done is to suggest that repetitive dreams and repetitive dream elements fit with such a conception.

More generally, I would conjecture that many dreams are a metaphorical attempt at problem resolving, with the use of the word *attempt* implying that they do not usually succeed. The use of the word *metaphorical* is in keeping with Hall's (1953b, 1953c,) cognitive theory of dreams and dream symbolism, which put a great deal of emphasis on metaphor. However, I would add that the exciting and very different metaphorical theory of language proposed by George Lakoff (1987), placing metaphor at the heart of language development and comprehension, provides an effective critique of all previous (overly rationalistic) theories of cognition and language, and an ideal framework for the study of dreams.

Still, as I said at the outset, I am not comfortable with functional explanations or the language of functionalism. I am therefore hesitant to say that evolution has bequeathed us a form of thinking during sleep that is "meant" to help us solve our personal problems. It may be that this "function" of dreams operates only in some cultures and for those who remember and study their dreams. In that sense, it might be better to talk about problem resolving as a possible "use" of dreams (cf., Hunt, 1986).

Put another way, perhaps dreams were not conserved by natural selection to be problem resolvers, or anything else for that matter, but they nonetheless can be used to understand our unfinished emotional business because they happen to express our conceptions of our preoccupations. Dreams as we are dreaming them, whether in REM or NREM sleep, may have no function, but dreams can be "useful" to waking consciousness in a variety of ways, and in that sense we have invented "functions" for them. From that angle dreams have an emergent function that develops through culture.

In closing my argument, I want to emphasize that I have not said that all dream content is repetitive and oriented to the past. I recognize that new elements appear in dreams and that we can dream about concerns in the future. The painful dreams about fouled-up weddings that some young unmarried women report spring to mind here (Hall, 1953a, pp. 134–135; Garfield, 1988, pp. 134–142), as do the anxious dreams about deformed babies and difficult labour suffered by many pregnant women (Van De Castle, 1971, pp. 39–40; 1986; Stukane, 1985; Maybruck, 1989). I have argued that the repetition dimension provides a big clue that one function of dreams may be an attempt at dealing with emotional preoccupations, but that does not preclude emotional preoccupation with the new as well as the old, or the trivial as well as the profound for that matter. Mine is a view consonant with Hall's metaphorical definition of dreams as the kaleidoscope of the mind:

Dreams objectify that which is subjective, they visualize that which is invisible, they transform the abstract into the concrete, and they make conscious that which is unconscious. They come from the most archaic alcoves of the mind as well as from the peripheral levels of waking consciousness. Dreams are the kaleidoscope of the mind (Hall and Nordby, 1972, p. 146).

The repetition dimension is but another pattern within the dream kaleidoscope. I offer it as an intriguing topic for future theorizing about dream meaning and dream function.

References

Antrobus, J. (1977). "The Dream as Metaphor: An Information Processing and Learning Model." *Journal of Mental Imagery*, 2: 327–338.

————. (1978). "Dreaming for Cognition." In A. Arkin, J. Antrobus, and S. Ellman (Eds.), *The Mind in Sleep: Psychology and Psychophysiology*, pp. 569–581. Hillsdale, N.J.: Lawrence Erlbaum Associates.

Baylor, G. (1981). "Dreams as Problem Solving." In W. Koella (Ed.), *Sleep 1980*, pp. 354–356. Basel: Karger.

———— and Deslauriers, D. (1985). "Understanding Dreams: Methods, Maps and Metaphors." *Dreamworks* 5: 46–57.

Bell, A., and Hall, C. (1971). *The Personality of a Child Molester: An Analysis of Dreams*. Chicago: Aldine Books.

Breger, L. (1967). "Function of Dreams." *Journal of Abnormal Psychology Monograph* 72, no. 5: 1–28.

Brown, R., and Donderi, D. (1986). "Dream Content and Self-Reported Well-Being Among Recurrent Dreamers, Past-Recurrent Dreamers, and Nonrecurrent Dreamers." *Journal of Personality aand Social Psychology* 50: 612–623.

Cartwright, R. (1977). *Night Life*. Englewood Cliffs, N.J.: Prentice-Hall.

————. (1979). "The Nature and Function of Repetitive Dreams: A Speculation." *Psychiatry* 42: 131–137.

———. (1986). "Affect and Dream Work from an Information Processing Point of View." *Journal of Mind and Behavior*. 7: 411–428.

——— and Romanek, I. (1978). "Repetitive Dreams of Normal Subjects." *Sleep Research* 7: 174.

D'Andrade, J. (1985). "On Recurrent Dreams." Unpublished term research paper for a course on dreams taught by G. William Domhoff, University of California, Santa Cruz.

Delaney, G. (1979). *Living Your Dreams*. New York: Harper and Row.

Dudley, L., and Fungaroli, J. (1987). "The Dreams of Students in a Women's College: Are they Different?" *ASD Newsletter* 4, no. 6: 6–7.

——— and Swank, M. (1990). "A Comparison of the Dreams of College Women in 1950 and 1990. ASD Newsletter 7, no. 5: 3, 16.

Fiss, H. (1986). "An Empirical Foundation for a Self Psychology of Dreaming." *Journal of Mind and Behavior* 7: 161–192.

Foulkes, D. (1982). *Children's Dreams*. New York: John Wiley and Sons.

———. (1985). *Dreaming: A Cognitive-Psychological Approach*. Hillsdale, N.J.: Lawrence Erlbaum Associates.

——— and Schmidt, M. (1983). "Temporal Sequence and Unit Composition in Dream Reports from Different Stages of Sleep." *Sleep* 6: 265–280.

French, T., and Fromm, E. (1964). *Dream Interpretation*. New York: Basic Books.

Freud, S. (1953). "The Interpretation of Dreams." In J. Strachey (Ed. and Trans.), *The Standard Edition of the Complete Psychological Works of Sigmund Freud*, vols. 4 and 5. London: Hogarth Press. [Original work published 1900].

———. (1955). "Beyond the Pleasure Principle." *The Standard Edition of the Complete Psychological Works of Sigmund Freud*, vol. 18, pp. 3–71. London: Hogarth Press. [Original work published 1920].

———. (1964). "New Introductory Lectures on Psychoanalysis." *The Standard Edition of the Complete Psychological Works of Sigmund Freud*, vol. 22, pp. 3–30. London: Hogarth Press. [Original work published 1933].

Garfield, P. (1988). *Women's Bodies, Women's Dreams.* New York: Ballantine Books.

Griffith, R., Miyago, O., and Tago, A. (1958). "The Universality of Typical Dreams: Japanese vs. Americans." *American Anthropologist* 60: 1173–1179.

Hall, C. (1951). "What People Dream About." *Scientific American* 184: 60–63.

———. (1953a). *The Meaning of Dreams.* New York: Harper.

———. (1953b). "A Cognitive Theory of Dream Symbols." *Journal of General Psychology* 48: 169–186.

———. (1953c). "A Cognitive Theory of Dreams." *Journal of General Psychology* 49: 273–282.

———. (1955). "The Significance of the Dream of Being Attacked." *Journal of Personality* 24: 164–180.

———. (1967). "Caveat Lector." *Psychoanalytic Review* 54: 655–661.

———. (1969). "Content Analysis of Dreams: Categories, Units, and Norms." In G. Gerbner (Ed.), *The Analysis of Communication Content,*" pp. 147–158. New York: John Wiley and Sons.

———. (1982). "T's Dreams: A Case Study." Unpublished monograph, Special Collections, McHenry Library, University of California, Santa Cruz.

———. (1984). " 'A Ubiquitous Sex Difference in Dreams' Revisited." *Journal of Personality and Social Psychology* 46: 1109–1117.

——— and Domhoff, B. (1962). "Friends and Enemies in Dreams." Unpublished paper, Special Collections, McHenry Library, University of California, Santa Cruz.

——— and Domhoff, B. (1963a). "A Ubiquitous Sex Difference in Dreams." *Journal of Abnormal and Social Psychology* 66: 278–280.

——— and Domhoff, B. (1963b). "Aggression in Dreams." *International Journal of Social Psychiatry* 9: 259–267.

——— and Domhoff, B. (1964). "Friendliness in Dreams." *Journal of Social Psychology* 62: 309–314.

—— and Domhoff, B. (1968), "The Dreams of Freud and Jung." *Psychology Today* (June): 42–45, 64–65.

——, Domhoff, B., Blick, K., and Weesner, K. (1982). "The Dreams of College Men and Women in 1950 and 1980: A Comparison of Dream Contents and Sex Differences." *Sleep*, 5: 188–194.

—— and Lind, R. (1970). *Dreams, Life and Literature: A Study of Franz Kafka.* Chapel Hill: University of North Carolina Press.

—— and Nordby, V. (1972). *The Individual and His Dreams.* New York: New American Library.

—— and Van De Castle, R. (1966). *The Content Analysis of Dreams.* New York: Appleton-Century-Crofts.

Harris, I. (1948). "Observations Concerning Typical Anxiety Dreams." *Psychiatry* 11: 301–309.

Hartmann, E. (1984). *The Nightmare.* New York: Basic Books.

Hunt, H. (1986). "Some Relations Between the Cognitive Psychology of Dreams and Dream Phenomenology." *Journal of Mind and Behavior* 7: 213–228.

Jones, E. (1953, 1955, 1957). *The Life and Work of Sigmund Freud*, 3 vols. New York: Basic Books.

Jung, C. (1974). *Dreams.* Princeton, N.J.: Princeton University Press.

Kramer, M. (1982). "The Psychology of the Dream: Art or Science? *Psychiatric Journal of the University of Ottawa* 7: 87–100.

——, Schoen, L., and Kinney, L. (1987). "Nightmares in Vietnam Veterans." *Journal of the American Academy of Psychoanalysis* 15: 67–81.

——, Winget, C., and Whitman, R. (1971). "A City Dreams: A Survey Approach to Normative Dream Content." *American Journal of Psychiatry* 127: 1350–1356.

Lakoff, G. (1987). *Women, Fire, and Dangerous Things.* Chicago: University of Chicago Press.

LaRue, R. (1970). "Recurrent Dreams." Unpublished term research paper for a course on dreams taught by G. William Domhoff, University of California, Santa Cruz.

Maybruck, P. (1989). *Pregnancy and Dreams* Los Angeles: J. P. Tarcher.

Moffitt, A., and Hoffman, R. (1987). "On the Question of the Functions of Dreaming." Paper presented at the annual meetings of the Association of Professional Sleep Societies, Copenhagen.

Moss, C., Thompson, M., and Nolte, J. (1962). "An Additional Study in Hysteria: The Case of Alice M." *International Journal of Clinical and Experimental Hyponosis* 10: 59–74.

Pivik, T. (1978). "Tonic States and Phasic Events in Relation to Sleep Mentation." In A. Arkin, J. Antrobus, and S. Ellman (Eds.), *The Mind in Sleep: Psychology and Psychophysiology*, pp. 245–271. Hillsdale, N.J.: Lawrence Erlbaum Associates.

Riechers, M., Kramer, M., and Trinder, J. (1970). "A Replication of the Hall-Van De Castle Character Scale Norms." *Psychophysiology* 7: 238.

Robbins, P., and Houshi, F. (1983). "Some Observations on Recurrent Dreams." *Bulletin of the Menninger Clinic* 47: 262–265.

Rupprecht, C. (1985). "The Common Language of Women's Dreams: Colloquy of Mind and Body." In E. Lauter and C. Rupprecht (Eds.), *Feminist Archetypal Theory: Interdisciplinary Re-Visions of Jungian Thought*, pp. 187–219. Knoxville: University of Tennessee Press.

Smith, M., and Hall, C. (1964). "An Investigation of Regression in a Long Dream Series." *Journal of Gerontology* 19: 66–71.

Stukane, E. (1985). *The Dream Worlds of Pregnancy*. New York: Quill Press.

Tonay, V. (1990–91). "California Women and their Dreams: A Historical and Sub-Cultural Comparison of Dream Content." *Imagination, Cognition, and Personality* 10: 83–97.

Van De Castle, R. (1971). *The Psychology of Dreaming*. New York: General Learning Press.

———. (1986). "Phases of Women's Dreams." Paper presented to the annual meetings of the Association for the Study of Dreams, Ottawa, Canada.

Wilmer, H. (1982). "Vietnam and Madness: Dreams of Schizophrenic Veterans." *Journal of the American Academy of Psychoanalysis* 10: 47–65.

9

David Koulack ▬▬▬▬▬▬▬▬▬▬

Dreams and Adaptation to Contemporary Stress

The discovery of rapid eye movement (REM) sleep (Aserinsky and Kleitman 1953, 1955) gave impetus to a vast amount of work on dreaming. A number of the early studies were conducted to ascertain if, in fact, REM sleep might be associated with dreaming (e.g., Dement and Kleitman, 1957; Foulkes, 1962; Goodenough et al., 1965; Goodenough et al., 1959; Hobson, Goldfrank, and Snyder, 1965; Rechtschaffen, Verdone, and Wheaton, 1963; Wolpert and Trosman, 1958).

In general, it was found that dreams could be obtained from abrupt awakenings during REM sleep about 80 percent of the time. It was also ascertained that dreams could be obtained from abrupt awakenings during nonrapid eye movement (NREM) sleep (Foulkes, 1962; Goodenough et al., 1959; Rechtschaffen et al., 1963) although less readily than from REM sleep. In short, it soon became apparent that rather than being random fleeting events, dreams are an inexorable part of the sleep cycle. These findings in turn led to renewed interest in the question of whether or not dreams might be altered by events occurring both prior to and during sleep.

Altering Dream Content

To explore whether dreams are altered by presleep or during sleep events, investigators resorted to using such stimuli as films (Cartwright, Bernick, Borowitz and Kling, 1969; Cartwright et al., 1972; Collins, Davison, and Breger, 1967; Foulkes et al., 1967; Foulkes and Rechtschaffen, 1964; Karacan et al., 1966; Goodenough et al., 1975; Goodenough et al., 1974; De Koninck and Koulack, 1975; Witkin and Lewis, 1967), social isolation (Wood, 1962), problem solving and exercise (Hauri, 1967), water deprivation (Bokert, 1967; Dement and Wolpert, 1958), stressful intellectual activities (Cohen and Cox, 1975; Koulack, Prevost, and De Koninck,

1985; Koulack and Wright, 1987), subliminal stimulation (Fisher, 1959), posthypnotic suggestion (Tart, 1964), sound stimulation (Berger, 1963; Castaldo and Holtzman, 1967, 1969; De Koninck and Koulack, 1975; Dement and Wolpert, 1958), light and water (Dement and Wolpert, 1958), and electrical stimulation (Koulack, 1969) .

In addition, some studies explored the effects of life experiences on dreaming such as group therapy (Breger, Hunter, and Lane, 1971), desensitization (Koulack, LeBow, and Church 1976), disabilities and ailments (Breger et al., 1971; Newton, 1970; Ryan, 1961; Sabini, 1981), the menstrual cycle (Schultz and Koulack, 1980; Sirois-Berliss and De Koninck, 1982; Swanson and Foulkes, 1968), gender (Domhoff, Blick and Weesner, 1982; Hall, 1984; Hall, et al., 1982; Kramer, Kinney, and Scharf, 1983), age (Blick and Howe, 1984), personality types (Hicks, Chancellor, and Clark, 1987), and even the first night in the laboratory itself (Dement, Kahn, and Roffwarg, 1965).

The specific results of these studies are as varied as the stimuli and experiences examined. However, in general, the data suggest that events, and particularly events of an unusual or stressful nature, occurring prior to or during sleep do influence the content of dreams. The nature of the influence can take a number of different forms. For example, elements of the experience can be incorporated directly into the dream narrative, the emotionality of the dreams can be modified, activity in the dreams can be changed, and the types of interactions in the dream can be altered.

The mounting evidence that dreams, in fact, are subject to modification by different sorts of events reopened speculation as to whether such modification reflected some sort of adaptive function. Freud (1953) had suggested that dreams permit the expression of unconscious, infantile fantasies and the primary purpose of incorporation of elements from the day serve only to mask the expression of these wishes. However, contemporary theorists (e.g., Breger, 1967; French and Fromm, 1964; Greenberg et al., 1970; Jones, 1962) expanded Freud's view and suggested that dreams serve an adaptive function in dealing with contemporary stress. Although the mechanism for adaptation is never precisely identified, the underlying theme of these notions is that dreaming provides an opportunity for the dreamer to integrate affectively charged material with past, similar material that has already reached a successful resolution. Dallett (1973) called these types of notions *mastery* hypotheses. Implicit to the various forms of the mastery hypothesis is the assumption that incorporation of the stressful event into the dream is necessary for the dream to serve its adaptive function. However, there is some difference of opinion as to whether or not the dream has to be remembered to aid in adaptation to a stressor. For example, Greenberg et al. (1970) suggest that adaptation is best served by unrecalled dreams whereas Breger et al. (1971) argue that dreams have to be remembered and worked through to aid in adaptation.

While the mastery notion has a number of adherents, a seemingly antithetical position rooted in Jung's (1960) notion of compensation gained some measure of support from a few of the early studies of the influence of presleep experience on dreams. As Dallett (1973) points out, compensation for Jung meant the restoration of intrapsychic balance. In the context of dreaming then, dreams that provide an opposing experience to that of the waking state may be considered compensatory in nature. Within this framework for example, the work of Wood (1962), who placed subjects in sensory isolation before sleep and observed an increase in social contact in their dreams, might be interpreted as supportive of the compensatory notion of dreaming. Similarly, Hauri's (1967) finding that subjects who were involved in problem solving tasks or physical activity prior to going to sleep dreamed less of those events could also be viewed as supporting the compensatory notion, as could Foulkes et al.'s (1967) results showing that following the presentation of a baseball film the dreams of male subjects were more aggressive than after they had seen a western film. In so far as such compensatory dreams restore balance to the ego (Jung, 1960), they too may be considered adaptive in nature.

Thus, although the mastery and compensation notions are antithetical to one another, their proponents could point to disparate findings to support their positions. That is to say, supporters of the mastery notion were able to provide a wealth of data indicating that incorporation of presleep events into dreams takes place, while proponents of the compensation notion could point to studies where dreams provide experiences different from, and apparently compensatory to, those of waking life.

The issue was still further clouded by a couple of REM deprivation studies whose findings could be interpreted as support for either notion. In one study (Greenberg, Pillard, Pearlman, 1972) three groups of subjects saw a stressful film just prior to bedtime and again the next morning. One group was REM-deprived, a second was awakened during non-REM sleep and the third was allowed to have uninterrupted sleep. It was found that the REM-deprived subjects were more distressed at the second viewing of the film than those from the other two groups. Similarly, Grieser, Greenberg and Harrison (1972) demonstrated that REM sleep facilitated the retention of material containing affective components whereas non-REM sleep facilitated retention of nonemotional material. For both of these studies, it might be argued that whatever the components of REM-sleep dreaming, they served to help the dreamer cope with affectively charged material. Unfortunately, because we have no access to the dreams, we can only speculate about the nature of the dream content. It is equally plausible to argue that the dreams aided adaptation to the stressful presleep material by providing a vehicle for subjects to "work through" the material as it is to argue that the dreams aided in adaptation by providing an experience that compensated for the stressful situation.

Investigations of Adaptation

To try to resolve this issue, some investigators began to examine dream content and its effects on waking mood (Cohen and Cox, 1975; De Koninck and Koulack, 1975; Koulack et al., 1985). They shifted the thrust of their research so that dreams which had previously been examined as dependent variables were now utilized as independent variables. Making the assumption that morning (waking) mood is a reasonable measure of adaptation to a presleep stressful situation, these studies essentially asked the question whether it is better to dream about a stressful event or dream about something else instead.

In the Cohen and Cox (1975) study, subjects were assigned to either a negative or positive presleep condition. In the negative condition, they were treated in a perfunctory manner and were given a difficult test just prior to going to sleep. In the positive condition, the subjects were treated in a friendly fashion and given an easy test to complete. It was found that subjects in the negative condition who incorporated elements from the presleep experience in their dreams exhibited an increase in positive affect in the morning, whereas nonincorporators and subjects in the positive condition did not. These findings were interpreted as being consistent with the mastery hypothesis, that is, subjects who were confronted by a stressful waking situation and subsequently dreamed about it, felt better in the morning than subjects in the same condition who exhibited no incorporation of the stressful stimulus.

De Koninck and Koulack (1975) utilized a worker's compensation film, *It Didn't Have to Happen*, as the stressful presleep stimulus. The film depicts three workshop accidents, the last one resulting in a death. Subjects saw the film both before going to bed and again upon awakening in the morning. Those subjects who exhibited an increase in anxiety after viewing the film a second time exhibited more film incorporations during the night than those subjects who exhibited no increase in anxiety after the morning presentation of the film. These results seem more consistent with the compensation hypothesis. That is, not dreaming about the stressor seemed to enable subjects to better cope with its second presentation.

Finally, a third study (Koulack et al., 1985) attempted to resolve the discrepancies just described. They felt that the disparate findings between the two studies might have resulted from procedural differences alone. In particular, they noted that the subjects in the Cohen and Cox (1975) study spent only one night in the laboratory whereas in the De Koninck and Koulack (1975) study subjects slept for three nights including one adaptation night. They speculated that the Cohen and Cox (1975) subjects may have been made so anxious by the combination of the stress manipulation and the first night in the laboratory that they reached an asymptote of negative affect and the only possible affective change was in a positive direction. This notion was bolstered somewhat by the fact that the control subjects in the Cohen and Cox (1975) study who had had a positive presleep experience exhibited no change in positive affect the following morning.

Koulack, Prevost, and De Koninck (1985) utilized a difficult intellectual task similar to the one used by Cohen and Cox (1975) as a presleep stressor and an easy intellectual task as a control. They found that subjects in the difficult test condition who exhibited an increase in morning anxiety had significantly more treatment incorporations than subjects who exhibited no increase in morning anxiety, a result consonant with the compensation hypothesis.

It should also be noted that the design of the Koulack, Prevost, and De Koninck (1985) study permitted the assessment of pre- and post-sleep mood surrounding a night of uninterrupted sleep after presentation of the stressor. This condition, which took place on the night just prior to the dream collection night, revealed a slight decrease in anxiety from night to morning, a finding somewhat consistent with those of Greenberg, Pillard, and Pearlman (1972) and Grieser, Greenberg and Harrison (1972) I mentioned earlier.

Incorporation and Adaptation

Recently Wright and Koulack (1987) advanced a disruption-avoidance-adaptation model to try to reconcile the disparate findings from the many studies described previously. According to their notion, dreams can play both mastery and avoidance roles in relation to contemporary stress.

In their view, mastery is an ongoing process that begins with the occurrence of a stressful event. Although stress can be defined as an environmental event that threatens the existence or the well-being of the individual (Baum, Singer, and Baum, 1981), the experience of such a threat is dependent on the individual's appraisal of it (Lazurus, 1966). Consequently, two components play a role in the duration of the mastery process. The first is the nature and extent of the stressor itself. The second is the personality of the individual and the personal relevance the stressor has for that individual.

Within this context, if the stressor is particularly potent or relevant to the individual, Wright and Koulack (1987) postulate the attempts at mastery should flow from the waking state into sleep and back again until some resolution of the situation (adaptation to the stressor) occurs. Adaptation is broadly defined to include "concepts as varied as habituation to a stressful stimulus to the dreaming of a solution to a pressing problem" (p. 173).

Wright and Koulack (1987) assumed the process of mastery is the same as that which occurs during the waking state. If during the waking state we are confronted by a stressful event or a problem, we think about it, perhaps even obsess about it, until we obtain a successful resolution of it, until we are inured of it, or until we have to put it aside because of the demands of our waking lives.

Thus, within the context of the disruption-avoidance-adaptation model, incorporation is taken as evidence of attempts at mastery. It is analogous to thinking about a stressful event while we are awake and trying to deal with it in some way. Avoidance, on the other hand, is pictured as a respite from the burdens of the problem. It is analogous to times in the waking state when we put aside our problems either to give ourselves some respite from them or because there are other, more pressing demands for our attention. It is a response, if you will, to the demands of our sleeping lives.

Redefining Avoidance Dreams

The notion of avoidance as espoused by Wright and Koulack (1987) is a term under which are subsumed compensation dreams (e.g., Wood, 1962), dreams with complementary affect to stressful waking or sleeping experiences (e.g., Koulack et al., 1976) or dreams which have no apparent relationship to the stressful experience (e.g., De Koninck and Koulack, 1975). Perhaps a more general, accurate, and ultimately more useful description of avoidance dreams would be that they are dreams devoid of disturbing affect. Such a description is more useful because, although still embracing the original dream categories described earlier, it now includes an additional dream type. Specifically dreams that incorporate the stressful presleep material *without* its concomitant affect. These various types of avoidance dreams may serve an important adaptive function in two distinct ways. First, they may help to maintain the integrity of sleep itself. Second, they may themselves actually provide a useful medium for the mastery of stressful events.

Avoidance Dreams and the Integrity of Sleep

The impact of taking our concerns to bed with us is beginning to become clearer. An examination of dream studies and sleep studies that utilized similar or identical presleep stressors is particularly instructive. They indicate that those presleep stimuli which have an impact on dream content or concomitant dream affect also have an impact on the structure of sleep itself.

For example, Browman and Cartwright (1980), Dement, Kahn, and Roffwarg (1965), and Hall (1967) found the first night in the laboratory altered the content of dreams. Agnew, Webb, and Williams (1966) and Webb and Campbell (1979) found the first night in the laboratory resulted in more time awake, more stage 1 sleep, less REM, more sleep stage changes, more arousal, and generally longer latencies.

Tart (1964) found hypnotic suggestion altered dream content and Stoyva (1965) found hypnotic suggestion reduced the total REM time. Bokert (1967) found water deprivation increased thirst-related dreams, and Koulack (1970) found water deprivation decreased REM period time, decreased REM period length, and increased body movements.

Koulack, LeBow, and Church (1976) found desensitization altered dream affect and altered the latency to sleep and REM density. Koulack, Prevost, and De Koninck (1985) found a stressful intellectual activity increased anxiety associated with dreams, also increased sleep latency, and decreased REM density.

Goodenough et al. (1974, 1975) found an increase in dream anxiety and an alteration of dream content following stressful presleep films. Baekeland, Koulack, and Lasky (1968), De Koninck and Koulack (1975), and Goodenough et al. (1975) found that stressful presleep films resulted in a greater proportion of REM periods being terminated by spontaneous awakening, a greater number of REM period awakenings, increase in REM density, increase in REM period respiratory irregularity, and increases in sleep latency.

In addition, Goodenough et al. (1975) found dreams containing high levels of anxiety were accompanied by more rapid respiratory rates and higher REM density than dreams containing relatively low levels of anxiety. And similarly, they found that dreams containing a relatively high level of hostility were accompanied by more rapid respiratory rates than were dreams containing a relatively low level of hostility.

In short, these data suggest that stressful or disturbing important events occurring during the waking state alter the content of dreams and their accompanying affect. Such alteration in turn is accompanied by a disturbance in the sleep cycle.

This is particularly interesting in light of the findings of sleep deprivation studies (e.g., Agnew, Webb, and Williams, 1967; Carskadon and Dement, 1979; Dement, 1960; Gulevich, Dement, and Johnson, 1966; Johnson and MacLeod, 1973; Sampson, 1965; Webb, 1973; Webb and Agnew, 1974). They demonstrate a need for the sleeper to obtain his or her normal compliment of sleep with its appropriate components. Artificial reduction in one or more of the stages of sleep is subsequently met by attempts to make up for the lost time when sleep is no longer interrupted.

Therefore it seems reasonable to assume that if the daytime stressor that effects the course of sleep continues, the individual has to find some way to bring about a proper course of sleep, to reestablish homeostasis. The disruptive dreams have to be "turned off" as it were. One obvious way of doing this is to replace the disturbing dreams with pleasant ones or at least with innocuous ones (Koulack, 1991).

In his book, Horne (1988) suggests that the most important part of sleep is what he calls *core sleep*. This sleep occurs in the first part of the night and is typified by non-REM sleep, particularly stage 4. Interestingly enough, in a study of mental activity during sleep, Rechtschaffen, Verdone, and Wheaton (1963) compared the content of reports obtained from REM and non-REM sleep. They found that "compared with REM mentation, subjects report NREM mentation as . . . less emotional and more pleasant." (p. 411). It seems reasonable to speculate then, in light of the previous discussion, that these relatively pleasant dreams are adaptive insofar as they provide no impetus for arousal on the part of the dreamer.

Avoidance Dreams and the Mastery of Stress

Although incorporation may logically be assumed to represent evidence for attempts at mastery of a stressful event, it does not necessarily follow that it is the most efficacious means to attain mastery. Indeed, there are some theorists (e.g., Greenberg et al., 1970) who suggest that nonremembered dreams may better serve in the mastery of contemporary stress. One of the important reasons for this may be derived from consideration of the process of dream recall itself.

The arousal-retrieval model of dream recall (Koulack and Goodenough, 1976, 1977) identifies some of the components necessary for successful dream recall. Although not all of the components have relevance for the present discussion (for example, the role of interference and distraction in morning dream recall failure) the elements that provide the necessary, although not sufficient, conditions for successful dream recall are of particular importance. Essentially, the arousal-retrieval model suggests that successful dream recall is contingent on a type of information processing strategy or encoding that makes the dream material amenable to subsequent waking retrieval.

The information processing is postulated to involve a two-stage process in which dream material is transferred from a short-term to a long-term storage. A number of authors (e.g., Goodenough, 1967, 1968; Goodenough et al., 1971; Hebb, 1949; Portnoff et al., 1966; Wolpert, 1972) have suggested that the transfer of information from short-term to long-term storage is impaired during sleep. The arousal-retrieval model takes this notion in a somewhat different direction. In essence it suggests that sleep impairs the transfer of information from short-term to long-term storage in a form amenable to subsequent retrieval on waking. It further suggests that arousal while the target material still resides in the short-term storage enhances immediate recall and subsequent recall (for example in the morning) because, first, it permits retrieval directly from the short-term store and second, a sufficient level of arousal provides the wherewithal for transfer of the material to the long-term store in a form compatible with subsequent waking thought.

The evidence for this notion comes from the findings of a number of sleep learning studies as well as studies of dream recall itself. For example, the sleep learning studies of Evans and Orchard (1969), Koukkou and Lehmann (1968), Jus and Jus (1972), and Jus et al. (1969) basically demonstrated that waking recall of stimuli presented during sleep is a function of arousal at or near the time of stimulation. Similarly, studies by Goodenough et al., (1971) and Portnoff et al., (1966) indicated that arousal levels during brief periods of wakefulness were crucial in determining the likelihood that incidental material would subsequently be recalled. Finally, the classical dream recall studies of Goodenough et al. (1959), Shapiro, Goodenough, and Gryler (1963), and Shapiro, Goodenough, Lewis, and Sleser (1965) demonstrated that abrupt awakenings in the midst of REM periods greatly enhances the likelihood of dream recall.

Interestingly, Baekeland, Koulack, and Lasky (1968) found that the frequency of arousal during the night, and particularly REM sleep arousal, increases as a result of presleep stress. In addition, both Baekeland (1969) and Cory (1975) reported that dream recall obtained by diary and questionnaire is significantly related to the number of awakenings subjects report having had during the course of the night.

In the framework of the arousal-retrieval model, it appears that dreaming about stressful material with its concomitant affect may not only result in arousal but may trigger an information processing system whereby dreams are both better recalled and also fitted into a framework of waking thoughts. The former consequence may have implications for the psychological well-being of the dreamer, whereas the latter may have information-processing implications.

As far as the well-being of the dreamer is concerned, it is not unreasonable to assume that recall of a dream related to a stressful event redintegrates the stressor. Insofar as such redintegration does *not* lead to a resolution of the stressful experience, it can hardly be considered adaptive. To put it another way, if sleep provides a respite from the day's cares, dreaming about them in a direct and disturbing manner would seem to be self-defeating.

In the information processing dimension, it seems reasonable to assume that a different type of information processing may take place during dreaming when there is no arousal (Koulack, 1983). Such processing would be unlikely to be subject to distraction or impaired by external stimuli. It would probably be relatively flexible in nature because it would not be bound by the constraints of waking thought.

In this context, it would appear that the type of dream which would be ideally suited for aiding in the mastery of a stressful event would be one in which the event is depicted without its concomitant affect. In this manner, the dreamer would be less likely to be aroused and yet could avail himself or herself of the more fluid encoding possibilities postulated to exist during uninterrupted sleep.

Unfortunately, the experimental literature has very little to tell us about such dreams. There are of course the REM deprivation studies of Greenberg et al., (1972), and Grieser, Greenberg and Harrison (1972) which tell us only that REM sleep seems to aid in adaptation. However, as I have already pointed out we have no information about the actual content of the dreams. Nevertheless, there is some presumptive evidence to be gleaned from the data of the study by Koulack et al. (1985). As I mentioned earlier, in that study, subjects exhibited a decrease in morning anxiety after a night of uninterrupted sleep following the presentation of a presleep stressful intellectual activity. Although there were some alterations in sleep parameters (specifically latency to sleep and REM density) there was no evidence of increased arousal during sleep. On the following night, when subjects in the stressful condition were subjected to experimental awakenings, those subjects who exhibited an increase in morning anxiety also exhibited more incorporation of the stressful stimulus and more anxiety in their dreams. Although it is reasonable to assume that subjects dreamed about the stressful event on the night of uninterrupted sleep the low levels of arousal suggest that such dreams were devoid of disturbing affect.

In any case, there can be no doubt that dreams of stressful events, devoid of affect, can and do occur. For example, Koulack et al. (1976) studied the dreams of a phobic subject undergoing desensitization over a period of eleven nights. The subject complained of two related fears—those of noise and closed spaces. Over the course of treatment and dream collection, the subject showed a diminution in both dream anxiety and depression although phobic elements appeared in at least some dreams of every dream collection night. Of course, whether or not these dreams aided in the process of mastery of the phobia is still an open question. Nevertheless, the results are suggestive and are worthy of future, more systematic research.

Dreams and Stress

The research that I have described in this chapter represents small bits and pieces of an intriguing puzzle. For reasons that I have discussed elsewhere (Koulack, 1984), dream research is fraught with difficulty. Not the least of the problems is the necessity of examining some of the most important questions in what can be described only as a roundabout fashion. Nevertheless, I think we can begin to make some modest statements and draw some inferences about the relationship between dreams and contemporary stress on the basis of the research I have described.

First, there seems to be no question that stressful (or unusual) presleep experiences (as well as such experiences occurring during sleep) can and do alter the content of dreams as well as their concomitant affect.

Second, although such stressful stimuli are able to alter sleep patterns in general, their incorporation into REM period dreams may result in increases in REM-period arousal.

Third, such arousal may result in better waking recall of the disturbing dream content but at the same time may inhibit a more fluid encoding process, which is postulated to be best suited for mastery of the stressful material.

Fourth, dream material that at once incorporates the stressor but is devoid of concomitant affect may be ideally suited for mastery by allowing the dreamer to experience the stressor without being aroused by it.

Within this context, then, avoidance dreams would seem to play an important role in coping with contemporary stress. By allowing the dreamer a respite from stressful events, such dreams may be conceived of as helping to restore the integrity of sleep and promoting the psychological well-being of the individual. Insofar as they contain elements of the stressor without the concomitant negative affect, they may also aid in the mastery process itself.

References

Agnew, H. W., Webb, W. B., and Williams, R. L. (1966). "The First Night Effect: An EEG Study of Sleep." *Psychophysiology* 2: 263–266.

———. (1967). "Comparison of Stage Four and 1-REM Deprivation." *Perceptual and Motor Skills* 24: 851–858.

Aserinsky, E., and Kleitman, N. (1953). "Regular Occurring Periods of Eye Motility and Concomitant Phenomena During Sleep." *Science* 118: 273–274.

———. (1955). "Two Types of Ocular Motility Occurring in Sleep." *Journal of Applied Physiology* 8: 1–10.

Baekeland, F. (1969). "Correlates of Home Dream Recall: Reported Home Sleep Characteristics and Home Dream Recall." *Comprehensive Psychiatry* 10: 482–491.

———, Koulack, D., and Lasky, R. (1968). "Effects of a Stressful Presleep Experience on Electro-Encephalograph-Recorded Sleep." *Psychophysiology* 4: 436–443.

Baum, A., Singer, J. E., and Baum, C. S. (1981). "Stress and the Environment." *Journal of Social Issues* 37: 4–35.

Berger, R. J. (1963). "Experimental Modification of Dream Content by Meaningful Verbal Stimuli." *British Journal of Psychiatry* 109: 722–740.

Blick, K. A., and Howe, J. B. (1984). "A Comparison of the Emotional Content of Dreams Recalled by Young and Elderly Women." *The Journal of Psychology* 116: 143–146.

Bokert, E. (1967). "The Effects of Thirst and a Related Verbal Stimulus on Dream Reports." *Dissertation Abstracts* 28: 4753B.

Breger, L. (1967). "Function of Dreams." *Journal of Abnormal Psychology Monograph* 72:, no. 5, Pt. 2, Whole No. 641.

———, Hunter, I., and Lane, R. W. (1971). "The Effects of Stress on Dreams." *Psychological Issues*, no. 3, Monograph 27.

Browman, C. P., and Cartwright, R. D. (1980). "The First-Night Effects on Sleep and Dreams." *Biological Psychiatry* 15: 809–812.

Carskadon, M. A., and Dement, W. C. (1979). "Effects of Total Sleep Loss on Sleep Tendency." *Perceptual and Motor Skills* 48: 495–506.

Cartwright, R. D., Bernick, N., Borowitz, E., and Kling, A. (1969). "Effects of an Erotic Movie on the Sleep and Dreams of Young Men." *Archives of General Psychiatry* 20: 262–271.

Cartwright, R. D., Kasniak, A., Borowitz, E., and Kling, A. (1972). "The Dreams of Homosexual and Heterosexual Subjects to the Same Movie." *Psychophysiology* 9: 117.

Castaldo, V., and Holtzman, P. S. (1967). "The Effects of Hearing One's Own Voice on Sleep Mentation." *Journal of Nervous and Mental Disease* 144: 2–13.

———. (1969). "The Effects of Hearing One's Own Voice on Dream Content: A Replication." *Journal of Nervous and Mental Disease* 148: 74–82.

Cohen, D. B., and Cox, C. (1975). "Neuroticism in the Sleep Laboratory: Implications for Representational and Adaptive Properties of Dreaming." *Journal of Abnormal Psychology*, 84: 91–108.

Collins, A. M., Davison, L., and Breger, L. (1967). "Dream Function in Adaptation to Threat: A Preliminary Study." Paper presented at the meeting of the Association for the Psychophysiological Study of Sleep, Santa Monica, Calif.

Cory, T. L. (1975). "Objective Factors in Dream Recall." *Dissertation Abstracts International* 34: 1042B.

Dallett, J. (1973). "Theories of Dream Function." *Psychological Bulletin* 79: 408–416.

De Koninck, J. M., and Koulack, D. (1975). "Dream Content and Adaptation to a Stressful Stimulus Situation." *Journal of Abnormal Psychology* 84: 250–260.

Dement, W. C. (1960). "The Effect of Dream Deprivation." Science 131: 1705–1707.

———, Kahn, E., and Roffwarg, H. P. (1965). "The Influence of the Laboratory Situation on the Dreams of the Experimental Subject." *Journal of Nervous and Mental Disease* 140: 119–131.

——— and Kleitman, N. (1957). "The Relation of Eye Movements During Sleep to Dream Activity: An Objective Method for the Study of Dreaming." *Journal of Experimental Psychology* 53: 339–346.

——— and Wolpert, E. A. (1958). "The Relation of Eye Movements, Body Motility, and External Stimuli to Dream Content." *Journal of Experimental Psychology* 55: 543–553.

Evans, F. J., and Orchard, W. (1969). "Sleep Learning: The Successful Waking Recall of Material Presented During Sleep." *Psychophysiology* 6: 269.

Fisher, C. (1959). "Subliminal and Supraliminal Influences on Dreams." *American Journal of Psychiatry* 116: 1009–1017.

Foulkes, D. (1962). "Dream Reports from Different Stages of Sleep." *Journal of Abnormal and Social Psychology* 65: 14–25.

Foulkes, W. D., Pivik, T., Steadman, H. S., Spear, P. S., and Symonds, J. D. (1967). "Dreams of the Male Child: An EEG Study." *Journal of Abnormal Psychology* 72: 457–467.

Foulkes, W. D., and Rechtschaffen, A. (1964). "Presleep Determinants of Dream Content: Effects of Two Films." *Perceptual and Motor Skills* 19: 983–1005.

French, T. M., and Fromm, E. (1964). *Dream Interpretation: A New Approach.* New York: Basic Books.

Freud, S. (1953). "The Interpretation of Dreams." In J. Strachey (Ed. and Trans.), *The Standard Edition of the Complete Psychological Works of Sigmund Freud*, Vol. 4. London: Hogarth. [Original work published 1900].

Goodenough, D. R. (1967). "Some Recent Studies of Dream Recall." In H. A. Witkin and H. B. Lewis (Eds.), *Experimental Studies of Dreaming.* New York: Random House.

———. (1968). "The Phenomena of Dream Recall." In L. E. Abt and B. F. Riess (Eds.), *Progress in Clinical Psychology*, vol. 8. New York: Grune and Stratton.

———, Lewis, H. B., Shapiro, A., Jaret, L., and Sleser, I. (1965). "Dream Reporting Following Abrupt and Gradual Awakenings from Different Types of Sleep." *Journal of Personality and Social Psychology* 2: 170–179.

———, Sapan, J., Cohen, H., Portnoff, G., and Shapiro, A. (1971). "Some Experiments Concerning the Effects of Sleep on Memory." *Psychophysiology* 8: 749–762.

———, Shapiro, A., Holden, M., and Steinschriber, L. G. (1959). "A Comparison of 'Dreamers' and 'Nondreamers': Eye Movements, Electroencephalograms, and the Recall of Dreams." *Journal of Abnormal and Social Psychology* 59: 295–302.

———, Witkin, H. A., Koulack, D., and Cohen, H. (1975). "The Effects of Stress Films on Dream Affect and on Respiration and Eye-Movement Activity During Rapid-Eye Movement Sleep." *Psychophysiology* 12: 313–320.

———, Witkin, H. A., Lewis, H. B., Koulack, D., and Cohen, H. (1974). "Repression, Interference, and Field Dependence as Factors in Dreaming Forgetting." *Journal of Abnormal Psychology* 83: 32–44.

Greenberg, R., Pearlman, C., Fingar, R., Kantrowitz, J., and Kawliche, S. (1970). "The Effects of Dream Deprivation: Implications for a Theory of the Psychological Function of Dreaming." *British Journal of Medical Psychology* 43: 1–11.

Greenberg, R., Pillard, R., and Pearlman, C. (1972). "The Effect of Dream Deprivation on Adaptation to Stress." *Psychosomatic Medicine* 34: 257–262.

Greiser, C., Greenberg, R., and Harrison, R. H. (1972). "The Adaptive Function of Sleep: The Differential Effects of Sleep and Dreaming on Recall." *Journal of Abnormal Psychology* 80: 280–286.

Gulevich, G., Dement, W. C., and Johnson, L. (1966). "Psychiatric and EEG Observations on a Case of Prolonged (264 h) Wakefulness." *Archives of General Psychiatry* 15: 29–35.

Hall, C. S. (1967). "Representation of the Laboratory Setting in Dreams." *Journal of Nervous and Mental Disease* 144: 198–206.

———. (1984). "'A Ubiquitous Sex Difference in Dreams' Revisited." *Journal of Personality and Social Psychology* 46: 1109–1117.

———, Domhoff, G. W., Blick, K. A., and Weesner, K. E. (1982). "The Dreams of College Men and Women in 1950 and 1980: A Comparison of Dream Contents and Sex Differences." *Sleep* 5: 188–194.

Hauri, P. (1967). "Effects of Evening Activity on Subsequent Sleep and Dreams." Ph.D. dissertation, University of Chicago.

Hebb, D. O. (1949). *The Organization of Behavior: A Neuropsychological Theory.* New York: John Wiley and Sons.

Hicks, R. A., Chancellor, C., and Clark, T. (1987). "The Valence of Dreams Reported by Type A-B College Students." *Perceptual and Motor Skills* 65: 748–750.

Hobson, J. A., Goldfrank, F., and Snyder, F. (1965). "Respiration and Mental Activity in Sleep." *Journal of Psychiatric Research* 3: 79–90.

Horne, J. (1988). *Why We Sleep: The Function of Sleep in Humans and Other Animals.* Oxford: Oxford University Press.

Johnson, L. C., and MacLeod, W. L. (1973). "Sleep and Awake Behavior During Gradual Sleep Reduction." *Perceptual and Motor Skills* 36: 87–97.

Jones, R. M. (1962). *Ego Synthesis in Dreams.* Cambridge, Mass.: Schnkman.

Jung, C. G. (1960). "On the Nature of Dreams." In Sir H. Read, M. Fordham, G. Adler, and W. McGuire. (Eds.), *The Structure and Dynamics of the Psyche, the Collected Works of C. G. Jung,* Vol. 8, pp. 281–297. New York: Princeton University Press.

Jus, K., and Jus, A. (1972). "Experimental Studies on Memory Disturbances in Pathological and Physiological Conditions." *International Journal of Psychobiology* 2: 205–218.

Jus, K., Kiljan, A., Kubacki, A., Losieczko, T., Wilczak, H., and Jus, A. (1969). "Experimental Studies on Memory During Slow Sleep Stages and REM Stages." *Electroencephalography and Clinical Neurophysiology* 27: 668.

Karacan, I., Goodenough, D. R., Shapiro, A., and Starker, S. (1966). "Erection Cycle During Sleep in Relation to Dream Anxiety." *Archives of General Psychiatry* 20: 183–189.

Koukkou, M., and Lehmann, D. (1968). "EEG and Memory Storage in Sleep Experiments with Humans." *Electroencephalography and Clinical Neurophysiology* 25: 455–462.

Koulack, D. (1969). "Effects of Somatosensory Stimulation on Dream Content." *Archives of General Psychiatry* 20: 718–725.

———. (1970). "Effects of Thirst on the Sleep Cycle." *Journal of Nervous and Mental Disease* 151: 143–145.

———. (1982). "Information Processing During Sleep." In W. P. Koella (Ed.), *Sleep 1982,* pp. 53–55. Basel: Karger.

———. (1984). "Dream Research and Methodology: A Perennial Problem." In M. Bosinelli and P. Cicogna (Eds.), *Psychology of Dreaming,* pp. 47–50. Bologna: Clueb.

————. (1991). *To Catch a Dream: Explorations of Dreaming* Albany: State University of New York Press.

———— and Goodenough, D. R. (1976). "Dream Recall and Dream Recall Failure: An Arousal Retrieval Model." *Psychological Bulletin* 83: 975–984.

———— and Goodenough, D. R. (1977). "Modèle de rappel, des rêves au réveil, proposé pour rendre compte des défauts de souvenir des rêves." *Annales Médicos-Psychologiques* 135: 35–42.

————, LeBow, M. D., and Church, M. (1976). "The Effect of Desensitization on the Sleep and Dreams of a Phobic Subject." *Canadian Journal of Behavioural Science* 8: 814–821.

————, Prevost, F., and De Koninck, J. (1985). "Sleep, Dreaming and Adaptation to an Ego-Threatening Intellectual Activity." *Sleep* 8: 244–253.

———— and Wright, J. (1987). "Dreams and Stress." Paper presented at the Fifth International Congress of Sleep Research, Copenhagen.

Kramer, M., Kinney, M. A., and Scharf, M. (1983). "Sex Differences in Dreams." *The Psychiatric Journal of the University of Ottawa* 8: 1–4.

Lazurus, R. S. (1966). *Psychological Stress and the Coping Process.* New York: McGraw-Hill.

Newton, P. M. (1970). "Recalled Dream Content and the Maintenance of Body Image." *Journal of Abnormal Psychology* 76: 134–139.

Portnoff, G., Baekeland, F., Goodenough, D. R., Karacan, I., and Shapiro, A. (1966). "Retention of Verbal Materials Perceived Immediately Prior to Onset of Non-REM Sleep." *Perceptual and Motor Skills* 22: 751–758.

Rechtschaffen, A., Verdone, P., and Wheaton, J. (1963). "Reports of Mental Activity During Sleep." *Canadian Psychiatric Association Journal* 8: 409–414.

Ryan, J. (1961). "Dreams of Paraplegics." *Archives of General Psychiatry* 5: 286–291.

Sabini, M. (1981). "Dreams as an Aid in Determining Diagnosis, Prognosis and Attitude Towards Treatment." *Psychotherapy and Psychosomatics* 36: 24–36.

Sampson, H. (1965). "Deprivation of Dreaming Sleep by Two Methods: I. Compensatory REM Time." *Archives of General Psychiatry* 13: 79–86.

Schultz, K. L., and Koulack, D. (1980). "Dream Affect and the Menstrual Cycle." *Journal of Nervous and Mental Disease* 168: 436–438.

Shapiro, A., Goodenough, D. R., and Gryler, R. B. (1963). "Dream Recall as a Function of Method of Awakening." *Psychosomatic Medicine* 25: 174–180.

Shapiro, A., Goodenough, D. R., Lewis, H. B., and Sleser, I. (1965). "Gradual Arousal from Sleep: A Determinant of Thinking Reports." *Psychosomatic Medicine* 27: 342–349.

Sirois-Berliss, M., and De Koninck, J. (1982). "Menstrual Distress and Dreams: Adaptation or Interference?" *Psychiatric Journal of the University of Ottawa* 7: 77–86.

Stoyva, J. M. (1965). "Posthypnotically Suggested Dreams and the Sleep Cycle." *Archives of General Psychiatry* 12: 287–295.

Swanson, E. M., and Foulkes, D. (1968). "Dream Content and the Menstrual Cycle." *Journal of Nervous and Mental Disease*, 145: 358–363.

Tart, C. J. (1964). "A Comparison of Suggested Dreams Occurring in Hypnosis and Sleep." *International Journal of Experimental and Clinical Hypnosis* 12: 263–289.

Webb, W. B. (1973). "Selective and Partial Sleep Deprivaton." In W. P. Koella (Ed.), *Sleep: Physiology, Biochemistry, Psychology, Pharmacology, Clinical Implications*, pp. 167–184. Basel: Karger.

—— and Agnew, H. W., Jr. (1974). "The Effects of a Chronic Limitation of Sleep Length." *Psychophysiology* 11: 265–274.

—— and Campbell, S. S. (1979). "The First Night Effect Revisited with Age as a Variable." *Waking Sleep* 3: 319–324.

Witkin, H. A., and Lewis, H. B. (1967). "Presleep Experiences and Dreams." In H. A. Witkin and H. B. Lewis (Eds.), *Experimental Studies of Dreaming*, pp. 148–201. New York: Random House.

Wolpert, E. A. (1972). "Two Classes of Factors Affecting Dream Recall." *Journal of the American Psychoanalytic Association* 20: 45–58.

—— and Trosman, H. (1958). "Studies in Psychophysiology of Dreams: I Experimental Evocation of Sequential Dream Episodes." *Archives of Neurological Psychiatry* 79: 603–606.

Wood, P. (1962). "Dreaming and Social Isolation." Ph.D. dissertation, University of North Carolina.

Wright, J., and Koulack, D. (1987). "Dreams and Contemporary Stress: A Disruption-Avoidance-Adaptation Model." *Sleep* 10: 172–179.

10

Carlyle Smith ━━━━━━━━━━━━━━━━━━━━━━━━━━━

REM Sleep and Learning: Some Recent Findings

The Animal Studies

Over the years my laboratory has been interested in the possible relation between sleep states and learning. Although there are more studies with animals than with humans on this topic, a general picture is emerging (McGrath and Cohen, 1978; Pearlman, 1979; Smith, 1985). It seems that the state of sleep most likely involved with learning-memory processes is rapid eye movement (REM) sleep rather than non-REM (NREM) sleep. It has been observed in the animal studies that if the training task is sufficiently difficult, animals exhibit posttraining increases in REM sleep above normal levels. These REM sleep increases can occur shortly after the end of the training session, but have also been observed many hours and days after the end of training as well. Further, if REM deprivation (REMD) is applied at times after training that coincide with these expected REM sleep increases, learning-memory deficits occur. These special time periods have been called *REM windows* (Smith, 1985).

One of the phenomena that surprised us was the persistence of REM sleep increases following the end of training. REM sleep increases over normal levels have been observed up to a week after the end of training. Depending on the number of training trials, REM windows have been found from 9–12 hours, 17–20 hours and 48–72 hours after the last training trial (Smith, 1985; Smith and Butler, 1982; Smith and Kelly, 1988; Smith and Lapp, 1986). For example, the training of Sprague-Dawley rats in a shuttle avoidance task, at fifty trials per day, results in REM sleep increases after the first fifty trials. After the second day of training (fifty trials again) the level of REM sleep following the session is not so elevated. However, surprisingly, if sleep recording is continued after all

341

training has ended, it is found that above normal REM sleep increases manifest again and persist for up to a week after the last training trial. These REM sleep increases are paralleled by actual increases in the number of REMs (Smith and Lapp, 1986). A graph of the REM sleep data can be seen in Figure 10.1. After training on day 1, REM sleep increases begin in the ninth hour after the last training trial and remain elevated for several hours. If selective REMD is applied between 9–12 hours after the last training trial, learning-memory deficits are induced that are relatively permanent in nature (Smith and Lapp, 1986). This vulnerable period is a REM window. Even more surprising is the fact that a REM window has been found to exist 48–72 hours after the training session on day 2 (Smith and Kelly, 1988). The fact that REM sleep increases appeared so long after the end of training and that they were vulnerable to REMD strongly suggested that quite prolonged learning-memory processing activity was occurring. These times are beyond the conventionally understood short- or intermediate-term memory consolidation time frames (Tarpy, 1982).

The Human Recording Studies

It was decided to see if these phenomena could be observed in humans at such long posttraining times. A variety of human recording studies have been done following learning tasks to examine sleep parameter changes. The focus, however, has been on the sleep changes occurring the same night as the learning situation (McGrath and Cohen, 1978). The examination of possible sleep parameter changes several days after the end of training has not been explored. One of the problems with the human recording studies is that the task given by the experimenter must ethically be moderate in size and difficulty. It is unfortunately also likely to be emotionally neutral and personally irrelevant to the subject (McGrath and Cohen, 1978). By contrast, the animal studies use naive subjects and the learning situation imposed is undoubtedly the most important and traumatic event in the life of the organism.

We tried to circumvent this problem by choosing a personally relevant, emotionally involving life situation of great importance to the subjects. It was decided to examine the sleep of Honors psychology students, both when relatively little learning was going on in their lives and shortly after substantial learning had taken place. It was hypothesized that the amount of REM sleep and number of REMs would be higher following this major learning event and that these sleep changes would

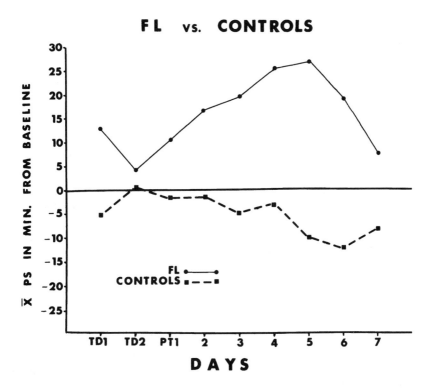

FIGURE 10.1. Comparison of fast learning (FL) vs. combined controls. Points represent the REM sleep (PS) differences from mean baseline values based on 24-hour REM sleep totals. TD1 and TD2 represent training days 1 and 2. PT1–7 represents the seven post-training days of sleep monitoring. REM sleep of the FL group was superior to that of the controls (p <.05). From Smith and Lapp (1986).

persist for at least several days after the end of acquisition as was seen in rats (Smith and Lapp, 1986; Smith, Young, and Young, 1980).

Method

The Test subjects (n = 6, ages 21–24) were chosen from successful applicants to our honors psychology program. This program is a fourth year of specialized university undergraduate study for those students who plan to enter graduate school. The academic year runs from September of one year to April of the next. Of approximately 200 psychology majors, 10–15 students are normally accepted into this program by the end of their third year. All participants were assessed to be relatively free of personal problems and clearly superior in terms of their academic ability. These subjects were given four consecutive nights of baseline EEG-EOG-EMG sleep recording during the summer holidays when none was currently taking any course or involved in any major learning situation.

These same subjects were again sleep recorded several days after (rather than immediately after) their Christmas exams. The start of the four consecutive days of the sleep recording began one to three days after the end of the last examination. Therefore subjects had completed their exams and had time to recover from any self imposed sleep deprivation—although none of the students was in the habit of staying up much beyond their normal bedtime. They all seemed well enough organized to avoid staying up all or part of the night to cram for their exams.

These same subjects were then asked to come in at least two months after the end of April (final) exams for a third recording session of four consecutive nights, when again relatively little learning was occurring. Thus both pre- and postlearning recording was carried out to provide a baseline for the sleep that followed the Christmas exams. For control subjects, it was possible to chose individuals of virtually the same age ($n = 5$, ages 21–27) who had completed the honors program the year before. These people had, for financial reasons, delayed their entry to graduate school and had found employment as teaching-research assistants in the Department of Psychology. Thus they were very comparable to the test subjects. Their three sleep recording sessions took place, as with the test subjects, during Summer 1, just before Christmas, and during Summer 2. None was assessed to have been involved in any major learning situation or to have any significant personal problems.

Sleep recording and scoring were done according to the standard method of Rechtschaffen and Kales (1968). For the recording, one EEG (C3/A2), two EOG, and one EMG (chin) channel were utilized. All records were scored by two scorers and the interrater reliability was always greater than 95 percent. Only the last two of the four recording nights were scored. It was assumed that any adjustment to the laboratory or any sleep-deprived condition would have passed by the time the third and fourth nights of recording had occurred. The REMs were counted manually and included only if at least one of the two traces showed a deflection of at least 25 microvolts amplitude. No distinction was made between bursts and single REMs, all were counted and added to the final total. The REM density was calculated by dividing the total number of REMs by the total number of minutes of REM sleep in the period.

Statistical analyses were done in the following way. Mean values were found for all subjects on nights 3 and 4. Then difference scores were calculated using the following formula: Mean Christmas score − (mean score for Summer 1 + mean score for Summer 2/2). The subtraction scores thus obtained were then compared in a one way ANOVA of test vs. control groups.

Results

The most obvious result in this study was the increase in the total number of REMs observed in the test subjects following the exam period, $F(1, 9) = 6.3, p < .05$. The mean number of REMs for both groups can be seen in Figure 10.2. Also significant was the increased REM density of the test group at the postexam time period, $F(1, 9) = 6.63, p < .05$. No other REM-related measure (minutes of REM sleep, percent REM sleep, or latency from stage 2 onset to any of the five REM periods) was found to be significant. Further, there were no changes in any of the other sleep parameters measured (i.e., latency to sleep onset, amounts of Stages 1, 2, 3, 4, or total sleep time) (Smith and Lapp, 1987; Smith, Lapp, and Dixon, 1984).

In an attempt to try to find out more precisely when, during the night of sleep, the extra REMs were concentrated, the two groups were compared on each of the five REM periods (REMP) separately. Analyses of variance revealed that the test subjects had significantly more REMs during the fifth or last REMP of the night, $F(1, 8) = 8.66, p < .05$. REM density (number of REMs/time in REM sleep in minutes) was found to be higher for the test group during the fourth REMP. Figure 10.3 shows the mean number of REMs for each REMP for both test and control groups.

Discussion

It was expected that there would be a very prolonged postlearning increase in REM sleep as well as an increase in the number of REMs. It was also expected that these increases would occur several days after the end of the learning situation. However, although there was an increase in the number of REMs that did appear three to five days after the end of the learning situation, the number of minutes of REM did not increase. Therefore there would appear to be some difference between the animal data and this human data, in terms of the exact changes in REM sleep/REMs measures.

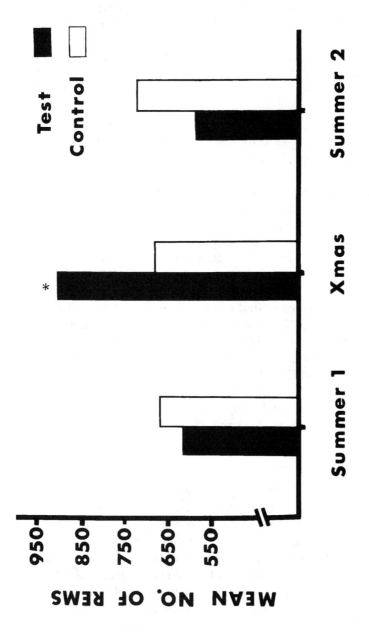

FIGURE 10.2. Mean Number of REMs for both Test and Control Subjects. Pre- and postbaseline values are shown at Summer 1 and Summer 2. The posttraining values of the test group and the nonlearning control group are shown at Xmas ($p < .05$).

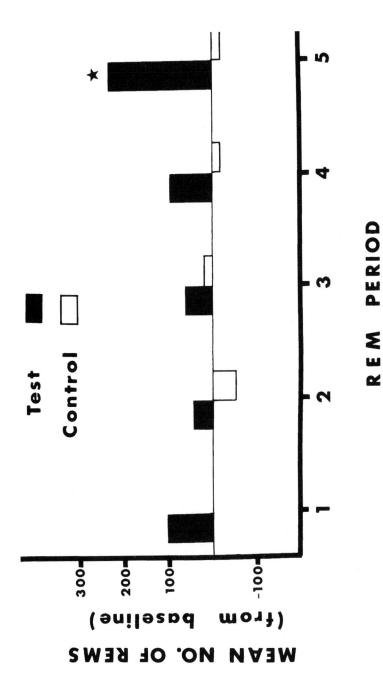

FIGURE 10.3. A Detailed Examination of the Two Groups at Christmas (Postlearning for the Test Grou) Showing the Mean Number of REMs Compared to the Subjects Own Pre- and Postbaseline Values for Each of the five REM Periods. Test subjects had significantly higher numbers of REMs than controls at REM period 5 ($p < .05$).

There does not seem to be much agreement in the literature as to what the increase in REM density reflects. Aserinsky (1969) considered it to be an index of sleep satiety, with densities increasing with each succeeding REMP of the night. Although we saw this same general phenomenon in our control subjects, the test subjects had REM densities increased above this normal amount to be at their highest during the fourth REMP. More interesting is the idea of REM density being a reflection of REM sleep intensity (Ellman et al., 1978). Increased REM densities may reflect increased learning-memory processing. Certainly, at least one group considers REM density to be independent of other REM sleep measures, such as REM sleep time or latency to REM onset (Antonioli et al., 1981).

There are no more human recording studies that have reported REMs/REM density increases so long after the end of acquisition. Thus, a comparison with the animal studies may be fruitful. Two major studies with rats (Smith and Lapp, 1986; Smith et al., 1980) showed prolonged increases in REM sleep time and percent of REM sleep. One of these studies also measured number of REMs (normally not done in rodent sleep studies) and an increase in number of REMs paralleling the increases in REM sleep time were observed (Smith and Lapp, 1986). The fact that the REM density measure was not significant in the animal study was undoubtedly due to the increases in both number of REMs and REM sleep time (numerator and denominator of the REM density calculation, respectively).

The fact that increases in amount of REM sleep time occurred in the animal studies, but not in the present human data may be a species difference. However, if one looks at other human recording studies it becomes clear that the exact nature of the REMs/REM sleep changes are apparently sensitive to the modality of sensory input as well (McGrath and Cohen, 1978). A look at those studies that examined sleep parameters the night of training, rather than several nights later, reveals that tasks, like the present study, with primarily a visual component have been reported to increase the REM density, but not the amount of REM sleep (Spreux et al., 1982). Auditory learning did not result in an increase in the number of REMs although there was an increase in the amount of REM sleep time (DeKoninck, Christ, and Lorrain, 1987; Verschoor and Holdstock, 1984). However, Verschoor and Holdstock (1984) reported both increased REMs and REM sleep time after visual learning, and Mandai et al. (1989) reported both increased amount of REM and number of REM periods following a task with both a visual and auditory component. Thus, the exact changes in REM sleep parameters following learning are not yet completely understood.

The Total Sleep Deprivation Studies

Experiment 1

It seems likely that REM sleep–learning correlations depend on tasks that are reasonably difficult (McGrath and Cohen, 1978; Smith, 1985). Therefore for comparison purposes, we chose two tasks, one of which was relatively easy and one which was more difficult (Lapp and Smith, 1986). The easy task chosen was a paired associate (PA) task. It was assumed that introductory psychology students would be able to learn this type of task without much problem as they had already had a great deal of memorizing experience in their lives. The more difficult task was the Wff'n'Proof task (Allen, 1966), which required the subjects to learn a set of logic rules and then apply them to a series of novel problems. The task required an understanding of the rules at a level beyond memorization.

Method. Twelve subjects (seven men, five women, aged 19–22) were first asked to complete the two tasks on the morning (10–11 a.m.) of the day that the test subjects were to be sleep deprived. Seven subjects were then asked to return to the lab that evening to stay up all night with the experimenter. The five control subjects were trained in exactly the same way, but were allowed to go to bed at their normal bedtime (both groups contained men and women). The total sleep deprivation (TSD) and control groups were asked on the following morning, to recall the missing member of the ten pairs of adjectives. They were also asked to create the largest logical sequence possible from each of nineteen strings of symbols. Subjects were given 30 seconds to complete each sequence and then asked to move on to the next string. One week later, all subjects were again tested on the paired adjectives and on their ability to generate symbol sequences from new symbol strings.

Results. The TSD and control groups both did equally well on the PA task, and the ANOVA revealed no differences between the groups at any time. On the other hand, the TSD group was inferior to the controls in their ability to generate symbol sequences both immediately and one week after the end of the sleep deprivation, $F(1, 10) = 14.24, p < .01$.

Experiment 2

The results indicated that TSD subjects had trouble applying the rules learned previous to the TSD, although they could recite the rules with no trouble. Although it could be argued that fatigue was a factor the night after the sleep deprivation, fatigue could not have been the reason for their poor performance seven days later. These preliminary findings indicated that sleep might well be involved in the facilitation of understanding and integration of material.

It was decided to try to replicate these findings involving the complex logic task. Along with the TSD group, several other groups were added. Because of the success in interfering with learning in rats 48–72 hours after the end of shuttle avoidance training (Smith and Kelly, 1986; 1988) and having observed such prolonged postlearning REMs changes in both humans (Smith and Lapp, 1987; Smith et al., 1984, the human recording study) and animals (Smith and Lapp, 1986; Smith et al., 1980), it was decided to include several delayed TSD groups.

Method. All groups were trained in the Wff'n'Proof logic task between 4– 6 P.M. and the various groups were as follows:

TSD-8. This group ($n = 10$) was subjected to a night of TSD (12 midnight–8 A.M.) the night of the training session.

TSD-4. This group ($n = 9$) was asked to stay up from 12 midnight until 4 A.M. the night of the training session, then were allowed to go home to bed. This group was included to see if simply staying up late (loss of the first half of the night of sleep) would affect learning.

TSD-24. This group ($n = 10$) was allowed to go home to bed the night of the training session but were then asked to stay up all night with the experimenter twenty-four hours later, or the night *after* the training session.

TSD-48. This group ($n = 9$) were deprived of a night of sleep two days (beginning forty-eight hours) following the day of the training session.

TSD-72. Subjects ($n = 8$) were deprived of a night of sleep three days (beginning seventy-two hours) after the day of the training session.

NSD. These non-sleep deprived control subjects ($n = 10$) were allowed normal sleep and never subjected to TSD.

All groups were retested one week later.

Results. It was predicted on the basis of the animal data, that TSD occurring either the same day, or two days after training (TSD-8 and TSD-48) would show learning deficits whereas the TSD-24 and TSD-72 groups as well as the NSD controls would not be impaired. It was further predicted that the TSD-4 group would also be impaired because the

TSD was at the beginning and thus most vulnerable time for the REM sleep–memory processing system. That is, in animals it had been observed that the times most vulnerable to REMD coincided with the first appearance of extra, above-normal levels of REM sleep following successful learning (beginning of a REM window) (Smith and Kelly, 1986; 1988; Smith and Lapp, 1986).

The overall ANOVA between groups tested one week later was significant, $F(5, 50) = 3.14$, $p < .05$. An orthogonal comparison between

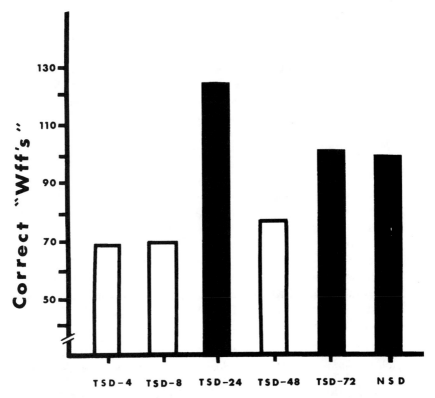

FIGURE 10.4. Groups Designated by Black Bars Had Significantly Higher Scores than Groups Designated by White Bars ($p < .01$).

TSD-4, TSD-8, and TSD-48 vs. TSD-24, TSD-72, and NSD showed the former three groups to be significantly poorer in posttest performance one week later, $F(1, 50) = 11.47$, $p < .01$, as predicted (Smith & Whittaker, 1987). These results can be seen in Figure 10.4.

Discussion. The data confirmed results seen in the previous experiment that TSD the same night as acquisition resulted in learning-memory deficits lasting at least one week. More interesting perhaps, was the fact that subjects need not stay up the entire night to reduce learning efficiency (TSD-4). We cannot be absolutely sure what the subjects did beyond their verbal assurance that they went home to bed after staying up until 4 A.M. However, it seems likely that they got much more sleep than did the TSD-8 group. Yet despite this fact, they were just as impaired as were the TSD-8 and TSD-48 groups. Even more surprising was the poor performance of the TSD-48 group. The idea that the learned material is still vulnerable several days after acquisition, however unusual, was predicted from the animal data (Smith and Kelly, 1986; 1988). The picture emerging is one of a rather prolonged processing mechanism that continues to work over a period of several days after acquisition. Interruption of this system at any of its vulnerable points results in learning-memory impairment.

The REM Sleep Deprivation Studies

Experiment 1

The aforementioned studies involved total sleep deprivation rather than REM sleep deprivation (REMD) as was done in the animal studies (Smith, 1985; Smith and Kelly, 1988; Smith and Lapp, 1986). It was decided to try to replicate the results of these TSD studies using both paired associate and logic tasks, substituting selective REMD for TSD.

Method. Subjects were ($N = 24$, aged 18–24 years, twelve men and twelve women) introductory psychology students who were asked to learn both the PA word task and the Wff'n'Proof logic task. There were four different experimental groups:

1. REMD. This group was polygraphically recorded in the sleep lab and selectively deprived of REM sleep on each and every occasion that it began to manifest during the night.

2. NREMD. This group was awakened from NREM sleep the same number of times as were the REMD subjects, with each NREMD subject being yoked to a REMD subject in terms of number of awakenings.

3. TSD. This group was asked to stay up all night with the experimenter, thus ensuring that they receive neither REM nor NREM sleep. This group was not polygraphically recorded.

4. NSD.: This group was allowed a normal night of sleep in the sleep lab following the learning tasks.

After the learning situation took place (6–7 p.m.), the subjects were asked not to drink alcoholic beverages or coffee before their return later that evening to sleep over in the sleep laboratory. Subjects had the standard EEG-EOG-EMG electrode hook up as previously described. The deprivation of REM sleep was carried out by having the experimenter enter the bedroom, turn on the lights and call to the sleeping subject at the first appearance of REMs on the EOG record accompanied by reduced muscle tonus on the EMG channel and 2–7 Hz activity on the EEG channel. The subjects were kept awake for at least five minutes by requesting them to do arithmetic sums during that time. The awakenings from NREM sleep were done in an identical fashion except that awakenings were always at least ten minutes from the end of a REM sleep period. Awakenings were made from the early, middle, and late portions of the subjects sleep night to correspond as much as possible to the REM sleep awakenings. The TSD group was not polygraphically recorded, but simply stayed in a comfortable room and allowed to do any kind of mental activity that they wished. Vigorous physical exercise as well as heavy coffee drinking and smoking were discouraged. The NSD group was never awakened during their sojourn in the sleep lab, although they were led to believe that they might be awakened. It has been suggested that REM sleep is important in the processing of emotionally charged material (Greenberg et al., 1983). Thus, along with the PA and logic task, a version of the Multiple Affect Adjective Check List (MAACL) was also included to measure possible changes in emotions following the two tasks (Zuckerman, Lubin, and Rinck, 1983).

As before, the polygraphic records were scored using the standard method of Rechtschaffen and Kales (1968). All scoring was done by two scorers and the interrater agreement was always at least 95 percent.

Results. For the REMD, NREMD, and NSD groups, ANOVAs indicated a difference in total sleep time, $F(2, 14) = 5.38, p < .05$. A Newman-Keuls post hoc test revealed that the REMD group had less sleep than did either the NSD group, $q(3, 14) = 12.20, p < .001$ or the NREMD group, $q(2, 14) = 11.59, p < .001$. There was no difference in total sleep time between the NREMD and NSD groups. This lower amount of total sleep in the REMD group was undoubtedly due to the REM sleep loss compared to the other groups, $F(2, 14) = 27.76, p < .001$. Individual comparisons showed the REMD group with less REM sleep than either the NSD group, $q(3, 14) = 9.31, p < .001$, or the NREMD group, $q(2, 14) = 7.79, p < .001$. There was no difference between the NREMD and NSD groups. Further ANOVAs revealed no significant differences between groups concerning time in Stage 1, 2, 3, or 4, nor in latencies to either Stage 1 or Stage 2. Subjects in the REMD group never received more than one minute of REM sleep before being awakened. The mean time spent in REM sleep before being awakened was 32.9 seconds (Pirolli, 1988).

For the learning scores, an ANOVA of the percentage of correct subunits revealed a significant pre- vs. posttest difference, $F(3, 20) = 5.86$, $p < .05$. A significant interaction between groups and time was also found with $F(3, 20) = 7.71$, $p < .01$. The Newman-Keuls procedure was then applied to all pre- and post test means. One pretest significant difference was found between the REMD and NREMD groups, $q(4, 20) = 4.80$, $p < .05$. No other significant differences were found at this pretest period. At posttest time, there was a significant difference between the NREMD and REMD groups, $q(8, 20) = 11.20$, $p < .001$, with the REMD group being much lower. The REMD group was also much lower than the NSD group, $q(7, 20) = 10.82$, $p < .01$. The TSD group was significantly lower than the NREMD, $q(7, 20) = 8.98$, $p < .001$, and the NSD group, $q(6, 20) = 8.60$, $p < .001$. There was also a significant drop from pre- to posttest for the REMD subjects, $q(3, 20) = 4.88$, $p < .01$, and for the TSD subjects $q(3, 20) = 5.33$, $p < .01$. These decreases in performance from pre to post test indicate a drop in correct performance. No comparable drop was seen in the scores of either the NSD or NREMD groups. Neither of the ANOVAs for the PA task or the MAACL test yielded significant differences between the test and control groups (Pirolli, 1988). The learning scores can be seen in Figure 10.5.

Experiment 2

The main hypothesis, that selective REMD would induce deficits in the logic task but not in the PA task, was generally confirmed. The results are slightly less powerful because of the pre-test difference found between the REMD and NREMD groups. However, weighed against the large drop seen in the REMD group as well as the TSD group from pre- to posttest, it seems likely that REM sleep deprivation as opposed to NREM awakenings are important in learning-memory processing. Further, it seems unlikely that NREM sleep plays any role in this process, because the TSD group was equally impaired in the logic task. Had NREM sleep played a part in learning over and above that of REM sleep, we might have expected a pre- to posttest drop for the TSD group that was even larger than for the REMD group. This did not happen.

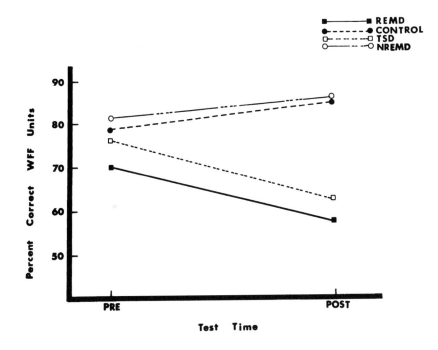

Figure 10.5. Mean Correct Percent of Wff Units for Pretest and Posttest, for All Groups. There was a significant decrement from pre- to posttest for the REMD and TSD groups ($p \leq$ .01) and the REMD and TSD groups differed significantly from the NREMD and Control (NSD) ($p < .01$) groups at posttest time.

Because REM sleep appeared to be the important phase of sleep for learning the logic task, the next question appeared to be whether all of the REM periods in the night were necessary. From the previously mentioned experiment, total sleep deprivation for four hours beyond normal bedtime seemed just as devastating as total sleep deprivation for eight hours (an entire sleep night). On the other hand, our recording study suggested that the extra REMs/REM densities were concentrated in the last two REMPs of the night (periods 4 and 5).

Method. It was decided to do a selective REMD study with the following groups:

1. FST2. These subjects were deprived of REM sleep at REM periods 1 and 2. Then for the rest of the night, they were allowed a normal night of sleep.

2. LST2. These subjects were allowed three uninterrupted REM periods for the first part of the night. Then they were deprived of REM sleep during REM periods 4 and 5 of the night.

3. NSD. These subjects were allowed a normal night of sleep and were never awakened.

All subjects were polygraphically recorded as previously described and the training of the logic task and the awakenings were done in the same manner.

Results. The overall ANOVA revealed a significant pre- to post-REMD difference, $F(1, 12) = 7.18$, $p < .01$. The post hoc Newman-Keuls test revealed that both the FST2, $q(3, 12) = 4.54$, $p < .05$, and LST2, $q(2, 12) = 4.02$, $p < .05$, groups had scores that were significantly inferior to the NSD group at the post-REMD test period. However, the two test groups, FST2 and LST2, were not different from each other. The data can be seen in Figure 10.6.

Thus it would seem that not only is REM sleep necessary for certain kinds of learning, but that apparently all REM periods are important for maximum efficiency.

Summary of the REM Sleep-Learning Studies

A picture of the relationship between REM sleep and learning processes is slowly emerging, based on both animal studies (Pearlman, 1979; Smith, 1985; Smith and Kelly, 1988; Smith and Lapp, 1986) and human studies (McGrath and Cohen, 1978) as well as the present data. Several facts seem to be emerging:

1. REM sleep increases or increases in number of REMs appear after substantial learning has taken place.

2. These REM sleep/REMs increases appear to persist for many hours and days after the end of acquisition.

3. At certain times, which seem to coincide with the beginning of expected REM sleep or REMs increase, application of REMD results in relatively permanent learning-memory deficits. These vulnerable time periods have been named *REM windows*.

4. Not all learning is sensitive to REMD. Material that is relatively simple and with which the subject is already generally familiar does not appear to be affected by REMD. More likely to be involved with REM sleep is material that requires the learning and understanding of new concepts that were previously unfamiliar.

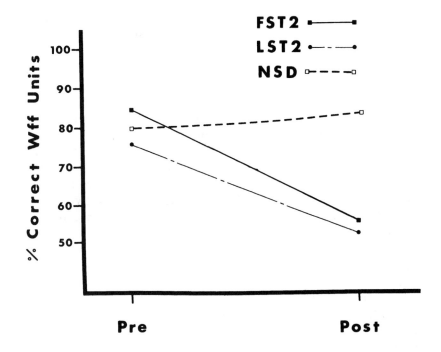

FIGURE 10.6. Both FST2 and LST2 Groups were Significantly Lower at the Post-REMD Retest Period Compared to the NSD Controls ($p < .05$).

Implications for the Study of Dreams

The possibility that dreams provide material for the solution of problems is a fascinating one. The literature has many anecdotal examples of scientific and artistic breakthroughs that apparently occurred in this manner (i.e., Dement, 1972; Sonnet, 1961). Unfortunately, the evidence is difficult to evaluate in terms of when the problem was first considered and when the subsequent breakthrough dream occurred.

Although REM sleep is not necessarily synonymous with dreaming, there is evidence that dreams often occur during REM sleep (Snyder, 1967). The possibility exists that above-normal levels of REMs and or amounts of REM sleep following learning experiences reflects both processing at a biological level and a parallel set of dreams whose content relates to that learning situation. Such an idea has already been expressed by Rossi in relation to personality growth (Rossi, 1972, 1973).

It is interesting to note that the success of the dream incubation process (Reed, 1976) is markedly enhanced by choosing only those subjects that have already had a dream about the problem they wish to dream more about. The timing of the more valuable dreams is several days later when often a much more helpful, comprehensive dream is then experienced. It is interesting to note that the timing of this experience is very close to the kinds of REM sleep increases reported in our recording experiments. Consistent with the idea that processing-problem solving is in progress, the first dream might indicate that the problem has been taken seriously enough and occupied enough of the individuals time to become a major learning experience. The processing of this experience continues and of course could be enhanced by further thought and related daytime activity. Dreams of events that have been in process for some time would be expected to contain more complete solutions or perspectives than the initial dreams of newly considered problems.

This idea has already been put forward in terms of the dreams within a single night of sleep by Cartwright (1977). In a series of studies she found that the first dreams of the night appeared to be directly related to present anxieties, whereas later dreams incorporated emotionally associated experiences from the past and final dreams of the night appeared to involve contemplation of possible problem solutions. Thus, within a single night and over a period of days, there would appear to be continual processing. This undoubtedly takes place whether or not the individual remembers his or her dreams.

What about incorporation over a period of days? Neilsen and Powell (1988, 1989) have recently reported that dream incorporation was reasonably high the same night as the material was introduced, then fell to much lower levels of recall by days 3 and 4, but was much higher again by days 5–6 after the original introduction of the material. In fact the curve of probability of recall is of a shape very similar to the REM sleep increases seen in the animal learning data (Figure 10.1) and the timing similar to the REM increases observed in the human recording study described previously.

An oscillatory disruption-avoidance-adaption model of dream function has recently been proposed that also predicts that intensification of REM sleep in some form will occur at times well after the event being dreamed. The model predicts that dreams (most of which occur during REM sleep) are actively involved in mastery (adaption) of emotionally charged environmental stimuli. Further, they suggest that dreams relevant to the mastery are themselves stressful and thus appear in an oscillatory manner (i.e., being present one night, absent a second because the content is too stressful, present again on a third night and so on) (Wright and Koulack, 1987).

In a speculative vein, the results indicate that following certain rules might maximize the possibility of finding the most useful dreams. Some suggested rules are as follows:

1. Examining dream material five to seven days after introduction to the problem may result in dream material that is related much more highly to the problem and its solution than was previously suspected. If processing has indeed occurred, the caliber of the dreams would be expected to be much higher in terms of possible solutions to problems, integration, understanding, and so forth than initial (same night as introduction of the problem) dreams.

2. If there was even modest REM sleep deprivation on the same night or forty-eight to seventy-two hours after the problem has been introduced, the likelihood that the material will be incorporated into dreams five to seven days later will be much less.

3. The time at which one goes to bed and gets up should vary as little as possible, in order that maximum processing efficiency occurs.

4. Because excessive use of drugs or alcohol seriously reduce REM sleep, drug abstinence would be the best course during serious dream incubation–problem solving periods.

References

Allen, L. (1966). *Wff'n'Proof: The Game of Modern Logic.* New Haven, Conn.: Aototalic Institutional Materials Publishers.

Antonioli, M., Solano, L., Torre, A., Violani, C., Costa M., and Bertini, M. (1981). "Independence of REM Density from Other Rem Sleep Parameters Before and After REM Deprivation." *Sleep* 4: 221–225.

Aserinsky, E. (1969). "The Maximal Capacity for Sleep: Rapid Eye Movement Density as an Index of Sleep Satiety." *Biological Psychiatry* 1: 147–159.

Cartwright, R. (1977). *Night Life: Explorations in Dreaming.* Englewood Cliffs, N.J.: Prentice-Hall.

DeKoninck, J., Christ, G., and Lorrain, D. (1987). "Intensive Language Learning and REM Sleep: More Evidence of a Performance Factor." *Sleep Research*, 16: 201.

Dement, W. C. (1972). *Some Must Watch While Some Must Sleep.* San Francisco: W. H. Freeman.

Ellman, S. J., Spielman, A. J., Luck, V., Steiner, S. S., and Halperin, R. (1978). "REM Deprivation: A Review." In A. M. Arkin, J. S. Antrobus, and S. J. Ellman (Eds.), *The Mind in Sleep*, pp. 419–457. Hillsdale, N.J.: Lawrence Earlbaum Associates.

Greenberg, R., Pearlman, C., Schwartz, W., and Grossman, H. (1983). "Memory, Emotion and REM Sleep." *Journal of Abnormal Psychology* 92: 378–381.

Lapp, L., and Smith, C. (1986). "The Effect of One Night's Sleep Loss on Learning and Memory in Humans." *Sleep Research* 15: 73.

Mandai, O., Guerrin, A., Sockeel, P., Dujardin, K. and Leconte, P. (1989). "REM Sleep Modifications Following a Morse Code Learning Session in Humans." *Physiology and Behavior* 46: 639–642.

McGrath, M. J., and Cohen, D. B. (1978). "REM Sleep Facilitation of Adaptive Waking Behavior: A Review of the Literature." *Psychological Bulletin* 85: 24–57.

Nielsen, T., and Powell, R. A. (1988). "Longitudinal Dream Incorporation: Preliminary Evidence of Cognitive Processes with a Supradian Period." *Sleep Research* 17: 112.

———. (1989). "The 'Dream-Lag' Effect: A Six Day Temporal Delay in Dream Content Incorporation." *Psychiatric Journal of the University of Ottawa* 14, no. 4: 561–565.

Pearlman, C. (1979). "REM Sleep and Information Processing: Evidence from Animal Studies." *Neuroscience and Biobehavioral Reviews* 3: 57–68.

Pirolli, A. (1988). "The Effect of Selective REM Deprivation in Humans on the Performance of a Logic Task Versus a Paired Associate Task." Honours Thesis, Trent University.

Rechtschaffen, A., and Kales, A. (1968). *A Manual of Standardized Terminology, Techniques and Scoring System for Sleep Scoring Stages of Human Subjects.* Bethesda, Md.: U.S. Dept. of Health, Education, and Welfare Public Health Services.

Reed, H. (1976). "Dream Incubation: A Reconstruction of a Ritual in Contemporary Form." *Journal of Humanistic Psychology*, 16: 53–70.

Rossi, E. L. (1972). "Dreams in the Creation of Personality." *Psychological Perspectives* 3: 122–134.

———. (1973). "Psychosynthesis and the New Biology of Dreams and Psychotherapy." *American Journal of Psychotherapy* 27: 34–41.

Smith, C. (1981). "Learning and Sleep States in the Rat." In W. Fishbein (Ed.), *Sleep, Dreams and Memory*, pp. 19–35. New York: Spectrum Book Publications.

———. (1985). "Sleep States and Learning: A Review of the Animal Literature." *Neuroscience and Biobehavioral Reviews* 9: 157–168.

——— and Butler, S. (1982). "Paradoxical Sleep at Selective Times Following Training Is Necessary for Learning." *Physiology and Behavior* 29: 971–997.

——— and Kelly, G. (1986). "PS Deprivation Several Days After the End of Training Retards Learning." *Sleep Research* 15: 77.

——— and Kelly, G. (1988). "Paradoxical Sleep Deprivation Applied Two Days After the End of Training Retards Learning." *Physiology and Behavior* 43: 213–216.

——— and Lapp, L. (1986). "Prolonged Increases in Both PS and Number of REMs Following a Shuttle Avoidance Task." *Physiology and Behavior* 36: 1053–1057.

——— and Lapp, L. (1987). "Increased Number of REMs Following an Intensive Learning Experience in College Students." *Sleep Research* 16: 211.

———, Lapp, L., and Dixon, M. (1984). "Increased REM Density Following Major Learning Experiences in Humans." *Sleep Research* 13: 99.

——— and Whittaker, M. (1987). "Effects of Total Sleep Deprivation in Humans on the Ability to Solve a Logic Task." *Sleep Research* 16: 536.

————, Young, J., and Young, W. (1980). "Prolonged Increases in Paradoxical Sleep Following Acquisition of an Avoidance Task." *Sleep*
3: 67–81.

Snyder, F. (1967). "In Quest of Dreaming." In H. A. Witkin and H. B.
Lewis (Eds.), *Experimental Studies of Dreaming*, pp. 3–75. New York:
Random House.

Sonnet, A. (1961). *The Twilight Zone of Dreams.* New York: Chilton Company.

Spreux, F., Lambert, C., Chevalier, B., Meriaux, H., Frexia I Baque, E.,
Grubar, G. C., Lancry, A., and Leconte, P. (1982). "Modification des
caracteristiques du SP consecutif a un apprentissage chez
l'homme." *Cahiers de Psychologie Cognitive* 2: 327–333.

Tarpy, R. M. (1982). *Principles of Animal Learning and Motivation.* Glen-
view, Ill.: Scott, Foresman and Co.

Verschoor, G. J., and Holdstock, T. L. (1984). "REM Bursts and REM
Sleep Following Visual and Auditory Learning." *South African Journal of Psychology* 14: 69–74.

Wright, J., and Koulack, D. (1987). "Dreams and Contemporary Stress: A
Disruption-Adaptation-Avoidance Model." *Sleep* 10: 172–179.

Zuckerman, M., Lubin, B., and Rinck, C. (1983). "Construction of Scales
for the Multiple Adjective Check List." *Journal of Behavioral Assessment* 5: 119–129.

11

Ramon Greenberg and Chester Pearlman ▬

An Integrated Approach to Dream Theory: Contributions from Sleep Research and Clinical Practice

W e will present a theory of dream function derived from sleep research which also suggests modifications of classical psychoanalytic dream theory. We will then illustrate this new, research-based theory with clinical examples. To accomplish this task, we will begin with a review of the sleep research that led to our theory of dream function and follow it with studies that have tested the theory with dreams collected under controlled conditions. Then, we will present material from therapeutic interviews in order to demonstrate the connection between our theoretical framework and clinical experience.

The Foundation: Research

The findings of recent sleep research suggest that information processing is a function of REM sleep and dreaming. This is a rather all-encompassing statement that should be more specifically defined. To do so, we must consider the meaning of *function* in relation to higher activity of the nervous system, the relationship between REM sleep and dreaming, and finally, what the studies of REM sleep and dreaming tell us about the nature of the information processed. Let us begin with some thoughts about the nervous system and function. Two authors will be of great help here. One is Luria, the Russian neurologist, and the other, Gallistel. In his book, *Higher Cortical Functions in Man*, Luria (1980) discussed the concept of function and functional systems. After considering the problems presented by attempts to understand function on the basis of anatomical localization in the nervous system, he suggested that function is organized in relation to tasks, such as locomotion, perception, or even intellectual activities. Because these acts can be performed in different ways, he postulated that they must be based on a dynamic constellation of connections situated at different levels of the nervous system. Gallistel (1981) expanded these ideas with the concept of interconnecting hierarchies of units of behavior, from simple motor units to units of activity. He suggested that such schemas organize the overall form but not the specifics of action. For example, we all have our own recognizable handwriting, whether it is on a small piece of paper or on a blackboard. Clearly, different sets of muscles and neurons are involved in these two writing samples. Yet, a basic interrelationship is maintained. An important question to be asked in relation to schemas is: how do they develop? We are going to suggest that when mammals go beyond their basic, hardwired patterns of behavior, REM sleep plays a significant role and that this role is reflected in dreams.

To develop this idea, we shall use evidence from studies of REM sleep and of dreams. We should note, therefore, that the psychological events in dreams and the physiological events in REM sleep represent different aspects of the same activity. An analogy would be the electrocardiogram and the sounds heard through the stethoscope, which are both manifestations of the heart beat and both assist our understanding of cardiac activity. Evidence for this assertion begins with the fact that dreams and REM sleep normally occur together. Awakenings from REM sleep lead to reports of mental activity that we recognize as dreams. In addition, although there have been a number of negative studies, some experiments have shown a clear relationship between dream content and such physiologic components of REM sleep as eye movements (Roffwarg et al., 1962), middle ear muscle activity (Roffwarg, Herman, and Lamstein, 1975), small muscle twitches (review by Pivik, 1978), and penile erections (Fisher, 1978). In view of this close relationship between REM sleep and dreaming, it is important to include evidence from studies of REM sleep physiology, REM deprivation, and dreams in the effort to develop a complete picture of the function of this activity. Because all mammals show similar physiologic activity during REM sleep, the results of animal experiments can also help us understand REM sleep and dreams in humans.

The brain is extremely active during REM sleep (Steriade and Hobson, 1976). Neurons are firing at a high rate but not at random. Some areas of the pons shut off while others increase their rate of discharge. Hippocampal recordings show a kind of activity seen only in the awake, aroused animal. Cortical activity is increased and also shows certain specific patterns of increased firing, such as in short interneurons, which may be involved in information processing (Steriade, 1978). Thus, although some investigators have suggested that the pons is the source for all this activity (Hobson and McCarley, 1977), these studies indicate a complicated interaction among different levels of the nervous system, which is consistent with the formulation of function by Luria noted earlier and with a recent discussion of the physiology (Hobson, Lydic, and Baghdoyan, 1986). Lesion studies have also contributed to this picture. In both humans (Greenberg, 1966) and animals (Jeannerod, Mouret, and Jouvet, 1965), destruction of certain cortical areas affects normal REM patterns, with marked diminution of eye movements following damage to the visual association areas. Thus, brain activity during REM sleep suggests a highly activated system with complex interconnections hard at work. To what end, we shall see.

Next we will consider the role of REM sleep in the interaction between the animal and its environment. Here, studies of REM deprivation have provided some interesting findings. A classical method for studying the nervous system has been to remove an area and observe the resultant behavioral deficits. In the case of REM deprivation (REMD), a particular form of nervous system activity is removed and the effects are noted (Pearlman, 1979, 1981; Smith, 1985). A number of studies have been conducted using different animals, different means for producing REMD, and different measurements of behavioral effects. Both positive and negative results have contributed to the picture we develop. Initial studies involving observation of the animals suggested heightened drive pressure following prolonged REMD as manifested by aggressiveness, hypersexuality, and ravenous hunger. When measures of drive intensity were used and artifactual effects of the REMD procedure were excluded, however, this idea was contradicted. Some aspects of emotionality (fear motivation) were actually reduced following REMD (Hicks and Moore, 1979). Subsequent experiments focused on the effects of REMD on learning. Simple tasks, such as one-way avoidance or position learning, were unaffected. More complicated tasks, such as difficult discriminations or learning sets, were clearly impaired when REMD followed learning trials. Particularly relevant to the development of complex behavioral patterns in humans was the impact of REMD on the effects of brief socialization for mice reared in social isolation (Watson and Henry, 1977). Isolation during infancy has profound disruptive effects on adult behavior. Brief periods of socialization prevent these effects, but when the socialization was followed by sleep (and REM) deprivation, the beneficial effects of socialization were abolished.

If certain tasks are sensitive to REMD, implying a need for REM sleep for mastery, will this phase respond to demand? Animals who were being trained in REMD-sensitive tasks showed increased REM sleep following training while they were learning. When the task was fully learned, REM sleep returned to baseline levels (Pearlman, 1979; Hennevin & Hars, 1985; Smith, 1985).

All these animal studies suggested involvement of REM sleep in the learning of unfamiliar tasks. Studies with humans have reported some similar findings with regard to REM sleep (Pearlman, 1982) and, as we will show, have an added dimension for study; that is, dreams. As mentioned earlier, the physiology in humans—including EEG, eye movements, and loss of muscle tone—is similar to that in animals. REMD can be produced by monitoring the EEG and waking subjects at the beginning of REM periods. Initial studies were observational, and as in animals, the first interpretation suggested increased drive pressure and tension. Later studies failed to confirm this impression and have focused on the performance of certain tasks or activities. Again, there have been negative as well as positive findings. Memory tests involving word lists have not shown any effect of REMD. A sophisticated test of recent memory scanning, the Sternberg paradigm, also showed no effect (Greenberg et al., 1983). On the other hand, tests of more complicated information processing have shown effects. Tasks requiring creative thinking and problem solving were impaired by prior REMD (Glaubman et al., 1978). Projective tests, such as the Rorschach, showed that REMD led to changes in the capacity to deal with recently aroused emotional material, suggesting that without REM sleep the usual mechanisms for dealing with such material were impaired (Greenberg et al., 1970). In a study using a modified TAT task, we found that connections to emotionally meaningful childhood memories were not developed without REM sleep (Greenberg et al., 1983). Another approach, involving adjustment to an unpleasant laboratory situation, also found decreased adaptation with REMD (Cohen and Cox, 1975). As in animals, human studies have shown a responsiveness of REM sleep to task demands. In an intensive foreign language course, students whose language performance improved showed increased REM sleep whereas those who failed to improve showed no such increase (DeKoninck et al., 1977). Shortening of REM latency (the time asleep from sleep onset to the first REM period) was found in a subject who was in a state of heightened need for processing emotional material, and greater total REM sleep was associated with a decrease in disturbance of emotional equilibrium from presleep to postsleep measurement (Greenberg and Pearlman, 1975).

As mentioned earlier, dreams are another source of data as well as the subject of our efforts to understand function. The REM sleep studies we have described provide us with a new framework for organizing our study of dreams because of the close association between dream mentation and REM sleep. The research we have described and the formulation of REM function we have presented led to some new approaches to the study of dreams.

This approach runs counter to the classical psychoanalytic view of dreams, which includes ideas about drive discharge, censorship, disguise, and indifferent manifest content. The foundation for the psychoanalytic view was Freud's hypothesis that the dream provided an opportunity for discharge of potentially sleep-disturbing drives through wish fulfillment. Although this seemed more possible in sleep, there was still, according to Freud, some barrier to the open expression of unacceptable wishes. The dream censor monitored the dream wishes and ensured that they could emerge only in a disguised fashion. Supposedly, this disguise took the form of attaching the unacceptable material to inconsequential experiences from the previous day, the so-called day residues. Thus, the manifest dream was considered to be composed of images from the previous day that had no emotional significance in themselves. The availability of extensive dream material collected in sleep laboratories provided an opportunity to test some of the ideas we have presented. Most striking was the finding that the manifest content is very meaningful in and of itself. The correspondence of manifest content and emotionally important waking experiences has become eminently clear. Such connections were demonstrated in a study of a patient in psychoanalysis (Greenberg and Pearlman, 1975), in a study of our own dreams (Greenberg and Pearlman, 1980), and also, without the benefit of a sleep laboratory, in a reexamination of Freud's Irma dream (Greenberg and Pearlman, 1978). Some examples of these findings are as follows. The psychoanalytic patient was struggling in one hour with painful feelings about his father's death. He was attempting to talk about this without getting too upset. That night he dreamed that he was involved in a process of transferring some of his father's possessions from one refrigerator to another. In our reconsideration of the Irma dream, we used Schur's (1966) material indicating references to a surgical procedure performed shortly before the dream on Freud's patient, Emma, by Wilhelm Fliess, who was Freud's confidante and major supporter. The operation and Freud's feelings about the complications were described in his letters to Fliess. The dream vividly portrayed many of Emma's postoperative complications, which can be readily understood as Freud's attempt to exonerate Fliess so as to maintain his highly important relationship with him. Other examples of the clear correspondence between waking concerns and manifest dreams have been shown in presurgical patients and subjects in intensive group therapy situations (Breger, Hunter, and Lane, 1971). For example, one patient was faced with an operation on a plugged artery. He dreamed of repairing plumbing.

A possible paradigm for the significance of the manifest content is seen in the posttraumatic nightmare. Here, the connection between the dream content and the emotionally important waking experience is portrayed literally. We would suggest that in these dreams only the problem is seen. On the basis of the research we have cited, we feel this represents an example of a failed dream; that is, no adaptation has occurred. In the usual dream, the problem is presented together with some evidence of efforts to deal with it in a more or less satisfactory fashion. The evidence of some processing or integration may be seen in the symbolism of the dream and in the attempts at resolution of the manifest problem in the dream.

We have reviewed a number of studies of dreams and REM sleep that suggest a role in adaptation to emotionally important situations. A more detailed discussion of this and related work can be found in Pearlman (1982). For purposes of this discussion, it should be noted that most of the studies cited have been replicated in more than one laboratory. We see, therefore, that REM sleep is an activity ideally suited for developing the type of complex interconnections proposed by Luria and Gallistel. Such interactions form the basis for schemas that guide tasks but not the specifics of action. To do this, memories must be connected with current experiences so that the animal or human can deal with the present by using past experience without being rigidly controlled by the past. Many of the studies we have cited showed impairment of this process when REM sleep was not available. Dreams, then, might be viewed as a printout that shows the dreamer's struggles to make effective connections. In the posttraumatic nightmare, there is obvious failure. Absence of integration is indicated by the dream, which shows only the traumata and no content from other aspects of the dreamer's life experience. In the nontraumatic dream, on the other hand, we can begin to look for evidence of integration. This understanding of the process suggests an approach to the content of the dream by a formulation of the problems in the dream and a consideration of how the dreamer is faring in the struggle to make meaningful connections for currently active problems in waking life. This approach to dreams is, we feel, more consistent with the findings from REM sleep studies than the traditional view of dreams as a vehicle for discharge of drive tension and attempts to disguise or censor. It is also consistent with two other recent theories of REM function. Rotenberg (1984), a Soviet investigator, has conducted some creative studies of REM sleep. He explored the role of REM sleep in resistance to toxic substances and in the lowering of seizure threshold. He also studied the role of REM sleep in students' ability to cope with the anxiety related to examinations. As a result of his findings, as well as those already mentioned in this chapter, he has developed a theory that suggests that REM sleep serves the function of restoring search activity to the nervous system. Search activity is a process involving the quest for solutions to problems, be they physical, intellectual, or emotional. Without this activity the animal or human is resigned, and therefore vulnerable to nervous or physiologic disorders. For example, anaphylactic edema of the muzzle of an animal after injection of an irritating substance was more severe in the absence of search behavior. Cobalt-induced seizures lasted longer when search behavior was reduced. A second researcher, Palombo (1978), used a somewhat different language to capture a similar idea. He saw REM sleep or dreaming as providing the opportunity to store recent memories by matching them with memories from the past, thus providing a sense of integration and continuity. Both these writers also discussed the problem of failure or success in the REM process or in dreams. Palombo introduced the idea of the correction dream as an event that occurs when a previous dream fails to make an appropriate match. Rotenberg considered the role of REM deprivation or REM exhaustion in the renunciation of search and therefore its role in the development of depression or neurotic disorders. We will discuss the issue of success or failure in dreams after discussing a more clinical perspective.

A theory of the adaptive function of dreaming has evolved from research in sleep laboratories. Although this work raised questions about the classical psychoanalytic formulations of dream function, we should note that some psychoanalytic thinkers have introduced modifications quite consistent with our perspective. In "The Dream Problem," Maeder (1916) went beyond Freud's view of dreams as drive discharge and introduced the idea of a prospective function for dreaming. He demonstrated how the dream showed evidence of the dreamer's struggle to find solutions to problems and that the nature of the solutions predicted subsequent waking behavior and affect. Thus, he considered the dream to be an accurate reflection of the dreamer's more or less successful efforts to come to terms with important emotional issues. Some years later, French and Fromm (1964) presented very similar ideas. These stemmed from French's concept of the focal conflict. These authors suggested that every dream showed evidence of a particular conflict that was closely related to the dreamer's current waking concerns. The dream also showed the dreamer's efforts to find a more or less comforting resolution of the conflict. While focusing on the dreamer's current life, Maeder and French and Fromm did not ignore the past. Both discussed how current concerns were related to unresolved issues from the past. Also of importance to our discussion of dreaming is how, within their theoretical framework, these authors dealt with the problem of understanding the dream and especially the fact that the manifest dream contains a great deal of useful information. This leads us to the next section, in which we will try to illustrate the relation of theory to dream interpretation and to the clinical use of the reported dream.

Jones (1965) discussed the importance of distinguishing between dream psychology and dream interpretation. He pointed out that dream psychology is the science of dreaming and can be subject to study, experimentation, and objective validation. Dream interpretation, on the other hand, is subjective and usually involves collaboration between two people attempting to understand the meaning of a dream to the dreamer. Our discussion up to now has been concerned with the work that provides the basis for a psychology of dreaming. We feel this offers a basis for dream interpretation and for the clinical work with dreams, but it does not tell the whole story. Work with dreams during psychotherapy takes place within an ongoing process of treatment that has its own theoretical framework. For effective treatment to take place, there has to be some congruence between the approach to dreams and the overall clinical orientation. Freud showed this clearly by first demonstrating the meaningfulness of dreams and then using his understanding of dreams toward a better understanding of the unconscious processes involved in patients' conflicts. Although we have questioned the validity of his orientation toward drive discharge, we feel the basic idea of the dream as a window through which one can see what the patient is struggling with is crucial. The thrust of the studies we have described underlines the centrality of the dream for understanding what is currently of major concern for the dreamer and also for how the patient is integrating or coping with these major issues. Furthermore, our research suggests that the manifest content should be taken seriously and should be seen as representing, in pictorial language, the problems of the dreamer (Greenberg and Pearlman, 1980). Recently, we have investigated this idea more extensively and have found that the manifest problems in the dream correlate very closely with those seen in analytic material and in that of a normal subject (Greenberg et al., 1992).

This work has involved the material we collected in the sleep laboratory from a patient who was also in psychoanalysis. We had transcripts of the analytic hours preceding and following the sleep lab night. During twelve of the nights we awakened the patient at the end of REM periods and tape recorded his dream reports. In our current study of this material, we have scored the dreams for the appearance of problems in the manifest dream, and we also scored the analytic hours for problems. We then compared the dream problems with the problems in the hours. Some examples of what we found will illustrate how much the dream problems corresponded to those in the analytic hours. One night the patient dreamed that he was making love with a young woman. A yakking dog kept interrupting them. He shooed the dog away. We formulated the problem as something interfering with his sexual activity. In the hour before this dream the patient had been talking about an impending trip, in the company of a woman friend. He kept bringing up concerns about possible problems in his sexual performance. In the hour, he dismissed each problem as it arose. As one can see, the problem and the solution in the dream are very similar to what occurred in the hour. Another example, referred to earlier in this paper, occurred on a night following an analytic hour in which the patient had been struggling with feelings about his dead father. He was having trouble containing his sadness. He then had a dream in which he was a prisoner of two men. They had the task of transferring his father's possessions from one refrigerator to another. As the dream progressed, he became part of a very efficient line that moved things from one refrigerator to the other. He was impressed by the smoothness of the operation. In this dream, the problem continues, but the solution feels much more satisfactory to the patient.

It should be clear at this point that we are discussing dreams in a manner that fits with a psychodynamic perspective. Although not totally consistent with a classical psychoanalytic understanding of the patient, it is consistent with more modern psychoanalytic approaches, such as those described by Kohut and his associates. Although it is not possible in this discussion to provide a detailed discussion of self-psychology, a few words might be appropriate. Kohut has introduced the idea that the development of a cohesive sense of self is superordinate in personality development. This occurs through the interaction of parental figures and the child and in the normal course of events, leads to the important psychologic functions of self-esteem, initiative, ambition, and life goals. Treatment is focused on enhancing the arrested development of these functions by the analysis of transferences that reflect past difficulties in the parental self-object functions. Thus, whereas the focus is away from traditional conflicts related to libidinal issues, it includes the importance of transference and the role that past experience plays in the understanding of present difficulties. Furthermore, Kohut emphasizes the idea that this theory is an experience-near one in contrast to the metapsychology of traditional psychoanalysis. The clinical application is thus much closer to the theoretical foundation. The role we have formulated for dreaming meshes perfectly with this clinical theory in that it considers the dream as a vivid portrayal of what the patient is experiencing in relation to self and to important self-objects. For a more complete discussion of this idea, see Greenberg (1987).

We will now present some clinical examples that illustrate the application of the ideas we have been discussing. A young woman had been in treatment for about a year and a half because of profound dissatisfaction with what life offered her, despite a successful career and marriage. She also suffered from periodic severe anxiety. She had improved considerably, and at the time of these dreams, her main concerns were her inability to get pregnant (she had one child) and her growing awareness of intense feelings about the therapist, which she found very discomforting. She began the hour by indicating that she had a post-cold cough. She took the day off and made stuffing and cookies with her daughter. The cookie making was hard work, and her daughter got tired of it. She then mentioned that she had a dream a couple of days ago. (She was looking in the mirror and looked very pregnant, more than when she had been actually pregnant. She said that she could not be and then realized that she was leaning back.) This was followed by the description of another dream she had the night before. (She came to her session and worked on a doll house. She was coughing. The therapist did not even comment on her cough. There were two other things they worked on but she couldn't remember them.) She then said that actually her daughter has a doll house that the whole family works on, building new parts for it. She felt the interpretation was obvious, and she did not like it. She had awakened irritated with the therapist and with herself for having the dream. She thought it meant that she wants to be his daughter and cannot be. "Why don't I pick someone else? This is an unreal relationship." She was really irritated after the dream. The therapist focused on the problem in the dream by noting the fact that she was irritated in the dream because of his failure to comment on the cough. She then proceeded to bring up a number of times that he had failed to comment on things about her and instead dealt only with what she brought up. This led to her talking about her disappointment in her father and father-in-law. Although disappointed, she had not given up completely on her father, but she had with her mother. It made her nervous to talk about this. She did not want to still be wanting a father. The therapist questioned whether her nervousness in general stemmed from the fact that she did not have a father who helped her feel safe from her mother's superstitions. The hour then proceeded with further material about her fantasies and mixed feelings about the therapist. In this hour, the therapist dealt with the dream by commenting on the problem. His assumption that this was of importance to the patient was borne out by the fact that the patient was able to talk more openly than before about her feelings about the therapist. By focusing on the problem in the dream, she was helped to move from an intellectual interpretation to much more affect-laden material that was currently active in the treatment process. The connection between past and present is clearly seen in the similarity of affect toward the therapist and her father, both in her sense of disappointment and in her reluctance to acknowledge such feelings.

The second patient is a single woman in her middle twenties. She began treatment about a year before because she was depressed and unable to find any direction for her life. She was involved in a long-term relationship with a man that did not seem to be going anywhere. She was not working and, although she had completed college, she had no idea about what she wanted to do. Of significance in her past history is the fact that her parents were divorced when she was six. Her mother developed cancer a couple of years later and, after a long illness, died when the patient was nine. The patient remembers little if any help in understanding what was happening and dealt with these events by denying they had any impact on her. She did not grieve and did not want anyone to feel sorry for her. She focused on looking good and trying to be popular. She described her father as being very involved in her life in a controlling and insensitive manner. The dream was reported in an hour that followed a two-week interruption resulting from a visit to her father and stepmother. The first of the two missed hours was cancelled at the last minute because of a sudden change in travel plans. Just before she left, she had been expressing dissatisfaction about the fact that she and the therapist had not been able to arrange a second hour to add to her regular weekly sessions. She began the hour by asking why she had been billed for the first of the two missed hours. She seemed to accept the explanation that it had been done at the last minute and was perhaps related to a discussion last time about her wanting to pull back because she felt the therapist did not want to give her an additional weekly hour. She talked about having had a good time socially while away but about feeling very aware of the lack of any good feeling about herself. She did not feel things went very well with her father. She was about to relate something she was telling him when she recalled a dream. She remarked that she rarely remembers dreaming.

Her parents [father and stepmother] were in their bedroom in the apartment in Florida. She was in the bathroom, in the shower, smoking. She is not allowed to smoke in the house. Robbers came in the house and started shooting. Suddenly the dream changed so that now her father was away in New York, and only her stepmother was in the house when the robbers came in. They came into the bathroom and started to shoot through the shower door. She was hiding behind the bathroom door and they did not see her. She then realized that father was coming back. The robbers were in the dining room so she was able to go out into the hall to meet father and stepmother, who was somehow still alive. She told her father he had better go downstairs and not risk his life by going into the apartment to try to save things from the robbers. She told him that if he went in she would get herself killed by going downstairs and getting herself run over. So he went downstairs. It was the only way to get him to listen, that is, to threaten him with the loss of her own life.

The therapist commented on the problem of not being able to get father to listen to her. She responded by relating it to what reminded her of the dream in the first place. She had been asking father about his life in the past, and he had dismissed her questions and her interest in getting to know him better. She also said that she had been thinking last night about whether she could survive if father were to die. The therapist continued to focus on the problem of getting through to father and of how important he is to her. She became more sad than she had ever been during an hour. She was surprised at the strength of her feelings. With the help of the therapist, she talked about her never feeling that what she felt was valid. She always had to hide her crying. The therapist commented on her having to hide in the dream. The issue of the robbery was also discussed, and in connection with this, the loss of her mother came up. Her sister had quit therapy when strong feelings about mother's death began to emerge. No one in the family had talked with the patient, who is the youngest, about mother's illness and death, and nothing had been explained. She expressed her sense of the unfairness of her life in a much more direct manner than she had ever done before.

Again, in this example, a manifest problem in the dream was connected to a central and active concern of the patient. This was expressed in the dream in a manner that was both overt and in a symbolic form that captured a great deal of affect. Work with the dream involved an understanding of the patient, including her past, and of the therapeutic process. Both these examples have been presented in a manner that we hope will allow the reader to develop some sense of how the theoretical framework we have presented can apply to the clinical situation and how the clinical work provides some sense of validity to the theory.

We have attempted to provide a theory of dream function developed from sleep research and to illustrate the application of this theory to clinical practice. The research points to a function of dreaming that can be formulated as the integration of current experiences into existing programs or memory systems, when such recent experiences require adaptation. We have also shown how this concept and the research on which it is based suggest modifications of classical psychoanalytic dream theory while retaining a psychodynamic framework. Other clinical theoreticians have presented ideas that match very well with this approach. We have also suggested that one must have not only a theory of dreaming but also a clinical theory within which it fits. With this in mind, we would like to spell out more clearly how this theory can be applied to psychotherapeutic work.

The main point is that the dream represents the dreamer's effort to cope with a currently meaningful issue. Thus, the manifest dream is the royal road to what is important to the dreamer and not a pastiche of insignificant day residues. Furthermore, we would suggest that a problem appearing in the manifest dream is a direct expression of the patient's problem and provides a schema with which to approach discussion of the dream. These problems are presented in the language used in the dream. Because this is perceptual, it is often not portrayed in an easily understood fashion, especially if one is thinking in waking verbal terms. Thus, some translation is required. From this perspective, the concept of disguise is of little relevance. Because the dreamer is also searching for ways to cope with the problems, solutions may also be apparent in the dream, and in fact the solutions, if successful enough, may even obscure the problem. This may also lead to the fact that the dream is not always readily understandable. The solutions in the dream may be new to the patient or may be the institution of old methods of coping; that is, defenses. The difference we see between our approach and the usual one is that the defenses are not there to hide meaning but are an example of the dreamer's method of coping with the problem.

To this point, we have considered the dream only as illustrative of a current problem. In our clinical examples, however, we also related the dreams to the patient's past. We feel this is important because it allows us to seek an understanding of why the present experience is a problem. It is here that the patient's associations to the dream become meaningful. Through them we can learn the significance of the problem in terms of the patient's unique life experiences. As we do this, we can appreciate the ways in which the dream integrates past and present in the dreamer's attempts to make sense out of what is happening. For example, although we did not discuss it during the hour, the robbery dream had some clear connections with the patient's past. She grew up in the New York area, and at the time of the original robbery, her mother's death, her father was not there because he had remarried and was living in a nearby suburb. Finally, this approach to dreams also helps us understand how dreams can be more or less successful and more or less direct in their expression of the dreamer's situation and experience of it. Thus, the two examples from our research present two solutions that differ greatly in their effectiveness. In the first, the ineffective denial during the hour is merely repeated as a shooing away of the dog, whereas in the second, an effective operation, in which the patient is an active participant, is instituted to keep his father's effects in cold storage. It is our opinion that the integration of research and clinical experience is an important model for any approach to dreaming. Clinical work requires a theory that is not derived purely from clinical experience and yet at the same time is consistent with clinical realities. Experimental proof in our field is rarely possible. If we find that we develop similar ideas from different data bases, however, we can begin to feel that they have some validity and are not just epiphenomena of current therapeutic fashion.

To summarize, we have tried to show how sleep research has pointed to a theory of the function of REM sleep and dreaming. We have presented evidence for the unique association of a special physiological state, REM sleep, and a special psychological state, dreaming. Studies of both of these phenomena led to similar conclusions about a process in which information is integrated into the nervous system to develop schemata for the performance of certain complicated activities of which the most important in humans is the management of emotional life and its interaction with the environment. We have illustrated this with clinical examples to demonstrate the meaningfulness and usefulness of this formulation.

References

Breger, L., Hunter, I., and Lane, R. (1971). "The Effect of Stress on Dreams." *Psychological Issues Monograph 27*, vol. 7, no. 3. New York: International Universities Press.

Cohen, D., and Cox, C. (1975). "Neuroticism in the Sleep Laboratory: Implications for Representational and Adaptive Properties of Dreaming." *Journal of Abnormal Psychology* 84: 91–108.

De Koninck, J., Proulx, G., King, W., and Poitras, L. (1977). "Intensive Language Learning and REM Sleep: Further Results." *Sleep Research* 7: 146.

Fisher, C. (1978). "Experimental and Clinical Approaches to the Mind Body Problem Through Recent Research in Sleep and Dreaming." In N. Rosenzweig and H. Grissom (Eds.), *Psychopharmacology and Psychotherapy*, pp. 61–99. New York: Human Sciences Press.

French, T., and Fromm, E. (1964). *Dream Interpretation.* New York: Basic Books.

Gallistel, C. (1981). "The Organization of Action: A New Synthesis." *Behavioral and Brain Sciences* 4: 609–619.

Glaubman, H., Orbach, I., Aviram, O., Frieder, I., Friedman, M., Pelled, O., and Glaubman, R. (1978). "REM Deprivation and Divergent Thinking." *Psychophysiology* 15: 75–79.

Greenberg, R. (1966). "Cerebral Cortex Lesions: the Dream Process and Sleep Spindles." *Cortex* 2: 357–366.

———. (1987). "Self-psychology and Dreams: the Merging of Different Perspectives." *Psychiatric Journal of the University of Ottawa* 12: 98–102.

Greenberg, R., and Pearlman, C. (1975). "A Psychoanalytic Dream Continuum: The Source and Function of Dreams." *The International Review of Psychoanalysis* 2: 441–448.

———. (1978). "If Freud Only Knew: A Reconsideration of Psychoanalytic Dream Theory." *The International Review of Psychoanalysis* 5: 71–75.

———. (1980). "The Private Language of the Dream." In J. Natterson (Ed.), *The Dream in Clinical Practice*, pp. 85–96. New York: Jason Aronson.

———, Katz, H., Schwartz, W., and Pearlman, C. (1992). "A Research Based Reconsideration of Psychoanalytic Dream Theory." *Journal of the American Psychonalytic Association* 40: 531–550.

———, Fingar, R., Kantrowitz, J., and Kawliche, S. (1970). "The Effects of REM Deprivation: Implications for a Theory of the Psychologic Function of Dreaming." *British Journal of Medical Psychology* 43: 1–11.

———, Schwartz, W., and Youkilis, H. (1983). "Memory, Emotion, and REM Sleep." *Journal of Abnormal Psychology* 92: 378–381.

Hennevin, E., and Hars, B. (1985). "Post-Learning Paradoxical Sleep: A Critical Period When New Memory is Reactivated?" In B. E. Will, P. Schmitt, and J. C. Dalrymple-Alford (Eds.), *Brain Plasticity, Learning, and memory*, pp. 193–203. New York: Plenum Press.

Hicks, R., and Moore, J. (1979). "REM Sleep Deprivation Diminishes Fear in Rats." *Physiology and Behavior* 22: 689–692.

Hobson, J. A., Lydic, R., and Baghdoyan, H. A. (1986). "Evolving Concepts of Sleep Cycle Generation: From Brain Centers to Neuronal Populations." *The Behavioral and Brain Sciences* 9: 371–400.

Hobson, J. A., and McCarley, R. (1977). "The Brain as a Dream-State Generator: An Activation-Synthesis Hypothesis of the Dream Process." *American Journal of Psychiatry* 134: 1335–1348.

Jeannerod, M., Mouret, J., and Jouvet, M. (1965). Étude de la motoricité oculaire au cours de la phase paradoxale du sommeil chez le chat." *Electroencephalography and Clinical Neurophysiology* 18: 554–566.

Jones, R. (1965). "Dream Interpretation and the Psychology of Dreaming." *Journal of the American Psychoanalytical Association* 13: 304–319.

Luria, A. (1980). *Higher Cortical Functions in Man.* New York: Basic Books.

Maeder, A. (1916). "The Dream Problem." *Nervous and Mental Disease Monograph,* no. 22. New York: New York Publishing Co.

Pearlman, C. (1979). "REM Sleep and Information Processing." *Neuroscience and Biobehavioral Reviews* 3: 57–68.

———. (1981). "Rat Models of the Adaptive Function of REM Sleep." In W. Fishbein (Ed.), *Sleep, Dreams, and Memory,* pp. 37–45. New York: Spectrum Publications.

———. (1982). "Sleep Structure Variation." In W. Webb (Ed.), *Biological Rhythms, Sleep and Performance,* pp. 143–173. London: John Wiley and Sons.

Palombo, S. (1978). *Dreaming and Memory.* New York: Basic Books.

Pivik, T. (1978). "Tonic States and Phasic Events in Relation to Sleep Mentation." In A. Arkin, J. Antrobus, and S. Ellman (Eds.), *The Mind in Sleep,* pp. 245–271. Hillsdale, N.J.: Lawrence Erlbaum Associates.

Roffwarg, H., Dement, W., Muzio, T., and Fisher, C. (1962). "Dream Imagery: Relationship to Rapid Eye Movements." *Archives of General Psychiatry* 7: 235–238.

Roffwarg, H., Herman, J., and Lamstein, S. (1975). "The Middle Ear Muscles: Predictability of Their Phasic Activity in REM Sleep and Dream Material." *Sleep Research* 7: 235–238.

Rotenberg, V. (1984). "Search Activity in the Context of Psychosomatic Disturbance of Brain Monoamines and REM Sleep Function." *The Pavlovian Journal of Biological Science* 19: 1–15.

Schur, M. (1966). "Some Additional 'Day Residues' of the Specimen Dream of Psychoanalysis." In R. Loewenstein, L. Newman, M.

Schur, and A. Solnit (Eds.), *Psychoanalysis—A General Psychology*, pp. 45–85. New York: International Universities Press.

Smith, C. (1985). "Sleep States and Learning: A Review of the Animal Literature." *Neuroscience and Biobehavioral Reviews* 9: 157–168.

Steriade, M. (1978). "Cortical Long-Axoned Cells and Putative Interneurons During the Sleep-Waking Cycle." *Behavioral and Brain Sciences* 3: 465–514.

——— and Hobson, J. (1976). "Neuronal Activity During the Sleep-Waking Cycle." *Progress in Neurobiology* 6: 155–376.

Watson, F., and Henry, J. (1977). "Loss of Socialized Patterns of Behavior in Mouse Colonies Following Sleep Disturbance During Maturation." *Physiology and Behavior* 18: 119–123.

12

Harry Fiss

The "Royal Road" to the Unconscious Revisited: A Signal Detection Model of Dream Function

Although much of psychoanalytic theory has inevitably come under dispute over the past five decades, the concept of the unconscious (ucs) has pretty much stood the test of time. For most practicing clinicians, it has proven to be an invaluable tool for understanding and treating psychiatric disorders. Furthermore, the concept's validity appears to have been firmly established. For one thing, research on the activity of the reticular formation has provided the concept with a biological underpinning whose importance can hardly be ignored. For example, the finding that impulse velocities in the nonspecific ascending reticular activating system are significantly slower than they are in the specific sensory pathways (Samuels, 1959) is clear indication that a stimulus may reach the cortex via specific pathways *before* any awareness of it occurs. However, by far the most persuasive verification of the existence of ucs mental processes comes from the experimental psychology laboratory. What this body of knowledge shows is (1) that stimuli may register without conscious awareness; (2) that they have a delayed and predictable effect on experience and behavior; and (3) that dreams are particularly responsive to the effects of subliminal stimulation. This brings me to the essential point of this chapter: that dreams have a unique capacity for detecting signals both exteroceptive and interoceptive. Because they have this property of fine tuning, they are indeed a "royal road" to the ucs. However, it is not the motivational ucs of drives and impulses that dreams are the "royal road" to, but, as Eagle (1987) suggests, a *cognitive* ucs of information processing and psychic structure building. I will first review the empirical foundation underlying this formulation of dream function. I will then point out how this formulation fits the framework of signal detection theory and sketch the outlines of a unified signal detection model in terms of which the effects of subliminal stimuli administered in the waking state (subliminal activation) are understood to be analogous to the effects of what normally would be considered to be supraliminal stimuli applied during sleep (sleep stimulation). I conclude this presentation by considering the implications of this model for further experimental research, clinical practice, and theory.

The Subliminal Activation Paradigm for the Experimental Study of Unconscious Mental Processes

Historical Origins

The idea that meanings, trace systems, or schemata can be activated by "subliminal," "incidental," or "indifferent" stimuli, that is, stimuli too weak to capture our attention, has a history that can be traced at least as far back as Binet, who, as far as we know, was the first behavioral scientist to suggest that ucs stimuli may affect normal consciousness (1896). Urbantschitsch (1907) took this notion a step further by having subjects adept at producing eidetic imagery describe in detail pictures they were viewing and then, after removing the pictures, asking them to call up images of them. He reported that many stimulus details appeared in the images that had not previously appeared in the direct perceptual reports that followed the actual viewing of the stimulus. Urbantschitsch also found that many of the originally unrecognized details that emerged in the images did so in strangely transformed ways reminiscent of primary process modes of thinking—an important point to which I will come back later. Related phenomena such as discrimination without awareness, perceptual "vigilance" and "defense," and hypnagogic reverie have been the objects of subsequent studies by Diven (1937), Kubie (1943), Lacey and Smith (1954), Lazarus and McCleary (1951), Miller (1939), Pustell (1957), and Razran (1955). They all indicate that "many more impingements upon receptor surfaces achieve subjective representation than is evident in the thought products and behavior of which the subject is fully or even partially aware" (Klein, 1970, p. 238).

The Phenomenon of Day Residues in Dreams

The phenomenon of the day residue involves the carry-over of incidental registrations of recent events, as described previously, into *dreams*. It was clearly Freud (1953; 1955) who first seized upon the significant role these transient, unnoticed registrations or "indifferent perceptions," as he called them, play in the formation of the dream. He often referred to his well-known botanical monograph dream to illustrate that "dreams have a preference for taking up unimportant details of waking life" (1953, p. 174), that in dreams fleeting, hardly noticed daytime experiences become conspicuous. As Klein states: "the general importance of the day-residue phenomenon is that it concerns the effect on thought of transient, momentarily unessential, even unnoticed stimuli that nevertheless are drawn into an independently active field of thought, the consequences of which appear not when the activation takes place but only later—in a dream" (1970, p. 273).

Experimental Evidence of Subliminal Activation

The concept of the day residue led to the first experimental demonstration of the effects of subliminal activation. Poetzl (1917) carried out the demonstration in an attempt to show that the manifest content of dreams draws upon exposures of stimuli too brief to attract notice. In his classical study, Poetzl showed his subjects landscapes very briefly by exposing them for only 1/100 of a second and had them describe and draw what they had seen. They were instructed to return the next day and to make a special effort to recall any dreams they might have in the meantime. The following day he asked them to report and draw their dreams. In these reports and drawings Poetzl found an abundance of unreported components of the original stimulus. He therefore arrived at the conclusion that what his subjects had failed to notice immediately after stimulation was more likely to appear in their subsequent dreams than what they *had* noticed. Poetzl's unique observations were soon after extended to drawings of spontaneously occurring *images* (Allers and Teler, 1924), but it took more than forty years for Poetzl's milestone experiment to find its way back into mainstream psychology. This renewed interest in experimentally verifying aspects of psychoanalytic dream theory is largely due to the efforts of Fisher (1954, 1956, 1957), Fisher and Paul (1959), Paul and Fisher (1959), Shevrin and Luborsky (1958), Bach and Klein (1957), Eagle (1959), Klein et al. (1958), Smith, Spence, and Klein (1959), and a host of other investigators who not only have replicated the phenomenon of registration without awareness under far more rigorous experimental conditions and with far more sophisticated controls than Poetzl employed, but have also demonstrated that many experiences other than dreams, such as spontaneous imagery, symbolic associations, thoughts, and percepts, could be influenced by stimuli not consciously perceived. In fact, as more recent work by Silverman and his associates has shown (Silverman, 1972; Silverman et al., 1972; Silverman et al., 1973; Silverman et al., 1978), the entire gamut of human experience can be affected by subliminal activation, including not only cognition but also mood and affect, speech, academic performance, competitive behavior, substance abuse, even sexual orientation. At least a dozen studies by Silverman and associates (see references) have demonstrated, for instance, that the subliminal symbiotic message "Mommy and I are one" significantly reduced pathological thinking in schizophrenics even under the most stringent double-blind conditions. Other studies by these authors show that subliminal activation can be effectively used as an adjunct in weight reduction, smoking cessation, and other therapeutic efforts (Silverman et al., 1978; Palmatier and Bornstein, 1980; Linehan and O'Toole, 1982). In short, the validity of the phenomenon of registration without awareness has been more than amply documented.

The Special Contribution of the Dream to the Recovery of Subliminally Registered Material

The fact that such a wide range of human experience and behavior can be influenced by stimuli that are not consciously perceived does not mean, however, that such influence can be detected or detected equally well in every mode of experience. We must be careful, as Klein (1970, p. 269) points out, to separate *activation* from the *varieties of experience* in which the effects of activation are embedded. A case in point is a study by Fiss, Goldberg, and Klein (1963), which shows that even when discrimination of a stimulus is not possible, the stimulus may still influence another kind of experience, namely imagery. The authors used two stimuli, a round clock face and a square double profile, and exposed these at exposure times well below the threshold of awareness of even the tiniest part. Following each exposure, the subjects were asked to report and draw any images that spontaneously occurred to them. The images and drawings were scored in a double-blind procedure requiring judges to assess quantitatively the degree of similarity between each drawing and the two stimuli. For this purpose they used two checklists, one of double profile and one of clock characteristics, similar to checklists developed earlier by Paul and Fisher (1959). In addition to drawing these images, the subjects were asked to discriminate the two stimuli by guessing after each exposure which of the two had been shown. For the discrimination test, the stimuli were presented at the same subliminal exposure level as during the imagery procedure. The results were decisive: although the subjects were unable to discriminate the clock and double profile figures, images produced after exposures of the double profile stimulus showed significantly more double profile checklist elements than images elicited by the clock stimulus. Thus, clearly, the activity of stimuli not discernible in a discrimination task may nonetheless register and contribute to the organization of thought in another variety of experience— imagery. It appears, therefore, that subliminal stimuli have differential effects on behavior, depending on the mode of experience of the subject.

The reason images and dreams, according to Klein, are especially responsive to subliminal activation is that they are relatively free of reality testing; that is, they are modes of experience in which critical judgment and reality requirements are bypassed. When this occurs, the prospects of incidentally registered material emerging to awareness increases and the effects of subliminal stimuli are highlighted (Klein, 1959a).

Compelling evidence lends support to the assumption that an inverse relationship exists between reality contact and the subliminal effect. Fisher and Paul (1959) experimentally varied reality contact by having their subjects, following subliminal stimulation, draw images, once in an upright position with the room illuminated, and once in a supine position with the room darkened. They found a stronger subliminal effect in the supine-dark condition, when postural supports were reduced, presumably inducing a state of passive receptiveness and lowered reality contact. In a study of positional choice behavior, Dondero (1959) found that subjects who had *not* been instructed to watch for visual cues were more responsive to these cues than subjects who *had* been alerted to them. Fox (1960) found that subjects who tend to be guided by feelings and fantasies in disregard of reality are more sensitive to subliminal stimuli than subjects who are more attuned to reality. Finally, a number of studies indicate that the further below threshold a stimulus is presented, the greater its effect (Bach, 1959; Eagle, 1959; Paul and Fisher, 1959). Because threshold reflects attentiveness to the outside world, these studies suggest that the subliminal effect is enhanced by reduced reality contact.

Not only does the mode of experience determine how registrations are worked over and recovered in awareness, but also "the controlling structures characterizing the *state of consciousness* of the moment" (Klein, 1959b). Thus, a state of consciousness in which reality contact is reduced should also enhance the effects of subliminal stimuli. This was directly demonstrated by Fiss (1966) in one of the few attempts not only to demonstrate but actually manipulate the phenomenon of registration without awareness. The subjects in this investigation were each subliminally stimulated once in an alert, attentive state and once in a nonalert, nonattentive state.

In the alert condition, the instructions which they were given served to *focus* their attention, induce *active* scanning of the visual field, and an *expectant, anticipating* attitude. In the nonalert condition, the same subjects were given instructions intended to induce a state of *diffuse* attention deployment, *passive* looking at the stimulus field, and a *nonexpectant, nonanticipating* attitude. For reasons of expediency, images rather than dreams were used to capture the effects of the subliminal stimulus, which was again the double profile. Alertness level was monitored and measured physiologically by means of basic skin resistance. The results of this study revealed that sensitivity to subliminal stimulation varied as a function of physiological arousal, but not invariably so: the subjects were indeed most responsive to subliminal stimulation when they were relaxed, but only while *imaging*; their state of arousal during *stimulation*, on the other hand, did not appear to be related to their responsiveness to subliminal cues. In other words, arousal interacted with subliminal stimulation only during the retrieval and not during the intake phase of the experimental procedure.

This finding is significant for two reasons. In the first place, it makes a contribution to cognitive theory: it clearly shows that a cognitive experience such as an image or a dream is not a single organized product, but *"an event over time, a process of organization that needs time to be prepared, evolved, and established"* (Smith, 1957). Investigations of brain mechanisms lend additional support to this "microgenetic" approach to cognition, just as they have supported the concept of the ucs. Lindsley (1958), for example, has been able to demonstrate that it requires at least 50 milliseconds for sensory impingements to consolidate themselves into percepts. In short, both the experimental psychology and the neurophysiology laboratories have yielded data consonant with the view that percepts, images, dreams, and so forth, are not instantaneously formed; rather they are the end-products of an emerging, complex organizing activity, a good deal of which unfolds without benefit of awareness. Thus, images, dreams, and so on, are not merely passive reproductions of past events, they are *purposeful constructions*. Because this is a unifying principle governing a wide range of experiences and states of consciousness, it calls for a close examination of the subliminal activation paradigm as it applies both to sleep and the waking state.

The finding by Fiss (1966) that state of consciousness (alertness-nonalertness) interacted with the unfolding of the cognitive process, in this case image formation, thus highlighting the effects of subliminal stimulation even further, is particularly relevant to the aim of this discussion, namely, that the dream, perhaps more than any other mental product, is uniquely sensitive to low-level stimuli, both internal and external. Because of this, the dream is especially capable of bringing to our awareness facts about ourselves and the world around us that would normally remain unnoticed.

The dream, it must be remembered, is both an experience and a state of consciousness in which reality testing and reality contact are minimized to an extent not observable in most experiences and states of consciousness. Using the language of a different conceptual framework—that of information processing—the dream should be especially adept at *detecting signals*, even the faintest ones, emanating from both within and outside ourselves. What follows is an attempt to construct an information processing model based on signal detection theory that would be applicable to a wide range of cognitive experiences in both waking and sleeping states of consciousness. As I will now show, the two models in question—subliminal activation and sleep stimulation—are virtually identical.

A Signal Detection Model of Dreaming and Waking

Traditional signal detection theory (SDT) does not actually have all that much to say about dreams, as it is a conceptual framework that grew out of the classical tradition of psychophysics, with its emphasis on precise, objective measurement. However, with the discovery of REM sleep and the ensuing capability to study dreaming objectively and scientifically, SDT, as I propose to show, offers new possibilities as a conceptual tool. This is hardly surprising in view of the fact that SDT came into existence precisely because traditional psychophysical methods proved too inflexible to do justice to the complexity of the human mind. As Candland and Mayer (1978) and Schiffman (1976) point out, and as I have suggested, SDT is the outcome of our growing awareness that a multitude of extraneous factors can cause an individual's discriminative capacity to fluctuate and bias or confound his or her response. These factors include degree of certainty, random neural activity, fatigue, lapses in attention span, and changing expectations. Swets (1964, 1973) in particular stressed the importance, for every threshold determination, of disentangling signal from noise, and rejected the traditional notion of the invariance of psychophysical measurement. Seen from the point of view of SDT, therefore, experiential modes and states of consciousness, such as dreams, constitute a class of intervening variables, analogous perhaps to Hull's (1943) "behavioral oscillation," which must be taken into consideration whenever stimulus-response contingencies are being investigated. For purposes of our discussion, SDT thus leads us, at the very least, to expect that the dream state modulates the magnitude of an individual's response to a stimulus too faint to be consciously perceived.

It should be noted, however, that nothing that has been said so far applies directly to the dream state *at the time it actually occurs.* The so-called dreams that we have been talking about up to this point are, after all, nothing more than verbal reports obtained in the waking state of subjective events that presumably took place in an earlier, sleeping state of consciousness. To truly encompass the mind in sleep, our subliminal activation-signal detection model must therefore be expanded to bridge both organismic states: sleep and wakefulness. Surprisingly, this turns out to be not all that difficult.

In Fig. 12.1 two schematic representations of ucs mental activity, one for the waking state and one for sleep, have been juxtaposed one on top of the other. The top part represents what Cohen (1981) has referred to as the (REM) sleep-stimulation paradigm, showing the effects of applying, *during* REM sleep, stimuli that in the waking state would be supraliminal but are subliminal when administered during sleep. The bottom half of the figure illustrates the subliminal-activation or registration-without-awareness paradigm (Fiss, 1988) which has already been described in depth. Note that the *two paradigms,* the upper and the lower, *are just about isomorphic.* For one thing, they have identical prestimulation or antecedent variables. Second, in both cases, the stimuli are not consciously perceived. They are operationally determined to be subliminal; yet, they have immediate measurable physiological effects (indicated by the wiggly lines), showing that they have indeed registered, are subsequently retrievable in dreams and other experiential modes, and affect waking, that is, poststimulation behavior, in ways that have major implications for adaptive functioning. Finally, both models employ very similar methodologies.

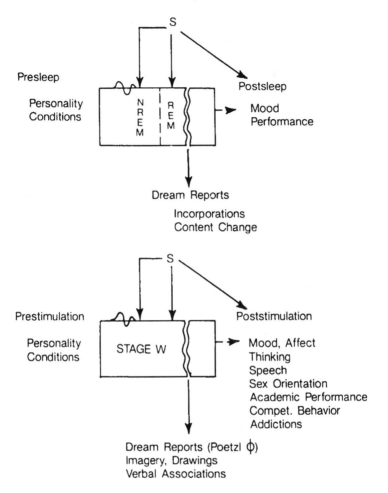

Figure 12.1. A Sleep-Waking Model of Subliminal Activation. The top portion is after Cohen (1981)

Pre-stimulation Variables

These constitute individual differences or personality variables, the adaptive requirements or demands made on the individual by the experimental task at hand, and the interactions between the two. In the Fiss (1966) study, for instance, I demonstrated not only that a relaxed state of consciousness enhanced the subliminal effect, but also that there were individual differences in responsiveness to subliminal stimulation.

An earlier study by Levy, Thaler, and Ruff (1958) suggests that the capacity to relax, to "regress" to a reverielike state of consciousness and suspend reality judgment, is not only state but also trait dependent; in other words, some people are just generally more relaxed than others. Eagle (1962), Fox (1960), Smith et al. (1959), and Spence and Paul (1959) have all demonstrated that there are indeed a variety of personality correlates of sensitivity to subliminal stimulation. The Fiss (1966) experiment, using a sampling of approximately 20 minutes of prestimulation (baseline) recordings of basal skin resistance level per subject, demonstrates that subjects who are characteristically relaxed show significantly more sensitivity to the effects of subliminal stimuli in their imagery than subjects who tend to be alert or vigilant.

Dream recall has similarly been shown to be a function of individual difference variables. Compared to poor recallers, good recallers have been reported to be less repressed (Goodenough et al., 1974), more anxious (Tart, 1962), more field independent (Schonbar, 1965), more inner-directed and more self-aware (Lewis et al., 1966; Cohen, 1974). Factors conducive to dream recall other than individual differences are known to include such variables as sleep stage, of course, with recall following REM awakenings being better than recall following non-REM awakenings (Foulkes, 1962); method of awakening, with abrupt awakenings yielding more dream reports than gradual awakenings (Goodenough, 1969; Shapiro, Goodenough, and Gryler, 1963); the desire and expectation to recall (Cartwright, 1977); and salience: dreams are more likely to be recalled if they are interesting, that is, if they are vivid and self-involving, and if they are accompanied by high levels of autonomic activity, such as penile erections, REM "density," respiratory irregularity, and other phasic sleep events (Cohen, 1974).

Subliminality

In both the waking and sleeping states, the subliminality of the stimulus can be operationally defined and empirically demonstrated. For the sleeping subject, the experimental task is considerably simpler: all that needs to be shown is that the sleep recording (polysomnogram or PSG) during and following stimulation contains no signs of arousal, such as alpha intrusions or body movements. Determinations of subliminality in the waking state, on the other hand, require far more sophisticated psychophysical threshold and discrimination procedures (see Goldberg and Fiss, 1959; Fiss et al., 1963, for details).

Registration without Awareness

Normally, registration is assumed to have occurred if aspects of an unperceived or undiscriminated stimulus can be recovered, usually after some delay, in dream reports, images, associations, and so forth. The evidence for such registration of subliminal stimuli applied during the waking state has already been extensively reviewed. In sleep, registration without awareness can be demonstrated if external or internal stimuli can be shown to influence dream content without arousing the subject. There is abundant evidence that dream content can be influenced by *pre*sleep stimuli: real-life stress situations (Breger, Hunter, and Lane, 1971), arousing films (Cartwright et al., 1969; Foulkes and Rechtschaffen, 1964; Witkin, 1969), drive states (Bokert, 1968; Fiss, 1980), wishes (Cartwright, 1974), and a host of suggestions, hypnotic and otherwise, to dream about specific topics (Barber, Walker, and Hahn, 1973; Fisher, 1953; Tart, 1964). These effects, however, are not subliminal. To be subliminal, the stimuli must be applied while the subject is *actually asleep*. This too has been demonstrated, though not as abundantly, with sprays of water (Dement and Wolpert, 1958), verbal stimuli (Berger, 1963), somatosensory stimuli (Koulack, 1969), and visual stimuli (Rechtschaffen and Foulkes, 1965).

Strictly speaking, however, even in these instances, evidence of registration is lacking. The acid test of registration would have to be some kind of neurophysiological change. In sleep, this is usually considered to be the "K-complex," a high-amplitude, low-frequency wave typically appearing in the EEG during stage 2 sleep. But as these K-complexes are primarily non-REM phenomena, they do not appear to be especially useful indicators for studies in which REM dreams are used to recover subliminal intake. The physiological change would have to appear mainly in REM sleep. Conceivably, phasic events such as PIPs (phasic integrated potentials) might be markers of this sort if their appearance could be shown to coincide with the onset of external stimulation during sleep. Work with PIPs has suggested that these phasic events, which may be the human equivalent of the pontine-geniculo-occipital (PGO) spikes found in the cat, are more specifically related to the experience of dreaming than the REM state itself (Watson, 1972). Whether they are also indicators of registration during sleep has yet to be explored.

On the other hand, the identity of the neurophysiological correlates of registration in the waking state seems to be more definite. Both heart rate deceleration (Spence, Lugo, and Youdin, 1974) and average evoked response (Shevrin, 1973) have been found to be markers for subliminal activation.

Post-stimulation Effects

That stimuli not consciously perceived are registered and retrievable in a variety of experiences and states of consciousness need not be pointed out again. What does need emphasizing, however, is that the recovery of these stimuli (in dreams, images, etc.) should not be confused with their even more delayed effects on mood, affect, thought, language, performance, and so on, as indicated on the lower right side of Figure 12.1.

For sleep, a parallel distinction needs to be made between the incorporation of an external or internal stimulus into dream content and the effects of this incorporation on postsleep behavior. A stimulus may get incorporated, but the incorporation may not necessarily affect us. That it often does, however, has been well documented. Cohen and Cox (1975) have shown, for example, that subjects who dreamed about a stressful presleep stimulus subsequently had a more positive attitude about it than those subjects who did not dream about it. Greenberg and Pearlman (1975) found that dreaming about a problem raised during a presleep psychoanalytic hour predictably influenced the degree of "defensive strain" evidenced by the analysand during a subsequent analytic session. Kramer and Roth (1972) and Kramer, Roehrs, and Roth (1976) report that improvement in mood from pre- to postsleep was significantly related to specific dream content. Fiss, Kremer, and Litchman (1977) have observed that dreaming about a verbal presleep stimulus facilitated its recall the following morning, and Fiss (1980) has demonstrated that the intensity with which recovering alcoholics crave alcohol is a function of how and how much they dream about drinking. Bokert (1968) reports that dreams about drinking influence postsleep thirstiness in a nonaddicted thirsty population. Thus, the incorporation of both external and internal stimuli into dream content can have adaptive value in terms of memory consolidation, drive and mood regulation, and so forth. There is room for a good deal more research in this area, however, especially involving "internal" stimuli, such as drive and mood states, that are present both during and before sleep. The clinical importance of this type of research strategy will be discussed shortly.

Methodology

Last but not least, the two paradigms illustrated in Figure 12.1 make use of very similar methodological strategies, principally the extensive use of experimental and control stimuli, to rule out chance factors. Thus, in a typical sleep-stimulation study, a control stimulus for a message recorded in the subject's own voice might be the same message recorded in another person's voice. In a typical subliminal stimulation study, the experimental stimulus is usually a visual one, while the control stimulus is usually a different visual stimulus or a blank.

To recapitulate: in both the sleeping and waking state, stimuli not consciously perceived do nevertheless register, are recoverable, and have predictable delayed effects. The quality and magnitude of these effects are modulated by preexisting situational and personality variables, by the nature of the stimuli used, by the mode of experience and state of consciousness in which the effects of the stimuli are captured, and finally by the type of ego function on which these effects have an impact. Clearly, the two activation models shown in Figure 12.1 so closely correspond to one another that one is justified in combining them into a single unified signal detection model applicable to both sleep and wakefulness. This has important implications for theory and research. For one thing, the idea of a unified sleep-wake model of subliminal activation is entirely consistent with the current view, based on extensive laboratory evidence, that dream mentation, far from being discontinuous, is very much *continuous* with waking mentation. Second, because the subliminal activation strategy has proven so valuable in our understanding not only of ucs mental activity but information processing in general, the extension of this strategy to the study of sleep should substantially add to our knowledge of this important area of investigation and advance the cause of dream research. Third, the concept of subliminal activation, when applied to sleep, combined with the fact that dreams have been shown to be particularly conducive to the recovery of subliminally registered input, has major implications for clinical practice and research, especially in the field of behavioral medicine. This will be discussed shortly.

Transformations in the Emergence of Subliminally Registered Material

Before proceeding to considerations of clinical application, however, let me briefly call the reader's attention to yet another particularly striking characteristic that the two activation models have in common, one I alluded to when I mentioned Urbantschitsch's (1907) early work on ucs mental activity. I am referring to the transformed ways in which subliminally registered stimuli typically make their appearance known.

These transformations are not unlike those observed when stimuli applied during sleep are incorporated into dream content.

It is a well-known fact that subliminal waking effects are rarely if ever a direct representation or exact likeness of the stimulus itself. This is why sorting and checklist techniques of the type employed by Fisher and Paul (1959) and Fiss (1966) are needed to measure not absolute but relative correspondence or identity between stimulus and response. I know of no study in which perfect correspondence has ever been found. What we usually obtain and measure in these studies is some kind of *indirect* effect or *transformation* of some sort. What is of special interest to us is that the characteristics of these transformations are extremely similar to the formal properties of dream work: concreteness, symbolization, bizarreness, and so on.

Let me illustrate this point by showing you two typical drawings obtained by a subject in a study of subliminal effects (Fiss, 1961). The subject had been stimulated by the double profile stimulus (Figure 12.2) and was asked to close his eyes, wait for an image or mental picture to pop into his mind, and then draw and describe it. The stimulus was presented tachistoscopically at a luminosity and speed well below the threshold of discrimination. Subjectively speaking, therefore, the stimulus appeared no different to the subject than the control blank stimulus: in both conditions, all the subject reported was a flash of light.

It should be pointed out that both drawings are "optimal" representations in the sense that they were given high checklist scores by the judges who rated them; that is, they both contained many elements of the double profile stimulus, such as roundness, facelike contours, the concept of twoness or doubleness, human properties, and so forth.

The image in Figure 12.3 was described by the subject as "two identical fat little fishes kissing." Note here the close, but not complete, correspondence between the drawing and the physical attributes of the double profile.

The image in figure 12.4 is of particular interest because even though it strongly resembles a face, it wasn't described as such. It was described by the subject as "two fried eggs, sunny side up, with strips of bacon." While reporting and drawing this, the subject did not have the slightest awareness of the striking resemblance it bore to a human face. This lack of awareness reminds one very much of the lack of insight and the uncritical acceptance of even the most bizarre content one generally observes in nonlucid dreamers, as noted by Rechtschaffen (1978).

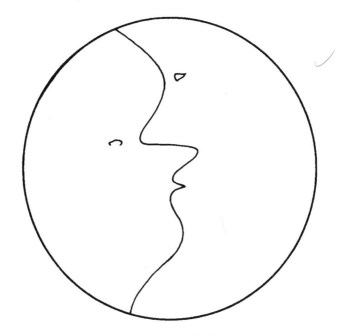

Figure 12.2. Double Profile Stimulus

In short, the effects of subliminal stimuli in the waking state resemble the effects of supraliminal stimuli administered during sleep in that they are both indirect and not recognized by the responders. This further underscores the "goodness of fit" of the two models I have presented.

Dreaming and the Early Detection of Illness

It is now time to consider some of the clinical applications of the subliminal activation paradigm. One idea that immediately comes to mind is the potential role of the dream in the early detection of illness. A recent study by Smith (1991) indicates that such a role is a distinct possibility. Using a sample of cardiology patients, Smith found a highly significant correlation between severity of cardiac illness and the frequency with which references to death and separation occurred in these patients' dreams approximately six to eight weeks prior to their admission to the hospital.

Studies relating somatic conditions to dreaming are nothing new, of course. The biological states and conditions found to be associated

Figure 12.3. Image Drawn After Subliminal Exposure of Double Profile Stimulus

with dream content include, among others, ulcers (Armstrong et al., 1965), hypertension (Saul et al., 1954), plasma free fatty acids (Gottschalk et al., 1966), pregnancy (Winget and Kapp, 1972), psychosomatic illness (Levitan, 1980), migraine headaches (Levitan, 1984), asthma (Levitan, 1983), cardiac disease (Schneider, 1973; Ziegler, 1962) and arthritis (French and Shapiro, 1949). What distinguishes the Smith (1991) study from most of these others is that it is prospective. It raises the exciting possibility of predicting a medical diagnosis from dream content, a possibility based on the rationale developed earlier in this paper that dreams are singularly sensitive detectors of interoceptive and exteroceptive signals. Thus, bodily changes may reveal themselves in dream content long before they manifest themselves as subjective complaints or objective symptoms. To paraphrase Haskell (1985), dreaming is a cognitive activity that monitors internal conditions, better perhaps than any

Figure 12.4. Image Drawn After Subliminal Exposure of Double Profile Stimulus

other information processing system, because it picks up cues too subtle to be processed consciously. In short, dreams do not conceal. On the contrary, they *reveal*, and they reveal extraordinarily well, despite the transformations these cues often undergo. There is no contradiction in this. As Greenberg (1987) points out, "the process of translating from a sensory mode of expressing ideas to a waking, verbal mode is more relevant to understanding dreams than the old ideas of disguise and latent content" (p. 100).

Unfortunately, the Smith (1991) study was not designed to test the validity of the signal detection model of dream function. For one thing, it failed to control for information input: we simply do not know how much awareness his subjects had of their condition. This leaves open the possibility that the dream content reported by them was determined not by subliminal but by supraliminal stimuli; that is, by conscious knowledge and concerns. To test the signal detection capacity of the dream more rigorously, a design would be required that would guarantee that all subjects are equally unaware of their diagnosis. A study by Schmale (1966) of the relationship between expressed hopelessness and cervical cancer in women offers a methodology that would make it possible to carry out such an investigation.

Schmale interviewed three samples of women at a time when they were at risk for cervical cancer; that is, the women had been referred for a cone biopsy following one or more abnormal Pap smears. It should be noted that these interviews took place *well before either the doctor or the patient knew the outcome of the biopsy*. During the interviews, Schmale tried to assess each patient's degree of hopelessness. The results of these three separate studies showed that the patient's degree of subjective hopelessness, as judged by Schmale, correlated significantly with the subsequently known outcome of the biopsy. Was Schmale, although ostensibly assessing hopelessness, actually reacting to latent, subtle signs of illness unwittingly communicated by his patients? Or do these findings merely reflect the effect stress has on illness?

To get around this ambiguity about the source of Schmale's predictions, Spence (1978) undertook a more rigorous test of this intriguing hypothesis by reexamining the transcripts of these earlier interviews of Schmale's. The published findings of this analysis were appropriately titled "Lexical Correlates of Cervical Cancer."

What Spence did essentially was to use a computer to calculate the frequency with which hope- and hopelessness-connoting words were used in the Schmale interviews. He did this separately for the interviewer and the interviewees. No other clues were looked at. Thus, the analysis was completely context free. His prediction was that a person's choice of words would be influenced by ucs mental processes and thus give rise to expressions of hopefulness or hopelessness, regardless of what the person may actually be talking about. Specifically, he hypothesized that patients who had used more hopeless and fewer hopeful words in their original interviews with Schmale were also more likely to be the ones whose subsequent biopsy results indicated ongoing cancer. He further predicted that lexical measures of hopelessness in the *interviewer's* language would predict biopsy outcomes.

Both hypotheses were confirmed. "Hope" words occurred significantly more often in the speech of the false-alarm (negative biopsy) patients than in the speech of the cancer patients, and "hopeless" words were used more often by the interviewer when talking to cancer patients than when talking to false-alarm patients. Thus, lexical choice appears to be a significant index of underlying pathology, even when neither speaker is aware of the specific diagnosis at the time of the interview! Furthermore, the speaker was frequently unaware that he or she was using "hope" or "hopeless" words. Because the analysis was context free, it often happened that the words used by the speaker evoked his or her mental state even when he or she was talking about something else. For example, where a hopeless individual might say "nothing ever came of it," a more hopeful person might use the phrase "it was only wishful thinking," regardless of the context. Spence appropriately likens this context-free analysis of an interview to a dream or fantasy. The point is well taken. The speech he analyzed was largely metaphoric, not unlike the fried eggs and bacon that look like a face (Figure 12.4), and metaphors are particularly characteristic of dream formation (Sharpe, 1937). Spence suggests that this "lexical leakage," as he calls it, comes about when bodily changes accompanying the onset of disease result in ucs mental changes which in turn produce a bias in word selection. Thus, the lexical changes which he picked up could have resulted from the patients' ability to detect faint, subliminal changes in their bodies.[*]

Now we come to the crux of the matter. If subliminal, or at least low-level, stimuli can be shown to affect plain, ordinary conversation, then does it not stand to reason that such stimuli would exert a much greater influence on dreams? Here then we have an opportunity not only to subject the dream's signal detection capacity to a rigorous test, but also to determine whether dreams are better predictors of illness than other modes of experience. Thus, by replicating the Schmale-Spence study and adding dream collection to the procedure, we could both test our model and enrich our clinical knowledge.

The Dream as Predictor of Response to Treatment

If, because of their sensitivity to internal cues, dreams can predict diagnoses, they should also be able to help us make *prognoses*. This is suggested by the aforementioned study of recovering alcoholics by Fiss (1980). The subjects for this investigation were twenty alcoholic inpa-

---

[*]There is, of course, an alternative explanation to Spence's findings, as he himself is quick to point out. Instead of bodily changes resulting in mental changes, which in turn trigger lexical changes (our hypothesis), it is entirely conceivable that both physical and lexical changes result from changes in mental state. Thus, a person who feels hopeless would be more likely to contract an illness and use hopelessness connoting words. No test of these two competing hypotheses has as yet been undertaken, largely because it would require a longitudinal design that would be extremely costly and time consuming (Spence, personal communication). My position on this issue is simply that either way we are dealing not with facts but with hypotheses, and if one of these rather than the other leads to experiments that advance our understanding of ucs mental activity, so be it.

tients who had just completed a week-long detoxification program. They were given tape-recorded dream interviews for five consecutive mornings. On the third day of dream collection, and again shortly before being discharged four weeks later, they were administered the Ludwig-Stark Craving Questionnaire, the Global Assessment Scale, and the Profile of Mood States. The dream protocols were blindly scored by two raters on a selected number of scales described by Winget and Kramer (1979). Analysis of the data revealed that nearly 20 percent of all the correlations between dream content, on the one hand, and mood and overall adjustment, on the other, turned out to be significant. It indicated that alcoholic patients are most likely to respond positively to treatment if their dream narratives are long and elaborate, if they themselves appear as active participants in their dreams, if the characters appearing in their dreams represent persons with whom they have close relationships in their waking lives, if their dreams contain sexual themes, if aggression in their dreams is directed outward rather than inward, and if the feelings expressed in the dreams are both intense and pleasant.

Of greatest interest, however, was the relationship we found between dream content and craving. A median split of the scores on the craving questionnaire revealed that more than 80 percent of the high cravers dreamed about drinking, whereas of the low cravers only 30 percent dreamed about drinking—a difference significant at the .03 level.

At first this finding, which obviously contradicts Freud's (1953; 1955) wish-fulfillment hypothesis, puzzled us, especially in view of Bokert's (1968) finding of an inverse relationship between dreaming about drinking and thirstiness in a normal population. However, a subsequent qualitative analysis of our data showed that there actually was no inconsistency between our data and Bokert's. His subjects in general all had gratifying dreams about drinking. Our subjects, on the other hand, had not only gratifying but also many conflictual dreams about drinking, as might be expected in view of the fact that, contrary to Bokert's subjects, ours were addicted to a noxious, socially disapproved substance. We therefore reanalyzed our data separately for gratifying and nongratifying dream content and found that the dreams of the low cravers all contained themes of drive gratification (e.g., drinking and feeling happy), whereas the dreams of the high cravers all contained defensive or conflictual themes (e.g., the loss of a love object as a result of being caught drinking).

Two principal conclusions can be drawn from these results. One is that an individual's response to an intensified drive state is determined not only by how much drive material gets incorporated into his or her dreams, but also by the manner in which this material is incorporated—an important guiding principle underlying all studies of dream function. The second conclusion is more germane to the issue under consideration here: by demonstrating that the quality of the dream experience may determine how people cope with the effects of withdrawing from a substance to which they have become addicted, in terms of their mood, general adjustment, and craving intensity, the Fiss (1980) study confirms that dream content may indeed be a valuable predictor variable in studying responsiveness to treatment. In terms of the proposed signal detection model of dream function, it suggests that indicators of change may appear in dream content before they manifest themselves in the waking state. It further suggests that *dreams are uniquely sensitive to subtle physical as well as mental and emotional cues.*

The Dream as Facilitator of Self-Understanding and Self-Awareness

We now come full circle to the premise we started out with, namely, that the dream is indeed the "royal road" to the ucs, but, as stated earlier, a cognitive ucs, an ucs of information processing. If dreams constitute an experiential mode in which the detection of faint, low-level internal cues, both physiological and psychological, is more likely to occur than in other modes of experience, then the dream does indeed become the vehicle of choice for achieving the capacity for self-understanding, self-awareness, and self-reflection.

One indication that the dream may be a promoter of self-knowledge is a recent finding reported by Purcell et al. (1986) that the content of REM dreams is characterized by greater self-reflectiveness (as measured by a nine-point scale developed by the authors) than the content of non-REM dreams. This suggests that attending to one's REM dreams should increase self-reflectiveness in waking life.

To test this hypothesis experimentally, one needs to design studies in which subjects are required to focus their attention on their dreams for long periods of time, to immerse themselves, so to speak, in their dream life. If this process results in a significant improvement in self-awareness, then the hypothesis would be confirmed. At least two studies have been carried out that lend convincing support to this formulation. One, by Cartwright, Tipton, and Wicklund (1980), shows that patients trained in attending to their REM dreams remained longer in treatment and made better progress than patients trained in attending to their non-REM dreams. Those subjects who made better progress showed more treatment-appropriate behavior and used the therapeutic hours more productively: they produced more personal material and expressed more affect. The other study on the effects of "enhanced" dream access, by Fiss and Litchman (1976), found that focusing on REM dreams resulted in significantly greater symptom relief and significantly higher levels of self-awareness than did focusing on non-REM dreams. This study involved fewer subjects than the Cartwright study; but it used subjects as their own controls, which the Cartwright study did not. It also exposed subjects to a more intensive experience: it was literally a "crash program" designed to maximize dream recall and minimize dream forgetting. The subjects were required to listen attentively to a playback of all the dreams recorded in the laboratory the night before and were encouraged to reflect on the meaning of these dreams during their waking hours. No dreams, however, were interpreted. Utilizing four commonly used clinical scales—the SCL-90, the Beck Depression Inventory, the State-Trait Anxiety Inventory, and Target Complaints—Fiss and Litchman found that on all measures subjects experienced significantly less symptom distress following three nights of REM-dream "enhancement" than after three nights of non-REM-dream "enhancement." Furthermore, on an objective measure of self-awareness based on subjects' free associations—the EXPeriencing Scale (Klein et al., 1970)—*subjects showed maximal insightfulness only during REM-dream "enhancement".*

Both studies strongly suggest that attending to one's dreams is most beneficial when this opportunity for picking up internal psychological cues is maximized. The results should encourage the extension of the dream immersion technique to many other areas of ego functioning. For example, would enhancing access to one's dreams *speed up* recovery from substance addiction? Instead of merely collecting dreams, as Fiss (1980) did, ETOH-dependent subjects could be asked to listen to a playback of their recorded dreams. Would they respond faster to treatment than subjects who merely report their dreams? Dream "enhancement," which after all is an experimental procedure as well as a therapeutic technique, could also be used to help subjects cope with stress, especially the stress of illness or injury or the stress of impending surgery. Thus, one might hypothesize that attending to one's dreams would alleviate one's anxiety before surgery and possibly even accelerate one's recovery from it. Again, the possibilities are numerous; they attest to the heuristic value of the signal detection paradigm of dream function.

Implications for a Self-Psychology of Dreaming

Elsewhere, (Fiss, 1986, 1989) I have proposed, along with Fosshage (1988), that dreaming serves a triple function: that of facilitating the development, maintenance, and restoration of the self. In support of this formulation, I have drawn extensively on sleep laboratory evidence that shows, among other things, that dream deprivation is causally related to maladaptive and regressive behavior and, conversely, that increased dreaming facilitates adaptive and self-preserving behavior, suggesting that dreaming plays a fundamental role in the process of building psychic structure. As Atwood and Stolorow (1984, p.103) so aptly put it, "dreams are the guardians of psychological structure." If this is so, then it should not surprise us, for example, that the newborn spends up to 50 percent of its total sleep time in dreaming sleep: it may well be that this high level of dream activity in the neonate serves the purpose of forming new psychic structures at a time in development when the need for structure formation is most urgent.

In this context it should be noted that self-reflection and self-awareness are indispensable to the development, maintenance and restoration of psychic structure. As Tolpin states, "once the self has been substantially formed, its contents are experienced as a reliable experiential configuration. . . . In some essential way *one knows one's self*" (Tolpin, 1980, p. 308). The case of Mr. E (Goldberg, 1978, p. 295) exemplifies this point: as the patient's self became more and more cohesive, his capacity for self-observation and insight developed correspondingly. "The proper working through of the analytic transference allowed him to realize the authenticity of his experience." In his discussion of normal and pathological narcissism, Kernberg (1975, p. 316) makes a similar assumption about the essential link between self-coherence and self-knowledge, only he looks at the other side of the coin: "a *lack* of an integrated self," he writes, "is characterized by . . . a marked incapacity to perceive oneself realistically as a total human being." Stolorow and colleagues (Stolorow, Brandchaft, and Atwood, 1987, p. 71) single out affects as the principal medium for achieving self-knowledge. "The modulation and containment of affects makes possible their use as self-signals." This presumably occurs at a time when self-experience has become differentiated and synthesized. Stolorow and his associates conceptualization raises an important question. Need affects be the sole or principal "self signals"? Could the dream not serve the same purpose, perhaps even more effectively?

Kohut's concept of the "self-state dream" (Kohut, 1977, p. 109) certainly provides an affirmative, albeit incomplete answer to this question. It is almost self-evident that dreams should portray the state of a person's self or state of mind, and that they do so in particularly vivid and salient terms. By viewing the dream as a singularly sensitive signal detector, hence as a particularly effective promoter of self-awareness, it stands to reason that the more internal signals we can detect, the greater would be our self-awareness; and because self-awareness facilitates psychic structure formation, dreaming can certainly be considered to be a major contributor to self-consolidation and integration. Furthermore, if we agree with Kohut that the need to maintain the integrity of the self is the primary motivating principle of psychic life (Kohut, 1971), and if the dream does indeed play a critical role in the consolidation of the self, then it would indeed be incumbent upon us to regard the dream once more as central to the workings of the human mind and restore it to its rightful eminent place in psychological theory.

The Signal Detection Model of Dream Function and Hartmann's Concept of "Boundaries in the Mind"

In his recent book, Hartmann (1991) proposes a new personality dimension on which our view of the dream as signal detector par excellence may have important bearing. He calls this dimension or individual difference variable "boundaries in the mind." The dimension is a continuum ranging from extremely "thin" boundaries to extremely "thick" boundaries, along which individuals vary as they do in terms of any other stable characteristic, such as "field-dependence-independence" or "introversion-extraversion." The concept of "boundaries in the mind" is an outgrowth of Hartmann's extensive work on nightmares, and his striking observation that nightmare sufferers, schizophrenics, and creative people all tend to have "thin" boundaries. Thus, for the first time, we are led to a fundamental understanding of the long suspected but never before so well-substantiated link between creativity and madness.

Hartmann defines "boundary" as an individual's capacity to distinguish mental structures. Among the different kinds of "boundaries" that can be distinguished are boundaries separating wakefulness from sleep, fantasy from reality, self from others, adult from child, male from female, past from present, ordinary sensory experience from extrasensory experience; and boundaries delineating body surfaces, memories, and many other dimensions. According to Hartmann, the relative thickness or thinness, density or permeability, rigidity or flexibility of an individual's "boundaries" is the result of both genetic and environmental factors, and constitutes a basic predisposition or vulnerability to the development of frequent nightmares, schizophrenia, or artistic or scientific creativity.

The evidence Hartmann marshals in support of this general organizing principle is impressive. Using a combination of psychological testing and depth interviews, he discovered that, in contrast to a control group of non-nightmare sufferers, persons with a lifelong history of frequent nightmares have the following characteristics in common: they are unusually sensitive, open, undefended, and expressive; they reveal a tendency toward schizophrenia on the MMPI; they tend to describe their night dreams as well as their daydreams as unusually real (the opposite of lucidity); they lose themselves in play and easily regress, the way children do; they tend to merge readily and overidentify with others, become too easily enmeshed with others, and are overly trusting; they tend to present a mixture of masculine and feminine characteristics rather than a stereotyped sexual identity; they show boundary deficits in their Rorschach scores; and they frequently have depersonalization, derealization, deja vu, and extrasensory experiences.

On the basis of this evidence Hartmann concludes that the same psychological makeup may make a person both artistic and vulnerable to mental illness. It enables an individual, for better or for worse, "to experience the world more directly, more painfully than others." Thus, if associated with the right combination of talent, intelligence, and support, thin boundaries may actually be a major asset: they could make one a better, more empathic writer, artist, teacher, or therapist. In the absence of these supports, however, these same thin boundaries are likely to become a major liability and overwhelm the vulnerable self.

While all this is highly speculative, it is extremely intriguing, because it all points toward a fundamental property of human nature whose importance has so far been insufficiently appreciated. It is especially appealing because it can be operationalized. Hartmann has begun to develop a questionnaire designed to quantify where on the boundary continuum a particular individual falls.

In looking over the different kinds of boundaries that Hartmann describes, I am particularly struck by the impression that many of them are in one way or another related to what the psychoanalytic literature refers to as the "stimulus barrier," "protective barrier against stimuli," or "Reitzschutz," which protects against excessive external and internal stimulation. Too permeable a barrier has been held accountable for both schizophrenic decompensation and precocious ego development (Bergman and Escalona, 1949). According to Freud (1955), the traumatic neurosis results from a breach in the stimulus barrier, and the dreams of those suffering from traumatic neurosis "are endeavoring to master the stimulus retrospectively." In his book, Hartmann reports that at least one subgroup of posttraumatic nightmare sufferers tended to form extremely close attachments to a buddy, whose death or injury often provided the trauma that later entered the nightmare. Hartmann speculates that this trauma constituted the loss of a self-object with whom the veteran had formed a narcissistic merger or mirror relationship.

As far as the stimulus barrier is concerned, Hartmann includes it among all the other types of boundary, both general (e.g., ego boundaries, "character armor," etc.) and specific (Rorschach-derived boundary measures, interpersonal boundaries, etc.). My point here is that "stimulus barrier" may be a more basic genotypical dimension, a common factor underlying the other more phenotypical ones.[*] I further propose that *a person's characteristic responsiveness to subliminal stimulation may be the most direct way of quantifying "boundary."* In essence, I envision it to be comparable to a person's response, say to the Embedded Figures Test, in determining his or her degree of field dependence or independence. Earlier I have presented evidence showing that responsiveness to subliminal stimulation is not only state but also trait related (Fiss, 1966). Admittedly, much of my reasoning here rests on face validity. There is, however, some evidence that supports my hypothesis. Mednick (1970), borrowing from Hullian learning theory, postulates that the predisposition to schizophrenia is characterized by excessively strong reactions to mild stress and excessive stimulus generalization, qualities all indicative of barrier insufficiency. Furthermore, the work of Silverman et al. (1982) strongly suggests that schizophrenics are particularly responsive to sub-

---

[*]A recently completed factor analysis of Hartmann's 146-item boundary questionnaire shows that the factor with the highest loading (called "Primary Process Thinking") describes a person who has many experiences of merging: merging of self with others, of imagery with reality, etc. Other factors with high loadings describe persons who feel like children, who are easily hurt, who profess to know others' unexpressed thoughts and feelings, who are open and trusting to the world, and who enjoy soaking up ambience. These initial findings are clearly consistent with my suggestion that stimulus barrier may be the principal component of the boundary concept.

liminal stimuli. Thus, the notion that *sensitivity to subliminal stimulation may be the marker of choice for Hartmann's boundary concept* does not seem too farfetched.

The boundary concept also has significant implications for self-psychology, especially in its interpersonal aspects of merging and mirroring. For example, persons whose boundaries are either too thick or too thin, too rigid or too flexible, may be prone to self-fragmentation. Conversely, there may be some optimal boundary qualities that characterize those individuals whom we would characterize as having cohesive or well-integrated selves.

Summary

This chapter concerns itself with the experimental study of ucs mental activity both in the waking state and during sleep. Historically, the experimental psychology laboratory has provided the most persuasive verification of the existence of ucs mental processes by demonstrating that stimuli may register without awareness and still affect our experience and behavior in predictable and clearly definable ways. In this endeavor, dreams have consistently been shown to be particularly responsive to the effects of subliminal activation.

Experimental studies showing that far more material registers in our minds than we are consciously aware of go back as far as the turn of the century, but not until 1917, after Freud's introduction of the concept of the day residue in dreaming, was an attempt to validate experimentally what has since become known as the *Poetzl phenomenon* seriously undertaken. Poetzl (1917) was the first person to demonstrate that the manifest content of dreams draws on exposures to stimuli too brief to attract notice: that which is *not* perceived immediately after stimulation is more likely to appear in subsequent dreams than that which is *is* perceived. Yet, despite the promise of this early work, forty years elapsed before it was replicated, this time, however, under much more rigorous control conditions than Poetzl originally employed. These later studies, by Fisher, Paul, Shevrin, Luborsky, Spence, Klein, Eagle, myself, and particularly Silverman and his associates, to name only a few, not only succeeded in validating the Poetzl phenomenon, but also in demonstrating that of all the possible human experiences, dreams are by far the most responsive to subliminal or low-level stimuli. This is because dreams are both an experiential mode as well as a state of consciousness in which reality contact is reduced to a minimum. When this occurs, response to subliminal activation has been shown to be maximal. Studies of subliminal activation have also significantly added to our conceptual understanding of information processing: they show that a cognitive experience is not an instantaneous event but a complex, multiphasic process of organization—a purposeful reconstruction, if you will—that takes time to evolve. Furthermore, a good deal of this process unfolds without benefit of awareness. Today, we even know many of the essential neurophysiological correlates of this extended process.

Because of the dream's exceptional facilitative role in the recovery of subliminally registered input, it makes sense to regard *the dream as a signal detector par excellence*, as an event far more likely to reveal than conceal something. According to signal detection theory, the dream can be understood to be an intervening variable that modulates the response to a stimulus too faint to be consciously perceived. Two signal detection models—a waking subliminal activation model and a sleep stimulation model—are described, compared, and found to be virtually identical: both have the same antecedent variables (personality and experimental condition); both employ similar methodologies (experimental and control stimuli, psychophysical threshold determinations, etc.); in both, the stimuli, although not consciously perceived, do nevertheless register, are retrievable in dreams and in other modes of experience and have delayed effects, adaptive as well as nonadaptive, on waking behavior; and in both models, the subliminally registered material emerges, not as a facsimile of the stimulus, but as a concretized, often symbolic transformation of it, having all the characteristics of primary process thinking. Subjects, however, usually fail to recognize that there is any correspondence between the original stimulus and the emerging end-product, even if this correspondence is striking. Several illustrations of these kinds of transformation are presented, suggesting that lack of lucidity is generally the norm for subliminally activated experiences both in sleep and in the waking state.

So closely does the sleep-stimulation model resemble the subliminal activation model that one appears justified in proposing a single unified signal detection model for both sleep and wakefulness. According to this unified model, the effects of subliminal stimuli administered during both sleep and wakefulness are modulated by preexisting situational and personality variables, by the type of stimulus used, by the mode of experience and state of consciousness in which the subliminally registered stimulus is recovered, and by the type of behavior on which these stimuli make their final impact.

One important heuristic value of this combined model is that it has major implications for research, theory, and clinical practice, especially in the area of behavioral medicine. Two examples are offered that show the value of focusing on dreams as signal detectors, especially as detectors of signals from within: one describes in detail how the experimental investigation of dream content may facilitate the early detection of physical illness, in this case cervical cancer; the other illustrates how dream content can be effectively used as a marker or predictor of response to treatment for substance addiction.

Not only physical but also psychological well-being can be enhanced by utilizing the dream's signal detection capacity. This is borne out by studies carried out by the author and others that show that focusing on one's dreams facilitates self-reflection and self-awareness and reduces distress caused by psychological symptoms. Because self-awareness is an indispensable precondition for the development, maintenance and restoration of psychic structure (see, for example, Tolpin, 1980; Goldberg, 1978; Stolorow et al., 1987), this finding has major implications for a self-psychology of dreaming, the empirical foundation of which has been described elsewhere (Fiss, 1986).

Finally, the signal detection model of dreaming proposed here is also theoretically relevant to Hartmann's recently formulated concept of "boundary." In fact, as I attempt to show, there is a good possibility that a person's characteristic way of responding to subliminal stimulation may constitute the most direct and effective way of "diagnosing" this fundamental personality dimension.

References

Allers, R., and Teler, J. (1924). "Ueber die Verwertung Unbemerkter Eindruecke bei Assoziationen." *Zeitschrift fur Neurologie und Psychiatrie* 89: 492–513.

Armstrong, R., Burnap, D., Jacobson, A., Kales, A., Ward, S., and Golden, J. (1965). "Dreams and Gastric Secretions in Duodenal Ulcer Patients." *New Physician* 14: 241–243.

Atwood, G. E., and Stolorow, R. D. (1984). *Structures of Subjectivity: Explorations in Psychoanalytic Phenomenology.* Hillsdale, N.J.: Lawrence Erlbaum Associates.

Bach, S. (1959). "The Symbolic Effects of Words in Subliminal, Supraliminal, and Incidental Presentation." Ph.D. dissertation, New York University.

———— and Klein, G. S. (1957). "The Effects of Prolonged Subliminal Exposures of Words." *American Psychologist* 12: 397–398.

Barber, T. X., Walker, P. C., and Hahn, K. W. (1973). "Effects of Hypnotic Induction and Suggestions on Nocturnal Dreaming and Thinking." *Journal of Abnormal Psychology* 82: 414–427.

Berger, R. J. (1963). "Experimental Modification of Dream Content by Meaningful Verbal Stimuli." *British Journal of Psychiatry* 109: 722–740.

Bergman, P., and Escalona, S. (1949). "Unusual Sensitivities in Very Young Children." *The Psychoanalytic Study of the Child* 3–4: 333–352.

Binet, A. (1896). *Alterations of Personality.* New York: Appleton.

Bokert, E. (1968). "The Effects of Thirst and a Related Verbal Stimulus on Dream Reports." Ph.D. dissertation, New York University.

Breger, L., Hunter, I., and Lane, R. (1971). "The Effect of Stress on Dreams." *Psychological Issues,* Monograph No. 27: 1–213.

Candland, D. K., and Mayer, R. S. (1978). *Psychology: The Experimental Approach.* New York: McGraw-Hill.

Cartwright, R. (1974). "The Influence of a Conscious Wish on Dreams." *Journal of Abnormal Psychology* 83: 387–393.

————. (1977). *Night Life.* Englewood Cliffs, N.J.: Prentice-Hall.

————, Bernick, N., Borowitz, G., and Kling, A. (1969). "Effect of an Erotic Movie on Sleep and Dreams of Young Men." *Archives of General Psychiatry* 20: 262–271.

Cartwright, R., Tipton, L., and Wicklund, J. (1980). "Focusing on Dreams." *Archives of General Psychiatry* 37: 275–277.

Cohen, D., (1974). "Toward a Theory of Dream Recall." *Psychological Bulletin* 81: 138–154.

————. (1981). "The Functional Significance of REM Dreaming." Paper presented at meeting of Association for the Psychophysiological Study of Sleep. Mexico City.

———— and Cox, C. (1975). "Neuroticism in the Sleep Laboratory: Implications for Representational and Adaptive Properties of Dreaming. *Journal of Abnormal Psychology* 84: 91–108.

Dement, W., and Wolpert, E. (1958). "The Relation of Eye Movements, Body Motility, and External Stimuli to Dream Content." *Journal of Experimental Psychology* 55: 543–553.

Diven, K. (1937). "Certain Determinants in the Conditioning of Anxiety Reaction." *Journal of Psychology* 3: 291–308.

Dondero, E. A. (1959). "Subliminal Perception and Set." Ph.D. dissertation, The Catholic University of America.

Eagle, M. N. (1959). "The Effects of Subliminal Stimuli of Aggressive Content Upon Conscious Cognition." *Journal of Personality* 27: 578–600.

————. (1962). "Personality Correlates of Sensitivity to Subliminal Stimulation." *Journal of Nervous and Mental Disease* 134: 1–17.

————. (1987). "The Psychoanalytic and the Cognitive Unconscious." In R. Stern (Ed.), *Theories of the Unconscious and Theories of the Self*, pp. 155–189. Hillsdale, N.J.: Analytic Press.

Fisher, C. (1953). "Experimental Induction of Dreams by Direct Suggestion." *Journal of the American Psychoanalytic Association* 1: 22–255.

————. (1954). "Dreams and Perception: The Role of Preconscious and Primary Modes of Perception in Dream Formation." *Journal of the American Psychoanalytic Association* 3: 389–445.

————. (1956). "Dreams, Images, and Perception: A Study of Unconscious-Preconscious Relationships." *Journal of the American Psychoanalytic Association* 4: 5–48.

————. (1957). "A Study of the Preliminary Stages of the Construction of Dreams and Images." *Journal of the American Psychoanalytic Association* 5: 5–60.

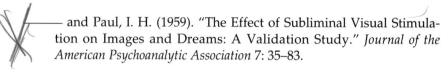 ———— and Paul, I. H. (1959). "The Effect of Subliminal Visual Stimulation on Images and Dreams: A Validation Study." *Journal of the American Psychoanalytic Association* 7: 35–83.

Fiss, H. (1961). "State of Consciousness and the Subliminal Effect." Ph.D. dissertation, New York University.

————. (1966). "The Effects of Experimentally Induced Changes in Alertness on Response to Subliminal Stimulation." *Journal of Personality* 34: 577–595.

————. (1980). "Dream Content and Response to Withdrawal from Alcohol." *Sleep Research* 9: 152.

————. (1986). "An Empirical Foundation for a Self Psychology of Dreaming." *Journal of Mind and Behavior* 7: 161–191.

————. (1988). "The Meaning of Dreams: Warning Function or Signal Detection Capacity?" Paper presented at meeting of the Association for the Study of Dreams, Santa Cruz, Cal.

————.(1989)"An Experimental Self Psychology of Dreaming: Clinical and Theoretical Applications." In A. Goldberg (Ed.), *Progress in Self Psychology*, vol. 5, pp. 13–23, 50–54. Hillsdale, N.J.: Analytic Press.

————, Goldberg, G. H., and Klein G. S. (1963). "Effects of Subliminal Stimulation on Imagery and Discrimination." *Perceptual and Motor Skills* 17: 31–44.

————, Kremer, E., and Litchman, J. (1977). "The Mnemonic Function of Dreaming." Paper presented at meeting of Association for the Psychophysiological Study of Sleep, Houston, Texas.

———— and Litchman, J. (1976). "Dream Enhancement: An Experimental Approach to the Adaptive Function of Dreams." Paper presented at meeting of the Association for the Psychophysiological Study of Sleep, Cincinnati, Ohio.

Fosshage, J. (1988). "Dream Interpretation Revisited." In A. Goldberg (Ed.), *Progress in Self Psychology*, vol. 3, pp. 161–175. Hillsdale, N.J.: Analytic Press.

Foulkes, D. (1962). "Dream Reports from Different Stages of Sleep." *Journal of Abnormal and Social Psychology* 65: 14–25.

——— and Rechtschaffen, A. (1964). "Presleep Determination of Dream Content: Effects of Two Films." *Perceptual and Motor Skills* 19: 983–1005.

Fox, M. (1960). "Differential Effects of Subliminal and Supraliminal Stimulation." PhD. dissertation, New York University.

French, T., and Shapiro, L. B. (1949). "The Use of Dream Analysis in Psychosomatic Research." *Psychosomatic Research* 11: 110–112.

Freud, S. (1953). "The Interpretation of Dreams." In J. Strachey (Ed. and Trans.), *The Standard Edition of The Complete Psychological Works of Sigmund Freud*, vol. 4. London: Hogarth [Original work published 1900.]

———. (1955). "Beyond the Pleasure Principle." In J. Strachey (Ed. and Trans.), *The Standard Edition of the Complete Psychological Works of Sigmund Freud*, vol. 18, pp. 3–64. London: Hogarth. [Original work published 1920.}

Goldberg, A. (1978). "Analysis of a Mirror Transference in a Case of Arrested Development." In A. Goldberg (Ed.), *The Psychology of the Self: A Casebook*, pp. 263–296. New York: International Universities Press.

Goldberg, F. H., and Fiss, H. (1959). "Partial Cues and the Phenomenon of Discrimination Without Awareness." *Perceptual and Motor Skills* 9: 22–26.

Goodenough, D. R. (1969). "The Phenomena of Dream Recall." In L. E. Abt and B. F. Riess (Eds.), *Progress in Clinical Psychology*, pp. 136–153. New York: Grune and Stratton.

———, Witkin, H. A., Lewis, H. B., Koulack, D., and Cohen, H. (1974). "Repression, Interference, and Field Dependence as Factors in Dream Forgetting." *Journal of Abnormal Psychology* 83: 32–44.

Gottschalk, L. A., Stone, W. N., Glesser, G. C., and Iacono, J. (1966). "Anxiety Levels in Dreams in Relation to Changes in Plasma Free Fatty Acids." *Science* 153: 654–657.

Greenberg, R. (1987). "Self Psychology and Dreams: The Merging of Different Perspectives." *Psychiatric Journal of the University of Ottawa* 12: 98–102.

————— and Pearlman, C. (1975). "REM Sleep and the Analytic Process: A Psychophysiologic Bridge." *The Psychoanalytic Quarterly* 44: 392–403.

Hartmann, E. (1991). *Boundaries in the Mind.* New York: Basic Books.

Haskell, R. (1985). "Dreaming, Cognition, and Physical Illness." *Journal of Medical Humanities and Bioethics* 6: 27–32.

Hull, C. (1943). *Principles of Behavior, An Introduction to Behavior Theory.* New York: Appleton–Century–Crofts.

Kernberg, O. (1975). *Borderline Conditions and Pathological Narcissism,* (p. 316). New York: Aronson.

Klein, G. S. (1959). On subliminal activation. *Journal of Nervous and Mental Disease,* 128, 293–301. (a)

————. (1959). Consciousness in psychoanalytic theory: Some implications for current research in perception. *Journal of the American Psychoanalytic Association,* 7, 5–34. (b)

————. (1970). *Perception, Motives, and Personality.* New York: Knopf.

————, Spence, D. P., Holt, R. R., and Gourevitch, S. (1958). Cognition without awareness: Subliminal influences upon conscious thought. *Journal of Abnormal and Social Psychology,* 57, 255–266.

Klein, M., Mathiew, P., Gendlin, E., and Kiesler, D. (1970). *The EXPeriencing Scale: A Research and Training Manual.* Madison: Wisconsin Psychiatric Institute.

Kohut, H. (1971). *The Analysis of the Self.* New York International Universities Press.

————. (1977). *The Restoration of the Self.* New York: International Universities Press.

Koulack, D. (1969). "Effects of Somatosensory Stimulation on Dream Content." *Archives of General Psychiatry* 20: 718–725.

Kramer, M., Roehrs, T., and Roth, T. (1976). "Mood Change and the Physiology of Sleep." *Comprehensive Psychiatry* 17: 161–165.

Kramer, M., and Roth, T. (1972). "The Mood Regulating Function of Sleep." In W. Koella (Ed.), *Sleep,* pp. 563–571. Basel: S. Karger.

Kubie, L. S. (1943). "The Use of Induced Hypnagogic Reveries in the Recovery of Repressed Amnesic Data." *Bulletin of the Menninger Clinic* 7: 172–182.

Lacey, J. I., and Smith, R. L. (1954). "Conditioning and Generalization of Unconscious Anxiety." *Science* 120: 1045–1052.

Lazarus, R. S., and McCleary, R. A. (1951). "Autonomic Discrimination Without Awareness: A Study of Subception." *Psychological Review* 58: 113–122.

Levitan, H. (1980). "Traumatic Events in the Dreams of Psychosomatic Patients." *Psychotherapy and Psychosomatics* 33: 226–232.

———. (1983). "Dreams Which Precede Asthma Attacks." In A. Krakowski and C. Kimball (Eds.), *Psychosomatic Medicine: Theoretical, Clinical and Transcultural Aspects*, pp. 79–85. New York: Plenum Press.

———. (1984). "Dreams Which Culminate in Migraine Headaches."*Psychotherapy and Psychosomatics* 41: 161–166.

Levy, E. Z., Thaler, V. H., and Ruff, G. E. (1958). "New Techniques for Recording Skin Resistance Changes." *Science* 128: 33–34.

Lewis, H. B., Goodenough, D. R., Shapiro, A., and Sleser, I. (1966). "Individual Differences in Dream Recall." *Journal of Abnormal Psychology* 71: 52–59.

Lindsley, D. B. (1958). "Perceptual Blanking: A Measure of Perception Time." Paper presented at meeting of Midwestern Psychological Association, Detroit.

Linehan, E., and O'Toole, J. (1982). "The Effect of Subliminal Stimulation of Symbiotic Fantasy on College Students' Self Disclosures in Group Counseling." *Journal of Counseling Psychology* 29: 151–157.

Mednick, S. A. (1970). "Breakdown in Individuals at High Risk for Schizophrenia: Possible Predispositional Perinatal Factors." *Mental Hygiene* 54: 50–63.

Miller, J. G. (1939). "Discrimination Without Awareness." *American Journal of Psychology* 52: 562–578.

Palmatier, J. R., and Bornstein, P. H. (1980). "The Effects of Subliminal Stimulation of Symbiotic Merging Fantasies on Behavioral Treatment of Smokers." *Journal of Nervous and Mental Disease* 168: 715–720.

Paul, I. H. and Fisher, C. (1959). "Subliminal Visual Stimulation: A Study of Its Influence on Subsequent Images and Dreams." *Journal of Nervous and mental Disease* 129: 315–340.

Poetzl, O. (1917). "Experimentell erregte Traumbilder in ihren Beziehungen zum indirekten Sehen." *Zeitschrift fur Neurologie und Psychiatrie* 37: 278–349.

Purcell, S., Mullington, J., Moffitt, A., Hoffman, R., and Pigeau, R. (1986). "Dream Self-Reflectiveness as a Learned Cognitive Skill." *Sleep* 9: 423–437.

Pustell, T. E. (1957). "The Experimental Induction of Perceptual Vigilance and Defense." *Journal of Personality* 25: 425–438.

Razran, G. (1955). "Conditioning and Perception." *Psychological Review* 62: 83–95.

Rechtschaffen, A. (1978). "The Single-Mindedness and Isolation of Dreams." *Sleep* 1: 97–109.

———— and Foulkes, D. (1965). "Effect of Visual Stimuli on Dream Content." *Perceptual and Motor Skills* 20: 1149–1160.

Samuels, I. (1959). "Reticular Mechanisms and Behavior." *Psychological Bulletin* 56: 1–25.

Saul, L., Sheppard, E., Selby, D., Lhamon, W., and Sacks, D. (1954). "The Quantification of Hostility in Dreams with Reference to Essential Hypertension." *Science* 119: 382–383.

Schiffman, H. R. (1976). *Sensation and Perception: An Integrated Approach.* New York: John Wiley and Sons.

Schmale, A. (1966). "The Affect of Hopelessness in the Development of Cancer: The Prediction of Uterine Cancer in Women with Atypical Cytology." *Psychosomatic Medicine* 28: 714–726.

Schneider, D. E. (1973). "Conversion of Massive Anxiety into Heart Attack." *American Journal of Psychotherapy* 27: 360–378.

Schonbar, R. A. (1965). "Differential Dream Recall Frequency as a Component of Life Style." *Journal of Consulting Psychology* 29: 468–474.

Shapiro, A., Goodenough, D. R., and Gryler, R. B. (1963). "Dream Recall as a Function of Method of Awakening." *Psychosomatic Medicine* 25: 174–180.

Sharpe, E. (1937). *Dream Analysis: A Practical Handbook for Psychoanalysts.* New York: Brunner-Mazel.

Shevrin, H. (1973). "Brain Wave Correlates of Subliminal Stimulation, Unconscious Attention, Primary and Secondary Process Thinking, and Repressiveness." *Psychological Issues,* Monograph No. 30: 56–87.

———— and Luborsky, L. (1958). "The Measurement of Preconscious Perception in Dreams and Images: An Investigation of the Poetzl Phenomenon." *Journal of Abnormal and Social Psychology* 56: 285–294.

Silverman, L. H. (1972). "Drive Stimulation and Pschopathology." In R. Holt and E. Peterfreund (Eds.), *Psychoanalysis and Contemporary Science,* vol. 1, pp. 306–326. New York: Macmillan.

————, Klinger, H., Lustbader, L., Darrell, J., and Martin, A. (1972). "The Effect of Subliminal Drive Stimulation on the Speech of Stutterers." *Journal of Nervous and Mental Disease* 155: 14–21.

————, Kwawer, J. S., Wolitzky, D., and Caron, M. (1973). "An Experimental Study of Aspects of the Psychoanalytic Theory of Male Homosexuality." *Journal of Abnormal Psychology* 82: 178–188.

————, Martin, A., Ungaro, R., and Mendelsohn, E. (1978). "Effect of Subliminal Stimulation of Symbiotic Fantasies on Behavior Modification Treatment of Obesity." *Journal of Consulting Psychology* 46: 432–441.

Silverman, L. H., Lachmann, F. M., and Milich, R. H. (1982). *The Search for Oneness.* New York: International Universities Press.

Smith, G. J. (1957). "Visual Perception: An Event over Time." *Psychological Review* 64: 306–313.

————, Spence, D. P., and Klein, G. S. (1959). "Subliminal Effects of Verbal Stimuli." *Journal of Abnormal and Social Psychology* 59: 167–176.

Smith, R. (1991). "The Meaning of Dreams: a Current Warning Theory." In Gackenbach and A. Sheikh (Eds.), *Dream Images: A Call to Mental Arms.* pp. 127–146.

Spence, D. P. (1978). "Lexical Correlates of Cervical Cancer." *Social Science and Medicine* 12: 141–145.

——— and Paul, I. H. (1959). "Importation Above and Below Awareness." Paper presented at meeting of American Psychological Association, Cincinnati, Ohio.

———, Lugo, M., and Youdin, R. (1974). "Cardiac Correlates of Cognitive Processing." *Psychosomatic Medicine* 36: 420–437.

Stolorow, R. D., Brandchaft, B., and Atwood, G. E. (1987). *Psychoanalytic Treatment: An Intersubjective Approach.* Hillsdale, N.J.: Analytic Press.

Swets, J. A. (1964). *Signal Detection and Recognition by Human Observers: Contemporary Readings.* New York: John Wiley and Sons.

———. (1973). "The Relative Operating Characteristic in Psychology." *Science* 182: 990–1000.

Tart, C. (1962). "Frequency of Dream Recall and Some Personality Measures." *Journal of Consulting Psychology* 26: 467–470.

———. (1964). "A Comparison of Suggested Dreams Occurring in Hypnosis and Sleep." *International Journal of Clinical and Experimental Hypnosis* 12: 263–289.

Tolpin, P. (1980). "The Borderline Personality: Its Makeup and Analyzability." In A. Goldberg, (Ed.), *Advances in Self Psychology*, pp. 299–316. New York: International Universities Press.

Urbantschitsch, V. (1907). *Ueber Subjektive Optische Anschauungsbilder.* Vienna: Deuticke.

Watson, R. (1972). "Mental Correlates of Periorbital Potentials During REM Sleep." Ph.D. dissertation, University of Chicago.

Winget, C., and Kapp, F. T. (1972). "The Relationship of the Manifest Content of Dreams to Duration of Childbirth in Primiparae." *Psychosomatic Medicine* 34: 312–320.

Winget, C., and Kramer, M. (1979). *Dimensions of Dreams.* Gainesville: University Presses of Florida.

Witkin, H. (1969). "Presleep Experiences and Dreams." In J. Fisher and L. Breger (Eds.), *The Meaning of Dreams: Recent Insights from the Laboratory*, pp. 1–37. Sacramento: California Mental Health Research, Monograph No. 3.

Ziegler, A. (1962). "A Cardiac Infarction and a Dream as Synchronous Events." *Journal of Analytic Psychology* 7: 141–148.

13

Don Kuiken and Shelley Sikora ━━━━

The Impact of Dreams on Waking Thoughts and Feelings*

You tossed a blanket from the bed,
You lay upon your back and waited;
You dozed and watched the night revealing
The thousand sordid images
Of which your soul was constituted;
They flickered against the ceiling.
And when all the world came back
And the light crept up between the shutters
And you heard the sparrows in the gutters,
You had such a vision of the street
As the street hardly understands . . .

(Eliot, 1934)

In Eliot's verse, the "sordid" dream images that "flickered against the ceiling" predispose the awakening dreamer to a "vision of the street." The dreamer's "vision" is sensitive to aspects of the "street" that are not understood in the busy, purposive "light" of day. Dreaming, in this view, sensitizes us to additional layers of significance; it alerts us to aspects of our life-worlds that we typically ignore.

Eliot's reference to "sordid" images is a reminder that the layers of significance to which dreams alert us are sometimes distinctly unsettling. Poetic renderings of this theme frequently suggest that the dreamer's "vision" includes a lingering sense of loss and melancholy. Emily Bronte writes:

*Correspondence may be addressed to Don Kuiken, Center for Advanced Study in Theoretical Psychology, Biological Sciences Building, University of Alberta, Edmonton, Alberta T6G 2E9. This research was supported by grant #410-87-1013 from the Social Sciences and Humanities Research Council.

> Sleep brings no joy to me,
> Remembrance never dies;
> My soul is given to misery
> And lives in sighs.
> Sleep brings no rest to me;
> The shadows of the dead,
> My waking eyes may never see,
> Surround my bed.
> Sleep brings no strength to me,
> In soundest sleep they come,
> And with their doleful imagery
> Deepen the gloom...
>
> (Bronte, 1985)

Neither Eliot's allusion to dreams' sensitizing effects nor Bronte's reference to dreams' lingering moods anticipate the drama in some portrayals of dreams' impact. For instance, in Dostoevsky's *The Brothers Karamazov*, Alyosha dozes near the coffin of Zossima, his spiritual mentor. He awakens from a dream that profoundly influences him:

> "He had only just been hearing [Zossima's] voice [in his dream], and that voice was still ringing in his ears. He was listening, still expecting other words. . . .
>
> . . . his soul, overflowing with rapture, yearned for freedom, space, openness. . . . The white towers and golden domes of the cathedral gleamed out against the sapphire sky. . . . The silence of the earth seemed to melt into the silence of the heavens.
>
> Alyosha stood, gazed, and suddenly threw himself down on the earth . . . he kissed it weeping, sobbing and watering it with his tears . . . in his rapture he was weeping even over those stars, which were shining to him from the abyss of space. . . ."
>
> (Dostoevsky, 1950)

Even after Alyosha awakens, the dreamed image of Zossima maintains a presence as though he might still speak. The lingering reality of this image is embedded in an enhanced aesthetic sensitivity—not a "vision of the [morning] street" but a vision of the nighttime sky. The lingering reality of Zossima's image is also part of extraordinary changes in Alyosha's feelings—not deepened gloom but complex, tearful rapture.

Aspects of dreams' impact on waking thoughts and feelings have been described by other authors: Rossetti, Muir, Pirandello, and so forth. But, it would be a mistake to regard subjective dream impact as an unusual concern of a few predisposed individuals. In a recent study, we administered a questionnaire to 168 young adults, asking them how frequently they experienced dreams that influenced their waking activities. For twelve of the sixteen types of influence that we asked about, Table 13.1 presents the reported frequency with which dreams affected waking events. For example, when asked how frequently they had dreams that made them feel like changing the way they were living, 13 percent indicated that they had such dreams at least twelve times during the past year, 25 percent indicated that they had such dreams at least four times during the past year, and 44 percent indicated that they had such dreams at least twice during the past year. (For comparison, when asked how frequently they had anxiety dreams, 10 percent indicated that they had such dreams at least twelve times during the past year, 26 percent indicated that they had such dreams at least four times during the past year, and 64 percent indicated that they had such dreams at least twice during the past year.) Although the accuracy of these questionnaire estimates is not assured, they suggest that impactful dreams, although not an everyday occurrence, certainly are not rare.

These data were also used to explore whether the several aspects of dream impact about which we asked could be understood as a smaller number of more basic dimensions. Factor analysis, with Varimax rotation, revealed three orthogonal factors. Table 13.1 presents each item and its loading on the factor with which it was most clearly associated. The first factor implies the penetration of waking thoughts by remembered dreams. References to daytime reminders of dreams, dreams recalled for the first time during the day, and dream deja vu suggest *spontaneous dream reminiscence*. The second factor implies deepened self-perception. References to influences on daytime mood, reminders of events from one's personal past, sensitivity to realities that are typically ignored, and readiness to change one's way of living suggest dream-induced *affective insight*. The third factor implies comprehension that is temporarily expanded beyond normal limits. References to foretelling the future, deliberate waking contact with dream characters, and recognition of spiritual or deceased dream figures suggest dream-induced *transcendent awareness*.

Table 13.1

The Frequency of Dreams' Influence on Thoughts, Feelings, and Actions During Wakefulness

	Number of Times Last Year		
	12 or More	4 or More	2 or More
Factor 1. *Spontaneous Reminiscence*			
How often does something that occurs later in the day remind you again of your dream? (.819)	11%	36%	64%
How often do you recall a dream during the day, a dream that you did not recall in the morning? (.766)	17%	36%	66%
How often do you find yourself in a place or situation that seems familiar from a dream (deja vu)? (.618)	30%	54%	76%
Factor 2. *Affective Insight*			
How often do you experience dreams that make you feel like changing the way you live? (.736)	8%	17%	29%
How often do your dreams remind you of events that occurred in your past? (.736)	11%	30%	70%
How often after a dream do you feel more sensitive to aspects of reality that you typically ignore? (.731)	9%	18%	44%
How often do you find that your dreams influence your mood during the day? (.635)	13%	25%	44%
Factor 3. *Transcendent Awareness*			
How often have you experienced dreams that foretell the future? (.713)	8%	12%	45%
How often do you deliberately seek contact with people because you dreamed about them? (.606)	7%	14%	31%
How often have you experienced dreams that involve a spiritual being or a deceased person? (.574)	5%	17%	35%
How often do your dreams help you solve a personal problem? (.432, Affective Insight; .643, Transcendent Awareness)	5%	13%	32%
How often do your dreams give you an artistic idea (e.g., for a painting, for a poem)? (.436, Affective Insight; .532, Transcendent Awareness)	6%	13%	20%

These three factors are based upon a limited array of items. Also, they are appropriately understood as variations among individuals rather than as variations among dreams per se. Nonetheless, they provide a preliminary scheme for discussing the impact of certain extraordinary dreams. In the present chapter, we will contrast this kind of dream impact with available conceptions of dream function, present results of a classificatory study of impactful dreams, and provide a framework for understanding the impact of different types of extraordinary dreams.

Dream Function: Beyond Uniformity and Utility

Whether as "flickering" reminiscences, "doleful" insights, or "rapturous" transcendence, the kinds of dream impact described by Eliot, Bronte, Dostoevsky, and so on—and by our research participants—have not been the object of systematic study by dream researchers. One reason is that theories of dream function guiding recent research have been quite limited in their conceptions of function. Consider the following representative hypotheses. From one perspective (Spear and Gordon, 1981), dream mechanisms have the effect of encoding aspects of a presleep event with elaboration; such encoding improves memory for features of the presleep event. From another perspective (Cohen, 1979), dream mechanisms have the effect of generating novel conceptions of a presleep problem; such reconstructions facilitate the dreamer's attempt to find a solution to the problem. From still another perspective (Jones, 1970), dreams have the effect of presenting an unconscious attitude that compensates for a one-sided conscious attitude; such presentations further the dreamer's continuing need to attain "self-perception in depth." Although seldom acknowledged explicitly, these perspectives share two problematic assumptions, specifically, that (1) dreaming uniformly functions in the hypothesized manner and (2) dreaming fulfills a utilitarian function.

Uniformity of Function

Typically, theories of dream function are stated in very general terms, that is, it is assumed that *all* dreams have the same function. For example, the theory that dreaming enables elaborative encoding of information (Spear and Gordon, 1981) does not differentiate between dreams that do and dreams that do not serve this mnemonic function. Although dreams may vary in the extent to which their elaboration provides cues that improve memory during the waking state, presumably all dreams are elaborative. Similarly, the theory that dreaming enables problem solving (Cohen, 1979) implies that all dreams generate novel conceptions of a problem. Although some dreams may generate more adaptive conceptions than others, presumably all dreams generate novel conceptions. Finally, the theory that dreaming facilitates self-perception in depth (Jones, 1970) implies that all dreams present attitudes that compensate for one-sided conscious attitudes. Although some dreams may be more readily recognized as compensating presentations than others, presumably all dreams present compensating attitudes.

The notion that all dreams function in the same manner is independent of whether dreams have more than one function. When more than one function is hypothesized for dreaming, such functions are typically integrated (sometimes quite loosely) into a theory that regards their integrated function as uniformly characteristic of all dreams (cf. Greenberg, 1981). To illustrate, condensation, as originally described by Freud (1953), is a dreamwork mechanism with two types of modus operandi. To create a collective image, condensation selects for inclusion into the manifest dream one dream element that represents several similar latent elements. To create a composite image, condensation fuses several similar latent dream elements—in the manner of superimposed photographic negatives—to form one manifest dream element. Conceived in this way, condensation may (1) encode a presleep event with elaboration by comparing it with similar past events (cf. Palombo, 1978), (2) generate a novel conception of the presleep event by forming a composite image (see Breger, 1967), *and* (3) construct an analogical ("symbolic") presentation of unconscious attitudes toward a presleep event by selecting a collective image or forming a composite image (see Hall, 1953). Therefore, if condensation is uniformly characteristic of dreaming, it could simultaneously serve several functions: (1) enhancing memory, (2) solving problems, and (3) compensating for one-sided conscious attitudes.

Perhaps dreaming *is* a sufficiently uniform phenomenon to consistently serve some function or integrated set of functions. On the other hand, perhaps dreaming is only *apparently* uniform because differences among kinds of dreaming—and among the functions of different kinds of dreaming—have not received sufficient research attention. By abandoning rigid assumptions about the uniformity of dream function, contrasting functions of different types of dreams may be found. Abandonment of this assumption may be especially important in studies of impactful dreams. At least, some available observations suggest that different types of impactful dreams have quite different functions. For example, Jung (1969) proposed that both archetypal and post-traumatic dreams are emotionally intense and profoundly unsettling. However, he concluded that the extraordinary figures and cosmic elements of archetypal dreams present compensatory unconscious attitudes; in contrast, the relived life-threatening events within post-traumatic dreams have the effect of "exhausting" through repetition the emotional impact of the trauma. Consistent with Jung's hypothesis, Hartmann (1984) observed that ordinary nightmares are common in creative individuals, whereas post-traumatic nightmares are not associated with creative activity. Such preliminary observations indicate the potential of contrasting the functions of different types of impactful dreams.

Function and Utility

Generally, contemporary theories of dream function reflect a utilitarian understanding of human needs and purposes. One contributing factor has been dream researchers' liaison with psychobiology—and implicitly with evolutionary biology. The result is a legacy of theories that elaborate on a biologically "adaptive" function for REM sleep to describe a psychological function for dreaming. For example, Snyder (1966) hypothesized that REM sleep provides preparatory activation prior to periodic awakenings. Such preparatory activation includes dreaming, especially about potential threats, and it allows the organism to more effectively cope with actual threats after awakening. Even when such preparatory activation involves dreaming about social predicaments, as in Ullman's (1973) similar proposal, the implication is that dreaming enhances adaptation vis-à-vis actual environmental challenges. The language of preparation and defense, vigilance and coping gives these theories of dream function their utilitarian flavor.

A second factor in dream researchers' utilitarian turn has been their liaison with cognitive psychology, both earlier experimental psychology and contemporary cognitive science. That association has left a legacy of theories that elaborate on models of learning, memory, and problem solving to describe dream function. For example, according to Pearlman (1981), "unprepared" learning, which involves unusual or complex behavioral adjustments, requires extensive "reprogramming" of "information processing systems." Such reprogramming, reflected in transformations within the dream narrative, facilitates retention of the newly acquired behavioral adjustment during wakefulness. A more recent notion in discussions of dream function is that dreaming reflects a process of "reverse learning" that dampens mnemonic "obsessions" and reduces subsequent confusion among memories (Crick and Mitchison, 1986). Although the unprepared learning hypothesis borrows from a model of animal learning and the reverse learning hypothesis adapts a connectionist model of human memory, both formulations depict dreaming as an "efficient" adjustment to environmental challenges, which contributes to their utilitarian tone.

A third factor in dream researchers' utilitarian orientation is perhaps the most influential: their affiliation with psychodynamically oriented therapist-investigators. That liaison has left a legacy of diverse perspectives within which dreaming is conceived as comparable to effective psychotherapy. Frequently subsuming the formulations of psychobiologists and cognitive psychologists, these theorists propose that dreaming regulates mood (Lowy, 1942; Kramer and Roth, 1973), embeds a recent emotional dilemma within a network of analogous problems and solutions (French and Fromm, 1964; Breger, Hunter, and Lane, 1971), and alternately provides defensive and revelatory resolution to emotional predicaments (Ullman, 1973; Greenberg and Pearlman, 1975). These formulations clearly emphasize self-mastery rather than environmental mastery, but the emphasis on achieving "therapeutic progress" is nonetheless utilitarian.

Unlike the preceding array of utilitarian conceptions, nonutilitarian theories of dream function have not been systematically and empirically investigated. Consider the following examples of such nonutilitarian hypotheses:

1. Conceptions of what is fundamentally "real" vary considerably — both within and between cultures. Such variations involve peoples' readiness to claim familiarity with something sacred, to affirm the reality of souls or spirits, and so forth. Anthropologists and folklorists have examined the possibility that these variations are affected by exceptional dream experiences (Hufford, 1982; Tylor, 1870). Similarly, among psychologists, Jung (1969) proposed that archetypal dreams change and even reverse conceptions of personal and extrapersonal reality. In our preliminary study, the transcendent awareness factor (see Table 13.1) hinted that this type of dream impact is salient in the experience of some people.

2. A compelling understanding of the fundamental attributes of "being-in-the-world" (Binswanger, 1963) occurs only irregularly during daily affairs. Only at certain times do people claim to fully recognize what is existentially "given" in their lives, including their "thrownness" within a specific historical place and time, their human finitude and mortality, or their separateness within relationships. Existential-analytic dream theorists (e.g., Boss, 1958; Craig, 1987) have often described dreams that, independent of subsequent interpretation, precipitate such

recognition. The affective insight factor identified in our preliminary study (see Table 13.1) suggests that this type of dream impact is familiar to numerous individuals.

3. Moments of "aesthetic arrest" (Joyce, 1964) also occur irregularly during daily affairs. Only at certain times are people able to attain even a limited appreciation of the sensuous presence of places, things, and persons around them. And yet, some dreams appear to announce this sensuous presence in a manner that lingers after awakening. Bachelard (1971) has commented on the capacity of dreamlike reverie to enable subsequent apprehension of a sensuous percept. Similarly, in response to an item that was part of both the transcendent awareness and affective insight factors, participants in our preliminary study alluded to the occasional aesthetic effects of their dreams (see Table 13.1).

It is hard to escape the impression that these nonutilitarian conceptions of dream function are too ideologically divisive to become the object of impartial empirical study. In contrast, studies of utilitarian dream functions are more acceptable because it is relatively difficult to argue with an ideology that emphasizes survival, environmental mastery, and psychological health. Perhaps the invidious ideological issues in this area could be neutralized somewhat by clearly differentiating the hypothetical *effects* of dreams from the equally hypothetical *needs* or *purposes* that make such effects "functional." For example, that certain dreams increase awareness of personal mortality is a hypothetical dream effect. Whether this effect is regarded as functional will depend upon the investigator's independent conception of how awareness of mortality influences self-development.

Methodological issues also seriously affect the prospects for systematic investigation of nonutilitarian dream functions. Nonutilitarian dream effects are typically precipitated by exceptionally impactful dreams that, as indicated earlier, occur infrequently and irregularly. Consequently, our current understanding of these effects is almost entirely dependent on case descriptions and literary accounts. Clarification and evaluation of nonutilitarian dream effects may depend upon the development of research procedures that are more systematic than case descriptions and yet sensitive to rather subtle changes in beliefs, attitudes, and feelings.

A Classificatory Study of Impactful Dreams

We recently completed a study that was designed to identify different types of impactful dreams and to examine their effects. Specifically, we obtained a sample of reports of impactful dreams, sorted them into natural classes according to their similarity, and then reviewed the resulting classes to identify the properties that defined each class. The procedures used are analogous to those of biological taxonomists who select a set of specimens (e.g., turtles), sort them into natural classes of similar entities (e.g., species of turtles), and then review the members of those classes in order to identify their characteristic features (e.g., the characteristics that define each turtle species). As applied to descriptions of experience, these methods provide systematic phenomenological methods in the tradition of Husserl and Merleau-Ponty (Kuiken, Schopflocher, and Wild, 1991). A rationale for application of these procedures in studies of dreams has been presented by Kuiken (1991).

Our classificatory research design was further constrained by the assumption that impactful dreams occur infrequently and irregularly. Thus, obtaining a sample of "specimens" (impactful dreams) within a sleep laboratory would have been impractical. Furthermore, preliminary observations (Kuiken, Nielsen, and Chahley, 1988) had indicated that systematic laboratory awakenings would interfere with the intense spontaneous arousals that are associated with some impactful dreams. Therefore, the dreams for our study were spontaneously recalled dreams recorded by telephone from participants' homes during a four-week period.

Participants were twenty-five volunteers who said that they typically had at least one dream per month that they regarded as impactful, for example: as affecting their mood during wakefulness, as changing the way they felt like living their lives, and so on. They were instructed to describe one impactful dream and the first dream recalled four days after the impactful one. The impactful dream was identified by the participants themselves. Specifically, each participant was told to report the first spontaneously recalled dream that was as impactful as the most impactful dream experienced during the preceding month. Their dreams could be impactful according to any one of several criteria: making the dreamer sensitive to typically ignored realities, affecting the dreamer's subsequent mood, motivating change in the dreamer's way of living, providing a reminder of events from the dreamer's personal past, hinting at some significant personal meaning, or providing an artistic idea. These criteria were associated with the affective insight factor in the factor analytic study reported earlier (see Table 13.1).

Both the impactful dream and the dream that was reported four days later were rated on a variety of scales, including an Emotions

Checklist (ECL) and a Morning Questionnaire (MQ). The ECL included independent scales from the Differential Emotions Scale (Izard et al., 1977) and the Profile of Moods Scale (McNair, Lorr, and Droppelman, 1971). The MQ included a variety of items regarding aspects of the dream experience that are not always described in open-ended dream reports, for example: sensory vividness, movement ineffectuality, and so on. Finally, one of us (SS) carefully read the dream reports and scored the presence or absence of descriptive comments that were present in some but not all dreams. This allowed identification of properties (hereafter called constituents) that had not been anticipated by the questionnaires but that might nonetheless distinguish among different types of dreams. For example, metamorphoses were detected in a number of the dream reports; so, every dream was evaluated for the presence or absence of metamorphoses.

Finally, each of the ratings was dichotomized (using a median split) and included with the judge's dichotomous judgments (constituents) to form a binary array of properties for each dream in the sample. Cluster analysis (Ward's Method with Euclidean distances) was then used to identify classes of similar dreams. Four clusters of dreams were identified and then compared to determine which properties were associated with cluster membership. (For a more complete description of these procedures and results, see Sikora, 1989.)

General Results

Three of the four clusters were characterized by the presence of distinct, often anomalous, qualities of sensation, affect, and action. The fourth cluster tended to include dreams reported on the fourth day following impactful dream experiences. Dreams in this cluster were characterized by the absence of many of the qualities that defined the first three clusters.

In general, these clusters were differentiable according to six categories of properties: (1) emotions and feelings; (2) goals and concerns; (3) movement style; (4) sensory phenomena; (5) dreamer perspective; and (6) dream endings. Each cluster exhibited distinct profiles of properties from these six categories. In the subsections that follow, properties that defined each of the four clusters will be described in detail. Also, a synopsis of the most prototypic member of each cluster will be presented to make the results of the classificatory analysis more concrete. A prototypic cluster member is one in which a large number of cluster-defining properties are represented. Finally, description of the subjective aspects of these dreams' impact will be summarized. These descriptions of dream impact rely on participants' ratings and comments in response to questions that did *not* contribute to identification of the clusters per se.

Description of Cluster 1

The emotions and feelings that identified dreams in the first cluster are summarized in Table 13.2, Part A. ECL ratings indicated that "surprise," "awe," and "ecstasy" were the most characteristic feelings within these dreams. Related statements within the dream reports described tears of joy, being "overcome with joy," and so on. That such affect was accompanied by enhanced sensibilities is suggested by responses to an MQ item indicating the experience of an "ineffable sense of significance"; that is, "a kind of knowing" that "[couldn't] be . . . put into words."

This ineffable significance seems attributable to quite extraordinary dream events. Just how extraordinary is indicated by the goals and concerns summarized in Table 13.2, Part B. In the constituent analysis, it was found that the dreamer-protagonist frequently possessed magical abilities (e.g., time travel, healing powers, the ability to fly). Not surprisingly, given these abilities, dreamers in this cluster rated themselves on an MQ item as relatively "successful in achieving [their] goals." A rereading of the dreams revealed that the attainment of goals and the possession of magical abilities tended to coincide; that is, magical abilities often enabled goal achievement. For example, one dreamer's acquaintance with "a spot that makes it possible for time travel" evoked praise from his father and promised future benefits to his family.

Dreamer-protagonists with magical abilities often met other equally exceptional dream figures. Specifically, according to MQ ratings, dreams in this cluster commonly involved (1) encounters with "spiritual beings" and (2) incidents in which "normally inanimate objects were . . . alive and aware." A rereading of these dreams indicated that such animism and spiritual significance sometimes coincided. For example, in one dream, fire was imbued with "consciousness" and with a "presence that permeated history."

The extraordinary feelings and abilities represented in dreams from this cluster were echoed in the stylistic qualities attributed to dream movements (see Table 13.2, Part C). These dreamers' ECL ratings of "vigor" were relatively high, and they reported on the MQ that they felt "bodily alive, energetic, and vital"—qualities one might expect during moments of rapture. Also, their MQ ratings indicated that they engaged in "vigorous physical activity" and that their movements in the dream were "exceptionally graceful and well balanced." Apparently these dreamers' magical abilities were reflected in vigorous actions executed with unusual ease and grace. For example, one dreamer was able to "glide . . . and land gracefully"—not once, but repeatedly.

Table 13.2

Cluster 1: Rapture and Mythic Capabilities (N=8)

	1	2	3	4
Part A. *Rapture and Ineffable Significance*				
Surprise	1.09	.13*	-.77*	-.28*
Awe	1.19	-.40*	-.32*	-.09*
Ecstasy	.63	-.16*	.32	-.25*
Ineffable Significance	.76	.56	-.56*	-.62*
Part B. *Magical Abilities and Goal Attainment:*				
Dreamer Magical Abilities**	.63	.20*	.17*	.06*
Dreamer Goal Attainment	.72	-.74*	.67	.08*
Spiritual Beings	.81	-.16*	-.25*	-.14*
Objects Alive and Aware	.93	-.06*	.02*	-.37*
Part C. *Graceful and Vigorous Movements:*				
Vigor	.40	-.10*	.31	-.21*
Bodily Felt Vitality	.47	-.13*	.18	-.16*
Vigorous Physical Activity:	.61	-.15*	.88	-.44*
Dreamer Grace and Balance	.89	-.06*	.28	-.44*
Part D. *Bodily Sensations and Extraordinary Sources of Light:*				
Spreading Warmth	.72	.10	-.46*	-.25*
Floating Sensations	1.27	-.34*	-.32*	-.17*
Bright Flashing Light	.85	.12*	-.39*	-.35*
Part E. *Transformations in Visuo-Spatial Perspective of the Dreamer:*				
Own Actions Strange	.54	.47*	-.70*	-.40*
External Self-Observation	.42	.58*	-.50*	-.50*
Shift in Dreamer Perspective	1.27	.06*	-.61*	-.41*
Part F. *Ending Not Distinctive*				

*Different from Cluster 1 at a preset criterion that takes into account both mean differences and variance.

**A constituent from the protocol analysis and, hence, a proportion (all others are standard scores for dreamer ratings).

Sensory events characterizing this cluster are summarized in Table 13.2, Part D. First, on the MQ, these dreamers reported that they experienced "spreading warmth" and "buoyant, floating, or uplifting sensations." These items seem to reflect diffuse or unlocalized changes in sensory experience, perhaps further components of the ecstatic feelings or graceful movements associated with this cluster. Second, on another MQ item, these dreamers reported experiencing a "bright, flashing, or ebbing light." Rereading the dreams revealed that such unusual forms of light tended to occur during moments of extraordinary significance. In the dream of the spiritually significant fire, the dreamer experienced a succession of images—flames in his bedroom, in a field, on a river, in a building.

Table 13.2, Part E, summarizes distinctive qualities of the dreamer's perspective within this cluster of dreams. Two items reflected a form of self-awareness within the dream. In particular, on the MQ, participants indicated that they regarded their own actions as "somehow strange or unfamiliar" and that they were aware of themselves "as if from outside." Rereading these dreams revealed events that may have been the origin of such ratings. These were events in which the dreamer temporarily became an observer of dream actions. For instance, one dreamer reported a scene in which he was "seeing these burning buildings in a pan shot, as if it was in a movie." Such moments, in which the dreamer assumes an external perspective on dream events, are also compatible with these dreamers' ratings of an MQ item indicating "shift(s)" of "perspective in the dream." However, whereas some perspective shifts transformed the dreamer from participant to external observer (as in the preceding example), other perspective shifts *more* directly implicated the dreamer in the dream actions. For instance, in one dream, the dreamer observed a young woman with telekinetic powers "zapping things in the room." Then the dreamer *became* "the finger that's zapping things in the room or her finger became the extension of mine." In these dreams, then, transformations in visuo-spatial orientation were accompanied by shifts in the dreamer's participation in the essential drama of the dream.

Finally, as indicated in Table 13.2, Part E, the endings of these dreams were not distinctive; that is, there was no characteristic emotional climax, intensification of dream imagery, or persistence of dream thoughts and feelings after waking.

A Protoypic Dream from Cluster 1. The dreamer-protagonist in the most prototypic dream from this cluster encountered a "fat man" who said that he was dying. An anonymous voice announced that the "fat man" was a "king" with "loosened intestines." Realizing the king's pain, the dreamer healed him by placing his hand on the king's abdomen and transmitting "energy into his stomach"—despite another anonymous but this time "evil" voice that expressed doubt about the dreamer's ability to heal. After the dreamer's accomplishment, he was suddenly (and briefly) accompanied by his proud family. When they disappeared, a dramatic change in perspective was reported:

> the whole galaxy . . . began to evolve in front of my eyes. It was a really beautiful, bluish color, very blue. And then slowly I saw a string of silver, bright starlike silver, just kind of glide through my eyes and twist and turn into almost like an infinity . . . the last scene I saw when I was kneeling down . . . was a bright spiral galaxy that's silvery in color and I felt really happy . . . a drop appeared, just one drop of tears formed in my eyes. . . .

Dream Impact in Cluster 1. In responses to an open-ended question regarding what made their dream "stand out from dreams that [they] typically have," comments associated with the more prototypic dreams of this cluster suggested an increased readiness to affirm some form of transcendent awareness. For example, one dream prompted the dreamer to "consider the human urge to . . . endow elements of nature with human or spiritual attributes." Another dream was "like a symbol" indicating to the dreamer that he was "growing spiritually." Comments such as these indicate that dreams in this cluster affirmed the importance of transcendent awareness, perhaps among individuals who were already predisposed.

Description of Cluster 2

The emotions and feelings that identified dreams in the second cluster are summarized in Table 13.3, Part A. In contrast to the rapture that was characteristic of Cluster 1, these dreams involved feelings of agony and distress. Specifically, ECL ratings of "agony," "discouragement," "distress," "anger," and "guilt" were higher in this cluster than in the other three clusters. Phrases within the dream reports referred to similarly diverse and keenly felt affect: "overwhelmed by . . . sadness," "a real feeling of disappointment and dissatisfaction," "just furious," etc. Also, these dreamers felt estranged, as indicated by MQ ratings of the extent to which they felt "lost" and "like . . . outsider[s] in the dream." Despite their negative tone, feelings in this cluster were accompanied by enhanced sensibilities; that is, on the MQ, these dreamers indicated the experience of an "ineffable sense of significance," "a kind of knowing" that "[couldn't] be . . . put into words".

Table 13.3
Cluster 2: Agony and Separation (N=15)

	1	2	3	4
Part A. *Agony and Ineffable Significance*				
Agony	-.38*	.75	-.36*	-.33*
Discouragement	-.31*	.69	-.45*	-.29*
Distress	-.56*	.94	-.43*	-.39*
Anger	-.02*	.74	-.14*	-.58*
Guilt	-.23	.82	-.57*	-.39*
Felt Lost/Like Outsider	-.01	.45	-.55*	-.19
Ineffable Significance	.76	.56	-.55*	-.62*
Part B. *Disillusionment, Separation, and Loss*				
(Absence of) Dreamer Achievement	.72*	-.74	.67*	.08*
Separation**	.25*	.67	.00*	.17*
Deceased Persons	-.34*	.54	-.34*	-.19*
Part C. *Bodily Felt Ineffectuality*				
Strong and Clear Bodily Feelings	-.21*	.68	.25	-.56*
Kinesthesia**	.00*	.27	.17	.00*
Awkward or Off Balance	-.25*	.66	-.25*	-.36*
Movement Inhibition	-.37*	.58	.63	-.53*
Fatigue	-.65*	.52	.00	-.14*
Part D. *Sensory Saturation and Contrasts*				
Lucid Darkness	.40	.45	-.42*	-.42*
Vivid Colors or Sounds	.60	.54	-.18*	-.65*
Part E. *Emergent Self-Awareness*				
Own Actions Strange	.54	.47	-.70*	-.40*
External Self-Observation	.42	.58	-.50*	-.50*
Emergent Self-Observation	.30	.56	-.42*	-.46*
Part F. *Movement-Induced Awakening*				
Awakened During Enactment	.14	.31	.04	-.34*

*Different from Cluster 2 at a preset criterion that takes into account both mean differences and variance.

**A constituent from the protocol analysis and, hence, a proportion (all others are standard scores for dreamer ratings).

The source of these significant feelings is suggested by the goals and concerns summarized in Table 13.3, Part B. In general, the agony and distress in this cluster was a reaction to dream events that involved disillusionment, separation, or loss. First, as indicated by ratings on the MQ, dreamers in Cluster 2 may have been disillusioned because they were relatively "[un]successful in achieving [their] goals." Second, the constituent analysis suggested that many of the dreams in this cluster involved some form of separation, i.e., events in which the dreamer was either the agent or object of actions intended to abandon, exclude, or reject. Third, ratings on the MQ indicated that these dreams involved persons who, in the dreamer's waking life, were actually deceased. This latter quality lends these dreams existential depth and, probably, their personal profundity.

The feelings and concerns of dreamers in Cluster 2 were embodied in their experience of dream movement, as indicated in Table 13.3, Part C. On the MQ, these dreamers rated their bodily feelings as comparatively "strong and clear." The constituent analysis of kinesthesia, that is, the explicit sense of body position or movement, provided elaboration of this finding. Specifically, in contrast to the unlocalized body sensations reported by dreamers in Cluster 1, dreamers in Cluster 2 referred to localized kinesthetic sensations associated with affect and movement. In one example involving movement, the dreamer felt "a kind of physical limpness" during her attempt to "push" and "pound" an attacker. In another example, this time involving affect, the dreamer felt sadness "coming out . . . from way down deep some place".

Not only were bodily feelings clear and localized, but related aspects of movement style were distinctive. Whereas dreamers in Cluster 1 rated their movements as exceptionally graceful and balanced, MQ ratings indicated that dreamers in Cluster 2 felt "awkward" or "off balance" during their movements. On another MQ item, they indicated that, at times, they felt "weak or unable to move." And, in contrast to the vigor that characterized dreams in Cluster 1, ECL ratings of "fatigue" were particularly high in these dreams. Rereading them suggested that ineffectuality and feelings of fatigue were commonly associated. In the clearest example, the dreamer said, "I was getting tired . . . and because I was getting tired I lost control of my ability to walk."

Sensory events characterizing Cluster 2 are summarized in Table 13.3, Part D. Color and sound appeared to have a palpable vividness. On the MQ, dreamers in this cluster reported feeling "as though [they] had entered a most lucid darkness," and they rated color and sound as "exceptionally vivid." Re-reading these dreams suggested that vivid colors were most common. For example, one dreamer referred to a room that was "really brightly sunlit" except for "shadows where this guy was standing." Another referred to a "bright" area that contrasted with the "dull and dark hallway" nearby. As these examples indicate, the sensory qualities of dreams in Cluster 2 seem to involve exceptional luminance or color contrasts in the appearance of familiar entities. This was different than in Cluster 1, which was characterized by extraordinary sources of light and color.

Attributes of dreamer perspective in Cluster 2 are described in Table 13.3, Part E. As in Cluster 1, two items from the MQ reflected a form of self-awareness within these dreams. In particular, dreamers (in both clusters) indicated that they regarded their own actions as "somehow strange or unfamiliar" and that they were aware of themselves "as if from outside." Whereas in Cluster 1 these ratings were traced to shifts in visuo-spatial perspective, in Cluster 2 they had a quite different significance. One interpretive hint was provided by an MQ item in which these dreamers reported that they *"felt* [themselves] *moving* outside of [their] bod[ies] *until* [they] could see [their bodies] as though [they were] spectator[s]." That these dreamers *felt* the *emergence* of this form of dream self-awareness is not only compatible with their acknowledgment that bodily feelings were "strong and clear"; it is also a suggestion that emergent self-awareness was an aspect of *shifts* in the strength and clarity of dream feelings. Consistent with this interpretation, rereading these dreams revealed examples in which dreamers described distinct feeling shifts: "my abhorrence . . . was building," "I started to feel a really strong sense of love," "I was . . . overwhelmed by the sadness."

The feeling shifts just described typically occurred immediately before the dream ending. Therefore, it is noteworthy that dreams in Cluster 2 frequently ended with an awakening that was apparently induced by enactive expression of dream feelings. On an MQ item described in Table 13.3, Part F, these dreamers reported that, as they awoke, they were "acting out some aspect of [their] dream[s]." This item did not quite meet our criterion for a defining property of a cluster, but examples of such awakenings were a common ingredient in the dream reports. For instance, one dreamer "just screamed louder for my sister to hurry up and then at that point I woke . . . crying." In another example, the dreamer reported that, in the dream, he was "really crying because nothing was working... and when I woke up I was really close to tears and I really felt sort of anger and frustration and everything that was in the dream." In both excerpts, the dreamer continued to experience and express feelings that emerged in the dream just prior to awakening.

A Protoypic Dream from Cluster 2. The dreamer described events in a room from a "secluded area of [a] hotel" in a foreign country. Because they had "dumped all their stuff" in her drawer, she "had to help" her "disorganized" family pack their belongings in preparation for departure. Then, after leaving the room briefly, she returned to find that her family "had gone". After relocating them, she "got . . . an overseas phone call" from her (actually deceased) father who informed her of an ailment that would "never heal." Then there was a heated argument, first with "some stupid person on the phone" and then with her sister. Their "practical" advice contradicted the dreamer's plan to gather all of her family together in the foreign country. The dreamer kept telling them to "shut up" because she was "overwhelmed . . . by the sadness" concerning her father's ailment and the fact that she "couldn't stay with him." The dreamer concluded, "I remember at the end of the dream [that] I just felt this . . . sadness . . . sort of coming . . . from way down deep . . . out of my soul . . . and waking me up."

Dream Impact in Cluster 2. Comments about the impact of these dreams described the emergence of feelings that the dreamer had been reluctant to acknowledge. One dream prompted the dreamer to "face" a "long-standing . . . conflict" that she would "prefer to shut out." Another dream "helped" the dreamer to become aware of "feelings . . . that [she] had not been aware [she] was carrying." Still another dreamer said that the dream was "an image that normally frightens me" but now "presented a kind of mothering nurturance," a change that hinted at a "reality" that was "as yet undefined." Consistent with these reports, MQ ratings indicated that affective insight was a consequence of dreams from this cluster. Specifically, we devised a scale that was based upon the four items associated with the affective insight factor identified in the preliminary study (see Table 13.1). Analysis of variance indicated that scores on this scale were higher in Cluster 2 than in the other clusters, $F(3, 43) = 6.84$, $p < .001$. (Note: In this and subsequent comparisons, ANOVA statistics are reported only when the assessed item was not among those included in the cluster analysis.)

Description of Cluster 3

The emotions and feelings identifying the third cluster are summarized in Table 13.4, Part A. Ratings on the MQ indicated that, "during the dream event that felt most significant," these dreamers experienced more "intense . . . emotions" than dreamers in any of the other clusters. In particular, ECL ratings of "fear" were especially high. In contrast to both Clusters 1 and 2, these feelings were *not* regarded as having an "ineffable significance."

Table 13.4
Cluster 3: Intense Fear and Harm Avoidance (N=6)

	1	2	3	4
Part A. *Intense Fear*				
Affective Intensity	-.19*	.29*	.92	-.47*
Fear	-.10*	.26*	.98	-.50*
(Absence of) Ineffable Significance	.76*	.56*	-.56	-.62
Part B. *Pervasive Avoidance of Harm*				
Harm Avoidance**	.38*	.33*	.83	.11*
Erotic Arousal	-.28*	.13*	.74	-.23*
Narrative Coherence**	.63	.47*	1.00	.50*
Part C. *From Passivity to Assertiveness*				
Assertion of Self-Control	-.21*	.13*	1.12	-.39*
Movement Inhibition	-.38*	.58	.63	-.53*
Vigorous Activity	.61	-.15*	.88	-.44*
Part D. *Primary Environmental Vigilance*				
Olfactory Phenomena	-.11*	.19*	.97	-.43*
Auditory Phenomena**	.25*	.27*	.67	.28*
Physical Metamorphoses**	.25	.07*	.50	.00*
Part E. *Unreflective Self-Participation*				
(Absence of) Own Actions Strange	.54*	.47*	-.70	-.40
(Absence of) External Self-Observation	.42*	.58*	-.50	-.50
Part F. *Fear-Induced Awakening*				
Intense Affect at Ending**	.25*	.47*	.67	.06*
Intense Ending with Awakening**	.25*	.40*	.83	.00*
Persistence of Affect**	.13*	.27	.50	.00*

*Different from Cluster 3 at a preset criterion that takes into account both mean differences and variance.

**A constituent from the protocol analysis and, hence, a proportion (all others are standard scores for dreamer ratings).

The goals and concerns defining Cluster 3 (see Table 13.4, Part B) directly reflect this intense fear. The constituent analysis revealed that most of these dream reports depicted actions that had as their goal harm avoidance, that is, avoidance of physical injury, illness, or death. Moreover, although ECL ratings indicated that mild "erotic arousal" was common, the predominance of harm avoidance made these dreams seem peculiarly unidimensional. The constituent analysis also indicated that these dreams were more coherent in their narrative structure than dreams in other clusters; that is, actions in these dreams were linked by a common goal so that the entire dream formed a coherent action sequence. Rereading these dreams indicated that harm avoidance was typically that common goal. For example, one dreamer's entire report described successive attempts to "ward off" a "decapitated head" by "screaming and screaming," then "looking away," and finally by throwing it "through the front window."

The qualities of movement that defined dreams in Cluster 3 (see Table 13.4, Part C) are compatible with the preceding emotions and concerns. Specifically, on the MQ, dreamers in this cluster rated themselves as attempting to "take control of dream events that [they] were not previously attempting to control." This shift from passivity to vigorous action was evident in the dream reports. For example, one dreamer, hiding on a roof from pursuants, reported that he was "getting pretty scared" and that he "just couldn't handle it." So, instead of waiting to be confronted by his attacker, he "rushed out and pushed him off the ladder." Such shifts from passivity to assertiveness may explain why these dreamers reported on the MQ that they were "weak or unable to move" *and* that they were "engaged in vigorous activity" in these dreams. In contrast with the ineffectuality and fatigue of Cluster 2, in Cluster 3, being "weak or unable to move" meant being temporarily frozen by fear *before* initiating vigorous evasive action.

Sensory events characterizing Cluster 3 are summarized in Table 13.4, Part D. Whereas dreams in Clusters 1 and 2 involved unusual visual imagery, dreams in Cluster 3 were more likely to involve intense olfactory and auditory phenomena. First, on the MQ, dreamers in Cluster 3 reported exceptionally vivid "scents or smells in the dream." Second, in the constituent analysis, these dreams more frequently involved distinct auditory phenomena, especially loud or unusual noises (e.g., the "snuffling and snorting" of a bear). In this example, the dreamer observed that the "snuffling and snorting" was the transformed incorporation of an actual environmental stimulus, specifically, the noise of "a basset hound who sleeps outside [the dreamer's] open window." This observation is noteworthy because physical transformations of objects in the dream "environment" also occurred *within* these dreams. Specifically, in the constituent analysis, physical metamorphoses were more common in dreams from Cluster 3 than in dreams from any other cluster. Physical metamorphoses were defined as changes in the physical appearance of objects and characters other than the dreamer. For example, one dreamer reported that a dream character's face "went . . . weird and impassive and she turned into Yoko Ono." Another indicated that a "small hovel had turned into a large Victorian house."

If it is assumed that attention may be directed toward either the environment or oneself, then the preceding emphasis on objects or characters in the dream environment is consistent with evidence indicating the *absence* of self-awareness in the dreams from Cluster 3 (see Table 13.4, Part E). MQ ratings of whether dreamers' actions were "strange or unfamiliar" and whether dreamers were aware of themselves "as if from outside" were distinctly *lower* in this cluster than in the others. These dreamers, then, were quite unreflectively involved in their dream actions.

The fearful environmental focus typical of these dreams marked their endings as well. As indicated in Table 13.4, Part F, the constituent analysis revealed that these dreams reached an intense emotional climax, that intense affect or compelling imagery awakened the dreamer, and that these dreamers continued to experience the dream feelings *after* awakening. A rereading of the dreams confirmed that the intense affect at the ending of these dreams was heightened fear-related arousal. Persistence of such arousal is perhaps most evident in a comment made by one participant, who observed that, given the "extraordinary terror that [she] woke with and retained . . . after [she awoke] . . . the entire room seemed sinister and fraught with possible danger. . . . Despite . . . recognizing its impossibility, [she] felt as though something was under the bed." In contrast with Cluster 2, where self-awareness and affect accompanied awakening (e.g., crying while awakening from a sad dream), in Cluster 3, fear-induced alertness to potential environmental danger apparently persisted.

A Prototypic Dream from Cluster 3. In the dream, a bear was trying to get into the dreamer's house. The dreamer managed to "get it out of there," but the bear's cub "had somehow gotten into the house." The dreamer "desperately [tried] to think how to shove this cub out without enraging the bear." Finally, it "became too much for [the dreamer and she] bolted out the front door." She fled to the roof of a nearby machine shed, but the roof was covered by "slippery . . . glazed stuff" and wasn't safe anyway because the bear could climb onto it with "no difficulty." So, the dreamer jumped off the roof and entered a small building that might provide refuge. There she warned some people who were casually listening to music that "this bear [was] attacking." When she awakened, the fear lingered and environmental vigilance continued, as described earlier.

Dream Impact in Cluster 3. The comments about impact that were provided for this cluster reiterated the intense fear during and immediately after awakening from the dream (see preceding). In general, these comments reflected a continuing preoccupation with the dream images and feelings per se—rather than with effects on waking activities. It is noteworthy that, in response to an MQ item, some of these dreams were reportedly accompanied by "intense panic" and recall of a "brief" story "involving extreme danger" (night terrors?) and others were accompanied by "distress" and an "emotionally powerful" story of "ordinary length" (anxiety dreams?). The proportion of dreams that fit one of these two descriptions was greater in this cluster than in any other, $F(3, 43) = 5.27$, $p < .01$. However, only one of the dreams in this cluster resembles the descriptions of night terrors in the literature, including reported disorientation after awakening, and we are inclined to regard this cluster as primarily anxiety dreams.

Description of Cluster 4

Members of the fourth cluster were generally identified by the *absence* of many of the features that characterized the first three clusters. Rather than present the (somewhat redundant) details of these observations, we will emphasize those that most clearly differentiated Cluster 4 from the other clusters. As indicated in Table 13.5, Part A, dreams in Cluster 4 were not affectively intense, and they lacked the ineffable significance associated with Clusters 1 and 2. Part B of this table presents the results of the constituent analysis indicating that the most distinctive goal property of these dreams was their relative lack of "aggression", that is, actions intended to annoy, injure, or dominate others. Part C summarizes observations indicating that dreams in this cluster were characterized neither by the vigorous activity nor by the inhibited actions that identified movement styles in the other clusters.

Part D describes the relative absence of unusual sensory events in these dreams, most clearly the absence of visual phenomena. Compared to Clusters 1 and 2, these dreams lacked visual vividness. Beyond ratings of the vividness of color and sounds, MQ ratings of how "distinctly and clearly" these dreamers experienced places and objects were relatively low, suggesting the absence of a total hallucinatory environment. Perhaps most important is the finding from the constituent analysis that the dream reports from Cluster 4 included infrequent visual *discontinuities,* that is, explicit looking behavior (e.g., "I looked outside"), visual anomalies (e.g., "all of a sudden I have an axe"), and sudden shifts in location (e.g., "and suddenly we were in a hotel"). We will have occasion to return to this pattern later in the discussion.

Table 13.5
Cluster 4: Mundane Experience (N = 18)

	1	2	3	4
Part A. *Moderate and Unclear Feelings*				
(Absence of) Affective Intensity	-.19	.29*	.92*	-.47
(Absence of) Ineffable Significance	.76*	.56*	-.56	-.62
Part B. *Motives Not Distinctive*				
(Absence of) Aggression**	.38*	.60*	.50*	.06
Part C. *Physical Inactivity*				
(Absence of) Vigorous Activity	.61*	-.15	.88*	-.44
(Absence of) Movement Inhibition	-.37	.58*	.63*	-.53
Part D. *Lack of Sensory Vividness*				
(Absence of) Vivid Colors or Sounds	.60*	.54*	-.18	-.65
(Absence of) Lucid Darkness	.40*	.45*	-.42	-.42
(Absence of) Sense of Place and Objects	.48*	.27*	-.21	-.37
(Absence of) Looking Behavior**	.63*	.53*	.67*	.22
(Absence of) Visual Intrusions**	.50*	.40*	.33	.06
(Absence of) Sudden Shifts in Location**	.88*	.73*	.67	.39
Part E. *Self-Participation*				
(Absence of) External Self-Observation	.42*	.58*	-.50	-.50
(Absence of) Own Actions Strange	.54*	.47*	-.70	-.40
Part F. *Mundane Ending*				
(Absence of) Intense Affect at Ending**	.25*	.47*	.67*	.06
(Absence of) Persistent Reality	.55*	.32*	.11	-.55

*Different from Cluster 4 at a preset criterion that takes into account both mean differences and variance.

**A constituent from the protocol analysis and, hence, a proportion (all others are standard scores for dreamer ratings).

Part E records the lack of self-awareness in these dreams compared to those in Clusters 1 and 2. Finally, Part F suggests that these dreams were lacking in the intense dream endings that marked each of the other three clusters. Specifically, the constituent analysis revealed that dreams in Cluster 4 lacked intense affect at their termination; and an MQ item indicated that features of these dreams seldom "seem[ed] real even after awakening."

A Prototypic Dream from Cluster 4. The most prototypic dream of this cluster confirms how mundane these dreams could be. The dreamer and her husband had "decided to open up a children's clothing store." (The dreamer had devised a "fabulous name" for the store within the dream, but could not recall it.) They discussed plans for the store's location, its advertising, its handmade goods, and so on. Then suddenly she and her husband were in a "hotel room . . . with two kids," but there was only one bed on which to sleep. (The dreamer acknowledged concerns about being crowded during sleep.) However, they were able to "work [it] out" in this case. The dreamer concluded by commenting that "it was all sort of vague."

Dream Impact in Cluster 4. These dreams were only infrequently (17 percent) those that participants identified as impactful as the most impactful dream experienced during the preceding month, $F(3, 43) = 3.86, p < .02$. For that reason, there were also few comments about dream impact.

Summary and Discussion

An overview of these clusters of dreams and of their dream effects is presented in Table 13.6. These results distinguish three types of impactful dreams from ordinary dreams. Each type of impactful dream differs not only in characteristic feelings, actions, sensory qualities, and so on, but also in its characteristic effects on waking thoughts and feelings. It is of concern, of course, that descriptions of the dream types and their respective dream effects depend on participants' ratings and reports. Also, because the judge's analysis of the dream reports was intended to include a wide variety of potentially discriminating properties, it was not practical to examine reliability at that time. However, it is now possible to more carefully assess those features that identify the dream types found in the present study. For example, given the importance of self-awareness in Clusters 1 and 2, in future classificatory studies it would be useful to assess dream self-awareness using the more

precise criteria developed by Purcell and colleagues (1986). In the meantime, validation of the present results is limited to the observed coherence of participants' self-reports in each cluster.

Table 13.6
Summary of Cluster Comparisons

Cluster 1	Cluster 2	Cluster 3	Cluster 4
Emotions and Feelings:			
Ecstasy	Agony	Fear	—
Intense Affect	Intense Affect	Intense Affect	—
Ineffable	Ineffable	—	—
Significance	Significance		
Goals and Concerns:			
Magical Success	Separation	Harm Avoidance	—
Movement Style:			
Vigorous Activity	—	Vigorous Activity	—
—	Movement Inhibition (Fatigue)	Movement Inhibition (Passivity)	—
Sensory Events:			
Exploratory Looking	Exploratory Looking	Exploratory Looking	—
Visual Intrusions	Visual Intrusions	—	—
Extraordinary Sources of Light	Sensory Saturation and Contrast	Olfactory/Auditory Phenomena	—
Dreamer Perspective:			
Self-Awareness	Self-Awareness	Environmental Focus	—
Visuo-Spatial Shifts	Affective Shifts	Physical Metamorphoses	—
Dream Endings:			
Intense Affect at Ending	Intense Affect at Ending (Enactment)	Intense Affect at Ending (Arousal)	—
Persistent Reality	Persistent Reality	Persistent Reality	—
Dream Effects:			
Transcendent Awareness	Affective Insight	Lingering Fear and Vigilance	—

The coherent pattern of features that defined Cluster 1 is related to
the conception of archetypal dreams described by Jung (1969) and sys-

tematically studied by Kluger (1975) and Brown and Donderi (1986). In Kluger's study, archetypal dreams were defined as involving (1) intense affect, (2) mythical themes, (3) events that are unfamiliar in everyday life, and (4) events that are unlikely or incompatible with natural laws. Parallel, but more specific, features defined Cluster 1: (1) moderately intense affect, specifically, awe and ecstasy; (2) the presence of animistic and spiritual figures, (3) unusual body sensations and perspective shifts, and (4) dreamer magical abilities. In Brown and Donderi's (1986) study, mythical themes were not included as a criterion of archetypal dreams because their judges lacked the expertise required to assess this quality. The present results suggest that the dreamer's reports of animistic or spiritual figures are sufficient to assess this aspect of archetypal dreams. However, for three reasons, we prefer to call the dreams in this cluster *transcendent dreams* rather than *archetypal dreams*. First, unlike *archetypal*, *transcendent* is a term that is not linked to a particular theory of these dreams' origin. Second, *transcendent* is a term that captures the subjective qualities actually reported by these dreamers, for example, the explicit reference to their ineffable spiritual significance. Third, the particular properties associated with the dreams in Cluster 1 define a somewhat more specific phenomenon than is portrayed in discussions of archetypal dreams.

The pattern of features that defines Cluster 2 has no clear precedent in the literature. Previously, Hendricks and Cartwright (1978) identified dreams that involved abundant feeling expression, but feeling expression was only one element in the profile of properties of dreams in Cluster 2. Similarly, these dreams were not simply bereavement dreams, although they frequently involved the deceased; they were not simply helplessness dreams, although they frequently involved fatigue and the inability to move; and they were not simply dysphoric dreams, although they involved agony, distress, anger, and guilt. Rather, the term *existential* captures the combination of subjective qualities reported for these dreams. Specifically, clear and distressing feelings occurred within the context of disillusionment, loss, and intimations of mortality, and the ineffable significance of these dreams included increased sensitivity to aspects of waking reality that typically had been ignored. These dreams seem to contain the uncanniness (Unheimlichkeit) that Heidegger (1962) associated with the emergence of authentic being within recognition of finitude and death.

The pattern of features that defines Cluster 3 is compatible with a fairly inclusive definition of "nightmares," one that emphasizes intense fearful awakenings (cf. Mack, 1970). Although such fearful awakenings can accompany either night terrors or anxiety dreams, we cannot be confident which type of nocturnal fright our participants experienced because we do not know the physiological conditions that would enable their more precise identification. Regardless of their linkage to sleep parameters, these nightmares lacked the self-awareness and ineffable significance characteristic of transcendent dreams and existential dreams. Instead, dreamers' comments suggested that the effect of these dreams was to induce lingering fear and *external* vigilance. Nightmares may be intense (e.g., emotionally powerful) but they are not necessarily significant.

In fact, transcendent dreams, existential dreams, and nightmares are *all* more "intense" than ordinary dreams. Specifically, all three of these dream types involve visual discontinuities (i.e., explicit looking behavior, visual anomalies, and sudden shifts in location); all three types involve relatively intense affect, especially at the end of the dream; and, the imagery of all three types seemed "real" to their dreamers even after awakening. Despite such evidence of their shared "intensity," each of these dream types had markedly different effects. The "intensity" of transcendent dreams seemed to influence dreamers' readiness to express their spiritual inclinations; the "intensity" of existential dreams seemed to influence dreamers' awareness of realities that they typically ignored; and, the "intensity" of nightmares seemed to influence dreamers' alertness to environmental dangers. If these observations are valid, the dream processes that determine dream impact require differentiation beyond that provided by the familiar language of dream intensity, emotionality, and bizarreness. This should give pause to the many investigators who discuss differences in dream "intensity" in relation to varying physiological or psychological conditions. We may be developing models of dream intensity that require considerable modification if they are to be relevant to the types of dream impact described by our participants.

Dream Intensity Reconsidered

Foulkes (1988) provides the following definition of dreaming:

an imagined experience misattributed as real-life experience; the possibility of multi-modal sensory and bodily imagery, of affective accompaniment, and of hallucinated self-participation; the presence, at minimum, of some "situation," and the possibility of that situation evolving thematically into related situations; and the inventiveness of these situations, that is, their failure to be simple memories or anticipations of real-life experiences of the dreamer.

This definition suggests that a qualitatively distinct profile of properties differentiates dreaming from nondreaming mentation. Acceptance of this differentiation need not obscure evidence that dreaming per se varies in the *degree* to which each of the properties in Foulkes's profile is manifest, for example: the vividness of sensory imagery, the strength of accompanying affect, or the extent of self-participation. Such variations are repeatedly (and loosely) referred to as variations in *dream intensity*, or as variations in the extent to which mentation is "dreamlike."

The most persistently pursued project in recent decades of dream research has been clarification of the relationship between dream intensity and sleep physiology. By the mid 1960s, it had become clear that qualitatively distinct dreaming is not confined to REM sleep, as predicted by the sleep stage model (Dement and Kleitman, 1957). Instead researchers began to differentiate REM from NREM mentation in degree; that is, when dreaming occurred, it was more intense (more vivid, more emotional) during REM sleep than during NREM sleep. By the mid 1970s, it had become clear that qualitatively distinct dreaming is also not precisely predicted by the phasic events described within the tonic-phasic model (Grosser and Siegal, 1971). Instead some evidence suggested that dreams reported after awakenings from phasically active sleep were relatively intense compared to dreams reported after phasically inactive sleep. During this research era, challenges to the presumed coherence among indices of dream intensity occurred but with little impact on many dream researchers who continued to regard dream intensity as though it was a set of highly correlated parameters. Because our study of impactful dreams suggested several different types of dream intensity, the present discussion provides an opportunity to review some of the evidence bearing on that issue.

In tests of the tonic-phasic model, phasic events that are associated with ponto-geniculo-occipital (PGO) spikes have been given special attention because (1) PGO spikes are implicated in the brain stem mechanisms that mark the onset of stage REM sleep and (2) PGO spikes and related phasic activity involve the visual and motor systems plausibly activated during dream construction (McCarley and Hobson, 1979). Also, the occurrence of PGO spikes during sleep in animals is, in some respects, analogous to the distribution of intense dreaming in humans. First, PGO spikes are concentrated in REM sleep where dreaming is most intense (see Foulkes, 1966); second, the frequency of PGO spikes increases within a REM period, as does the intensity of dreaming (cf. Kramer, Roth, and Czaya, 1975); third, REM deprivation increases the density of PGO spiking within REM sleep, just as REM deprivation increases REM-dream intensity (cf. Ingmundson and Cohen, 1981).

Consequently, a cluster of peripheral phasic events that seem to be triggered by a common PGO mechanism have been identified for use in studies of dream intensity in humans. These include eye movements (EMs), twitches of the limb and facial musculature, phasic integrated potentials (PIPs), phasic EMG suppression, and middle ear muscle activity (MEMAs). Despite considerable care in the selection of these PGO analogues, attempts to establish a close correspondence between such phasic events and dream intensity have been disappointing. One reason is that PGO analogues fall well short of one-to-one correspondence with PGO spikes. For example, only about 41 percent of PGO spikes are accompanied by EMG suppression (Glenn and Dement, 1982). Also, although 81 percent of PGO spikes are accompanied by PIPs during REM sleep, that figure drops to 32 percent during NREM sleep (Rechtschaffen, 1978). In addition, asynchrony of the various PGO analogues argues against the simple assumption that they are methodologically different indices of a single underlying mechanism. For example, in humans, PIPs are several times more frequent than MEMAs (Benson and Zarcone, 1979). Such loose linkage among phasic events makes it very unlikely that these hypothetical PGO analogues will be uniformly related to dream intensity.

A second reason for the meagre correspondence between PGO analogues and dream intensity is that the dimensions defining dream intensity are not as closely related as they are often portrayed to be. Use of the term *intensity* to subsume bizarreness, vividness, and so forth, obscures what should be quite clear, dream intensity is not a unitary dimension. Consider, for example, that the correspondence between phasic events and dream intensity has been assessed using criteria that include bizarreness, primary visual experience, self-participation, and hostility. Consider also that Hauri, Sawyer, and Rechtschaffen (1967) found that each of these dimensions was factorially independent of the others! Not surprisingly, at least in retrospect, attempts to study the linkages between an amorphous collection of dream intensity dimensions and an asynchronous set of PGO analogues produced a perplexing array of results (Pivik, 1978).

To address these conflicting results, it may be useful to abandon the assumption that PGO analogues are simply imperfect indices of a single mechanism. An alternative assumption is that forebrain modulation of originating PGO activity produces *psychologically significant patterns* of peripheral phasic events. Pivik (1986) has recently presented an analysis compatible with this alternative. He noted that PGO spikes typically follow EMs during wakefulness and precede EMs during REM sleep. He reasoned that these different patterns may reflect activity of a system that signals the internal or external origin of visual images. If so, dream imagery that is experienced as having an external origin (e.g., nightmares) may be accompanied by a phasic pattern, comparable to wakefulness, in which PGO analogues (e.g., PIPs) *follow* EMs. On the other hand, when dream imagery is experienced as having an internal origin (e.g., during REM onset episodes in narcoleptics), dreams would be accompanied by a phasic pattern in which PIPs *precede* EMs.

Pivik's hypothesis provides an example of how a carefully delimited psychological description may enable articulation of specific patterns of phasic events. One instructive aspect of his analysis is that he relied on observations of phasic activity not only during sleep but also during wakefulness. The advantage is that, during wakefulness, the psychological significance of a pattern of phasic events may be more directly assessed than during sleep. Then, occurrence of that same pattern during sleep may more precisely predict features of the accompanying dream. A second instructive aspect of Pivik's analysis is that he related a specific physiological pattern to a specific feature of dream phenomenology. Rather than associating one of several roughly equivalent PGO indices with qualities as diffuse as dream intensity, a particular physiological pattern was associated with a particular quality of the dream.

Extension of this type of analysis may contribute to a model in which the intensification of different patterns of phasic events accompany different types of impactful dreams. For example, the nightmares in our study may be understood as Pivik describes, that is, dream imagery experienced as unmitigated perception of an external reality. If so, not only will nightmares be accompanied by intensified phasic activity in which PIPs *follow* EMs, but carry-over of that physiological pattern may be an ingredient of the environmental vigilance that our participants reported after awakening. This extension of Pivik's analysis indicates that articulation of the physiological substrate of certain forms of dream intensity may also enhance comprehension of their specific psychological effects. In what follows, we will provide such an account of the different types of impactful dreams identified in our study.

Orienting Activity and Dream Phenomenology

We found that visual discontinuities were evident in all three types of impactful dreams: transcendent dreams, existential dreams, and nightmares. Descriptions of all three dream types included references to explicit looking behavior, visual anomalies, and sudden shifts in location. Evidence of such discontinuities in all three dream types is reminiscent of one reasonably reliable finding in research on PGO analogues and dream intensity. Specifically, as Pivik (1978) pointed out, the only dream dimension that consistently is associated with PGO analogues in both REM and NREM sleep is *discontinuity* (Bliwise and Rechtschaffen, 1978; Foulkes and Pope, 1973; Ogilvie et al., 1982; Watson, 1972; Watson et al., 1978). The modesty of this conclusion—in comparison with the expected correspondence between phasic events and dream intensity—should not undercut its importance. This particular dream dimension may be pivotal in understanding the psychological significance of PGO activity during sleep.

In recent years, Morrison (Morrison, 1979; Morrison and Bowker, 1975) has argued that PGO waves are part of the orienting response (OR), that is, the neurocognitive adjustment to stimulus change. By suggesting a parallel between orienting activity during sleep and orienting activity during wakefulness, Morrison has enabled a liaison with theoretical developments that relate components of the OR to other physiological and psychological processes. Our extension of Morrison's hypothesis will suggest that the orienting processes reflected in PGO waves adjust sensorimotor, affective, and cognitive systems to stimulus change and that evidence of spontaneous orienting activity is found in *discontinuities* within the imagery of impactful dreams. The outline of our argument is as follows:

1. Spontaneous PGO activity during sleep, especially during REM sleep, indicates that the individual is predisposed to respond as though adjusting to stimulus change. Such spontaneous orienting activity creates equally spontaneous shifts (discontinuities) in the concepts that shape dream imagery.

2. Three different patterns of PGO waves and related phasic events reflect different types of OR: to initially presented stimuli, to novel stimuli, or to aversive stimuli. Each of these types of OR is prominent in a

different affective reaction involving surprise (initially presented stimuli), distress (novel stimuli), and fear (aversive stimuli).

3. Frequent and intense orienting activity of a particular type (e.g., the OR to aversive stimuli) results in (a) the activation of concepts that reflect the sensitivities of the corresponding affective reaction (e.g., the system involving fear) and (b) more frequent and abrupt discontinuities in the dream imagery that is shaped by those concepts (e.g., images of frightening events).

4. The carry-over effects on thoughts, feelings, and actions after awakening correspond to the orienting and affective reactions that were prominent during the preceding dream. Such carry-over is the basis for the impact of different types of intense dreams.

Orienting Processes and Dream Discontinuities

Morrison's interpretation of PGO waves as a component of orienting activity is supported by several observations. First, animals in which the familiar atonia of REM sleep has been disrupted by pontine tegmental lesions display a variety of overt investigative activities (e.g., staring, searching, etc.) that are accompanied by spontaneous PGO spikes (Henley and Morrison, 1974; Bowker and Morrison, 1976). Second, PGO waves induced by auditory or tactile stimulation during sleep decline in frequency and amplitude with repeated stimulus presentations (Ball, Morrison, and Ross, 1989). Such habituation to repetitive stimulation is one defining feature of the OR (Sokolov, 1975). Third, during wakefulness, waveforms resembling PGO spikes in shape and amplitude accompany overt investigative activities and also habituate to repetitive stimulation (Bowker, 1980).

If PGO waves are a component of orienting activity, their prevalence during REM sleep suggests either (1) that there *are* more endogenous stimulus changes during REM than during NREM sleep or (2) that, during REM sleep, the individual is predisposed to respond *as though* stimulus changes have occurred. The latter interpretation is supported by studies indicating that, although PGO spikes can be induced by auditory stimuli during either REM or NREM sleep, the habituation of PGO spikes is slower during REM than during NREM sleep (Ball et al., 1989; Morrison and Bowker, 1975). Apparently, during REM sleep, repetitive stimuli continue to elicit responses that are associated with novel stimuli during NREM sleep or wakefulness. By implication, "spontaneous" PGO activity during REM sleep may reflect a state-dependent lowering of the threshold for the OR.

Spontaneous PGO activity during sleep, especially during REM sleep, may participate in the same processes that constitute the OR during wakefulness. Generally, OR processes reflect the adjustment of a neurocognitive system to a discrepancy between a presented stimulus and the kind of stimulus for which the system was prepared. When such a discrepancy occurs, the orienting process adjusts the system so that it "expects" a conceptual neighbor of the stimulus for which it was originally prepared. In a connectionist model of this adjustment, an orienting subsystem may temporarily introduce "noise" into a mnemonic subsystem so that it wanders and settles into a neighboring stable state in the network, thereby becoming prepared for a different stimulus configuration (see Carpenter and Grossberg, 1988, for a connectionist model that functions in roughly this manner). To understand the relevance of this orienting process to dreaming, it is necessary to consider that, when no stimuli are actually presented, as effectively occurs during sleep, the kind of stimulus for which the mnemonic subsystem is prepared determines the experienced image. Thus, spontaneous adjustment of the mnemonic subsystem, as indicated by PGO activity, may result in a shift to a conceptual neighbor of the stimulus for which it was originally prepared—and a shift from the original dream image to a conceptual neighbor of that image.

In the dreams from our study, visual discontinuities may have been precipitated by this process. To illustrate, one dreamer (also a proud tomato grower during wakefulness) described an initial dream image that was shaped by her conception of one kind of plant-infesting insect: "tomato plants . . . just covered in aphids." By the present account, when the mnemonic subsystem was adjusted, prompting her to "look more closely," the conceptual neighbor shaping subsequent dream imagery became *another* kind of plant-infesting insect, i.e., "one plant [with] a spider . . . that's a little bit like a beetle." In a different example, the initial dream scene was shaped by a conception of one kind of house: one apparently remodeled to provide work space for professionals. When the mnemonic subsystem was adjusted, prompting a sudden scene shift, the conceptual neighbor shaping the dream imagery was *another* kind of house: i.e., a residential home or family dwelling.

It should be noted that, even though the orienting process introduces noise into the mnemonic subsystem, the consequence is not random visual "intrusions" that must be woven into the dream by an artful dream planner. Instead, the proposed adjustment prompts discontinuities that are comprehensible shifts to a conceptual neighbor of the preceding dream image. Nonetheless, during the sensory restrictions of sleep, the "neighborly" proximity of the conception to which the shift occurs *is* dependent on the amount of noise introduced into the mnemonic subsystem by the orienting process. If the orienting process introduces large amounts of noise into the mnemonic subsystem, the effect is to increase the likelihood that a distant rather than near conceptual neighbor will be selected.

Different OR Types, Affective Reactions, and Dream Impact

More precise identification of the discontinuities that occur during intense dreams depends on familiarity with the particular concepts represented in the mnemonic subsystem when the orienting adjustment occurs. However, connectionist models (e.g., Crick and Mitchison, 1986) and psychobiological models (e.g., McCarley and Hobson, 1979) have been silent regarding the nature of the concepts that are relevant to discussions of dreaming—beyond emphasizing that they involve sensory information. The visual discontinuities present in the intense dreams in our study are superficially compatible with that emphasis, but to account for different types of intense dreams, it is necessary to be more precise about different aspects of the orienting process and the different kinds of mnemonic material affected by orienting activity.

To address this issue, it is important to emphasize that a great deal of evidence contradicts any unitary conception of the OR. Frequent fractionation (differential responding) has been observed among the several slow and nonspecific responses traditionally utilized in studies of orienting (e.g., skin conductance, heart rate deceleration, etc.) and among the faster and more specific components of event-related potentials (ERP) recently used in studies of orienting activity (cf. Rohrbaugh, 1984). Some sense can be made of such fractionation if it is seen as the result of three different types of OR: (1) the initial OR, a response to a stimulus presented for the first time; (2) the change OR, a response to a deviant or novel stimulus within a series; and (3) the defense reaction, a response to aversive stimulation (Graham, 1979).

Furthermore, intense and repeated occurrences of one of these types of OR may evoke the concepts and sensitivities related to a basic affective reaction. The basis for this suggestion is that each OR type is associated with a characteristic pattern of visceral, muscular, and cognitive activity. *When intensely and recurrently activated*, each of these patterns resembles a basic affective reaction (cf. Panksepp, 1982). Therefore, depending on which OR type is involved, one of three affective reactions may occur: surprise (initially presented stimuli), distress (novel stimuli), or fear (aversive stimuli). The occurrence of a particular affective reaction entails activation of corresponding concepts and sensitivities; that is, the mnemonic subsystem becomes prepared for stimulus configurations characteristic of that particular affective reaction. Subsequent orienting processes will produce discontinuities in these affect-specific concepts—and produce corresponding discontinuities in dream imagery.

In what follows, we will demonstrate the implications of these hypotheses for the types of impactful dreams identified in our study. That is, for each type of impactful dream, we will describe (1) the correspondence between a pattern of PGO-related phasic events and an established index of one type of orienting process, (2) the affective reaction implicated when that particular orienting process is intense and recurrent, (3) the effects of the orienting process on discontinuities in dream imagery when mnemonic material related to a particular affective system is active, and (4) the carry-over effects of each type of orienting and affective process immediately after awakening.

The Initial OR and Transcendent Dreams

The initial OR is a response to the first presentation of a stimulus. In ERP studies, the initial OR has been identified with the N1 waveform (Naatanen and Picton, 1987). The N1 marks the onset of processes that adjust the current representation of primary sensory configurations to locate and represent a newly introduced sensory configuration. For example, when a multifeatured visual stimulus is presented for the first time, the negativities that follow N1 reflect an overlapping progression of processes for representing its location, contours, spatial frequency, orientation, and the conjunction of such stimulus features (Harter and Guido, 1980). These processes (1) provide spatiotemporal integrity for this feature cluster independent of peripheral (e.g., retinal) stimulation and (2) mark the location of this integral feature cluster in relation to the perceiver (Pylyshyn, 1989). These processes are preattentive and preconceptual, although they *enable* subsequent coordination of attentional adjustments or investigative movements.

In sleep studies, an index of the initial OR analogous to N1 may be a pattern including a PGO spike and a (simultaneous) transient EMG suppression. Three observations support this parallel. First, in response to auditory stimuli during sleep, latencies of PGO spikes with EMG suppression are in the same range (20–50 ms) as would be expected for the N1 component of the feline ERP (Wu, Mallick, and Siegel, 1988; Csepe,

Karmos, and Molnar, 1987). Second, prepulse stimulation consistently inhibits acoustically induced PGO waves with EMG suppression (Wu et al., 1988), just as it does N1 waveforms (Hackley, Woldorff, and Hillyard, 1987). Third, although PGO spikes with EMG suppression occur in response to either moderate- or high-intensity stimuli, very brief EMG excitation, suggestive of primary startle, precedes this pattern when high intensity stimuli are presented (Wu et al., 1988). Similarly, although stimuli of varying intensity will initiate the N1, at high stimulus intensities, this waveform occurs simultaneously with the startle blink (Putnam and Roth, 1988).

Because the initial OR is associated with startle, intense orienting activity of this type precipitates the startle-surprise affective reaction. Physiologically, startle includes heart rate acceleration, cephalic vasodilation, and diffuse muscular activation. Subjectively, startle involves momentary interruption of thought and transient feelings of surprise. Surprise may be associated with memories related to achievement. When asked to remember a time when they were surprised, young adults most frequently recall events that involve unexpected success or failure, events that involve mistakes, and events that involve creativity or originality (Izard, 1977).

Therefore, when the initial OR is prominent during sleep, as indicated by intense and recurrent PGO activity with EMG suppression, dreaming will accentuate the sensorimotor, affective, and cognitive processes characteristic of the startle-surprise reaction. Such dreams will not only include aspects of the startle-surprise reaction, but also reflect the preattentive processes that represent integral clusters of sensory features and locate such clusters in relation to the perceiver. Transcendent dreams, such as those identified in our study, are dreams of this kind.

1. Because intense PGO waves and concomitant EMG suppression reflect startle, subjective reactions include feelings of surprise. (Feelings of awe may reflect the temporal density of recurrent startle-surprise reactions.) Because the memories associated with surprise are related to achievement, the mnemonic material enlisted in dream formation is frequently related to success and failure.

2. Because startle involves transient and diffuse muscular excitation, dreamer actions are experienced as vigorous and bodily involving. And, because such muscular activation is unlocalized, it influences images of other dream entities (cf. Koulack, 1969) so that even inanimate objects seem alive.

3. Dreamer feelings of spreading warmth may reflect the persistent cephalic vasodilation associated with recurrent startle reactions. Another sensory anomaly in these dreams, the experience of bright light, may be related to the occasional reports of "brightness" during startle (Landis and Hunt, 1968).

4. When intensified, the preattentive processes that create clusters of sensory features and locate such clusters in the visuo-spatial perspective of the dreamer have distinct subjective effects. One effect is dream discontinuities in which configurations of primary visual features are transformed. For example, one dreamer in our study experienced a bright light in the form of fire. If the orienting process adjusts the mnemonic subsystem while such a visual configuration is active, a shift to a neighboring configuration of visual features occurs. To continue the example, the dreamer experienced the fire as flashing and ebbing in such a way that it appeared insubstantial. In another example of such visual transformations, the dreamer experienced a "string of silver" that began to "twist and turn into . . . infinity". A second effect is dream discontinuities in which the visuo-spatial perspective of the dreamer is transformed. The dreamer may experience a particular visuo-spatial perspective within the dream, and if the orienting process adjusts the mnemonic subsystem while such a visuo-spatial perspective is represented, a shift to a neighboring visuo-spatial perspective occurs. For example, one of our dreamers experienced a shift from an ordinary perspective (looking ahead while walking) to an unusual perspective on that same dream scene (looking down while flying). In another example, the dreamer initially observed a young woman exercising her telekinetic powers and then experienced a sudden shift in which *she* became the figure that was exercising such powers.

5. Since the dream processes that carry over into wakefulness reflect their physiology and psychology, one lingering effect of transcendent dreams may be enhanced sensitivity to primary visual features and their conjunctions. Because this effect involves preattentive processes, it is independent of the conceptions by which objects are recognized. Such preconceptual perception immediately after transcendent dreams may compare with the effects of meditation (cf. Hunt, 1989). Advanced meditators apparently provide Rorschach responses that explicitly refer to shapes, edges, colors, and shading (Brown and Engler, 1980). Also, after intensive meditation, they do not recognize tachistoscopically presented letters that were readily recognized before meditation (Brown, 1987). The same kind of preconceptual perception, embedded within feelings

of awe and bodily vigor, may contribute to the lingering aesthetic and spiritual effects of transcendent dreams.

The Change OR and Existential Dreams

Whereas the initial OR is a reaction to the first presentation of a stimulus, the change OR is a response to a novel item within a series of stimulus presentations. In ERP studies, the change OR has been identified with the N2a waveform, also known as the mismatch negativity (MMN; Naatanen and Gaillard, 1983). The MMN (1) signals a discrepancy between a preceding configuration of sensory features and a current configuration of sensory features in the same modality and location and (2) marks the onset of processes that adjust the mnemonic subsystem so that it becomes prepared to recognize the current sensory configuration as a particular kind of entity. The latter processes, typically associated with the P3 waveform, involve adjusting ("updating") the current conceptual model until the novel sensory configuration is recognized as a particular kind of entity (Donchin et al., 1986). An example of this kind of adjustment occurs during illusory reversals of the Necker cube (O'Donnell, Hendler, and Squires, 1988), where there is an adjustment in the conceptual model by which the perceiver recognizes the figure as a cube in a particular orientation. As another example, during reversals in identification of the familiar old hag–young woman figure, there is an adjustment in the conceptual model by which the perceiver recognizes the figure as a particular kind of feminine form.

We propose that, during sleep, the change OR is indicated by a pattern involving PGO activity, extended EMG suppression in the postural musculature, and selective EMG excitation in the limb and facial musculature. Although this phasic pattern has not been directly studied, our conjecture is plausible for several reasons. First, Ball and colleagues (1989) reported latencies of acoustically induced PGO spikes of up to 200 ms, which is longer than expected for N1 but in the same range as expected for the MMN. Second, Csepe and colleagues (1987) found that the amplitudes of the feline MMN are greater when the stimuli are deviants in a tone series, indicating that the change OR *can* be elicited during sleep in a form that is differentiable from the initial OR. Together, these observations suggest that *some* PGO waves may correspond to the MMN. (See Rechtschaffen, 1978, regarding the plausibility of a second generator of PGO activity.)

Moreover, the change OR during wakefulness is accompanied by a visceral and neuromuscular pattern clearly different from that associated with the initial OR (Graham, 1979). Specifically, the change OR consistently involves (1) heart rate deceleration, (2) the suppression of eyeblinks, (3) relaxation of the musculature around the mouth, and (4) inhibition of the postural musculature (Obrist, 1981). Paradoxically perhaps, this integrated inhibitory pattern coincides with enhanced reflexive responding when (1) the reflex probe is presented in an attended channel (Graham, 1979; Hackley and Graham, 1984) and (2) the observed reflexive behavior is consistent with the modality of the stimulus (e.g., sniffing in response to olfactory stimulation; Siegel et al., 1987). Therefore, by analogy, the change OR during sleep may be indicated by extended EMG suppression in the postural musculature and by selective EMG excitation in the limb and facial musculature associated with modality-specific behavior. Such selective EMG excitation may be contrasted with the diffuse EMG excitation associated with startle; only the former has the kind of specificity that is related to particular dream movements (Gardner et al., 1975) or to dream gaze (Herman et al., 1984).

In sum, the change OR may be reflected in the following pattern of phasic events: PGO waves, extended EMG suppression in the postural musculature, and selective EMG excitation in the limb and facial musculature. If so, intense orienting activity of this type may precipitate the separation-sadness affective reaction identified by Panksepp (1982). That is, the visceral and neuromuscular aspects of the change OR are similar to those that identify this affective reaction. Most important is the common parasympathetic inhibition of HR and postural musculature. When intense and recurrent, this aspect of the change OR may contribute to the sinking feelings and slumped posture associated with separation and sadness (Riskind and Gottay, 1982). Furthermore, selectively enhanced responses compatible with this affective modality include the respiratory hesitations, tears, and facial expressions that accentuate subjective sadness and anguish. Sadness may be associated with memories related to separation. When asked to remember a time when they were sad, young adults most frequently recall events that involve heterosexual problems, events that involve death or illness among friends or family, and events that involve separation or loneliness (Izard, 1977).

Therefore, when the change OR is prominent during sleep, as indicated by intense and recurrent PGO activity with extended EMG suppression and selective EMG excitation, dreaming will accentuate the subjective correlates of the separation-sadness reaction and of the cognitive processes by which a novel stimulus configuration is conceived as a particular kind of entity. Existential dreams are dreams of this kind.

1. Because extended inhibition of the postural musculature is associated with the initial OR, subjective correlates include inhibited or awkward dreamer movements and accompanying feelings of ineffectuality and fatigue. Also, such movement characteristics are associated with unsuccessfully executed attempts to achieve dream goals.

2. Indirectly because of the connotations of ineffectuality (e.g., frustration, disappointment) and directly as a consequence of persistent inhibition of the postural musculature, dream feelings are negative and have an inactive quality; for example, distress, guilt, and discouragement. Because the memories associated with such anguish are related to separation, dream representations enlist mnemonic material related to actual or anticipated rejection and loss.

3. When intensified, the conceptual processes that enable recognition of a stimulus configuration as a particular kind of entity will influence dream imagery. One effect is dream discontinuities involving transformations of the concepts related to the separation-sadness reaction. These include conceptions of affectively significant action episodes—what we have elsewhere called *affective scripts* (cf. Kuiken, 1986). For example, one dreamer in our study experienced dream imagery in which she took a room in a "secluded area of [a] hotel" that was otherwise filled to capacity. She said to herself that she "must be brave" because of "rapists in the hall and that sort of thing," although "it seemed to work out." By the current account, if the orienting process adjusts the mnemonic subsystem while the conception shaping this imagery is prominent, the result is a neighboring conception of that affective episode. To continue the example, the dreamer was suddenly in a *another* hotel in a foreign country (a conceptual neighbor of the hotel in the first scene). She reported that she and her family "were all in a room together" (a conceptual neighbor of being filled to capacity). Only the dreamer was "organized" and had finished packing (a conceptual neighbor of being brave alone), but she felt that she "had to" help her less organized family (a conceptual neighbor of coercive intruders in the hallway). Finally, "it turned out" that she was able to help others in her family and simultaneously "get a bag or two" that she needed (a conceptual neighbor of things working out). In sum, the second scene was a shift to a conceptual neighbor of the first scene—a shift to a another kind of affective event in which the isolated dreamer copes with coercive others and attains a minimally satisfactory outcome.

4. A shift to a neighboring conception of an affectively significant action episode will be accompanied by amplification of feelings that are

common to both the original and the neighboring conceptions. That is because the sensorimotor pattern associated with the change OR enables selective EMG excitation, for instance, excitation of the facial musculature expressive of dreamer feelings (Gerne and Strauch, 1985). In our example, the affective connotations of the second, crowded-hotel room episode may have been accompanied by EMG excitation congruent with the feelings that were salient in the first hotel episode. The subjective effect may have been the emergence of an increasingly clear, strong, kinesthetic sense of the feelings that were common to both episodes. Accordingly, in this example, there was evidence of greater affective intimacy in the second episode, such as a more elaborate description of feelings and explicit reference to family members rather than stranger-rapists. Such increased affective intimacy may progress until the dream concludes with an emotionally poignant expression of the feelings uniting the sequence of affective episodes. In the current example, the final scene also occurred in the crowded hotel room. The dreamer's father was indirectly present because he called by telephone to report that he had an ailment that "will never heal." The dreamer proposed a solution to a complication that threatened to separate the family at this critical time (a conceptual neighbor of being brave alone and of having already packed), but her sister insisted in threatening tones that the dreamer's solution was not "practical" (a neighboring conception of coercive intruders and demanding family members). In this final variation, there is no neighboring conception of things working out because the dream was interrupted; the despair associated with separation from her father induced awakening to agonizing and tearful sadness. In sum, the progression in these scenes provided increasing clarity of bodily feelings, the emergence of kinesthetically sensed feeling-awareness, and an awakening accompanied by affectively expressive movement.

5. One lingering carry-over effect of existential dreams is persistence of the kinesthetically sensed feeling-awareness that emerged during the dream. Also, because affectively similar episodes are represented in existential dreams, they readily remind the dreamer of affectively similar personal memories after awakening (McGregor, 1988). A less obvious effect of these dreams is that the progression from one conception to a neighboring conception of an affective episode increases the dreamer's emotional intimacy (States, 1988) with the theme that is transformed within the dream. Dreamers describe that intimacy as increased sensitivity to aspects of their lives that they had previously ignored. By successively activating neighboring conceptions of affectively significant

episodes, existential dreams may alert the dreamer to the several layers of significance in similar events during wakefulness. The dreamer in our example may have become more alert to the sense in which she is metaphorically alone in an isolated hotel room even when she is with her family. Or she may have become more alert to the sense in which she metaphorically grieves the loss of fatherly nearness even when she is in a lonely hotel.

The Defense Reaction and Nightmares

As recently described by Turpin (1986), the defense reaction (DR) is a response to presentation of a noxiously intense stimulus. The DR in this sense can be distinguished from either the initial OR or the change OR. Only the DR includes heart rate acceleration with a long peak latency (about 30 sec). The potential relevance of this conception is that (1) the peak latency of the DR is comparable to the latency of heart rate increases during night terrors (Kahn, Fisher, and Edwards, 1978), (2) heart rate increases suggestive of the DR occur in response to auditory stimuli during sleep (Berg, Jackson, and Graham, 1975), and (3) among night terror sufferers, night terrors occasionally are induced by intense auditory stimuli (Broughton, 1968). However, in our study, all but one of the reported nightmares clearly resembled anxiety dreams rather than night terrors. Therefore, the relevance of the defense reaction as Turpin described it is doubtful.

More relevant perhaps is the conception of the DR presented by Graham (1979). She also described the DR as a response to intense stimulation, but she was concerned with a relatively short latency heart rate increase (3 to 5 sec) associated with response preparation. This conception of the DR may be best understood as a late manifestation of the change OR. In fact, the DR in this sense is comparable to the processes that have been associated with a late component of the ERP, specifically, the slow wave, also called the *O-wave* to indicate its relationship to the OR (cf. Rohrbaugh, 1984). Slow waves are sensitive to processes that relate a recently recognized stimulus to other conceptual entities by (1) comparing the representation of a novel stimulus with a representation of another stimulus (e.g., in a mental rotation task; Perronet and Farah, 1987), (2) manipulating the representation of a novel stimulus in relation to another stimulus according to a rule (e.g., adding or dividing two numbers; Ruchkin et al., 1988), (3) searching memory for representations that are anticipated or cued by the novel stimulus (Johnston, Miller, and Burleson, 1986); and so forth. In general, these processes may be regarded as appraisals of the significance of a recently recognized stimulus configuration.

There is some evidence that a *shift* from parasympathetic to sympathetic activation accompanies the late manifestations of the change OR that Graham conceives as the DR. For example, Gogan (1970) described three phases in the EMG response to novel stimuli: early EMG excitation peaking at 20–40 msec (comparable to the initial OR), a middle period of relative EMG suppression (comparable to the change OR), and then late EMG excitation peaking at about 2 seconds (comparable to the DR and associated with response preparation). A similar sequence has been observed for the H-reflex (Brunia, 1979). Also, Hodes, Cook, and Lang (1985) found that, in a conditioning paradigm, heart rate deceleration to the conditioned stimulus typically preceded acceleration, but that, among individuals fearful of the conditioned stimulus (e.g., a picture of a snake), heart rate acceleration obscured the decelerative response. Although these studies are more suggestive than conclusive, they indicate that the DR is associated with the appraisal of stimulus significance and involves sympathetic somatomotor activation that follows or even displaces parasympathetic somatomotor inhibition.

To draw the parallel, the DR during sleep may involve the same phasic pattern as the change OR *except* that extended inhibition of the postural musculature is followed or, in some cases, displaced by excitation of that musculature. If so, intense and recurrent activation of the DR may precipitate the threat-fear affective reaction identified by Panksepp (1982). The visceral and neuromuscular aspects of the DR are sufficiently similar to those that identify the fear reaction that the conceptions and sensitivities associated with that reaction will be activated. Most important is the common duality of inhibition and then excitation. Subjectively, fear is often associated with "freezing" *and* the feeling of needing or wanting to escape (Bull, 1951). And, selectively enhanced responses compatible with this affective modality include the rapid respiration, tension, and facial expressions that accentuate subjective fear. Fear may be associated with memories related to danger and moral transgression. When asked to remember a time when they were frightened, young adults most frequently recall events that involve moral wrongdoing, events that involve danger, and events that involve threats to self-esteem (Izard, 1977).

Therefore, when the DR is intense and recurrent, the prevalent phasic pattern will include PGO waves and, in the postural musculature, EMG suppression that is either interrupted or displaced by EMG excitation. Dreaming accompanying this pattern will reflect aspects of the fear-escape reaction and aspects of the cognitive processes by which the appraisal of stimulus significance occurs. Nightmares, such as those identified in our study, are dreams of this kind:

1. Since the DR involves intense sympathetic activation, the feelings will involve intense fear. The progression from "freezing," a momentary inability to move, to vigorous activity may reflect the duality of momentary suppression and then excitation of the postural musculature. Because the memories associated with fear are related to danger and moral transgression, dream representations enlist such memories to depict the avoidance of harm and the moral risks of erotic arousal.

2. Because stimulus appraisal entails judgments about the rule-governed and anticipatory relations between one conceived event and another, the dream narrative is a relatively coherent sequence of actions linked by a common conception of their intended consequences. For example, one dreamer was rather single-mindedly committed to a sequence of attempts to resist or elude the members of an aggressive street gang holding him captive.

3. Fear-induced vigilance entails concepts and sensitivities related to dangerous circumstances and morally risky erotic interests—both of which must be avoided. Because these conceptions are prominent in the mnemonic subsystem when orienting processes precipitate dream transformations, nightmares include more frequent metamorphoses involving those external dangers and erotically conceived others. For example, one dreamer described a "white lady" who was helping her to escape from a crude mental institution. Her apparent benefactor "turned into" a black lady who was a "very beautiful" stripper and the object of several men's attentions but who had to be shunned so that the dreamer could persist in her escape attempts.

(4) The progressive intensification of sympathetic arousal eventually results in awakening. The carry-over effects include lingering fear and environmental vigilance. Recall, for example, the dreamer whose room "seemed sinister and fraught with danger" after awakening. The persistent sensitivity to, appraisal of, and reaction to potential dangers is the legacy of these dreams.

A Note on Our Classificatory and Explanatory Goals

In the preceding account, we have taken some care not to provide a reductionistic description of impactful dreams. First, we have tried to be sensitive to different levels of analysis. For example, our reference to the orienting subsystem is intended to convey that the orienting process may cause dream discontinuities (e.g., sudden scene changes). Our reference to basic affective systems is intended to convey that the occurrence of a particular affective reaction (e.g., sadness) may cause activation of concepts and sensitivities related to that reaction (e.g., conceptions of significant separation episodes). Furthermore, the interaction among these processes is an integral and higher-level process. That is, when the orienting process precipitates discontinuities in the concepts activated by a particular affective reaction, the combination causes a result (e.g., a shift from an original separation episode to a conceptual neighbor of that episode) that could not be predicted from either process alone. It has not always been possible to explicitly and briefly clarify the relations among different levels of analysis in our discussion, but that is required to maintain a proper perspective on these dream phenomena.

Second, our discussion of causes has been restricted to levels of analysis that account for specific *properties* of each type of impactful dream. We have *not* commented on the processes that cause the occurrence of those types of dreams per se. That is, we have not commented on the causes of the *structured complex of properties that constitute each dream type.* To confuse these different levels of causal analysis would be wrong and a disservice to these experiences. It would also be a misunderstanding of our intentions. Our efforts may be regarded as analogous to the efforts of a biological taxonomist. Biological taxonomists locate the morphological properties, characteristic behaviors, and physiological processes that define a species. Defining a species, however, is quite separate from attempts to understand the evolutionary origins of that species. Similarly, we are trying to locate the properties and processes that separately and in interactive combination define each "species" of impactful dream. That is quite different from the kind of study that would help us understand the origin of those dream species (see Kuiken, 1991, for a more detailed rationale for this classificatory research strategy).

Implications and Elaborations

In the preceding discussion, the impact of each type of dream "species" was portrayed as a particular carry-over effect. For each dream type, emphasis was given to postawakening carry-over of affect and affect-related sensitivities and concepts. However, our descriptions of these dream effects remain rather undifferentiated. In our study, we focused on the qualities of the dreams per se rather than on the qualities of those dreams' *experienced impact.* Although our participants answered a brief series of questions about the impact of their dreams, it would be useful to do a much more detailed phenomenological study of the experienced impact of each dream type. Nonetheless, we have provided a general outline of these dreams' impact, which, in our judgment, is a clearer outline than has characterized previous discussions. At least, by setting aside the assumption that all dreams have a similar function, the contrasting effects of transcendent dreams, existential dreams, and nightmares have become clearer.

The emphasis on carry-over effects is intended to suggest that assessment of dream impact can involve more than simply asking people to describe it. The few available studies of carry-over effects demonstrate that some subtle perceptual, cognitive, and affective dream effects can be assessed independently of linguistic descriptions. For example, after transcendent dreams, sensitivity to preconceptual sensory configurations could be assessed using tasks that juxtapose preconceptual and conceptual aspects of apparent movement (cf. Anstis, 1980). Or, after existential dreams, enhanced affective-kinesthetic awareness could be assessed using human movement responses to the Rorschach (Nielsen, Kuiken, and McGregor, 1989). This type of investigation is possible if researchers chose to study impactful dreams as they sometimes have studied nightmares, by selecting individuals who frequently have such dreams, recording the spontaneous occurrence of such dreams in the laboratory, and assessing their immediate effects through self-reports, projective techniques, perceptual tasks, and so on. It may be more practical to compare the carry-over effects of spontaneous laboratory dreams that are classified according to their match with a particular type of impactful dream. This would be comparable to studying nightmares by examining dreams dominated by fearful feelings—and ecological validity similarly becomes problematic.

The study of *uninterrupted* impactful dreams—either in the lab or at home—seems critical because, for all three types of impactful dreams (see Table 13.6), the endings are typically moments of particular significance. It is difficult to imagine the impact of some of these dreams from our study without their powerful endings, such as (1) when one dreamer awakened after his ecstatic image of a "bright spiral galaxy that's silvery in color," (2) when another dreamer awakened to sadness that came from "way down deep . . . out of [her] soul" in reaction to news of her father's ailment that "would never heal," or (3) when still another dreamer awakened to an "intense physical shock to [her] body" while watching someone being assaulted with a "syringe with a short fat needle." Although all three types of impactful dreams involved awakenings with intense affect, this was especially so for awakenings from existential dreams, which were frequently movement-induced, and for awakenings from nightmares, which were typically arousal-induced. Because of the apparent importance of dream endings, such contrasting forms of spontaneous awakening merit closer study.

Even prior to their powerful endings, each type of impactful dream is accompanied by a characteristic movement style, by distinctive body sensations, and by a particular affective quality. These qualities reveal that dreamers become fully embodied in their activities, especially during transcendent dreams and existential dreams. In transcendent dreams, movements and bodily sensations enliven the experience in a manner that contributes to their ineffable significance. On the one hand, this enlivenment is "objective." Normally inanimate dream *objects* are attributed vitality and consciousness. Perhaps simultaneously, this enlivenment is "subjective." In a manner reminiscent of Bachelard's (1971) description of dynamic imagination, these dreamers do not simply move gracefully and physically; they *feel in themselves* "the force of gracefulness." The bodily felt vitality, the floating sensations, and the spreading warmth contribute to a separate sense of self in the dream space, providing intimations of dreamer self-awareness.

In existential dreams, movements and bodily sensations accentuate subjectivity (but apparently not objectivity). Movements are kinesthetically felt—sometimes as excruciatingly awkward and effortful. That same kinesthetic accentuation is evident in the clarity and strength of affective reactions within these dreams. The progressive clarity of these feelings often culminates in a dream ending that awakens the dreamer to a movement expressive of dream feelings. In these dreams, then, the intimations of dreamer self-awareness reach a climax in moments of pronounced subjectivity. These climactic moments involve the kind of bodily felt shift (Gendlin, 1981) that sometimes occurs during intensive self-reflection (Kuiken, Carey, and Nielsen, 1987).

Both transcendent dreams and existential dreams can be contrasted with nightmares in which subjectivity seems to be lacking and objectivity seems paramount. The vigorous bodily activity of nightmares is not accompanied by either bodily felt vitality or clearly embodied affect. Also, the intimations of self-awareness found in transcendent and existential dreams are absent in nightmares. The absence of subjectivity in nightmares emphasizes that existential dreams and nightmares must be clearly differentiated in discussions of "bad dreams" (cf. Starker, 1985). The lingering effects of existential dreams include the not entirely unwelcome awakening of personal memories and the positive affirmation of feelings that are typically ignored but subjectively "real." Nightmares, at least those reported in our study, include an objective vigilance that may linger after awakening without such redeeming subjective features. Perhaps nightmares evoke the terror whereas existential dreams evoke the terror and the pity of tragic catharsis (Aristotle, 1952).

References

Anstis, S. M. (1980). "The Perception of Apparent Movement." *Philosophical Transactions of the Royal Society of London* B 290: 153–158.

Aristotle (1952). "Poetics." In B. Jowett and T. Twining (Eds. and Trans.), *Aristotle's Politics and Poetics*, pp. 223–265. New York: Viking Books.

Bachelard, G. (1971). *On Poetic Imagination and Reverie*, trans. C. Gaudin. Indianapolis: Bobbs-Merrill.

Ball, W. A., Morrison, A. R., and Ross, R. J. (1989). "The Effects of Tones on PGO Waves in Slow Wave Sleep and Paradoxical Sleep." *Experimental Neurology* 104, no. 3: 251–256.

Benson, K., and Zarcone, V. P. (1979). "Phasic Events and REM Sleep: Phenomenology of Middle Ear Muscle Activity and Periobital Integrated Potentials in the Same Normal Population." *Sleep* 2: 199–213.

Berg, W. K., Jackson, J. C., and Graham, F. K. (1975). "Tone Intensity and Rise-Decay Time Effects on Cardiac Response During Sleep." *Psychophysiology* 12: 254–261.

Binswanger, L. (1963). *Being-in-the-World*. New York: Basic Books.

Bliwise, D., and Rechtschaffen, A. (1978). "Phasic EMG in Human Sleep: III. Periorbital Potentials and NREM Mentation." *Sleep Research* 7: 58.

Boss, M. (1958). *The Analysis of Dreams*. New York: Philosophical Library.

Bowker, R. M. (1980). "The Awakening of the Sleeping Ponto-Geniculo-Occipital Wave." In W. Koella (Ed.), *Sleep 1980*, pp. 304–306. Basel: Karger.

———— and Morrison, A. R. (1976). "The Startle Reflex and PGO Spikes of Sleep." *Brain Research* 102: 185–190.

Breger, L. (1967). "Function of Dreams." *Journal of Abnormal Psychology* 72: 1–28.

————, Hunter, I., and Lane, R. W. (1971). *The Effect of Stress on Dreams*. New York: International Universities Press.

Bronte, E. (1985). "Sleep Brings No Joy." In E. Chitham and T. Winnifrith (Eds.), *Selected Bronte Poems*. New York: Basil Blackwell. [Original work published 1846.]

Broughton, R. (1968). "Sleep Terrors: Disorders of Arousal?" *Science* 159: 1070–1078.

Brown, D. P. (1987). "The Transformation of Consciousness in Meditation." Paper presented at a Conference on Exceptional Abilities sponsored by the Institute of Noetic Sciences, Washington, D.C.

———— and Engler, J. (1980). "The Stages of Mindfulness Meditation: A Validation Study." *Journal of Transpersonal Psychology* 12: 143–192.

Brown, R. J., and Donderi, D. C. (1986). "Dream Content and Self-Reported Well-Being Among Recurrent Dreamers, Past-Recurrent Dreamers, and Nonrecurrent Dreamers." *Journal of Personality and Social Psychology* 50: 612–623.

Brunia, C. H. M. (1979). "Some Questions About the Motor Inhibition Process." In H. D. Kimmel, E. H. van Olst, and J. F. Orlebeke (Eds.), *The Orienting Reflex in Humans*, pp. 241–258. Hillsdale, N.J.: Lawrence Erlbaum Associates.

Bull, N. (1951). *The Attitude Theory of Emotion*. Nervous and Mental Disease Monographs, no. 81, New York: Nervous and Mental Disease Monographs.

Carpenter, G. A., and Grossberg, S. (1988). "A Massively Parallel Architecture for a Self-Organizing Neural Pattern Recognition Machine." In S. Grossberg (Ed.), *Neural Networks and Natural Intelligence*, pp. 251–315. Cambridge, Mass.: MIT Press.

Cohen, D. B. (1979). *Sleep and Dreaming: Origins, Nature, and Functions.* Oxford: Pergamon Press.

Craig, P. E. (1987). "The Realness of Dreams." In R. Russo (Ed.), *Dreams Are Wiser than Men*, pp. 34–57. Berkeley, Cal., North Atlantic Books.

Crick, F., and Mitchison, G. (1986). "REM Sleep and Neural Nets." *Journal of Mind and Behavior* 7: 229–250.

Csepe, V., Karmos, G., and Molnar, M. (1987). "Evoked Potential Correlates of Stimulus Deviance During Wakefulness and Sleep in Cat-Animal Model of Mismatch Negativity." *Electroencephalography and Clinical Neurophysiology* 66: 571–578.

Dement, W. C., and Kleitman, N. (1957). "The Relation of Eye Movements During Sleep to Dream Activity: An Objective Method for the Study of Dreaming." *Journal of Experimental Psychology* 53: 339–346.

Donchin, E., Karis, D., Bashore, T. R., Coles, M. G. H., and Gratton, G. (1986). "Cognitive Psychophysiology and Human Information Processing." In M. G. H. Coles, E. Donchin, and S. W. Porges (Eds.), *Psychophysiology: Systems, Processes, and Applications*, pp. 244–267. Amsterdam: Elsevier.

Dostoevsky, F. (1950). *The Brothers Karamazov*, trans. C. Garnett, New York: Random House. [Original work published 1880.]

Eliot, T. S. (1934). "Preludes." In *The Wasteland and Other Poems.* New York: Harcourt, Brace and World.

Foulkes, D. (1966). *The Psychology of Sleep.* New York: Charles Scribner and Sons.

———. (1988). "Dreaming and Consciousness." Paper presented to Verleihung des Dr. Margrit Egner-Preises, Zurich.

——— and Pope, R. (1973). "PVE and SCE in Stage REM: A Modest Confirmation and Extension." *Sleep Research* 1: 103.

French, T., and Fromm, E. (1964). *Dream Interpretation: A New Approach.* New York: Basic Books.

Freud, S. (1953). "The Interpretation of Dreams." In J. Strachey (Ed. and Trans.), *The Standard Edition of the Complete Psychological Works of*

Sigmund Freud, vols. 4–5. London: Hogarth Press. [Original work published 1900.]

Gardner, R. A., Grossman, W., Roffwarg, H., and Weiner, H. (1975). "The Relationship of Small Limb Movements During REM Sleep to Dreamed Limb Action." *Psychosomatic Medicine* 37: 147–159.

Gendlin, E. T. (1981). *Focusing*, 2d ed. New York: Bantam Books.

Gerne, M., and Strauch, I. (1985). "Psychophysiological Indicators of Affect Patterns and Conversational Signals During Sleep." In W. Koella, E. Ruther, and H. Schulz (Eds.), *Sleep 1984*, pp. 367–369. Stuttgart: Gustav Fischer Verlag.

Glenn, L. L., and Dement, W. C. (1982). "Motoneuron Properties During Electomyogram Pauses in Sleep." *Brain Research*, 243: 11–23.

Grogan, P. (1970). "The Startle and Orienting Reactions in Man: A Study of Their Characteristics and Habituation." *Brain Research* 18: 117–135.

Graham, F. K. (1979). "Distinguishing Among Orienting, Defense, and Startle Reflexes." In H. D. Kimmel, E. H. van Olst, and J. F. Orlebeke (Eds.), *The Orienting Reflex in Humans*, pp. 137–167. Hillsdale, N.J.: Lawrence Erlbaum Associates.

Greenberg, R. (1981). "Dreams and REM Sleep: An Integrative Approach." In W. Fishbein (Ed.), *Sleep, Dreams, and Memory*, pp. 125–133. New York: Spectrum.

———— and Pearlman, C. A. (1975). "A Psychoanalytic Dream Continuum: The Source and Function of Dreams." *International Review of Psychoanalysis* 2: 441–448.

Grosser, G., and Siegal, A. (1971). "The Emergence of a Tonic-Phasic Model for Sleep and Dreaming: Behavioral and Psychological Observations." *Psychological Bulletin* 75: 60–72.

Hackley, S. A., and Graham, F. K. (1984). "Early Selective Attention Effects on Cutaneous and Acoustic Reflexes." *Physiological Psychology* 11: 235–242.

Hackley, S. A., Woldoroff, M., and Hillyard, S. A. (1987). "Combined Use of Micro-Reflexes and Event-Related Potentials in Measures of Auditory Selective Attention." *Psychophysiology* 24: 632–647.

Hall, C. S. (1953). "A Cognitive Theory of Dream Symbols." *Journal of General Psychology* 48: 169–186.

Harter, M. R., and Guido, W. (1980). "Attention to Pattern Orientation: Negative Cortical Potentials, Reaction Time, and the Selection Process." *Electroencephalography and Clinical Neurophysiology* 49: 277–290.

Hartmann, E. (1984). *The Nightmare: The Psychology and Biology of Terrifying Dreams*. New York: Basic Books.

Hauri, P., Sawyer, J., and Rechtschaffen, A. (1967). "Dimensions of Dreaming: A Factored Scale for Dream Reports." *Journal of Abnormal Psychology* 72: 16–22.

Heidegger, M. (1962). *Being and Time*, trans. J. Macquarrie and E. Robinson. Oxford: Basil Blackwell. [Original work published in 1927.]

Henley, K., and Morrison, A. R. (1974). "A Re-Evaluation of the Effects of Lesions of the Pontine Tegmentum and Locus Coeruleus on Phenomena of Paradoxical Sleep in the Cat." *Acta Neurobiologiae Experimentalis* 34: 215–232.

Hendricks, M., and Cartwright, R. D. (1978). "Experiencing Level in Dreams: An Individual Difference Variable." *Psychotherapy, Theory, Research and Practice* 15: 292–298.

Herman, J. H., Erman, M., Boys, R., Peiser, L., Taylor, M. E., and Roffwarg, H. (1984). "Evidence for a Directional Correspondence Between Eye Movements and Dream Imagery in REM Sleep." *Sleep* 7: 52–63.

Hodes, R. L., Cook, E. W., III, and Lang, P. J. (1985). "Individual Differences in Autonomic Response: Conditioned Associations or Conditioned Fear?" *Psychophysiology* 22: 545–560.

Hufford, D. J. (1982). *The Terror that Comes in the Night*. Philadelphia: University of Pennsylvania Press.

Hunt, H. (1989). *The Multiplicity of Dreams: Memory, Imagination, and Consciousness*. New Haven, Conn.: Yale University Press.

Ingmundson, P., and Cohen, D. B. (1981). "The Effects of REM Deprivation on Dream Mentation." *Sleep Research* 10: 259.

Izard, C. E. (1977). *Human Emotions*. New York: Plenum Press.

————, Dougherty, F. E., Bloxom, B. M., and Kotsch, W. E. (1974). "The Differential Emotions Scale: A Method of Measuring the Subjective Experience of Discrete Emotions." Unpublished manuscript, Vanderbilt University.

Johnston, V. S., Miller, D. R., and Burleson, M. H. (1986). "Multiple P3s to Emotional Stimuli and Their Theoretical Significance." *Psychophysiology* 23: 684–694.

Jones, R. M. (1970). *The New Psychology of Dreaming.* New York: Grune and Stratton.

Joyce, J. (1964). *A Portrait of the Artist as a Young Man.* New York: Grune and Stratton.

Jung, C. G. (1969). "The Structure and Dynamics of the Psyche." In H. Read, M. Fordham, G. Adler, and W. McGuire (Eds.), *The Collected Works of C. G. Jung,* vol. 8, 2d ed. Princeton, N.J.: Princeton University Press.

Kahn, E., Fisher, C., and Edwards, A. (1978). "Night Terrors and Anxiety Dreams." In A. M. Arkin, J. S. Antrobus, and S. J. Ellman (Eds.), *The Mind in Sleep,* pp. 533–542. Hillsdale, N.J.: Lawrence Erlbaum Associates.

Kluger, H. Y. (1975). "Archetypal Dreams and 'Everday' Dreams: A Statistical Investigation into Jung's Theory of the Unconscious." *Israel Annals of Psychiatry* 13: 6–47.

Koulack, D. (1969). "Effects of Somatosensory Stimulation on Dream Content." *Archives of General Psychiatry* 20: 718–725.

Kramer, M., and Roth, T. (1973). "The Mood-Regulating Function of Sleep." In W. Koella (Ed.), *Sleep 1972,* pp. 563–571.

———— and Czaya, J. (1975). "Dream Development Within a REM Period." In W. Koella (Ed.), *Sleep 1974,* pp. 406–408. Basel: Karger.

Kuiken, D. (1986). "Dreams and Self-Knowledge." In J. Gackenbach (Ed.), *Sleep and Dreams: A Sourcebook,* pp. 225–250. New York: Garland Press.

————. (1991). "Interdisciplinary Studies of Dreams: Finding a Common Ground." In J. Gackenbach and A. Sheikh (Eds.), *Dream Images: A Call to Mental Arms.* pp. 185–202. Farmingdale, N.Y.: Baywood.

————, Carey, R., and Nielsen, T. A. (1987). "Moments of Affective Insight: Their Phenomenology and Relations to Selected Individual Differences." *Imagination, Personality, and Cognition* 6: 341–364.

————, Nielsen, T. A., and Chahley, S. (1988). "Orientation-Induced Movement Inhibition and the Influence of Dreams on Waking Activities." *Sleep Research*, 17: 103 (abstract).

————, Schopflocher, D., and Wild, T. C. (1989). "Numerically Aided Phenomenology: A Demonstration." *Journal of Mind and Behavior* 10: 373–392.

Landis, C., and Hunt, W. A. (1968). *The Startle Pattern.* New York: Johnson Reprint Co. [Original work published 1939.]

Lowy, S. (1942). *Foundations of Dream Interpretation.* London: Kegan Paul.

Mack, J. E. (1970). *Nightmares and Human Conflict.* Boston: Little, Brown and Company.

McCarley, R. W., and Hobson, J. A. (1979). "The Form of Dreams and the Biology of Sleep." In B. Wolman (Ed.), *Handbook of Dreams: Research, Theories, and Applications*, pp. 76–130. New York: Van Nostrand Reinhold.

McGregor, D. (1988). "Dreams and Waking Events: Evidence for an Affective and Motivational Correspondence." Master's thesis, University of Alberta.

McNair, D. M., Lorr, M., and Droppleman, L. F. (1971). *Profile of Mood States.* San Diego: Educational and Industrial Testing Service.

Morrison, A. R. (1979). "Brainstem Regulation of Behavior During Sleep and Wakefulness." In J. M. Sprague and A. W. Epstein (Eds.), *Psychobiology and Psychophysiology*, pp. 91–131. New York: Academic Press.

———— and Bowker, R. M. (1975). "The Biological Significance of PGO Spikes in the Sleeping Cat." *Acta Neurobiologiae Experimentalis* 35: 821–840.

Näätänen, R., and Gaillard, A. W. K. (1983). "The Orienting Reflex and the N2 Deflection of the ERP." In A. W. K. Gaillard and W. Ritter (eds.), *Tutorials in Event-Related Potential Research: Endogenous Components*, pp. 119–140. Amsterdam: Elsevier.

———— and Picton, T. (1987). "The N1 Wave of the Human Electric and Magnetic Response to Sound." *Psychophysiology* 24: 375–425.

Nielsen, T. A., Kuiken, D., and McGregor, D. (1989). "Effects of Dream Reflection on Waking Affect: Awareness of Feelings, Rorschach Movement, and Facial EMG." *Sleep* 12: 277–286.

Obrist, P. A. (1981). *Cardiovascular Psychophysiology: A Perspective*. New York: Plenum Press.

O'Donnell, B. F., Hendler, T., and Squires, N. K. (1988). "Visual Evoked Potentials to Illusory Reversals of the Necker Cube." *Psychophysiology* 25: 137–143.

Oglivie, R., Hunt, H., Sawicki, C., and Samahalskyi, J. (1982). "Psychological Correlates of Spontaneous Middle Ear Muscle Activity During Sleep." *Sleep* 5: 11–27.

Palombo, S. R. (1978). *Dreaming and Memory: A New Information-Processing Theory*. New York: Basic Books.

Panksepp, J. (1982). "Toward a General Psychobiological Theory of Emotions." *Behavioral and Brain Sciences* 5: 407–422.

Pearlman, C. A. (1981). "Rat Models of the Adaptive Function of REM Sleep." In W. Fishbein (Ed.), *Sleep, Dreams, and Memory*, pp. 37–45. New York: Spectrum.

Perronet, F., and Farah, M. J. (1987). "Mental Rotation: An ERP Study with a Validated Mental Rotation Task." In M. Kutas and B. Renault (Eds.), *Proceedings of the Fourth International Congress on Neuroscience*, pp. 49–52. Paris: Dourdan.

Pivik, T. (1978). "Tonic States and Phasic Events in Relation to Sleep Mentation." In A. M. Arkin, J. S. Antrobus, and S. J. Ellman (Eds.), *The Mind in Sleep*, pp. 245–271. Hillsdale, N.J.: Lawrence Erlbaum Associates.

————. (1986). "Sleep: Physiology and Psychophysiology." In M. G. H. Coles, E. Donchin, and S. W. Porges (Eds.), *Psychophysiology: Systems, Processes, and Applications*, pp. 378–406. Amsterdam: Elsevier.

Purcell, S., Mullington, J., Moffitt, A., Hoffman, R., and Pigeau, R. (1986). "Dream Self-Reflectiveness as a Learned Cognitive Skill." *Sleep* 9: 423–437.

Putnam, L. E., and Roth, W. T. (1988). "Distinguishing Between Orienting, Defense, and Startle: Heart Rate, Event Related Potentials, and Eyeblink Responses to Intense Stimuli." *Psychophysiology* 25: 427 (abstract).

Pylyshyn, Z. (1989). "The Role of Location Indexes in Spatial Perception: A Sketch of the FINST Spatial-Index Model." *Cognition* 32: 5–79.

Rechtschaffen, A. (1978). "Phasic EMG in Human Sleep: I. Relation of EMG to Brainstem Events." *Sleep Research* 7: 56.

Riskind, J. H., and Gottay, C. C. (1982). "Physical Posture: Could It Have Regulatory or Feedback Effects on Motivation and Emotion?" *Motivation and Emotion* 6: 273–298.

Rohrbaugh, J. W. (1984). "The Orienting Reflex: Performance and Central Nervous System Manifestations." In R. Parasuraman and D. R. Davis (Eds.), *Varieties of Attention*, pp. 323–373. Orlando, Fla.: Academic Press.

Ruchkin, D. S., Johnson, R., Mahaffey, D., and Sutton, S. (1988). "Toward a Functional Categorization of Slow Waves." *Psychophysiology* 25: 339–353.

Siegel, M. A., Sananes, C. B., Gaddy, J. R., and Campbell, B. A. (1987). "Dissociation of Heart Rate and Somatomotor Orienting Responses to Novel Stimuli in Preweanling Rats." *Psychobiology* 15: 122–127.

Sikora, S. (1989). "A Classificatory Study of Impactful Dreams." Master's thesis, University of Alberta.

Snyder, F. (1966). "Toward an Evolutionary Theory of Dreaming." *American Journal of Psychiatry* 123: 121–142.

Sokolov, E. N. (1975). "The Neural Mechanisms of the Orienting Reflex." In E. N. Sokolov and O. S. Vinogradova (Eds.), *Neural Mechanisms of the Orienting Reflex*, pp. 217–235. New York: John Wiley and Sons.

Spear, N. E., and Gordon, W. C. (1981). "Sleep, Dreaming, and the Retrieval of Memories." In W. Fishbein (Ed.), *Sleep, Dreams, and Memory*, pp. 183–203. New York: Spectrum.

Starker, S. (1985). "Daydreams, Nightmares, and Insomnia: The Relation of Waking Fantasy to Sleep Disturbances." *Imagination, Cognition, and Personality* 4: 237–248.

States, B. O. (1988). *The Rhetoric of Dreams.* Ithaca, N.Y.: Cornell University Press.

Turpin, G. (1986). "Effects of Stimulus Intensity on Autonomic Responding: The Problem of Differentiating Orienting and Defense Reflexes." *Psychophysiology* 23: 1–14.

Tylor, E. B. (1870). *Researches into the Early History of Mankind and the Development of Civilization.* London: John Murray.

Ullman, M. (1973). "A Theory of Vigilance and Dreaming." In Z. Zikmund (Ed.), *The Oculomotor System and Brain Function*, pp. 453–465. London: Butterworths Books.

Watson, R. (1972). "Mental Correlates of Periorbital PIPs During Sleep." *Sleep Research* 1: 116.

———, Bliwise, D., Friedman, L., Wax, D., and Rechtschaffen, A. (1978). "Phasic EMG in Human Sleep: III. Periorbital Potentials and REM Mentation." *Sleep Research* 7: 57.

Wu, M. F., Mallick, B. N., and Siegel, J. M. (1988). "Lateral Geniculate Spikes, Muscle Atonia, and Startle Response Elicited by Auditory Stimuli Are a Function of Stimulus Parameters and Sleep-Waking State." *Sleep Research* 17: 20.

14

Waud H. Kracke ━━━━━━━━━━━━

Reasons for Oneiromancy: Some Psychological Functions of Conventional Dream Interpretation

$\mathbb{S}$peculation about dreaming is virtually universal in human societies—hardly surprising, considering how intriguing are the regular nocturnal experiences we all undergo and occasionally recall. But what is more striking is how widely similar are the *forms* that this speculation often takes. Certain ideas recur with great frequency among the notions of dreaming held in different cultures: many cultures observe that what you are preoccupied with during the day is likely to appear in your dreams, or hold that nightmares are the product of spirits who accost the dreamer (sexually or aggressively) while he or she sleeps.

Of particularly wide distribution is the notion of dreams as symbolic predictors. There are few societies—"primitive," peasant, or industrialized—that do not in some way regard dreams as privileged vistas on the future and develop a traditional apparatus for interpreting them. This may be a simple rule that dreams tend to come true. Frequently it is a rule of reversal that "dreams mean their opposite," or—most commonly—an elaborate exegesis in terms of conventional equivalences based on metaphor and metonymy. Such systems of dream exegesis, or oneiromancy, are encountered in all of the peasant cultures of Europe in oral traditions passed on in the family, and even in our sophisticated and literate industrial society, in the form of popular "dream books" that offer "the meaning of your dreams." Even Freud (1953, pp. 3–4) traced the genealogy of his method of interpreting dreams to this tradition of oneiromancy, as represented in its apex in the work of Artemidorus of Daldis (Kilborne, 1987).

How can we explain the widespread similarity of at least certain beliefs about dreams, among completely unrelated cultures in all parts of the world? Such prevalence bespeaks some powerful functions to such beliefs.

Research using free-associative interpretation of dreams in depth interviews, among the Kagwahiv Indians of Brazil, suggests some ways in which dreamers use such interpretations to regulate affective reactions to the content of their own dreams. Further conversations with people brought up in other traditions of oneiromantic dream interpretations suggest that such functions are widespread.

Theories of the Function of Dreaming

If beliefs about dreams do have some functions, it seems likely that they are related to the functions of dreaming itself. Therefore, we need to start with some ideas about the functions of dreaming, and see how these traditional interpretations of dreams relate to those functions.

The hunting and fishing people who live on the Andaman Islands, in the Bay of Bengal to the southwest of Burma, put forward the theory that a dream is the wandering of a part of the self, the *ene tia* ("body internal"), as it wanders at night to collect the smells—emanations of one's self—in all the places the dreamer left them during the day. Then the *ene tia* returns to the sleeper and weaves the regathered smells into a *dane kurale*, "spider home" (Pandya, 1986).

Let us take this beautiful metaphor as a theory of dreaming. The function of dreaming, it seems to suggest, is to gather up all the occurrences of the remembered day—the places and people one has touched —and weave them into the fabric, like a spider's web, that is where one lives—one's lived-constructed life. For the theory implicit in the Andaman beliefs, the process of linking the day's concerns with past ones, by all kinds of associational links, is an essential task of dreaming itself. The dream does not simply contain or express transferences, the dream is a part of the process of *creating* transferences—of investing current experiences with deep meaning derived from associations with past experiences and tendencies.

This theory implicit in Andaman beliefs about dreams is essentially that which has been put forward by Stanley R. Palombo (1978), who argues that dreaming serves to integrate short-term memory of current experiences with past experiences in long-term memory. Affect plays an important part in this process, for it is affect (like smell for the Andamaners?) that the mind uses as a key to the emotional significance of the experience, to determine just where it should be woven into the web of past memories. What part then does traditional dream interpretation—oneiromancy—play in respect to this function of dreaming? My research with personal use of such dream interpretations in talking about dreams suggests a multiple function: cultural ways of dealing with dreams both facilitate and implement the process of translating emotionally important daytime experiences into meaningful life events.

Other theorists have suggested related functions for dreaming, more directly derived from Freud's interpretation of dreams, though differing from Freud's theoretical analysis. One concept of the function of dreaming was put forward in its initial form by Thomas M. French and Erika Fromm (French and Fromm, 1964) and elaborated in an Eriksonian vein by Richard M. Jones (1962, 1978, pp. 171–183) that dreaming is a problem-solving thought process directed toward resolving emotional conflict. Several contributors to this volume provide more sophisticated elaboration and extension of this concept. All of these theories exactly invert Freud's basic premise on the function of dreaming. For Freud, the dream called up significant images from the past to weave the current day's concerns, which disturb sleep, into a wish-fulfilling hallucination that could be "played" once and then dismissed from the mind to permit it to go on sleeping. In these theories, the wish expressed in the dream is that which gives rise to the conflict whose resolution is the essential function of dreaming. Or, in the Andaman-Palombo theory, the weaving of current memories into the web of past memory is a basic function of dreaming, not just a means to preserve sleep.

Functions of Dream Beliefs

Beliefs that Delineate and Organize Dream Experience

Some beliefs may simply encapsulate perceptive observations of dreaming, identifying elements of the dreaming process and types of dreams. Such beliefs help the individual control the dream experience by understanding it; therefore, the widespread belief that dreams are a continuation of thinking about something into sleep. For example, carrying the thought into sleep with you, as the Parintintin put it (Kracke, 1979, pp. 135-136), or, as Barbadians hold, the belief that dreaming about something is a consequence of "studying" it during the day (Fisher, 1973) are based on accurate observation of the process of dream formation. This belief points to the role of day residues in dreams and frequently enables the dreamer to identify day residues. To give just one of many examples: one day I received a letter from my mother describing a hair-raising adventure in which my aunt was narrowly saved from driving into a flooded river, which I recounted to the Indian family in whose settlement I was staying. The next day, my elderly informant Catarina told me a dream she had that night, of a flood engulfing the settlement and surrounding area. She identified my story as the day residue for her dream, saying she was thinking about my story as she was falling asleep, brought it into sleep with her and it turned into her dream.

Another widespread belief based on accurate observation is that nightmares are caused by visitation of an incubus who attacks the sleeper, sometimes sexually or often by choking. The term *nightmare*— which was originally applied to night terrors, although it has come to be broadened to include any anxiety dream, originally referred to "a female monster supposed to settle on people and animals in their sleep producing a feeling of suffocation" (*Shorter Oxford English Dictionary* 1964). This belief recognizes the night terror as a distinct type of phenomenon from the ordinary dream, a phenomenon with a far more vivid sense of reality than the usual dream, accompanied by suffocating feelings of anxiety (see Hartmann, 1984, p. 21).

Such beliefs as these encode real aspects of the dream experience in such a way as to enable the dreamer to understand something of the dream mechanism and fit it into a larger scheme of things, perhaps even to gain some insight into the content of the dream. Parintintin dreamers, for example, frequently use the first-mentioned belief, to identify the day residue of a dream, what they were thinking about during the day that led to their forming that particular dream image.

Symbolic Predictions in Dreams

What is intriguing is the near universal occurrence of one particular way of explaining dreams, the notion that the dream presents a future state of affairs, either directly or, more often, through the mediation of metaphorically based conventional indexical symbols. Certain dream images indicate, to those who know the code, the imminent occurrence of some particular kind of event or state. The particular equations vary radically from culture to culture, as do the classes of events predicted; and even within a culture, as Bruce Mannheim (1987) has shown, the particular interpretations of a dream image may change fairly rapidly—much more rapidly than ritual or myth, for example. But what is interesting is the fact that so many cultures have a system of interpreting dreams that characterizes them as metaphorically expressed prognostications. The widespread occurrence of this phenomenon suggests that such predictive interpretations of dreams may have some function.

Parintintin Dream Prognostications

In studying the dreams and dream beliefs of a Brazilian indigenous culture in the Amazon, the Parintintin, Tupí-speaking hunter-fisher-horticulturists who live near the Madeira River in the southern Amazon region, I have recorded a reasonable number of such dream glosses, either in lists provided by informants in the abstract or, better, in explanations of particular dreams. In their belief system, it is possible for a dream to be directly predictive—you may dream that you will bag peccary when you go hunting, or of the arrival of a visitor—but more commonly such predictions are mediated by a metaphorically constructed indexical symbol of the event predicted.

The dream images are related to the things they predict in a variety of ways, mostly by metonymy or metaphor. The great majority of Parintintin dream prognostications pertain to two areas of concern: results of the hunt and illness or death. Thus, to dream of fighting, or of a snake or jaguar, predicts that a hunter (if one goes hunting) will bag game. To dream of a party predicts killing peccary, a social animal that runs in packs; an old man with a white beard is white-lipped peccary. To dream of a hammock means one will encounter a jaguar (because the open, net-like weave of the hammock resembles the spots of the jaguar). To dream of fire predicts fever, by an obvious analogy; to dream of paddling a canoe means death, because the motion of paddling resembles digging a grave. To dream of an old, broken-down house also foreshadows death, because a house is customarily abandoned on the death of one of its occupants. Some connections are mediated by mythical references: to dream of making love with a woman foretells the successful ambush of a tapir, referring to a myth in which the tapir is the lover of a married woman and is ultimately ambushed and slaughtered by the jealous husband.

Game and illness are not the only things predicted in dreams. To dream of water, or of paddling in a canoe, may forecast rain. Often people dream of the arrival of visitors, though I have not heard of any specific equations in this regard.

A particularly intriguing group of symbolic predictions in this regard are several that share one striking characteristic: they appear to embody some of those equations of childhood thinking that are sometimes referred to as "Freudian symbols," but they do so *in reverse*. That is, whereas the "symbols" that Freud and other early analysts discussed are relatively neutral images that occur in dreams representing experiences that are highly charged with ambivalent or disturbing emotion, these dream glosses take an emotionally charged dream image and reinterpret it as something *less* prone to provoke anxiety—but something that might be described in the analytic literature as a symbol for that particular image. Thus, although in a boy's childhood fantasies the female genitals may be thought of fearfully as a wound, and the vagina with its connotations of castration might thus be represented in a man's dream as a wound in some less cherished part of the anatomy, in Parintintin dream explication a dream of a vagina predicts that one will be wounded. Similarly, to dream of kissing (an act considered rather perverse in Parintintin society) means one will encounter wasps or a snake, and to dream of pregnancy means that one will find honey. In all these instances, the dream represents openly the experience that is deeply invested with conflictful or anxious emotion, and the gloss translates it into an innocuous or at least a more banal or obvious danger.

Psychological Functions of the Prognostications

My research with the dreams of Parintintin Indians and their use of traditional dream glosses to elucidate them, reveals two functions of such traditional glosses of dreams. They may be used directly to represent a preoccupation of the dreamer, as if forming a kind of code for the expression of emotional concerns in dreams; or conversely, they may be used to deflect attention from the dream's content, as a kind of reassuring denial that the dream does not mean what it seems to.

My research with the Parintintin Indians has included, since 1968, personal interviews with individuals in which they are encouraged to tell their dreams and free associate to them. In these interviews, naturally, they also gave me their own explanations of their dreams. With this methodology, it was possible to get at the personal concerns and emotional conflicts expressed in dreams and the dreamers' attempts to resolve them. At the same time it was possible to see the dreamer's explanation of his or her dream in terms of the person's own dream beliefs and explicatory system, and how these explanations and interpretations of the dream were related to the dream's dynamics.

In some cases, the glosses themselves represent intensely significant and affectively charged situations, as in the dream images that are glossed as foreseeing the death of a close relative. Not infrequently such images are used by the dreamer, in constructing the dream, as a kind of language to refer to the distressing situation in his or her dream thoughts. Thus one man, who had never been able to fully mourn his mother's death five years earlier and who continued to be preoccupied with his grief for her, opened a dream that dealt with longings for his mother with the image of an old, broken-down house—a dream image traditionally glossed as referring to death.

More frequently, however, such traditional dream glosses are used to *ward off* anxiety-arousing dream thoughts that occur too openly in a dream, by being able to reinterpret the dream image as predicting something benign, or at least less anxiety arousing than the dream image. Thus, a fight in a dream is interpreted as predicting that a hunter will kill game; sexual intercourse in a dream, or the image of a penis, can be glossed to mean one will kill tapir (an animal with a proverbially large penis, who also figures as a lover in a classic adultery myth). My most insightful informant had a dream about sexual intercourse that carried incestuous overtones for him and involved the castration of the man who was making love in the dream (Kracke, 1979, pp. 143–145, 1980, pp. 256-259). He first glossed the dream as predicting that someone would bag tapir; but then when that failed to contain the anxiety (partly because my questioning led him to recall childhood memories of sexual curiosity directly related to the penis image in the dream) he reinterpreted the dream as predicting that he would be injured—the vagina in the dream predicting a wound—and confirmed his new gloss by referring to the fact that he had, that morning, jarred the scab of a machete-cut on his leg and started it bleeding again.

This same informant later made explicit the anxiety-controlling function that such dream glosses have for him. Talking about a dream about a violent marital fight, he said:

> At first when I was little I was afraid when I had dreams like that, I didn't know what it was. I told Papa. I thought it was an *añang* [ghost or malevolent spirit] that I had dreamed of.—Sometimes you dream of a woman, and it is game. When you dream of a man, his prick, it is a tapir you are going to kill. All this Papa told me.

So the traditional glosses of dreams, in these instances, serve for him as reassurance that an intensely emotional and anxiety-provoking dream "really" refers to something quite different, something agreeable (success in the hunt) but not quite so intensely invested with emotion. In other words, a segment of the system of dream interpretations—those interpretations that take a highly charged dream image and interpret it as something relatively benign or banal, or at least something everyday —can be understood as acting as a kind of culturally constituted denial or displacement. Or it may be thought of as a culturally constituted *secondary elaboration*.

The frequently occurring device of reversal of meaning, whereby the dream "means" the opposite of what it says, may in some cases be an ideal vehicle for such an anxiety-soothing mechanism. A Brazilian woman who grew up in a Corsican family, and whose mother had frequent recourse to traditional Corsican dream glosses, related to me a childhood experience much like my Parintintin informant's, involving the use of reversal. She had repeated dreams of the death of a close relative, which disturbed her greatly, until her mother explained to her that each time you dream of someone's death, you add a day to the person's life. After that, she told me, she was very much relieved. Such culturally standardized secondary elaboration may, paradoxically, permit the more open expression of disturbing fantasies in dreams.

Another use of dream glosses is prescriptive than rather predictive: one dreams what one *should do*, taking the dream as the annunciation of a decision or resolution of a dilemma. The Pakistani "initiation dreams" of call to a pir (a sufi saint) as one's personal saint, described by Kathy Ewing (1990), are of this type, as are the Guajiro annunciation dreams described by Watson (1981), where a supernatural figure appears to the dreamer in a stock framework and instructs him or her on the course of action to follow in a difficult or contentious situation. (These often endorse the dreamer's wishes contrary to those of an authority figure.) Erika Bourguignon (1954) reported a beautiful example of such a dream in Haiti which I have discussed extensively elsewhere (Kracke, 1987).

Among the Parintintin, such dreams occur, but without the supernatural figures. A good example are the dreams reported by Arlete, a young woman who had returned to Canavial to take care of her aged grandfather after much travel as a maid to a Brazilian family. She reported several dreams that she had in Canavial before leaving again to the nearby city of Humaitá, including dreams of traveling by water and by bus, and of the city—or rather, of the cemetery, which she said referred to the city. (This information was provided by Suzanne Oakdale).

The efficacy of such dreams in bringing about action is due to the belief that dreams not only predict future circumstances, but also recommend a course of action that will have a favorable outcome. (Indeed, dreams that predict game are of this sort, as they in essence recommend that a hunter go out after a particular type of game, predicting that if he does so he will be successful.) The function of such a belief is most clearly tied in with the problem-solving function of dreams, as articulated by Thomas French and Erika Fromm, referred to earlier. Bourguignon's Haitian girl's dream resolved a conflict between her duty of accompanying Bourguignon on a visit to her family in the country, and her longing for the city, in favor of returning to the latter—to care for the saints as they instructed her. The appearance of the saint, in the guise of a man of her acquaintance, suggests a possible further motive for this resolution. Similarly, moving to Humaitá resolved a difficult situation for Arlete, involving a conflict between her sense of duty to her grandfather Paulino whom she had come back to care for, and friction with his son who displaced her from the caretaking role when he moved back into the household at a time when Paulino was sick.

The belief that dreams of a certain type provide prescriptions for behavior is a validation of the solution provided by the dream to a conflict. Indeed, as Ewing comments (1990, p. 68), "dreaming can become an *active* effort to resolve conflict, a form of social action, only in societies where dreams are believed to be significant" (italics added). Thus, the use of dreams to prescribe a certain course of action might be seen as a culturally constituted extension, or validation, of the problem-solving nature of dreams.

Conclusions

Thus, many of the beliefs about dreams that are widespread among world cultures enhance the regular functioning of dreaming. Some provide theories of dreams that enable the dreamer to understand the dream process, or to better understand his or her her own dreams— perhaps to derive insight from them, or to tune into them as a thinking process. Other beliefs provide a ready-made denial of the manifest content of the dream, reinforcing the dreamer's defenses and permitting fairly open dreaming about conflictual subjects. Conversely, however, some of the conventional dream glosses provide a kind of language of dream symbols for expressing some basic concerns in dreams. And still other beliefs legitimate the outcome of dreams as a problem-solving form of thought.

These functions of dream beliefs are not automatic; their fulfillment of the functions mentioned is a potential available to each dreamer, but not necessarily utilized equally by all. In my experience with Kagwahiv dreamers, different individuals used the beliefs in different ways and to different degrees. One man was particularly good at using traditional symbols to express his conflicts, another was especially effective in using dream glosses to allay his anxiety, or in identifying day residues in dreams, guided by the belief that dreams are a continuation of thinking about something as you go to sleep. Others had recourse to the system of dream glosses, but did not seem to use them nearly so regularly in these psychological ways (Kracke, 1979). However, for those who are prepared to utilize the potential of the system, the various beliefs I have discussed offer ways to enhance the problem-solving capacity of dreams, and to deal with deep concerns in a relatively open way in dreams while controlling the anxiety and other disturbing feelings that such open expression of these concerns may arouse.

References

Bourguignon, E. (1954). "Dreams and Dream Interpretation in Haiti."*American Anthropologist* 56: 262–268.

Ewing, K. (1990). "The Dream of Spiritual Initiation and the Organization of Self Representations Among Pakistani Sufis." *American Ethologist* 17: 56–74.

Fisher, L. E. (1973). "The Imagery of Madness in Village Barbados." Ph.D. dissertation, Northwestern University.

French, T. M., and Fromm, E. (1964). *Dream Interpretation: A New Approach.* New York: Basic Books. [Reprinted 1986, New York: International Universities Press.]

Freud, S. (1953). "The Interpretation of Dreams." In J. Strachey (Ed. and Trans.), *The Standard Edition of the Complete Psychological Works of Sigmund Freud*, Vols. 4 and 5. London: Hogarth Press.

Hartmann, E. (1984). *The Nightmare.* New York: Basic Books.

Jones, R. M. (1962). *Ego Sythesis in Dreams.* Cambridge, Mass.: Schenkman.

————. (1978). *The New Psychology of Dreaming.* New York: Penguin Books.

Kilborne, B. (1987). "On Classifying Dreams." In B. Tedlock (Ed.), Dreaming: *Anthropological and Psychological Interpretations*, pp. 171–193. Cambridge: Cambridge University Press.

Kracke, W. (1979). "Dreaming in Kagwahiv: Dream Beliefs and their Psychic Uses in an Amazonian Indian Culture." *Psychoanalytic Study of Society* 8: 119–171.

―――. (1980). "Amazon Interviews: Dreams of a Bereaved Father." *Annual of Psychoanalysis* 8: 249–267.

―――. (1987). "'Everyone Who Dreams has a Bit of Shaman': Cultural and Personal Meanings of Dreams—Evidence from the Amazon." *Psychiatric Journal of the University of Ottawa* 12: 65–72.

Mannheim, B. (1987). "A Semiotic of Indian Dreams." In B. Tedlock (Ed.), *Dreaming: Anthropological and Psychological Interpretations*, pp. 132–153. Cambridge: Cambridge University Press.

Palombo, S. (1978). *Dreaming and Memory.* New York: Basic Books.

Pandya, V. (986). "Hunting Bodies with Smell: A Study in Andamanese Cosmology." Paper presented at the University of Illinois at Chicago, 1986, and at the South Asia Seminar, University of Chicago, 1987.

Watson, L. C. (1981). "Dreaming as World View and as Action in Guajiro Culture." *Journal of Latin American Lore* 7: 239–254.

15

**Robert Knox Dentan and
Laura J. McClusky** ━━━━━━━━━━━━━

"Pity the Bones by Wandering River Which Still in Lovers' Dreams Appear as Men"

Introduction

Dreams as the Focus of a Cultural System

The chief goal of this chapter is to sketch a preliminary description of how Han Chinese people, particularly the ruling class intelligentsia or "scholar-bureaucrats," *shi da fu*, have used and still use dream accounts.[1] The topic is therefore not "dreams," internal and usually nocturnal psychic experiences, but how Han gentry talk about dreams. Nor is there space to deal in detail with the importance of dreams in, say, folk religion as opposed to gentry ideology (Sangren, 1988).

Our description focuses on two periods in Han history: (1) a classic period from late Zhou times to early Sung dynasty, about 500 B.C. to A.D. 1000 (see Table 15.1), and (2) a modern period from the Great Proletarian Cultural Revolution to 1985. Han literature provides the basis for the first section. The primary materials for the second section are seventy-eight dream narratives and five interviews with four students. The narratives were collected from Beijing college and high school students by Myrna Walters and Dentan in 1985 (Walters and Dentan, 1985a, 1985b). McClusky conducted the interviews with Han students attending the State University of New York at Buffalo during the 1987–1988 school year. This dual focus requires addressing questions of continuity and discontinuity, persistence and change, in the content, structure and function of dream accounts.

These concerns require setting dream narratives in their context as part of a series of interwoven "cultural systems," within which each part may affect and be affected by any other in continuous but ever-changing patterns of mutual feedback (Geertz, 1973, 1983; Sangren, 1988, pp. 677, 683, 685). Thus many classical Han dream narratives had social and political functions. Indeed, many narratives seem to grow out of political infighting or rhetorical imperatives rather than out of nocturnal psychic experiences.

Table 15.1
Chinese Dynasties

NAME*		DATES	FEATURES
Pinyin	Wade-Giles	(Traditional)	
Xia	Hsia	(2205–1766 B.C.)	scapulimancy
Shang	Shang	c. 1500–1040 B.C.	oneiromancy
		(1766–1122 B.C.)	
Zhou	Chou	(1122–256 B.C.)	first record of shamans & spirit mediums
(political fragmentation)			
Qin	Chin	221–206 B.C.	Legalist despotism
Han	Han	B.C. 206–220 A.D.	Confucianism est'd
(political fragmentation)		220–265	Daoist rebellion
Jin	Tsin	265–420	Buddhism spreads to all classes
(political fragmentation)		420–589	
Sui	Sui	589–618	
Tang	Tang	618–907	Zen (Daoist) Buddhism
(political fragmentation)		907–960	Buddhism repressed
Sung	Song	960–1280	San Jiao (3 teachings)
Yuan	Yuan	1280–1364	politicization of folk religion vs. Mongols
Ming	Ming	1363–1644	Nestorians and Catholics

* There are several ways of translating Han words. The official system of the People's Republic of China is pinyin. The old system, with which some readers may be familiar, is Wade-Giles.

Finally, the notion of a "cultural system" should not obscure the fact that segments of society (e.g., age sets, classes, genders, occupations) hold different notions of how the world works (K. Mannheim, 1936). Depending on the social or psychological context, a single person will approach the same experience in a number of different ways (e.g., Cheung, 1982; Cheung and Lau, 1982). Moreover, no one in daily life is obsessively concerned with consistency, parsimony, or coherence of thought (Dentan, 1988c; Levy-Bruhl, 1935). Contradictions or mutually incongruous notions are the rule between or within individuals in China as in the United States.

This variation may be particularly marked in China compared to other peoples of the world. The Han intelligentsia pay little public attention to dreams. People even in classic times were reluctant to take an interpreted dream as revelatory unless confirmation was available from another source (Palmer et al., 1986, pp. 112–113). Under such circumstances, one might expect that people have little incentive to remember or talk about dreams. In fact, however, students in 1985 seem to have done so, suggesting that although official ideology may not facilitate dream recall (e.g., Kuiken et al., n.d.) it does not inhibit it (Cernovsky, 1984). Therefore, the Han cultural system of which dream accounts are part is complex and not internally consistent, like most cultural systems (Sangren, 1988; Dentan 1988c; Guenther, 1979).

Approaches

A discursive account like this chapter requires a vocabulary, which in turn necessitates some definitions. Because the parts of cultural systems interpenetrate, however, readers must recognize that defining terms is simply a convenience that breaks a continuous and living reality into handy packages suitable for transmission from China to the reader. Western social science tends to objectify and reify ideas, separating and classifying them as if they were apples and oranges, tidying up phenomena that in fact are amorphous and fluid (Dentan, 1988c; Guenther, 1979; Pedersen and Baruffati, 1985; B. Tedlock, 1987). With this caveat, we use the terms *dream theory* and *oneirology* interchangeably to refer to Han answers to questions like "Why do we dream?" or "How can we tell good dreams from bad ones?" The terms *oneirocriticism* or *dream interpretation* refer to Han methods for assessing the meaning of dreams and *oneiromancy* refers to the use of dream narratives. *Attitudes toward dreams* is shorthand for Han answers to questions like "Are dreams significant?" and "Why do some people take dreams more seriously than others?"[2]

Similarly, Han need a vocabulary to talk about dreams. In the second part of this chapter we stress the words Han in classic times used to talk about dreams for two reasons: first, the dream accounts available to us are primarily verbal narratives; and second, words are clues to the ways people conceptualize their world. This approach falls into the old anthropological tradition of "emic" studies or "ethnoscience" (e.g., Baziak and Dentan, 1965; Mathiot, 1979; Sturtevant, 1964), now a concern of "interpretive" anthropology (e.g., Geertz, 1973, 1983; Ricoeur, 1981; D. Tedlock, 1983). The basic assumption is that the "common images that a people has of any situation is necessarily sketched in by, but not necessarily limited by, the horizons of the language" (Bohannan, 1963, p. 32). The idea is neither that words are isomorphic with cognitive categories so that knowing the one implies knowing the other; nor that lack of vocabulary implies that people cannot think about or express complex or abstract ideas, though they may have to resort to metaphor or long-winded exposition to do so. Therefore we agree with those who reject the idea that poverty of vocabulary explains the prevalence of somatization in the accounts that Han psychiatric patients give of their trouble (e.g., Kleinman, 1977; Tseng, 1975; for a lengthy colloquial Han vocabulary for emotions and personality, see Zeng, 1986, pp. 83–90, pp.108–115). The explanation lies in their "ethnopsychiatry;" that is, the way they conceptualize their problems (e.g., Cheung, 1982; Cheung, and Lau, 1982; Kleinman, 1982). A careful examination of the words and contexts in which they occur does provide an entree into how the Han think about dreams and ultimately into the cultural systems of which dream narratives are a manifestation. Failure to attend to such linguistic details can lead to confusion in practice as well as scholarship (e.g., Dentan, 1983; Lourie and Mikhalev, 1989; Tao-Kim-Hai, 1965).[3]

The modern dream narratives discussed in the third section of this paper, however, were first written in English; and the interviews also took place in English. Moreover, spoken Chinese, *putonghua*, is a "restricted code" compared with classical written Chinese (J. Hsu, 1985, p. 105; Tseng, 1975). That is, it does not facilitate the elaboration or explication of dream narratives as well as classical written Mandarin. This sort of restricted code is characteristic of social situations that downplay individuality and stress group solidarity (Bernstein, 1964, pp. 59–60; Dentan, 1988c, pp. 859, 872; Douglas, 1973, pp. 44–58). The relative crudity of the language, especially in translation, does not mean that the words have simple meanings. To paraphrase Empson (1961, p. 236), it means that the narrator, distanced by time and Communist ideology from traditional oneirology and oneirocriticism, must use a restricted vocabulary to refer to a vague and complex mass of ideas that he or she apprehends only in part. In this case, it seems appropriate to enlarge the mesh of our linguistic net and look for themes that seem to survive translation and recur in the narratives (cf. Kracauer, 1947; Wolfenstein and Leites, 1950).

Classic Oneirology

There are normal dreams, and dreams due to alarm, thinking, memory, rejoicing, fear. These six happen when the spirit connects with something. People who don't see where dreams come from do not know why; if you know why, nothing will startle you.

A body's *qi* fluctuates in correlation with the cosmos. Therefore, when *Yin qi* is strong, you are frightened by dreams of walking through great waters. When *Yang qi* is strong, you are roasted by dreams of walking through great fires. When *Yin* and *Yang* are both strong, you dream of killing or sparing. When you overeat, you dream of giving presents; when you starve, of receiving them. For the same reason, when you're dizzy, you dream of floating in the air; from a sinking, congested feeling, of drowning. When you fall asleep lying on your belt, you dream of snakes; when a flying bird pecks your hair, of flying. As it turns dark, you dream of fire, falling ill you dream of eating. . . . The spirit chances on it, and we dream; the body encounters it, and it seems to happen. Hence by day we imagine and by night dream what spirit and body chance upon. That is why, when your spirit is concentrated, imagination and dreaming automatically diminish. What people who trust the time they awake do not understand is the constant change and transformation of empirical phenomena. It is no empty saying that the True Men of olden times were unaware of themselves when awake and did not dream when asleep. (Liezi, modified from Lie, 1990, pp. 66–67)

Words and Ancient Dream Theory

One of the best ways to understand dream theory is to attend to the words people use when discussing dreaming (Dentan, 1984). This section primarily discusses Mandarin words the Han use and have used when discussing dreams. However, because there is disparity between written and spoken Mandarin (Hsu, J., 1985, p. 105; Tseng, 1975) and because the information about modern Han rests on oral interview data, this lexical emphasis applies more to ancient than modern Han usage.

Our procedure is first roughly to define (gloss) the Mandarin word, then to analyze the ideograph for the term. Finally, we specify some contexts in which the word is used. Knowing the context highlights subtleties glosses hide. Among the contexts to which we refer most often are *chengyu*, or "set phrases." These are idioms or proverbs, usually four syllables in length, which even today pervade Han speech and writing (Table 15.2).

Table 15.2

Han "Idioms" (*Chengyu*) Relating to Dreams

Han + Literal Gloss	Free Gloss	Ref#	Lai	WU
1. *chiren shuo meng* demented person talk dream	idiotic nonsense, lunatic ravings	0686		
2. *Handan* meng jue* Handan dream wake	unrealized ambition rude awakening		46	66
3. *hao meng bu chang* good dream not long	life's joys are fleeting pipe dream	*Straits Times,* 1983, p. iii:	56	
4. *hungling meimeng** golden millet beautiful dream		1919	59	
5. *hudie meng*** butterfly dream	illusory nature of reality			
6. *meng bi sheng hua **** dream pen birth flower	poetic inspiration		88	
7. *menghuan paoying***** dream illusion bubble shadow	bubble,illusion, pipe dream	2863		65
8. *mengmei yi qiu* dream sleep result crave	yearn so much for something you dream of it	2864		
9. *nan ke yi meng** south tributary- state 1 drm	illusory joy, fondest dreams	3013	91	66
10. *ru meng chu xing* like dream begin wake	beginning to see the light	3652		
11. *qingting dian shui*** dragonfly dot water	ephemeral beauty skillful touches	3440	28	
12. *ri you suo si* day there's place yearn *ye you suo meng* night there's place dream	what you think about or long for during the day you dream about at night			65
13. *shenghua miao bi**** born flower brush pen	poetic inspiration	3866	88 108	
14. *tongchuang yimeng* shared bed, different dream	make strange bedfellows	4352	135	
15. *yi zhen huangliang** one pillow golden millet	brief illusion of grandeur (see #2)	5425		

Table 15.2 *(Continued)*

Sources: (1) Beijing Weiguoyu Xueyuan Zubian [Peking Foreign Language University English Department Editorial Committee], 1982. Each *chengyu* is numbered, and those numbers are listed in "Ref #" column. (2) T. C. Lai, 1970b. (3) Wu Zuguang, 1985. The Lai and Wu columns list page numbers.

* From the well–known story by a Tang dynasty writer, Shen Jiji (c. 750–800 A.D.), about a poor scholar who fell asleep in Handan while a pot of millet was cooking. He dreamed of his life as an important scholar-bureaucrat but awoke before the millet was completely cooked; also called the "Handan dream" (Pu, 1984). Modified versions of this story recur in Han literature, beginning "Southern Tributary State," by another Tang Dynasty author, Li Gongzuo (c. 770–850 A.D.). This story is about a man who dreams of his life as governor of a state tributary to the ant kingdom (Li, 1980). Similarly, the last two plays of the great Ming Dynasty playwright who wrote "The Peony Pavilion" and other "dream plays" were versions of Shen's and Li's stories (Hsia, 1970).

** The phrase *butterfly dream*, not a *chengyu*, nevertheless, recurs throughout Chinese history. It refers to the dream of a butterfly, from which the great Daoist Zhuangzi awoke, unable to decide whether he was Zhuangzi who had dreamed of being a butterfly or if he was a butterfly dreaming he was Zhuangzi (Watson, 1958, p. 49; Dentan, 1988a). For instance, there is a play by that name, dating to one of the convulsive periods in Chinese history (Arlington and Acton, 1937, pp. 226–229); a playwright describes a moment of satori in 1937 by referring to the butterfly dream (Wu, 1985, p. 67); and Wang Meng, a writer whose career has taken him from obscurity to fame to revilement to power, has a semi-autobiographical story called "The Butterfly" (1983).

The great Tang Dynasty poet Du Fu presumably had Zhuangzi's dream in mind when he wrote the almost untranslatable couplet:

> *chuan hua hudie shen shen jian*
> *dian shui qingting e e fei*

A literal word by word gloss:

> wearing ornaments butterflies hard hard to see
> dotting water dragonflies pip! pip! fly

A *chengyu* based on these lines (*qingting dianshui*) refers to a literary style full of "delicate allusions and recondite obscurities" or to "ephemeral beauty" (Lai, 1970a, p. 28) or to just scratching the surface of a topic (Beijing Weiguoyu Xueyuan Yingyushi Zubian, 1982, #3340). Lai (1970a, pp. 48, 86, 132) gives two similar allusions to the butterfly dream [##63, 127].

*** These *chengyu* refer to two dreams of the painter and poet Jiang Yan (444–505 A.D.), reported in Wang Renyu's "Kaiyuan Tianbao Yishi," very roughly glossable as "Open Garden Treasury of Lost Histories," from Five Dynasty times (907–960 A.D.). Jiang became a poet after dreaming that someone gave him

Table 15.2 (*Contnued*)

a five-colored brush, but he lost his poetic ability after a dream in which a Jin dynasty poet, Guo Pu (276–324 A.D.), demanded the brush back. A Ming dynasty poet modified the story by alleging that he became a poet after he dreamt that a man gave him a brush from which lotuslike flowers grew. In another version, the poet involved is the Tang dynasty genius Li Bai (Lai, 1976, pp. 75, 76). The story is a poetic staple (Chaves, 1986, pp. 162, 183).

**** From the conclusion of the Diamond Sutra or Vagrakkhedika (Muller, 1969, p. 144):

> Stars, darkness, a lamp, phantom, dew, a bubble.
> A dream, a flash of lightning, and a cloud - thus
> we should look upon the world (all that was made).

See, e.g., Wu (1985); Walters and Dentan (1985b).

Meng (Dreams)

The Han call dreams in general *meng*. The top part of the unsimplified ideograph stands for "confused vision" or "bad eyesight," the bottom for "evening." The reference to distorted vision reflects the low esteem in which literate Han held dreams. Set phrases suggest that dreams merely reflect the day's events or unsatisfied desires (Table 15.2, nos. 8, 12). Han poetry refers often to yearning (nostalgia, love) as a cause for dreams (Lee, 1979, pp. 132–140; see section entitled "Using Dream Accounts"). To "Dream-think of," *mengxiang*, is to hope in vain. This meaning suggests that only silly people talk about dreams (Table 15.2, no. 1).

Yan and Gui (Nightmares and Demons)

The ideograph for "nightmare," *yan*, incorporates the ideograph for *gui*, which is often misleadingly glossed as "ghost" or "devil" as in "foreign devil" (Wieger, 1965, p. 808). The *gui* ideograph connotes deceptiveness, as in the ideograph for the obsolete word *huo*, glossable as "spell, delusion, misguided judgment" (Kung, 1979, pp. 114, 116; Wieger, 1965, p. 808; for discussion, see Fingarette, 1972, pp. 22–23). The word *gui* occurs in expressions meaning stealthy, surreptitious, sneaky, deceptive, lying, furtive, plotting and scheming. Therefore in nightmares or other delusions, *gui* deceive and scare victims. The phrases equivalent to English words ending in the derogatory -*ard* (e.g., sluggard, drunkard, coward), in Han end with the word *gui*. The word also occurs in phrases for ugly things: grimaces, mandrills, lumpfish. In slang expressions, it means "smart" or "clever," as in English "he's a clever devil" or "smart as the dickens."

The *gui* ideograph seems initially to have represented a floating head with a disquieting appendage. Han philologists speculated this appendage might be a tail or a whirlwind. However, it also resembles the dangling intestines of Malay penanggalan, manjang, or tenggelung.[4] These are floating female vampire heads that, like *gui*, associate with puerperal death and will o'the wisps (Embun, 1959, pp. 15–18; Endicott, 1970, pp. 60–63; Gimlette and Thompson, 1971, pp. 79, 182; McHugh, 1955, pp. 82–84, 123; Wilkinson, 1901, pp. ii, 106, 233–234, 239–240, 567). Penggalan, like *gui*, fall into the *yin* (female) category of creatures. Because Malay culture originated in South China, the two monsters may be cognate.

Gui, like gods in Han folk religion, are often ghosts of the dead, particularly of suicides and other "restless dead who died unjustly or whose bodies are not properly cared for" (Overmyer, 1986, p. 52). This funeral connection may be the source of their power and efficacy, which Han call *ling* (see section later entitled *"Hunpo* (Soul)" and Table 15.2) and anthropologists call *mana*. *Gui* appear as man-eating tigers, incubi or succubi, werewolves, and so on. They live (Latourette, 1934, p. 163):

> in old trees, or in clothes, in objects of furniture, or in mountains and stones. Leaves driven before the wind may each be a kuei [gui] ... They lurk in ponds and rivers to draw people in and drown them. Indeed, one theory has it that the kuei of a drowned person remains in the place of the tragedy and can obtain release only by luring some hapless wight to a similar fate. The kuei of a mother who dies in childbirth wins surcease from anguish by bringing on some other woman the same demise. Insane persons are controlled by kuei. An epidemic of kuei may visit a city - in the old days cutting queues, and striking people on the streets.

So far, Westerners might be comfortable with the concept of *gui*, thinking of it as "evil spirit, " "demon" or "ghost." You could say "demons cause nightmares." Indeed, the character for the entity that most often appears in Han discussions of dreams is the character for *gui*, with a modifier indicating that it should be pronounced differently, like the word for "cloud." That entity is the *hun*, "soul," which in Chinese dualism is paired with another entity, *po*. The ideograph for *po* is the same as for *hun* or *gui*, except for a modifier indicating that it should be pronounced like the word for "white."

Hunpo (Soul)

Cosmology and Souls: Central to ancient Han dream theory is the concept of *hunpo*, which we gloss as soul. Educated ruling-class men in the late Zhou to the early Sung dynasties believed *hunpo* responsible for dream experiences. Today, evidence for this belief seems to appear in students' discussions of dreams.

The reader may want to refer throughout this discussion to Table 15.3, which represents crudely some ways in which ancient Han discussed souls. A linguist might read the table as a taxonomy. That is, you could refer to *hun* as *hunling*; to *hunling* as *ling*; to *ling* as *shen*; and *shen* as *yang*. In the same way you can refer to your pet pig as "Porky"; to Porky as a duroc or Poland white; to a duroc as a pig; and to a pig as an animal. Thus to call *hun* and *po shen* and *gui* is proper (De Groot, 1912, pp. 13, 282).

The traditional Han, however, read this taxonomy as a cosmic hierarchy in which higher levels infused or energized lower levels and were in turn affected by them. Thus one sense of *hun* is "*shen* individuated in a person." Similarly, *shen* interacts with the One that divides into *yang* and *yin*; the result is *ling*, according to the DAODE JING, (chapter 42).[5]

Table 15.3 represents dialectics, not static dichotomies. Therefore, no matter which column an entity fits into, it contains both *yang* and *yin*. Zuo Quiming in the late Zhou gave the classic description (ZUO ZHUANG, adapted from Ong, 1985, pp. 21–22; cf. Watson, 1989): When a person is born, what first forms is *po*. When this is produced, its *yang* gives rise to *hun*. Using things increases the vital force [*qi*]. *Hun* and *po* are thus strengthened and become refined and bright."

Preliminary Definitions: A quick run-through of the notions in Table 15.3 may be useful, although readers should recognize the glosses are only preliminary. We will develop them further as needed. *Qi* is the basic stuff of the cosmos; both matter and energy animate it. It is a force ancient Han conceived of as the same sort of gaseous material as "breath," the original meaning of the word. *Yang* and *yin* are the positive and negative aspects of *qi*, and are thus gaseous material forces. These characters initially referred to sunlight and shadow.

Yang is universal *shen*, which is deposited as individual *shen* among living and supernatural beings. *Shen* are *yang* equivalents of *yin gui*. They are heavenly deities as opposed to ghosts or demons. Both *shen* and *gui* are products of the interaction of *yang* and *yin*. The ideograph for *shen* comes from an ancient form depicting the alternation between dominance by *yang* and by *yin*.

Table 15.3
Matter-energy (*qi*, Breath) Taxonomy

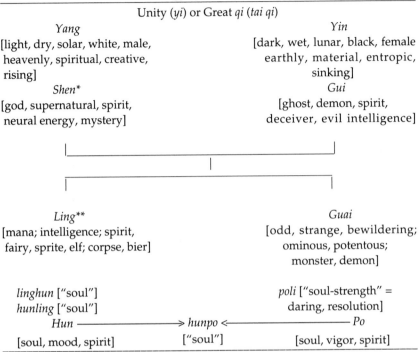

Unity (*yi*) or Great *qi* (*tai qi*)

Yang	*Yin*
[light, dry, solar, white, male, heavenly, spiritual, creative, rising]	[dark, wet, lunar, black, female earthly, material, entropic, sinking]
*Shen**	*Gui*
[god, supernatural, spirit, neural energy, mystery]	[ghost, demon, spirit, deceiver, evil intelligence]

*Ling***	*Guai*
[mana; intelligence; spirit, fairy, sprite, elf; corpse, bier]	[odd, strange, bewildering; ominous, potentous; monster, demon]

linghun ["soul"]		*poli* ["soul-strength" =
hunling ["soul"]		daring, resolution]
Hun ⟶	*hunpo* ⟵	*Po*
[soul, mood, spirit]	["soul"]	[soul, vigor, spirit]

From top to bottom, these categories go from greater to lesser inclusivity. Readers may think of members of lower categories as participating in, having affinities to, or being a local manifestation of higher ones. Lines indicate that *Guai* and *Ling* bear these relationships to both superior categories, although they are normally associated with the one in their column. Readers should remember that Han dualism is not dichotomous but dialectic. That is, categories are not mutually exclusive but in the world of experience refer to aspects of reality in tension with thus dependent on each other.

* One derivative is witch, *shenpo*, from *shen* + *po* [old woman, not the same as the word for "female soul"]. *Posuo*, whirling dancing, may refer to dancing into trance. Another derivative is *shensi*, from *shen* and *si*, thought, craving, reverie (see text). Although the usual meaning is "state of mind," Liu Xie (1983, pp. 115–121, 180–181) uses it to describe poetic imagination (Wong, 1983, p. 121) in which one's *si* rises high enough to participate in *shen*.

** The old ideograph for *Ling* consists of the ideograph for shaman, *wu*, under the ideographs for rain and big drops. The ideograph for *wu* shows two rainmaking shamans dancing, again presumably into trance.

Ling seems equivalent to the anthropological notion of mana, a supernatural impersonal energy or potency concentrated in particular things or activities in particular societies (Day, 1940, pp. 47, 171–175.). Thus it refers to being clever, intelligent or effective; to fresh corpses, a main focus; and to supernatural beings, fairies, sprites, and so on. It occurs in compounds meaning "inspiration" (note that the English word also has a "spirit" in it), mind, insight, quickness (of skill, intelligence) as well as in compounds referring to funerals. The old character shows two dancing shamans successfully bringing on a heavy rain (for an extensive discussion, see Sangren, 1988, pp. 681, 683–687).

Chapter 39 in the DAODE JING describes the relationship between *shen* and *ling* by analogy. Readers would profit by looking at several translations (e.g. Blakney, 1955, p. 92; Ch'u, 1973, p. 53; Day, 1940, p. 174; Lau, 1963, p. 100).

> Sky got the One and became *qing*
> [*qing*: pure, clear, limpid, translucent blue-black-green
> (of water or sky)]
> Earth got the One and became *ning*
> [*ning*: settled, tranquil, peaceful, firm, in repose]
> Shen got the One and became *ling* . . .
> 10,000 creatures got the One and became alive.

Hun and *Po:* In ancient Han systemics, *hun* is the *yang* aspect of the *hunpo*, and therefore is associated with heart (*xin*) and blood, light, productivity, and life, as well as with heaven, rising, the South, warmth, summer, fire, bitter tastes, blue, joy, and *shen*. It dwells in the eyes and tongue. *Po* is *yin*, and therefore associated with lungs and kidneys, dark, entropy, and death, as well as with earth, sinking, the West, autumn, dryness, metal, acrid tastes, white, sorrow, and *guai* or *gui*. It dwells in the ears, nose and mouth (De Groot, 1912, pp. 13, 169; Ong, 1985, pp. 20–29). *Po*, being somatic, appears at conception; hun at birth. Harmless *hun* animate moral, conscious personality; dangerous *po* amoral, unconscious vitality. On death *hun* go to Heaven, perhaps riding white deer or cranes; *po* sink to the Yellow Springs, Chinese Hades, or become *gui*. Folk Daoism contrasts three *hun* and seven *po* (Osgood, 1974, p. 1144). There are a lot of other variations on this scheme (see Table 15.3; MacNair, 1946, p. 237; Ong, 1985, p. 23), but the opposition is clear.

A late Zhou commentator wrote in the LI JI, one of the Five Classics: (adapted from a quote in Ong, 1985, p. 28)

Hun can't ride the clouds and ascend to Heaven, but their ling can rise and float and go anywhere. They may enjoy sacrificial offerings or enter new womb [for rebirth]. Their mutations are limitless. . . . *Po* don't sink without trace into the Yellow Springs. *Po ling* adheres to the corpse and hovers around the coffin and does not leave the grave. Thus, when the [dead person's] descendants come to sacrifice at the grave, it may enjoy the offerings.

When the corpse decomposes and the grave deteriorates, *po* become nothing. For *po* are composed of father's sperm and mother's blood. Returned to their origin, they do not come back to life. . . . Life comes from the union of *hun* and *po*, and death from their separation. But the *hun* existing and the *po* not yet dissipated are still inextricably linked and sympathetic, much as leaves and branches are related to roots.

During the Zhou and Han dynasties, Han seem to have thought that most dreams were due to out-of-body experiences by *hun*, often in response to strong emotion or desire. Later on, as the influence of Buddhism made desire seem more earthly (*yin*) and less spiritual (*yang*), some commentators began to attribute dreams to travels of the *po*. The change from virile and spiritual to womanish and fleshly reflects the increasing tendency for intellectuals to dismiss the significance of dreams. A Ming dynasty essayist reflects this change:

Hun live in people's hearts and roam in the eyes, generating all states of wakefulness. *Po* roam the kidneys and live in the liver, generating all dream states.

But then why does waking seem solid and dreaming vacuous? Because *hun* transmigrate from epoch to epoch, their habits are set, their ideas fixed. Hence the states of consciousness they generate are hard to rarify or destroy. But *po* grow with the body, with superficial habits and evanescent ideas; hence the states of consciousness they generate vanish as soon as they arise. All *hun* cognition partakes of Reality, so waking states are alike. But *po* states evolve from specific fetal *qi*, so that dream states vary from person to person (Adapted from quote in Ong, 1985, pp. 24–25).

Hunpo can temporarily depart the body, typically as part of a startle reaction, causing "soul loss," a familiar affliction for East Asian peoples. The set phrases for being scared out of one's wits (Beijing Weiguoyu Xueyuan Yingyushi, 1982, ## 1960–1961, p. 3905) are

Hun bu fu ti: Soul not close to body
Hunfei posan: Hun fly po disperse
Shihun luopo: Lose hun sink po

They can also be attracted out of the body when one *si* (thinks of, yearns for, remembers) a loved person, as implied in a Tang dynasty poet's song (Wei Zhuang, quoted in Fusek, 1982, pp. 5–6):

Bu zhi hun yi duan: Not know soul already snap-in-two
Kong you meng xiang sui: empty are dream together follow
chu que tian bian yue: except but sky edge moon
Mei ren zhi: there's no person know

We didn't know our hearts would be torn apart,
That only empty dreams of being together would follow.
Except for the moon on the horizon,
No one knew.

Hun, split from each other like this or from their home, fly to the person or place they love and appear in lovers' dreams, as discussed later. The *po* of suicides, of the drowned or of people who died during childbirth, like po not treated with respect at funerals, may turn into ghosts (*gui*) that demand redress in dreams (Ong, 1985, pp. 30–36).

Using Dream Accounts

Divination During The Late Zhou to Early Sung Dynasties

This section discusses how ruling-class men used dream accounts for divination from the Zhou to the Sung dynasty. All forms of divination, including oneiromancy, were important during this period. Thus the emperor Wu, who overthrew a former dynasty to found the Zhou, supposedly had a dream confirmed by scapulimancy, justifying his treachery (e.g., Palmer et al., 1986, p. 113). The Legalist prime minister of the totalitarian Qin dynasty that followed Zhou ordered the burning of all poetry, songs, philosophical treatises, and histories not focused on Qin, but made an exception for books on medicine, agronomy, and divination (Sima, 1979, pp. 178, 181).

Words For Divination: The Han phrase for interpreting dreams was *zhan meng*. *Zhan* refers to many forms of divination; for example, *zhanxing*, cast a horoscope; or *zhanke*, divine by tossing coins. The character for *zhan* combines the one for scapulimancy and the one for mouth, suggesting "to ask about an enterprise by singeing a turtle shell or shoulder bones." The "scapulimancy" (*bu*) character is a vertical line with a short line (later a dot) extending from its midpoint to the right, representing the lengthwise and widthwise cracks in the tortoise shell. The "mouth" character is a square.

The word for "outside" or "foreign" (*wai*) combines the characters for evening and *bu*, reflecting an ancient ritual rule. Oneiromancy by means of scapulimancy had to occur the day after the dream. "Evening divination" was "outside" these ritual limits (Wieger, 1965, p. 151). As will become clear, Han oneiromancy almost always requires verification by using forms of divination unrelated to dreams. Dreams are not reliable just by themselves.

General Divinatory Theory: What interest did agnostic ruling class men have in dreams? The answer seems to be that, from Han dynasty times on, oneiromancy and other forms of divination served political ends. There was no safe way for bureaucrats to criticize the emperor's policies directly. Han dynasty bureaucrats devised several indirect ways of doing so; for example, in 120 B.C., during the reign of Wu Di when the influence of shamans (*wu*) and magicians (*fangshi*) was at its peak (DeWoskin, 1983; Henricks, 1983, pp. 60n–61n). It was they who set up the Music Bureau (*Yuefu*), a conservatory that collected the songs in which ordinary people expressed their feelings (Hung, 1985, pp. 21–22). They could then present the emperor creatively edited copies of songs which reflected popular dissatisfaction with imperial policies.

They also worked out a theory of omens and portents, for which they found or created evidence by a retrospective interpretation of unusual events in earlier times (De Groot, 1912, pp. 256, 273-277). The HAN SHU, the Han book, usually translated as *The History of the Former Han Dynasty*, is a rich source of material on this theory of omens, which incorporates oneiromancy. The theory modified the traditional notion that anomalies (*guai*, Table 15.3) or strange dreams were *shen guang, shen* revealed, as expressed in the set phrase *gui shi shen chai* (Beijing Weiguoyu Yingyushi, 1982, p. 113), "sent as messages or on errands by *gui* and *shen*." The premise was this: "The genesis of all such portents and wonders is errors in the state," according to a leading Han dynasty Confucian historian quoted by De Bary, Chan, and Watson (1960, p. 171). The times at which the *Han Shu* reports a proliferation of ominous dreams and scary portents were precisely the times that scholar bureaucrats had the most reason to be upset with government policy (De Bary, Chan, and Watson 1960, vol. 1, pp. 170–178). Therefore dream accounts in the ancient Han literature reflect bureaucratic infighting at least as much as they reflect psychic events (De Groot, 1912, pp. 251–253; Dentan, 1988a).

Intellectuals propagated this theory retrospectively. Sima Qian, the Han dynasty Herodotus, recalls several portents that the emperor of the dynasty overthrown by the founder of the Han dynasty allegedly refused to heed (Sima, 1979, p. 182). Among them was a dream:

> The emperor dreamed that he had a fight with a sea god which had assumed human form. He consulted his scholars about this dream and they said, "The gods of the sea are invisible but they may take the form of giant fish, sea-serpents or dragons. Though you have taken such care to offer prayers and sacrifice, this evil spirit has appeared. It must be driven away so that good spirits will come in its place."
>
> Then the emperor ordered sailors to prepare implements to catch a great fish, and he waited with a repeating crossbow for the monster to appear so that he might shoot it himself. . . . he saw some great fish and shot and killed one of them. Then he . . . fell ill.
>
> Since the emperor could not bear to talk of death, his ministers dared not mention the subject either (Sima, 1979, pp. 184–185).

The great historian's account is a clear if subtle rebuke of emperors who do not heed omens as interpreted by scholar-bureaucrats, who intimidate scholar-bureaucrats or otherwise undermine their influence. Thus oneiromancy became one of the many weapons scholar-bureaucrats used to solidify their position (cf. section later on "Modern Dream Theory").

Discussing or even having dreams that did not serve such ends was frivolous. Thus even after the great Sung dynasty philosopher Zhu Xi (1130–1200) leavened sociological Confucianism with Buddhist psychologism, he questioned the propriety of dreaming. His "Jin Si Lu," a neo-Confucian anthology, avers (Zhu and Lu, 1967, pp. 148–149):

> 54. One can judge by his sleep whether his learning is profound or shallow. If in his sleep or dreams he is restless, it means his mind is not settled and his effort to preserve his mind is not firm.
>
> 55. Question: When one's mind is attached to something that is good and he dreams about it, is that not harmless?
>
> Answer: Although the thing is good, nevertheless the mind is aroused. There is no harm if one dreams of something which is an omen. Otherwise, the mind is aroused erroneously. . . . One's mind must be calm. It should think only when it is directed to do so. But today people let their minds operate without direction.

A thirteenth century commentator on this work (Ye Zai, quoted in Zhu and Lu, 1967, p. 149) adds: "Omens refer to fortune and misfortune.

When they are revealed in dreams, it means that the mind is acting according to the principle of influence and response. There is no harm in this. But if one dreams for no particular reason, it is all due to the mind's erroneous activity."

The only nonprognostic dream accounts that might prove acceptable to these Confucians would be those that justified Confucian goals (Lu, 1983, pp. 133, n. 12), as in the following self-serving report by one of the earliest literary critics, Liu Xie:

> When I was seven, I once dreamt of a cloud, colorful as brocade [a good omen, see Table 15.4], and in my dream I climbed to pluck it. At thirty, I had another dream, in which I saw myself carrying ritual vessels of wood and bamboo, walking behind Confucius. . . . Waking up early in the morning, I was overjoyed thinking how extraordinary it was for the Sage, not easily accessible to a mortal's eyes, to come into the dream of so undistinguished a person as I. I could not but reflect how the Sage overtowered all mankind in its entire history (Liu, 1983, pp.126, cf.180)

Of course, in Lui's time (c.465–c.532 A.D.) dreams were not as fully discredited as they were in the neo-Confucian Sung dynasty of Zhu and Ye.

The "Heart" Reacts But Does Not Create: Zhu and Ye express a corollary of the sociocentric theory of divination the Confucian scholar bureaucrats had devised. Proper dreams, "culture pattern dreams" (Dentan, 1987; Lincoln, 1936), can predict the future because they are sensitive to psychology. Personal influences would obscure the "message from *gui* and *shen*." The Chinese word *xin*, usually translated "mind" and denoted by the ideograph for "heart" (Wieger, 1965, p. 258), can be used in the sense of "individual psychology." The goal of the "Three Teachings," the Daoist-Buddhist-Confucian syncretism that served the gentry as religion, is to relieve the *xin* of the suffering caused by active striving to control the uncontrollable world and bring the *xin* to a completely reactive state, so that, rather than initiating anything, it simply "goes with the flow" of Dao, the way the world runs. Worthwhile dreams thus come from outside and are part of a healthy *xin*'s uneffortful attunement to reality. It is that attunement which makes the dreams predictive.

It is worth stressing, perhaps, that the traditional Han notion of *xin* does not stress creativity the way the Angloamerican notion of mind has since the Romantic era. General Lu Ji (261–303 A.D.) did write (Lu, 1983, p. 173) that poets "embrace" (*lan*) the *hun* dream-soul while trying to vivify imagination. But his central assumption is the traditional one, that poetry like dreams results from the right circumstances, which stimulate the right feelings. Only then does the mind (*xin*) or imagination (*shensi*, Table 15.3) become active, to pick the right words (Wong, 1983, pp. xviii, 52, 115, 121). Thus, although the Han recognized the connection between poetry and dreams, they took neither to be creative. Inspiration proverbially appears in a dream and disappears the same way, independent of the dreamer (Table 15.2, nos. 6, 13).

Table 15.4

A Sampling of Oneiromantic Equivalences from Han Texts

Heavens and Weather:

Rising or shining sun	+ (see note)	Palmer
or moon	+	Lip
Setting sun/moon	Servants cheat	Palmer
Thunder	+, thunder king calls	Palmer
Thunder	-	Lip
Clouds, dark ,drizzle	Someone's death	Palmer
	due to strong *yin*?	Lie
Storm, wind, rain	- due to strong *yin*?	Lip
		Lie
Walking through great	Strong yin	Lie
waters (nightmare)		
Phoenix	Letter from far away	Palmer
	(see LIVING CREATURES)	
Heaven's soldiers seen	Nobleman will aid you	Palmer
through sky door		
Shooting star	Sickness in your family	Palmer
	or legal problems	
Multicolored cloud	+, for whole family	Palmer,
		Lip
Cloudless starry sky	+	Palmer
Star enters cloud	You'll have a child	Palmer
Clouds coming from the	+, for business	Palmer
4 directions		
Star enters womb	Boy will be born	Eberhard
Holding star	Obtain high rank	Eberhardt
Flying to heaven	+	Lip
Snow falls on your body	+	Lip
Struck by lightning	+	Lip
Floating on air	You're dizzy	Lie

* Passage from song #189 in the SHI JING, "Book of Odes," ancient songs collected after 600 B.C. supposedly by Confucius (Birch, 1965, pp. 14–15)

** Passage from song #190 in the SHI JING (Ong, 1985, p. 12).

** Fox spirits are beautiful succubi (Eberhardt, 1986, pp. 117—118).

Table 15.4 (*Contnued*)

Flying	A flying bird is pecking your hair	Lie
House, Garden, Forest, Etc.:		
Healthy bamboo in forecourt	+	Palmer
Lying on large stone	+	Palmer
Playing with small stones	You'll have a child	Palmer
Trees die, new growth appears	Many and lucky decendents	Palmer
Grass and trees flourish	Happy family	Palmer
Trees and plants dry up	-	Lip
Falling tree	-	Lip
Crossing bridge hand in hand	Wife pregnant	Palmer
Walking to market with wife	Soon you buy property	Palmer
Damaged bridge	Legal problems	Palmer
Empty town	– – (you may be murdered)	Palmer
Empty house or city	-	Lip
Monk gives you cash	Job goes well	Palmer
Giving presents	You've eaten well	Lie
Getting presents	You're hungry	Lie
Orchard full of fruit	Decendents safe and well	Palmer
Garden growing well	+	Palmer, Lip
Standing under a tree	Nobleman will help you	Palmer
Broken sleeping platform	Someone will die	Palmer
You collect clear well water	+	Palmer
You collect cloudy well water	Danger	Palmer
New tomb and coffin	+ [pun: coffin = windfall]	Palmer
New coffin taken from tomb	+ [pun as previously]	Palmer
Bright soil around tomb	+	Palmer
Dark soil around tomb	-	Palmer
Putting body in coffin	+ [pun as previously]	Palmer
Dead or dying people	+ [pun as previously]	Lip
Funeral in house	+ [pun as previously]	Lip
Dead revive in house	+ [pun as previously]	Lip
Fire	Night is falling	Lie
Hill fire	Promotion because *yang* is strong	Palmer
House or woods afire	+, because *yang* is strong	Lip, Lie
Leaves falling from tree	- [see note]	Palmer
Repairing building, dike, etc	+	Lip

Table 15.4 (*Continued*)

Digging a well by a building	+	Lip
Building or tree collapses	-	Lip
Kitchen afire	-	Lip
	Yang (in woman area?)	Lie
Front door wide open	+	Lip
Gods, Fairies, Spirits, Etc.		
Visit temple	++ [good Buddhism or Daoism]	Palmer, Lip
Statues of Buddha on altar	++	Palmer
Dead person leaves coffin	+, wealth [pun as previously]	Palmer
Monk, nun or guru recite sutras	+	Palmer
You're with a goddess (devi)	Wife will bear fine son	Palmer
Dragon [see also snake]	+	Lip
Talking with *xian* (immortal)	+	Lip
Kilun (fabulous beast)	+	DeG 274
Human Body:		
Honoring parents or elders	++ [good Confucianism]	Palmer, Lip
Naked person	++	Palmer
No teeth, new teeth growing	Many descendents	Palmer
Man with wife in water	+	Palmer
Female genitals	Fight with kin or neighbor	Palmer
Your wife is pregnant	Her adultery	Palmer
You & wife honor each other	Divorce	Palmer
White or falling hair	Grief over male descendent	Palmer
Hand or foot with bleeding boil	+	Palmer, Lip
Teeth falling out	Parents are in danger	Palmer
Saying goodbye to brother	Quarrel	Palmer
Going with a woman	Lose money	Palmer
Sex with any woman	Dirty mind	Palmer
Eating	You're falling ill	Lie
Eating only vegetables	– –	Palmer
Being tied up	+	Lip
Washing or combing hair	+	Lip
Studying or learning	+ [good Confucianism]	Lip
Disharmony:		
Blowing flute, banging drum	Party	Palmer
Sick person cries or laughs	Sickness will be cured	Palmer
Killing or sparing	Yang and yin both strong	Lie
Killing chicken, duck, goose, or pig	++	Palmer
Killing lamb	-	Palmer

Table 15.4 *(Continued)*

You are killed	++	Palmer
Kill self with knife or ax	++	Palmer
Family quarrels at home	Family splits, some leave	Palmer
You drown	You have bad congestion	Lie
Living Creatures:		
Snakes or lizards	= dragon, +, or	Mrg 129
	since dragon = Yin, treachery	
Snakes	Girl children	*
	You fell asleep on	
	your belt	Lie
Snake becomes dragon	Nobleman comes to help	Palmer
Dying snake or lizard	Death of emperor	DeG 274
Lizard in well	Plotting bureaucrats	DeG 274
Many snakes	You plot deviously	Palmer
Snake bites you	Wealth	Palmer
Snake or centipede bites you	+	Lip
Snake indoors	+	Lip
Snake indoors	Insurrection or madness	DeG 276, 18
Turtle enters well	+ [turtle is longlived]	Lip
Crane, stork, heron	+	Mrg 128
Heron flies to heaven	You quarrel	Palmer
Stork or crane flies away	- [crane = long life]	Bkh 112
Parrot calls you	Major quarrel	Palmer
Swallow	- [= *Yin*]	Mrg 127
Swallow flies to you	Friend from far away visits	Palmer
Door with dragons	++	Palmer
Phoenix	Noble comes to help	Palmer
[see also *Heaven and Weather*]	+	DeG 274
Peacock	+ (= phoenix)	Palmer
Peacock	+ (= phoenix)	Mrg 126
Reeves pheasant	+ (= phoenix)	Mrg 125
Bird flies at your belly	You'll have a son	Palmer
Bird flies into your home	-	Palmer
Hen hatches egg	+	Palmer
Hen stands on tree	Wealth	Palmer
Cock	Yang, i.e. success	Mrg 127
Red cock	As previously, vs. fire	Bkh 113
White cock	Overcome bad horoscope	Bkh 167
Cock on rooftree	-	Mrg 127
Goose	+ [= *yang*]	Mrg 128
Pair of geese	Conjugal fidelity	Mrg 128
Mandarin ducks	Conjugal fidelity	Mrg 128

Table 15.4 (Continued)

Cat catches rat	+	Lip
Barking dog	-	Lip
Strange dog	Wealth	Bkh 168
Dying pig	-	Lip
Catching fish	+	Lip
Fish becomes shrimp	-	Lip
Carp	+ [fish are longlived]	Bkh 30
Cow enters house	+	Lip
Horse	Speed, stamina	Bkh 64
Hare	Long life	Lip
White rabbit	+	DeG 276
Deer	Long life	Bkh 140
Riding white horse or deer	Death [take soul to heaven]	Bkh 112
Ride a tiger	Obtain high rank	Eberhard
White tiger	Courage, wealth	Mrg 19
Roaring lion	+	Lip
Bear	Bravery	Mrg 65
	Boy children	*
Macaque	Success esp. by trickery	Mrg 66
Bat	Long life [pun: character	Mrg 67
	resembles that for "joy"]	Bkh 113
Wolf	Lose Mandate of Heaven	DeG 18, 227
Elephant	Wisdom	Bkh 142
Fox	Wealth	Bkh 139
Fox indoors	Sexual depravity endangers owner of house [a]	DeG 18, 277 ***
Chinese raven-crow	-	Mrg 128
Quail	+/- poverty or courage	Mrg 129
Magpie	+, pun on word for "merriment"	Mrg 130 Bkh 112
Bees	Lose war	DeG 277
Locusts	+	**
Clothes, Jewelry, Etc.:		
Ship or boat sailing fast	You become a rich noble	Palmer
Your clothes are muddy	Hard pregnancy for your wife	Palmer
Fish smashes boat	-	Palmer
Vehicles do not move	Your application rejected	Palmer
Boat under bridge	+	Palmer
Lamp or candle lit	+	Palmer
Cloudy mirror	-	Palmer
Rattle expensive hairpins	Your wife leaves you	Palmer
You have bamboo-leaf roof	Worry	Palmer

Table 15.4 (*Continued*)

Your belt or sash falls off	+	Palmer
Lying on a boat	-	Palmer
Your vehicle is broken	-	Palmer
or running backwards	-	Palmer
Patient but in ambulance	– –	Palmer
Any vehicle moves off	+	Palmer
Picking up money	+	Palmer
Needle and thread	Everything succeeds	Palmer
Bright gold hairpin	You'll have a noble son	Palmer
Flags, banners	Many descendents	**

Source: Texts used include the following:

1. Duke of Zhou (traditionally, c. 1020 B.C.). "Commentary on the Yi Jing," preserved in the LI SHU, "Alamnac," as "Old Mr. Zhou's Book of Lucky and Unlucky Dreams," of which Palmer et al. (1986, pp. 112–116) gives the first third. Eberhard (1952, p. 34) gives some other excerpts from an almanac, and many of Lip's (1985) interpretations are from almanacs.

2. Ban Gu (32–92 A.D.), HAN SHU, "History of the former Han Dynasty." Most references from Morgan (1942) [Mrg], DeGroot (1912) [DeG], and some from Lip (1985) are from this book, written in the second half of the Han dynasty.

3. Burkhardt (1954) [Bkh]

4. Liezi (Lie 1990, pp. 66–67) the third great Taoist book, after the Do De Jing and the Zhuangzi, and the one most closely connected with folk Daoism [Lie].

Note: The topical arrangement in this table follows that of the Duke of Zhou. + indicates general good luck, e.g. a rising sun or moon means "your family will be fine, prosperous, well educated and have important jobs" (Palmer et al., 1986, p. 114); ++ is for very good luck.

– indicates danger, e.g., leaves falling from a tree suggest your family is in danger of, e.g., being murdered (Palmer et al., 1986, p. 114); – – is for extreme danger

"You" = dreamer

Still, the traditional Han oneirology recognized the part individual psychology plays in creating dreams. The most important word here is *si*, the character that combines brain and heart, apparently on the theory that when one is thinking, the vital "material force" (*qi*) goes from heart (*xin*) to the brain (Weiger, 1965, p. 111). The ideograph for brain may be cognate with the one in the ideograph for *gui*, which means "head." Because Han psychological concepts do not split thought from feeling in the bizarre but compulsory Western manner, *si* resists translation: think (of), consider, deliberate, long for, yearn. What you *si* in the day, you dream of at night (Table 15.2, no. 12). The Han equivalent of "he wants it so much he can taste it" is "he wants it so much he dreams about it" (Table 15.2, no. 8). But si, being "private" (the Han word for "private" is a homonym), gives rise to dreams unworthy of scholar bureaucrats exquisitely attuned to social welfare. The same holds true for *yuan*, to have one's feelings hurt, to be aggrieved, and thus to be resentful.

Love, particularly in poetry, was a prime cause of the *si* and *yuan* that made the Han dream, as in the poem that titles this chapter (for love and dreams in East Asian poetry, see Lee, 1979, pp. 132–140). Tang poets associated this *si* and *yuan* with spring (*chun*) or a woman's boudoir (*gui*) and noted that these emotions caused dreams (e.g., Y. Li 1984; F. Liu, 1984; Y. Liu, 1984; Jia, 1984; Wang Changling, 1984a, 1984b). In poetry, abandoned women were reluctant to wake from such dreams (e.g., B. Zhang, 1984; Z. Zhang, 1984; Jin, 1984a, 1984b).

The great Tang poet Li Bai (1984) writes in "Chang Xiang Si" (Long Yearnings for Each Other):

> *Tian chang di yuan hun fei ku*: Heaven long earth far soul
> fly bitter
> *Meng hun bu dao guan shan*: Dream soul not arrive pass
> mountain difficult
> *Chang xiang si cui xin gan*: Long each-other yearn urge
> heart courage

> The sky too vast, the earth too huge for suffering hun to fly
> In dreams my hun cannot cross the harsh mountain passes
> Long we've loved each other; be brave, heart.

But because Buddhists and Daoists teach that desire, always ultimately frustrated, causes all human misery, dreams that come from *si* or *yuan* exemplify the stupidity of human striving. Wei Zhuang (1984), a Tang poet (see section above entitled Hunpo), looking at a picture of Jinling, which served as capital for six dynasties, comments:

> *Jiang yu feifei jiang cao q*i: River rain pelt river grass
> alike
> *Liu chao ru meng niao kong ti*: Six dynasties like dream
> bird empty caw

> The river rain falls heavily on river and grass alike;
> Six dynasties are gone like dreams; birds vainly cry.

Ancient Attitudes Toward Dreams

Introduction

Han dream praxis (putting theory into practice) was never internally undifferentiated. For example, peasant women seem to have been more involved with dreams and other altered states of consciousness, like spirit possession, than their men were, a pattern that continues today (e.g., Potter, 1974; Sangren, 1988; Shanzhu, 1983, pp. 174; Shi, 1983, see section later entitled "Modern Dream Theory"). Han from the south seem to have been more interested in dreams than Northerners. Because dream praxis was never undifferentiated, attitudes toward dreams are not and never were uniform. Generally, as we will discuss, Confucians (or Maoists) and urban bureaucrats tended to doubt the significance of dreams, whereas Daoists (or Buddhists) and rural peasants were more credulous. Oneiromancy peaked during the Han dynasty (206 B.C.–220 A.D.) and declined thereafter. Except where indicated, due to considerations of space and relative accessibility of material, this section focuses on the dream praxis and the attitudes toward dreams of ruling class intellectual men, the scholar-bureaucrats. Modern dream praxis and attitudes of ruling-class women, which share many similarities with those discussed here, will be discussed later.

Dealing only with the attitudes and praxis of the ruling class has consequences. The cultural gulf between Han gentry, especially highly literate scholar-bureaucrats, and the rest of the people, especially illiterate peasants, has been almost unbridgeable (but cf. Sangren, 1988). Bureaucrats might romanticize or sympathize with peasants; a few might try to bridge the gap, like the Tang dynasty poet Bai Juyi, who reportedly chanted his poetry to an old peasant woman and deleted any passages she did not understand; but none of them, including Bai, wanted peasants as friends or thought of themselves as being in any important way like peasants.

Although Nationalist folklorists recognized how oral folk tradition inspired ruling-class literature (e.g. Hung, 1985, pp. xii, 4–7), they stressed the antagonism between the two streams. And although Mao Zedung repeatedly railed against the alienation of the intelligentsia from the people (e.g., 1967a, 1967b, 1967c), and although the national trauma of the Great Proletarian Cultural Revolution was ostensibly about smashing such "contradictions," we have noticed a tendency, even among dedicated Communist bureaucrats, still to wrinkle their noses or sneer slightly when talking about peasants. Peasants and workers, in turn, still resent intellectuals. As late as 1985, workers in Beijing beat up teachers whose school had added an extra story, so that it overshadowed the workers area, an attack that intellectuals told Dentan reflected class antagonisms that flourished during the Cultural Revolution.

Variation by Class and Gender

At first, during the late Zhou and early Han dynasties, the conflict between the visionary and the intellectual streams of Chinese thought had not taken on its class and gender structure. There seem to have been three main reasons for this disjuncture: empiricism, xenophobia, and politicization.

Empiricism: First, the focus on Dao, the way things work, led intellectuals into an intense empiricism about how things did work. Concern with proper categorization ("calling things by their right names") and enumeration became almost obsessive: the five poisonous creatures, sense organs and Classics; the eight syndromes, trigrams; and so forth. Scientific observation required a degree of rigor impossible for oneiromancy. Horoscopy or geomancy thus promised better results. Quantifiable or enumerative research was good, interpretation unscientific. This attitude is familiar to students of dreams today (De Woskin, 1983, pp. 7–9).

The constant, increasingly vicious internecine warfare that characterized the late Zhou dynasty made people cynical about traditional praxes of all kinds. Wandering intellectuals with no firm political loyalties traveled from state to state peddling new ideas, like the ancient Greek Sophists, and involving themselves in intrigue and treachery. The military theoretician SUNZI (13, p. 4) summed up what the warlords had learned: "What is called 'foreknowledge' cannot be elicited from spirits, nor from gods, nor by analogy with past events, nor from calculations. It must be obtained from men who know the enemy situation" Sun, 1963, p. 145). The great Confucian Xunzi summed up the equivalent scholar bureaucrat attitude in his "Essay on Heaven" (Watson, 1958, p. 85): "You pray for rain and it rains. Why? For no particular reason, I say. It is as though you had not prayed for rain and it rained anyway . . . it is not as though you could hope to accomplish anything by such ceremonies. They are done merely for ornament. Hence the gentlemen regards them as ornaments, but the common people regard them as supernatural. He who considers them ornaments is fortunate; he who considers them supernatural is unfortunate."

This empiricism pervaded Han oneiromancy. Dream interpretation assumed that dreams reflected reality more or less literally, just like waking perception, also unreliable: sleep on a belt, dream of a snake. Thus in 70 A.D. the story of a Han emperor's dream of a huge Buddha rationalized putting up a huge statue of Buddha, marking the bureacracy's willingness to accommodate the foreign religion (H. Yang, 1984, pp.

4–5). A big Buddha means a big Buddha, in what semanticists call an "indexical" interpretation: what you see is what you get. To preserve flexibility in their maneuvres, however, the scholar-bureaucrats could refer to symbolic equivalences drawn from *Yin-Yang* theory or established by precedent in the extensive annals of bureaucratic infighting (see Table 15.4).

Xenophobia: The second reason for the divergence of visionaries from intellectuals was that *wu,* shamans (see Table 15.2), who claimed contact with spirits and the ability to cure the sick, seem to have come mainly from outside the Han heartland, especially from the huge southern state of Chu along the Yangtze River, from Yi country in modern Sichuan and from the small states of Yan and Chi in the northeast (Creel, 1970, p. 12; DeWoskin, 1983, p. 3). Han feared, hated, and despised the non-Han. "Outsider" warriors helped rebels topple Chinese dynasties and often held sway over parts of the central country; for example, during the Liao dynasty. Indeed, the last Chinese dynasty was Manchu, not Han, and Mongols, not Han, incorporated the southern tribes into the central country. Han battled Northerners into the 1940s (Mao Zedung, 1967a, p. 255) and in a number of officially unacknowledged uprisings in the 1970s and 1980s.

Even today official tours of Bai country in Yunnan are likely to elide the fact that the "Tang dynasty" monuments there were built by non-Han peoples and to bypass the "Tomb of Ten Thousand Men" (Wan ren zhong) near Xiaguan, where lie the Tang troops slaughtered by the Bai soldiers of Nanzhao in 754. The Tang poet Bai Juyi's great antiwar poem "Xinfeng zhebei weng" about draft resistance memorializes the terror ordinary Chinese felt at the prospect of fighting in the south (Alley, 1981, pp. 56–58; Waley, 1941, pp. 89–192; Yang and Yang, 1984, p. 119; cf. Stover, 1974, p. 72). Chinese poetry recurrently describes the bloody horror of endless futile warfare along the frontiers, century after century (e.g. Alley, 1981, pp. 59, 60, 86, 114–120, 137, 175–182; Xu, 1984, pp. 17–19, 87–90, 154–156). The Tang poet Li Bai's grisly antiwar poems describe tribal people: "tigers and wolves," "fierce tigers, great snakes, which each day grind their teeth and drink the blood of those they meet" (Alley, 1981, pp. 21, 116; Yang and Yang, 1984, p. 22). As Mencius said, Han could conceive of using the Han culture to change barbarians, but not the other way around.

Politicization: In early Han dynasty times, when the influence of magicians and shamans was at its height, they read and wrote books of arcana and vied for power with Han scholar-bureaucrats who stressed

Confucian virtues in reaction against the book-burning Legalists of the dynasty they had overthrown. Badmouthing alien superstitions came easily to the embattled bureaucrats. Confucius himself never talked of prodigies, force, disorder, gods or spirits (ANALECTS, 7:21). Asked what wisdom was, he said: "To work for the things the common people have a right to and to keep one's distance from the gods and spirits while showing them reverence can be called 'wisdom'" (ANALECTS, 6:22; Lau, 1979, p. 84). Dreams, as the experiences of the "soul," were not proper subjects of conversation. By the end of the Han dynasty the influence of visionaries (*fangshi*) in ruling circles was mostly confined to people's private lives.

Around this time Daoism split into two schools. Intellectuals followed the example of the great Daoist teacher Zhuangzi, who made elaborate mock of *wu*, shamans (ZHUANGZI, 3:17a–18b; Zhuang, 1968, pp. 94–97). Their Daoism was a contemplative, back-to-nature, mystical but atheistic philosophy oriented toward maintaining serenity in trying times. Dreams became metaphors for the unreality and stupidity of striving (Dentan, 1988a). Folk Daoist priests, by contrast, made *wu* visionary practices their own and became devoted to the pursuit of immortality (Creel, 1970).

Folk Daoism celebrates an enormous divine bureaucracy that replicates the Chinese state, staffed by divinities encountered in dreams and visions (Overmyer, 1986, pp. 51–53; Sangren, 1988; Seaman, 1987). Since the sixteenth century, the central figure in many variants of folk religion is the Great Mother, perhaps reflecting the importance of women in popular religion (Overmyer, 1986, p. 54).

Peasant women could be folk Daoist priestesses, although male priests were in charge. Women could also be spirit mediums, and several obtained a good deal of power through their revolutionary visions. An early nineteenth century Han commentator observes that folk religion: "does not call itself a teaching (*jiao*) but . . . there is no one who does not practice it. Even women and children—illiterates—frequently see and hear (it performed). It is their teaching, and compared with Confucianism, Buddhism and Taoism, it is more widespread" (quoted in Ropp, 1981, p. 53; Seaman, 1987, p. 13). Cults in which spirits, working through a medium, write messages in sand are still popular among the overseas Han (Sangren, 1988; Seaman, 1978; Seiwart, 1981; Thompson, 1982).

Folk religion, continually both refreshed and ideologically fragmented by visionary experiences (including dreams) was a constant threat to the ruling class. The scholar bureaucrats might despise it, but they also feared it enough to outlaw it, particularly after the Mongol conquest that established the Yuan dynasty and made folk religion a rallying point for anti-Mongol sentiments. Thus visionary folk religion fostered secret societies, some of which degenerated into gangster organizations such as the Triads. Nevertheless, the worry of the bureaucrats about folk religion was justified. In the middle of the Han dynasty, a Daoist immortality movement worshipping Xi Wangmu, the Queen Mother of the West, flourished briefly. They were followed by the explicitly revolutionary Yellow Turban movement (Taiping Dao), put down by the government, and the Five Bushels of Rice Way (Tianshi Dao) which was instrumental in the fall of the Han rulers (Overmyer, 1986, pp. 33–39). Later on, such movements were active in overthrowing the Manchu regime (Comber, 1961), and even today the Nationalists on Taiwan seek to coopt folk Daoist "mother goddess" cults (Sangren, 1988).

Dreams remained of significance in such movements at least until the final collapse of the Nationalists in the 1940s (and probably thereafter):

> [O]ne of the local soothsayers had dreamed that a baby was to be born in the district who would some day restore the empire and become the founder of a new dynasty. The dream and the talk about it were seized upon by enemy agents, who used handbills and a whispering campaign to proclaim the royal birth and inspire revolt against the [Nationalist] Central Government. Within a few days this farfetched story had gained hundred of supporters. Groups began to discuss the great wealth and prestige possible if they were to rise up and place this babe on the throne, an instance of how new dynasties had risen from just such beginnings were cited as local feelings became intense. The local leaders had to step in, stop the meetings, and arrest a few of the leaders before the incident quieted down (Winfield, 1948, p. 199)

Folk religion, and thus most oneiromancy, became a class and gender marker. It was all right for women and children, peasants and merchants, unless it threatened the state. Perhaps one might indulge in it oneself in private. But in public, ruling-class men were ostensibly too sophisticated and worldly for such superstitious nonsense. The only exception was for oneiromancy affecting state matters.

Modern Dream Theory

In the suburbs [towns around Beijing], older people are usually superstitious whereas their children are Marxist, or less superstitious as they are in the different times. My grandmother, aged 74, believes in gods and does what we regard as superstitious. She would not eat meat on the first day of the lunar calendar and says people born at a certain year should not marry those born at another year [who] are characteristically different. My parents are pure Communists, and they never say and do what ever they think is not socialist. They call those fancy dressed youngsters dandies and believe they are not honest. My sister and I, the third generation, know more modern terms and [W]estern life. We don't believe what our grandmother says and think our parents are too monotonous. (College man, 19 years old, Beijing, 1985)

Introduction

During the Great Proletarian Cultural Revolution, when most of the students who reported dreams were growing up, Maoism stressed rejecting all old cultural systems like oneiromancy, without offering substitutes (Wee, 1988, p. 24). After the Revolution, Maoism stressed public and political life over private life and devalued irrational experience other than "revolutionary fervor." Life was real and earnest, not metaphorically a dream. Dreams were therefore too private and too irrational to be of interest to Maoists. A study of 271 Han and 340 American students indicates that relatively few Han say they like dreaming ($p <$ .001), and few (12.6 percent) agree with Americans (80.7 percent, $p <$. 001) that dreaming is good for one's health (Walls, 1985, p. 9; Walters and Dentan, 1985b). As the foregoing account shows, this materialist attitude toward dreams was not a sharp break with the pre-Revolutionary past.

Skepticism, however, did not permeate the whole society. It became, instead, another facet of Han oneirology, the congeries of disparate ideas people use to explain how and why dreams happen. Like most other peoples' dream theory, Han oneirology lets people interpret dreams more or less as they see fit (Dentan, 1987, p. 321, 1988c). Many of the eighty-one dream narratives collected in Beijing use two or more principles to make sense of a single dream. This flexibility is not infinite, however, as all the principles address the question of how dreams relate to waking life. Thus, although the Han describe the first and last principles we present as mutually opposite, they seem to be opposite sides of the same coin. Each contributes to the ambivalence modern Chinese students express about dreams. Discussing dreams seems to keep these notions both alive and in conflict.

In this half of the chapter, numbers and numbers preceded by TC refer to written Beijing narratives, of which only a few have been published (Walters and Dentan, 1985a, 1985b). Letters refer to the four students in Buffalo with whom McClusky discussed dreams. These students prefer to remain anonymous. McClusky conducted the interviews in English and transcribed them according to the method popularized by Dennis Tedlock (1983), which preserves nuances lost in standard prose transcriptions (Scheff, 1986). The quotes from Tung (1986), a Taiwanese woman oneiromancer, put in lowercase the capital letters she uses for dream accounts.

Principle 1: Dreams Reflect Emotions from Everyday Life

"What you think about or long for during the day is what you dream about at night" (Table 15.2, no. 12).

All the Buffalo students and most of the Beijing narratives concur with the traditional notion that dreams are not creative but reflective (see section earlier entitled "Using Dream Accounts").

> I just believe that
> [softly] when something is on people's mind
> [softly] they dream about it. (XM)

According to my experience, dreams are related to activities recently taking place and emotions. (37)

Chinese classical literature had kept dream very mysterious until recently. Now modern sciences reveal that dreams are a sort of reflection of people's daily lives. It is a normal psychological phenomenon of the human brain. (28)

[M]y dreams are almost the reflection of daily events. (71)

Maoist modernism apparently succeeded in eradicating traditional oneiromancy to the extent that students attributed this ancient oneiromantic principle (Lie, 1990, pp. 66-67) to "modern science" or "personal experience." The transformation in rhetoric obscures the continuity in function. Dreams remain in Han theory reflections of daily life, the result of thinking a lot, experiencing events, feeling strong emotions or desires. After a nightmare, a Beijing woman student writes: "I began to think of the reason for having such a dream. I tried to associate it with something dreadful which might have happened to me during the day. Unfortunately I found none." This procedure is traditional. Tung (1986, p. 1) writes that, after a dream, she will "recall freely what happened the last three or four days, then try hard to find out what I was thinking before I slept last night." Purposive recall turns up events or emotions that dreamers can then interpret as explaining the dream, thus reinforcing the oneiromantic credibility of the reflective principle by using it. This feedback loop probably in part accounts for the persistence of the principle on the Chinese mainland.

Despite revolutionary changes, similar unacknowledged persistence of traditional practice under a modified or absent rationale characterizes modern Han life. A Hong Kong reporter, for example, describes a woman spirit-medium who before the Revolution achieved political influence by narrating her visionary experiences and dreams but afterward retained it by talking "frequently and systematically on the new political line" (quoted in C. K. Yang, 1959, p. 132). The inspirational rationale is different; but, as Han women have traditionally done (see sections entitled "Using Dream Accounts" and "Ancient Attitudes Toward Dreams"), this woman continues to use her inspiration to influence community affairs.

The similarity of the reflective principle to Freud's "day residue" merits discussion. The Han version is not hermeneutic. Events in waking life repeat themselves in dreams because they make a "deep impression" on dreamers. I dreamed about taking a test because I was nervous about upcoming exams. I dreamed about a race because I attended a track meet. The dream is an "index," it replicates reality; it is not an "icon," a representation of reality (B. Mannheim, 1987).[6] There is no hidden meaning. A footrace is just a footrace, not a metaphor for, say, sexual activity or competition with my father.

Furthermore, the emotions that give rise to dreams are conscious. Like the widows of ancient times in the quote we use for the title of the chapter, modern Han students attribute their dreams to conscious feelings (especially *si*). The students assertion that, in dreams, what you see is what you get, may be a way of denying dissociated impulses by excluding iconic or predictive interpretations.

Such denial would be consistent with the emotional reserve that the Han attribute to themselves and that shows up in Song's (1985) interpretation of Han MMPI profiles (cf. Jiobu, 1976; Kleinman, 1977; Kuo, 1979; Suzuki, 1977; Tseng, 1975). Moreover, it might partially explain the traditional tendency of Han intellectuals to play down the significance of dreams. But the same reluctance to communicate feelings directly may make talking about dreams a way to express otherwise private desires, worries, thoughts, and experiences (cf. Cheung, 1982; Cheung and Lau, 1982; Ruel, 1970, pp. 348–349). Of the seventy-eight Beijing dream narratives, the average contained 2.25 references to emotion, about three times the American average of 0.70 reported by Hall and Van de Castle (1966).

McClusky therefore asked Han students in Buffalo to whom they told their dreams, that is, which relations are most appropriate for this indirect discussion of personal feelings and experiences. They said they rarely discuss dreams, for fear that people will think them egoistic; not a Maoist or Confucian virtue. The dreams they tell for amusement are not those they attribute to emotions they felt during the day, they said. One would tell such dreams only to close friends or, better, a close kinswoman, preferably one's father's mother, the closest senior woman in one's patrilineage. The traditional notion persists that dreams are too trivial to merit men's attention, only "old women" pay attention to such "small things." As one student said, she would talk with her father about dreams, but he is generally not interested in such minor manners. The modern day emphasis on "old" folks' interest in dreams as a means to express negativity about dreams may reflect the Maoist attempt to divorce oneself from the feudal ways of the past. But it also embodies the ancient belief that women are more involved than men in dreams and visions (Potter, 1974; Shanzhu, 1983, p. 174; Shi, 1983; Shilang, 1983; see section earlier entitled "Ancient Attitudes Toward Dreams").

Actual behavior seems to match these expressed norms. The women interviewed all volunteered a dream account, the men did not. Although McClusky's own gender may have influenced the responses of the people she talked with, most (71 percent) Beijing students who volunteered dream accounts were women. Indeed, both American and Han women are more likely to say they talk about dreams than the men are ($p < .001$) (Walls, 1985, p. 9; cf. Eberhard, 1986). A woman would normally tell her dream to a woman friend, who would then interpret it for her (e.g., dream account TC 10). Telling dreams thus may reflect and cement ties among women. Because men narrate dreams less often, they have less access to this reinforcement for dream narration; lacking that reinforcement, they narrate dreams less often. This sort of closed feedback is cross culturally characteristic of cultural systems that segregate social categories, particularly where gender is involved (Bateson, 1958, pp. 175–197).

The following recurrent dream by a women in the senior class at Beijing teachers' college is typical.

After I took the post-graduate exams, I had a dream like this:

I was asked to take a series of exams, I failed in all of them. I was very depressed and disappointed with myself. When I went back to school, lots of students sneered at me and teased me. When I got home, my father said I was useless and stupid, and all the money he had spent on me was in vain. I cried and cried and asked myself what to do. My mother came and soothed me. She told me that it did not matter and there were many chances. She asked me to go to another exam the next day. But I don't know why I had the dream just like the previous one once again (7, TC 7)

Since the Han Dynasty instituted open civil service exams in 196 B.C., passing tests has been one of the main ways Han gain power and prestige. Test scores were a main reason for fluctuations in the power and wealth of families (F. L. K. Hsu, 1967, pp. 3n, 292, 300). Most Han valued education primarily as a means to wealth rather than an end in itself, and drop-out rates, especially in the country, remain high (F. L. K. Hsu, 1967, pp. 237–239; Butterfield, 1982, pp. 196–197; Wei and Li, 1983, pp. 21–22). Nowadays, along with party membership or military promotion, education is what a young person needs to move up socially. Most people, however, reject the Confucian notion that education is valuable in and of itself: "What use is studying? Scribblers are not even as good as beggars. You can't eat culture, and you can't put ideas in the bank" (Wu Dunn, 1989, p. 18).

Although 220 million Han are illiterate, and the average adult has only about five years of schooling, there seems no question that, after the Revolution, school enrollments increased substantially, thereby greatly increasing competition (Geddes, 1963, pp. 45–46; Kessen, 1975, p. ix; Zhou, Cai, and Liu, 1983, pp.11–14, 25; Wu Dunn, 1989). Only about 3 percent of college-age Han can go to college. The key to success, since Mao's death, is passing the national university entrance exams, twelve and a half hours of tests in six subjects spread over three days. In 1980, of the 3.3 million students who qualified to sit for the tests, only 285,000 were admitted. Americans are familiar with college boards—the competition, the pressure, the anxiety, but the Chinese exams involve even more tension (Butterfield, 1982, p. 198). Parents and teachers pressure students to do well in school. Failure reflects badly not only on the students but on their families (Suzuki, 1979).

The most common theme in the eighty-one dream narratives is test anxiety (e.g., Walters and Dentan, 1985a). Tung's temple charity group also dreams of exams (1986, p. 16). Sharing dream reports, like talking about upcoming tests, may both relieve the anxiety by sharing it and also reinforce the notion that school is stressful, creating a closed feedback loop of tension and release. This socially acceptable and pervasive emotion shows up in socially acceptable dream accounts.

As noted previously (see section entitled "Using Dream Accounts"), homesickness and longing for those from whom one is parted are traditional themes in classic Han poetry. Modern Han college students usually attend school away from their families. Family remains a central concern. Dream narratives of homesickness and family members reflect this socially acceptable and pervasive emotion, which is also explicable in terms of the second common principle of explanation, that dreams reflect social connections.

Principle 2: Dreams Reflect Attachments

> *For* example, uh
> your next of kin
> your parents especially
> *If* they are elderly
> and uh
> you are away from home
> far away from home
> and
> they are about to [softly] die
> and sometimes
> you *dream*
> * * *
> It comes through
> that message comes through in your dream. (F)

F, a young man, suggests that dreams may provide information about crises in the affairs of distant family members. Several other Han proposed that a "wave" or "connection" exists between family and close friends. This notion recalls Zhu Xi's already mentioned twelfth century comments on the role of "attachment" in dreaming. This connection keeps people in touch with those emotionally significant to them despite the distance between them. As young people in a system still fundamentally patriarchal they stressed the ties between father and child (cf. F. L.

K. Hsu, 1967) but also mentioned ties between husband and wife and a woman and her roommates.

Such connections last beyond death. Several Beijing accounts concern a dead relative, usually a father's mother, who says she is fine but misses the dreamer. She may suggest that the dreamer should not loose touch with her family. Unlike principle 1, the explanation of such dreams requires no preexisting emotion, like longing or nostalgia; the dreamer is completely passive, as in classical oneirology.

The dreamer who reports such visitation dreams may be referring to some of the ideas surrounding *hunpo* discussed earlier. A dream report that a deceased relatives says they are fine may signal that the image of the deceased is *hun*, rather than *po* or *gui* (ghost) (see section "Classic Oneirology"). Such reports suggest that the narrators and their families have expressed enough respect for the deceased to prevent a transformation to *gui*. Telling such a dream may relieve whatever narrators feel about the death.

The oneiromantic principle of connection may draw on Han folk sociology, according to which society is a web of *guanxi*, glossable as tie, connection, relationship, significance, or concern. The equivalent of English "You're welcome" is *mei guanxi*, "no obligation," which, like many polite phrases around the world, may connote the opposite of what it suggests. Han students consciously "network" by creating *guanxi* and assume that only by *guanxi* can one get good jobs (Butterfield, 1982, pp. 48–49). The only people on whom one can securely rely, however, are family and close friends. Therefore their *guanxi* is special.

F makes the kinship connection explicit:

> I I remember
> somebody told me that
> there was this man
> who
> dreamt about speaking a language
> that he NEVER encountered before
> * * *
> uh
> [McC: was he a linguist?]
> no no
> I don't think so
> and then
> * * *
> he found that his

FATHER
was a linguist and knew this language
so
[laughs]
there might be a connection between dream
and genetic make-up, (F)

Telling these dream accounts both reflects and reinforces ties between family members and close friends. The oneiromantic equation of close friends and family reflects and reinforces Han notions of friendship, which involve: "assurances and an intimacy that we have abandoned in America . . . psychic as well as material rewards that we have lost . . . the constant gift-giving and obligations left us uneasy" (Butterfield, 1982, pp. 47–48). In other words, kinship is the model for Han friendship, and close friends are by Han definition brought "inside" (*nei*) the circle of kinship (cf. Sangren, 1988, p. 687). The requirements are so steep that Han have few close friends. As one Beijing woman student wrote explaining her nightmares while growing up during the Cultural Revolution of 1966–76: "Many students, especially boys, did something awful. Many parents often told their children some horrible stories because they wanted their kids to know what there were some evil things in the world and let kids maintain sharp vigilance. I was really afraid." This "sharp vigilance" makes it hard to make friends, and the only ones mentioned in connection with principle 2 were roommates.

Principle 3: Dreams as Moral Messages

Thousands of people are gathering at a square where the awarding ceremony is being held. The head of the English Department is presenting the award to the several top students in our grade. These students, who deserve the honor of the awards, smile when they receive a gold medal and something that I can hardly remember. I feel ashamed of myself because I am not among them. It's mainly because I didn't try my best in the past years. I have the ability to be a top student but I didn't study hard. Several years passed and I didn't make any progress. At this time, I hear the awarded students give speeches, talking about their experiences, their study methods, and their way of life. After the speech, the head is giving his speech. He says that those who have the ability to get good grades but don't try their best should feel ashamed of themselves. They are no better than those who are not intelligent enough to be top students. The former are clear. And I am one of the former group. How could I wish I could start a brand new life in which I will take the advantage of any potential abilities . . .

> That's the dream I had a year ago. It indicated that I wasn't leading a satisfactory life. It is a kind of warning. Although I could sleep no more after the dream and felt quite bitter, that dream really affected my future life in some way. I don't want to analyze this dream. The only [thing] I want to say is that: it's my nature to take life as a game, which is not serious. I don't know how to do my best in life (42, TC 13).

This 20-year-old man's interpretation of his dreams seems to hark back to the traditional idea, first promulgated by Han dynasty bureaucrats, that dreams could be warnings to mend one's ways (see section earlier entitled "Using Dream Accounts," cf. ZUO ZHUANG, Watson, 1989, pp. 23, 28, 33). A few other Beijing students made similar interpretations (Walters and Dentan, 1985b). Oneiromancy in these cases tends to be iconic rather than indexical; that is, people recount these dreams as more surreal and symbolic than those interpreted by the first two principles.

Tung (1986, p. 5) also interprets a couple of her dreams as moral messages, for example, one of walking around the temple with a hat on her head: "This dream is trying to remind me that I was too proud to worship GODS in the temple with a hat on my head. Generally we should feel humble and take off the hat when we are in a temple or church. This dream is to correct my attitude." Sometimes, however, the message is confusing, as in this 19-year-old woman's dream.

> I used to have the same horrible dream not infrequently when I was in my early teens. But now I no longer dream that dream. Now the dream. Somehow my mother and I were watching a tiger. Then all of a sudden, the tiger rushed to my mother and opened its mouth to try to devour her. Being very much frightened I just watched that tiger and my mother. I was aware that moment that I should help her in any way I could. But I just remained where I was, not because my legs were unable to move, but because I didn't want to be confronted with that beast. Somehow, I couldn't see how[,] the tiger ate my mother but I only knew my mother was gone.
>
> I once told this dream to some of my classmates, and one of them said jokingly, "Oh, don't make friend[s] with her. She doesn't even help her mother." And this remark hurted not a little. Although during that time, I was sometimes impatient with my mother . . . I was far from disliking her. Did that dream tell me something which lurked in my unconsciousness? Did it mean my mother and I have any emotional split? Or what did it really mean? I'm eager to know. Could you help me? (3, no TC #)[7]

The classmate thus used principle 1 to condemn the appearance of unfilial behavior, which violates a central Han value (see principle 2). The dreamer's nervous denial of unfilial emotions fits the Han emotional behavior discussed earlier. Thus the response simultaneously uses the dream account to teach a moral lesson and reinforces the practice of not telling people dreams that might reveal socially disapproved emotions. Conversely, traditional accounts of how one dreamed of Confucius both celebrated Confucian virtues and raised the status of the dreamer (see section entitled "Using Dream Accounts"; Ong, 1985, pp. 65–67).

The reluctance, even in dream narratives, to express socially unacceptable emotions may in part account for the absence from our sample of dream accounts of becoming an animal. Such transformations may reflect ambivalence or internal conflict, (Ruel, 1970, pp. 348–349), which Han students in Beijing vehemently rejected as an element in their dreams or lives. Perhaps this same intolerance of ambiguity underlies the apparent rarity with which Han admit using dream narratives to resolve situations of uncertainty (Firth, 1967, pp. 293–294).

Even before the Revolution, a person who took his dreams as serious personal adjurations ran the risk of derision.

> In the southern Manchurian village where I grew up, one man aspired to obey the daily will of the gods by seeking to live out his dreams of the previous night. Each morning he would wander around his yard and roam to other parts of the neighborhood to which he supposed the gods had directed him, turning up stones in search of money and other valuables which the gods said lay hidden there. His conviction that personal rapport with the gods would bring him wealth was generally regarded by the villagers as the idea of a ne'er-do-well or the slightly insane. The only other persons who could commune with the spirits were the sick and women allegedly possessed by the essence of foxes [female succubae]. These persons were subjected to various treatments often involving physical torture. (F. L. K. Hsu, 1981, pp. 243-244)

This sort of "crazy" behavior also suggests Principle 4, that dreams reflect future as well as past experiences, to which we now turn.

Principle 4: Dreams Predict the Future

> Sometimes I dreamed
> and then
> the dream Really came True. (R)

I was feeling blue. Because just the day before we went to Bejing University, I had a strange and horrible dream, that dream seemed to me something aweful would happen . . . The result of going to the university was I bumped into another bike. My bike was heavily "hurt," while, fortunately, only my elbow and knee had a scratch (*TC14)

[S]ome people say dreams are unbelievable, and still others say dreams are prediction[s] of what will happen on the following day . . . (19, no TC #)

Last month, my boyfriend lost his wallet. On one Friday morning I dreamed that I saw it on the floor of our dining hall and picked it up. I was very glad because I heard that all dreams are not true except those you dream on Fridays. However, I still have not seen his wallet yet. Wish me good luck. (6, TC 61)

If it [a dream] is not concerned in the past or present, I have to wait for some time to prove my dreams. In [g]eneral it takes a few days or weeks or months to clarify the meanings of my dreams . . . Personally I have spent two years just in remembering my dream first, then awaited patiently to see what happen[s] next (Tung, 1986, p. 2)

People report that they usually tell predictive dreams after the predicted event happens, in part, as Tung suggests, because one cannot be sure what the dream predicts until the event occurs. Retrospective prophesy is, of course, not subject to disconfirmation or falsification and thus constitutes proof that dreams do predict. This principle recalls Ye Zai's thirteenth century "principle of influence and response," a modification of the principle of connection or attachment (see section entitled "Using Dream Accounts").

Therefore, in addition to the dream-fear in the nightmare, the Han feel uneasy about what a bad dream might mean, once interpreted. Telling nightmares before the obscurely predicted disaster occurs, mobilizes social support and thus partially relieves the anxiety that nightmares produce by definition. Moreover, at least in the country, the Han have a comforting interpretive principle that they can use, as follows.

Principle 5: Dreams Mean the Reverse of What They Suggest

[D]reams that I have alway[s] turn out contrary to the real result in daily life. For example, four years ago after taking the entrance examination, I was very eager to know whether or not I could pass it, and I was very afraid that I might [have] failed. And in [a] dream, I was told that I failed the examination. I told my dream to my mother who said to me that dreams were contrary to the truth. Then, I got the information that I was enrolled as a freshman ... (69, TC 8).

> there
> is this kind of super s t i [wrinkles nose] t i o n
> that if you have a good
> you you you explain
> or interpret dreams in the opposite way
> ifitsa g o o d dream that means that bad isgoing to happen
> [section of interview omitted]
> ESPEcially in the countryside people have this
> if you dream of
> uh something b a d
> the people will c o n s o l e you
> and so OH YOU know that
> that you know
> a BAD dream means something GOOD is going to happen
> if you dreamed that someone
> died
> then uh
> people will say ofcourse
> this person who dreamed
> who had the dream is kinda s c a r e d
> or you know and you say OH YOU know that
> people interpret dreams in
> just the opposite way (XM)

The Han students we talked to in Bejing and Buffalo rarely invoked the traditional principle that "Evil in a dream means good in reality" (Yi and Xu, 1984, p. 60). Although this principle is cross-culturally widespread (Dentan, 1986, p.330), we have shown that the main thrust of traditional Han oneiromancy is that dreams are automatic and straightforward responses of a sleeping body to fluctuating psychological and physical energies, just as perceived experiences are automatic and straightforward responses of a waking body to the same variables (DeWoskin, 1983, pp. 7–9; Lie, 1990, pp. 66–67; Watson, 1958, p. 85). Therefore, in an old cautionary tale from Guilin in South China, events disprove a professional oneiromancer's optimistic interpretation by this principle of a dream in which a beloved but unfilial son drowns; the son really does drown (Yi and Xu, 1984, pp. 53–62). As XM suggests, and unlike most of the Beijing students, the woman who has invoked the oneiromantic principle of reversal in the preceding example comes from the countryside. The implication is that people, at least in the country, do fear that dreams come true and seek reassurance that they come true in reverse. Thus the reversal principle functions as Malinowski (1948) thought magical belief in general does: to reduce anxiety. As noted previously, the apparent Han rejection of ambiguity may prevent dream accounts themselves from fulfilling that function.

Analysis and Conclusions

Two conclusions emerge from this material. First, as expected, dream accounts, particularly those preserved in classic literature, reflect their social and political context as well as nocturnal experiences of the narrator. Second, individual interest in dreams seems rather independent of systemic cultural constraints. These conclusions have methodological, theoretical and political implications.

Dream Narratives Are Social

The first point emerges most clearly from the classic material. Although dream narratives ostensibly emerge from individuals' nocturnal experiences, narrators often fashion them, sometimes probably out of whole cloth, to suit private or social ends. Dream narratives constitute a literary genre, not a body of faithful reportage.

Edel (1982) and others suggest literary ways to approach dream accounts. But many of such approaches suffer from too rigid a distinction between "dreams" (i.e., dream *narratives*,) and "literature." This distinction seems to reflect more the current Western division of the academy into the "two cultures" (Snow, 1963) of "science" and "humanities" or, more narrowly, of Freudians versus Jungians (e.g., Rupprecht, 1987) and behaviorists versus Rogerians (Olson, 1982, pp. 1–7). Yet to limit attention to the "purely literary" quality of dream accounts as literary constructs that stand on their own would impoverish investigation as much as treating them like scientific reports does. Snow's "third culture," social science, should also play a role.

In a social analysis, no dream narrative should be taken at face value without explicit consideration of the social relationships between (1) narrator(s); (2) dreamer(s), if different from the narrator, as in many accounts of the dreams of powerful people; (3) audience and social context. Courtiers told the emperor dream stories they thought he wished to hear—unless they wanted to change imperial policies (cf. Olson, 1982, p.

39). The process is precisely analogous to that by which Jungian or Freudian analysts produce from their analysands the genre of dream narratives the analysts prefer (Calestro, 1974; Munroe, 1957; Whitman, 1963).

In the case of the Han students, being asked to submit a written report of any dream they remembered to a teacher (*laoshi*, a status more respected in China than in the United States) from a country then widely admired probably improved the literary value of the reportage, as opposed, say, to the notoriously boring character of lab dream reports (cf. Dentan, 1987, pp. 318–319). Moreover, this permissive atmosphere, which contrasted with some students' experiences about recounting dreams to their peers, may have resulted in the students' feeling freer about reporting or inventing dreams than they would otherwise have felt. On the other hand, except for dreams reported as occurring during the week of the assignment, it probably had little effect on recall. Our inability to collect comparable dream narratives from local oneiro-mancers or to observe discussions of dreams among Han students renders these speculations undemonstrable but also suggests research that needs doing.

In short, investigators who accept dream narratives as accounts of "real dreams" risk misreading them badly. This misreading in turn can vitiate sophisticated interpretations of dreaming and oneiromancy, like B. Mannheim's (1987, pp. 147–149) analysis of Quechua dream interpretation, which assumes a unilinear development of dream narratives from dreams alone.

Cultural Hegemony Has Limits

The Cultural System: Dreams Are Meaningless

For over a millennium Han intellectuals have paid at least lip service to the attitude that being concerned with dreams is womanish silliness, peasant superstition or barbarian craziness, although they continued to use dreams to proclaim their own virtues, push their own policies or create poetic metaphors for longing or worldly vanity (e.g., Bai Junyi, quoted in Lee, 1979, p. 114). Disbelief in the significance of dreams thus became a marker for belonging to the ruling gender, class, ethnic group. Like most such markers, it both embodied and created the reality it purported to reflect. For indeed Han women have been prominent as priestesses in folk Daoism and as dream-inspired leaders of millenarian religions (Potter, 1974; Sangren, 1988; Shanzhu, 1983, pp. 174; Shi, 1983; Shilang, 1983). Dreams indeed remain important in Han folk religion, the flexible congeries of beliefs to which Han peasants, proletarians, artisans, and petty bourgeois outside the People's Republic still officially subscribe. And the peoples who once surrounded Han but are now incorporated into the nation include despised and feared southern shamanist tribes and nations (Creel, 1970, pp. 2; DeWoskin, 1983, p. 3) as well as the Tungusic speakers who gave the world the word *shaman* (Qiu, 1985).

Maoist doctrine and economic rationalism further eroded the traditional public and political functions of narrating dreams. Oneiromancy and oneirology were part of the "old culture" that Maoists were determined to expunge entirely, especially during the Great Proletarian Cultural Revolution, during which the Beijing students who reported dreams to Walters and Dentan grew up (Wee, 1988, p. 24). Dream accounts do not warn political leaders or trigger revolutionary movements, as they did less than half a century ago (e.g., Chesneaux, 1971; cf. Compilation Group, 1976, pp.15–16; Clarke and Gregory, 1982). But although traditional oneirology with its complex array of souls and spirits seems moribund, individuals continue to puzzle over their dreams, to talk about them despite derision and to try to interpret at least some of them.

Why Do Individuals Remain Concerned with Dreams?

One reason for this persistence may be that a major function of telling dreams is to reinforce traditional praxis, even while modifying it. An interpreted dream narrative becomes an exemplar of the interpretive principle used. A persistent and imaginative Han sifting through the myriad waking experiences that precede and follow a dream can almost always find something which in some way fits some element in the dreams by the principle of reflection, connection, moral judgment, prediction, or contradiction. Even if not, as Malinowski (1948, p. 82) remarks: "in human memory the testimony of a positive case always overshadows the negative one. One gain easily outweighs several losses. Thus the instances which confirm magic [or oneiromancy] always loom more conspicuously than those which deny it."

B. Mannheim's (1987) ethnohistory of Andean oneiromancy suggests a more subtle reason for the persistence of Han oneiromancy among people who reject traditional oneirology. Comparing the modern oneiromantic lexicon with sixteenth century manuscripts on the same topic from the same village, he found a complete reversal of meaning. His explanation is that Andean dream interpretation is semantic. That is, it concerns relationship between signs (elements in dream narratives) and meanings. It does not concern syntactic relationships, between signs and other signs, or pragmatic ones, between signs and waking experience. By contrast, myths work on the two semiotic levels (semantics and syntactics); so do rituals (syntactics and pragmatics). Andean dream interpretation is therefore not rooted in other spheres of Andean life and, being independent, undergoes change readily.

Classic Han oneiromancy also involved semantic element-meaning relationships (Table 15.4), most of which are now moribund. Moreover, contemporary Han oneirology has lost most of its syntactic dimension, about which the Han have always been dubious anyway. As an intellectual activity, oneirology seems rudimentary. The meaning of dreams is typically indexical, a literal reflection of waking events or connections or a literal (or inverted) prediction of future ones. Meaning and experience, semantics and pragmatics, remain closely intertwined. The feedback loops we have described within and between these levels may account for what might strike American intellectuals as a paradox: that Han continue in practice what they have largely rejected as theory.

Some Implications of This Obduracy

A common tacit assumption in talking or writing about "Chinese" or "American" systems, for example, national oneirologies, is the following: although such societies are "complex" in the sense that they comprise many mutually contrastive and even mutually opposed social segments like classes, genders, ethnicities, and so on, nevertheless all share an overreaching set of concepts and values (but see Wee, 1988). Depending on theoretical and political bias scholars call this presumptive shared ideology "mainstream" or "hegemonic" culture.

Intellectuals like the Han scholar-bureaucrats often articulate and systematize such cultural systems. The intelligentsia thus, in theory, maintains cultural hegemony in tandem with the ruling class or gentry, which maintains political dominance (Fei, 1953, pp. 33–58). Hegemony is, in the realm of intellectual life, what dominance is in the realm of politics. In this sense hegemony means the "'spontaneous' consent given by the great masses of the population to the general direction imposed on social life by the dominant . . . group; this consent is 'historically' caused by the prestige (and consequent confidence) which the dominant group enjoys" (Gramsci, 1971, p. 12). A hegemonic cultural system sets the limits of common sense and makes it hard for people to entertain alternatives to the dominant political order or the mainstream cultural systems that are its hegemonic counterpart (Williams, 1973).

But this study of the functions of dream narratives in Han society suggests that, throughout Chinese history, the attitude of the Han gentry toward dreams has never been hegemonic. Women, peasants, workers, and national minorities have simply ignored it. The blanket Maoist rejection of "old" superstitions does not prevent the elite students in training from working out their own indexical oneiromancy, much of which resembles its classical counterpart. The intelligentsia has not in over a thousand years been able to convince "the great masses" that experiences which *feel* as meaningful as some dreams do are in fact meaningless.

In this sense, Han student attitudes toward dreams in 1985 foreshadow the events in Tiananmen Square in June 1989 and suggest that, however repressive the political dominance of the ruling clique, it will be unable to establish ideological hegemony. Proponents of irrationality, pluralism, or freedom should take heart.

Notes

1. Han are the "ethnic" Chinese, who today dominate the People's Republic of China (PRC) politically. In 1982, Han numbered almost 937 million people, about 93 percent of the PRC population (Z. Chen, 1985, p. 25). The name *Han* comes from the Han Dynasty (206 B.C. - A.D. 220) For the relationship between the traditional intellectual class of scholar-bureaucrats and the politically dominant class or "gentry," *shen shi*, see Fei (1953) and the "Conclusion" of this chapter.

For more on the distinction between dreams and dream accounts, see Dentan (1988a). For the distinction between folk as opposed to gentry responses to dreams and other altered states of consciousness, see Creel (1970); Sangren (1988); Seaman (1978, 1987); Thompson (1982). For a detailed rationale of studying only the functions of dream accounts, the public residue of private dreams, not the functions of dreaming itself, see Dentan (1988a) and the "Conclusion" of this chapter.

2. Oneirology, oneirocriticism, and oneiromancy vary from place to place and over time. For example, women of Atjeh in Sumatra recount dreams to enhance their status (Siegel, 1978). Aguaruna and Semai men may use dreams to gain political influence (Brown, 1987; Dentan, 1988b).

The basic reference for ancient Han oneirology and oneiromancy is R. K. Ong's "Interpretation of Dreams in Ancient China" (1985). His work is invaluable but suffers from the common fault of equating dream accounts with dreams (Dentan, 1987). He relies heavily on Zhuang Fengyi's "Oneiromantic Systemics," *Mengzhan Leikao*, a Ming dynasty compilation dated after 1585. Another main source for Ong is "Duke Zhou Interprets Dreams." A version of this text, traditionally dated c. 1020 B.C., is available in the almanacs that used to hang as amulets in Han homes (e.g., Palmer et al., 1986, pp. 112–116; see Table 15.2).

Finally, he uses *biji xiaoshuo*, "collections of short anecdotes," a Han literary genre.

3. The section entitled Classic Oneinology relies heavily on the "Han-yin Cidian" and the "Han-Yin Chengyu Cidian" compiled by the Beijing Weiguoyu Xueyuan Yingyushi Zubian [Peking Foreign Language University English Department Editorial Committee], 1985; the *Straits Times* (1980, 1982, 1983) collection of characters; and a translation of the fourth edition of L. Wieger's "Chinese Characters." Our main sources for *chengyu* is the collection by T. C. Lai. For details, see Table 15.2.

4. Malays originated in southeastern China, where some minority people still speak related languages.

5. References to classic Han texts, available in several translations are in small capital letters; references to particular translations follow the standard format.

6. One of the few iconic symbols the Han identified in dreams was the snake: "The snake [in her nightmare] may be the image of love, which probably won't be very smooth" (#TC 19). Snakes are the only symbols Tung (1986, p. 2) tries to define, as follows:

   a. Sex organ; especially men's.
   b. Sin, evil . . . [biblical interpretation, cf. De Groot, 1912, pp. 274, 276; Morgan, 1942, p. 29; Palmer et al., 1986, p. 115].
   c. Area gods who take care of money; if you dream it, you ...might have some unexpected money coming soon . . . [cf. Lip, 1985, p. 37; Palmer et al., 1986, p. 115]
   d. Sickness; if you dream the snake to tight[en around] your body and you can't move, perhaps you might be ill soon. [One Beijing student had such a dream.]
   e. Power; if you dream the snake in your hand or on your head without fear, it might mean that you are going to have the power on what you are doing or on what you will do soon [the snake here may stand for dragon, as often happens in Chinese mythology; cf. Anonymous, 1980, pp. 188–124; Werner, 1922, pp. 208–235].

7. "A dream of wolves" by Pu, the Han equivalent of Edgar Allen Poe (Pu, 1981), exemplifies how Han would deal with such a transformation; the dream, says Pu, turns out to be completely correct.

References

Alley, R. (ed. and Trans.). (1981). *Li Pai: 200 Selected Poems*. Hong Kong: Joint Publishing Company.

Anonymous. (1980). *The Rites and Mysteries Connected with the Origin, Rise, and Development of Serpent Worship in Various Parts of the World.* Toronto: Tutor Press.

Arlington, L. C., and Acton, H. (Eds. and Trans.). (1937). *Famous Chinese Plays.* Beijing: Henri Vetch.

Bateson, G. (1958). *Naven. A Survey of the Problems Suggested by a Composite Picture of the Culture of a New Guinea Tribe Drawn from Three Points of View*, 2d. ed. Stanford, Cal.: Stanford University Press.

Baziak, A. T., and Dentan, R. K. (1965). "The Language of the Hospital and Its Effects on the Patients." In J. K. Skipper, Jr., and R. C. Leonard (Eds.), *Social Interaction and Patient Care.* Philadelphia: J. B. Lippencott Co.

Beijing Weiguoyu Xueyuan Yingyushi Zubian [Peking Foreign Language University English Department Editorial Committee]. (1982). *Hanying chengyu cidian. A Chinese English Dictionary of Idioms.* Beijing: Shangwu Yinshuguan.

———. (1985). *Hanying chengyu cidian. A Chinese English Dictionary of Idioms.* Beijing: Shangwu Yinshuguan.

Bernstein, B. (1964). "Social Class and Psycho-Therapy." *British Journal of Sociology* 15: 54–64.

Birch, C. (Ed.), (1965). *Anthology of Chinese Literature.* New York: Grove Press.

Blakney, R. B. (Trans.). (1955). *The Way of Life. Lao Tzu.* New York: Mentor Books.

Bohannan, P. (1963). *Social Anthropology.* New York: Holt Rinehart Winston.

Brown, M. F. (1987). "Ropes of Sand: Order and Imagery in Aguaruna Dreams." In B. Tedlock (Ed.), *Dreaming: Anthropological and Psychological Perspectives.* Cambridge: Cambridge University Press.

Burkhardt, V. R. (1954). *Chinese Creeds and Customs.* Hong Kong: South China Morning Press.

Butterfield, F. (1982). *China: Alive in the Bitter Sea.* New York: Bantam Books.

Calestro, K. M. (1974). "Psychotherapy, Faith Healing and Suggestion." *International Journal of Psychiatry* 10: 83–113.

Cernovsky, Z. Z. (1984). "Dream Recall and Attitude Toward Dreams." *Perceptual and Motor Skills* 58: 911–914.

Chaves, J. (Ed. and Trans.). (1986). *The Columbian Book of Later Chinese Poetry. Yuan, Ming and Ch'ing Dynasties (1279–1911).* New York: Columbia University Press.

Chen, T. (1984). "Longxi Hang. The Riverside Battleground." In Xu Yuan-zhong (Ed. and Trans.), *Tangshi yi bai wushi shou. 150 Tang Poems.* Shaanxi: People's Publishing House.

Chen, Z. (1985). *Life and Lifestyles.* China Handbook Series. Beijing: Foreign Languages Press.

Chesneaux J. (1971). *Secret Societies in China in the Nineteenth and Twentieth Centuries.* Ann Arbor: University of Michigan Press.

Cheung, F. M. (1982). "Psychological Symptoms Among Chinese in Urban Hong Kong." *Social Science and Medicine* 16: 1339–1344.

———— and Lau, B. W. K. (1982). "Situational Variations of Help-Seeking Behavior Among Chinese Patients." *Comprehensive Psychiatry* 23: 252–262.

Ch'u, Ta-Kao (1973). *Tao Te Ching.* New York: Samuel Weiser.

Clarke, P., and Gregory, J. S. (1982). *Western Reports on the Taiping.* Honolulu: University of Hawaii Press.

Comber, L. (1961). *The Traditional Mysteries of Chinese Secret Societies in Malaya.* Singapore: Eastern Universities Press.

Compilation Group for the "History of Modern China" (1976). *The Taiping Revolution.* Beijing: Foreign Languages Press.

Creel, H. J. (1970). *What Is Taoism? and Other Studies in Chinese Cultural History.* Chicago: University of Chicago Press.

Day, C. B. (1940). *Chinese Peasant Cults.* Shanghai: Kelly and White.

De Bary, W. T., Chan W. T. and Watson, B. (1960). *Sources of Chinese Tradition*, 2 vols. New York: Columbia University Press.

De Groot, J. J. M. (1912). *Religion in China.* New York: Putnam.

Dentan, R. K. (1983). *A Dream of Senoi.* Council on International Studies, Special Study 150, Albany: SUNY Press.

———. (1984). "Techniques and Antecedents: A Response to Geisler." *Lucidity Letter* 3: 5–7.

———. (1987). "Ethnographic Considerations in the Cross-Cultural Study of Dreaming." In J. Gackenbach (Ed.), *Sleep and Dreams: A Sourcebook*, pp. 317–358. New York: Garland.

———. (1988a). "Butterflies and Bughunters: Reality and Dreams, Dreams and Reality." *Psychiatric Journal of the University of Ottawa* 13: 51–59.

———. (1988b). "Lucidity, Sex, and Horror in Senoi Dreamwork." In J. Gackenbach and S. LaBerge (Eds.), *Conscious Mind, Sleeping Brain*, pp. 37–63. New York: Plenum Press.

———. (1988c). "Ambiguity, Synedoche and Affect in Semai Medicine." *Social Science and Medicine* 27: 857–877.

DeWoskin, K. J. (1983). *Doctors, Diviners, and Magicians of Ancient China. Biographies of Fang Shih.* New York: Columbia University Press.

Douglas, M. (1973). *Natural Symbols. Explorations in Cosmology.* New York: Vintage Press.

Eberhard, W. (1952). *Chinese Festivals.* New York: Henry Shuman.

———. (1986). *A Dictionary of Chinese Symbols. Hidden Symbols in Chinese Life and Thought*, trans. G. L. Campbell. London: Routledge.

Edel, L. (1982). *Stuff of Sleep and Dreams: Experiments in Literary Psychology.* London: Chapto and Windus.

Embun, A. B. (1959). *Hantu dengan kerja-nya*, vol. 2. Penang: Sinaran Brothers.

Empson, W. (1961). *Seven Types of Ambiguity.* Harmondsworth: Penguin Books.

Endicott, K. M. (1970). *An Analysis of Malay Magic.* Oxford: Claredon Press.

Fei, X. (1953). *China's Gentry. Essays in Rural-Urban Relations by Haiao-tung Fei*, rev. ed. ed. M. P. Redfield. Chicago: Chicago University Press.

Fingarette, H. (1972). *Confucius–The Secular World as Sacred.* New York: Harper Books.

Firth, R. (1967). "Individual Fantasy and Social Norms: Seances with Spirit Mediums." In R. Firth (Ed.), *Tikopia Ritual and Belief.* Boston: Beacon Press.

Fusek, L. (trans.). (1982). *Among the Flowers. The Hua-chien chi.* New York: Columbia University Press.

Geddes, W. R. (1963). *Peasant Life in Communist China Monograph 6*, Itha-ca, N.Y.: Society for Applied Anthropology.

Geertz, C. (1973). *The Interpretation of Cultures.* New York: Basic Books.

———. (1983). *Local Knowledge. Further Essays in Interpretative Anthropology.* New York: Basic Books.

Gimlette, J. D., and Thompson, H. W. (1971). *A Dictionary of Malay Medicine.* Kuala Lumpur: Oxford University Press.

Gramsci, A. (1971). *Selections from the Prison Notebooks of Antonio Gramsci*, trans. and ed. Q. Hoare and G. N. Smith. New York: International publishers.

Guenther, M. G. (1979). "Bushman Religion and the (Non)sense of Anthropological Theory of Religion." *Sociologus* 29: 102–132.

Hall, C. S., and Van de Castle, R. L. (1966). *The Content Analysis of Dreams.* New York: Appleton-Century-Crofts.

Henricks, R. G. (Ed. and Trans.). (1983). *Philosophy and Argumentation in Third-Century China: The Essays of Hsi Kang.* Princeton, N.J.: Princeton University Press.

Hsia, C. T. (1970). "Time and the Human Condition in the Plays of T'sang Hsien-Tsu." In W. T. DeBary, (Ed.) *Self and Society in Ming Thought.* New York: Columbia University Press.

Hsu, F. L. K. (1967). *Under the Ancestor's Shadow. Kinship, Personality, and Social Mobility in Village China*, rev. ed. Garden City, N.Y.: Natural History Library, Doubleday.

————. (1981). *Americans and Chinese. Passage to Differences*, 3d. ed. Honolulu: University of Hawaii Press.

Hsu, J. (1985). "The Chinese Family: Relations, Problems and Therapy." In W. Tseng and D. Y. H. Wu (Eds.), *Chinese Culture and Mental Health*. Orlando, Fla.: Academic Press.

Hung, C. (1985). *Going to the People. Chinese Intellectuals and Folk Literature, 1918–1937.*Cambridge, Mass.: Harvard University Press.

Jai, Z. (1984). "Chun si." In Xu Yuan-zhong (Ed. and Trans.). *Tangshi yi bai wushi shou. 150 Tang Poems*. Shaanxi: People's Publishing House.

Jiobu, R. M. (1976). "Earning Differentials Between Whites, and Ethnic Minorities: The Cases of Asian Americans, Blacks, and Chicanos." *Sociology and Social Research* 61: 24–38.

Jin, C. (1984a). "Chung yuan." In Xu Yuan-zhong (Ed. and Trans.), *Tangshi yi bai wushi shou. 150 Tang Poems*. Shaanxi: People's Publishing House.

————. (1984b). "Spring Grievance." In B. Watson (Ed.), *The Columbia Book of Chinese Poetry. From Early Times to the Thirteenth Century*. New York: Columbia University Press.

Kessen, W. (1975). *Childhood in China*. New Haven, Conn.: Yale University Press.

Kleinman, A. M. (1977). "Depression, Somatization and the 'New Cross-Cultural Psychiatry.'" *Social Science and Medicine* 11: 3–11.

————. (1982). "Neurathenia and Depression: A Study of Somatization and Culture in China." *Culture, Medicine and Psychiatry* 6: 117–190.

Kracauer, S. (1947). *From Caligari to Hitler, a Psychological History of the German Film*. Princeton, N.J.: Princeton University Press.

Kuiken, D., Sharp, C., Jaques, A. and Leendert, M. (n.d.). "Awakening to Dreams: Sleep Patterns Dream Recall, and Dream Use Among Native Canadian and Euro-Canadian Young Adults." Manuscript, Center for Advanced Study in Theoretical Psychology, University of Alberta.

Kung, Chiu [Confucius], (1979). *The Analects (Lun yu)*, trans. D. C. Lau. New York: Dorset.

Kuo, W. H. (1979). "Colonized Status of Asian Americans." *Ethnic Groups* 3: 227–251.

Lai, T. C. (1970a). *Chinese Couplets,* 2d ed. Hong Kong: University Bookstore.

——. (1970b). *Selected Chinese Sayings.* Hong Kong: University Bookstore.

——. (1976). *Treasurers of a Chinese Studio (Ink-Brush-Inkstone-Paper).* Hong Kong: Swidon Book Co.

Lau, D. C. (1963). *Lao Tzu, Tao te ching.* Harmondsforth, New York: Penguin Books.

Lau, D. C. (trans.) (1979). *Confucius: The Analects.* Hamondsforth: New York, Penguin Books.

Latourette, K. S. (1934). *The Chinese: Their History and Culture,* vol. 2. New York: Macmillan Company.

Lee, P. H. (1979). *Celebration of Continuity. Themes in Classic East Asian Poetry.* Cambridge, Mass.: Harvard University Press.

Levy-Bruhl, L. (1935). *La mythologie primitive.* Paris: Alcan.

Li, B. (1984). "Chang xiang si." In Xu Yuan-zhing (Ed. and Trans.), *Tang-shi yi bai wushi shou. 150 Tang Poems.* Shaanxi: People's Publishing House.

Li, G. (1980). "Governor of the Southern Tributary State." In Yang Xianyi and Gladys Yang (trans.). *The Dragon King's Daughter, Ten Tang Dynasty Stories.* Third Edition, Beijing: Foreign Languages Press.

Li, Yi (1984). "Gong Yuan." In Xu Yuan-zhing (Trans. and Ed.), *Tangshi yi bai wushi shou. 150 Tang Poems.* Shaanxi: People's Publishing House.

Lie. (1990). *"The Book of Lieh-tzu, a Classic of Tao,* trans. A. C. Graham. New York: Columbia University Press.

Lincoln, J. S. (1936). *The Dream in Primitive Culture.* Baltimore: Williams and Wilkins.

Lip, E. (1985). *Chinese Beliefs and Superstitions.* Singapore: Graham Brash.

Liu, F. (1984). "Chun yuan." In Xu Yuan-zhong (Ed. and Trans.), *tangshi yi bai wushi shou. 150 Tang Poems.* Shaanxi: People's Publishing House.

Liu X. (1983). "A Postscript to Wenxin Diaolong." In Wong Siu-kit (Ed. and Trans.), *Early Chinese Literary Criticism.* Hong Kong: Joint Publishing Co.

Liu, Y. (1984). "Chun ci." In Xu yuan-zhong (Ed. and Trans.), Tangshi yi bai wushi shou. 150 Tang Poems. Shaanxi: People's Publishing House.

Lourie, R., and Mikhalev, A. (1989). "Why You'll Never Have Fun in Russian." *New York Times Book Review,* 18 (June): 1, 38.

Lu, Ji (1983). "A Descriptive Poem on Literature [Wen fu]." In Wong siu-kit (Ed. and Trans.), *Early Chinese Literary Criticism.* Hong Kong: Joint Publishing Co.

MacNair, H. F. (1946). *China: The land and People.* Berkeley and Los Angeles: University of California Press.

Malinowski, B. (1948). *Magic, Science and Religion and Other Essays.* Garden City, N.Y.: Doubleday Archer.

Mannheim, B. (1987). "A Semiotic of Andean Dreams." In B. Tedlock (Ed.), *Dreaming: Anthropological and Psychological Interpretations.* Cambridge: Cambridge University Press.

Mannheim, K. (1936). *Ideology and Utopia. An Introduction to the Sociology of Knowledge,* trans. L. Firth and E. Shils. New York: Harvest Book.

Mao Zedung, (1967a). *On Coalition Government. Selected Works,* vol. 3. Beijing: Foreign Languages Press. [Originally published in 1945.]

———. (1967b). *Reform Our Study. Selected Works of Mao Tse-Tung,* vol. 3. Peking: Foreign Languages Press.

———. (1967c). *Rectify the Party's Style of Work. Selected Works of Mao Tse-Tung,* vol. 3. Peking: Foreign Languages Press.

Mathiot, M. (1979). "Folk Definitions as a Tool for the Analysis of Lexical Meaning." In M. Mathiot (Ed.), *Ethnolinguistics.* The Hague: Mouton.

McHugh, J. N. (1955). *Hantu Hantu: An Account of Ghost Belief in Modern Malaya.* Singapore: Donald Moore.

Morgan, H. T. (1942). *Chinese Symbols and Superstitons.* South Pasadena, Cal.: Perkins.

Muller, F. M. (1969). "The Vagrakkhedika." In E. B. Cowell and others (Eds.), *Buddhist Mahayana Texts.* New York: Dover Books. [Originally published in 1894.]

Munroe, R. L. (1957). "Other Psychoanalytic Approaches (Adler, Jung, Rank)." In S. Arieti (Ed.), *American Handbook of Psychiatry.* New York: Basic Books.

Olson, R. (1982). *Science Deified and Science Defied. The Historical Significance of Science in Western Culture from the Bronze Age to the Beginnings of the Modern era ca. 3500 B.C. to ca. A.D. 1640.* Berkeley: University of California Press.

Ong, R. K. (1985). *The Interpretation of Dreams in Ancient China.* Bochum: Studienverlag Brockmayer.

Osgood, C. (1974). *The Chinese: A Study of a Hong Kong Community.* Tucson: University of Arizona Press.

Overmyer, D. L. (1986). *Religions of China. The World as a Living System.* San Francisco: Harper and Row.

Palmer, M., Chung M. H., Kwok, M. H., and Smith, A. (1986). *T'ung shu. The Ancient Chinese Almanac.* Boston: Shambala.

Pedersen, D., and Baruffati, V. (1985). "Health and Traditional Medicine Cultures in Latin America and the Carribean." *Social Science and Medicine* 21: 5–12.

Potter, J. M. (1974). "Cantonese Shamanism." In A. P. Wolf (Ed.), *Religion and Ritual in Chinese Society.* Stanford, Cal.: Stanford University Press.

Pu, S. (1981). "A Dream of Wolves." In S. Pu (Ed.), *Selected Tales of Laiozhai.* Beijing: Panda Books.

————. (1984). *Huang Liang yi meng. A Golden Millet Dream.* Beijing: Zhaohua.

Qui, P. (Ed.) (1985). *Samanjiao Yanju.* Shanghai: People's Press.

Ricoeur, P. (1981). *Hemenutics and the Human Sciences.* Cambridge: Cambridge University Press.

Ropp. P. S. (1981). *Dissent in Early Modern China*. Ann Arbor: University of Michigan.

Ruel, M. (1970). "Wereanimals and the Inverted Witch." In M. P. Douglas (Ed.), *Witchcraft Confessions and Accusations*. Association of Social Anthropologists Monograph 9, London: Travistock.

Rupprecht, C. S. (1987). "Dreams and Literature: A Reader's Guide." In J. Gackenbach (Ed.), *Sleep and Dreams: A Sourcebook*. New York and London: Garland.

Sangren, P. S. (1988). "History and the Rhetoric of Legitimacy: The Ma Tsu Cult of Taiwan." *Comparative Studies in Society and History* 30: 674–697.

Scheff, T. J. (1986). "Towards Resolving the Controversy over 'Thick Description'." *Current Anthropology* 27: 408–410.

Seaman, G. (1978). *Temple Organization in a Chinese Village*. Taipei: Asian Folklore and Social Life Monographs.

————. (1987). *Journey to the North. An Ethnohistorical Analysis and Annotated Translation of the Chinese Folk Novel Pei-yu chi*. Berkeley: University of California.

Seiwart, H. (1981). "Religious Response to Modernization in Taiwan: The Case of I-kuan Tao." *Journal of the Hong Kong Branch of the Royal Asiatic Society* 21: 43–70.

Shanzhu. (1983). "On Market Day" and "The Burning of Busy Incense." In S. Cochran and A. C. K. Hsieh with J. Cochran (Trans. and Ed.), *One Day in China. May 21, 1936*. New Haven, Conn.: Yale University Press.

Shi, P. (1983). "The Temple Fair for the God of Good Sight in Zhengzhou." In S. Cochran and A. C. K. Hsieh with J. Cochran (Trans. and Ed.), *One Day in China, May 21, 1936*. New Haven, Conn.: Yale University Press.

Shilang. (1983). "Possesed by the Bodhisattva." In S. Cochran and A. C. K. Hsieh with J. Cochran (Trans. and Ed.), *One Day in China. May 21, 1936*. New Haven, Conn.: Yale University Press.

Siegel, J. (1978). "Curing Rites, Dreams and Domestic Politics in a Sumatran Society." *Glyph* 3: 18–31.

Sima, Q. (1979). *Selections from Records of the Historian Written by Szuma Chien*, trans. Yang Xianyi and G. Yang. Beijing: Foreign Languages Press.

Snow, Sir C. P. (1963) *The Two Cultures: A Second Look.* Cambridge: Cambridge University Press.

Stover, L. E. (1974). *The Cultural Ecology of Chinese Civilization. Peasants and Elites in the Last of the Agrarian States.* New York: PICA Press.

Straits Times (Eds.). (1980). *Fun with Chinese Characters*, vol. 1. Singapore and Kuala Lumpur: Federal Publications.

———. (Eds.). (1982). *Fun with Chinese Characters*, vol 2. Singapore and Kuala Lumpur: Federal Publications.

———. (Eds.). (1983). *Fun with Chinese Characters*, vol. 3. Singapore and Kuala Lumpur: Federal Publications.

Sturtevant, W. C. (1964). "Studies in Ethnoscience." *American Anthropologist*, 66, no. 3, part 8: 99–131.

Sun, W. (1963). *Sun Tzu. The Art of War.* S. B. Griffiths (Trans. and Ed.). Oxford: Oxford University Press.

Suzuki, B. H. (1977). "Education and the Socialization of Asian-Americans: A Revisionist Analysis of the "Model Minority" Thesis." *American Journal* 4: 23–52.

Tao-Kim-Hai, A. M. (1965). "Orientals Are Stoic." In J. K. Skipper, Jr., and R. C. Leonard (Eds.), *Social Interaction and Patient Care.* Philadelphia: J. B. Lippincott Co.

Tedlock, B. (1987). "An Interpretative Solution to the Problem of Humoral Medicine in Latin America." *Social Science and Medicine* 24: 1069–1083.

Tedlock, D. (1983). *The Spoken Word and the Work of Interpretation.* Philadelphia: University of Pennsylvania Press.

Thompson, L. G. (1982). "The Moving Finger Writes: A Note on Revelation and Renewal in Chinese Religion." *Journal of Chinese Religions* 10: 91–107.

Tseng, W. S. (1975). "The Nature of Somatic Complaints Among Psychiatric Patients: The Chinese Case." *Comprehensive Psychiatry*, 16: 237–245.

Tung, Y. C. A. (1986). "My Dreams—How I Work My Own Dreams." Manuscript, in possession of Robert K. Dentan.

Waley, A. (1941). *Translations from Chinese*. New York: Alfred A. Knopf.

Walls, J. (1985). "Dream Content, Experience and Attitudes Towards Dreams in Chinese and American University Students." *Association for the Study of Dreams Newsletter* 1: 8–9.

Walters, M. and Dentan, R. K. (1985a). "Are Lucid Dreams Universal? Two Unequivocal Cases of Lucid Dreaming Among Han Chinese University Students in Beijing, 1985." *Lucidity Letter* 4, no. 2: 12–14.

———. (1985b). "'Dreams, Illusions, Bubbles, Shadows': Awareness of 'Unreality' While Dreaming Among Chinese College Students." *Lucidity Letter* 4, no. 2: 86–93.

Wang C. (1984a). "Gui yuan." In Xu Yuan-zhing (Ed. and Trans.), *Tangshi yi bai wushi shou. 150 Tang Poems*. Shaanxi: People's Publishing House.

Watson, B. (Ed. and Trans.). (1958). *Basic Writings of Mo Tzu, Hsun Tzu and Han Fei Tzu*. New York: Columbia University Press.

———. (1989). *The Tso Chuan. Selections from China's Oldest Narrative History*. New York: Columbia University Press.

Wee, V. (1988). "What Does 'Chinese' Mean? An Exploratory Essay." National University of Singapore Sociology Department, Working Paper #90.

Wei, L., and Li, Y. (1983). "From Kindergarten to College." In Su Wenming (Ed.), *A Nation at School, China Today, 5*. Beijing: Beijing Review.

Wei, Z. (1984). "Jingling tu." In Xu Yuan-zhing (Ed. and Trans.), *Tangshi yi bai wushi shou. 150 Tang Poems*. Shaanxi: People's Publishing House.

Werner, E. T. C. (1922). *Myths and Legends of China*. London: Harrap.

Whitman, R. M. (1963). "Which Dream Does the Patient Tell?" *Archives of General Psychiatry* 8: 277–282.

Wieger, L. (1965). *Chinese Characters. Their Origin, Etymology, History, Classification and Signification. A Thorough Study from Chinese Docu-*

ments, trans. L. Davrout. New York: Dover Books. [Originally published 1927.]

Wilkinson, R. J. (1901). *A Malay-English Dictionary*, 2 vols. Singapore: Kelly and Walsh.

Williams, R. (1973). "Base and Superstructure in Marxist Cultural Theory." *New Left Review* 82: 3–16.

Winfield, G. F. (1948). *China: The Land and People*. New York: William Sloane.

Wolfenstein, M., and Leites, N. (1950). *Movies: A Psychological Study*. Glencoe, Ill.: The Free Press.

Wong, S. (Ed. and Trans.) (1983). *Early Chinese Literary Criticism*. Hong Kong: Joint Publishing Co.

Wu, Z. (1985). "Sleep and Dreams." *Chinese Literature* (Summer): 64–67.

Wu Dunn, S. (1989). "China's Intense Love of Education Cools Off." *New York Times*, (9 April), p. 18.

Xu, Y. (1984). *Tangshi yi bai shou. 150 Tang Poems*. Shaanxi: People's Publishing House.

Yang, C. K. (1959). *The Chinese Family in the Communist Revolution*. Cambridge, Mass.: MIT Press.

Yang, H. (1984). *A Record of Buddhist Monasteries in Lo-Yang*, trans. Y. Wang. Princeton, N.J.: Princeton University Press.

Yang, X., and Yang, G. (Eds. and Trans.). (1984). *Poetry and Prose of the Tang and Song*. Beijing: Panda Books.

Yi, Q. and Xu, J. (1984). *Elephant Trunk Hill. Tales from Scenic Guilin*. Beijing: Foreign Languages Press.

Zhang, B. (1984). In Xu Yuan-zhing (Ed. and Trans.), *Tangshi yi bai wushi shou. 150 Tang Poems*. Shaanxi: People's Publishing House.

Zhang, Z. (1984). "Chun gui si." In Xu Yuan-zhing (Ed. and Trans.), *Tangshi y bai wushi shou. 150 Tang Poems*. Shaanxi: People's Publishing House..

Zeng, Z. (1986). *Colloquial Cantonese and Putonghua Equivalents*. Hong Kong: Joint Publishing Co.

Zhou, Y., Cai, G., and Liu, H. (1983). *Education and Science.* The China Handbook Series, Beijing: Foreign Languages Press.

Zhuuang, Z. (1968). *The Complete Works of Zhuangzi,* trans. B. Watson. New York: Columbia University Press.

Zhu, X., and Lu Z. (1967). *Reflections on Things at Hand. The Neo-Confucian Anthology Compiled by Chu Hsi and Lu Tsu-Ch'ien,* trans. Wing-tsit Chan. New York: Columbia University Press.

16

John Antrobus ━━━━━━━━━━━━━━━

Dreaming: Could We Do Without It?

The question of whether dreaming has a function arises so often that it reminds me of the equally frequent question of whether there is a God. In both cases, there is, I think, a pressing motive to invent an affirmative answer even in the absence of supporting evidence. I think that those of us that have spent a substantial part of our lives studying dreaming, and the larger domain of what I call sleep mentation, often feel that if this stuff doesn't have any function, then we really have no business wasting all this time studying it. But the striking advances of neuropsychology, cognitive science and neurophysiology in the past twenty years allow us now to put the study of dreaming in a new perspective. Despite the great cost and methodological difficulties of studying dreaming, the phenomena do provide us with a unique window on the neurocognitive processes that we call the human mind-brain. There is no other time in the diurnal cycle where such large variations in the qualities of thought and imagery have been found to vary so systematically with the characteristics of the central nervous system. There is no other time when the brightness and color saturation of visual images so closely approximates that of waking perception even though dream images are produced in the absence of any external visual stimulus (Antrobus et al., 1987).

As the cognitive and neurosciences continue to grow in sophistication and scope, and as their models begin to cope with the size and complexity of the organization of the human mind-brain we will find, I believe, that both cognitive and neuropsychological research on sleep and dreaming will become increasingly informative about how dreams are created. Then perhaps that knowledge of how these perceptual-like phenomena are produced in the absence of external stimuli, will in turn, shed some light on some of the major issues in these neighboring fields. Conversely, I am persuaded that the study of dreaming outside of the cognitive and neurosciences context will retard our ability to understand this most fascinating state of consciousness. It is for this reason that I think that the question of the function of dreaming is unlikely to be solved before more headway is made on the question of the function of waking consciousness, and the problem of measurement of subjective or private events continues to hold up progress in that quarter.

Turning to the question at hand, the function, if any, of dreaming, I would first like to define how I understand the question. By *function*, I shall mean that the process of dreaming has some instrumental value to the individual. That is, at least some part of the individual is either better or worse off as a consequence of the amount of time devoted to the process of dreaming. For example, people have proposed that the process of dreaming protects the sleep state (Freud, 1955), solves problems (Cartwright, 1986), makes the individual better integrated (Fiss, 1986), transforms sensory or autonomic stimuli so as to maintain sleep, and more recently, reduces the risk of gridlock in neural nets and thus permits more efficient waking cognitive processing (Crick and Mitchison, 1983, 1986). Both Crick and Mitchison and Evans and Newman (1964) proposed that dreaming involved a random process that served to dump information from memory. The dream as a cognitive event is a throw away. The state of the system is enhanced by its loss. For Crick and Mitchison, the PGO spikes are a random generator that reduces the possibility of netlock among cortical neural nets, but the information processed by the neural nets in REM sleep has no particular functional value for the sleeper. I recently suggested that PGO spikes are the output of an oculomotor, saccade controlling neural circuit, and the frequency of the output is proportional to the angular deflection of the eye (Antrobus, 1990). If this activity is indeed nonrandom, then it cannot serve as a random generator for the neural net clearing process.

The remaining positions generally propose that the cognitive process of dreaming serves some function for the individual regardless of whether the dream event is remembered on awakening or experienced as a "lucid" event within sleep.

The question of the function of dreaming does not apply, as I understand it, to those instances where an individual has stored the dream experience in memory and then subsequent to the original experience, examines, analyzes, or meditates on the recalled event. Also excluded from consideration here is the function, or consequence, of daytime rumination on one's dreams as well as the lucrative function of interpreting the dreams of others.

Now let us briefly consider the body-mind issue. I take a monist position; namely, that the body and mind belong to the same physical domain even though we only poorly understand the nature of this unity. But the mind-brain identity position is an article of faith. We do not, in fact, know the precise relation between the mental and physiological measures that we study and the mind-brain identity that I espouse, and in that sense, as the late Heintz Pagels (1988) argued in *The Dreams of Reason*, I am a monist by faith and perhaps a dualist by practice.

This monist position implies that the experience and reports of dreaming and the electroneurophysiological measures carried out during sleep measure different characteristics of the same mind-brain processes. To represent the simultaneous action of mental and neurophysiological processes associated with dreaming, I have proposed (Antrobus, 1991) a laminar model in which the constructs or measurements of each domain can be mapped onto one other. In this connection, the recent work on parallel distributed processes (Rumelhart and McClelland, 1986; McClelland and Rumelhart, 1986) in which the individual neuron, or a cluster of neurons, organized in extremely large neural networks is the basic unit for a model of cognitive processes, provides a major theoretical breakthrough for neurocognition and provides a new vehicle for approaching the body-mind problem. My laminar model has five layers. The macro-neurophysiological models layer maps onto the micro neural net models layer, which in turn maps onto one of several alternative mathematical models. On the other side, the macro cognitive models layer (e.g., of mental imagery), maps onto a micro cognitive units layer, which in turn, maps onto the same central mathematical models as do the neural net models.

These new distributed neural net models (Rumelhart and McClelland, 1986; McClelland and Rumelhart, 1986) have profound implications for theories of the function of dreaming that propose that dream images themselves are the units by which information is processed in the dream state. If the fundamental units that create the dream image are orders of magnitude smaller than the conceptual feature units that people typically use to describe their dreams, and if a particular configuration of network activity across millions of such units is necessary to produce the images, then the dream images are the consequence of this distributed network activity and are not the basic units of information processing. In fact, many quite dissimilar processes might be able to create the same image.

In passing, it may be noted that, whatever the nature of the information processing operations that produce the dream, information can be processed quite effectively without creating any form of imagery. No one, for example, would assume that a commuter's daydreams while driving to work are in any way descriptive of the cognitive processes of driving a car. In short, dream imagery does not necessarily identify the cognitive processes that create it, and moreover, the information processed during dreaming sleep need not be represented in the form of imagery.

Now let us examine the very plausible assumption that a class of information processing must serve some function for the human organism otherwise the process will be discontinued. It might drop out in the course of species evolution or in the course of individual development. If true, the argument goes that inasmuch as the production of dream imagery represents some form of information processing, the process by which the imagery is produced must have some value to the dreamer. It does *not* follow, however, that every instance of that class, or even of an entire subclass, of information processing has such a function. If dreaming is a subclass of perception and thought processes, then it follows that dreaming might have no function for an individual and yet fail to drop away because the larger cognitive class, perception and thought, has considerable functional value to the individual in the waking state. The only remaining puzzle is why this rather large cognitive subclass of dreaming does not drop out entirely, and it is to this issue that I now turn.

REM sleep is a cluster of neurophysiological processes that occur periodically within the sleep of mammals. Although we may assume that at least one class of REM sleep has some functional value to the mammal, and we do not as yet know what that function is, we need not assume that all classes do. In particular, the cortical processes that support certain aspects of perception and thought are unusually active in REM sleep. But if the motor output of these processes were not drastically inhibited during REM sleep, everyone would be periodically up and about each night acting out their dreams. An entire world of stage 2 sleepwalkers and sleeptalkers would be a mild affair compared to a night world of REM sleep actors and actresses!

And so there are convincing reasons to assume that the inhibition of the motor execution of the motor commands that are produced in the process of dreaming must be inhibited (Hobson and McCarley, 1977). The interesting question is, "Why in the process of mammalian evolution were the cognitive processes activated in the first place?" And I hear my colleagues on the other side of the table shout, "Because dreams serve a function for the individual." Proposed explanations for evolutionary decisions are often, of course, quite speculative. But having acknowledged that I would like to propose my own speculation; namely, that some of the processes of REM sleep may have an instrumental function, but not the imaginal and thought processes, the production of dreams. Moreover, perceptual and cognitive processes have perhaps many functions, but not the processing subclass of dreaming.

Consider the sleep of a reptile, who awakens from sleep as the light and heat of the morning sun warms and activates its cortical cells. In the absence of such an external *on* switch the animal might never again awaken. Humans like all other mammals have an internal clock whose phase is modulated by external light but can also run independent of it. The timing of the sleep period is achieved by an active process that we now identify with the REM-NREM sleep cycle. We have excellent local neurotransmitter explanations (McCarley and Massaquoi, 1986) for how this ninety minute timing cycle occurs in humans and how other mammals generate different cycles, but we have no satisfying functional explanation for phase duration. One suggestion here it that, although both REM and NREM processes enhance the survival and satisfaction of the mammal in the waking state, they also have additional semi-independent functions. One of these functions, the relative phase length of REM and NREM sleep within a given night, is a function of the shifting relative values of the two states as the sleep cycle moves toward awakening.

Two general classes of sleep function may be proposed: restoration or recovery, and preparation or readiness for the next day. One might expect the former to be dominant in the early part of sleep, and the second in the latter. Indeed, a restorative process has often been attributed to stage 4, which dominates the early hours of sleep. But why then does stage 4 and the rest of NREM sleep not continue until the restoration process is complete and then leave the remainder of the sleep period for REM sleep and the functional process of preparation for waking? Although this restoration-preparation conception is an oversimplification, it does suggest that there may be a function not only for REM sleep, but a function for the phase duration of the REM period.

More specifically, I would like to propose that the brain stem components of REM sleep constitute a neurocognitive process that keeps the associative and motor executive cortex in a minimally active state, so that they can quickly be brought to full working capacity upon awakening, but not so active that it engages the sensory, autonomic and motor systems that also benefit from restorative sleep. As the reader will note, this proposal is similar to the neural tonus metaphor that Berger and Walker (1972) introduced for the oculomotor system and that Roffwarg, Muzio, and Dement (1966) proposed for the development of the fetal nervous system.

Let us suppose that the beneficial effects of a sleep stage are initially rapid but that increasing time brings decreased benefits. Further, suppose that these benefits fall off slowly when the system shifts to another stage of sleep. Thus maximum benefit to the system at large would be realized by alternating back and forth between states. The phase duration and shift would depend on the rate at which benefits accrued in each state, and the rate at which they decayed when the state was off.

But the nervous system was not constructed from human theories so it is unlikely that any structure in the system serves only one particular function. So saying, I would like to propose yet another reason why mammalian sleep consists of the alternation between at least two phases, rather than letting the various sleep processes proceed simultaneously. In keeping with the Berger and Walker (1972) and Roffwarg et al. (1966) proposal just described, let us assume that all of the neurocognitive processes employed in the waking state must be given intermittent activation even when not in use; that is, in sleep. If all of the components of the system were activated simultaneously, the individual would be, by definition, awake. Inhibition of the motor system might eliminate motor behavior but all perceptual, thought and emotional processes would be unchanged. Consider the advantage of activating one-half of the system at a time. Thus in one state the individual might register external stimuli but not interpret or elaborate on them. In the alternate state, the individual might have the ability to elaborate on percepts, but no percepts would be available from perceptual channels so the elaboration would be restricted to memorial material and the output would be a quasi-perceptual output that we have come to call dreams. So external information would never be fully processed in either state, yet every part of the system would receive some form of activation every ninety minutes.

For example, the locus coeruleus and related noradrenergic, pontine bodies that are very active in NREM sleep also play a major role in the selective aspects of waking perception (Aston-Jones and Bloom, 1981; Bloom, 1980). In sleep, this noradrenergic, NREM component goes into ninety-minute oscillations with the REM sleep, cholinergiccholinoceptive, medial reticular formation based component (McCarley and Hobson, 1975; Hobson, Lydic, and Baghdoyan, 1986). Upon awakening, however, the two systems appear to collaborate quite intimately. Milliseconds after sensory information is selected in the cortex with the help of the locus coeruleus based component it is passed on for elaborative processing by the mRF supported associative cortex and finally to the motor cortex that produces the commands for skeletal motor execution.

In other words, when the two systems are activated either simultaneously or in close sequence, the entire perceptual-association-motor system is active and the individual is awake. Putting the two components into oscillation to achieve sleep is a rather neat way of turning off the perceptual-association-motor system, while giving each half of the system sufficient stimulation so that the start-up time in the morning, when they are brought back into close synchrony, is at a minimum. Within this conception, dreaming is the output of the association cortex (1) when it has no sensory input, because the sensory or recognition component controlled by the locus coeruleus is off, and (2) when the motor efferent neurons are also inhibited so that the commands of the motor cortex cannot be executed. In summary, as long as no sensory information is processed and no association-motor commands are executed, it makes no difference what the association cortex does. Sleep imagery and thought might have been reduced to zero in the process of natural selection, except that dreaming has no specific maladaptive consequences, so it has survived at the level we all know.

Yet another reason why I am not inclined to assume that dreaming has a function of its own, beyond that of any function of REM sleep, is that the cognitive output of the association cortex is so inferior during REM sleep relative to what the same part of the cortex can do in a fraction of the time in the waking state, that, in my judgment, the cognitive output we know as dreaming can have little or no value to the individual either during sleep or following recall upon awakening.

Another common argument against the dream-function position is that people who typically recall none of the one to two hours per night of their dreaming sleep seem to function as well, if not better during the day, as those who do recall their dreams. Even the latter, however, rarely recall more than a fraction of 1 percent of their dreams. In support of the dreaming-function position, however, it could be argued, perhaps, that even if the information processed during REM dreaming is never recalled, the periodic activation of certain patterns of neural networks during sleep is necessary for them to be readily reactivated upon awakening. In cognitive terms, some fragment of a presleep problem may need to be periodically reactivated during sleep for the memory of the problem to survive and be available for further processing on the following day. However Verdone's (1965) work on the temporal reference of dreams does not support this position. The concerns of the preceding day in one's dreams tend to fade away as the night progresses.

Related to this conception is the position advanced here of a positive function for the periodic activation during sleep of the neurophysiological structures that produce dreaming. Nevertheless, in this position, the temporal order of the activation of the neurocognitive microstructure that constitutes the neural substrate of the dream is of no consequence to the individual.

The chief limitation of this position is that we do not as yet have enough hard evidence about how much activation different cortical structures need, how often, and how diffuse or focused its distribution should be. Although the brain-stem origin of cortical activation suggests that it is rather diffuse (Hobson et al., 1986), the network of synaptic links among the activated cortical neurons might rapidly organize the pattern of activation around the personal concerns and goal structures of the sleeper, and this pattern of activation may, in turn, prepare or bias the course of cognitive processes upon awakening. If such were the case, I should conclude that such dreaming thought served an instrumental function for the individual.

Finally, I must add my usual exhortation that dreaming is not a univariate concept or a unidimensional process. The question of function must be raised separately for the amount of information processed in the dream, the hallucinatory quality or belief in the dream fantasy, the thematic and meaningful qualities of the mentation, and finally, the qualities of the imagery, the sensory modality, verbal or visual, and within the latter, the brightness, hue, and clarity of focus.

In conclusion, dreaming is one quite fascinating component of one phase of a cyclical sleep process. This process, one component of which is dreaming sleep, may function to give the non-central nervous system part of the organism a break for restorative purposes and to keep the cognitive engine warm so that it will be ready to run efficiently when the sun rises. However, I suspect that we could do quite well without it.

References

Antrobus, J. (1990). The Neurocognition of Sleep Mentation: Rapid Eye Movements, Visual Imagery and Dreaming." In R. Bootzin, J. Kilstrom, and D. Schacter (Eds.), *Sleep and Cognition* pp. 3–24. Washington, D.C.: American Psychological Association.

————. (1991). "Dreaming: Cognitive Processes During Cortical Activation and High Afferent Thresholds." *Psychological Review* 98: 96–121.

————, Hartwig, P., Rosa, D., and Reinsel, R. (1987). "Brightness and Clarity of REM and NREM Imagery: Photo Response Scale." *Sleep Research* 16: 240.

Aston-Jones. G., and Bloom, F. E. (1981). "Norepinephrine-Containing Locus Coeruleus Neurons in Behaving Rats Exhibit Pronounced Responses to Non-Noxious Environmental Stimuli." *Journal of Neuroscience* 1: 998–900.

Berger, R. J., and Walker, J. M. (1972). "Oculomotor Coordination Following REM and Non-REM Sleep Periods." *Journal of Experimental Psychology* 94: 216–234.

Bloom, F. E. (1980). "How Neurotransmitters May Differentiate a Cell's Role in Sensorimotor Integration and Behavioral State Control." *Neurosciences Research Program Bulletin* 18: 19–21.

Cartwright, R. (1986). "Affect and Dream Work from an Information Processing Point of View." *Journal of Mind and Behavior* 7: 411–428.

Crick, F., and Mitchison, G. (1983). "The Function of Dream Sleep." *Nature* 304: 111–114.

————. (1986). "REM Sleep and Neural Nets." Journal of Mind and Behavior 7: 229–249.

————, Evans, O. R., and Newman, E. A. (1964). "Dreaming: An Analogy from Computers." *New Scientist* 419: 577–580.

Fiss, H. (1986). "An Empirical Foundation for a Self Psychology." *Journal of Mind and Behavior* 7: 161–192.

Freud, S. (1955). *The Interpretation of Dreams.* New York: Basic Books.

Hobson, J. A., Lydic, R., and Baghdoyan, H. A. (1986). "Evolving "Concepts of Sleep Cycle Generation: From Brain Centers to Neuronal Populations." *Behavioral and Brain Sciences* 9: 371–448.

Hobson, J. A., and McCarley, R. W. (1977). "The Brain as a Dream State Generator: An Activation-Synthesis Hypothesis of the Dream Process." *American Journal of Psychiatry* 134: 1335–1348.

McCarley, R. W., and Hobson, J. A. (1975). "Neuronal Excitability Modulation over the Sleep Cycle: A Structural and Mathematical Model." *Science* 189: 58–60.

McCarley, R. W., and Massaquoi, S. G. (1986). "A Limited Cycle Mathematical Model of REM Sleep Oscillator System." *American Journal of Physiology* 251: R1001–R1029.

McClelland, J. L., and Rumelhart, D. E. (Eds.). (1986). *Parallel Processes; Explorations in the Microstructure of Cognition,* vol. 2. Cambridge, Mass.: MIT Press, Bradford Books.

Pagels, H. (1988). *The Dreams of Reason.* New York: Simon and Schuster.

Roffwarg, H. P., Muzio, J. N., and Dement, W. C. (1966). "Ontogenetic Development of the Human Sleep-Dream Cycle." *Science* 152: 604–619.

Rumelhart, D. E., and McClelland, J. L. (Eds.). (1986). *Parallel Distributed Processes: Explorations in the Microstructure of Cognition,* vol. 1. Cambridge, Mass.: MIT Press, Bradford Books.

Verdone, P. (1965). "Temporal Reference of Manifest Dream Content." *Perceptual and Motor Skills* 20: 1253–1268.

INDEX

abandonment, 435
absorption in dream, 127, 200, 209, 212. *See also* involvement in dream
absorption states, 24
abstract concepts/thought, 64–65, 80
academic performance, 384
accommodative functions of dreams, 141, 187
achievement, 268, 269, 455. *See also* goals; success
achievement motivation, 265, 268, 269, 273
achievement striving in dreams, 165
acquired languages, 57, 71, 72
acting, vs noticing, 216
action layer of C-network, 120, 123
action(s), 71, 72, 238. *See also* behavior
activation, 280, 384
   preparatory, 425
   random, 128, 129, 133, 134
activation-deactivation scales, 163–164
activation-synthesis hypothesis, 3, 4, 200–201, 244
active-defense behavior, 272, 274, 280
activities
   daytime, 171–172, 358
   in dreams, 169, 177, 294, 309, 322
   as phase attributes, 32

activity level, and dream control, 218, 219
adaptation
   and dreams, 4, 5, 321–332, 368–371, 375, 403–405 and search activity, 272. *See also* functional adaptation
adaptive dream function, theory of, 140–141
adaptive functioning, 98, 99, 388, 392
adaptive processing, 31
addictive substances, withdrawal from, and dream contents, 392, 399–401, 409
Adelson, J., 202–203
adjustment, overall, and dream contents, 400, 401
adolescents, dreams among, 298, 300, 308
adrenal cortex, 265
"aesthetic arrest," 427
aesthetic effects of dreams, 427, 457
affect
   and C-networks, 123, 124
   and dream functions, 5, 478
   and dream interpretation, 478
   in dreams, 144, 330
      lack of, 327, 330, 331, 332
      and stressful/unusual events on, 322, 324, 326–328, 332

effects of dreaming on, 8, 220, 478
and impactful dreams, 431–434,
    438, 440–447, 466
and intentionality, 24
in nightmares, 144
in recurrent dreams, 298
as self-signal, 403–404
and subliminal stimulation, 384,
    392. *See also* emotions; feelings;
    mood; selective mood regulatory
    function of dreaming
affective insight, dream-induced,
    421, 422, 427–428, 437, 444
affective reactions, and orienting
    response, 451, 455, 458–460, 462,
    464
affective scripts, 459
affective shifts, 436, 444
affective states
    dreaming and, 142, 148–150, 173,
        220
    gender differences in, 154–155
    sleep and, 150–163. *See also* emo-
        tions; mood
affective tuning, 124, 127, 134
afferent system of orienting
    response, 66–67
afunctional/antifunctional theories
    of dreaming, 3–5. *See also* nonutili-
    tarian theories of dreaming
age
    and dream accounts, 490
    and dream contents, 165, 293, 296,
        298, 302–303, 308, 309, 312, 313,
        322. *See also* developmental
        changes; ontogeny
age change/regression in dreams,
    304, 305–306, 308, 309
aggression
    as form of search behavior, 262
    and nightmares, 477, 480
aggression in dreams, 280, 300, 323,
    400

demographic variations in, 165,
    310, 312
direction of, 311, 312, 400
aggressiveness
    and dream contents, 176, 181
    and dream scales, 203
    and impactful dreams, 441, 442
    and performance, 164
    and psychosomatic diseases, 265
    and sleep/sleep deprivation,
        151–163 *passim,* 180, 280, 365
agitated behavior, 271, 274, 281
agony, 433, 434, 435, 444, 445
Aguarauna, 534n2
alcohol/alcoholism
    and dream contents, 392, 399–400
    and REM sleep-learning, 353, 359
    and search activity, 264, 272
    and state-dependent retrieval, 80
alertness, and subliminal stimula-
    tion, 386, 387
alpha intrusions, 390
alpha rhythms, 63
alpha-two adrenoreceptors, 277
altered states of consciousness, dis-
    crete, 205–206
ambiguity, intolerance of, 527, 530
ambition, 372
ambivalence, 482, 518–519, 527
amnesia, 34–35, 81
analyzing dream while dreaming,
    210
anaphylactic shock, 264
Andaman Islanders, 478, 479
Andean (Quechua) culture, 531,
    532–533
anger, 301, 433, 434, 445
anguish, 458, 459
anhedonia, 266
animals
    and dreaming, 6, 12, 17
    in dreams, 298, 300, 304, 308, 312,
        481, 509–510, 527
    and REM sleep, 14, 341–342, 345,

348, 351, 358, 364–366
animism, 430, 431, 445, 455, 466
annunciation dreams, 484
answer
    ability of dream to provide, 221,
        224
    and cycle of communication,
        58–60
    and orienting response, 66, 67
    See also behavior
anthropology, and dream accounts,
    491–492
antidepressants, 174, 178, 271
antifunctional/afunctional theories
    of dreaming, 4–5. *See also* nonutili-
    tarian theories of dreaming
antistructural nature of warps, 33
anxiety
    and dream contents, 176, 325, 331
    and dream enhancement, 402
    and dream interpretation, 482,
        483–484, 485, 486, 530
    and dream narration, 523, 528
    and nightmares, 301
    and NREM sleep/dreams, 402
    and presleep experience, 325, 331
    productive/normal, 264, 274
    and REM sleep, 273, 274, 279, 280,
        283, 369, 402
    and search activity, 264, 270, 271
    and sleep/sleep deprivation, 151–
        163 *passim*, 179, 181
    trait, 273, 390
    unproductive/neurotic, 264, 270,
        271, 273, 274, 279, 280, 283
    See also apprehension; fear
anxiety dreams, 295–296, 298, 315,
    328, 480, 523
    as form of impactful dream, 441,
        446, 461
    frequency of, 421
    functions of, 15
    See also "bad dreams"; nightmares;
        night terrors

anxiety in dreams, 174, 178, 300, 327,
    328, 331
apathy, 266
appetence, 262
apprehension in dreams, 166, 312.
    See also anxiety; fear
archetypal dreams, 424–425, 426,
    444–445
archetypes, undeveloped, 294
arousal
    at end of REM sleep period, 142,
        144, 145, 150
    and dreaming, 15–16, 144, 148,
        149, 328
    and dream recall, 330, 332
    during REM period, 327, 328, 332
    and impactful dreams, 438, 439,
        440
    and information processing, 66,
        70, 329–330
    and mood, 181
    and pre-attentive processes, 86–87
    and presleep stress, 330
    shift toward during sleep, 91–92
    and sleep laboratories, 327
    and state-dependent retrieval, 81
    and state-shift hypothesis, 200
    and subliminal stimulation, 386,
        390
    and tunings, 133–134
arousal-induced awakenings, 466
arousal-retrieval model, 329, 330
Artemidorus of Daldis, 477
arthritis, 396
artificial intelligence, as model for
    dream studies, 18, 201
artists/artistic inspiration, and
    dreaming, 3–4, 422, 428
asleep, defined, 32, 38
assertiveness, 311, 438, 439. *See also*
    feeling expressiveness-assertive-
    ness
assimilative functions of dreams,
    141, 148, 187, 248

association, semantic, 52, 59, 87
associations, 376, 383, 391, 402
associative cortex, 553–554, 555
asthma, 396
asymmetry of cerebral functions, 22, 28
athletes, 272
attachments, 131, 132–133, 406, 523–525, 528
attack dreams, 298, 300, 301, 312, 477, 480. *See also* nightmares
attacking behavior, 274
attention, 33, 66, 67–68, 69–70, 77. *See also* subliminal stimulation
attentional deficiencies, 215
attentional skills, 221–247
attention patterning schemata, 213
attention response, defined, 78
attention span, 387–388
attention to dreams/dream processes
    and dreaming to waking transfer effects, 221–226, 237–239, 242, 246
    and self-awareness/insight, 208, 209, 213, 401–403
    and waking to dreaming transfer effects, 220, 225–227, 230, 233, 235, 239–241, 243, 245
attitudes
    and dreams, 222, 423, 424
    toward dreams, 491, 512–517
attractors, 122, 126, 129
attributes, phase, 32–33
audience, and dream narratives, 530–531
auditory learning tasks, and REM sleep, 348–349
auditory phenomena in dreams, 438, 439, 444
auditory stimuli during sleep, 454–455, 457, 461
authentic being, emergence of, 445
authority figures, 484

automatic information-processing mode, 58, 61, 68–70, 74, 76, 87, 91–92
automaticity, 67–70, 87, 92
automatized attention response, 70, 76, 87, 91
automatized behavior/responses, 62, 69–70, 80, 87, 92
autonomic activity, 145, 148, 390
autopoiesis, 22–23, 25, 30–31, 199, 247
autosuggestion, 214
average evoked response, 392
aversion/aversive stimuli, 262, 277–278. See also defense reaction
avoidance
    active, 262, 283
    of failure, 269, 271, 273
    of harm, 438, 439, 444
    passive, 263, 274, 283
avoidance dreams, 326–331, 332
avoidance tasks, and REMD, 365
awake, defined, 32, 38
awakening(s), 155, 217, 554
    abrupt vs gradual, 390
    arousal-induced, 466
    and dream recall, 12, 63, 390
    fear-induced, 438, 440, 444, 445–446, 463, 466
    movement-induced, 434, 436–437, 444, 466
    number of, 180, 327–328, 330
awareness
    and automatic processes, 69
    and control, 33
    defined, 31
    in dream phases, 38–39
    and information processing, 58
    and intentionality, 24, 33
    levels of, 209–210, 216. *See also* self-reflection
    and memory, 16
    multilevel, 209, 210
    of warps, 33

See also consciousness; lucid dreaming; subliminal stimulation; transcendent awareness; unconscious (ucs), the
awe, 430, 431, 445, 455, 457
awkwardness, 434, 435, 466

babies, in dreams, 302, 315
"bad dreams," 467. *See also* anxiety dreams; nightmares; night terrors
balance, 431, 434, 435
Bali, 3–4
banality, 202, 208, 219
Barbados, 479
barrier insufficiency, 404–407
Beck Depression Inventory, 402
bedtime, 359
behavior
    active-defense, 272, 274, 280
    agitated, 271, 274, 281
    and brain functional states, 87
    coordination/organization of, 12, 55–70, 76, 77–79
    coping, 271
    correct responses during sleep, 62
    and cycle of communication, 55–70
    defense, 262
    defined, 52, 57, 60
    and dream manipulations, 222
    dreams as prescriptions for, 484–485
    efficacy of, 60
    exploratory, 274, 275
    integral, 261
    looking, 442, 444, 446, 450
    maladaptive, 403
    motor, 263
    neurotic, 54
    and noticing, 224, 225, 244
    orientative-exploratory, 262, 263, 271, 274, 280
    and orienting response, 66, 67
    panicky, 262, 263, 270, 271

positional choice, 385
    psychotic, 54
    regressive, 403
    self-preserving, 403
    sleep, 70
    stereotyped, 262, 264, 268, 271
    See also answer; search behavior(s)
behavioral adaptation, 14, 425
behavioral choices, 208, 214, 224, 225
behavioral medicine, 393, 409
behavioral oscillation, 388
behavioral systems, primitive, 12
behavior classification, 261–262
behaviorists, 530
"being-in-the-world," 426
beliefs, 222, 477–486
benzodiazepines, 271
bereavement dreams, 445
bilateral asymmetry of cerebral functions, 22, 28
Binet, A., 382
biochemical mechanisms of search behaviors, 269–270, 276–277
biochemical transductions, 30
biogenetic structural theory, 38, 41n10
biological functions
    of brain, 55, 56
    of sleep, 38
biological processes, and dreams, 2, 4, 5
biology, evolutionary, 425
bizarreness
    as dream characteristic, 202, 304, 446
    as indicator, 208, 210
    vs intensity, 448
    and self-reflectiveness scaling, 211, 212
    and subliminal stimulation, 394
    and waking to dreaming transfer effects, 243, 244
black holes, 122
bodily functions/sensations in

dreams, 307, 430–431, 434, 435, 445, 466
body, dream, 217
body internal (*ene tia*), 478
body-mind issue, 551
body movements, 390
body temperature, core, 26
Bokert, E., 392, 400
Boltzmann machine model, 4
boredom, 24
botanical monograph dream, Freud's, 383
bottom-up processes, 244
boundaries, 301, 404–407, 409
brain
    biological function of, 55
    evolution of, 41*n*10
    functional adaptation of, 55–56, 59
    functional state of, 52, 79–88
    as organizer of human behavior, 56, 57
    psychological function of, 55
    and REM sleep, 15
    and search behavior, 269
    See also catecholamines; electrophysiology; event-related brain potentials; nervous system, central
brain processes, 52. *See also* cycle of communication; information processing
brain science, 119
Brazil, 37, 478, 479, 480, 481–486
breakthrough dreams, 357
breath taxonomy, 498, 499
Brenneis, C., 217–218
brevity of dreams, 202
brothers in dreams, 306
Brown, F., 217
bu (scapulimancy), 490, 502–503
Buddhism, 490, 501, 504, 505, 508, 512, 513, 516
buoyant sensations, 432
burglars in dreams, 298
"butterfly dream," 495

cancer, 397–399, 409
cardiac disease, 396
cardiac rhythm, 264. *See also* heart rate
carry-over effects. *See* transfer effects
Cartesian world-view, 139
catecholamines, 269, 270–271, 276–277, 278, 279, 281
categorization, 514
catharsis, tragic, 467
Catholics, 490
cats, 391
CDPTSD. *See* chronic delayed post-traumatic stress disorder
censorship, 93, 367
centrality-involvement, 218. *See also* involvement in dream
central nervous system, 55, 58–59, 60, 65–66. *See also* brain
cephalic vasodilation, 455, 456
cerebral cortex, 21
cerebral functions, bilateral asymmetry of, 22, 28
certainty, 387
cervical cancer, 397–399, 409
change, 422, 428, 489
change OR, 453, 457–461, 462
chanting, 34
chaos, 33
chaotic activity, 263
character armor, 406
characters in dreams, 169, 216
    across REM periods, 168, 170, 183, 186
    and dreaming to waking transfer effects, 421, 422
    extraordinary, 430, 431
    frequency of, 294, 307–308, 309, 312
    metamorphoses in, 438, 439–440
    number of, 165, 166, 176, 177, 182, 187
    relationship of to dreamer in waking life, 400

repeated, 294, 298
type of, 178, 182, 183, 187
chase dreams, 294, 298, 300–301
chengyu ("set phrases"), 493, 494–496
childbirth, in dreams, 315
childish information-processing
    strategies. *See* primary process
    rules
child molester, dreams of, 307–309
children
    and dreaming, 12, 81, 88, 91,
    95–96, 295, 296
    in dreams, 307
    and recurrent/repetitive
    dreams/nightmares, 294, 298, 300,
    301, 307, 308, 312
    See also infants
Chinese, dreaming among, 489–534
Chinese dynasties, 490
choking, 480
cholinergic-cholinoreceptive compo-
    nent of sleep, 554–555
chronic delayed post-traumatic
    stress disorder (CDPTSD)
    and dream contents, 166, 181, 295–
    298
    and dream repression, 5
    and nightmares, 149–150, 368, 406
    and traumatic dreams, 295–298,
    300
chronobiology, 25–27. *See also* circa-
    dian cycles/rhythms
chun (spring), 512
circadian cycles/rhythms, 25–27,
    31–35, 38, 97
circadian system, 27
clarity, waking, 238, 242
class, social, 165, 490, 513, 514–517,
    531, 533
climax, dream, 432, 438, 440, 466
clinical practice, 363–377, 393,
    395–407. *See also* psychotherapy

clock-dependent (spontaneous) state
    shifts, 91, 92
Clyde Mood Scale, 151, 156, 164, 175,
    176, 177, 179, 181
C-networks, 120, 121, 123–130,
    133–134
coffee, 353
cognition, 21–50, 59, 71, 384
cognitive abilities in dreams, 217
cognitive activation, 12, 553–556
cognitive associations, 30
cognitive deficiencies. *See* deficiency
    views of dreaming
cognitive differences, and dream
    contents, 165–166
cognitive effects of dreaming, 8
cognitive-emotional analysis, system
    of, 56, 57
cognitive-emotional interpretation,
    60–61, 63–65, 68–69
cognitive-emotional strategies, 69,
    75, 76
    defined, 72
    during sleep, 91, 92, 99
    state-dependency of, 81–82
cognitive-emotional style, 63–65, 81,
    83, 94
cognitive experiences, 386, 408
cognitive functions, 5, 55
cognitive interpretive system, 14–15
cognitive output, 555
cognitive processes/processing,
    77–79, 550
cognitive psychology, 17–18, 58,
    425–426
cognitive science(s), 1, 4, 119, 139,
    201, 207, 425
cognitive theory of dreaming,
    Foulkes's, 206
cognitive unconscious, 381, 401
cognitive variables in wakefulness,
    142
cognized environment
    and autopoiesis, 22–23, 25
    and circadian cycles, 31–35

defined, 23, 38
and dreaming, 21, 29
and entrainments, 27, 28
intentionality of, 23–25
and operational environment, 27,
    28
reality as, 21–22
and symbolic function, 29–30
See also external environment;
    internal environment
Cohen, D.B., 324, 325, 392
coherence
    between dreams and waking, 15,
        16, 169–170
    of dream accounts, 490–491
    of dreams, 129–130, 131, 133, 218,
        463
collective image, 424
color, in dreams/dream reports, 222,
    434, 435, 436, 441, 442
communication. *See* cycle of commu-
    nication
Communism, 492, 513, 518
compensation dreams, 326
compensation hypothesis, 323, 325,
    423, 424, 425
competence of dream ego, 197–198
compliance, 225
composite image, 424
comprehension, 24, 39, 421, 422. *See
    also* meaning(s)
computational energy, 121
computational modeling, 18, 201, 207
computer simulation, 18
conative processes, 203, 204. *See also*
    dream control; lucid dreaming;
    self-reflectiveness
conceptualization of problems, 492
conceptual neighbor, 452–453, 456,
    459, 460, 464
concerns, and dreams, 429, 430, 431,
    434, 435, 438, 439, 441, 442, 444.
    See also emotional preoccupations
concreteness, 394, 408

condensation, 93, 126, 424
conductance, skin, 453
conflict
    focal, 370
    inner, 268, 269, 273, 527
conflict resolution, 479, 485, 486
conflictual dream themes, 400–401
Confucianism, 490, 504, 505, 508, 513,
    516, 521, 522, 527
confusion, 237–238, 242, 247, 425, 526
connectedness, 169–170
connectionism, 5, 119–135, 426, 452,
    453
connections, 368–369, 523–525, 528,
    532
connection weights, 120, 123, 124,
    129
conscious episodic recollection, 16,
    33–34
conscious experience, 65
consciousness
    content of, 77
    and cross-phasing, 34–35
    cycles of, 31–35
    dream, 14–17
    and dream creation, 17
    and dream functions, 12, 14–15
    equated with waking, 200, 202
    flow of, 34
    functions of, 16–17
    and information processing,
        16–17, 69
    levels of, 58, 76–77
    nature of, 247–248
    phases of, 31–37, 38
    source of, 247
    states of, 205–206, 385–386, 387,
        388, 389–390, 407
    stream of, 33, 34
    waking, 14, 15, 16, 550
    warps of, 31–35. *See also* cross-
        phasing; hypnagogic warp;
        hypnopompic warp
    See also awareness; discrete

altered states of consciousness model; intentionality; lucid dreaming; polyphasic consciousness; wakefulness; waking state
conscious network, 24, 31, 40
consistency, 203, 490–491
constituents of impactful dreams, 429, 430, 431, 434, 435, 438–443 *passim*
constraint satisfaction, 120, 124, 127–128
contents of dreams. *See* dream contents
context, 80, 87, 123, 134
context-free analysis, 398–399
context information. *See* knowledge sets
continuity
across sleep-wake boundary, 202, 208, 209, 245, 393
of behavioral organization, 60
and consciousness, 31, 34
and dream accounts, 489
and dreams/dream states, 29, 130–133, 369
and intentionality, 24, 39
See also cross-phasing; discontinuity
contradiction principle, 532. *See also* reversal, rule of
contradictions, 491
contrasts, color, 434, 436, 444
control, 69, 265, 269. *See also* dream control
control in vs control over dreams, 216, 217, 218, 219
control elements of signal representations, 73
controlled information-processing mode, 58, 61, 68, 69, 70, 74, 76, 87, 92
control systems approach, 246
conversation, 397–399

coordination, system of, 56, 58, 59, 67. *See also* feedback control loops
coping, 66, 67, 75, 93, 99, 271, 371, 376, 425
core body temperature, 26
core sleep, 328
Cornell Medical Index, 148
corpses, 500, 501
correction dreams, 369
corrective goal, 141, 182
correctness of dreams, 7
correct responses during sleep, 62
Corsican dream glosses, 484
cortex
adrenal, 265
associative, 553–554, 555
cerebral, 21
motor executive, 553–554, 555
prefrontal, 23–24, 28, 30, 31, 32
and REM sleep, 364–365, 553–556
sensorial, 23–24, 28, 30, 31, 32, 33
cosmic dream elements, 424–425
cosmologies, 36–37, 498–499
courage, 216
Cox, C., 324, 325, 392
craving, 392, 400, 401
creative activity, 265, 268, 271, 273, 366
creativity
and boundaries, 404–407
and dreaming, 3–4, 203–204, 245, 314, 422, 428, 506
Han beliefs about, 505–506, 519
and impactful dreams, 422, 428
and madness, 404
and nightmares, 301, 425
creodes, 25, 27–28, 30
Crick, F., 4–5, 119, 128–133, 201, 244
critical attitude, 211, 213
critical judgment, 385
cross-phasing, 34–35, 39. *See also* continuity
Cuddy, M., 4
cultural hegemony, 531–534

Cultural Revolution, Great Proletarian, 513, 518, 525, 532
"culture pattern dreams," 505
culture(s)
    defined, 25
    and dream contents, 293, 310
    and dreaming, 2, 5, 35–37, 293, 489–490, 492, 531–534
    and dream interpretation, 6–7, 477–486
    and functional significance of dreaming/dream recall, 4, 5, 7, 315, 426
    monophasic, 35–36, 39
    and phases of consciousness, 32–33, 39–40
    polyphasic, 36–37, 39–40
    in Western academy, 530
cycle of communication, 55–70
    and acquired knowledge, 59–60, 67, 71, 97
    in children, 95
    defined, 51–52
    and emotions, 78
    and information processing, 60–61, 61–65, 67–70
    nature of, 56–60, 57, 65–67, 71
    operations of, 59–60
    and sleep, 52–53, 89–90, 91, 92, 95, 97

Dallett, J., 322–323
dane kurale ("spider home"), 478
danger, 441, 446, 462, 463, 482, 511
Dao, defined, 505, 514
Daoism, 490, 500, 505, 508, 512, 513, 516–517, 531–534
darkness, lucid, 434, 435, 442
data, units of, 71–72, 75
data constraints, 11–20
day dreaming, 29, 53, 65, 88, 248. See also fantasies
day residue, 131, 167–168, 220, 367, 375, 382–383, 407, 479–480, 486, 520
daytime activities, 171–172, 358

daytime mood, 163–164
death, 262, 439, 445, 458, 481, 482–483, 497
death anxiety, 165
debriefing, 224
deceased figures in dreams, 421, 422, 434, 435, 445, 524
decision making, 75, 484–485
decompensation, schizophrenic, 406
defecating in dreams, 307
defense behaviors, 262
defense reaction, 453, 461–463
defense(s), 301, 376, 382, 425, 426, 485
defensive dream themes, 400–401
defensive strain, 392
deficiency views of dreaming, 197, 199–201, 203, 205, 211, 215. See also activation-synthesis hypothesis; state-shift hypothesis
deities, Han Chinese, 498
deja vu, 210, 405, 421, 422
De Koninck, J.M., 324–325
Delaney, G., 221
delirium, 264
delta sleep, 274
demographic variables, and dream contents, 165–167, 170, 181, 310, 312
demons. See gui; guai
denial, 482, 484, 485, 520, 527
depersonalization, 405
depression
    and dream contents, 166, 174, 178–179, 181, 331
    and learning/memory, 80, 83, 283
    and psychosomatic disease, 265
    and REM sleep/dreams, 180, 273, 274, 278–279, 280, 369, 402
    and renunciation of search, 271
    and search activity, 264, 269, 270–271, 276
    and sleep deprivation, 279, 280
    and sleep physiology, 181
derealization, 405

descriptive elements in dreams, 169, 177

desensitization, 322, 327, 331

desire, 501, 511–512, 519

despair, 460

detachment, 202, 213, 216. *See also* involvement in dream; observer, dreamer as

developmental changes
in dreaming, 4, 5, 7, 88. *See also* age; ontogeny
in memory, 16
in neurognostic structures, 22

developmental functions
of dreaming, 38
of search behavior, 272

developmental stages, regression during sleep to earlier, 90–91, 98, 200

diagnoses, medical, and dream contents, 395–399, 409

dialecticism, 498, 499

dialogues, 210

dichotomies, 498, 499

Differential Emotions Scale, 429

disabilities, 322

disappointment, 433, 434, 459

discontinuity, 201, 205, 489

discontinuity, dream
and connectionism, 127, 129–133
and sleep physiology, 450, 451, 454, 456
and state-shift hypothesis, 92

discouragement, 433, 434, 459

discrepancy enhancement, 246

discrete altered states of consciousness model, 205–206

discrimination, 62, 365, 382, 384–385, 387–388, 390

disentrainment, 24, 33

disguise, 367, 376, 397

disillusionment, 434, 435, 445

disorientation, 15

displacement, 93, 126–127, 484

disruption-avoidance-adaptation model, 325–326, 358–359

dissatisfaction, 433, 434

dissociation, 14–15, 79–80, 520–521

distortion, 93

distraction, 329

distress
and impactful dreams, 433, 434, 435, 441, 445
and orienting response, 451, 454, 459
vs stress, 265

distributed neural net models, 551

disturbance structure, 123

disturbing dreams. *See* dream(s), disturbing

disturbing motives, 183, 184

diurnal animals, 26, 38

diurnal temperature curve, 163, 164

divination, 502–512

dizziness (anxiety), 151–163 *passim*, 176, 179, 181

dolphins, 283–284

dominance, political, 533–534

Domino, G., 203

dopamine, 270

"Dorothea" (dream subject), 302–303

double profile stimulus, 394–395

dream accounts, 489–534

dream action, carriers of, 216

dream competence, 221

dream composition, 217

dream consciousness, 14–17

dream construction, 140, 447

dream content(s), 11
across-night variations in, 145, 168, 170, 183, 186, 187, 358
and affective state, 165–179, 181
age variations in, 310
and arthritis, 396
and asthma, 396
and cardiac disease, 396
daytime activities and, 171–172
demographic variations in, 29,

165–167, 170, 181, 310–311, 312
dream interpretation and, 478
drive states and, 391
drugs and, 174, 175
emotionally significant material
during dream-REM process and,
174–175
emotionally significant waking
experiences and, 171–174, 175
films and, 321, 323–324, 324–325,
327, 391
future orientation of, 315
and headaches, 396
of homosexuals, 311–312
and hypertension, 396
and hypnotic suggestion, 327
and illness, 167, 170, 178–179, 395–
399
incubation. See dream incubation
individual variations in, 167–168,
170
influences on, 92, 93, 96, 140, 141–
142, 170–179
and information processing, 14,
332
and intentionality/awareness, 38–
39
and migraines, 396
mood and, 165–179, 181, 182, 400
new/nonrepetitive, 315
norms for, 294, 310–311, 312
and oneiromancy, 480
and plasma free fatty acids, 396
predictability of, 167
and pregnancy, 396
presleep/during-sleep events and,
321–332, 391
vs process, 207
and recurrent dreams, 298, 299,
300
REM-period variations in, 145,
168, 183, 186
significance of, 367–369
and sleep laboratories, 327

and sleep maintenance, 148
and sleep physiology, 364
and sleep stages, 401
and somatic conditions, 395–399
and stress, 321–322, 359, 391
and subliminal stimulation, 322,
391, 392, 399, 401
suggestions and, 327, 391
symbolic nature of, 30–31
systematic variability of, 156
and ulcers, 396
and waking life/thought, 13, 168–
170, 197
and water deprivation, 327
wishes and, 391
See also manifest content; repetition of dreams/dream elements
dream control, 198–199, 214–216
and attention to dreams/dream
processes, 225, 226, 233, 235, 239,
240, 241
and awareness, 38–39, 216
and behavioral choice, 225
by experimenter, 214
and creativity, 202–203
and deficiency views of dreaming,
199–201, 214–215
defined, 214
development of, 213, 214, 215,
216–217, 222, 233, 239, 243
differences in, 204, 216
and dream competence, 221
and dreaming to waking transfer
effects, 199
and dream recall, 226, 233–235,
239, 241, 243
and dream self-reflectiveness, 210,
212, 216, 240
gender differences in, 233, 242
learning/practice and, 214, 233,
243
and lucidity, 198, 207, 213, 214,
215–216, 217, 218, 219, 230, 243
and oneiromancy, 479–480

and pleasurable dreams, 221
prelucid forms of, 215, 216
as quasi-continuous (not dichotomous) variable, 213
scaling, 214, 216–219, 240
spontaneous occurrence of, 240
and waking to dreaming transfer
effects, 199, 233–235, 239
without lucidity, 216, 219
See also conative processes; intentional dreaming
Dream Control Scale, 213, 216–219,
222, 224, 225, 226, 240, 247
dream deprivation, 403
dream diary, 223
dream ego, 39, 197–198, 202–203,
209, 210
dream elements, repeated, 294, 295,
309–314, 315
dream endings, 429, 431, 432, 434,
436–437, 438, 440, 442, 443, 444,
446, 465–466
dream enhancement, 401–403
dreamer
vs dream narrator, 530
perspective of in dream, 429, 431,
432, 434, 436, 438, 440, 442, 444,
445, 456
presence/role of in dream, 219,
298, 400, 432
dream events, extraordinary, 430,
445
dream exegesis. *See* oneiromancy
dream forgetting, 5, 7, 13, 329, 402
dream formation, 54, 140, 217,
479–480
dream gaze, 458
dream generation
afunctional theories of, 549–556
in childhood, 12, 95
mechanisms of, 88–89, 207, 244,
549–550
and state-shift hypothesis, 52, 54,
88, 89–96

dream glosses, 481, 482–486, 506–511
dream imagery, 13, 17, 432, 551–552,
556. *See also* imagery
dream immersion, 402
dream impacts, 419–467
dream incubation, 33–34, 221, 358,
359. *See also* presleep experiences
dreaming
and brain micro-states, 65
as continuous process, 93
defined, 2, 11–12, 446–447
dimensions of, 2
effects of, 13–14
as form of existence, 17
functional significance of, 1–8,
549–556
and homeomorphogenesis, 30
psychological, functions of, 139–
140
and search activity, 261–284
as symbolic activity, 30–31
dreaming to waking transfer effects,
204, 220–226, 235–238, 239, 242,
243–244, 247, 419–467, 556
and attention to dreams/dream
processes, 225, 226, 237, 239
and dream recall, 226, 235, 237,
239, 242, 245–246
gender differences in, 222, 237, 242
and impactful dreams, 429–430,
432, 433, 437, 441, 443, 444, 446
and lucid dreaming, 232, 237–238,
239, 242, 247
dream intensity, 446–450
dream interpretation, 29, 54
among Han Chinese, 491, 502–512
and connectionist theory, 126, 133
vs dream psychology, 370
functions of, 477–486, 550
metaphorical (symbolic), 309, 315–
316
relation of theory to, 370–377
dream isolation, 197, 200, 201, 207,
220, 243

dream mechanics, 219
dream movements. *See* movement
  style
dream narrative(s)
  vs actual dreams, 531, 534*n*1
  characteristics of, 93
  coherence of, 438, 439
  and connectionism, 129, 130
  and defense reaction, 463
  length of, 400
  transformations within, 425
  uses for, 489–534
dream organization, 140
dream patterns, gender differences
  in, 154–155
dream phases, 32–33
dream phenomenology, 207, 450–463
dream planning processor, 202
dream praxis, Han Chinese, 512–517,
  532–534
dream process, vs content(s), 207
dream protocols, 225
dream psychology, 370
dream recall, 148, 202, 204, 212, 221,
  245–246, 390
  and arousal, 63, 330, 332
  and brain's functional state, 94–95
  in children, 12, 95, 296
  cross-phasing and, 34–35
  and dream control, 226, 233–235,
    241, 243
  and dream functions, 145, 148, 187,
    550
  and dreaming to waking transfer
    effects, 13–14, 226, 235, 237, 238,
    239, 242, 245–246, 555–556
  and dream self-reflectiveness, 200,
    225–226, 227, 241, 243
  dysfunctionality of, 201
  frequency of, 555
  functions of, 4–5
  influences on, 29, 172–173, 390,
    402, 491
  and information processing, 81,
    329, 332

and lucid dreaming, 227, 232, 239,
  241
process of, 329
quality of, 89
and redintegration, 330
and REM sleep, 89, 94–95, 96, 276,
  279
and sleep stages, 89, 390
and state-shift hypothesis, 54, 94–
  95, 99
and stress, 323, 329
and waking to dreaming transfer
  effects, 221, 222, 227, 230, 232, 239
  See also arousal-retrieval model
dream reminiscence, spontaneous,
  421, 422
dream reports
  contents of, 11, 225, 429
  differences in, 53, 89, 94–95, 144–
    145
  and dreaming to waking transfer
    effects, 237
  interpersonal situation and, 172–
    173, 531
  skills in providing, 222, 224
  and waking to dreaming transfer
    effects, 237
  word count of, 225, 227
dream-report variables, 11
dream repression, 5, 7, 13, 329
dream residues. *See* dreaming to
  waking transfer effects
dream retrieval. *See* dream recall
dream(s)
  cognitive processes and, 386
  common/typical, 294
  as data source, 367
  defined, 89
  as dependent variable, 140, 142,
    171–175, 324
  disturbing, 144, 148, 187. *See also*
  nightmares
  and illness, 395–399
  as independent variable, 140, 142,
    205, 324

length of, 202
as purposeful constructions, 386
reactivity/proactivity of, 170
recurrent. *See* recurrent dreams
and responsiveness to treatment,
    399–401, 409
and search activity, 274, 275–276
and self-understanding/self-
    awareness, 401–403
as signal detectors, 381–409
and sleep physiology, 450, 451,
    454, 456, 459, 464, 551
and state-dependent retrieval, 80
and state-shift hypothesis, 54
and subliminal stimulation, 384–
    387, 407
types of, 294, 444–446, 479. *See also*
    annunciation dreams; anxiety
    dreams; archetypal dreams;
    attack dreams; avoidance
    dreams; "bad dreams"; bereave-
    ment dreams; breakthrough
    dreams; chase dreams; compensa-
    tion dreams; dysphoric dreams;
    entrapment dreams; existential
    dreams; falling dreams; flying
    dreams; helplessness dreams;
    impactful dreams; intellectual
    dreams; invasion dreams; lucid
    dreaming; mythic dreams; night-
    mares; night terrors; NREM
    dreaming; nudity dreams;
    painful dreams; pleasurable
    dreams; post-traumatic dreams;
    punishment dreams; recurrent
    dreams; REM dreaming; thirst-
    related dreams; transcendent
    dreams; traumatic dreams;
    unpleasant dreams; visitation
    dreams; "war neurosis" dreams
    as warnings, 395–399
    See also meng
dream scales, 203, 211–219, 240–241.
    See also Dream Control Scale;
    Dream Self-Reflectiveness Scale

Dream Self-Reflectiveness Scale, 212,
    213, 218, 222, 224, 225, 226,
    240–241, 247
dream self. *See* dream ego
dream series, 294, 302–309, 310,
    311–312, 314
dream specialists, 36. *See also* oneiro-
    critics
dream themes
    and automatized responses, 92–93
    awareness/control of, 29
    discontinuity/continuity of, 127,
        129–133
    and dream narratives, 492
    patterns of, 183–187
    progressive-sequential patterns
        of, 183–185, 186, 187
    and recurrentdreams/
        nightmares, 298, 300–301,
        303, 309
    repetitive, 294, 295, 298, 302–309,
        314, 315
    repetitive-traumatic patterns of,
        183, 185–186, 187
    and responsiveness to treatment,
        400
    and traumatic dreams, 303, 309
    zero/near-zero frequency of
        expected, 307–308, 309
dream theory, Han Chinese, 491,
    498, 501, 518–530
dream-think (*mengxiang*), 496
dream translation, 188
dream trips to multiple realities, 36
dream within a dream, 210, 212
dream workers, 208, 220
"dream work" (Freud's concept of),
    92, 93, 140, 424
dream yogis. *See* Tibetan yogis
drinking, in dreams, 392, 400
drive, and C-networks, 123
drive discharge, 367, 369, 370
drive gratification, 400–401
drive intensity, 365

drive material, 400–401
drive pressure, 365, 366
drive regulation, 392
drivers, 33, 34
drive states, 391
drugs
    and dream contents, 174, 175, 177
    and imagery, 88
    and mood, 155, 164
    and phases of consciousness, 36, 37
    and REM sleep/dreaming, 278, 359
    and state-dependent retrieval, 79–80
drumming, 34
dualism, Han Chinese, 498, 499
dualistic world-view, 139, 551
dulled-out states, 24
dynamical systems, 120–121, 127
dynamic functional theories, 3
dynamic imagination, 466
dynasties, Chinese, 490
dysphoric dreams, 300, 445

eating, in dreams, 302, 493, 508
ECL (Emotions Checklist), 428–429
economic rationalism, 532
ecstasy, 430, 431, 432, 444, 445
Edel, L., 530
education, 35, 296
EEG-EOG-EMG sleep recording, 344
EEG events, phasic, 91
EEG patterns
    and brain's functional state, 79, 91, 200
    developmental changes in, 73, 83, 84
    during REM sleep, 366
    during sleep, 91
    and information processing, 61, 63–65, 76
    and sleep walking, 62–63
    and state-dependent retrieval, 80–84, 96

and states of consciousness, 52, 53, 63, 67
    and subliminal stimulation, 391
EEG reactivity, and orienting response, 59, 61–62, 65–67, 70, 76
effectiveness
    of actions in dreams. See dream control
    of problem-solving in dreams, 183–187, 376
effects of dreams/dreaming, 13–14, 427. See also dreaming to waking transfer effects
efferent system of orienting response, 66–67
efficacy (ling), 497, 498, 499, 500, 501
effort/exertion, 216, 218, 219, 267, 268, 466
ego-absent dreams, 209
ego boundaries, 406
ego control(s), 179, 199, 200, 207, 215, 243
ego development, 406
egoism, 521
ego style, 217–218
Eich, J.E., 79–80
eidetic imagery, 382
E/I. See excitatory-inhibitory ratio
elaboration, 423, 484, 554, 555
electrical stimulation, 322
electroneurophysiological measures, 551
electrophysiology, 58, 61–65, 244, 263, 269–270
EMs. See eye movements
EMC (empirical modification cycle), 25
Embedded Figures Test, 406
emergent self-awareness/self-observation, 434, 436
EMG excitation, 455, 457, 458, 460, 462–463
EMG suppression, 454, 455, 457, 458, 462
emic studies, 491–492

emotional climax in dreams, 432, 438, 440

emotional conflict, and dream function, 479

emotional experiences, intensity of, 171, 174, 342, 353, 358–359

emotional functions, 55

emotionality, 365, 446

emotional languages, 57, 72, 77, 78

emotionally charged dream images, 482, 483–484

emotionally charged/significant experiences, and dream contents, 171–175, 478–479, 482

emotional material, and REM deprivation, 366

emotional preoccupations
and dream contents, 173, 174, 182, 183–187, 294–316, 367–368, 370–377, 426, 477, 519–523, 556
and dream interpretation, 482
See also concerns

emotional reserve, Han Chinese, 520–521, 527

emotional responsivity, 148, 149. *See also* arousal

emotional significance, of dream contents, 367

emotional state, and dream functions, 148–149

emotional surge during REM sleep, 145–150, 182, 187

emotional tension, 264, 270, 272

emotion(s)
and acquired knowledge, 71
and behavioral organization, 61, 77–79
as cause of dreams, 501, 511–512, 519–523
and cycle of communication, 59
and dream contents, 167, 171–172
and dream reports, 222
in dreams, 88, 90, 165–166, 309
and impactful dreams, 429, 430, 431, 433, 434, 436–438, 440, 441, 442, 443, 444, 445–446
and orienting response, 67
as phase attributes, 32
and pre-attentive processes, 58, 87
See also affect; affective states; cognitive-emotional interpretation

Emotions Checklist (ECL), 428–429

empirical data, 11–20

empirical modification cycle (EMC), 25

empiricism, 514–515

encoding, 423

endings. *See* dream endings

endocrinal tissues, 24

energetic quality of impactful dreams, 430–431

energy landscape, 121–122, 126

energy. *See* qi

ene tia (body internal), 478

Engel, G., 264, 271

enhanced sensibilities, 430, 433, 434

enlivenment, 466

entertainment, 201

entrainment(s), 23, 27, 28, 38, 41n7, 213, 221

entrapment dreams, 300

environmental mastery, 426. *See also* mastery hypotheses

environmental press, 169

environmental vigilance, 438, 440, 444, 446, 449, 467

environment. *See* cognized environment; external environment; internal environment; hallucinatory environment; operational environment; reality

epilepsy, 80, 264

epinephrine, 269–270

epiphenomenon, 2–4, 7, 130

episodes of experience, cognized, 31

epistemic functions of dreaming, 5

epistemological functions of dreaming, 1, 247, 248

equations between dreams and pre-

dicted events, 480, 481–482, 506–511, 515
erections, penile, 364, 390
ERPs. *See* event-related brain potentials
error(s)
 dreaming as source of, 4, 7, 201
 and dream interpretation, 503
escape, desire to, 462, 463
estrangement, 433, 434
ethnicity, 531, 533
ethnopsychiatry, 492
ethnoscience, 491–492
ETOH-dependent subjects, 402
Euroamericans, 28, 29
evaluation, 75
event-related brain potentials (ERPs), 61, 64, 453, 454, 457, 461
evocators, 30
evolutionary biology, 425
evolution of REM cognitive processes, 552–556
exams
 in dreams, 522–523, 528–529
 and REM sleep, 344, 369
excitation, 77
 EMG, 455, 457, 458, 460, 462–463
 of postural musculature, 462
excitatory connections, 120, 121, 122
excitatory-inhibitory ratio (E/I), 122–123, 124, 125, 128
exclusion, 435
exercise, 321, 353
existential-analytic dream theorists, 426–427
existential depth, 435
existential dreams, 445, 446, 450, 457–461, 465, 466–467
expectancy, 61–62, 66
expectations, 388
expectedness, 65
experience, 7, 24, 31, 41n9, 41n10
EXPeriencing scale, 402
experiential functions of dreaming, 5

experiential modes, 388, 407
experimental psychology, 425
experimenter control, 214
exploitation fantasies, 171
exploration/exploratory behavior, 24, 274, 275, 444, 446. *See also* orientative-exploratory behavior
expression, object as, 30
expressiveness, 216, 219. *See also* feeling expressiveness-assertiveness
external environment, 55, 56, 57, 67. *See also* cognized environment; operational environment
external origin, visual images of, 449
external self-observation, 431, 432, 436, 438, 440, 442
external vigilance, 438, 440, 444, 446, 449, 463
extraordinary dream events, 430, 445
extraordinary dream figures, 424–425, 430, 431
extraordinary sources of light, 431, 432, 444
extrasensory experiences, 405
eye, angular deflection of, 550
eyeblinks, 458
eye movements (EMs), 145, 364, 365, 366, 448, 449

facial expressions, 458, 460
failure
 of dreams, 368, 376
 in dreams, 528–529
 and impactful dreams, 434, 435, 459
 and REM sleep, 272, 369
 and renunciation of search, 267–268, 271, 283
failure. *See also* success
failure-success, 218, 219, 455
faithfulness of models, 15
falling dreams, 232, 294
familiarity
 and automatic information processing, 69, 70

and EEG reactivity, 61–62, 66
and orienting response, 65
and pre-attentive processes, 86, 87
and self-reflectiveness, 212
and working memory, 75
family enculturation, 35
family members in dreams, 166, 178,
    460, 523–525
fangshi (magicians), 503, 515–516
fantasies/fantasizing, 29, 30, 58, 67,
    77, 94, 264, 306. *See also* day
    dreaming
fasting, 36
fathers in dreams, 304, 305, 306, 307,
    460
father substitutes in dreams, 308
fatigue
    and impactful dreams, 434, 435,
        439, 444, 445, 459
    and performance, 350, 387
fear
    and impactful dreams, 438, 439,
        440, 441, 444, 445–446, 454, 465
    and orienting response, 451, 462,
        463
    and renunciation of search, 266,
        271, 274
    and search requirement, 267
    See also anxiety; apprehension;
    nightmares
fear-induced awakenings, 438, 440,
    444, 445–446, 463, 466
fear motivation, 365
feedback
    between dreaming and waking
    consciousness, 208, 244–245, 245–
        246
    and dream narratives, 490
    and search activity, 270, 277, 278
    and stereotyped behavior, 262
feedback control loops, 55, 58–59. *See
    also* system of coordination
feeling expressiveness-assertiveness,
    218, 219

feeling(s)
    and dream control, 219
    and impactful dreams, 429, 430,
        431, 432, 433, 434, 436–438, 440,
        441, 442, 443, 444, 445–446
    and orienting response, 67
    and pre-attentive processes, 58
    and responsiveness to treatment,
        400
    and working memory, 75
    See also affect; mood
field dependence-independence, 390,
    404, 406
fighting, in dreams, 481, 483, 504
films, and dream contents, 321,
    323–324, 324–325, 327, 391
finitude, 426, 445
fire, in dreams, 298, 430, 432, 456,
    481, 493, 507
Fishbein, H., 2–3, 8
Fiss, H., 386, 387, 392, 394, 399–401
5HT (serotonin), 125, 128
fixations, 314
floating, in dreams, 431, 432, 466, 506
floods, in dreams, 298
flying dreams, 214, 232, 294, 430, 493,
    506
flying shamans, 36
focal conflict, 370
folk religion, 489, 497, 500, 516–517,
    531–534
folk sociology, 524
food, in dreams, 302, 493, 508
forgetting dreams. *See* dream repres-
    sion
Fosshage, J., 403
Foucault, M., 17
Foulkes, D., 203, 206, 207, 220,
    446–447
fractionation, 453
free associations, 402
freezing, 262, 263, 264, 462, 463
French, T., 309, 370, 479
Freudians, vs Jungians, 530, 531

Freudian symbols, 481–482
Freud, S.
 and deficiency views of dreaming, 199, 202, 207, 215
 and dream functions, 140, 142, 150, 322, 367–368, 369, 370, 382–383, 400, 407, 424, 520
 and dream interpretation, 477, 479
 dreams of, 313
 and traumatic dreams, 267, 295–296, 406
friendliness, 151–164 *passim*, 176, 177, 180, 181
friendly interactions in dreams, 310
friends, and dream interpretation, 524–525
Fromm, E., 309, 370, 479
frontal brain lobe, 269
frustration, 268, 271, 282, 459
fulfillment, object as, 30
fullness references in dreams, 166
fully polyphasic cultures, 36–37
function, concept of, 139–140, 363–364, 423–427
functional adaptation, 55–56, 68–69, 76. *See also* habituation
functional arguments/explanations, 293, 315
functionalism, language of, 315
functional states of brain, 79–88, 91, 94–95, 98. *See also* state-shift hypothesis
functional theories of dreaming, 3
functions of beliefs about dreaming, 477–486
functions of dreaming, and dream interpretation, 478–479
further cognitive-emotional interpretation, 60–61
future, dreams as predictors of, 421, 422, 480–485, 505, 527–528, 532
future challenges/concerns, dreams as way of dealing with, 294, 315

Gaines, R., 3–4

Gallistel, C., 363, 364, 368
gamma-amino butyric acid (GABA), 125, 128
gender
 and affective state, 154–155
 and dream accounts/theory/interpretation, 490, 514–517, 531, 533
 of dream characters, 310, 312
 and dream contents, 165–166, 173, 293, 309–310, 313–314, 322
 and dream control, 233, 242
 and dreaming to waking transfer effects, 222, 237, 242
 and dream recall, 245, 246
 and dream self-reflectiveness, 227, 242
 and lucid dreaming, 239, 242
 and mood changes across the night, 155
 and nightmares, 4
 and repetitive dream elements, 310, 313–314
 and sleep patterns, 154–155
 and waking to dreaming transfer effects, 227, 242
gender change/confusion, in dreams, 304, 305, 307
genetics, 22
gentry, Han, 489, 505, 513, 533–534
geomancy, 514
gestalts, incomplete, 294
ghosts, 497, 498, 502. *See also gui*
give-up[-]giving up reaction, 264
Global Assessment Scale, 400
goals
 and behavior, 56
 and C-networks, 123
 cognitive processes and, 77
 and controlled information-processing mode, 68
 and development of self, 372
 and further cognitive-emotional interpretation, 60
 and impactful dreams, 429, 430,

431, 434, 435, 438, 439, 441, 442, 444, 459
and orienting response, 67
and phases of consciousness, 34
and pre-attentive processes, 58
gods, 497, 504, 508, 516, 518. *See also shen*; spiritual figures; supernatural figures
Gottschalk[-]Gleser content scoring system, 165
gracefulness, 431, 432, 435, 466
Great Mother, 516
Great Proletarian Cultural Revolution, 513, 518, 525, 532
Greenberg, R., 275–276
Green, C., 203
groups in dreams, 174
group support, 214
group therapy, 322, 368
guai (odd, strange, monster, demon), 499, 500, 503
Guajiro annunciation dreams, 484
guanxi (tie, connection, relationship, significance, concern), 524
gui (ghost, demon, spirit), 496–499, 500, 502, 505, 511, 512, 524
guilt, 301, 308, 433, 434, 445, 459

habits, acquisition of, 72
habituation, 52, 59, 62, 66, 326, 451. *See also* functional adaptation
Haiti, 484, 485
Hall, C., 294, 302–316
hallucinations, hypnagogic, 53, 65
hallucinatory emotional experiences, 264
hallucinatory environment, 442
hallucinatory quality of dreams, 556
Hall[-]Van de Castle dream content scoring system, 165, 169, 175, 176, 218, 310. *See also* quantitative content analysis system
Han Chinese, dreaming among, 489–534

happiness. *See* unhappiness
harm avoidance, 438, 439, 444
harmony principle, 121, 134
Hartmann, E., 199–200, 296–297, 300–301, 404–407, 409, 425
Hauri, P., 323
headaches, 396
healing powers, 430
heart rate
acceleration of, 455, 461, 462
deceleration of, 391–392, 453, 458, 462
hegemony, cultural, 531–534
Heidegger, M., 445
helplessness
learned, 265, 268, 269, 282
primary, 266
and REM sleep/dreams, 274, 279
and renunciation of search, 266–267, 277–278
helplessness dreams, 445
heterosexuality in dreams, 174, 178
heterosexual problems, 458
heterosexuals, dreams of, 305
Higher Cortical Functions in Man (Luria), 363–364
Hinton, G., 4, 244
hippocampus, 263, 269, 274, 364
Hobbesian materialistic world-view, 139
Hobson, A., 200–201
holes in dreams, 307
holistic world-view, 139
homeomorphogenesis, 30–31, 38, 42n12
homeostasis, 328
homeostatic conditions, 60
homeostatic factors, 97
homesickness, 523
homosexuals, dreams of, 311–312
homosexuals/homosexuality, in dreams, 304, 305–306
hopelessness, 397–399
hormonal conditions/states, 60, 83

Horne, J., 328
horoscopy, 514
hostility in dreams, 174, 178, 328, 448
H-reflex, 462
humanities, vs science, 530
hun (soul, mood, spirit), 497, 498,
　500, 501, 502, 505, 524
hunger, 365
hunling (soul), 498, 499
hunpo (soul), 498, 499, 500, 501, 524
hunting, 481, 484–485
hyperintentionality, 24, 39
hyperreactivity, 80
hyperresponsivity, 148, 149–150, 179
hypersexuality, 365
hypertension, 264, 396
hypnagogic hallucinations, 53, 65
hypnagogic period, 221
hypnagogic reverie, 382
hypnagogic warp, 37
hypnopompic warp, 37
hypnosis/hypnotic suggestion, 81,
　327, 391
hypointentionality, 24, 28–29, 38, 39
hyporesponsivity, 179
hypothalamus, 265, 269, 272

iconic symbols, 520, 526, 535n6
ideology, 489, 491, 492, 533–534
idioms. *See chengyu*
illness
　and dream contents, 166, 322, 395–
　　399, 409, 481
　and dream enhancement, 402–403
　and impactful dreams, 439, 458
　as repetitive dream theme, 302
image formation, 387
image (right-hemispheric) thinking,
　277, 279
imagery
　and homeomorphogenesis, 30
　cognitive processes and, 77, 386
　drug-induced, 88
　during sleep, 94

and EEG patterns, 64–65, 449
eidetic, 382
vs existence/experience, 17
and impactful dreams, 446, 459
normal, 88
pathological, 88
schizophrenic, 88
and self-reflectiveness, 210
spontaneous, 383
and subliminal stimulation, 383,
　384–385, 391
and wakeful mentation, 53, 88, 90,
　549
See also dream imagery
imagery mode of information pro-
　cessing, 65
images, collective vs composite, 424
imaginary death, 262
imagination, 200, 202
imipramine, 281
immortality, 516, 517
impactful dreams, 419–467
　defined, 428
　effects of, 429–430, 432, 433, 437,
　　441, 443, 444, 446
　frequency of, 421, 422, 428
　and sleep physiology, 449–450,
　　453–464
　types of, 444–446
importance of information, 65, 66,
　91–92
imprinting, 266–267
incidental stimuli. *See* subliminal
　stimulation
incoherence of models, 16
incomprehension, 7
incongruity, 491
incorporation, 322–323, 324, 325–326,
　329, 331, 332, 358–359, 392
incubation. *See* dream incubation
incubi, 480, 497
independence, 267
indexical approaches to dreaming, 2,
　3–4, 5
indexical symbols, 480–481, 515, 520,
　526, 533, 534

indifferent perceptions, 383
indifferent stimuli. *See* subliminal
    stimulation
induced state shifts, 91, 92
industrialized cultures, oneiromancy
    in, 477
ineffable significance, 430, 431, 434,
    438, 441, 442, 444, 445, 446, 466
ineffectuality, 429, 434, 435, 459
infantile wishes, 294
infants, 6, 12, 17, 22, 403. *See also* chil-
    dren
influence and response, principle of,
    528
information evaluation processes.
    See pre-attentive processes
information generator, brain as, 55
information processing
    and arousal, 329–330, 332
    and consciousness, 14–17
    and dream imagery, 551–552
    and dreaming, 14, 128, 200, 202,
        363, 556
    electrophysiology of, 61–65
    and emotions, 77
    and environment, 62
    and REM sleep, 14, 363, 365, 550,
        555–556
    and subliminal activation, 393, 408
    unconscious, 202, 381, 401
    without imagery, 552
    See also signal detection model
information-processing modes,
    64–65, 67–70, 70, 78, 86–88, 94. *See*
    also automatic information-pro-
    cessing mode; controlled informa-
    tion-processing mode
information-processing operations,
    53, 98
information-processing paradigm,
    51, 56
information-processing strategies,
    53, 54, 57, 65, 68, 69, 90–91, 329
information-processing systems, 55,
    425

information storage, 55, 81–82, 329.
    See also memory
inhibition
    of behavior, 263, 270, 275
    decreased, 126
    of postural musculature, 458, 459
    semantic, 52, 59, 68, 82, 86, 87
inhibitory connections, 120, 121, 122
initial interpretation of information.
    See pre-attentive processes
initially presented stimuli. *See* initial
    OR
initial OR, 453, 454–457, 458
initiation dreams, 484
initiative, 266, 372
injuries, 266–267, 301, 402–403, 439
innate responses. *See* reflexive stimu-
    lus-response relationships
inner-directedness, 390
inputs, 60, 121, 123, 124, 126. *See also*
    sensory input
insight, 294, 394
    and attention to dreams, 208, 402
    dream-induced, 221, 421, 422, 427,
        428, 437, 444
    and oneiromancy, 480, 485
insomnia, 26, 125, 181, 278
inspiration, creative, 422, 428, 500,
    506
instinct theory, Freud's, 296
instinctual tuning, 123, 124, 127, 134
instrumental value of dreaming, 550
integrated self, 403–404, 407
integration, and dreams, 368–369,
    371, 375, 377
integrative function of dreaming,
    148–150, 478–479, 550. *See also*
    sleep maintenance
integrity of self, 403–404
integrity of sleep. *See* sleep mainte-
    nance
intellectual dreams, 314
intellectual stream, in Chinese
    thought, 514–517

intelligence. *See ling*; representational intelligence
intelligentsia, Han, 489, 513, 533, 534
intensity
  of affect, 155, 164, 177, 182, 400
  of dreaming, 144–145, 150
  of emotional experiences, 171, 174
intensity references in dreams, 166
intentional deficiencies, 215
intentional dreaming, 204, 205, 206, 209, 214, 215, 240. *See also* dream control
intentionality
  and automatic processes, 69
  and awareness, 24, 33, 216
  circadian cycles of, 32
  and C-networks, 123, 124
  and cognized environment, 23–25, 28, 29
  and cross-phasing of consciousness, 39
  defined, 24
  and dream control, 38–39, 198–199, 200, 218
  and dream ego, 202, 203, 207
  in dream generation mechanism, 207
  and dream recall, 245
  intensity of, 24, 28
  and nightmares, 205
  and phases of consciousness, 33
  quality of, 28
  scaling of, 213–214
  and state-shift hypothesis, 243
  and waking self-exploration/insight, 205
  and warps of consciousness, 33
  See also hyperintentionality; hypointentionality; will
intentional processes, 207
intentional tuning, 123, 124, 127, 134
interacting with dream experience, 214
interactions in dreams, 309, 310, 322
interest in dreams, 237, 238

interference, 329
intermittent activation of neurocognitive processes, 554
internal environment, 55, 56, 57, 67. *See also* cognized environment
internal origin, visual images of, 449
interpersonal boundaries, 406, 407
interpersonal relations, 221, 296, 530–531
interpersonal situations, 172–174
The Interpretation of Dreams (Freud), 295, 313
interpretation of information, 56–61. *See also* cycle of communication; information processing; pre-attentive processes
interpretive anthropology, 492
intimacy in dreams, 174, 178, 460
intolerance of ambiguity, 527
invasion dreams, 302
involvement in dream, 213, 216. *See also* absorption in dream; centrality-involvement; detachment; observer, dreamer as; self-involvement in dream
Irma dream, Freud's, 367–368
irrationality, 518, 534
ischemic heart disease, 265
isolation in dreams, 302–303
isomorphism of symbolic models, 41n8

Jeffrey (dream series subject), 310–311
jiao (teaching), 516
Jivaro (Equador), 37
Jones, R., 370
Jones, R.M., 479
joy, 430
Jung, C.G., 217, 309, 323, 424–425, 426, 444
Jungians, vs Freudians, 530, 531

Kafka, F., dreams of, 312–313
Kagwahiv Indians (Brazil), 37, 478, 485–486

Kalapalo (Brazil), 37
Kales, A., 344, 353
Kaminer, H., 5
Kappa complexes, 91
K complex, 64, 391
kinesthesia, 434, 435, 460, 465, 466
kinship, 524–525
Klein, G.S., 382, 383, 384, 385
Kluger, H.Y., 445
knowing, 18, 22
knowledge
　acquisition of, 55, 70–77, 83
　basis of, 72
　and controlled information-pro-
　　cessing mode, 68
　and dream functions, 247
　and experience, 31
　factual, 72, 75–76. *See also* data,
　　units of
　innate, 97
　integration/reconstruction of, 53
　new, 53
　procedural, 72, 76. *See also* strate-
　　gies
　reorganization of, 98, 99
　selection of, 13
　and sleep, 53, 98, 99, 124
　and state-dependent brain mecha-
　　nisms, 52
　updating/use of, 55, 58, 67, 71, 72
knowledge, accessible
　and behavior, 52, 55, 87
　and cycle of communication, 57,
　　59–60, 67, 97
　and dreaming, 93, 95, 98, 127
　state-dependency of, 81–82, 90
　See also working memory
knowledge, acquired
　and automatic information-pro-
　　cessing mode, 69, 70
　and behavior, 52, 70–71
　in children, 95–96
　and cycle of communication, 59–
　　60, 67, 71, 97

defined, 71
　and dreaming, 91
　and emotions, 77–78
　and sleep/sleep stages, 53, 99
　and state-dependent retrieval, 80–
　　81, 82, 84
　uses of, 71
　See also working memory
knowledge-implemented brain oper-
　ations, 52, 59–60
knowledge sets (context
　information), 53
Kohut, H., 372, 404
Koukkou, M., 200, 243–244
Koulack, D., 324–326
Kracke, W., 37
Kramer, M., 1, 5, 400

LaBerge, S., 205–206
labor, in dreams, 315
laboratories. *See* sleep laboratories
Lakoff, G., 315
laminar model, 551
lan (embrace), 505
language, 41n10
　and dream accounts, 491–492
　metaphorical theory of, 315
　and subliminal stimulation, 392
language performance, 366
languages
　acquired, 57, 71, 72
　emotional, 57, 72, 77, 78
　symbolic, 57, 72
laoshi (teacher), 531
latency, 327
　REM, 180, 181, 348, 366
　sleep, 180, 327, 328, 331
lateness in dreams, 302
latent content, 397
lateral logic, 28
Lavie, P., 5
learned helplessness, 265, 266–267,
　268, 269, 277–278, 282
learning

and depression, 283
dissociation of, 79–80
and dream function, 4, 425
and EEG reactivity, 61–62, 66
and empirical modification cycle,
    25
and information-processing
    modes, 68
and sleep, 282–283, 329–330, 341–
    359, 365–366
See also reverse learning hypothe-
    sis
learning-memory deficits, 341, 342,
    349–352, 352–356
learning-memory processes,
    341–359, 365–366
learning tasks, 342, 348, 349–350, 356,
    365
left out, dreams of being, 302–303
Legalism, 516
Lehmann, D., 200, 243–244
length of dreams, 202
lesion studies, 365
lexical choice, 398–399
libidinal cathexes, 133, 134
life-history variables, 11
lifelong nightmares. *See* nightmares,
    recurrent/lifelong
light(s)
    and dream contents, 322
    flickering, 34
    and impactful dreams, 431, 432,
        436, 444, 456
liminality/liminal event, 33
ling (power, efficacy, *mana*, intelli-
    gence, spirit), 497, 498, 499, 500,
    501
linghun (soul), 499
literalness of dream meaning, 533
literary approaches to dream
    accounts, 530–531
location, shifts in, 442, 446, 450, 464
locus coeruleus, 270, 274–275, 554,
    555

logic, 28, 201
logical constraints, 29
logical representation, 28
logical-sign thinking, 277
logic tasks, 349–350, 352, 354
loneliness, 458
longing, 523
long sleepers, 273
long-term memory, 56, 57, 75
looking behavior, 442, 444, 446, 450
loss
    in dreams, 131, 132, 302
    and impactful dreams, 419–420,
        434, 435, 445, 459
    and search behavior, 266, 268
lost, dreams in which one feels, 433,
    434
lucid control, 205, 214–215, 218
lucid darkness, 434, 435, 442
lucid dreaming
    and attention to dream processes,
        225, 232
    correctness of, 7
    development/induction of, 213,
        239, 241
    and dream control, 213, 214, 215–
        216, 217, 243
    and dream functions, 550
    and dreaming to waking transfer
        effects, 232, 237–238, 242
    and dream recall, 227, 232, 239,
        241
    and dream self-reflectiveness, 209,
        210, 213, 230–232, 240, 247
    electrophysiology of, 244
    frequency of, 29, 205, 206, 218, 314
    and gender, 239, 242
    and hyperintentionality, 24, 29,
        198–199
    incidence of, 29, 230, 242–243, 314
    ontogeny of, 7
    prevalence of, 205
    pursuit of, 36
    research into, 203, 204–209

and sleep stage, 6
and waking to dreaming transfer
  effects, 227, 230, 232
See also conative processes; self-
  reflection, in dreams
lucidity
  as continuous process, 213
  and deficiency theories of dream-
    ing, 201
  defined, 39
  development/learning of, 205,
    206, 214, 222, 245
  and dream control, 198, 207, 215–
    216, 219, 230
  and dream self-reflectiveness, 212,
    230
  empirical observations of, 214–215
  and falling dreams, 232
  lack of, 199, 200, 408
  literature on, 206
  and nightmares, 205
  and out-of-body dream
    experiences, 232
  and recurring dream sequences,
    232
  scaling, 205
  signaling onset of, 204–205, 206
  and stress, 232
  and subliminal stimulation, 408
  triggers to, 232, 240
  and waking self-
    exploration/insight, 205
lucid phenomena, 205–206
Ludwig-Stark Craving
  Questionnaire, 400
luminance, 431, 436
luminosity (peak experiencing), 216
Luria, A., 363–364, 365, 368

MAACL, 353
machine model, Boltzmann, 4
macro cognitive models layer, 551
macro-neurophysiological models
  layer, 551

macro-states, brain, 65. *See also* sleep;
  sleep stages; wakefulness
madness, 404
Maeder, A., 369–370
Mae Enga (New Guinea), 36
magical abilities in dreams, 430, 431,
  444, 445
magical belief, 530, 532
magicians (*fangshi*), 503, 515–516
maladaptive behavior, 403
mana (power, efficacy), 497, 499, 500.
  See also ling
mania, 273
manic depressive illness, 178–179
manifest content of dreams
  denial of, 482, 485
  significance of, 367–368, 369–370,
    371, 372–377, 383, 407
  See also dream contents
manjang, 497
MAO inhibitors, 269, 274
Maoism, 513, 518, 519, 521, 532, 534
maps, 64–65
Maria (dream series subject), 310
marital status, 165
Marxism, 518
masochistic dreams, 178
masquerade, 41*n*10
mastery, 216, 326, 365–366
mastery hypotheses, 322–323, 324,
  326, 327, 329–331, 332, 358–359,
  406, 425–426
materialist attitude toward dreams,
  518
materialistic cultures, 39
materialist(ic) world-view, 35, 139
mathematical models, 551
matter–energy (breath) taxonomy,
  498, 499
Maturana, H., 247
meaning(s)
  activation of, 382
  and C-networks, 123, 124
  cognitive associations and, 30
  and dream contents, 175

of dreaming, 4. *See also* dreaming, functional significance of
of dream narrative, 93
of dreams, 127–128. *See also* oneiromancy
and EEG reactivity, 61–62, 66
and hypointentionality, 28
and intentional creodes, 30
and objects, 30
and signs, 532
and subliminal stimuli, 382
and symbolic function, 29–30
and tuning, 123, 124
and tuning bias, 133–134
See also comprehension; semiosis; significance
measurement of subjective/private events, 550
medical diagnoses, 395–399
meditation/meditators, 39, 456
meditation objects, 34
meditation techniques, 36
meditative-contemplative states, 24
Mednick, S.A., 406
melancholy, 419–420
MEMA, 364, 448
memorable dreams, 7
memories
    and past experiences, 368, 369, 375
    and pre-attentive processes, 58
    spurious, 129
memory
    and automatized response patterns, 69–70
    and awareness, 16
    constituents of, 57–58, 73
    coordination in, 68
    and dream function, 425, 478, 479, 550
    dreaming and, 13, 423, 424
    functions of, 74–75
    and information processing, 14
    and knowledge acquisition, 70–77
    long-term, 56, 57, 75
    and orienting response, 66–67,

452–453, 454, 457, 459, 461–462, 463
    and REM sleep/dreaming, 6, 341–359, 365, 366, 556
    search/access to. *See* retrieval processes
    sleep and, 282
    typologies of, 16
    working. *See* working memory
    See also cross-phasing; dream recall; knowledge, acquisition of; mnemonic categories; mnemonic representations; recall; remembering
memory accesses, 65
memory consolidation, 342, 392
memory-driven brain operation, 52
memory levels, 73–74. *See also* memory storages
memory material, 57–58
memory recall, 129
memory representations. *See* mnemonic representations
memory sets (mnemonic elements), 57, 59
memory space, 73–74, 83, 84
memory storages
    access to, 92
    arrangement of, 73
    inputs to, 74
    installation of, 54
    opening/closing of, 82–83
    and pre-attentive processes, 84–85
    retrieval from, 74–75
    and sleep, 54, 77, 90, 91–92, 93, 94, 98, 99, 329
    and state-dependent brain mechanisms, 52, 82–83, 87, 92, 329
    storage in, 74
    system of, 84–85
    See also memory levels
memory system, human, 70–77. *See also* knowledge
men

dream contents of, 165–166, 310
in dreams, 310, 312
meng (dreams), 496, 502
mengxiang (dream-think), 496
menstrual cycle, 322
mental activity during sleep, 15–16,
52–53, 54
mental causation in dreaming, 139,
150
mental imagery, 551
mentation. *See* cognitive-emotional
style
merging, and boundaries, 405, 406,
407
metabolic conditions, 60
metacognitive dreaming, 198, 203,
204, 216. *See also* lucid dreaming;
self-reflectiveness; self-regulation
meta-epistemic functions of dreaming, 5
metamorphoses, 210
and impactful dreams, 429, 438,
439–440, 444, 463
as repetitive dream theme, 304,
305
See also transformations
metaphorical attempt at problem-
solving, dreams as, 314–315
metaphorical representation, and
hypointentionality, 28
metaphorical (symbolic) interpretations of dreams, 309, 315–316
metaphoric content, of recurrent
dreams, 300
metaphor(s)
and dream accounts, 492
dream elements as, 310
dreaming as, 202
and oneiromancy, 477, 480–481,
516, 520
and subliminal activation model,
399
traumatic dreams as, 297
metapsychology, 372

methodology, 388, 392–393, 408, 427
metonymy, 477, 481
mice, 365
micro cognitive units layer, 551
microgenetic approach to cognition,
386
micro neural net models layer, 551
micro-states of brain activity, 64–65,
86
middle ear muscle activity (MEMA),
364, 448
migraines, 396
millenarian religions, 531
mind, 119, 120
mind-brain, 549, 551
minimally polyphasic cultures, 36
minimal re-entrainment, 34
mirroring, 406, 407
misfortunes in dreams, 312
mismatch negativity (MMN), 457
missing buses/trains in dreams, 302
Mitchison, G., 4–5, 119, 128–133, 201,
244
MMPI profiles/scales, 148, 181, 273,
278–279, 520
mnemonic categories, 71–73. *See also*
data; mnemonic representations;
skills; strategies
mnemonic elements (memory sets),
57, 59
mnemonic functions. *See* memory
storage
mnemonic obsessions, 425
mnemonic representations, 62, 68,
69–70, 72, 74, 77–78. *See also*
mnemonic categories
mnemonics, 34
mnemonic subsystems, 452–453, 454,
457, 459, 463
models
and cognized environment, 38
contradictory, 29
creation of, 57
defined, 22–23, 40*n*2

and empirical modification cycle,
   25
structure of, 41n8
symbolic, 21, 22–23
system of, 38
of world, 15, 16
See also neuronal models
Mongols, 490, 517
monist position on body-mind issue,
   551
monophasia, 34
monophasic 24-hour-cycle, 96
monophasic cultures, 35–36, 39
monophasic egos, 39
monsters in dreams, 298, 300
mood
   and dreaming to waking transfer
      effects, 220, 237, 238, 324–325,
      331, 392, 401, 419–420, 421, 422,
      426, 428
   and sleep/sleep deprivation, 162–
      163, 179, 280
   state aspect of, 156, 158–159, 160,
      162
   and subliminal stimulation, 384,
      392
   trait aspect of, 156, 158, 161–162
   and waking to dreaming transfer
      effects, 165–179, 181, 182, 400
   See also affect; affective states;
      emotions; hun; selective mood
   regulatory function of dreaming
mood difference
   across the day, 162, 163–164, 170
   across groups, 170
   across individuals, 170, 177
   across the night, 154–164, 166, 170,
      177, 179–182
mood intensity, across sleep, 182
mood predictability, across the
   night, 156–162, 170, 177, 180
mood regulation, dreams/sleep and,
   6, 139–188, 392
mood-sleep interaction, 151–163,

   164, 170, 177, 179–182
mood stability, 156, 158, 161–162
mood states, and EEG states, 83
mood variability
   across sleep, 182
   day-to-day, 156, 158–159, 160, 162
moral messages, dreams as, 525–527,
   532
moral transgression, 462, 463
Morning Questionnaire (MQ), 429
morning (waking) mood. See mood,
   and dreaming to waking transfer
   effects
Moroccans, dreaming among, 36
morphogenesis, 6
mortality, awareness of, 426, 427, 445
"mother goddess" worship, 516, 517
mothers in dreams, 302, 304–305,
   306, 307, 526
motility in dreams, 174
motivating change, 422, 428
motivation, 60, 62
   fear, 365
motivational state, 69, 75, 93
motivational unconscious, 381
motives, disturbing, 183, 184
motor behavior, 263
motor execution, skeletal, 555
motor executive cortex, 553–554, 555
motor output, inhibition of, 128, 552,
   554, 555
movement-induced awakening, 434,
   436–437, 444, 466
movement ineffectuality, 429, 439
movement inhibition
   during REM sleep, 552, 554
   and impactful dreams, 434, 435,
      439, 440, 441, 442, 444, 445, 463
movement style, and impactful
   dreams, 429–432 passim, 434, 435,
   438–441 passim, 444, 455, 458, 459,
   466
MQ (Morning Questionnaire), 429
Mr. E. (analysand), 403

multidimensional response pattern (answer), 58
multilevel awareness, 209, 210, 211, 212
multimodal pattern formation, 57–58
Multiple Affect Adjective Check List (MAACL), 353
multiple personality, 80
multiple perspectives, 202, 210, 211
multiple states of being, 210, 211
multi-state basis of dreaming, 12
muscle relaxation, 458
muscle tone, 366
muscle twitches, 364
muscular activation, 455, 457, 458
myocardial infarction, 264, 265
myth, 41n10, 480, 481, 483, 533
mythic dreams, 430, 445

N1 waveform, 454, 455
N2a waveform, 457
narcissism, 403
narcissistic merger/mirror relationships, 406
narcolepsy, 273, 449
narrative coherence, 438, 439
narrator, vs dreamer, 530
Nationalists, Han Chinese, 513, 517
natural forces in recurrent attack/chase dreams, 298, 300
Necker cube, 457
need-press variables, 169
needs, 427
neighboring conceptions. *See* conceptual neighbor
neocortex, 57
nervous system
  central, 55, 58–59, 60, 65–66
  and cognition, 21–22
  non-central, 556
  symbolic function of, 29–30
  See also brain
Nestorians, 490
netlock, 550

networks. *See* neural networks; neural net theories; distributed neural net models; social networks
neural activity, 387
neural coordinations. *See* entrainments
neural models. *See* models
neural net models, distributed, 551
neural net theories, as afunctional/antifunctional theories of dreaming, 3, 201, 207, 244, 550, 555–556
neural networks, 23, 119, 551
neural networks, connectionist. *See* C-networks
neural structures, 28
neural tonus metaphor, 554
neurobiology, 5, 21
neurocognition/neurocognitive processes, 551, 553–554
neuroendocrinal processes/systems, 26, 29, 30
neurognosis/neurognostic structures, 22, 25–27, 31, 32, 35, 40n4
neuroimmunological transductions, 30
neuromodulators, 125–126
neuronal activity, 364–365
neuronal models (multimodal/multidimensional), 57, 58, 60, 73, 76, 78, 89, 90, 95–96. *See also* models; pattern formation
neuronal sets, 57
neurophysiological correlates of registration, 391–392
neurophysiological processes, REM sleep as cluster of, 552
neuroscientists, 18
neuroses, 267, 276, 279
neurosis, traumatic, 406
neurotic anxiety, 264, 270, 271
neurotic behavior, 54
neurotic disorders, 369

neurotransmitters, 553
newborns, 403. *See also* infants
nightmares
  among Han Chinese, 496, 506,
    519–520, 525, 528
  beliefs about, 477, 480
  and boundaries, 301, 404–407, 409
  characteristics of, 445–446, 450
  content of, 148
  and defense reaction, 461–463
  and dream control, 217
  and dream's success, 187
  and ego control, 199
  and emotional responsivity, 149
  as form of impactful dream, 445–
    446, 465, 466–467
  and gender/sexual abuse, 4
  and intensity of affect, 144, 145
  and openness, 405
  post-traumatic, 368, 406, 425
  predispositional factors in, 148–
    149, 425
  recall of, 148
  recurrent/lifelong, 7, 217, 300–301,
    314, 404–407, 409
  and regression, 405
  and sensitivity, 405
  and sleep physiology, 449
  vs traumatic dreams, 301
  vs vivid dreams, 148
  See also anxiety dreams; attack
  dreams; chronic delayed post-
  traumatic stress disorder; dreams,
  disturbing; night terrors; traumatic
  dreams
night residue, 140
night-shift workers, 26
night terrors, 15, 441, 446, 461, 480.
  See also anxiety dreams;
  nightmares
ning (settled, tranquil, peaceful), 500
nocturnal animals, 26–27
nodes, 73, 119, 120, 121, 123–124. *See
  also* C-networks; neural networks

noise, 122, 126–127, 201, 388, 452–453
noises, in dreams, 438, 439
nonalertness, 386, 387
nondetermined thinking, 139
nonordinary dreaming, 205, 213, 247
nonrecall, dream. *See* dream repression
nonutilitarian theories of dreaming,
  426–427. *See also* afunctional/anti-
  functional theories of dreaming
nonvisual information-processing
  mode, 65
noradrenergic bodies/systems, 125,
  277, 554–555
Nordby, V., 309, 310, 311
norepinephrine (NE), 125, 128,
  269–270, 271, 276, 277, 278
noticing, 207, 208, 209, 216, 217
  and dreaming to waking transfer
    effects, 224
  oddities within dream, 211, 212,
    213, 224, 227, 232
  opportunities for behavioral
    choice, 224, 225, 244
  See also awareness; lucid dream-
    ing; perception(s); subliminal
    stimulation
novelty/novel stimuli, 65, 66, 450,
  453. *See also* change OR
NREM awakenings, 63
NREM dreaming, 6, 7, 15, 65, 96, 200,
  315, 321, 402
  characteristics of, 125, 328
NREM dream reports, 53, 89, 94–95,
  447
NREM sleep
  characteristics of, 124, 125, 127
  in children, 296
  and connectionist theory, 124–128,
    134
  and dream recall, 390
  EEG patterns in, 84, 448, 450, 451
  functions of, 15–16, 128, 328, 553,
    554–555

and learning-memory processes, 341
lucid dreaming and, 6
and mood, 180, 182
and search activity, 277
in shift workers, 27
and subliminal stimulation, 391
NREM sleep deprivation, 281, 282, 323–324, 352–354. *See also* sleep deprivation; total sleep deprivation
NREM sleep reports, 53, 328
nudity dreams, 294

objectivity, 466–467
objects, perceived, 32
objects in dreams
alive/aware, 430, 431, 445, 455, 466
frequency of, 309
repeated, 294
observer, dreamer as, 209–210, 212, 219, 432. *See also* detachment; involvement
obsessions, 126, 129, 134, 326, 425
obstacles, 267, 269
occupation, 490
olfactory phenomena in dreams, 438, 439, 444
omens, 503–504
oneirocritics/oneirocriticism, 36, 491, 492, 534n2
oneirology, 491, 492, 493, 518–530, 532, 533, 534n2
oneiromancy
Han Chinese, 490, 491, 502, 503, 504, 513, 514–517, 518–530, 532, 533, 534n2
reasons for, 477–486
ontogeny
and dream control, 216
of dream experience, 12, 17, 95–96, 99
and dream functions, 2
and EEG changes, 83, 84

and neurognosis, 22
and REM sleep, 12, 274
and search/renunciation of search, 266–268, 274
and waking/sleeping states, 6, 7
See also age; developmental changes
ontology
and dream control, 216
and dream functions, 1, 247
and systemic reflection, 248
openings in dreams, 307
openness, 405
operational environment, 29, 31, 32
and cognized environment, 27, 28
defined, 23, 38
external vs internal, 32
and structure of models, 41n8
See also cognized environment; external environment; reality
ordeals, 36
orderliness of dreaming, 5
orientative-exploratory behavior, 262, 263, 271, 274, 280
orienting activity, 450–463
orienting response (OR)
and affective reactions, 453–463
and automatized attention response, 70
biological significance of, 67
and cycle of communication, 57, 65–67, 71
defined, 65, 450
and dream impact, 453–463, 464
EEG components of, 59, 61–62, 65–67, 70, 76
and functional adaptation of brain, 59, 85, 86
functional/structural nature of, 57, 65–67, 71
habituation of, 52, 59, 66
and memory, 66–67
and pre-attentive processes, 65, 67, 76
structural nature of, 57

to aversive stimuli (defense reaction), 450, 453
to initially presented stimuli (initial OR), 450, 453
to novel stimuli (change OR), 450, 453
types of, 450–451, 453
and waking to dreaming transfer effects, 243–244
See also change OR; defense reaction; initial OR
oscillation, behavioral, 388
out-of-body experiences, 232, 436, 501
outputs, 60
outsider, feeling like an, 433, 434
overlearning, 62
overwhelming stimuli, 296, 297
O-waves, 461
"ownership" of dream, 217

P300 (EEG phenomenon), 76
P3 waveform, 457
painful dreams, 315
paired associate (PA) task, 349, 352, 354
Pakistani initiation dreams, 484
"paleo" logic, 28
Palombo, S., 369, 478, 479
panic/panicky behavior, 83, 262, 263, 270, 271, 441
parallel distributed processes, 119, 120, 551
parasympathetic somatomotor activation, 462
Parintintin (Brazil), 479, 480, 481–485
Parkinsonism, 279
Parkinsonlike neuroleptic syndrome, 264
parsimony of thought, 490–491
parsing of experience, 7
participation in dream, dreamer's, 219, 400, 432
passive reaction, 266, 267

passive receptiveness, 385
passivity in dreams, 29, 438, 439, 444
past experiences, 370, 376, 421, 422, 428
pathogenesis, 279
pathological thinking, 384
pathology, 203
patient-therapist dyads, 173
pattern formation, 58, 60, 71
pattern recognition, 4, 24, 31, 58, 60, 71
peak experiencing (luminosity), 216
Pearlman, C., 275, 425
peasant cultures, 477, 531–532, 534
peasant women, 512–513, 516–517
penanggalan, 497
penetration, 29–30, 34
penile erections, 364, 390
penises in dreams, 483
People's Republic of China, 489–534
perception(s)
    cognitive processes and, 77, 386
    dreaming as subclass of, 552
    and information processing, 57, 58
    organization/control of, 71
    and pre-attentive processes, 58
    and sleep, 62, 552, 554
    waking, 554, 555
    and working memory, 75
    See also noticing
percepts, 383–384, 427
perceptual-association-motor system, 555
perceptual layer of C-network, 120, 123
performance, 164, 366, 384, 392
permissive information-processing strategies of childhood. See primary process rules
persistence
    cultural, and dream accounts, 489, 532–534
    of dream thoughts/feelings upon waking, 432, 438, 440–444 *passim*, 446

personality types/variables, 322, 389–390

perspective. *See* dreamer, perspective of in dream

PGO activity/spikes, 127, 391, 447–449, 457, 550

PGO analogues, 448–449, 450

phase attributes of consciousness, 32–33

phase duration/alternation, sleep, 553, 554

phasic EMG suppression, 448

phasic integrated potentials (PIPs), 391, 448, 449

phasic sleep events, 390, 391, 447–450, 454–463

phenomenal objects, 23

phenomenal states/conditions, 11

phenomenological literature/methods, 41n10, 204, 428

phenomenology, dream, 14, 17. *See also* dream content(s)

philosophy, 215

phobias, 331

physical activity, 323, 353, 431, 438, 439

physical environment. *See* environment; external environment

physical sensations, 32

physiological changes during sleep, 54

physiological significance of dreams/sleep, 54

physiological states/conditions, 11

physiology
    and orienting response, 67
    sleep, 96, 179–182, 447–450

Piaget, J., 248

pilgrimages, 36

PIPs, 391, 448, 449

pituitary body, 265

pity, 467

plans/planning, 29, 67, 77, 264

plasma free fatty acids, 396

play, 29, 41n10, 215

pleasantness, of dream feelings, 400

pleasurable dreams, 221

pluralism, 534

po (soul, vigor, spirit), 497, 498, 499, 500, 501, 502, 524

poetry, 202

Poetzl, O., 383, 407

Poetzl phenomenon, 407

poli (soul-strength), 499

political context, 530, 533–534

political dominance, 533–534

political functions of dream narratives/interpretation, 490, 503–505, 530, 534n2

politicization, 514, 515–517

polyphasia, 35

polyphasic consciousness, 34

polyphasic cultures, 36–40

polyphasic egos, 39–40

polyphasic entrainment, 35

polyphasic experience, 35

polyphasic temporal organization, 96

polysemy, 28, 30. *See also* meaning(s)

polysomnogram (PSG), 390

pons, 364, 365

ponto-geniculo-occipital activity. *See* PGO activity/spikes/analogues

Porsolt Test, 263

portaling experience, 39

portents, 503–504

positional choice behavior, 385

possession cults/states, 35, 513

posthypnotic suggestion, 141, 213, 322

poststimulation effects, 388, 392

posttests, 223, 224, 237–238, 242

post-traumatic dreams, 424, 425

post-traumatic nightmares, 368, 406, 425

post-traumatic stress disorder. *See* chronic delayed post-traumatic stress disorder

postural musculature, 458, 459, 462
posuo (whirling dancing), 499
power, 34, 36, 37, 216, 497. *See also ling*
practice, 67, 72
pragmatic dream interpretation, 532–533
pre–attentive processes
and brain's functional state, 65, 86–88
and characteristics of answer, 59
defined, 58
during sleep, 70
and emotions, 58, 87
ERP mapping of, 61
and information-processing mode, 58, 68, 70
and multi-dimensional response pattern, 58
and orienting response, 65, 67, 76, 454, 456
parallel functioning of, 58
and pattern formation/recognition, 58
See also cycle of communication
preconceptual processes, 454, 456, 465
predictions in dreams, 480–484, 505, 520, 527–528, 532
prefrontal cortex, 23–24, 28, 30, 31, 32
pregnancy, 372, 396, 482, 508
prelucid control, 214, 215–216, 217
prelucidity, 210, 211, 212, 215
preoccupations. *See* emotional pre-occupations
preparation, as function of sleep, 553
preparatory activation, 425
prepulse stimulation, 455
prescriptions for behavior, dreams as, 484–485
presleep experiences, and dreams, 141, 214, 321–332, 391, 392. *See also* dream incubation; waking to

dreaming transfer effects
prestimulation variables, 388, 389–390, 408
presurgical patients, 368
Price-Williams, D., 3–4
primary process, 125, 126, 128
primary process dream mechanisms, 203
primary process rules, 53, 90–91, 94, 98
primary process thinking, 382, 406, 408
primary visual experience, 448
priming, 74. *See also* tuning
priming, semantic, 52, 59, 67, 86, 87
primitive cultures, oneiromancy in, 477
principal current concern. *See* emotional preoccupation
proactivity of dreams, 170
problem solving
and dream incubation, 221, 358, 359
and dreaming to waking transfer effects, 238, 242
functional significance of dreaming in, 6, 7, 93, 128, 182–187, 275–276, 314, 315, 368, 370, 371, 375–377, 422–426 *passim*, 479, 485, 486, 550
and recurrent dreams/dream elements, 299–300, 314–315
and REM sleep/dreaming, 6, 168, 272, 273, 275–276, 282–283, 357–359, 366, 369, 556
and renunciation of search, 283
and stress, 326
and waking to dreaming transfer effects, 321, 323
problem solving patterns in dreams
progressive-sequential, 183–185, 186, 187
repetitive-traumatic, 183, 185–186, 187

procedural knowledge. See strategies
process, dream, vs dream content, 207
processing principles, 119, 120, 551
process levels, 219
Profile of Moods Scale, 429
Profile of Mood States, 400
prognoses, dreams and, 399–401, 409
prognostications, dreams as, 480–485, 527–528, 532
programs of responses. *See* skills
progressive-sequential dream pattern, 183–185, 186, 187
projective tests, 366
prospective function of dreams, 369–370
protagonist, dreamer as, 219
protective barrier against stimuli, 406
proverbs. *See chengyu*
PSG (polysomnogram), 390
psychiatrists, 18
psychic structure building, 381, 403–404, 409
psychoanalysis/psychoanalytic theory, and dreams, 93, 200, 363, 367–372, 375, 383
psychobiological brain processes, 51
psychobiological models, 453
psychobiological priorities, 60, 67, 75, 87, 89, 93, 97
psychobiology, 51, 425, 426
psychodrama, 214
psychological differentiation, 208, 210, 245, 262
psychological dreaming, functions of, 139–188
psychological functions
    of brain, 55, 56
    of dream interpretation, 477–486
psychological processes, dreaming as index of, 5
psychological theory of dreaming, 216

psychology, individual, and dreams, 505, 511–512
psychology of dreaming, basis for, 370–371
psychometry, 203, 205
psychoneuroimmunology, 30
psychopathology
    and dream contents, 167, 170, 186
    and dream functions, 148, 149–150, 186
psychophysical measurement, 387, 388, 390
psychophysical theories, 261
psychophysics, 387
psychophysiology, 51, 54, 215, 282–283. *See also* electrophysiology; sleep physiology
psychosis/psychotic behavior, 54, 273
psychosomatic diseases/illnesses, 265, 267, 279, 396
psychotherapy
    and dream control, 214, 215
    dreams as form of, 426
    working with dreams in, 93, 370–377
    See also clinical practice
puerperal death, 497
Pukapuka, 32
punishment, 263, 267, 282
punishment dreams, 296
purpose/purposefulness, 56, 427
pursuit. *See* chase dreams

qi (matter-energy), 493, 498, 499, 501, 511
qing (pure, clear, limpid), 500
quantitative content analysis system, 309–310, 312, 314. See also Hall[-] Van de Castle dream content scoring system
Quechua (Andean) dream interpretation, 531, 532–533
questions, dreams' ability to answer, 221, 224

race, 165
randomness of dreaming, 3, 4
rape fantasies, 171
rapid eye movement (REM) sleep.
   See REM sleep
rapture, 431
rational comprehension, 24
rationalism, economic, 532
rationality, 201
rats, 348, 350
reactive motives, 183, 184
reactivity, 170, 171–179, 273
readiness, 553
realities
   internal/external, 55, 56, 57, 67
   typically ignored, 421, 422, 428,
      437, 445, 446, 467
reality
   and cognitive-emotional style, 83
   as a cognized environment, 21–22
   cultural conceptions of, 426
reality contact, 385–386, 407
reality judgment, 390
reality requirements, 385
reality testing, 385
reassurance, 482–484
recall
   dream. *See* dream recall
   of information received during
      sleep, 62–63
   See also memory; remembering
receptiveness, 385
Rechtschaffen, A., 200, 207, 281–282,
   344, 353
recognition, 24, 31, 457
recollection, 31
recovery
   from substance addiction, 392,
      399–401, 402, 409
   from surgery, 402–403
   as function of sleep, 553
recurrent dreams, 294, 295, 298–302,
   303, 314, 526–527
   content of, 298, 299, 300
   frequency of, 298

function of, 7
   and mood changes, 179
   and repetitive dream themes, 303,
      309
   vs traumatic dreams, 300
   See also nightmares
recurring dream sequences, 232
redintegration, 330
reductionism, 207, 244, 463
reductive goal, 141, 187
re-entrainment, 24, 31, 33, 34, 41n7
reflection principle, 519–523, 532
reflectiveness, 202. *See also* self-
   reflectiveness
reflexive responding, 458
reflexive stimulus-response relationships, 68–69
registration without awareness, 381,
   383, 384–385, 388, 391–392, 407,
   554. *See also* sleep stimulation; subliminal stimulation
regression
   and dream deprivation, 403
   and nightmares, 405
   and problem solving, 168, 170,
      183–184, 185
   and renunciation of search, 267
   and state-shift hypothesis, 90, 93,
      98, 200, 243, 244
   See also age change/regression in
      dreams
rehearsal, 242
"Reitzschutz" (stimulus barrier), 406
rejection, 435, 459
relaxation, 29, 268, 386, 389, 390
relearning, 4
relief, 268
religious training, 35
REM density, 181, 327, 344, 345, 348,
   390
REM dreaming, 65, 391, 401, 402
   characteristics of, 16, 328, 332
   functions of, 315
   ontogeny of, 7

and subliminal stimulation, 391
REM dream reports, 53, 89, 94–95,
212, 447. *See also* REM sleep, and
dream recall
REMD. *See* REM sleep deprivation
remembering, 31. *See also* memory
remembering dreams. *See* dream
recall
REM latency, 180, 181, 348, 366
REM–NREM sleep cycle, 553
REM onset, 181
REM periods, dream changes across,
186, 448
REM sleep
absence of in dolphins, 283–284
and achievement motivation, 273
and anxiety, 273, 274
awakenings from, 12, 63
characteristics of, 124, 125, 127, 142
cognitive output during, 555
and connectionist theory, 124–128
and depression, 273, 274, 278–279
distribution of, 142
and dreaming, 6, 88, 95–96, 142,
144–145, 168, 293, 315, 321, 357,
364–369
dreaming not limited to, 11–13,
200, 447
and dream recall, 89, 94–95, 96,
276, 390. *See also* REM dream
reports
and dream theory, 197
EEG patterns in, 84, 447–448, 449,
450, 451
emotional surge during, 145–150,
182
functional significance of, 6, 12, 13,
15–16, 99, 128–129, 133–134, 261–
284, 293, 324, 331, 369, 425, 550,
552, 553–556
and helplessness, 274, 279
and hypnotic suggestion, 327
increases in, 341–342, 345, 350, 356
influences on, 96–97
and information processing, 14, 96
and learning-memory processes,
273, 341–359
and lucid dreaming, 244
mechanisms for limiting, 277
and mood, 280
neurochemical changes in, 125–
126, 128
and perception, 552
and problem solving, 6, 168, 272,
273, 275–276, 282–283
and renunciation of search, 272,
273–274, 277, 278, 279, 281, 282,
283
and search activity, 261–284, 272–
275 *passim*, 278, 283
in shift workers, 27
and signal detection theory, 387
and sleep laboratory, 327
storage of, 53
and stress, 272, 273, 278
and subliminal stimulation, 391
and thought, 552
and traumatic dreams, 297
and water deprivation, 327
and working memory, 77
REM sleep deprivation
effects of, 14, 142, 179, 180, 220,
323–324, 331, 365–366
on dream intensity, 448
on learning–memory processes, 341–342, 352–357, 359,
365–366
on search activity, 273–276 *passim*,
279, 280–284, 369
timing of, 355–356, 359
REM sleep deprivation. *See also* sleep
deprivation; total sleep deprivation
REM sleep intensity, 348
REM sleep periods, number of, 342,
345, 348, 356
REM sleep physiology, 12, 142–145,
179, 180–181, 200–201, 364–365. *See
also* sleep physiology

REM sleep reports, 53, 328
REM sleep time
  percentage of, 348
  total, 180–181, 342, 345, 348, 353–354, 356, 366–367
REM windows, 341, 351, 356
renunciation of search. *See* search, renunciation of
repeated dreams. *See* recurrent dreams
repellors, 122
repetition dimension, 294
repetition of dreams/dream elements, 293–316. *See also* nightmares; recurrent dreams
repetitive stimuli, 451
repetitive-traumatic dream pattern, 183, 185–186, 187. *See also* traumatic dreams
reporter, dreamer as, 219
representational intelligence, 12, 13, 15
repression, 93–94, 173, 264, 299, 390
reprogramming, 425
resignation. *See* search, renunciation of
resistance, body's, 264, 265–266, 268, 369
respiratory hesitations, 458
respiratory irregularity, 390
respiratory rates, 328, 462
response preparation, 461, 462
responses, 60, 90. *See also* behavior; skills
responsiveness
  to subliminal stimulation, 385–386, 389–390, 406–407, 409
  to treatment, 399–401, 409
restoration, as function of sleep, 553, 554, 556
restorative synthetic functions of sleep, 98
rethinking, 264
reticular formation, 381
retrieval cues, 74

retrieval processes, 70, 74, 78–79, 386. *See also* memory; state-dependent retrieval
reverie, 382, 390, 427
reversal, rule of (contradiction principle), 477, 481–482, 484, 528–530, 532, 533
reverse learning hypothesis, 425–426
rhetorical imperatives, 490
right-hemispheric (image) thinking, 277, 279
rites of passage, 33
rituals/ritualization, 33–34, 35, 36, 41n10, 480, 533
Rogerians, 530
role changes, 210
rooms, in dreams, 302
Rorschach tests, 366, 405, 406, 456, 465
Rossi, E., 208–216 *passim*, 218, 245
Rotenberg, V., 379
"royal road" to unconscious, 381–409
ruling class, 489, 513, 533–534

sadness, 433, 434, 458, 459, 460, 464
salience, 390
San Jiao (Three Teachings), 490
satisfaction, 268, 271
scales/scaling. *See* Clyde Mood Scale; Cornell Medical Index; Differential Emotions Scale; dream scales; EXPeriencing scale; Global Assessment Scale; MMPI profiles/scales; Profile of Moods Scale; self-reflectiveness, scaling
scapulimancy (*bu*), 490, 502–503
SCE, 203
scents/smells in dreams, 438, 439
schema induction, cross-state, 244, 245
schemata, 224, 244, 245, 248, 364, 368, 377, 382
schizophrenia/schizophrenics, 404, 405

and dream contents, 166, 167, 181
and subliminal stimulation, 384,
     406–407
schizophrenic decompensation, 406
schizophrenic imagery, 88
Schmale, A., 397–398
scholar-bureaucrats (*shi da fu*), Han
     Chinese, 489–534
science, vs humanities, 530
SCL-90, 402
SDT. *See* signal detection theory
search activity, 261–284, 369
search behavior(s)
     biochemical mechanisms of, 269–
          270
     categorization of, 262–264
     electrophysiological correlates of,
          263
     vs exploratory behavior, 263
     and motor behavior, 263
     physiological mechanisms of, 269
     and REM sleep, 6, 272, 274, 275,
          283
     and search requirement, 267–268
     weakening/cessation of, 264,
          265–266, 268
search, renunciation of, 262, 263, 264,
     265–266, 272, 276
     reasons for persistence/emergence
          of, 266–268, 269, 270, 271
     and REM sleep, 272, 273–274, 277,
          278, 279, 281, 282, 283, 369
     results of, 271, 276, 277, 279, 283
search requirement, 267, 268
secondary cognitive elaboration
     (SCE), 203
secondary elaboration, 484
secondary process, 125
seizure threshold, 369
Sejnowski, T., 4, 244
selective aspects of waking percep-
     tion, 554, 555
selective mood regulatory function
     of dreaming, 139–188

self
     dreaming and, 5, 6, 403–404
     dream. *See* dream ego
     generation of. *See* autopoiesis
     organization/functioning of, 5,
          119, 120, 121–122, 134
     theoretical primacy of, 16
self-actualization, 208
self-awareness
     and dream recall, 390
     dreams as facilitators of, 401–403,
          404, 409
     and impactful dreams, 432, 434,
          436, 440, 442, 443–444, 446, 466–
          467
     importance of, 403
     and sleep, 14–15
self-coherence, 403
self-cohesion, 407
self-confidence, 311
self-conservation, 30–31
self-consistency, 121, 134
self-consolidation, 404
self-control, 438, 439
self-esteem, 372, 462
self-fragmentation, 407
self-generation, 30–31, 403–404
self-images, 210, 221
self-integration, 403–404
self-involvement in dream, 203, 390,
     438, 440. *See also* involvement
self-knowledge, 401–403
self-mastery, 426
self-objects, loss of, 406
self-observation, external, 431, 432,
     434, 436, 438, 440, 442
self-organization, 5, 119, 120,
     121–122, 134
self-participation, 438, 440, 442, 447,
     448
self-perception, 421, 422, 423, 424
self-preserving behavior, 403
self-psychology, 372, 403–404, 407,
     409
self-realization, 272

self-reflection, 208, 403
    in dreams, 197–198. *See also* lucid
        dreaming
    dreams as facilitators of, 401–403,
        409, 466
    and intentionality, 24, 198
    See also awareness, levels of
self-reflectiveness, dream, 199, 200,
        202, 203, 206, 209–210
    and attention to dream processes,
        225, 226–227, 230, 240
    and deficiency views of dreaming,
        199–201, 215
    defined, 209
    development of, 208, 209–210, 226,
        239, 243
    differences in, 204, 216, 227, 242
    and dream control, 210, 212, 216,
        240
    and dreaming to waking transfer
        effects, 199
    and dream recall, 225–226, 227,
        241, 243
    frequency of, 213, 240
    and impactful dreams, 438, 440
    increasing, 213, 227, 243, 245
    and lucid dreaming, 209, 210, 213,
        230–232, 240, 245
    scaling, 211–213, 216
    and sleep stage, 401
    and state-shift hypothesis, 243
    and waking to dreaming transfer
        effects, 199, 226–230, 239
    See also conative processes; dream
        control; lucid dreaming; Rossi, E.
self-regulation, 3, 4, 14–15, 197–249
self-representation, 203
self-restoration, 403–404
self-signals, 403–404
self-state dreams, 404
self-stimulation, 262–263, 272, 274,
        280
self-transformations, 202
self-understanding, 401–403
Semai, 534*n*2

semantic association, 52, 59, 87
semantic dream interpretation,
        532–533
semantic inhibition, 52, 59, 68, 82, 86,
        87
semantic priming, 52, 59, 67, 86, 87
semiosis, 42*n*11
semiotic levels, 532–533
sensations, physical, 32
sensibilities, enhanced, 430, 433, 434
sensitivity
    and impactful dreams, 421, 422,
        428, 437, 445, 446, 456, 465
    and nightmares, 301, 405
    and REM sleep/dreaming, 273,
        276
    to subliminal stimulation, 385–386,
        389–390, 406–407, 409
sensorial cortex (sensorium), 23–24,
        28, 30, 31, 32, 33
sensorimotor adaptation, 248
sensory cues, 32
sensory input, 124, 128, 348, 555
sensory isolation, 323
sensory phenomena, 429, 431–432,
        434, 435–436, 438–442 *passim*, 444,
        447, 465
sensory saturation, 434, 444
sensory vividness, 429, 556
separation, 434, 435, 444, 458, 459,
        464
serial local processes, 119, 120
serotonergic systems, 125
serotonin (5HT), 125, 128
set phrases (*chengyu*), 493, 494–496
settings, dream, 309
setting (sleep location), 154
sex dreams, 307, 311, 400, 483
sex roles, 301
sexual abuse, 4
sexual attacks, 477, 480
sexual interactions, 307
sexual orientation, 384
shamans, 36, 37, 499, 503, 515–516,
        532

shen (god, supernatural, spirit), 498, 499, 500

shen guang (*shen* revealed), 503

shenpo (witch), 499

shen shi (gentry), 534*n*1

shensi (state of mind, poetic imagination), 499, 506

shi da fu (scholar-bureaucrats), 489–534

shift(s)

    of attention, 67

    in dream affect, 436, 444, 466

    in dreamer activity level, 438, 439

    in dreamer perspective, 431, 432, 436, 444, 445

    from parasympathetic to sympathetic activation, 462

    in location, 442, 446, 450, 464

shift workers, 26–27, 31, 40

Shmale, A., 264, 271

short sleepers, 273

shuttle avoidance training, 341–342, 350

si (thought, craving, reverie), 499, 502, 511–512, 520

siblings in dreams, 306, 307, 460

signal, vs noise, 388

signal detection, 6

signal detection model

    of dream function, 381–409

    of dreaming and waking, 387–393

    unified, 382, 388, 408

signal detection theory (SDT), 382, 387, 408

signal information, 70, 87

signal-noise ratio (S/N), 122, 124, 125, 128

significance, 68, 76, 94, 419

    and impactful dreams, 428, 430–434 *passim*, 438, 441, 442, 444, 445, 446, 460–461, 466

    and orienting response, 65, 67, 460–461, 462, 463

    and state-dependent retrieval, 83

    and working memory, 75, 76

See also emotionally charged/significant experiences; meaning(s)

signs, 532–533

single-mindedness in dreams, 127, 200, 202, 209, 211, 227

single waves, 64

sisters in dreams, 307, 460

skeletal motor execution, 555

skills

    and automaticity, 62, 68, 69

    as mnemonic category, 71, 72

    rehearsal of, 221

    transfer of across sleep-wake boundary, 221–247

    and working memory, 75, 76

    See also responses

skin conductance, 453

sleep

    and accessibility of knowledge, 82

    and affective state, 150–155

    and change OR, 457

    in children, 95–96

    C-networks during, 124–128

    and connectionist theory, 119–135

    coordination of, 52, 54

    core, 328

    and cycle of communication, 57

    defined, 54

    depth of, 61, 70

    determinants of, 96–98

    dreaming not limited to, 11–13

    EEG patterns in, 83–84, 91

    effects on wakefulness, 150, 151, 155

    effects of wakefulness on, 150–151

    equated with unconsciousness, 199, 202, 207

    functional significance of, 27, 328, 553–556

        and connectionist theory, 119–135

        and selective mood regulatory theory, 150–151

        and state-shift hypothesis, 53, 54, 84, 90, 91, 93, 97, 98–99

and information processing, 61,
    62, 69, 70
and learning, 282–283
and memory, 62, 77, 90–94 *passim*,
    98, 99, 329
organization of behavior during,
    62
shift from/to, 87, 89–90
vs wakefulness, 90, 91, 93, 95–96
sleep continuity. *See* sleep mainte-
    nance
sleep cycles, 553
sleep deprivation
    and aggressiveness, 162–163, 280
    and depression, 279, 280
    effects of, 281, 282, 283, 328, 350–
        351, 352
    and mood change, 162–163, 179
    and Parkinsonism, 279
    and performance, 164
    timing of, 350–351, 355–356
    See also NREM sleep deprivation;
        REM sleep deprivation; total sleep
        deprivation
sleep disturbances, 26–27. *See also*
    insomnia; sleeptalking; sleepwalk-
    ing
sleep fragmentation, 27
sleepiness, 151–164 *passim*, 176, 177,
    179–182 *passim*
sleeping state, nature of, 6–7
sleep initiation, 97
sleep integrity. *See* sleep
    maintenance
sleep laboratories, 197
    effects of, 171–174, 322, 325, 327,
        344
sleep latency, 180, 327, 328, 331
sleep learning, 282–283, 329–330
sleep loss. *See* sleep deprivation
sleep maintenance, 97, 98
    and avoidance dreams, 327–328,
        332
    as function of dreaming, 142–145,
        148, 479, 550

and information processing, 53,
    61, 91, 94, 98
sleep maintenance insomnia, 26, 181
sleep mentation, 88, 89, 91, 93, 94–95
sleep-mood interaction, 151–163,
    164, 170, 177, 179–182
sleep necessity, 93, 98 97. *See also*
    sleep, functional significance of
sleep onset insomnia, 26, 181, 278
sleep patterns, gender differences in,
    154–155
sleep physiology, 96, 179–182,
    447–450. *See also* REM sleep physi-
    ology
sleep preservation. *See* sleep mainte-
    nance
sleep psychology, 182
sleep recordings, 390
sleep regulation, 96–98
sleep-related deficits, 26–27
sleep reports, NREM vs REM, 53
sleep research, 363–377
sleep satiety, 348
sleep stages
    and behavioral responses, 62
    dreaming and, 6, 11–13, 52, 88–89,
        94, 447
    and dream recall, 390
    and dream self-reflectiveness, 401
    EEG patterns in/within, 91
    functional significance of, 6, 98,
        553–556
    influences on, 96–97
    and information-processing mode,
        87
    and learning-memory processes,
        341
    maintenance/change of, 90, 91
    as regressions, 53
    relationship to mood/mood
    change, 179–181
    in shift workers, 27
    and sleep laboratories, 327
    and traumatic dreams, 297
    See also REM sleep; stage 1 sleep;

stage 2 sleep; stage 3 sleep; stage 4 sleep
sleep stimulation, 382, 392, 393, 454–455
sleep stimulation model, 387, 388–393, 394, 408
sleeptalking, 296, 552
sleep time
  minimum, 98
  total, 26–27, 179, 180, 181, 273, 353
sleep-wake boundary, 6–7, 202, 207, 208, 209, 221–247, 245, 393
sleep-wake cycle, 26
sleepwalking, 62–63, 69, 552
slow waves, 461
slow wave sleep, 27, 62
Smith, R., 395, 396, 397
smoking, 353
smoking cessation, 384
Snow, C.P., 530
S/N. *See* signal-noise ratio
Snyder, F., 203, 425
social class, 165, 490, 513, 514–517, 531, 533
social connections, 523–525, 528
social contact in dreams, 323
social context, and dream accounts, 530–531
social environment. *See* external environment
social functions, of dream narratives, 490
social interactions. *See* interactions in dreams; interpersonal relations; interpersonal situations
socialism, 518
social isolation, 321, 365
socialization, 365
social networks, 524
social predicaments, 425
social science, 530
sociocultural variables, 11
soliloquies, 210
somatic functions, 55

somatic responses, 69
somatic system, 66
somatomotor activation, 462, 463
somatosensory stimuli, 391
somnambulistic episodes. *See* sleep-walking
somnolence, 24
soul. *See hun; hunling; hunpo; linghun; po;* spirit(s)
"soul loss," 501
sound in dreams, 434, 435–436, 440, 441, 442
sound stimulation, 322
speech, 222, 227, 384
Spence, D.P., 398–399
"spider home" (*dane kurale*), 478
spirit mediums, 516, 520, 527
spirit possession, 513
spirit(s), 477. *See also guai; gui; hun; ling; po; shen;* supernatural figures
spiritual figures, 421, 422, 430, 431, 433, 445, 457
spontaneous (clock-dependent) state shifts, 91, 92
spontaneous dream reminiscence, 421, 422
spontaneous imagery, 383
spreading activation, 74
spreading warmth, 431, 432, 456, 466
spring (*chun*), 512
stage 1 sleep, 327, 354
stage 2 dream reports, 212
stage 2 sleep, 180, 354, 391, 552
stage 3 sleep, 180, 354
stage 4 dream reports, 212
stage 4 sleep, 179, 180, 328, 354, 553
stage REM sleep. *See* REM sleep
startle, 455, 456, 458, 501
startle-surprise affective reaction, 455
state aspect of mood, 156, 158–159, 160, 162
state-dependent brain mechanisms, 52

state-dependent information processing, 53, 56, 81
state-dependent lowering of OR
threshold, 451
state-dependent retrieval, 57–58,
79–88
asymmetry of, 70, 74, 82, 85, 92
characteristics of, 79–80
state-dependent storage, 81
state interdependence of dreaming
and waking, 245
state relationship between dreaming
and waking, 169, 170
state-shift hypothesis, 51–118, 200,
243–244
state shifts
induced, 91, 92
spontaneous (clock-dependent),
91, 92
state-specific memory. See state-
dependent retrieval
State-Trait Anxiety Inventory, 402
static functional theories, 3
status, 527, 534n2
stereotyped behavior, 262, 264, 268,
271
Sternberg paradigm, 366
stimuli
auditory, 454–455, 457, 461
aversive, 262, 277–278, 450, 453.
See also defense reaction
initially presented, 450, 453. See
also initial OR
novel, 65, 66. See also change OR
overwhelming, 296, 297
protective barrier against, 406
registration of without conscious
awareness. See subliminal stimulation
repetitive, 451
somatosensory, 391
subliminal, 382
verbal, 391
visual, 391

stimulus appraisal, 462, 463
stimulus barrier, 406
stimulus generalization, 406
storage spaces. See memory storages
storms in dreams, 298
story lines, dream, 15
strangeness of own actions in dream,
431, 432, 434, 436, 438, 440, 442
strangers in dreams, 166, 178, 300,
301, 460
strategies
as mnemonic category, 71, 72
and working memory, 75, 76
See also cognitive-emotional strategies; information-processing
strategies
stress
adaptive response of dreaming to,
6, 321–332
appraisal of, 326
and blocked cross-phasing, 35
and body's resistance, 265–266
and circadian cycles, 31
contemporary, 321–332
defined, 326
vs distress, 265
and dream contents, 321–322, 359,
391, 392
and dream enhancement, 402–403
and illness, 398
and lucid dreams, 232
and memory retrieval, 83
and personality, 326
and personal relevance, 326
and productive emotional tension,
264
and recurrent dreams, 298–302
and REM sleep/dreams, 272, 273,
278, 279–280, 359
and renunciation of search, 264,
265–266, 267, 270
and repetitive dream themes, 303
and search activity, 264–265, 266,
270, 271, 278
and search requirement, 268

and sleep latency, 327, 328, 331
and traumatic dreams, 295, 297
striving, 165, 512, 516
structure of dreams, 11
subcortical tissues, 24
subjective aspects of dream impacts,
    429–430, 433, 437, 441, 443, 446,
    464–465
subjective state. *See* affective states
subjectivity, 466–467
subliminal activation
    evidence for, 383–384, 407
    markers for, 391–392
subliminal activation
    model/paradigm, 382–384, 387,
    388–393, 408
subliminality, 388, 390
subliminal stimulation
    and boundaries, 406–407, 409
    and dream contents, 322, 381, 391,
        392, 399, 401, 407
    effects of, 381, 382, 392, 393, 394–
        395
    personality correlates of, 389–390,
        393
    and state of consciousness, 385–
        386, 387, 388, 389–390, 393
    See also registration without
    awareness
subliminal stimuli, defined, 382
substance addiction, dreaming and,
    392, 399–401, 402, 409
success, 268. *See also* failure
    in dream, 216, 430, 444
    of dream, 145, 148–150, 183–187,
        275, 314, 368, 369, 376
    and dream control, 216, 218, 221
success-failure, 218, 219, 455
succubi, 497, 527
suffocation, 480
suggestion(s), 391. *See also* hypno-
    sis/hypnotic suggestion
suicides, 497, 502
summary representations, 71–72
supernatural figures, 484, 498, 500,

508. *See also guai;* gods; *gui; shen*
superstition, 516, 518, 534
suppression, 173
supraliminal stimulation, 382, 395
surgery, 368, 402–403
surprise, 430, 451, 454, 455
surrealistic dreams, 526
surrender, 263, 264, 267, 268–269,
    275, 277–278
survival value of dreams, 2. *See also*
    dreaming, functional significance
    of
symbolic activity, dreaming as,
    30–31
symbolic associations, 383
symbolic function, 21, 27–31
symbolic languages, 57, 72
symbolic models. *See* models
symbolic predictors, dreams as, 477,
    480–485
symbolic processes, systems of,
    13–14
symbolism, dream, 36, 131, 132–133,
    309, 315–316, 368, 515, 526
symbolization, 394, 408
symbol(s), 30, 34, 41n10
    Freudian, 481–482
    indexical, 480–481, 485, 515
sympathetic somatomotor activa-
    tion, 462, 463
symptomatology, 203
syncretism, 505
syntactic dream interpretation,
    532–533
system of coordination, 56, 58, 59, 67.
    See also feedback control loops
systemic reflection, 248–249
systems approach, 55–70
systems perspective, 209, 246

tai qi (Great *qi*), 499
Taoism. *See* Daoism
Target Complaints, 402
Tart, C., 205, 206

TAT, 168, 366
taxonomy
  of dreams, 428
  matter-energy (breath), 498, 499
  "T" (dream series subject), 303–307, 309
teacher (*laoshi*), 531
teaching (*jiao*), 516
tears, 458
technology, 41*n*10
teleology, 12–13
temperature, core body, 26
temporal reference of dreams, 556
tenggelung, 497
tension, 168, 170, 183–184, 366, 462
terror, 440, 467. *See also* night terrors
tests, 324, 325, 522–523. *See also*
  Embedded Figures Test; Porsolt
  Test; posttests; projective tests;
  Rorschach tests; Thematic Apperception Test
textual criteria, 218
Thematic Apperception Test (TAT), 168, 366
thematic similarities, between
  dreaming and waking thought, 169–170, 182, 183, 187
themes
  in dream narratives, 492
  dream. *See* dream themes
therapist-patient dyads, dreaming among, 173
theta rhythms, 274
thinking
  clarity of, 151–164 passim, 176, 179, 180, 181
  creative, 366
  dreaming as aspect/form of, 21, 293
  in dreams, 166
  image (right-hemispheric), 277, 279
  logical-sign, 277
  and mastery process, 326

nondetermined, 139
pathological, 384
primary process, 382, 406, 408
and working memory, 75
See also thought
third culture, 530
thirstiness, 392, 400
thirst-related dreams, 327
thought
  atoms of, and EEG patterns, 65
  Chinese, 514–517
  cognitive processes and, 77
  and dream recall, 227
  and orienting response, 67
  parsimony of, 490–491
  and pre-attentive processes, 58
  and problem solving, 358
  qualities of, 32
  and REM sleep, 552
  and subliminal stimulation, 383–384, 392
  See also abstract concepts/thought;
    cognitive-emotional interpreta
    tion; *si*; thinking; waking thought
thought layer of C-network, 120, 123
threat
  and orienting response, 462
  and recurrent dreams, 301
  and REM sleep, 272, 425
  and search behavior, 263, 268, 271
Three Teachings (San Jiao), 490, 505
threshold of awareness, 385, 390
Tibetan yogis, dreaming among, 32, 37, 39
time travel, 430
tonic-phasic model, 447
tonic-phasic research paradigm, 202
top-down processes, 244
total sleep deprivation (TSD), 349–356. *See also* sleep deprivation
toxic substances, 369
trace, concept of, 76
trace systems, 382
tragic catharsis, 467

training. *See* learning tasks

trait aspect of mood, 156, 158, 161–162

trait relationship, between dreaming and waking thought, 169, 170

trait variables, 11

trance states, 24, 30, 36

tranquilizers, 271

Transcendental Experience, 37

transcendental nature of world, 23

transcendental polyphasic cultures, 37, 39

transcendent awareness, dream-induced, 421, 422, 426, 427, 433, 444

transcendent dreams, 445, 446, 450, 454–457, 465, 466

transductions, biochemical/neuroimmunological, 30

transductive logic, 28

transfer effects
    dreaming to waking, 204, 220–226, 235–238, 242, 243, 247, 419–467, 556
    waking to dreaming, 204, 221, 226–235, 239, 242, 243, 321–332

transferences, 372, 403, 478

transfer of information, 329

transformations
    and consciousness, 31, 33
    in dreamer, 202, 212, 244, 527, 535*n*7
    image, 275
    and impactful dreams, 431, 432, 456, 459, 463
    and subliminal stimulation, 382, 393–395, 397, 408
    and unprepared learning hypothesis, 425
    See also metamorphoses

transformative goal, 187–188

transitions, 205

transpersonal experiences, 36, 41*n*10

traumatic dreams, 294, 295–298, 300, 301, 303, 309, 314. *See also* repetitive-traumatic dream pattern

traumatic experiences, 301, 303, 305–306, 307–309

traumatic neurosis, 406

traveling, in dreams, 302, 484

treatment, responsiveness to, 399–401, 409

tricyclic antidepressants, 271

TSD. *See* total sleep deprivation

tumors, 264, 265, 268

tuning, 123–124, 134

tuning bias, 119, 133–134

tunnels, in dreams, 307

Turing machine, 119

Turner, Victor, 33

twitches, muscular, 448

"two cultures," 530

type A individuals, 273

ucs (unconscious), 381–409

ulcers, 265, 268, 396

Ullman, M., 425

uncanniness, 445

uncertainty, resolution of, 527

unconscious mental processes
    during sleep, 92
    and lexical choice as predictor of illness, 398–399
    schematic representations of, 388, 389
    and subliminal activation paradigm, 382–384, 393

unconsciousness, sleep equated with, 199, 202, 207, 215

unconscious (ucs), the
    dreams as "royal road" to, 381–409
    motivational vs cognitive, 381

understanding, 38–39, 238, 376, 485

unexpectedness, 65, 66, 86–87

unfinished business, 294, 314

unhappiness
    and dream contents, 176–177, 178, 181, 182, 183, 186, 187

and sleep physiology, 180, 181
and sleep/sleep deprivation, 151–164 *passim*, 177
Unheimlichkeit (uncanniness), 445
uniformity of function, 423–425
unimportance, 65
units of data, 71–72, 75
unlearning, 129, 134
unpleasant dreams, 314
unprepared learning, 282–283, 425
uplifting sensations, 432
Urbantschitsch, V., 382, 393
urinating, in dreams, 307
utilitarianism, 423, 425–427

vaginas, in dreams, 482, 483
Van De Castle, R., 294, 309, 310, 314
Varela, F.J., 247
varieties of experience, 384–385
vasodilation, cephalic, 455, 456
vegetative responses, 69
vegetative system, 66
verbal associations, 210
verbal stimuli, 391
Vertes, R., 15
vertex spikes, 91
Vietnam veterans, 166, 294, 296–297
vigilance, 60, 425
    environmental, 438, 440, 444, 449, 463, 467
    perceptual, 382
vigor/vigorous activity, and impactful dreams, 430, 431, 435, 438, 439, 440, 441, 442, 444, 455, 457, 463, 466
visionary stream, in Chinese thought, 514–517
visitation dreams, 524
visual anomalies, 442, 446, 450
visual association areas, 365
visual cues, 385
visual discontinuities, 442, 446, 450, 452, 456
visual imagery, 439, 440, 441, 449

visual intrusions, 442, 444, 446, 452–453
visualization, 88
visual learning tasks, 348–349
visual stimuli, 391
visuo-spatial perspective, 431, 432, 436, 444, 456
vitality, 430, 431, 466
vivid dreamers, 148–149
vividness
    and dream recall, 390
    and impactful dreams, 429, 434, 435–436, 440, 441, 442, 447
    vs intensity, 448
    of night terrors, 480
vocabulary, 492
volitional processes in dreams. *See* dream control; intentionality; self-regulation

wake-dream-wake paradigm, 141, 170, 183, 187
wakefulness
    EEG patterns in, 83–84
    effects of on mood, 162–163
    effects of on sleep, 150–151
    effects of sleep on, 150, 151
    increased, 96–97
    and information processing, 68, 81, 201
    and memory retrieval, 82
    shift to/from, 87, 89–90
    vs sleep, 90, 91, 93, 95–96
    See also waking state
wake-sleep-wake continuum, 142, 170
wake-sleep-wake paradigm, 169, 187
waking concerns. *See* emotional preoccupations
waking-dreaming connection, 168–170
waking experiences, and signs, 533
waking (morning) mood. *See* mood
waking state
    characteristics of, 124–125

effects of on dreaming, 7, 14, 142.
See also waking to dreaming transfer effects
effects of dreaming on, 7–8, 13–14,
142, 419–467. *See also* dreaming
to waking transfer effects
equated with consciousness, 200,
202, 207
nature of, 6–7
and prefrontal cortex, 24
and process of mastery, 326
simulated by dreaming, 13
See also consciousness, waking
waking thought, relation to dreaming, 168–170, 197
waking to dreaming transfer effects,
204, 221, 226–235, 239, 242, 243,
321–332
Wallin, J., 221
warmth, and impactful dreams, 431,
432, 456, 466
"war neurosis" dreams, 296
warnings, dreams as, 395–399,
525–527
warps. *See* consciousness, warps of
water/water deprivation, 321, 322,
327, 391, 481
waveforms, 27, 64, 454, 455, 457, 461
weakness, and impactful dreams,
435, 439
weddings, in dreams, 315
weight reduction, 384
werewolves, 497
Wff'n'Proof task, 349–350, 352
will, exercise of in dreams, 29. *See
also* intentionality
will o' the wisps, 497
Winget, C., 400
wish fulfillments, dreams as, 294,
295–296, 367, 391, 400, 479, 484
withdrawal
from addictive substances, 392,
399–401, 409
and surrender, 277

women
and dream accounts, 521
and dream contents, 165–166, 309,
310, 315
and dream interpretation, 516, 517,
520, 521, 531, 534
in dreams, 310, 312
Wood, P., 323
words
in dream reports, 235, 237, 491–492
in dreams, 210
as predictors of illness, 398–399
working memory
access to, 58, 75–77
and attention response, 78
and behavioral organization, 75
and brain's functional state, 93
contents of, 59, 67, 68, 73, 75–76,
77, 86
and cycle of communication, 56,
57, 58
dynamic nature of, 76
and information-processing
modes, 76
and knowledge, 75–77
and orienting response, 76
roles of, 75
and sleep, 77, 93
and state-dependent brain mechanisms, 52, 86
updating of, 59, 67. *See also* semantic association; semantic inhibition; semantic priming
world-awareness, 15
world-views, materialist, 35
Wright, J., 325–326
wu (shamans), 499, 503, 515–516

xenophobia, 514, 515
xin (mind, heart), 500, 505, 506, 511

yang, 493, 498, 499, 500, 501, 507, 508
yan (nightmares), 496
yi, 499

yin, 493, 497, 498, 499, 500, 501, 506, 508
yin-yang theory, 515
yogis. *See* Tibetan yogis
yuan (hurt feelings, resentment), 512

zeitgebers ("time-givers"), 25–26, 27, 31

Zen (Daoist) Buddhism, 490
zero/near-zero frequency of expected dream themes/characters, 307–308, 309
zhan (divination), 502
zhan meng (dream interpretation), 502
Zuckerman, M., 270